International Criminal Law Documents

This carefully edited text collects the major documents on International Criminal Law, through the early practice after the First World War, the Nuremberg and Tokyo International Military Tribunals up to the present. It includes the statutes of the ad hoc Tribunals for the former Yugoslavia and Rwanda, as well as the Rome Statute of the International Criminal Court and its associated documents, including the elements of crimes that were adopted to assist the Court, and its Rules of Procedure and Evidence. The book also includes the main treaty provisions that provide the basis of the subject.

Edited by a specialist in the field with more than twenty years' experience of teaching international criminal law, this book is designed for practical use by students and practitioners. For students it is ideal as a companion for both study and examination.

Robert Cryer is Professor of International and Criminal Law at the University of Birmingham. He has spoken widely around the world on issues of international law (including international crimes such as genocide, crimes against humanity and war crimes), criminal law more generally, and criminal co-operation (including extradition) in both academic and media contexts. His previous publications include *An Introduction to International Criminal Law and Procedure* (2019) (with Darryl Robinson and Sergey Vasiliev) and *The Tokyo International Military Tribunal: A Reappraisal* (with Neil Boister)(2008).

International Criminal Law Documents

EDITED BY **ROBERT CRYER**
University of Birmingham

CAMBRIDGE
UNIVERSITY PRESS

Shaftesbury Road, Cambridge CB2 8EA, United Kingdom

One Liberty Plaza, 20th Floor, New York, NY 10006, USA

477 Williamstown Road, Port Melbourne, VIC 3207, Australia

314–321, 3rd Floor, Plot 3, Splendor Forum, Jasola District Centre, New Delhi – 110025, India

103 Penang Road, #05–06/07, Visioncrest Commercial, Singapore 238467

Cambridge University Press is part of Cambridge University Press & Assessment, a department of the University of Cambridge.

We share the University's mission to contribute to society through the pursuit of education, learning and research at the highest international levels of excellence.

www.cambridge.org
Information on this title: www.cambridge.org/9781108729086

DOI: 10.1017/9781108678926

First published 2019

A catalogue record for this publication is available from the British Library

Library of Congress Cataloging-in-Publication data
Names: Cryer, Robert, editor.
Title: International criminal law documents / edited by Robert Cryer, University of Birmingham.
Description: Cambridge, United Kingdom ; New York, NY, USA : Cambridge University Press, 2019. | Includes index.
Identifiers: LCCN 2018053755 | ISBN 9781108729086
Subjects: LCSH: International criminal law – Sources. | LCGFT: Treaties.
Classification: LCC KZ7026 .I583 2019 | DDC 345/.00261–dc23
LC record available at https://lccn.loc.gov/2018053755

ISBN   978-1-108-72908-6   Paperback

Contents

EDITOR'S PREFACE

The purpose of this book can be stated fairly simply. It is to collect together the major international criminal law documents in one physical place. Even in the internet era, I believe that there is room for such a work not only for students, for both classroom and examination purposes, but also for practitioners and scholars, if nothing else for practical ease of use (often 'on the road', in the classroom, or in the courtroom). International criminal law (as is understood here) is now a broad and popular area of study and practice, so it was felt that it would be of assistance to provide a 'one stop' place where the documents were available for easy reference.

Conceptual Matters

Of course, international criminal law is not a self-defining term, it means different things to different people, and no one definition can claim even to be *primus inter partes*.[1] The one adopted here, solely for the purposes of ensuring a manageable and coherent book, is those crimes covered by the statement of the Nuremberg International Military Tribunal (IMT): 'crimes against international law are committed by men, not abstract entities, and only by punishing individuals who commit such crimes can the provisions of international law be enforced ... individuals have international duties which transcend the national obligations of obedience imposed by the individual state'.[2] These crimes are aggression, crimes against humanity, genocide and war crimes.

Others would define international criminal law more broadly as including those treaties which, whilst not creating direct liability for individuals, create obligations on States to criminalise conduct that they define in their domestic legal orders. These tend to be known as transnational criminal law conventions.[3] The various Drug Trafficking Conventions fall into this category, as do, although the matter is not beyond controversy, treaties on torture or terrorism. The two categories are not hermetically sealed, however, and there are those who believe that terrorism and individual acts of peacetime torture are direct liability international crimes.[4] There is no conceptual reason that conduct has to be considered, by its nature, as either an international or a transnational crime, it is simply how States wish to classify it.[5] Partially for these reasons, as well as to provide a counterpoint to the international criminal law documents, this book includes a small number

---

[1] See Robert Cryer, Håkan Friman, Darryl Robinson and Elizabeth Wilmshurst, *An Introduction to International Criminal Law and Procedure* (4th edn, Cambridge University Press 2019) 4.

[2] Nuremberg IMT: Judgment and Sentences (1947) 41 *AJIL* 172 at 221.

[3] Neil Boister, *An Introduction to Transnational Criminal Law* (2nd edn, Oxford University Press 2012) especially chapters 1–2.

[4] See, e.g., Antonio Cassese and Paola Gaeta *et al.*, *Cassese's International Criminal Law* (3rd edn, Oxford University Press 2013) chapter 8.

[5] Neil Boister, 'Transnational Criminal Law?' (2003) 14 *EJIL* 953, 954–6.

of transnational criminal law documents. However, there are literally hundreds of such conventions, so for reasons of space (and to keep the cost to the reader reasonable) this book largely keeps strictly to the more limited understanding of international criminal law identified above.

Criteria for Inclusion

For the most part, this book limits itself to the treaty law related to its understanding of international criminal law; however, international criminal law is not only made up of and developed by treaty law, so some General Assembly and Security Council Resolutions and Reports (including of the Secretary-General of the United Nations (UN) and the International Law Commission (ILC)) have also been reprinted. One issue that arose was the question of whether to include excerpts from selected, hugely important cases that are foundational in international criminal law (for example, the Nuremberg IMT's Judgment, mentioned above, and the well-known 1995 International Criminal Tribunal for the Former Yugoslavia (ICTY) 1995 decision in the *Tadić* Interlocutory Appeal[6] were both primary candidates for inclusion). However, on balance it was considered that it would increase the length of the book too much, and would risk making it into an *ersatz* cases and materials book (and there are already a number of examples of good collections of cases and materials available[7]), and reduce the likelihood of it being permitted in examinations. If readers think differently, I would very much like to hear from them.

Reasons of space, and the view being taken that the book should in essence reflect the universal aspects of international criminal law,[8] mean that regional treaties have not been included. It is, of course, the case that very few of the treaties included herein are universally ratified (only the Geneva Conventions of 1949 could make such a claim) so they are not in some respects truly universal (although they may reflect customary law, and many do). That said, including the specific parties to each treaty would make the book unwieldy. Furthermore, any such list of parties is likely to very quickly become out of date. Here is one area where the internet can be used to supplement the material in this book.

As a quick note on the organisation of materials, the arrangement is, with very small deviations (which relate to the manifest links between the documents) chronological. This seemed to be the most logical way to order the materials. It would have been possible to take a different view, and group documents (or even parts of them) conceptually. However, this route was not taken, as it relies on a pre-existing conceptual understanding that matches that of the editor, which may not always be shared. However, there is also an index to assist in identifying provisions in a more thematic manner.

Brief Notes on the Documents

The purpose of this section is to explain briefly the context of the various documents, some of the reasons for their inclusion, and the relationships they have to one another. It

---

[6] *Prosecutor v Tadić*, Decision on the Defence Interlocutory Appeal on Jurisdiction, IT-1-4-AR72, 2 October 1995.
[7] For examples from both sides of the Atlantic see: Antonio Cassese *et al.*, *International Law: Cases and Commentary* (Oxford University Press 2011); Beth van Schaak and Ronald Slye, *International Criminal Law and its Enforcement: Cases and Materials* (3rd edn, St Paul, MN: Foundation Press 2014).
[8] Which is not to denigrate regional or pluralist approaches, on which see Elies van Sliedregt and Sergey Vasiliev (eds), *Pluralism in International Criminal Law* (Oxford University Press 2014).

does not pretend to be anything like a detailed analysis of the documents, so it ought not to be taken as one.

The book begins with excerpts of the 1919 Report of the Commission on the Responsibility of the War, and on Their Punishment. This Commission was set up by the victorious Allies in the aftermath of World War I to decide on what to do with the defeated powers. In this they looked at the responsibility for starting the various conflicts that made up World War I. Unsurprisingly, this was placed firmly at the door of Germany and States aligned to it. However, the Commission also decided that there was no direct criminal liability in international law for aggression, although there was for war crimes and crimes against humanity. As such, the Report is probably the best place to identify the genesis of modern international criminal law. There were two dissents, however, one from the United States' (US) members, who argued that aggression was best left to the judgement of historians rather than lawyers, and that crimes against humanity were not international crimes. The Japanese representatives, on the other hand, queried whether international criminal law existed at all.

The Report had a considerable influence on the 1919 Treaty of Versailles, between the Allies and Germany. Article 227 dealt with the way in which the Kaiser was to be handled. He was to be arraigned before an international tribunal for an offence against morality and the sanctity of treaties (notably not an international crime – reflecting the Commission's views). As is well known, this provision was never put into effect, as the Kaiser fled to the Netherlands, who refused to extradite him on the basis that he was accused of a political offence.

Those suspected of war crimes or crimes against humanity were to be handed over to the Allied powers for domestic trials pursuant to Article 228. This provision was, for political reasons, never enforced, and the only outcome was the Leipzig trials, undertaken by Germany on the basis of German law, and notoriously lenient to the defendants. Even so, both provisions are included here, with others, for historical context.

From here we move to probably the first practical use of international criminal law. That was in 1945, and the Nuremberg IMT Statute (strictly speaking, an annex to a treaty, the London Agreement, that created the Tribunal (which was also adhered to by nineteen Latin American States – who derived no rights under it)). The Nuremberg IMT Statute was negotiated in London, amidst difficult discussions between France, the Soviet Union, the United Kingdom (UK) and the US. The Statute not only set up the Tribunal, but also defined the law it was to apply, including for the first time defining crimes against humanity. Very controversially, the Statute criminalised aggression (or, as it was called in Nuremberg 'crimes against peace'), the existence of which prior to 1945 was deeply controversial. We cannot overestimate the importance of the Nuremberg proceedings to the development of international criminal law.

The conduct of the proceedings was sometimes criticised for insufficiently protecting the rights of the defence, but the general view is that the proceedings were basically fair, especially when the mores of the time (which was prior to modern human rights law) are taken into account. This is part of the reason leading to the inclusion of the Tribunal's Rules of Procedure and Evidence, but it is also because of their brevity. It is interesting to compare them to the often exceptionally detailed Rules of Procedure and Evidence in the modern international criminal courts and tribunals. Also included here is Control Council Law No. 10, which was strongly linked to the Allied attempt to prosecute Nazis.

The Control Council was the joint body through which the Allies ruled Germany, and Law No. 10 was intended to co-ordinate the Allied efforts. Some consider that the US courts which sat pursuant to Law No. 10 were international courts,[9] but they are best seen, at most, to be an early example of 'hybrid' or 'internationalised' courts.

Although it is less well known, the Nuremberg Tribunal had a sibling in Tokyo, the IMT for the Far East. Rather than on the basis of a treaty, this was created by a proclamation of General Douglas MacArthur, the Supreme Commander of the Allied Powers. It was largely drafted by the prosecution, on the basis of the Nuremberg Tribunal's Statute (the borrowing of language in international criminal law, as in international law more generally, is common). MacArthur then willed it into being. However, three days before the Tribunal received the indictment MacArthur altered the Statute, to add India and the Philippines to the Proceedings, and, at the behest of the prosecution, to alter the definition of crimes against humanity to allow the prosecution to run the argument that all killings in an aggressive war were just murder. The argument for the rectitude of adding two new nations to the bench and prosecution is probably on balance one that can be made. The acceptability of altering a definition of a crime to the detriment of the defence is less so. The Rules of Procedure and Evidence are also reprinted. Even though they drew heavily on the Nuremberg Tribunal's rules, the conduct of the Tokyo Tribunal's proceedings have been almost universally criticised, showing that irrespective of the rules, those interpreting them still matter immensely.

The first major multilateral international criminal law treaty was the 1948 Genocide Convention, which was promulgated through the (then new) UN system a mere four years after the term was first coined by Raphaël Lemkin in his *Axis Rule in Occupied Europe* in 1944.[10] The Convention was preceded by General Assembly Resolution No. 96(I) of 1946, but was the first treaty of its type to create a generally applicable international crime in the pure sense (the Nuremberg and Tokyo Tribunal's jurisdictions were limited to the losing powers in World War II). A key provision, which differentiates it from transnational criminal law conventions, is Article I, which provides that 'genocide is a crime under international law', thus creating direct individual criminal liability. It has also been taken to imply that there is State responsibility flowing from the convention.[11] It is a key treaty in international criminal law, and its definition of genocide (in Article II) has since been repeated essentially verbatim in all international criminal courts and tribunals with jurisdiction over genocide.

Only a year later (in 1949), the Geneva Conventions were finalised. These contained the famous 'Grave Breaches' provisions (excerpted here), which create a form of mandatory universal jurisdiction over such breaches. It is often thought that Grave Breaches are a – if not the – quintessential example of war crimes, for which there is direct liability under international law. That may now be generally accepted (and it is and, as such, is the law on point) but the provisions read more like those of a transnational criminal law treaty. For example, there is nothing like Article I of the Genocide Convention in the Geneva Conventions, and the duty is to criminalise them domestically, and to extradite

---

[9] *Prosecutor* v *Erdemović*, Dissenting Opinion of Judge Cassese, IT-96–22-A, 7 October 1997, para. 21.

[10] Raphaël Lemkin, *Axis Rule in Occupied Europe* (Washington, DC: Carnegie Endowment for International Peace 1944) p. 79.

[11] *Case concerning the Application of the Convention on the Prevention and Punishment of the Crime of Genocide* (Bosnia and Herzegovina v Serbia and Montenegro) ICJ 26 February 2007, paras 162–6.

or prosecute suspects. Indeed the term 'Grave Breaches' was deliberately chosen because it was not 'war crimes'. Although it is now universally accepted that these provisions are war crimes, they do not, however, exhaust the law of war crimes, which are comprised of all serious violations of international humanitarian law. It would not be possible to include all of the relevant treaties on point; the standard reference guide runs to more than 750 pages.[12]

By the time of the Geneva Conventions, the Cold War had begun, and this largely stymied further development of international criminal law for almost two decades. By the late 1960s, however, a problem had arisen: prosecutions of Nazis in Germany – who had been undertaking such prosecutions under domestic law since the early 1960s – were approaching being time barred. Nazis had few powerful friends on either side of the Iron Curtain, and so the 1968 Convention on the Non-applicability of Statutory Limitations to War Crimes and Crimes against Humanity came from the UN General Assembly. This was rather sparsely ratified.[13] The Convention is well described by its title, although at the international level was not really necessary. As liability for international crimes comes from international law, no domestic jurisdiction can exclude that liability, and international criminal law knows of no doctrine of statutory limitation (other than to exclude it). It is notable, however, that although it was drafted with Nazis in mind, it was framed as universally applicable, but it remains a rare document on international crimes from the era.

Universality cannot quite be said of the next document included here: the 1973 International Convention on the Suppression and Punishment of the Crime of *Apartheid*, which, by its own terms, applied to '"the crime of apartheid", which shall include similar policies and practices of racial segregation and discrimination as practised in southern Africa, shall apply to the following inhuman acts committed for the purpose of establishing and maintaining domination by one racial group of persons over any other racial group of persons and systematically oppressing them ...'. (Article II). It also declares *Apartheid* to be a crime against humanity (Article I). Naturally, during the *Apartheid* era there was no possibility of South Africa ratifying it, and there have never been any prosecutions referable to it. That said, it has been quite broadly ratified (it currently has 107 parties), and its existence influenced the drafters of the Rome Statute of the International Criminal Court to include *Apartheid* as a crime against humanity in Article 7 of that treaty.

During this period perhaps the most influential document on international criminal law was not, in fact, binding at all. This was UN General Assembly Resolution No. 3314, that assembly's 1974 definition of aggression. Although intended primarily as a guide to the UN Security Council when exercising its powers under Chapter VII of the UN Charter, and differentiating a war of aggression (described as an international crime) from an act of aggression (which is the language of Article 39 of the UN Charter), it has hugely influenced the debate on aggression generally, and the definition of aggression for the purposes of the International Criminal Court.

States returned to update international humanitarian law relatively soon after (in particular in the aftermath of the Vietnam War, and owing to the fact that most armed

---

[12] Adam Roberts and Richard Guelff (eds), *Documents on the Law of War* (3rd edn, Oxford University Press 1999).
[13] Fifty-five as of 2018.

conflicts were non-international in nature and thus at the time relatively unregulated). This book includes the provisions on Grave Breaches in the 1977 Additional Protocol I to the 1949 Geneva Conventions, which apply to international armed conflicts, expand (in Article 85) the list of Grave Breaches to include certain violations of that Protocol (including *Apartheid*), and for the first time (in Articles 86–7) create a treaty basis for the very important international criminal law principle of command responsibility.[14] In contrast, Additional Protocol II, which applies to non-international armed conflicts, says nothing about criminal liability for breaches of its provisions. States at the time had no appetite for that.

This book's next treaty is the 1984 UN Convention against Torture. This is, strictly speaking, a transnational criminal law convention in that it does not create a crime in and of itself, but requires States to criminalise the conduct in their domestic law (and creates various other obligations surrounding crime and torture in general). In the first, 'Siracusa', draft of the Torture Convention, the drafters (who were not State representatives) included an article very similar to Article I of the Genocide Convention, declaring that torture was a crime under international law. When this draft was presented to States, it was immediately deleted. We have included the Torture Convention owing to the fact that there is a clear overlap between international and transnational crimes. For example, torture can be a means of committing international crimes in the narrow sense (war crimes, crimes against humanity and genocide) and, as mentioned above,[15] there are those that argue that individual acts of torture are direct liability international crimes. It is also useful to compare and contrast the Torture Convention with, for example, the Genocide Convention to see how the methods of drafting have changed.

This brings us to the renaissance era of international criminal law, the 1990s. The first document began the leap forward. This is the Report the Secretary-General of the UN was asked to write (and wrote in an astonishingly quick – for the UN – sixty days[16]) proposing a Statute for an international criminal tribunal to deal with the offences committed in the former Yugoslavia (i.e. the ICTY). This report, and the Statute it contained, was adopted by the UN Security Council in Resolution No. 827 (which is included here as it is, amongst other things, the foundation of the powers of the ICTY). The Report's commentary acts almost as the *travaux préparatoires* of the ICTY Statute. This book also includes, separately, an updated version of the ICTY Statute, for two reasons: first, for ease of use (unlike the Report, which intersperses the articles of the Statute with the commentary on them), and second, the Statute has been amended quite a few times since it was promulgated, so this book includes the most up-to-date version.

When the ICTY was created (and in part owing to the breakneck pace with which the Statute was adopted) not everything was fully thought through. One of the thornier issues that was passed over was what would happen when the Tribunal closed. Sentences still have to be supervised, decisions on parole have to be made, or new facts could require cases to be reopened. As a result, in 2010 the UN Security Council issued Resolution No. 1966 (also included), which set up a skeletal form of the Tribunal to perform these functions (the same applies to the International Criminal Tribunal for Rwanda (ICTR)). This

---

[14] Because of its connection to the 1949 Geneva Conventions, Additional Protocol I appears in Chapter 6 of this book, although chronologically this is not its place.

[15] Above, n 4.

[16] For the avoidance of doubt, as anyone who has worked with or for the UN will attest, this is not sarcasm.

goes by the name of the Residual Mechanism for the International Criminal Tribunals (and the unglamorous acronym MICT) and has now become the replacement for the Tribunals. A year after the creation of the ICTY, the most unambiguous example of genocide in the post-war era occurred in Rwanda. It was thought that it would be at the least Eurocentric, and perhaps racist, to have a Tribunal for a European conflict which had genocidal aspects, but not for an African genocide. Therefore the UN Security Council issued Resolution No. 955, which created the ICTR, the ICTY's conjoined twin, and annexed its Statute to that Resolution. The Statute, which is reproduced here, was clearly modelled, *mutatis mutandis*, on the ICTY Statute, although it was drafted by members of the UN Security Council rather than the Office of Legal Affairs of the UN Secretary-General. It is for this reason that the Report of the Secretary-General on the ICTR has not been included here; it does not quite perform the same role as the one that was written on the ICTY, as it does not contain the words of the drafters.

In the same year as the ICTR was created (1994), the International Law Commission (ILC) issued its second draft Statute for an (note the indefinite article) International Criminal Court. It had released its first in 1993. The second, whilst still bearing the strong imprimatur of its predecessor, also showed the influence of the then very recent ICTY Statute. What is notable is the mixing, to a fair extent, of international and transnational crimes and the strong emphasis on State consent. It is useful to compare this with the Rome Statute discussed below. For substantive law, it is also worth comparing the Rome Statute with another project of the ILC, the 1996 Draft Code of Crimes against the Peace and Security of Mankind. Although with the creation of the International Criminal Court, the project is essentially now defunct (though the ILC remains involved in projects that overlap with it), it is a useful artefact to show not only what could have been but also the porous border between international and transnational crimes.

The largest number of documents on any one institution in this book are on one institution in particular: the (the definite article is telling) International Criminal Court. This is because it is the most important (and soon to be perhaps the only) international criminal court or tribunal. The ICTY and the ICTR have closed and been replaced with the MICT, and (to the extent to which it is international) the Special Court for Sierra Leone (SCSL, discussed below) has also closed its doors. The first document, both chronologically and as the Court's foundational document, is the Rome Statute, negotiated in a tense and heated atmosphere in its titular city. The disagreements were numerous and deep, legal and political, principled and self-interested, and everything in between. Indeed, delegates supportive of the Court were by no means certain, even minutes before the final vote in the Committee of the Whole (not strictly the final vote of the Conference, but the one that would, to all intents and purposes, decide the matter), whether the final compromise draft would go through. When it did spontaneous joy broke out amongst supportive delegates, to the consternation of those who would have preferred the opposite conclusion.

The task facing the delegates was to create a court system (albeit not an entire criminal justice system (the Court has no police or other formal enforcement powers)) from scratch that would be strong enough to work, yet respectful enough of sovereignty that States would accept it. In addition they had to draft its substantive law (which is not coterminous with international criminal law *tout court*) and its processes as well as its institutional structure. That they managed to get a text which was tolerable to a large majority of States is extraordinary. Whether they achieved their (often differing) aims is a separate issue that can only be understood with reference to the Rome Statute and two accompanying documents, adopted by the Assembly of States Party of the International Criminal Court (itself a creature of the Rome Statute) in 2002. These are the Rules of Procedure and Evidence and the Elements of Crimes (which are detailed (albeit non-binding) further definitions of the crimes in the Rome Statute). Hence the inclusion of all three documents. Furthermore, in 2010 the Assembly of States Parties adopted two amending protocols to the Rome Statute, one applying additional offences to non-international armed conflicts, the other – which many thought to be the Holy Grail of international criminal law – a definition of aggression.[17] The final document that has made its way into the pages that follow about the Court is the Relationship Agreement, that is the agreement concerning the relationship the Court has with the UN. In spite of often expressed (or assumed) views to the contrary, the International Criminal Court is not a UN organ; it is a separate international organisation with its own international legal personality. Even so, for obvious reasons (including the relationship it has with the UN Security Council), both bodies were keen to formalise their institutional relationship in detail. The agreement is often forgotten in discussions about the Court and the UN, but it is an important part of it.

Leaving the Court, in a serendipitous confluence of concept and chronology, the next three chapters relate to 'hybrid' tribunals. These disparate tribunals are neither fully national nor fully international, but have a mixture of both elements, albeit with different blends. The most 'international' is the SCSL, which was created to deal with the Sierra Leonean conflict and based on a treaty between the UN and Sierra Leone. In spite of the Secretary-General's view that the Court was 'a treaty-based sui generis court of mixed jurisdiction and composition',[18] the Court considered itself to be fully international.[19] This book includes both the Statute of the SCSL and, since it has completed its work, the Residual Mechanism for the SCSL.

A different model is encapsulated in the next treaty, the 2003 Agreement between the UN and Cambodia relating to the Extraordinary Chambers in the Courts of Cambodia, which was created, after difficult negotiations between the UN and Cambodia, to prosecute members of the Khmer Rouge. The Chambers are essentially Courts of Cambodia to which international Judges and prosecutors are appointed alongside their Cambodian counterparts. The two sets of appointed people (national and international) have a complex relationship, best understood by reading the Agreement itself. The practice of the Chambers has been mixed and subject to critique from both within and without.

The final hybrid tribunal included is the Special Tribunal for Lebanon, created in 2007 to deal with the assassination of Lebanese Prime Minister Rafik Hariri. It is the first time an international tribunal has been created to deal solely with one incident. It was originally intended that a treaty including the Statute would be agreed between the UN and the Lebanese government, which would then be ratified by the Lebanese Parliament. The first step was successful, but the Parliament refused to ratify the agreement. As a result, the UN Security Council passed Resolution No. 1757, which brought the agreement (and Statute) into force. Both the Statute and the Resolution are included here. Interestingly,

---

[17] These 'Kampala Amendments' are included in the version of the Rome Statute set out in this book. Amendments not in force have been omitted.

[18] Report by the Secretary-General on the Establishment of a Special Court for Sierra Leone, UN Doc. S/2000/915 of 4 October 2000, para. 9.

[19] *Prosecutor* v *Taylor*, Decision on Immunity from Jurisdiction, SCSL 03–01-I, 31 May 2004.

owing to the view being taken that there is no international crime of terrorism (as opposed to various transnational conventions dealing with aspects of terrorism) the drafters of the Statute referred instead to the Lebanese domestic definition. In a deeply controversial decision, the Special Tribunal for Lebanon decided that there was, in fact, a customary law crime of terrorism.[20]

The final document that made the cut for inclusion is one of the (more) recent substantive conventions that relate to international criminal law. This is the 2008 International Convention for the Protection of All Persons from Enforced Disappearances. This is rather like a modern version of the Torture Convention in that it deals primarily with transnational crime concerns, such as the obligation to criminalise disappearances at the national level and the obligation to extradite or prosecute, but does so in a more modern fashion (although the issue of enforced disappearances had arisen in the *Apartheid* Convention). For instance, Article 5 of the 2008 Convention expressly states that 'the widespread or systematic practice of enforced disappearance constitutes a crime against humanity as defined in applicable international law and shall attract the consequences provided for under such applicable international law', and Article 6 applies the principle of command responsibility to enforced disappearances although command responsibility is more usually associated with international crimes. It ought to be said, however, whether someone is prosecuted for a domestic, transnational or international crime often matters less to victims than the fact they are prosecuted at all.

Final Word

I hope that this work assists in the understanding of international criminal law amongst students, practitioners and those in the field. All selections of documents of this type are, by their nature, subjective, and not everyone will agree with all of the decisions on inclusions or exclusions. Any suggestions for subsequent editions are very welcome (r.cryer@bham.ac.uk). Thanks are due to Rhiannon Blake for help in collating the documents.

---

[20] *Prosecutor* v *Ayyash*, Interlocutory Decision on the Applicable Law, STL-11–01 16 February 2011.

1919 Report of the Commission on the Responsibility of the War, and on Their Punishment (excerpts)

Commission on the Responsibility of the Authors of the War and on Enforcement of Penalties Report Presented to the Preliminary Peace Conference
March 29, 1919

...

The Commission was charged to inquire into and report upon the following points:
1. The responsibility of the authors of the war.
2. The facts as to breaches of the laws and customs of war committed by the forces of the German Empire and their Allies, on land, on sea, and in the air during the present war.
3. The degree of responsibility for these offences attaching to particular members of the enemy forces, including members of the General Staffs, and other individuals, however highly placed.
4. The constitution and procedure of a tribunal appropriate for the trial of these offences.
5. Any other matters cognate or ancillary to the above which may arise in the course of the enquiry, and which the Commission finds it useful and relevant to take into consideration.

...

CHAPTER I: RESPONSIBILITY OF THE AUTHORS OF THE WAR

On the question of the responsibility of the authors of the war, the Commission, after having examined a number of official documents relating to the origin of the World War, and to the violations of neutrality and of frontiers which accompanied its inception, has determined that the responsibility for it lies wholly upon the Powers which declared war in pursuance of a policy of aggression, the concealment of which gives to the origin of this war the character of a dark conspiracy against the peace of Europe.

...

Conclusions
1. The war was premeditated by the Central Powers together with their Allies, Turkey and Bulgaria, and was the result of acts deliberately committed in order to make it unavoidable.
2. Germany, in agreement with Austria-Hungary, deliberately worked to defeat all the many conciliatory proposals made by the Entente Powers and their repeated efforts to avoid war.

II: Violation of the Neutrality of Belgium and Luxemburg

...

Conclusion

The neutrality of Belgium, guaranteed by the treaties of the 19th April, 1839, and that of Luxemburg, guaranteed by the treaty of the 11th May, 1867, were deliberately violated by Germany and Austria-Hungary.

CHAPTER II: VIOLATIONS OF THE LAWS AND CUSTOMS OF WAR

On the second point submitted by the Conference, the facts as to breaches of the laws and customs of war committed by the forces of the German Empire and their allies on land, on sea, and in the air, during the present war, the Commission has considered a large number of documents.

... [they] ... supply abundant evidence of outrages of every description committed on land, at sea, and in the air, against the laws and customs of war and of the laws of humanity.

In spite of the explicit regulations, of established customs, and of the clear dictates of humanity, Germany and her allies have piled outrage upon outrage. Additions are daily and continually being made. By way of illustration a certain number of examples have been collected in Annex I [not included here]. It is impossible to imagine a list of cases so diverse and so painful. Violations of the rights of combatants, of the rights of civilians, and of the rights of both, are multiplied in this list of the most cruel practices which primitive barbarism, aided by all the resources of modern science, could devise for the execution of a system of terrorism carefully planned and carried out to the end. Not even prisoners, or wounded, or women, or children have been respected by belligerents who deliberately sought to strike terror into every heart for the purpose of repressing all resistance. Murders and massacres, tortures, shields formed of living human beings, collective penalties, the arrest and execution of hostages, the requisitioning of services for military purposes, the arbitrary destruction of public and private property, the aerial bombardment of open towns without there being any regular siege, the destruction of merchant ships without previous visit and without any precautions for the safety of passengers and crew, the massacre of prisoners, attacks on hospital ships, the poisoning of springs and of wells, outrages and profanations without regard for religion or the honor of individuals, the issue of counterfeit money reported by the Polish Government, the methodical and deliberate destruction of industries with no other object than to promote German economic supremacy after the war, constitute the most striking list of crimes that has ever been drawn up to the eternal shame of those who committed them. The facts are established. They are numerous and so vouched for that they admit of no doubt and cry for justice. The Commission, impressed by their number and gravity, thinks there are good grounds for the constitution of a special commission, to collect and classify all outstanding information for the purpose of preparing a complete list of the charges under the following heads:

The following is the list arrived at:

(1) Murders and massacres; systematic terrorism.

(2) Putting hostages to death.

(3) Torture of civilians.

(4) Deliberate starvation of civilians.

(5) Rape.

(6) Abduction of girls and women for the purpose of enforced prostitution.

(7) Deportation of civilians.

(8) Internment of civilians under inhuman conditions.

(9) Forced labor of civilians in connection with the military operations of the enemy.

(10) Usurpation of sovereignty during military occupation.

(11) Compulsory enlistment of soldiers among the inhabitants of occupied territory.

(12) Attempts to denationalize the inhabitants of occupied territory.

(13) Pillage.

(14) Confiscation of property.

(15) Exaction of illegitimate or of exorbitant contributions and requisitions.

(16) Debasement of the currency, and issue of spurious currency.

(17) Imposition of collective penalties.

(18) Wanton devastation and destruction of property.

(19) Deliberate bombardment of undefended places.

(20) Wanton destruction of religious, charitable, educational, and historic buildings and monuments.

(21) Destruction of merchant ships and passenger vessels without warning and without provision for the safety of passengers or crew.

(22) Destruction of fishing boats and of relief ships.

(23) Deliberate bombardment of hospitals.

(24) Attack on and destruction of hospital ships.

(25) Breach of other rules relating to the Red Cross.

(26) Use of deleterious and asphyxiating gases.

(27) Use of explosive or expanding bullets, and other inhuman appliances.

(28) Directions to give no quarter.

(29) Ill-treatment of wounded and prisoners of war.

(30) Employment of prisoners of war on unauthorized works.

(31) Misuse of flags of truce.

(32) Poisoning of wells.

The Commission desires to draw attention to the fact that the offences enumerated and the particulars given in Annex I are not regarded as complete and exhaustive; to these such additions can from time to time be made as may seem necessary.

Conclusions

1. The war was carried on by the Central Empires together with their allies, Turkey and Bulgaria, by barbarous or illegitimate methods in violation of the established laws and customs of war and the elementary laws of humanity.

2. A commission should be created for the purpose of collecting and classifying systematically all the information already had or to be obtained, in order to prepare as complete a list of facts as possible concerning the violations of the laws and customs of war committed by the forces of the German Empire and its Allies, on land, on sea and in the air, in the course of the present war.

1

CHAPTER III: PERSONAL RESPONSIBILITY

The third point submitted by the Conference is thus stated:

The degree of responsibility for these offences attaching to particular members of the enemy forces, including members of the General Staffs and other individuals, however highly placed.

For the purpose of dealing with this point, it is not necessary to wait for proof attaching guilt to particular individuals. It is quite clear from the information now before the Commission that there are grave charges which must be brought and investigated by a court against a number of persons.

In these circumstances, the Commission desire to state expressly that in the hierarchy of persons in authority, there is no reason why rank, however exalted, should in any circumstances protect the holder of it from responsibility when that responsibility has been established before a properly constituted tribunal. This extends even to the case of heads of states. An argument has been raised to the contrary based upon the alleged immunity, and in particular the alleged inviolability, of a sovereign of a state. But this privilege, where it is recognized, is one of practical expedience in municipal law, and is not fundamental. However, even if, in some countries, a sovereign is exempt from being prosecuted in a national court of his own country the position from an international point of view is quite different.

We have later on in our Report proposed the establishment of a high tribunal composed of judges drawn from many nations, and included the possibility of the trial before that tribunal of a former head of a state with the consent of that state itself secured by articles in the Treaty of Peace. If the immunity of a sovereign is claimed to extend beyond the limits above stated, it would involve laying down the principle that the greatest outrages against the laws and customs of war and the laws of humanity, if proved against him, could in no circumstances be punished. Such a conclusion would shock the conscience of civilized mankind.

...

Conclusion

All persons belonging to enemy countries, however high their position may have been, without distinction of rank, including Chiefs of States, who have been guilty of offences against the laws and customs of war or the laws of humanity, are liable to criminal prosecution.

CHAPTER IV: CONSTITUTION AND PROCEDURE OF AN APPROPRIATE TRIBUNAL

The fourth point submitted to the Commission is stated as follows:

The constitution and procedure of a tribunal appropriate for the trial of these offences (crimes relating to the war).

On this question the Commission is of opinion that, having regard to the multiplicity of crimes committed by those Powers which a short time before had on two occasions at The Hague protested their reverence for right and their respect for the principles of humanity, the public conscience insists upon a sanction which will put clearly in the light that it is not permitted cynically to profess a disdain for the most sacred laws and the most formal undertakings.

Two classes of culpable acts present themselves:
(a) Acts which provoked the world war and accompanied its inception.
(b) Violations of the laws and customs of war and the laws of humanity.

(a) Acts which Provoked the World War and Accompanied Its Inception

In this class the Commission has considered acts not strictly war crimes, but acts which provoked the war or accompanied its inception, such, to take outstanding examples, as the invasion of Luxemburg and Belgium.

The premeditation of a war of aggression, dissimulated under a peaceful pretence, then suddenly declared under false pretexts, is conduct which the public conscience reproves and which history will condemn, but by reason of the purely optional character of the institutions at The Hague for the maintenance of peace (International Commission of Inquiry, Mediation and Arbitration) a war of aggression may not be considered as an act directly contrary to positive law, or one which can be successfully brought before a tribunal such as the Commission is authorized to consider under its terms of reference.

Further, any inquiry into the authorship of the war must, to be exhaustive, extend over events that have happened during many years in different European countries, and must raise many difficult and complex problems which might be more fitly investigated by historians and statesmen than by a tribunal appropriate to the trial of offenders against the laws and customs of war. The need of prompt action is from this point of view important. Any tribunal appropriate to deal with the other offences to which reference is made might hardly be a good court to discuss and deal decisively with such a subject as the authorship of the war. The proceedings and discussions, charges and counter-charges, if adequately and dispassionately examined, might consume much time, and the result might conceivably confuse the simpler issues into which the tribunal will be charged to inquire. While this prolonged investigation was proceeding some witnesses might disappear, the recollection of others would become fainter and less trustworthy, offenders might escape, and the moral effect of tardily imposed punishment would be much less salutary than if punishment were inflicted while the memory of the wrongs done was still fresh and the demand for punishment was insistent.

We therefore do not advise that the acts which provoked the war should be charged against their authors and made the subject of proceedings before a tribunal ... The Commission is ... of the opinion that no criminal charge can be made against the responsible authorities or individuals (and notably the ex-Kaiser) on the special head of these breaches of neutrality, but the gravity of these gross outrages upon the law of nations and international good faith is such that the Commission thinks they should be the subject of a formal condemnation by the Conference.

Conclusions

1. The acts which brought about the war should not be charged against their authors or made the subject of proceedings before a tribunal.
2. On the special head of the breaches of the neutrality of Luxemburg and Belgium, the gravity of these outrages upon the principles of the law of nations and upon international good faith is such that they should be made the subject of a formal condemnation by the Conference.

3. On the whole case, including both the acts which brought about the war and those which accompanied its inception, particularly the violation of the neutrality of Belgium and Luxemburg, it would be right for the Peace Conference, in a matter so unprecedented, to adopt special measures, and even to create a special organ in order to deal as they deserve with the authors of such acts.

4. It is desirable that for the future penal sanctions should be provided for such grave outrages against the elementary principles of international law.

(b) Violations of the Laws and Customs of War and of the Laws of Humanity

Every belligerent has, according to international law, the power and authority to try the individuals alleged to be guilty of the crimes of which an enumeration has been given in Chapter II on Violations of the Laws and Customs of War, if such persons have been taken prisoners or have otherwise fallen into its power. Each belligerent has, or has power to set up, pursuant to its own legislation, an appropriate tribunal, military or civil, for the trial of such cases. These courts would be able to try the incriminated persons according to their own procedure, and much complication and consequent delay would be avoided which would arise if all such cases were to be brought before a single tribunal.

There remain, however, a number of charges:

(a) Against persons belonging to enemy countries who have committed outrages against a number of civilians and soldiers of several Allied nations, such as outrages committed in prison camps where prisoners of war of several nations were congregated or the crime of forced labor in mines where prisoners of more than one nationality were forced to work;

(b) Against persons of authority, belonging to enemy countries, whose orders were executed not only in one area or on one battle front, but whose orders affected the conduct of operations against several of the Allied armies;

(c) Against all authorities, civil or military, belonging to enemy countries, however high their position may have been, without distinction of rank, including the heads of states, who ordered, or, with knowledge thereof and with power to intervene, abstained from preventing or taking measures to prevent, putting an end to or repressing, violations of the laws or customs of war (it being understood that no such abstention should constitute a defence for the actual perpetrators);

(d) Against such other persons belonging to enemy countries as, having regard to the character of the offence or the law of any belligerent country, it may be considered advisable not to proceed before a court other than the high tribunal hereafter referred to.

For the trial of outrages falling under these four categories the Commission is of opinion that a high tribunal is essential and should be established …

Conclusions

The Commission has consequently the honor to recommend:

1. That a high tribunal be constituted as above set out.

2. That it shall be provided by the treaty of peace:

(a) That the enemy governments shall, notwithstanding that peace may have been declared, recognize the jurisdiction of the national tribunals and the high tribunal, that all enemy persons alleged to have been guilty of offences against the laws and customs of war and the laws of humanity shall be excluded from any amnesty to which the belligerents may agree, and that the governments of such persons shall undertake to surrender them to be tried.

(b) That the enemy governments shall undertake to deliver up and give in such manner as may be determined thereby:

  (i) The names of all persons in command or charge of or in any way exercising authority in or over all civilian internment camps, prisoner-of-war camps, branch camps, working camps and "commandoes" and other places where prisoners were confined in any of their dominions or in territory at any time occupied by them, with respect to which such information is required, and all orders and instructions or copies of orders or instructions and reports in their possession or under their control relating to the administration and discipline of all such places in respect of which the supply of such documents as aforesaid shall be demanded;

  (ii) All orders, instructions, copies of orders and instructions, General Staff plans of campaign, proceedings in naval or military courts and courts of inquiry, reports and other documents in their possession or under their control which relate to acts or operations, whether in their dominions or in territory at any time occupied by them, which shall be alleged to have been done or carried out in breach of the laws and customs of war and the laws of humanity;

  (iii) Such information as will indicate the persons who committed or were responsible for such acts or operations;

  ...

ANNEX II: MEMORANDUM OF RESERVATIONS PRESENTED BY THE REPRESENTATIVES OF THE UNITED STATES TO THE REPORT OF THE COMMISSION ON RESPONSIBILITIES

April 4, 1919.

The American members of the Commission on Responsibilities, in presenting their reservations to the report of the Commission, declare that they are as earnestly desirous as the other members of the Commission that those persons responsible for causing the Great War and those responsible for violations of the laws and customs of war should be punished for their crimes, moral and legal. The differences which have arisen between them and their colleagues lie in the means of accomplishing this common desire. The American members therefore submit to the Conference on the Preliminaries of Peace a memorandum of the reasons for their dissent from the report of the Commission and from certain provisions for insertion in treaties with enemy countries, as stated in Annex IV, and suggestions as to the cause of action which they consider should be adopted in dealing with the subjects upon which the Commission on Responsibilities was directed to report.

Preliminary to a consideration of the points at issue and the irreconcilable differences which have developed and which make this dissenting report necessary, we desire to express our high appreciation of the conciliatory and considerate spirit manifested by our colleagues throughout the many and protracted sessions of the Commission. From the first of these, held on February 3, 1919, there was an earnest purpose shown to compose the differences which existed, to find a formula acceptable to all, and to render, if possible, a unanimous report. That this purpose failed was not because of want of effort on the part of any member of the Commission. It failed because, after all the proposed means of adjustment had been tested with frank and open minds, no practicable way could be found to harmonize the differences without an abandonment of principles which were fundamental. This the representatives of the United States could not do and they could not expect it of others.

In the early meetings of the Commission and the three Sub-Commissions appointed to consider various phases of the subject submitted to the Commission, the American members declared that there were two classes of responsibilities, those of a legal nature and those of a moral nature, that legal offences were justiciable and liable to trial and punishment by appropriate tribunals, but that moral offences, however iniquitous and infamous and however terrible their results, were beyond the reach of judicial procedure, and subject only to moral sanctions.

While this principle seems to have been adopted by the Commission in the report so far as the responsibility for the authorship of the war is concerned, the Commission appeared unwilling to apply it in the case of indirect responsibility for violations of the laws and customs of war committed after the outbreak of the war and during its course. It is respectfully submitted that this inconsistency was due in large measure to a determination to punish certain persons, high in authority, particularly the heads of enemy states, even though heads of states were not hitherto legally responsible for the atrocious acts committed by subordinate authorities. To such an inconsistency the American members of the Commission were unwilling to assent …

With the manifest purpose of trying and punishing those persons to whom reference has been made, it was proposed to create a high tribunal with an international character, and to bring before it those who had been marked as responsible, not only for directly ordering illegal acts of war, but for having abstained from preventing such illegal acts.

Appreciating the importance of a judicial proceeding of this nature, as well as its novelty, the American representatives laid before the Commission a memorandum upon the constitution and procedure of a tribunal of an international character which, in their opinion, should be formed by the union of existing national military tribunals or commissions of admitted competence in the premises. And in view of the fact that "customs" as well as "laws" were to be considered, they filed another memorandum, attached hereto, as to the principles which should, in their opinion, guide the Commission in considering and reporting on this subject.

The practice proposed in the memorandum as to the military commissions was in part accepted, but the purpose of constituting a high tribunal for the trial of persons exercising sovereign rights was persisted in, and the abstention from preventing violations of the laws and customs of war and of humanity was insisted upon. It was frankly stated that the purpose was to bring before this tribunal the ex-Kaiser of Germany, and that the jurisdiction of the tribunals must be broad enough to include him even if he had not directly ordered the violations.

To the unprecedented proposal of creating an international criminal tribunal and to the doctrine of negative criminality the American members refused to give their assent.

…

II

The second question submitted by the Conference to the Commission requires an investigation of and report upon "the facts as to breaches of the laws and customs of war committed by the forces of the German Empire and their Allies, on land, on sea, and in the air, during the present war." ... The duty of the Commission was, therefore, to determine whether the facts found were violations of the laws and customs of war. It was not asked whether these facts were violations of the laws or of the principles of humanity. Nevertheless, the report of the Commission does not, as in the opinion of the American representatives it should, confine itself to the ascertainment of the facts and to their violation of the laws and customs of war, but, going beyond the terms of the mandate, declares that the facts found and acts committed were in violation of the laws and of the elementary principles of humanity ... The laws and customs of war are a standard certain, to be found in books of authority and in the practice of nations. The laws and principles of humanity vary with the individual, which, if for no other reason, should exclude them from consideration in a court of justice, especially one charged with the administration of criminal law. The American representatives, therefore, objected to the references to the laws and principles of humanity, to be found in the report, in what they believed was meant to be a judicial proceeding, as, in their opinion, the facts found were to be violations or breaches of the laws and customs of war, and the persons singled out for trial and punishment for acts committed during the war were only to be those persons guilty of acts which should have been committed in violation of the laws and customs of war.

...

III

The third question submitted to the Commission on Responsibilities requires an expression of opinion concerning "the degree of responsibility for these offences attaching to particular members of the enemy forces, including members of the General Staffs, and other individuals, however highly placed." The conclusions which the Commission reached, and which is stated in the report, is to the effect that "all persons belonging to enemy countries, however high their position may have been, without distinction of rank, including chiefs of states, who have been guilty of offences against the laws and customs of war or the laws of humanity, are liable to criminal prosecution." The American representatives are unable to agree with this conclusion, in so far as it subjects to criminal, and, therefore, to legal prosecution, persons accused of offences against "the laws of humanity," and in so far as it subjects chiefs of states to a degree of responsibility hitherto unknown to municipal or international law, for which no precedents are to be found in the modern practice of nations.

Omitting for the present the question of criminal liability for offences against the laws of humanity, which will be considered in connection with the law to be administered in the national tribunals and the high court, whose constitution is recommended by the Commission, and likewise reserving for discussion in connection with the high court the question of the liability of a chief of state to criminal prosecution, a reference may properly be made in this place to the masterly and hitherto unanswered opinion of Chief Justice Marshall in the case of the Schooner Exchange v. McFaddon and Others (7 Cranch, 116), decided by the Supreme Court of the United States in 1812, in which the reasons are given for the exemption of the sovereign and of the sovereign agent of a state from judicial process. This does not mean that the head of the state, whether he be called emperor, king, or chief executive, is not responsible for breaches of the law, but that he is responsible not to the judicial but to the political authority of his country. His act may and does bind his country and render it responsible for the acts which he has committed in its name and its behalf, or under cover of its authority; but he is, and it is submitted that he should be, only responsible to his country, as otherwise to hold would be to subject to foreign countries, a chief executive, thus withdrawing him from the laws of his country, even its organic laws, to which he owes obedience, and subordinating him to foreign jurisdictions to which neither he nor his country owes allegiance or obedience, thus denying the very conception of sovereignty.

But the law to which the head of the state is responsible is the law of his country, not the law of a foreign country or group of countries; the tribunal to which he is responsible is the tribunal of his country, not of a foreign country or group of countries, and the punishment to be inflicted is the punishment prescribed by the law in force at the time of the commission of the act, not a punishment created after the commission of the act.

These observations the American representatives believe to be applicable to a head of a state actually in office and engaged in the performance of his duties. They do not apply to a head of a state who has abdicated or has been repudiated by his people. Proceedings against him might be wise or unwise, but in any event they would be against an individual out of office and not against an individual in office and thus in effect against the state.

The American representatives also believe that the above observations apply to liability of the head of a state for violations of positive law in the strict and legal sense of the term. They are not intended to apply to what may be called political offences and to political sanctions.

These are matters for statesmen, not for judges, and it is for them to determine whether or not the violators of the treaties guaranteeing the neutrality of Belgium and of Luxemburg should be subjected to a political sanction.

However, as questions of this kind seem to be beyond the mandate of the Conference, the American representatives consider it unnecessary to enter upon their discussion.

IV

The fourth question calls for an investigation of and a report upon "the constitution and procedure of a tribunal appropriate for the trial of these offences." Apparently the Conference had in mind the violations of the laws and customs of war, inasmuch as the Commission is required by the third submission to report upon "the degree of responsibility for these offences attaching to particular members of the enemy forces, including members of the General Staffs and other individuals, however highly placed." The fourth point relates to the constitution and procedure of a tribunal appropriate for the investigation of these crimes, and to the trial and punishment of the persons accused of their commission, should they be found guilty.

The Commission seems to have been of the opinion that the tribunal referred to in the fourth point was to deal with the crimes specified in the second and third submissions, not with the responsibility of the authors of the war, as appears from the following statement taken from the report:

On the whole case, including both the acts which brought about the war and those which accompanied its inception, particularly the violation of the neutrality of

Luxemburg and of Belgium, the Commission is of the opinion that it would be right for the Peace Conference, in a matter so unprecedented, to adopt special measures, and even to create a special organ in order to deal as they deserve with the authors of such acts.

This section of the report, however, deals not only with the laws and customs of war – improperly adding "and of the laws of humanity" – but also with the "acts which provoked the war and accompanied its inception," which either in whole or in part would appear to fall more appropriately under the first submission relating to the "responsibility of the authors of the war."

Of the acts which provoked the war and accompanied its inception, the Commission, with special reference to the violation of the neutrality of Luxemburg and of Belgium, says: "We therefore do not advise that the acts which provoked the war should be charged against their authors and made the subject of proceedings before a tribunal." And a little later in the same section the report continues: "The Commission is nevertheless of opinion that no criminal charge can be made against the responsible authorities or individuals, and notably the ex-Kaiser, on the special head of these breaches of neutrality, but the gravity of these gross outrages upon the law of nations and international good faith is such that the Commission thinks they should be the subject of a formal condemnation by the Conference." The American representatives are in thorough accord with these views, which are thus formally stated in the first two of the four conclusions under this heading:

The acts which brought about the war should not be charged against their authors or made the subject of proceedings before a tribunal.

On the special head of the breaches of the neutrality of Luxemburg and Belgium, the gravity of these outrages upon the principles of the law of nations and upon international good faith is such that they should be made the subject of a formal condemnation by the Conference.

If the report had stopped here, the American representatives would be able to concur in the conclusions under this heading and the reasoning by which they were justified, for hitherto the authors of war, however unjust it may be in the forum of morals, have not been brought before a court of justice upon a criminal charge for trial and punishment. The report specifically states: (1) that "a war of aggression may not be considered as an act directly contrary to positive law, or one which can be successfully brought before a tribunal such as the Commission is authorized to consider under its terms of reference"; the Commission refused to advise (2) "that the acts which provoked the war should be charged against their authors and made the subject of proceedings before a tribunal"; it further holds (3) that "no criminal charge can be made against the responsible authorities or individuals, and notably the ex-Kaiser, on the special head of these breaches of neutrality." The American representatives, accepting each of these statements as sound and unanswerable, are nevertheless unable to agree with the third of the conclusions based upon them:

On the whole case, including both the acts which brought about the war and those which accompanied its inception, particularly the violation of the neutrality of Belgium and Luxemburg, it would be right for the Peace Conference, in a matter so unprecedented, to adopt special measures, and even to create a special organ in order to deal as they deserve with the authors of such acts.

The American representatives believe that this conclusion is inconsistent both with the reasoning of the section and with the first and second conclusions, and that "in a matter so unprecedented," to quote the exact language of the third conclusion, they are relieved from comment and criticism. However, they observe that, if the acts in question are criminal in the sense that they are punishable under law, they do not understand why the report should not advise that these acts be punished in accordance with the terms of the law. If, on the other hand, there is no law making them crimes or affixing a penalty for their commission, they are moral, not legal, crimes, and the American representatives fail to see the advisability or indeed the appropriateness of creating a special organ to deal with the authors of such acts. In any event, the organ in question should not be a judicial tribunal.

...

The fourth and final conclusion under this heading declares it to be "desirable that for the future penal sanctions should be provided for such grave outrages against the elementary principles of international law." With this conclusion the American representatives find themselves to be in substantial accord. They believe that any nation going to war assumes a grave responsibility, and that a nation engaging in a war of aggression commits a crime. They hold that the neutrality of nations should be observed, especially when it is guaranteed by a treaty to which the nations violating it are parties, and that the plighted word and the good faith of nations should be faithfully observed in this as in all other respects. At the same time, given the difficulty of determining whether an act is in reality one of aggression or of defence, and given also the difficulty of framing penal sanctions, where the consequences are so great or may be so great as to be incalculable, they hesitate as to the feasibility of this conclusion, from which, however, they are unwilling formally to dissent.

With the portion of the report devoted to the "constitution and procedure of a tribunal appropriate for the trial of these offences," the American representatives are unable to agree, and their views differ so fundamentally and so radically from those of the Commission that they found themselves obliged to oppose the views of their colleagues in the Commission and to dissent from the statement of those views as recorded in the report. The American representatives, however, agree with the introductory paragraph of this section, in which it is stated that "every belligerent has, according to international law, the power and authority to try the individuals alleged to be guilty of the crimes" constituting violations of the laws and customs of war, "if such persons have been taken prisoners or have otherwise fallen into its power." The American representatives are likewise in thorough accord with the further provisions that "each belligerent has, or has power to set up, pursuant to its own legislation, an appropriate tribunal, military or civil, for the trial of such cases." The American representatives concur in the view that "these courts would be able to try the incriminated persons according to their own procedure," and also in the conclusion that "much complication and consequent delay would be avoided which would arise if all such cases were to be brought before a single tribunal," supposing that the single tribunal could and should be created.

...

In a matter of such importance affecting not one but many countries and calculated to influence their future conduct, the American representatives believed that the nations should use the machinery at hand, which had been tried and found competent, with a law and a procedure framed and therefore known in advance, rather than to create an international tribunal with a criminal jurisdiction for which there is no precedent, precept, practice, or procedure. They further believed that, if an act violating the laws and customs of war committed by the enemy affected more than one country, a tribunal could be formed of the countries affected by uniting the national commissions or courts thereof, in which event the tribunal would be formed by the mere assemblage of the members, bringing with them the law to be applied, namely, the laws and customs of war, and the procedure, namely, the procedure of the national commissions or courts.

...

While the American representatives would have preferred a national military commission or court in each country, ... they were willing to concede that it might be advisable to have a commission of representatives of the competent national tribunals to pass upon the charges, as stated in the report:

(a) Against persons belonging to enemy countries who have committed outrages against a number of civilians and soldiers of several Allied nations, such as outrages committed in prison camps where prisoners of war of several nations were congregated or the crime of forced labor in mines where prisoners of more than one nationality were forced to work.

(b) Against persons of authority, belonging to enemy countries, whose orders were executed not only in one area or on one battle front, but whose orders affected the conduct towards several of the Allied armies.

The American representatives are, however, unable to agree that a mixed commission thus composed should, in the language of the report, entertain charges:

(c) Against all authorities, civil or military, belonging to enemy countries, however high their position may have been, without distinction of rank, including the heads of states, who ordered, or, with knowledge thereof and with power to intervene, abstained from preventing or taking measures to prevent, putting an end to or repressing, violations of the laws or customs of war, it being understood that no such abstention shall constitute a defence for the actual perpetrators.

In an earlier stage of the general report, indeed, until its final revision, such persons were declared liable because they "abstained from preventing, putting an end to, or repressing, violations of the laws or customs of war." To this criterion of liability the American representatives were unalterably opposed. It is one thing to punish a person who committed, or, possessing the authority, ordered others to commit an act constituting a crime; it is quite another thing to punish a person who failed to prevent, to put an end to, or to repress violations of the laws or customs of war. In one case the individual acts or orders others to act, and in so doing commits a positive offence. In the other he is to be punished for the acts of others without proof being given that he knew of the commission of the acts in question or that, knowing them, he could have prevented their commission. To establish responsibility in such cases it is elementary that the individual sought to be punished should have knowledge of the commission of the acts of a criminal nature and that he should have possessed the power as well as the authority to prevent, to put an end to, or repress them. Neither knowledge of commission nor ability to prevent is alone sufficient. The duty or obligation to act is essential. They must exist in conjunction, and a standard of liability which does not include them all is to be rejected. The difficulty in the matter of abstention was felt by the Commission, as to make abstention punishable might tend to exonerate the person actually committing the act. Therefore the standard of liability to which the American representatives objected are modified in the last sessions of the Commission, and the much less objectionable text, as stated above, was adopted and substituted for the earlier and wholly inadmissible one.

There remain, however, two reasons, which, if others were lacking, would prevent the American representatives from consenting to the tribunal recommended by the Commission. The first of these is the uncertainty of the law to be administered, in that liability is made to depend not only upon violations of the laws and customs of war, but also upon violations "of the laws of humanity." The second of these reasons is that heads of states are included within the civil and military authorities of the enemy countries to be tried and punished for violations of the laws and customs of war and of the laws of humanity. The American representatives believe that the Commission has exceeded its mandate in extending liability to violations of the laws of humanity, inasmuch as the facts to be examined are solely violations of the laws and customs of war. They also believe that the Commission erred in seeking to subject heads of states to trial and punishment by a tribunal to whose jurisdiction they were not subject when the alleged offences were committed.

As pointed out by the American representatives on more than one occasion, war was and is by its very nature inhuman, but acts consistent with the laws and customs of war, although these acts are inhuman, are nevertheless not the object of punishment by a court of justice. A judicial tribunal only deals with existing law and only administers existing law, leaving to another forum infractions of the moral law and actions contrary to the laws and principles of humanity. A further objection lies in the fact that the laws and principles of humanity are not certain, varying with time, place, and circumstance, and according, it may be, to the conscience of the individual judge. There is no fixed and universal standard of humanity. The law of humanity, or the principle of humanity, is much like equity, whereof John Selden, as wise and cautious as he was learned, aptly said:

> Equity is a roguish thing. For Law we have a measure, know what to trust to; Equity is according to the conscience of him that is Chancellor, and as that is larger or narrower, so is Equity. 'Tis all one as if they should make the standard for the measure we call a "foot" a Chancellor's foot; what an uncertain measure would this be! One Chancellor has a long foot, another a short foot, a third an indifferent foot. 'Tis the same thing in the Chancellor's conscience.

While recognizing that offences against the laws and customs of war might be tried before and the perpetrators punished by national tribunals, the Commission was of the opinion that the graver charges and those involving more than one country should be tried before an international body, to be called the High Tribunal

...

The American representatives felt very strongly that too great attention could not be devoted to the creation of an international criminal court for the trial of individuals, for which a precedent is lacking, and which appears to be unknown in the practice of nations. They were of the opinion that an act could not be a crime in the legal sense of the word, unless it were made so by law, and that the commission of an act declared to be a crime by law could not be punished unless the law prescribed the penalty to be inflicted ... The American representatives know of no international statute or convention making a violation of the laws and customs of war – not to speak of the laws or principles of humanity – an international crime, affixing a punishment to it, and declaring the court which has jurisdiction over the offence. They felt, however, that the difficulty, however great, was not insurmountable, inasmuch as the various states have declared certain acts violating the laws and customs of war to be crimes, affixing punishments to their commission, and providing military courts or commissions within the respective states possessing jurisdiction over such offence. They were advised that each of the Allied and Associated states could create such a tribunal, if it had not already done so. Here then was at hand a series of existing tribunal or tribunals that could lawfully be called into existence in each of the Allied or Associated countries by the exercise of their sovereign powers, appropriate for the trial and punishment within their respective jurisdictions of persons of enemy nationality, who during the war committed acts contrary to the laws and customs of war, in so far as such acts affected the persons or property of their subjects or citizens, whether such acts were committed within portions of their territory occupied by the enemy or by the enemy within its own jurisdiction.

The American representatives therefore proposed that acts affecting the persons or property of one of the Allied or Associated Governments should be tried by a military tribunal of that country; that acts involving more than one country, such as treatment by Germany of prisoners contrary to the usages and customs of war, could be tried by a tribunal either made up of the competent tribunals of the countries affected or of a commission thereof possessing their authority. In this way existing national tribunals or national commissions which could legally be called into being would be utilized, and not only the law and the penalty would be already declared, but the procedure would be settled.

It seemed elementary to the American representatives that a country could not take part in the trial and punishment of a violation of the laws and customs of war committed by Germany and her Allies before the particular country in question had become a party to the war against Germany and her Allies; that consequently the United States could not institute a military tribunal within its own jurisdiction to pass upon violations of the laws and customs of war, unless such violations were committed upon American persons or American property, and that the United States could not properly take part in the trial and punishment of persons accused of violations of the laws and customs of war committed by the military or civil authorities of Bulgaria or Turkey.

...

[I]t will be observed that the American representatives did not deny the responsibility of the heads of states for acts which they may have committed in violation of law, including, in so far as their country is concerned, the laws and customs of war, but they held that heads of states are, as agents of the people, in whom the sovereignty of any state resides, responsible to the people for the illegal acts which they may have committed, and that they are not and that they should not be made responsible to any other sovereignty.

The American representatives assumed, in debating this question, that from a legal point of view the people of every independent country are possessed of sovereignty, and that that sovereignty is not held in that sense by rulers; that the sovereignty which is thus possessed can summon before it any person, no matter how high his estate, and call upon him to render an account of his official stewardship; that the essence of sovereignty consists in the fact that it is not responsible to any foreign sovereignty; that in the exercise of sovereign powers which have been conferred upon him by the people, a monarch or head of state acts as their agent; that he is only responsible to them; and that he is responsible to no other people or group of people in the world.

The American representatives admitted that from the moral point of view the head of a state, be he termed emperor, king, or chief executive, is responsible to mankind, but that from the legal point of view they expressed themselves as unable to see how any member of the Commission could claim that the head of a state exercising sovereign rights is responsible to any but those who have confided those rights to him by consent expressed or implied.

The majority of the Commission, however, was not influenced by the legal argument. They appeared to be fixed in their determination to try and punish by judicial process the "ex-Kaiser" of Germany. That there might be no doubt about their meaning, they insisted that the jurisdiction of the high tribunal whose constitution they recommended should include the heads of states, and they therefore inserted a provision to this effect in express words in the clause dealing with the jurisdiction of the tribunal.

In view of their objections to the uncertain law to be applied, varying according to the conception of the members of the high court as to the laws and principles of humanity, and in view also of their objections to the extent of the proposed jurisdiction of that tribunal, the American representatives were constrained to decline to be a party to its creation. Necessarily they declined the proffer on behalf of the Commission that the United States should take part in the proceedings before that tribunal, or to have the United States represented in the prosecuting commission charged with the "duty of selecting the cases for trial before the tribunal and of directing and conducting prosecutions before it." They therefore refrained from taking further part either in the discussion of the constitution or of the procedure of the tribunal.

It was an ungracious task for the American representatives to oppose the views of their colleagues in the matter of the trial and punishment of heads of states, when they believed as sincerely and as profoundly as any other member that the particular heads of states in question were morally guilty, even if they were not punishable before an international tribunal, such as the one proposed, for the acts which they themselves had committed or with whose commission by others they could be justly taxed. It was a matter of great regret to the American representatives that they found themselves subjected to criticism, owing to their objection to declaring the laws and principles of humanity as a standard whereby the acts of their enemies should be measured and punished by a judicial tribunal. Their abhorrence for the acts of the heads of states of enemy countries is no less genuine and deep than that of their colleagues, and their conception of the laws and principles of humanity is, they believe, not less enlightened than that of their colleagues. They considered that they were dealing solely with violations of the laws and customs of war, and that they were engaged under the mandate of the Conference in creating a tribunal in which violations of the laws and customs of war should be tried and punished. They therefore confined themselves to law in its legal sense, believing that in so doing they accorded with the mandate of submission, and that to have permitted sentiment or popular indignation to affect their judgment would have been violative of their duty as members of the Commission on Responsibilities.

They submit their views, rejected by the Commission, to the Conference, in full confidence that it is only through the administration of law, enacted and known before it is violated, that justice may ultimately prevail internationally, as it actually does between individuals in all civilized nations.

Memorandum on the Principles which should Determine Inhuman and Improper Acts of War

To determine the principles which should be the standard of justice in measuring the charge of inhuman or atrocious conduct during the prosecution of a war, the following propositions should be considered:

1. Slaying and maiming men in accordance with generally accepted rules of war are from their nature cruel and contrary to the modern conception of humanity.
2. The methods of destruction of life and property in conformity with the accepted rules of war are admitted by civilized nations to be justifiable and no charge of cruelty, inhumanity, or impropriety lies against a party employing such methods.
3. The principle underlying the accepted rules of war is then necessity of exercising physical force to protect national safety or to maintain national rights.
4. Reprehensible cruelty is a matter of degree which cannot be justly determined by a fixed line of distinction, but one which fluctuates in accordance with the facts in each case, but the manifest departure from accepted rules and customs of war imposes upon the one so departing the burden of justifying his conduct, as he is prima facie guilty of a criminal act.
5. The test of guilt in the perpetration of an act, which would be inhuman or otherwise reprehensible under normal conditions, is the necessity of that act to the protection of national safety or national rights measured chiefly by actual military advantage.
6. The assertion by the perpetrator of an act that it is necessary for military reasons does not exonerate him from guilt if the facts and circumstances present reasonably strong grounds for establishing the needlessness of the act or for believing that the assertion is not made in good faith.
7. While an act may be essentially reprehensible and the perpetrator entirely unwarranted in assuming it to be necessary from a military point of view, he must not be condemned as wilfully violating the laws and customs of war or the principles of humanity unless it can be shown that the act was wanton and without reasonable excuse.
8. A wanton act which causes needless suffering (and this includes such causes of suffering as destruction of property, deprivation of necessaries of life, enforced labor, &c.) is cruel and criminal. The full measure of guilt attaches to a party who without adequate reason perpetrates a needless act of cruelty. Such an act is a crime against civilization, which is without palliation.
9. It would appear, therefore, in determining the criminality of an act, that there should be considered the wantonness or malice of the perpetrator, the needlessness of the act from a military point of view, the perpetration of a justifiable act in a needlessly harsh or cruel manner, and the improper motive which inspired it.

ANNEX III: RESERVATIONS BY THE JAPANESE DELEGATION

April 4, 1919

The Japanese Delegates on the Commission on Responsibilities are convinced that many crimes have been committed by the enemy in the course of the present war in violation of the fundamental principles of international law, and recognize that the principal responsibility rests upon individual enemies in high places. They are consequently of opinion that, in order to re-establish for the future the force of the principles thus infringed, it is important to discover practical means for the punishment of the persons responsible for such violations.

A question may be raised whether it can be admitted as a principle of the law of nations that a high tribunal constituted by belligerents can, after a war is over, try an individual belonging to the opposite side, who may be presumed to be guilty of a crime against the laws and customs of war. It may further be asked whether international law recognizes a penal law as applicable to those who are guilty.

In any event, it seems to us important to consider the consequences which would be created in the history of international law by the prosecution for breaches of the laws and customs of war of enemy heads of states before a tribunal constituted by the opposite party.

Our scruples become still greater when it is a question of indicting before a tribunal thus constituted highly placed enemies on the sole ground that they abstained from preventing, putting an end to, or repressing acts in violation of the laws and customs of war, as is provided in clause (c) of section (b) of Chapter IV.

It is to be observed that to satisfy public opinion of the justice of the decision of the appropriate tribunal, it would be better to rely upon a strict interpretation of the principles of penal liability, and consequently not to make cases of abstention the basis of such responsibility.

In these circumstances the Japanese Delegates thought it possible to adhere, in the course of the discussions in the Commission, to a text which would eliminate from clause (c) of section (b) of Chapter IV both the words "including the heads of states," and the provision covering cases of abstention, but they feel some hesitation in supporting the amended form which admits a criminal liability where the accused, with knowledge and with power to intervene, abstained from preventing or taking measures to prevent, putting an end to, or repressing acts in violation of the laws and customs of war.

The Japanese Delegates desire to make clear that, subject to the above reservations, they are disposed to consider with the greatest care every suggestion calculated to bring about unanimity in the Commission.

ANNEX IV: PROVISIONS FOR INSERTION IN TREATIES WITH ENEMY GOVERNMENTS

Article I

The Enemy Government admits that even after the conclusion of peace, every Allied and Associated State may exercise, in respect of any enemy or former enemy, the right which it would have had during the war to try and punish any enemy who fell within its power and who had been guilty of a violation of the principles of the law of nations, as these result from the usages established among civilized peoples, from the laws of humanity and from the dictates of public conscience.

Article II

The Enemy Government recognizes the right of the Allied and Associated States, after the conclusion of peace, to constitute a High Tribunal composed of members named by the Allied and Associated States in such numbers and in such proportions as they may think proper, and admits the jurisdiction of such tribunal to try and punish enemies or former enemies guilty during the war of violations of the principles of the law of nations as these result from the usages established among civilized peoples, from the laws of humanity and from the dictates of public conscience. It agrees that no trial or sentence by any of its own courts shall bar trial and sentence by the High Tribunal or by a national court belonging to one of the Allied or Associated States.

Article III

The Enemy Government recognizes the right of the High Tribunal to impose upon any person found guilty the punishment or punishments which may be imposed for such an offence or offences by any court in any country represented on the High Tribunal or in the country of the convicted person. The Enemy Government will not object to such punishment or punishments being carried out.

Article IV

The Enemy Government agrees, on the demand of any of the Allied or Associated States, to take all possible measures for the purpose of the delivery to the designated authority, for trial by the High Tribunal or, at its instance, by a national court of one of such Allied or Associated States, of any person alleged to be guilty of an offence against the laws and customs of war or the laws of humanity who may be in its territory or otherwise under its direction or control. No such person shall in any event be included in any amnesty or pardon.

Article V

The Enemy Government agrees, on the demand of any of the Allied or Associated States, to furnish to it the name of any person at any time in its service who may be described by reference to his duties or station during the war or by reference to any other description which may make his identification possible and further agrees to furnish such other information as may appear likely to be useful for the purpose of designating the persons who may be tried before the High Tribunal or before one of the national courts of an Allied or Associated State for a crime against the laws and customs of war or the laws of humanity.

Article VI

The Enemy Government agrees to furnish, upon the demand of any Allied or Associated State, all General Staff plans of campaign, orders, instructions, reports, logs, charts, correspondence, proceedings of courts, tribunals or investigating bodies, or such other documents or classes of documents as any Allied or Associated State may request as being likely to be useful for the purpose of identifying or as evidence for or against any person, and upon demand as aforesaid to furnish copies of any such documents.

2

1919 Treaty of Versailles (excerpts)

Treaty of Peace with Germany (Treaty of Versailles)

...

Article 227

The Allied and Associated Powers publicly arraign William II of Hohenzollern, formerly German Emperor, for a supreme offence against international morality and the sanctity of treaties.

A special tribunal will be constituted to try the accused, thereby assuring him the guarantees essential to the right of defence. It will be composed of five judges, one appointed by each of the following Powers: namely, the United States of America, Great Britain, France, Italy and Japan.

In its decision the tribunal will be guided by the highest motives of international policy, with a view to vindicating the solemn obligations of international undertakings and the validity of international morality. It will be its duty to fix the punishment which it considers should be imposed.

The Allied and Associated Powers will address a request to the Government of the Netherlands for the surrender to them of the ex-Emperor in order that he may be put on trial.

Article 228

The German Government recognises the right of the Allied and Associated Powers to bring before military tribunals persons accused of having committed acts in violation of the laws and customs of war. Such persons shall, if found guilty, be sentenced to punishments laid down by law. This provision will apply notwithstanding any proceedings or prosecution before a tribunal in Germany or in the territory of her allies.

The German Government shall hand over to the Allied and Associated Powers, or to such one of them as shall so request, all persons accused of having committed an act in violation of the laws and customs of war, who are specified either by name or by the rank, office or employment which they held under the German authorities.

Article 229

Persons guilty of criminal acts against the nationals of one of the Allied and Associated Powers will be brought before the military tribunals of that Power.

Persons guilty of criminal acts against the nationals of more than one of the Allied and Associated Powers will be brought before military tribunals composed of members of the military tribunals of the Powers concerned.

In every case the accused will be entitled to name his own counsel.

Article 230

The German Government undertakes to furnish all documents and information of every kind, the production of which may be considered necessary to ensure the full knowledge of the incriminating acts, the discovery of offenders and the just appreciation of responsibility.

3

1945 Nuremberg International Military Tribunal Statute; 1945 Nuremberg International Military Tribunal Rules of Procedure and Evidence and 1945 Control Council Law No. 10

1945 Charter of the International Military Tribunal (Nuremberg)

I. CONSTITUTION OF THE INTERNATIONAL MILITARY TRIBUNAL

Article 1
In pursuance of the Agreement signed on the 8th day of August 1945 by the Government of the United States of America, the Provisional Government of the French Republic, the Government of the United Kingdom of Great Britain and Northern Ireland and the Government of the Union of Soviet Socialist Republics, there shall be established an International Military Tribunal (hereinafter called "the Tribunal") for the just and prompt trial and punishment of the major war criminals of the European Axis.

Article 2
The Tribunal shall consist of four members, each with an alternate. One member and one alternate shall be appointed by each of the Signatories. The alternates shall, so far as they are able, be present at all sessions of the Tribunal. In case of illness of any member of the Tribunal or his incapacity for some other reason to fulfill his functions, his alternate shall take his place.

Article 3
Neither the Tribunal, its members nor their alternates can be challenged by the prosecution, or by the Defendants or their Counsel. Each Signatory may replace its members of the Tribunal or his alternate for reasons of health or for other good reasons, except that no replacement may take place during a Trial, other than by an alternate.

Article 4
(a) The presence of all four members of the Tribunal or the alternate for any absent member shall be necessary to constitute the quorum.
(b) The members of the Tribunal shall, before any trial begins, agree among themselves upon the selection from their number of a President, and the President shall hold office during the trial, or as may otherwise be agreed by a vote of not less than three members. The principle of rotation of presidency for successive trials is agreed. If,

however, a session of the Tribunal takes place on the territory of one of the four Signatories, the representative of that Signatory on the Tribunal shall preside.

(c) Save as aforesaid the Tribunal shall take decisions by a majority vote and in case the votes are evenly divided, the vote of the President shall be decisive: provided always that convictions and sentences shall only be imposed by affirmative votes of at least three members of the Tribunal.

Article 5

In case of need and depending on the number of the matters to be tried, other Tribunals may be set up; and the establishment, functions, and procedure of each Tribunal shall be identical, and shall be governed by this Charter.

II. JURISDICTION AND GENERAL PRINCIPLES

Article 6

The Tribunal established by the Agreement referred to in Article 1 hereof for the trial and punishment of the major war criminals of the European Axis countries shall have the power to try and punish persons who, acting in the interests of the European Axis countries, whether as individuals or as members of organizations, committed any of the following crimes.

The following acts, or any of them, are crimes coming within the jurisdiction of the Tribunal for which there shall be individual responsibility:

(a) CRIMES AGAINST PEACE: namely, planning, preparation, initiation or waging of a war of aggression, or a war in violation of international treaties, agreements or assurances, or participation in a common plan or conspiracy for the accomplishment of any of the foregoing;

(b) WAR CRIMES: namely, violations of the laws or customs of war. Such violations shall include, but not be limited to, murder, ill-treatment or deportation to slave labor or for any other purpose of civilian population of or in occupied territory, murder or ill-treatment of prisoners of war or persons on the seas, killing of hostages, plunder of public or private property, wanton destruction of cities, towns or villages, or devastation not justified by military necessity;

(c) CRIMES AGAINST HUMANITY: namely, murder, extermination, enslavement, deportation, and other inhumane acts committed against any civilian population, before or during the war; or persecutions on political, racial or religious grounds in execution of or in connection with any crime within the jurisdiction of the Tribunal, whether or not in violation of the domestic law of the country where perpetrated.

Leaders, organizers, instigators and accomplices participating in the formulation or execution of a common plan or conspiracy to commit any of the foregoing crimes are responsible for all acts performed by any persons in execution of such plan.

Article 7

The official position of defendants, whether as Heads of State or responsible officials in Government Departments, shall not be considered as freeing them from responsibility or mitigating punishment.

Article 8

The fact that the Defendant acted pursuant to order of his Government or of a superior shall not free him from responsibility, but may be considered in mitigation of punishment if the Tribunal determines that justice so requires.

Article 9

At the trial of any individual member of any group or organization the Tribunal may declare (in connection with any act of which the individual may be convicted) that the group or organization of which the individual was a member was a criminal organization.

After the receipt of the Indictment the Tribunal shall give such notice as it thinks fit that the prosecution intends to ask the Tribunal to make such declaration and any member of the organization will be entitled to apply to the Tribunal for leave to be heard by the Tribunal upon the question of the criminal character of the organization. The Tribunal shall have power to allow or reject the application. If the application is allowed, the Tribunal may direct in what manner the applicants shall be represented and heard.

Article 10

In cases where a group or organization is declared criminal by the Tribunal, the competent national authority of any Signatory shall have the right to bring individuals to trial for membership therein before national, military or occupation courts. In any such case the criminal nature of the group or organization is considered proved and shall not be questioned.

Article 11

Any person convicted by the Tribunal may be charged before a national, military or occupation court, referred to in Article 10 of this Charter, with a crime other than of membership in a criminal group or organization and such court may, after convicting him, impose upon him punishment independent of and additional to the punishment imposed by the Tribunal for participation in the criminal activities of such group or organization.

Article 12

The Tribunal shall have the right to take proceedings against a person charged with crimes set out in Article 6 of this Charter in his absence, if he has not been found or if the Tribunal, for any reason, finds it necessary, in the interests of justice, to conduct the hearing in his absence.

Article 13

The Tribunal shall draw up rules for its procedure. These rules shall not be inconsistent with the provisions of this Charter.

III. COMMITTEE FOR THE INVESTIGATION AND PROSECUTION OF MAJOR WAR CRIMINALS

Article 14

Each Signatory shall appoint a Chief Prosecutor for the investigation of the charges against and the prosecution of major war criminals.

The Chief Prosecutors shall act as a committee for the following purposes:
(a) to agree upon a plan of the individual work of each of the Chief Prosecutors and his staff,
(b) to settle the final designation of major war criminals to be tried by the Tribunal,
(c) to approve the Indictment and the documents to be submitted therewith,
(d) to lodge the Indictment and the accompanying documents with the Tribunal,
(e) to draw up and recommend to the Tribunal for its approval draft rules of procedure, contemplated by Article 13 of this Charter. The Tribunal shall have the power to accept, with or without amendments, or to reject, the rules so recommended.

The Committee shall act in all the above matters by a majority vote and shall appoint a Chairman as may be convenient and in accordance with the principle of rotation: provided that if there is an equal division of vote concerning the designation of a Defendant to be tried by the Tribunal, or the crimes with which he shall be charged, that proposal will be adopted which was made by the party which proposed that the particular Defendant be tried, or the particular charges be preferred against him.

Article 15

The Chief Prosecutors shall individually, and acting in collaboration with one another, also undertake the following duties:
(a) investigation, collection and production before or at the Trial of all necessary evidence,
(b) the preparation of the Indictment for approval by the Committee in accordance with paragraph (c) of Article 14 hereof,
(c) the preliminary examination of all necessary witnesses and of all Defendants,
(d) to act as prosecutor at the Trial,
(e) to appoint representatives to carry out such duties as may be assigned them,
(f) to undertake such other matters as may appear necessary to them for the purposes of the preparation for and conduct of the Trial.

It is understood that no witness or Defendant detained by the Signatory shall be taken out of the possession of that Signatory without its assent.

IV. FAIR TRIAL FOR DEFENDANTS

Article 16

In order to ensure fair trial for the Defendants, the following procedure shall be followed:
(a) The Indictment shall include full particulars specifying in detail the charges against the Defendants. A copy of the Indictment and of all the documents lodged with the Indictment, translated into a language which he understands, shall be furnished to the Defendant at a reasonable time before the Trial.
(b) During any preliminary examination or trial of a Defendant he will have the right to give any explanation relevant to the charges made against him.
(c) A preliminary examination of a Defendant and his Trial shall be conducted in, or translated into, a language which the Defendant understands.
(d) A Defendant shall have the right to conduct his own defense before the Tribunal or to have the assistance of Counsel.
(e) A Defendant shall have the right through himself or through his Counsel to present

evidence at the Trial in support of his defense, and to cross-examine any witness called by the Prosecution.

V. POWERS OF THE TRIBUNAL AND CONDUCT OF THE TRIAL

Article 17
The Tribunal shall have the power
(a) to summon witnesses to the Trial and to require their attendance and testimony and to put questions to them,
(b) to interrogate any Defendant,
(c) to require the production of documents and other evidentiary material,
(d) to administer oaths to witnesses,
(e) to appoint officers for the carrying out of any task designated by the Tribunal including the power to have evidence taken on commission.

Article 18
The Tribunal shall
(a) confine the Trial strictly to an expeditious hearing of the cases raised by the charges,
(b) take strict measures to prevent any action which will cause reasonable delay, and rule out irrelevant issues and statements of any kind whatsoever,
(c) deal summarily with any contumacy, imposing appropriate punishment, including exclusion of any Defendant or his Counsel from some or all further proceedings, but without prejudice to the determination of the charges.

Article 19
The Tribunal shall not be bound by technical rules of evidence. It shall adopt and apply to the greatest possible extent expeditious and nontechnical procedure, and shall admit any evidence which it deems to be of probative value.

Article 20
The Tribunal may require to be informed of the nature of any evidence before it is entered so that it may rule upon the relevance thereof.

Article 21
The Tribunal shall not require proof of facts of common knowledge but shall take judicial notice thereof. It shall also take judicial notice of official governmental documents and reports of the United Nations, including the acts and documents of the committees set up in the various allied countries for the investigation of war crimes, and of records and findings of military or other Tribunals of any of the United Nations.

Article 22
The permanent seat of the Tribunal shall be in Berlin. The first meetings of the members of the Tribunal and of the Chief Prosecutors shall be held at Berlin in a place to be designated by the Control Council for Germany. The first trial shall be held at Nuremberg, and any subsequent trials shall be held at such places as the Tribunal may decide.

Article 23

One or more of the Chief Prosecutors may take part in the prosecution at each Trial. The function of any Chief Prosecutor may be discharged by him personally, or by any person or persons authorized by him.

The function of Counsel for a Defendant may be discharged at the Defendant's request by any Counsel professionally qualified to conduct cases before the Courts of his own country, or by any other person who may be specially authorized thereto by the Tribunal.

Article 24

The proceedings at the Trial shall take the following course:

(a) The Indictment shall be read in court.

(b) The Tribunal shall ask each Defendant whether he pleads "guilty" or "not guilty."

(c) The prosecution shall make an opening statement.

(d) The Tribunal shall ask the prosecution and the defense what evidence (if any) they wish to submit to the Tribunal, and the Tribunal shall rule upon the admissibility of any such evidence.

(e) The witnesses for the Prosecution shall be examined and after that the witnesses for the Defense. Thereafter such rebutting evidence as may be held by the Tribunal to be admissible shall be called by either the Prosecution or the Defense.

(f) The Tribunal may put any question to any witness and to any defendant, at any time.

(g) The Prosecution and the Defense shall interrogate and may cross-examine any witnesses and any Defendant who gives testimony.

(h) The Defense shall address the court.

(i) The Prosecution shall address the court.

(j) Each Defendant may make a statement to the Tribunal.

(k) The Tribunal shall deliver judgment and pronounce sentence.

Article 25

All official documents shall be produced, and all court proceedings conducted, in English, French and Russian, and in the language of the Defendant. So much of the record and of the proceedings may also be translated into the language of any country in which the Tribunal is sitting, as the Tribunal is sitting, as the Tribunal considers desirable in the interests of justice and public opinion.

VI. JUDGMENT AND SENTENCE

Article 26

The judgment of the Tribunal as to the guilt or the innocence of any Defendant shall give the reasons on which it is based, and shall be final and not subject to review.

Article 27

The Tribunal shall have the right to impose upon a Defendant, on conviction, death or such other punishment as shall be determined by it to be just.

Article 28

In addition to any punishment imposed by it, the Tribunal shall have the right to deprive the convicted person of any stolen property and order its delivery to the Control Council for Germany.

Article 29

In case of guilt, sentences shall be carried out in accordance with the orders of the Control Council for Germany, which may at any time reduce or otherwise alter the sentences, but may not increase the severity thereof. If the Control Council for Germany, after any Defendant has been convicted and sentenced, discovers fresh evidence which, in its opinion, would found a fresh charge against him, the Council shall report accordingly to the Committee established under Article 14 hereof, for such action as they may consider proper, having regard to the interests of justice.

VII. EXPENSES

Article 30

The expenses of the Tribunal and of the Trials, shall be charged by the Signatories against the funds allotted for maintenance of the Control Council of Germany.

1945 Nuremberg International Military Tribunal Rules of Procedure and Evidence

Rule 1. Authority to Promulgate Rules

The present Rules of Procedure of the International Military Tribunal for the trial of the major war criminals (hereinafter called "the Tribunal") as established by the Charter of the Tribunal dated 8 August 1945 (hereinafter called "the Charter") are hereby promulgated by the Tribunal in accordance with the provisions of Article 13 of the Charter.

Rule 2. Notice to Defendants and Right to Assistance of Counsel

(a) Each individual defendant in custody shall receive not less than 30 days before trial a copy, translated into a language which he understands, (1) of the Indictment, (2) of the Charter, (3) of any other documents lodged with the Indictment, and (4) of a statement of his right to the assistance of counsel as set forth in sub-paragraph (d) of this Rule, together with a list of counsel. He shall also receive copies of such rules of procedure as may be adopted by the Tribunal from time to time.

(b) Any individual defendant not in custody shall be informed of the indictment against him and of his right to receive the documents specified in sub-paragraph (a) above, by notice in such form and manner as the Tribunal may prescribe.

(c) With respect to any group or organization as to which the Prosecution indicates its intention to request a finding of criminality by the Tribunal, notice shall be given by publication in such form and manner as the Tribunal may prescribe and such publication shall include a declaration by the Tribunal that all members of the named groups or organizations are entitled to apply to the Tribunal for leave to be heard in accordance with the provisions of Article 9 of the Charter. Nothing herein contained shall be construed to confer immunity of any kind upon such members of said groups or organizations as may appear in answer to the said declaration.

(d) Each defendant has the right to conduct his own defense or to have the assistance of counsel. Application for particular counsel shall be filed at once with the General Secretary of the Tribunal at the Palace of Justice, Nuremberg, Germany. The Tribunal will designate counsel for any defendant who fails to apply for particular counsel or, where particular counsel requested is not within ten (10) days to be found or available, unless the defendant elects in writing to conduct his own defense. If a defendant has requested particular counsel who is not immediately to be found or available, such counsel or a counsel of substitute choice may, if found and available before trial be associated with or substituted for counsel designated by the Tribunal, provided that (1) only one counsel shall be permitted to appear at the trial for any defendant, unless by special permission of the Tribunal, and (2) no delay of trial will be allowed for making such substitution or association.

Rule 3. Service of Additional Documents.

If, before the trial, the Chief Prosecutors offer amendments or additions to the Indictment, such amendments or additions, including any accompanying documents shall be lodged with the Tribunal and copies of the same, translated into a language which they each understand, shall be furnished to the defendants in custody as soon as practicable and notice given in accordance with Rule 2(b) to those not in custody.

Rule 4. Production of Evidence for the Defense

(a) The Defense may apply to the Tribunal for the production of witnesses or of documents by written application to the General Secretary of the Tribunal. The application shall state where the witness or document is thought to be located, together with a statement of their last known location. It shall also state the facts proposed to be proved by the witness or the document and the reasons why such facts are relevant to the Defense.

(b) If the witness or the document is not within the area controlled by the occupation authorities, the Tribunal may request the Signatory and adhering Governments to arrange for the production, if possible, of any such witnesses and any such documents as the Tribunal may deem necessary to proper presentation of the Defense.

(c) If the witness or the document is within the area controlled by the occupation authorities, the General Secretary shall, if the Tribunal is not in session, communicate the application to the Chief Prosecutors and, if they make no objection, the General Secretary shall issue a summons for the attendance of such witness or the production of such documents, informing the Tribunal of the action taken. If any Chief Prosecutor objects to the issuance of a summons, or if the Tribunal is in session, the General Secretary shall submit the application to the Tribunal, which shall decide whether or not the summons shall issue.

(d) A summons shall be served in such manner as may be provided by the appropriate occupation authority to ensure its enforcement and the General Secretary shall inform the Tribunal of the steps taken.

(e) Upon application to the General Secretary of the Tribunal, a defendant shall be furnished with a copy, translated into a language which he understands, of all documents referred to in the Indictment so far as they may be made available by the Chief

Prosecutors and shall be allowed to inspect copies of any such documents as are not so available.

Rule 5. Order at the Trial

In conformity with the provisions of Article 18 of the Charter, and the disciplinary powers therein set out, the Tribunal, acting through its President, shall provide for the maintenance of order at the Trial. Any defendant or any other person may be excluded from open sessions of the Tribunal for failure to observe and respect the directives and dignity of the Tribunal.

Rule 6. Oaths; Witnesses

(a) Before testifying before the Tribunal, each witness shall make such oath or declaration as is customary in his own country.

(b) Witnesses while not giving evidence shall not be present in court. The President of the Tribunal shall direct, as circumstances demand, that witnesses shall not confer among themselves before giving evidence.

Rule 7. Applications and Motions before Trial and Rulings during the Trial

(a) All motions, applications or other requests addressed to the Tribunal prior to the commencement of trial shall be made in writing and filed with the General Secretary of the Tribunal at the Palace of Justice, Nuremberg, Germany.

(b) Any such motion, application or other request shall be communicated by the General Secretary of the Tribunal to the Chief Prosecutors and, if they make no objection, the President of the Tribunal may make the appropriate order on behalf of the Tribunal. If any Chief Prosecutor objects, the President may call a special session of the Tribunal for the determination of the question raised.

(c) The Tribunal, acting through its President, will rule in court upon all questions arising during the trial, such as questions as to admissibility of evidence offered during the trial, recesses, and motions; and before so ruling the Tribunal may, when necessary, order the closing or clearing of the Tribunal or take any other steps which to the Tribunal seem just.

Rule 8. Secretariat of the Tribunal

(a) The Secretariat of the Tribunal shall be composed of a General Secretary, four Secretaries and their Assistants. The Tribunal shall appoint the General Secretary and each Member shall appoint one Secretary. The General Secretary shall appoint such clerks, interpreters, stenographers, ushers, and all such other persons as may be authorized by the Tribunal and each Secretary may appoint such assistants as may be authorized by the Member of the Tribunal by whom he was appointed.

(b) The General Secretary, in consultation with the Secretaries, shall organize and direct the work of the Secretariat, subject to the approval of the Tribunal in the event of a disagreement by any Secretary.

(c) The Secretariat shall receive all documents addressed to the Tribunal, maintain the records of the Tribunal, provide necessary clerical services to the Tribunal and its Members, and perform such other duties as may be designated by the Tribunal.

(d) Communications addressed to the Tribunal shall be delivered to the General Secretary.

Rule 9. Record, Exhibits, and Documents

(a) A stenographic record shall be maintained of all oral proceedings. Exhibits will be suitably identified and marked with consecutive numbers. All exhibits and transcripts of the proceedings and all documents lodged with and produced to the Tribunal will be filed with the General Secretary of the Tribunal and will constitute part of the Record.

(b) The term "official documents" as used in Article 25 of the Charter includes the Indictment, rules, written motions, orders that are reduced to writing, findings, and judgments of the Tribunal. These shall be in the English, French, Russian, and German languages. Documentary evidence or exhibits may be received in the language of the document, but a translation thereof into German shall be made available to the defendants.

(c) All exhibits and transcripts of proceedings, all documents lodged with and produced to the Tribunal and all official acts and documents of the Tribunal may be certified by the General Secretary of the Tribunal to any Government or to any other tribunal or wherever it is appropriate that copies of such documents or representations as to such acts should be supplied upon a proper request.

Rule 10. Withdrawal of Exhibits and Documents

In cases where original documents are submitted by the Prosecution or the Defense as evidence, and upon a showing (a) that because of historical interest or for any other reason one of the Governments signatory to the Four Power Agreement of 8 August 1945, or any other Government having received the consent of said four signatory Powers, desires to withdraw from the records of the Tribunal and preserve any particular original documents and (b) that no substantial injustice will result, the Tribunal shall permit photostatic copies of said original documents, certified by the General Secretary of the Tribunal, to be substituted for the originals in the records of the Court and shall deliver said original documents to the applicants.

Rule 11. Effective Date and Powers of Amendment and Addition

These Rules shall take effect upon their approval by the Tribunal. Nothing herein contained shall be construed to prevent the Tribunal from, at any time, in the interest of fair and expeditious trials, departing from, amending, or adding to these Rules, either by general rules or special orders for particular cases, in such form and upon such notice as may appear just to the Tribunal.

Control Council Law No. 10: Punishment of Persons Guilty of War Crimes, Crimes against Peace and against Humanity

In order to give effect to the terms of the Moscow Declaration of 30 October 1943 and the London Agreement of 8 August 1945, and the Charter issued pursuant thereto and in order to establish a uniform legal basis in Germany for the prosecution of war criminals and other similar offenders, other than those dealt with by the International Military Tribunal, the Control Council enacts as follows:

Article I

The Moscow Declaration of 30 October 1943 "Concerning Responsibility of Hitlerites for Committed Atrocities" and the London Agreement of 8 August 1945 "Concerning

Prosecution and Punishment of Major War Criminals of European Axis" are made integral parts of this Law. Adherence to the provisions of the London Agreement by any of the United Nations, as provided for in Article V of that Agreement, shall not entitle such Nation to participate or interfere in the operation of this Law within the Control Council area of authority in Germany.

Article II
1. Each of the following acts is recognized as a crime:
    (a) Crimes against Peace. Initiation of invasions of other countries and wars of aggression in violation of international laws and treaties, including but not limited to planning, preparation, initiation or waging a war of aggression, or a war of violation of international treaties, agreements or assurances, or participation in a common plan or conspiracy for the accomplishment of any of the foregoing.
    (b) War Crimes. Atrocities or offenses against persons or property constituting violations of the laws or customs of war, including but not limited to, murder, ill treatment or deportation to slave labour or for any other purpose, of civilian population from occupied territory, murder or ill treatment of prisoners of war or persons on the seas, killing of hostages, plunder of public or private property, wanton destruction of cities, towns or villages, or devastation not justified by military necessity.
    (c) Crimes against Humanity. Atrocities and offenses, including but not limited to murder, extermination, enslavement, deportation, imprisonment, torture, rape, or other inhumane acts committed against any civilian population, or persecutions on political, racial or religious grounds whether or not in violation of the domestic laws of the country where perpetrated.
    (d) Membership in categories of a criminal group or organization declared criminal by the International Military Tribunal.
2. Any person without regard to nationality or the capacity in which he acted, is deemed to have committed a crime as defined in paragraph 1 of this Article, if he was (a) a principal or (b) was an accessory to the commission of any such crime or ordered or abetted the same or (c) took a consenting part therein or (d) was connected with plans or enterprises involving its commission or (e) was a member of any organization or group connected with the commission of any such crime or (f) with reference to paragraph 1(a) if he held a high political, civil or military (including General Staff) position in Germany or in one of its Allies, co-belligerents or satellites or held high position in the financial, industrial or economic life of any such country.
3. Any persons found guilty of any of the crimes above mentioned may upon conviction be punished as shall be determined by the tribunal to be just. Such punishment may consist of one or more of the following:
    (a) Death.
    (b) Imprisonment for life or a term of years, with or without hard labor.
    (c) Fine, and imprisonment with or without hard labour, in lieu thereof.
    (d) Forfeiture of property.
    (e) Restitution of property wrongfully acquired.
    (f) Deprivation of some or all civil rights.Any property declared to be forfeited or the restitution of which is ordered by the Tribunal shall be delivered to the Control Council for Germany, which shall decide on its disposal.

4.

(a) The official position of any person, whether as Head of State or as a responsible official in a Government Department, does not free him from responsibility for a crime or entitle him to mitigation of punishment.

(b) The fact that any person acted pursuant to the order of his Government or of a superior does not free him from responsibility for a crime, but may be considered in mitigation.

5. In any trial or prosecution for a crime herein referred to, the accused shall not be entitled to the benefits of any statute of limitation in respect to the period from 30 January 1933 to 1 July 1945, nor shall any immunity, pardon or amnesty granted under the Nazi regime be admitted as a bar to trial or punishment.

Article III

1. Each occupying authority, within its Zone of Occupation,

(a) shall have the right to cause persons within such Zone suspected of having committed a crime, including those charged with crime by one of the United Nations, to be arrested and shall take under control the property, real and personal, owned or controlled by the said persons, pending decisions as to its eventual disposition.

(b) shall report to the Legal Directorate the name of all suspected criminals, the reasons for and the places of their detention, if they are detained, and the names and location of witnesses.

(c) shall take appropriate measures to see that witnesses and evidence will be available when required.

(d) shall have the right to cause all persons so arrested and charged, and not delivered to another authority as herein provided, or released, to be brought to trial before an appropriate tribunal. Such tribunal may, in the case of crimes committed by persons of German citizenship or nationality against other persons of German citizenship or nationality, or stateless persons, be a German Court, if authorized by the occupying authorities.

2. The tribunal by which persons charged with offenses hereunder shall be tried and the rules and procedure thereof shall be determined or designated by each Zone Commander for his respective Zone. Nothing herein is intended to, or shall impair or limit the Jurisdiction or power of any court or tribunal now or hereafter established in any Zone by the Commander thereof, or of the International Military Tribunal established by the London Agreement of 8 August 1945.

3. Persons wanted for trial by an International Military Tribunal will not be tried without the consent of the Committee of Chief Prosecutors. Each Zone Commander will deliver such persons who are within his Zone to that committee upon request and will make witnesses and evidence available to it.

4. Persons known to be wanted for trial in another Zone or outside Germany will not be tried prior to decision under Article IV unless the fact of their apprehension has been reported in accordance with Section 1(b) of this Article, three months have elapsed thereafter, and no request for delivery of the type contemplated by Article IV has been received by the Zone Commander concerned.

5. The execution of death sentences may be deferred by not to exceed one month after the sentence has become final when the Zone Commander concerned has reason to

believe that the testimony of those under sentence would be of value in the investigation and trial of crimes within or without his zone.

6. Each Zone Commander will cause such effect to be given to the judgments of courts of competent jurisdiction, with respect to the property taken under his control pursuant thereto, as he may deem proper in the interest of Justice.

Article IV

1. When any person in a Zone in Germany is alleged to have committed a crime, as defined in Article II, in a country other than Germany or in another Zone, the government of that nation or the Commander of the latter Zone, as the case may be, may request the Commander of the Zone which the person is located for his arrest and delivery for trial to the country or Zone in which the crime was committed. Such request for delivery shall be granted by the Commander receiving it unless he believes such person is wanted for trial or as a witness by an International Military Tribunal, or in Germany, or in a nation other than the one making the request, or the Commander is not satisfied that delivery should be made, in any of which cases he shall have the right to forward the said request to the Legal Directorate of the Allied Control Authority. A similar procedure shall apply to witnesses, material exhibits and other forms of evidence.

2. The Legal Directorate shall consider all requests referred to it, and shall determine the same in accordance with the following principles, its determination to be communicated to the Zone Commander.

   (a) A person wanted for trial or as a witness by an International Military Tribunal shall not be delivered for trial or required to give evidence outside Germany, as the case may be, except upon approval by the Committee of Chief Prosecutors acting under the London Agreement of 8 August 1945.

   (b) A person wanted for trial by several authorities (other than an International Military Tribunal) shall be disposed of in accordance with the following priorities:

   (1) If wanted for trial in the Zone in which he is, he should not be delivered unless arrangements are made for his return after trial elsewhere;

   (2) If wanted for trial in a Zone other than that in which he is, he should be delivered to that Zone in preference to delivery outside Germany unless arrangements are made for his return to that Zone after trial elsewhere;

   (3) If wanted for trial outside Germany by two or more of the United Nations, of one of which he is a citizen, that one should have priority;

   (4) If wanted for trial outside Germany by several countries, not all of which are United Nations, United Nations should have priority;

   (5) If wanted for trial outside Germany by two or more of the United Nations, then, subject to Article IV 2(b)(3) above, that which has the most serious charges against him, which are moreover supported by evidence, should have priority.

Article V

The delivery, under Article IV of this law, of persons for trial shall be made on demands of the Governments or Zone Commanders in such a manner that the delivery of criminals to one jurisdiction will not become the means of defeating or unnecessarily delaying the carrying out of justice in another place. If within six months the delivered person has not been convicted by the Court of the Zone or country to which he has been delivered, then such person shall be returned upon demand of the Commander of the Zone where the person was located prior to delivery

3

1946 Tokyo International Military Tribunal Statute and Rules of Procedure and Evidence

Special Proclamation—Establishment of an International Military Tribunal for the Far East (19 January 1946)

Whereas, the United States and the Nations allied therewith in opposing the illegal wars of aggression of the Axis Nations, have from time to time made declarations of their intentions that war criminals should be brought to justice;

Whereas, the Governments of the Allied Powers at war with Japan on the 26th July 1945 at Potsdam, declared as one of the terms of surrender that stern justice shall be meted out to all war criminals including those who have visited cruelties upon our prisoners;

Whereas, by the Instrument of Surrender of Japan executed at Tokyo Bay, Japan, on the 2nd September 1945, the signatories for Japan, by command of and on behalf of the Emperor and the Japanese Government accepted the terms set forth in such Declaration at Potsdam;

Whereas, by such Instrument of Surrender, the authority of the Emperor and the Japanese Government to rule the state of Japan is made subject to the Supreme Commander for the Allied Powers, who is authorized to take such steps as he deems proper to effectuate the terms of surrender; Whereas, the undersigned has been designated by the Allied Powers to carry into effect the general surrender of the Japanese armed forces;

Whereas, the Governments of the United States, Great Britain and Russia at the Moscow Conference, 26th December 1945, having considered the effectuation by Japan of the Terms of Surrender, with the concurrence of China have agreed that the Supreme Commander shall issue all orders for the implementation of the Terms of Surrender.

Now, therefore, I, Douglas MacArthur, as Supreme Commander for the Allied Powers, by virtue of the authority so conferred upon me, in order to implement the Term of Surrender which requires the meting out of stern justice to war criminals, do order and provide as follows:

Article 1. There shall be established an International Military Tribunal for the Far East for the trial of those persons charged individually, or as members of organizations, or in both capacities, with offenses which include crimes against peace.

Article 2. The Constitution, jurisdiction and functions of this Tribunal are those set forth in the Charter of the International Military Tribunal for the Far East, approved by me this day.

Article 3. Nothing in this order shall prejudice the jurisdiction of any other international, national or occupation court, commission or other tribunal established or to be established in Japan or in any territory of a United Nation with which Japan has been at war, for the trial of war criminals. Given under my hand at Tokyo, this 19th day of January, 1946.

Douglas MacArthur, General of the Army, United States Army, Supreme Commander for the Allied Powers.

CHARTER OF THE INTERNATIONAL MILITARY TRIBUNAL FOR THE FAR EAST

Article 1. Tribunal Established
The International Military Tribunal for the Far East is hereby established for the just and prompt trial and punishment of the major war criminals in the Far East. The permanent seat of the Tribunal is in Tokyo.

Article 2. Members
The Tribunal shall consist of not less than six members nor more than eleven members, appointed by the Supreme Commander for the Allied Powers from the names submitted by the Signatories to the Instrument of Surrender, India, and the Commonwealth of the Philippines.[1]

Article 3. Officers and Secretariat
a. President. The Supreme Commander for the Allied Powers shall appoint a Member to be President of the Tribunal.
b. Secretariat
...

Article 4. Convening and Quorum, Voting and Absence.
a. Convening and Quorum. When as many as six members of the Tribunal are present, they may convene the Tribunal in formal session. The presence of a majority of all members shall be necessary to constitute a quorum.
b. Voting. All decisions and judgments of this Tribunal, including convictions and sentences, shall be by a majority vote of those Members of the Tribunal present. In case the votes are evenly divided, the vote of the President shall be decisive.
c. Absence. If a member at any time is absent and afterwards is able to be present, he shall take part in all subsequent proceedings; unless he declares in open court that he is disqualified by reason of insufficient familiarity with the proceedings which took place in his absence.

II. JURISDICTION AND GENERAL PROVISIONS

Article 5. Jurisdiction over Persons and Offenses
The Tribunal shall have the power to try and punish Far Eastern war criminals who as individuals or as members of organizations are charged with offenses which include Crimes against Peace.

---

[1] Originally, the Article read '... The Tribunal shall consist of not less than six members nor more than eleven members, appointed by the Supreme Commander for the Allied Powers from the names submitted by the Signatories to the Instrument of Surrender.' It was altered on 26 April 1946 by General Order No. 20 to the text above.

The following acts, or any of them, are crimes coming within the jurisdiction of the Tribunal for which there shall be individual responsibility:

a. Crimes against Peace: Namely, the planning, preparation, initiation or waging of a declared or undeclared war of aggression, or a war in violation of international law, treaties, agreements or assurances, or participation in a common plan or conspiracy for the accomplishment of any of the foregoing;

b. Conventional War Crimes: Namely, violations of the laws or customs of war;

c. Crimes against Humanity: Namely, murder, extermination, enslavement, deportation, and other inhumane acts, before or during the war, or persecutions on political or racial grounds in execution of or in connection with any crime within the jurisdiction of the Tribunal, whether or not in violation of the domestic law of the country where perpetrated. Leaders, organizers, instigators and accomplices participating in the formulation or execution of a common plan or conspiracy to commit any of the foregoing crimes are responsible for all acts performed by any person in execution of such plan.[2]

Article 6. Responsibility of Accused

Neither the official position, at any time, of an accused, nor the fact that an accused acted pursuant to order of his government or of a superior shall, of itself, be sufficient to free such accused from responsibility for any crime with which he is charged, but such circumstances may be considered in mitigation of punishment if the Tribunal determines that justice so requires.

Article 7. Rules of Procedure

The Tribunal may draft and amend rules of procedure consistent with the fundamental provisions of this Charter.

Article 8. Counsel

a. Chief of Counsel. The Chief of Counsel designated by the Supreme Commander for the Allied Powers is responsible for the investigation and prosecution of charges against war criminals within the jurisdiction of this Tribunal, and will render such legal assistance to the Supreme Commander as is appropriate.

b. Associate Counsel. Any United Nation with which Japan has been at war may appoint an Associate Counsel to assist the Chief of Counsel.

III. FAIR TRIAL FOR ACCUSED

Article 9. Procedure for Fair Trial

In order to insure fair trial for the accused the following procedure shall be followed:

a. Indictment. The indictment shall consist of a plain, concise, and adequate statement of each offense charged. Each accused shall be furnished, in adequate time for defense, a

---

[2] The Charter originally read '... (c) Crimes against Humanity: Namely, murder, extermination, enslavement, deportation, and other inhumane acts *against any civilian population*, before or during the war, or persecutions on political or racial grounds in execution of or in connection with any crime within the jurisdiction of the Tribunal, whether or not in violation of the domestic law of the country where perpetrated. Leaders, organizers, instigators and accomplices participating in the formulation or execution of a common plan or conspiracy to commit any of the foregoing crimes are responsible for all acts performed by any person in execution of such plan' [emphasis added], but was altered on 26 April 1946 by General Order No. 20.

copy of the indictment, including any amendment, and of this Charter, in a language understood by the accused.

b. Language. The trial and related proceedings shall be conducted in English and in the language of the accused. Translations of documents and other papers shall be provided as needed and requested.

c. Counsel for Accused. Each accused shall have the right to be represented by counsel of his own selection, subject to the disapproval of such counsel at any time by the Tribunal. The accused shall file with the General Secretary of the Tribunal the name of his counsel. If an accused is not represented by counsel and in open court requests the appointment of counsel, the Tribunal shall designate counsel for him. In the absence of such request the Tribunal may appoint counsel for an accused if in its judgment such appointment is necessary to provide for a fair trial.

d. Evidence for Defense. An accused shall have the right, through himself or through his counsel (but not through both), to conduct his defense, including the right to examine any witness, subject to such reasonable restrictions as the Tribunal may determine.

e. Production of Evidence for the Defense. An accused may apply in writing to the Tribunal for the production of witnesses or of documents. The application shall state where the witness or document is thought to be located. It shall also state the facts proposed to be proved by the witness of the document and the relevancy of such facts to the defense. If the Tribunal grants the application the Tribunal shall be given such aid in obtaining production of the evidence as the circumstances require.

Article 10. Applications and Motions before Trial
All motions, applications, or other requests addressed to the Tribunal prior to the commencement of trial shall be made in writing and filed with the General Secretary of the Tribunal for action by the Tribunal.

IV. POWERS OF TRIBUNAL AND CONDUCT OF TRIAL

Article 11. Powers
The Tribunal shall have the power:
a. To summon witnesses to the trial, to require them to attend and testify,
b. To question them, to interrogate each accused and to permit comment on his refusal to answer any question,
c. To require the production of documents and other evidentiary material,
d. To require of each witness an oath, affirmation, or such declaration as is customary in the country of the witness, and to administer oaths,
e. To appoint officers for the carrying out of any task designated by the Tribunal, including the power to have evidence taken on commission.

Article 12. Conduct of Trial
The Tribunal shall:
a. Confine the trial strictly to an expeditious hearing of the issues raised by the charges,
b. Take strict measures to prevent any action which would cause any unreasonable delay and rule out irrelevant issues and statements of any kind whatsoever,

c. Provide for the maintenance of order at the trial and deal summarily with any contumacy, imposing appropriate punishment, including exclusion of any accused or his counsel from some or all further proceedings, but without prejudice to the determination of the charges,

d. Determine the mental and physical capacity of any accused to proceed to trial.

Article 13. Evidence

a. Admissibility. The Tribunal shall not be bound by technical rules of evidence. It shall adopt and apply to the greatest possible extent expeditious and non-technical procedure, and shall admit any evidence which it deems to have probative value. All purported admissions or statements of the accused are admissible.

b. Relevance. The Tribunal may require to be informed of the nature of any evidence before it is offered in order to rule upon the relevance.

c. Specific Evidence Admissible. In particular, and without limiting in any way the scope of the foregoing general rules, the following evidence may be admitted:

(1) A document, regardless of its security classification and without proof of its issuance or signature, which appears to the Tribunal to have been signed or issued by any officer, department, agency or member of the armed forces of any government.

(2) A report which appears to the Tribunal to have been signed or issued by the International Red Cross or a member thereof, or by a doctor of medicine or any medical service personnel, or by an investigator or intelligence officer, or by any other person who appears to the Tribunal to have personal knowledge of the matters contained in the report.

(3) An affidavit, deposition or other signed statement.

(4) A diary, letter or other document, including sworn or unsworn statements which appear to the Tribunal to contain information relating to the charge.

(5) A copy of a document or other secondary evidence of its contents, if the original is not immediately available.

d. Judicial Notice. The Tribunal shall neither require proof of facts of common knowledge, nor of the authenticity of official government documents and reports of any nation nor of the proceedings, records, and findings of military or other agencies of any of the United Nations.

e. Records, Exhibits and Documents. The transcript of the proceedings, and exhibits and documents submitted to the Tribunal, will be filed with the General Secretary of the Tribunal and will constitute part of the Record.

Article 14. Place of Trial

The first trial will be held at Tokyo and any subsequent trials will be held at such places as the Tribunal decides.

Article 15. Course of Trial Proceedings

The proceedings at the Trial will take the following course:

a. The indictment will be read in court unless the reading is waived by all accused.

b. The Tribunal will ask each accused whether he pleads "guilty" or "not guilty."

c. The prosecution and each accused (by counsel only, if represented) may make a concise opening statement.

d. The prosecution and defense may offer evidence and the admissibility of the same shall be determined by the Tribunal.

e. The prosecution and each accused (by counsel only, if represented) may examine each witness and each accused who gives testimony.

f. Accused (by counsel only, if represented) may address the Tribunal.

g. The prosecution may address the Tribunal.

h. The Tribunal will deliver judgment and pronounce sentence.

V. JUDGMENT AND SENTENCE

Article 16. Penalty

The Tribunal shall have the power to impose upon an accused, on conviction, death or such other punishment as shall be determined by it to be just.

Article 17. Judgment and Review

The judgment will be announced in open court and will give the reasons on which it is based. The record of the trial will be transmitted directly to the Supreme Commander for the Allied Powers for his action thereon. A sentence will be carried out in accordance with the order of the Supreme Commander for the Allied Powers, who may at any time reduce or otherwise alter the sentence except to increase its severity ...

RULES OF PROCEDURE OF THE INTERNATIONAL MILITARY TRIBUNAL FOR THE FAR EAST

The present rules of procedure of the International Military Tribunal for the Far East (hereinafter called the Tribunal) as established by the special proclamation of the 19th of January 1946 of the Supreme Commander for the Allied Powers and by the charter of the Tribunal of the same date and the amendments thereto are promulgated by the Tribunal in accordance with the provisions of Article 7 of the Charter, this 25th date of April 1946.

Rule 1. Notice to accused

(a) Each individual accused in custody shall receive not less than 14 days before the Tribunal begins to take evidence a copy, translated into a language which he understands, (1) of the Indictment, (2) of the Charter, (3) of any other documents lodged with the Indictment.

(b) Any individual accused not in custody shall be informed of the indictment against him and of his right to receive the documents specified in sub-paragraph (a) above by notice in such form and manner as the Tribunal may prescribe.

(c) Only one counsel shall be heard at the trial for any accused unless by special permission of the Tribunal.

Rule 2. Service of additional documents

(a) If, before the Tribunal commences to take evidence, the Chief Prosecutor offers amendments or additions to the indictments, such amendments or additions, including any accompanying documents, shall be lodged with the Tribunal and copies of the same translated into a language which they each understand shall be furnished to the accused in custody as soon as practicable and notice shall be given in accordance with Rule 1b to those not in custody.

(b) Upon application to the General Secretary, an accused shall be furnished with a copy translated into a language which he understands of all documents referred to in the indictment so far as they may be made available by the Chief Prosecutor, and shall be allowed to inspect copies of any such documents as are not made available.

Rule 3. Order at the trial

In conformity with the provisions of Article 12 of the Charter, and the disciplinary powers therein set out, the Tribunal, acting through its President, shall provide for the maintenance of order at the trial. Any accused or other person may be excluded from open session of the Tribunal for failure to observe and respect the directives or dignity of the Tribunal.

Rule 4. Witnesses

(a) Prior to testifying before the Tribunal, each witness shall make such oath or declaration or affirmation as is customary in his own country.

(b) Witnesses, while not giving evidence, shall not be present in the court without the permission of the Tribunal. The President shall direct, as circumstances demand, that witnesses shall not confer among themselves before giving evidence.

Rule 5. Applications and motions before the taking of evidence by the tribunal and rulings during the trial

(a) Any motion, application or other request addressed to the Tribunal prior to the commencement of the taking of evidence by the Tribunal, shall be communicated by the Secretary General to the Chief Prosecutor or to the accused concerned, or his counsel, as the case may be, and if no objection be made, the President may make an appropriate order on behalf of the Tribunal. If any objection be made, the President may call a special session of the Tribunal for the determination of the question raised.

(b) The Tribunal, acting through the President, will rule upon all questions arising during the trial, including questions of admissibility of evidence, as to recesses and upon motions, and before so ruling the Tribunal may, when necessary, order the closing or clearing of the court and take any other steps which to the Tribunal seem just.

Rule 6. Records, exhibits, and documents

(a) A record shall be maintained of all oral proceedings. Exhibits will be suitably identified and marked with consecutive numbers. So much of the record and proceedings may be translated into Japanese as the Tribunal considers desirable in the interest of justice and for the information of the public.

(b) As far as practicable, a copy of every document intended to be adduced in evidence by the prosecution or the defense will be delivered to the accused concerned or his counsel or to the prosecution, as the case may be, and also to the officer in charge of the Language Section of the Secretariat of the Tribunal, not less than twenty-four hours before such document is to be tendered in evidence. Every such copy shall have plainly marked thereon the part or parts upon which the prosecution or the defense, as the case may be, intends to rely, and every such copy shall be accompanied by a translation thereof into English or into Japanese, as the case may be, of the said part or parts. If the document is in a language other than English or Japanese, it shall be sufficient for the purpose of this provision if a translation into English or Japanese, as the case may be, of such document or such part or parts, is delivered to the prosecution or the accused concerned or his counsel, and to such officer.

(c) If, during the trial, counsel for the prosecution or any accused or his counsel receives or is apprised of any additional document which he intends to use at the trial, he will at once notify the opposing counsel concerned, or the accused concerned, as the case may be, and furnish him with a copy thereof as soon as practicable.

(d) All exhibits and transcripts of proceedings, all documents lodged with or produced to the Tribunal, and all official acts and documents may, with the consent of the Tribunal, be certified by the General Secretary to any government or to any other Tribunal or whenever it is appropriate that copies or representations as to such acts should be supplied upon a proper request.

(e) In cases where original documents are submitted by the prosecution or the defense in evidence, and upon showing (1) that because of historical interest or any other reason one of the signatories which has received the consent of all the said signatories desires to withdraw from the records of the Tribunal and preserve any particular original documents, and (2) that no substantial injustice will result, the Tribunal shall permit photostatic copies of the said original documents certified by the General Secretary, to be substituted for the originals in the records of the courts, and shall deliver the said original documents to the applicants.

Rule 7. Seal

(a) The Tribunal shall have a seal which shall be affixed to all summonses and certificates and to such other documents as the President from time to time directs.

(b) The Seal shall be kept in the custody of the General Secretary and shall be in a form approved by the President.

Rule 8. Forms of oath and affirmation

(a) The General Secretary and all personnel of the Secretariat of the Tribunal, and secretaries, stenographers, interpreters, and other persons in attendance on the members of the Tribunal, shall sign and lodge with the Tribunal an affirmation in the following form or to the like effect: 'I, (name and designation), will not disclose or discover any matter coming to my knowledge in the course of my employment in connection with the International Military Tribunal for the Far East, except to another person entitled to be informed of any such matter or to a member of such Tribunal.'

(b) Every official court reporter and interpreter shall, before commencing his duties, take an oath or make an affirmation according to the forms hereunder set out: (1) Reporter's Form of Oath (other than Japanese): 'I swear that I will faithfully perform the duties of reporter to this Tribunal. So help me God!' (2) Reporter's Form of Affirmation (other than Japanese): I affirm that I will faithfully perform the duties of reporter to this Tribunal.' (3) Interpreter's Form of Oath (other than Japanese):

'I swear that I will truly interpret in the case now in hearing. So help me God!' (4) Interpreter's Form of Affirmation (other than Japanese): 'I affirm that I will truly interpret in the case now in hearing.' (5) Japanese Reporters: 'I swear according to my conscience that I will faithfully perform the duties of reporter to this Tribunal.' (6) Japanese Interpreters: 'I swear according to my conscience that I will truly interpret in the case now in hearing.'

Rule 9. Effective date and powers of amendment and addition

Nothing herein contained shall be construed to prevent the Tribunal at any time, in the interest of a fair and expeditious trial, from departing from, amending or adding to these rules, either by general rules or special order for any particular case in such form and upon such notice as may appear just to the Tribunal.

1948 Convention on the Prevention and Punishment of the Crime of Genocide

Convention on the Prevention and Punishment of the Crime of Genocide, 9 December 1948.

The Contracting Parties,

Having considered the declaration made by the General Assembly of the United Nations in its resolution 96 (I) dated 11 December 1946 that genocide is a crime under international law, contrary to the spirit and aims of the United Nations and condemned by the civilized world

Recognizing that at all periods of history genocide has inflicted great losses on humanity, and

Being convinced that, in order to liberate mankind from such an odious scourge, international co-operation is required,

Hereby agree as hereinafter provided:

Article 1

The Contracting Parties confirm that genocide, whether committed in time of peace or in time of war, is a crime under international law which they undertake to prevent and to punish.

Article 2

In the present Convention, genocide means any of the following acts committed with intent to destroy, in whole or in part, a national, ethnical, racial or religious group, as such:

(a) Killing members of the group;
(b) Causing serious bodily or mental harm to members of the group;
(c) Deliberately inflicting on the group conditions of life calculated to bring about its physical destruction in whole or in part;
(d) Imposing measures intended to prevent births within the group;
(e) Forcibly transferring children of the group to another group.

Article 3

The following acts shall be punishable:

(a) Genocide;
(b) Conspiracy to commit genocide;
(c) Direct and public incitement to commit genocide;

(d) Attempt to commit genocide;

(e) Complicity in genocide.

Article 4
Persons committing genocide or any of the other acts enumerated in article III shall be punished, whether they are constitutionally responsible rulers, public officials or private individuals.

Article 5
The Contracting Parties undertake to enact, in accordance with their respective Constitutions, the necessary legislation to give effect to the provisions of the present Convention, and, in particular, to provide effective penalties for persons guilty of genocide or any of the other acts enumerated in article III.

Article 6
Persons charged with genocide or any of the other acts enumerated in article III shall be tried by a competent tribunal of the State in the territory of which the act was committed, or by such international penal tribunal as may have jurisdiction with respect to those Contracting Parties which shall have accepted its jurisdiction.

Article 7
Genocide and the other acts enumerated in article III shall not be considered as political crimes for the purpose of extradition.

The Contracting Parties pledge themselves in such cases to grant extradition in accordance with their laws and treaties in force.

Article 8
Any Contracting Party may call upon the competent organs of the United Nations to take such action under the Charter of the United Nations as they consider appropriate for the prevention and suppression of acts of genocide or any of the other acts enumerated in article III.

Article 9
Disputes between the Contracting Parties relating to the interpretation, application or fulfilment of the present Convention, including those relating to the responsibility of a State for genocide or for any of the other acts enumerated in article III, shall be submitted to the International Court of Justice at the request of any of the parties to the dispute.

Article 10
The present Convention, of which the Chinese, English, French, Russian and Spanish texts are equally authentic, shall bear the date of 9 December 1948.

Article 11
The present Convention shall be open until 31 December 1949 for signature on behalf of any Member of the United Nations and of any non-member State to which an invitation to sign has been addressed by the General Assembly.

The present Convention shall be ratified, and the instruments of ratification shall be deposited with the Secretary-General of the United Nations.

After 1 January 1950, the present Convention may be acceded to on behalf of any Member of the United Nations and of any non-member State which has received an invitation as aforesaid. Instruments of accession shall be deposited with the Secretary-General of the United Nations.

Article 12

Any Contracting Party may at any time, by notification addressed to the Secretary-General of the United Nations, extend the application of the present Convention to all or any of the territories for the conduct of whose foreign relations that Contracting Party is responsible.

Article 13

On the day when the first twenty instruments of ratification or accession have been deposited, the Secretary-General shall draw up a *procès-verbal* and transmit a copy thereof to each Member of the United Nations and to each of the non-member States contemplated in article 11.

The present Convention shall come into force on the ninetieth day following the date of deposit of the twentieth instrument of ratification or accession.

Any ratification or accession effected, subsequent to the latter date shall become effective on the ninetieth day following the deposit of the instrument of ratification or accession.

Article 14

The present Convention shall remain in effect for a period of ten years as from the date of its coming into force.

It shall thereafter remain in force for successive periods of five years for such Contracting Parties as have not denounced it at least six months before the expiration of the current period.

Denunciation shall be effected by a written notification addressed to the Secretary-General of the United Nations.

Article 15

If, as a result of denunciations, the number of Parties to the present Convention should become less than sixteen, the Convention shall cease to be in force as from the date on which the last of these denunciations shall become effective.

Article 16

A request for the revision of the present Convention may be made at any time by any Contracting Party by means of a notification in writing addressed to the Secretary-General.

The General Assembly shall decide upon the steps, if any, to be taken in respect of such request.

Article 17

The Secretary-General of the United Nations shall notify all Members of the United Nations and the non-member States contemplated in article XI of the following:

(a) Signatures, ratifications and accessions received in accordance with article 11;

(b) Notifications received in accordance with article 12;

(c) The date upon which the present Convention comes into force in accordance with article 13;

(d) Denunciations received in accordance with article 14;

(e) The abrogation of the Convention in accordance with article 15;

(f) Notifications received in accordance with article 16.

Article 18

The original of the present Convention shall be deposited in the archives of the United Nations.

A certified copy of the Convention shall be transmitted to each Member of the United Nations and to each of the non-member States contemplated in article XI.

Article 19

The present Convention shall be registered by the Secretary-General of the United Nations on the date of its coming into force.

1949 Geneva Conventions (excerpts) and 1977 Additional Protocol I to the 1949 Geneva Conventions (excerpts)

Geneva Convention I: for the Amelioration of the Condition of the Wounded and Sick in Armed Forces in the Field

Article 49

The High Contracting Parties undertake to enact any legislation necessary to provide effective penal sanctions for persons committing, or ordering to be committed, any of the grave breaches of the present Convention defined in the following Article.

Each High Contracting Party shall be under the obligation to search for persons alleged to have committed, or to have ordered to be committed, such grave breaches, and shall bring such persons, regardless of their nationality, before its own courts. It may also, if it prefers, and in accordance with the provisions of its own legislation, hand such persons over for trial to another High Contracting Party concerned, provided such High Contracting Party has made out a 'prima facie' case.

Each High Contracting Party shall take measures necessary for the suppression of all acts contrary to the provisions of the present Convention other than the grave breaches defined in the following Article.

In all circumstances, the accused persons shall benefit by safeguards of proper trial and defence, which shall not be less favourable than those provided by Article 105 and those following of the Geneva Convention relative to the Treatment of Prisoners of War of August 12, 1949.

Article 50

Grave breaches to which the preceding Article relates shall be those involving any of the following acts, if committed against persons or property protected by the Convention: wilful killing, torture or inhuman treatment, including biological experiments, wilfully causing great suffering or serious injury to body or health, and extensive destruction and appropriation of property, not justified by military necessity and carried out unlawfully and wantonly.

Geneva Convention II: for the Amelioration of the Condition of the Wounded and Sick and Shipwrecked Members of Armed Forces at Sea

Article 50

The High Contracting Parties undertake to enact any legislation necessary to provide effective penal sanctions for persons committing, or ordering to be committed, any of the grave breaches of the present Convention defined in the following Article.

Each High Contracting Party shall be under the obligation to search for persons alleged to have committed, or to have ordered to be committed, such grave breaches, and shall bring such persons, regardless of their nationality, before its own courts. It may also, if it prefers, and in accordance with the provisions of its own legislation, hand such persons over for trial to another High Contracting Party concerned, provided such High Contracting Party has made out a prima facie case.

Each High Contracting Party shall take measures necessary for the suppression of all acts contrary to the provisions of the present Convention other than the grave breaches defined in the following Article.

In all circumstances, the accused persons shall benefit by safeguards of proper trial and defence, which shall not be less favourable than those provided by Article 105 and those following of the Geneva Convention relative to the Treatment of Prisoners of War of August 12, 1949.

Article 51

Grave breaches to which the preceding Article relates shall be those involving any of the following acts, if committed against persons or property protected by the Convention: wilful killing, torture or inhuman treatment, including biological experiments, wilfully causing great suffering or serious injury to body or health, and extensive destruction and appropriation of property, not justified by military necessity and carried out unlawfully and wantonly.

Geneva Convention III: relative to the Treatment of Prisoners of War

Article 129

The High Contracting Parties undertake to enact any legislation necessary to provide effective penal sanctions for persons committing, or ordering to be committed, any of the grave breaches of the present Convention defined in the following Article .

Each High Contracting Party shall be under the obligation to search for persons alleged to have committed, or to have ordered to be committed, such grave breaches, and shall bring such persons, regardless of their nationality, before its own courts. It may also, if it prefers, and in accordance with the provisions of its own legislation, hand such persons over for trial to another High Contracting Party concerned, provided such High Contracting Party has made out a prima facie case.

Each High Contracting Party shall take measures necessary for the suppression of all acts contrary to the provisions of the present Convention other than the grave breaches defined in the following Article.

In all circumstances, the accused persons shall benefit by safeguards of proper trial and defence, which shall not be less favourable than those provided by Article 105 and those following of the present Convention.

Article 130

Grave breaches to which the preceding Article relates shall be those involving any of the following acts, if committed against persons or property protected by the Convention: wilful killing, torture or inhuman treatment, including biological experiments, wilfully causing great suffering or serious injury to body or health, compelling a prisoner of war to serve in the forces of the hostile Power, or wilfully depriving a prisoner of war of the rights of fair and regular trial prescribed in this Convention.

Geneva Convention IV: relative to the Protection of Civilian Persons in Time of War

Article 146
The High Contracting Parties undertake to enact any legislation necessary to provide effective penal sanctions for persons committing, or ordering to be committed, any of the grave breaches of the present Convention defined in the following Article.

Each High Contracting Party shall be under the obligation to search for persons alleged to have committed, or to have ordered to be committed, such grave breaches, and shall bring such persons, regardless of their nationality, before its own courts. It may also, if it prefers, and in accordance with the provisions of its own legislation, hand such persons over for trial to another High Contracting Party concerned, provided such High Contracting Party has made out a 'prima facie' case.

Each High Contracting Party shall take measures necessary for the suppression of all acts contrary to the provisions of the present Convention other than the grave breaches defined in the following Article.

In all circumstances, the accused persons shall benefit by safeguards of proper trial and defence, which shall not be less favourable than those provided by Article 105 and those following of the Geneva Convention relative to the Treatment of Prisoners of War of August 12, 1949.

Article 147
Grave breaches to which the preceding Article relates shall be those involving any of the following acts, if committed against persons or property protected by the present Convention: wilful killing, torture or inhuman treatment, including biological experiments, wilfully causing great suffering or serious injury to body or health, unlawful deportation or transfer or unlawful confinement of a protected person, compelling a protected person to serve in the forces of a hostile Power, or wilfully depriving a protected person of the rights of fair and regular trial prescribed in the present Convention, taking of hostages and extensive destruction and appropriation of property, not justified by military necessity and carried out unlawfully and wantonly.

1977 Protocol Additional to the Geneva Conventions of 12 August 1949, and Relating to the Protection of Victims of International Armed Conflicts (Protocol I)

Article 11
1. The physical or mental health and integrity of persons who are in the power of the adverse Party or who are interned, detained or otherwise deprived of liberty as a result of a situation referred to in Article 1 shall not be endangered by any unjustified act or omission. Accordingly, it is prohibited to subject the persons described in this Article to any medical procedure which is not indicated by the state of health of the person concerned and which is not consistent with generally accepted medical standards which would be applied under similar medical circumstances to persons who are

nationals of the Party conducting the procedure and who are in no way deprived of liberty.

2. It is, in particular, prohibited to carry out on such persons, even with their consent:
    (a) physical mutilations;
    (b) medical or scientific experiments;
    (c) removal of tissue or organs for transplantation,
    except where these acts are justified in conformity with the conditions provided for in paragraph 1.

3. Exceptions to the prohibition in paragraph 2(c) may be made only in the case of donations of blood for transfusion or of skin for grafting, provided that they are given voluntarily and without any coercion or inducement, and then only for therapeutic purposes, under conditions consistent with generally accepted medical standards and controls designed for the benefit of both the donor and the recipient.

4. Any wilful act or omission which seriously endangers the physical or mental health or integrity of any person who is in the power of a Party other than the one on which he depends and which either violates any of the prohibitions in paragraphs 1 and 2 or fails to comply with the requirements of paragraph 3 shall be a grave breach of this Protocol.

...

Article 37

1. It is prohibited to kill, injure or capture an adversary by resort to perfidy. Acts inviting the confidence of an adversary to lead him to believe that he is entitled to, or is obliged to accord, protection under the rules of international law applicable in armed conflict, with intent to betray that confidence, shall constitute perfidy. The following acts are examples of perfidy:
    (a) the feigning of an intent to negotiate under a flag of truce or of a surrender;
    (b) the feigning of an incapacitation by wounds or sickness;
    (c) the feigning of civilian, non-combatant status; and
    (d) the feigning of protected status by the use of signs, emblems or uniforms of the United Nations or of neutral or other States not Parties to the conflict.

2. Ruses of war are not prohibited. Such ruses are acts which are intended to mislead an adversary or to induce him to act recklessly but which infringe no rule of international law applicable in armed conflict and which are not perfidious because they do not invite the confidence of an adversary with respect to protection under that law. The following are examples of such ruses: the use of camouflage, decoys, mock operations and misinformation.

Article 57

...

2. With respect to attacks, the following precautions shall be taken:
    (a) those who plan or decide upon an attack shall:
        ...
        (iii) refrain from deciding to launch any attack which may be expected to cause incidental loss of civilian life, injury to civilians, damage to civilian objects,

or a combination thereof, which would be excessive in relation to the concrete and direct military advantage anticipated.

...

Article 85: Repression of Breaches of this Protocol

1. The provisions of the Conventions relating to the repression of breaches and grave breaches, supplemented by this Section, shall apply to the repression of breaches and grave breaches of this Protocol.
2. Acts described as grave breaches in the Conventions are grave breaches of this Protocol if committed against persons in the power of an adverse Party protected by Articles 44, 45 and 73 of this Protocol, or against the wounded, sick and shipwrecked of the adverse Party who are protected by this Protocol, or against those medical or religious personnel, medical units or medical transports which are under the control of the adverse Party and are protected by this Protocol.
3. In addition to the grave breaches defined in Article 11, the following acts shall be regarded as grave breaches of this Protocol, when committed wilfully, in violation of the relevant provisions of this Protocol, and causing death or serious injury to body or health:
   (a) making the civilian population or individual civilians the object of attack;
   (b) launching an indiscriminate attack affecting the civilian population or civilian objects in the knowledge that such attack will cause excessive loss of life, injury to civilians or damage to civilian objects, as defined in Article 57, paragraph 2(a)(iii);
   (c) launching an attack against works or installations containing dangerous forces in the knowledge that such attack will cause excessive loss of life, injury to civilians or damage to civilian objects, as defined in Article 57, paragraph 2(a)(iii);
   (d) making non-defended localities and demilitarized zones the object of attack;
   (e) making a person the object of attack in the knowledge that he is 'hors de combat';
   (f) the perfidious use, in violation of Article 37, of the distinctive emblem of the red cross, red crescent or red lion and sun or of other protective signs recognized by the Conventions or this Protocol.
4. In addition to the grave breaches defined in the preceding paragraphs and in the Conventions, the following shall be regarded as grave breaches of this Protocol, when committed wilfully and in violation of the Conventions or the Protocol:
   (a) the transfer by the Occupying Power of parts of its own civilian population into the territory it occupies, or the deportation or transfer of all or parts of the population of the occupied territory within or outside this territory, in violation of Article 49 of the Fourth Convention;
   (b) unjustifiable delay in the repatriation of prisoners of war or civilians;
   (c) practices of 'apartheid' and other inhuman and degrading practices involving outrages upon personal dignity, based on racial discrimination;
   (d) making the clearly-recognized historic monuments, works of art or places of worship which constitute the cultural or spiritual heritage of peoples and to which special protection has been given by special arrangement, for example, within the framework of a competent international organization, the object of attack, causing as a result extensive destruction thereof, where there is no evidence of the violation by the adverse Party of Article 53, sub-paragraph (b), and when such historic

6

monuments, works of art and places of worship are not located in the immediate proximity of military objectives;

(e) depriving a person protected by the Conventions or referred to in paragraph 2 of this Article of the rights of fair and regular trial.

5. Without prejudice to the application of the Conventions and of this Protocol, grave breaches of these instruments shall be regarded as war crimes.

Article 86

1. The High Contracting Parties and the Parties to the conflict shall repress grave breaches, and take measures necessary to suppress all other breaches, of the Conventions or of this Protocol which result from a failure to act when under a duty to do so.

2. The fact that a breach of the Conventions or of this Protocol was committed by a subordinate does not absolve his superiors from penal or disciplinary responsibility, as the case may be, if they knew, or had information which should have enabled them to conclude in the circumstances at the time, that he was committing or was going to commit such a breach and if they did not take all feasible measures within their power to prevent or repress the breach.

Article 87

1. The High Contracting Parties and the Parties to the conflict shall require military commanders, with respect to members of the armed forces under their command and other persons under their control, to prevent and, where necessary, to suppress and to report to competent authorities breaches of the Conventions and of this Protocol.

2. In order to prevent and suppress breaches, High Contracting Parties and Parties to the conflict shall require that, commensurate with their level of responsibility, commanders ensure that members of the armed forces under their command are aware of their obligations under the Conventions and this Protocol.

3. The High Contracting Parties and Parties to the conflict shall require any commander who is aware that subordinates or other persons under his control are going to commit or have committed a breach of the Conventions or of this Protocol, to initiate such steps as are necessary to prevent such violations of the Conventions or this Protocol, and, where appropriate, to initiate disciplinary or penal action against violators thereof.

...

1968 Convention on the Non-applicability of Statutory Limitations to War Crimes and Crimes against Humanity

Convention on the Non-Applicability of Statutory Limitations to War Crimes and Crimes against Humanity Adopted and Opened for Signature, Ratification and Accession by General Assembly Resolution 2391 (XXIII) of 26 November 1968

Preamble

The States Parties to the present Convention,

Recalling resolutions of the General Assembly of the United Nations 3 (I) of 13 February 1946 and 170 (II) of 31 October 1947 on the extradition and punishment of war criminals, resolution 95 (I) of 11 December 1946 affirming the principles of international law recognized by the Charter of the International Military Tribunal, Nürnberg, and the judgement of the Tribunal, and resolutions 2184 (XXI) of 12 December 1966 and 2202 (XXI) of 16 December 1966 which expressly condemned as crimes against humanity the violation of the economic and political rights of the indigenous population on the one hand and the policies of apartheid on the other,

Recalling resolutions of the Economic and Social Council of the United Nations 1074 D (XXXIX) of 28 July 1965 and 1158 (XLI) of 5 August 1966 on the punishment of war criminals and of persons who have committed crimes against humanity,

Noting that none of the solemn declarations, instruments or conventions relating to the prosecution and punishment of war crimes and crimes against humanity made provision for a period of limitation,

Considering that war crimes and crimes against humanity are among the gravest crimes in international law,

Convinced that the effective punishment of war crimes and crimes against humanity is an important element in the prevention of such crimes, the protection of human rights and fundamental freedoms, the encouragement of confidence, the furtherance of co-operation among peoples and the promotion of international peace and security,

Noting that the application to war crimes and crimes against humanity of the rules of municipal law relating to the period of limitation for ordinary crimes is a matter of serious concern to world public opinion, since it prevents the prosecution and punishment of persons responsible for those crimes,

Recognizing that it is necessary and timely to affirm in international law, through this Convention, the principle that there is no period of limitation for war crimes and crimes against humanity, and to secure its universal application,

Have agreed as follows:

Article I

No statutory limitation shall apply to the following crimes, irrespective of the date of their commission:

(a) War crimes as they are defined in the Charter of the International Military Tribunal, Nürnberg, of 8 August 1945 and confirmed by resolutions 3 (I) of 13 February 1946 and 95 (I) of 11 December 1946 of the General Assembly of the United Nations, particularly the "grave breaches" enumerated in the Geneva Conventions of 12 August 1949 for the protection of war victims;

(b) Crimes against humanity whether committed in time of war or in time of peace as they are defined in the Charter of the International Military Tribunal, Nürnberg, of 8 August 1945 and confirmed by resolutions 3 (I) of 13 February 1946 and 95 (I) of 11 December 1946 of the General Assembly of the United Nations, eviction by armed attack or occupation and inhuman acts resulting from the policy of apartheid, and the crime of genocide as defined in the 1948 Convention on the Prevention and Punishment of the Crime of Genocide, even if such acts do not constitute a violation of the domestic law of the country in which they were committed.

Article II

If any of the crimes mentioned in article I is committed, the provisions of this Convention shall apply to representatives of the State authority and private individuals who, as principals or accomplices, participate in or who directly incite others to the commission of any of those crimes, or who conspire to commit them, irrespective of the degree of completion, and to representatives of the State authority who tolerate their commission.

Article III

The States Parties to the present Convention undertake to adopt all necessary domestic measures, legislative or otherwise, with a view to making possible the extradition, in accordance with international law, of the persons referred to in article II of this Convention.

Article IV

The States Parties to the present Convention undertake to adopt, in accordance with their respective constitutional processes, any legislative or other measures necessary to ensure that statutory or other limitations shall not apply to the prosecution and punishment of the crimes referred to in articles I and II of this Convention and that, where they exist, such limitations shall be abolished.

Article V

This Convention shall, until 31 December 1969, be open for signature by any State Member of the United Nations or member of any of its specialized agencies or of the International Atomic Energy Agency, by any State Party to the Statute of the International Court of Justice, and by any other State which has been invited by the General Assembly of the United Nations to become a Party to this Convention.

Article VI

This Convention is subject to ratification. Instruments of ratification shall be deposited with the Secretary-General of the United Nations.

Article VII

This Convention shall be open to accession by any State referred to in article V. Instruments of accession shall be deposited with the Secretary-General of the United Nations.

Article VIII

1. This Convention shall enter into force on the ninetieth day after the date of the deposit with the Secretary-General of the United Nations of the tenth instrument of ratification or accession.
2. For each State ratifying this Convention or acceding to it after the deposit of the tenth instrument of ratification or accession, the Convention shall enter into force on the ninetieth day after the date of the deposit of its own instrument of ratification or accession.

Article IX

1. After the expiry of a period of ten years from the date on which this Convention enters into force, a request for the revision of the Convention may be made at any time by any Contracting Party by means of a notification in writing addressed to the Secretary-General of the United Nations.
2. The General Assembly of the United Nations shall decide upon the steps, if any, to be taken in respect of such a request.

Article X

1. This Convention shall be deposited with the Secretary-General of the United Nations.
2. The Secretary-General of the United Nations shall transmit certified copies of this Convention to all States referred to in article V.
3. The Secretary-General of the United Nations shall inform all States referred to in article V of the following particulars:
   (a) Signatures of this Convention, and instruments of ratification and accession deposited under articles V, VI and VII;
   (b) The date of entry into force of this Convention in accordance with article VIII;
   (c) Communications received under article IX.

Article XI

This Convention, of which the Chinese, English, French, Russian and Spanish texts are equally authentic, shall bear the date of 26 November 1968.

In witness whereof the undersigned, being duly authorized for that purpose, have signed this Convention.

1973 International Convention on the Suppression and Punishment of the Crime of *Apartheid*

International Convention on the Suppression and Punishment of the Crime of *Apartheid*

The States Parties to the present Convention,

Recalling the provisions of the Charter of the United Nations, in which all Members pledged themselves to take joint and separate action in co-operation with the Organization for the achievement of universal respect for, and observance of, human rights and fundamental freedoms for all without distinction as to race, sex, language or religion,

Considering the Universal Declaration of Human Rights, which states that all human beings are born free and equal in dignity and rights and that everyone is entitled to all the rights and freedoms set forth in the Declaration, without distinction of any kind, such as race, colour or national origin,

Considering the Declaration on the Granting of Independence to Colonial Countries and Peoples, in which the General Assembly stated that the process of liberation is irresistible and irreversible and that, in the interests of human dignity, progress and justice, an end must be put to colonialism and all practices of segregation and discrimination associated therewith,

Observing that, in accordance with the International Convention on the Elimination of All Forms of Racial Discrimination, States particularly condemn racial segregation and *apartheid* and undertake to prevent, prohibit and eradicate all practices of this nature in territories under their jurisdiction,

Observing that, in the Convention on the Prevention and Punishment of the Crime of Genocide, certain acts which may also be qualified as acts of *apartheid* constitute a crime under international law,

Observing that, in the Convention on the non-applicability of statutory limitations to war crimes and crimes against humanity, "inhuman acts resulting from the policy of *apartheid*" are qualified as crimes against humanity,

Observing that the General Assembly of the United Nations has adopted a number of resolutions in which the policies and practices of *apartheid* are condemned as a crime against humanity,

Observing that the Security Council has emphasized that *apartheid* and its continued intensification and expansion seriously disturb and threaten international peace and security,

Convinced that an International Convention on the Suppression and Punishment of the Crime of *Apartheid* would make it possible to take more effective measures at the international and national levels with a view to the suppression and punishment of the crime of *apartheid*,

Have agreed as follows:

Article I

1. The States Parties to the present Convention declare that *apartheid* is a crime against humanity and that inhuman acts resulting from the policies and practices of *apartheid* and similar policies and practices of racial segregation and discrimination, as defined in article II of the Convention, are crimes violating the principles of international law, in particular the purposes and principles of the Charter of the United Nations, and constituting a serious threat to international peace and security.
2. The States Parties to the present Convention declare criminal those organizations, institutions and individuals committing the crime of *apartheid*.

Article II

For the purpose of the present Convention, the term "the crime of *apartheid*", which shall include similar policies and practices of racial segregation and discrimination as practised in southern Africa, shall apply to the following inhuman acts committed for the purpose of establishing and maintaining domination by one racial group of persons over any other racial group of persons and systematically oppressing them:

(a) denial to a member or members of a racial group or groups of the right to life and liberty of person:
  (i) by murder of members of a racial group or groups;
  (ii) by the infliction upon the members of a racial group or groups of serious bodily or mental harm, by the infringement of their freedom or dignity, or by subjecting them to torture or to cruel, inhuman or degrading treatment or punishment;
  (iii) by arbitrary arrest and illegal imprisonment of the members of a racial group or groups;
(b) deliberate imposition on a racial group or groups of living conditions calculated to cause its or their physical destruction in whole or in part;
(c) any legislative measures and other measures calculated to prevent a racial group or groups from participation in the political, social, economic and cultural life of the country and the deliberate creation of conditions preventing the full development of such a group or groups, in particular by denying to members of a racial group or groups basic human rights and freedoms, including the right to work, the right to form recognized trade unions, the right to education, the right to leave and to return to their country, the right to a nationality, the right to freedom of movement and residence, the right to freedom of opinion and expression, and the right to freedom of peaceful assembly and association;
(d) any measures, including legislative measures, designed to divide the population along racial lines by the creation of separate reserves and ghettos for the members of

a racial group or groups, the prohibition of mixed marriages among members of various racial groups, the expropriation of landed property belonging to a racial group or groups or to members thereof;

(e) exploitation of the labour of the members of a racial group or groups, in particular by submitting them to forced labour;

(f) persecution of organizations and persons, by depriving them of fundamental rights and freedoms, because they oppose *apartheid*.

Article III

International criminal responsibility shall apply, irrespective of the motive involved, to individuals, members of organizations and institutions and representatives of the State, whether residing in the territory of the State in which the acts are perpetrated or in some other State, whenever they:

(a) commit, participate in, directly incite or conspire in the commission of the acts mentioned in article II of the present Convention;

(b) directly abet, encourage or co-operate in the commission of the crime of *apartheid*.

Article IV

The State Parties to the present Convention undertake:

(a) to adopt any legislative or other measures necessary to suppress as well as to prevent any encouragement of the crime of *apartheid* and similar segregationist policies or their manifestations and to punish persons guilty of that crime;

(b) to adopt legislative, judicial and administrative measures to prosecute, bring to trial and punish in accordance with their jurisdiction persons responsible for, or accused of, the acts defined in article II of the present Convention, whether or not such persons reside in the territory of the State in which the acts are committed or are nationals of that State or of some other State or are stateless persons.

Article V

Persons charged with the acts enumerated in article II of the present Convention may be tried by a competent tribunal of any State Party to the Convention which may acquire jurisdiction over the person of the accused or by an international penal tribunal having jurisdiction with respect to those States Parties which shall have accepted its jurisdiction.

Article VI

The States Parties to the present Convention undertake to accept and carry out in accordance with the Charter of the United Nations the decisions taken by the Security Council aimed at the prevention, suppression and punishment of the crime of *apartheid*, and to co-operate in the implementation of decisions adopted by other competent organs of the United Nations with a view to achieving the purposes of the Convention.

Article VII

1. The States Parties to the present Convention undertake to submit periodic reports to the group established under article IX on the legislative, judicial, administrative or other measures that they have adopted and that give effect to the provisions of the Convention.

2. Copies of the reports shall be transmitted through the Secretary-General of the United Nations to the Special Committee on *Apartheid*.

Article VIII

Any State Party to the present Convention may call upon any competent organ of the United Nations to take such action under the Charter of the United Nations as it considers appropriate for the prevention and suppression of the crime of *apartheid*.

Article IX

1. The Chairman of the Commission on Human Rights shall appoint a group consisting of three members of the Commission on Human Rights, who are also representatives of States Parties to the present Convention, to consider reports submitted by States Parties in accordance with article VII.
2. If, among the members of the Commission on Human Rights, there are no representatives of States Parties to the present Convention or if there are fewer than three such representatives, the Secretary-General of the United Nations shall, after consulting all States Parties to the Convention, designate a representative of the State Party or representatives of the States Parties which are not members of the Commission on Human Rights to take part in the work of the group established in accordance with paragraph 1 of this article, until such time as representatives of the States Parties to the Convention are elected to the Commission on Human Rights.
3. The group may meet for a period of not more than five days, either before the opening or after the closing of the session of the Commission on Human Rights, to consider the reports submitted in accordance with article VII.

Article X

1. The States Parties to the present Convention empower the Commission on Human Rights:
   (a) to request United Nations organs, when transmitting copies of petitions under article 15 of the International Convention on the Elimination of All Forms of Racial Discrimination, to draw its attention to complaints concerning acts which are enumerated in article II of the present Convention;
   (b) to prepare, on the basis of reports from competent organs of the United Nations and periodic reports from States Parties to the present Convention, a list of individuals, organizations, institutions and representatives of States which are alleged to be responsible for the crimes enumerated in article II of the Convention, as well as those against whom legal proceedings have been undertaken by States Parties to the Convention;
   (c) to request information from the competent United Nations organs concerning measures taken by the authorities responsible for the administration of Trust and Non-Self-Governing Territories, and all other Territories to which General Assembly resolution 1514 (XV) of 14 December 1960 applies, with regard to such individuals alleged to be responsible for crimes under article II of the Convention who are believed to be under their territorial and administrative jurisdiction.
2. Pending the achievement of the objectives of the Declaration on the Granting of Independence to Colonial Countries and Peoples, contained in General Assembly

resolution 1514 (XV), the provisions of the present Convention shall in no way limit the right of petition granted to those peoples by other international instruments or by the United Nations and its specialized agencies.

Article XI

1. Acts enumerated in article II of the present Convention shall not be considered political crimes for the purpose of extradition.
2. The States Parties to the present Convention undertake in such cases to grant extradition in accordance with their legislation and with the treaties in force.

Article XII

Disputes between States Parties arising out of the interpretation, application or implementation of the present Convention which have not been settled by negotiation shall, at the request of the States Parties to the dispute, be brought before the International Court of Justice, save where the parties to the dispute have agreed on some other form of settlement.

Article XIII

The present Convention is open for signature by all States. Any State which does not sign the Convention before its entry into force may accede to it.

Article XIV

1. The present Convention is subject to ratification. Instruments of ratification shall be deposited with the Secretary-General of the United Nations.
2. Accession shall be effected by the deposit of an instrument of accession with the Secretary-General of the United Nations.

Article XV

1. The present Convention shall enter into force on the thirtieth day after the date of the deposit with the Secretary-General of the United Nations of the twentieth instrument of ratification or accession.
2. For each State ratifying the present Convention or acceding to it after the deposit of the twentieth instrument of ratification or instrument of accession, the Convention shall enter into force on the thirtieth day after the date of the deposit of its own instrument of ratification or instrument of accession.

Article XVI

A State Party may denounce the present Convention by written notification to the Secretary-General of the United Nations. Denunciation shall take effect one year after the date of receipt of the notification by the Secretary-General.

Article XVII

1. A request for the revision of the present Convention may be made at any time by any State Party by means of a notification in writing addressed to the Secretary-General of the United Nations.

2. The General Assembly of the United Nations shall decide upon the steps, if any, to be taken in respect of such request.

Article XVIII

The Secretary-General of the United Nations shall inform all States of the following particulars:

(a) signatures, ratifications and accessions under articles XIII and XIV;

(b) the date of entry into force of the present Convention under article XV;

(c) denunciations under article XVI;

(d) notifications under article XVII.

Article XIX

1. The present Convention, of which the Chinese, English, French, Russian and Spanish texts are equally authentic, shall be deposited in the archives of the United Nations.

2. The Secretary-General of the United Nations shall transmit certified copies of the present Convention to all States

1974 Definition of Aggression
(General Assembly Resolution No. 3314)

The General Assembly,

Having considered the report of the Special Committee on the Question of Defining Aggression, established pursuant to its resolution 2330(XXII) of 18 December 1967, covering the work of its seventh session held from 11 March to 12 April 1974, including the draft Definition of Aggression adopted by the Special Committee by consensus and recommended for adoption by the General Assembly,

Deeply, convinced that the adoption of the Definition of Aggression would contribute to the strengthening of international peace and security,

1. Approves the Definition of Aggression, the text of which is annexed to the present resolution;

2. Expresses its appreciation to the Special Committee on the Question of Defining Aggression for its work which resulted in the elaboration of the Definition of Aggression;

3. Calls upon all States to refrain from all acts of aggression and other uses of force contrary to the Charter of the United Nations and the Declaration on Principles of International Law concerning Friendly Relations and Cooperation among States in accordance with the Charter of the United Nations;

4. Calls the attention of the Security Council to the Definition of Aggression, as set out below, and recommends that it should, as appropriate, take account of that Definition as guidance in determination, in accordance with the Charter, the existence of an act of aggression.

2319th plenary meeting
14 December 1974

ANNEX

Definition of Aggression

The General Assembly,

Basing itself on the fact that one of the fundamental purposes of the United Nations is to maintain international peace and security and to take effective collective measures for the prevention and removal of threats to the peace, and for the suppression of acts of aggression or other breaches of the peace,

Recalling that the Security Council, in accordance with Article 39 of the Charter of the United Nations, shall determine the existence of any threat to the peace, breach of the peace or act of aggression and shall make recommendations, or decide what measures shall be taken in accordance with Articles 41 and 42, to maintain or restore international peace and security,

Recalling also the duty of States under the Charter to settle their international disputes by peaceful means in order not to endanger international peace, security and justice,

Bearing in mind that nothing in this Definition shall be interpreted as in any way affecting the scope of the provisions of the Charter with respect to the functions and powers of the organs of the United Nations,

Considering also that, since aggression is the most serious and dangerous form of the illegal use of force, being fraught, in the conditions created by the existence of all types of weapons of mass destruction, with the possible threat of a world conflict and all its catastrophic consequences, aggression should be defined at the present stage,

Reaffirming the duty of States not to use armed force to deprive peoples of their right to self-determination, freedom and independence, or to disrupt territorial Integrity,

Reaffirming also that the territory of a State shall not be violated by being the object, even temporarily, of military occupation or of other measures of force taken by another State in contravention of the Charter, and that it shall not be the object of acquisition by another State resulting from such measures or the threat thereof,

Reaffirming also the provisions of the Declaration on Principles of International Law concerning Friendly Relations and Cooperation among States in accordance with the Charter of the United Nations,

Convinced that the adoption of a definition of aggression ought to have the effect of deterring a potential aggressor, would simplify the determination of acts of aggression and the implementation of measures to suppress them and would also facilitate the protection of the rights and lawful interests of, and the rendering of assistance to, the victim,

Believing that, although the question whether an act of aggression has been committed must be considered in the light of all the circumstances of each particular case, it is nevertheless desirable to formulate basic principles as guidance for such determination,

Adopts the following Definition of Aggression:

Article I

Aggression is the use of armed force by a State against the sovereignty, territorial integrity or political independence of another State, or in any other manner inconsistent with the Charter of the United Nations, as set out in this Definition.

Explanatory note: In this Definition the term "State":

(a) Is used without prejudice to questions of recognition or to whether a State is a member of the United Nations;

(b) Includes the concept of a "group of States" where appropriate.

Article 2

The First use of armed force by a State in contravention of the Charter shall constitute prima facie evidence of an act of aggression although the Security Council may, in conformity with the Charter, conclude that a determination that an act of aggression has been committed would not be justified in the light of other relevant circumstances, including the fact that the acts concerned or their consequences are not of sufficient gravity.

Article 3

Any of the following acts, regardless of a declaration of war, shall, subject to and in accordance with the provisions of article 2, qualify as an act of aggression:

(a) The invasion or attack by the armed forces of a State of the territory of another State, or any military occupation, however temporary, resulting from such invasion or attack, or any annexation by the use of force of the territory of another State or part thereof,

(b) Bombardment by the armed forces of a State against the territory of another State or the use of any weapons by a State against the territory of another State;

(c) The blockade of the ports or coasts of a State by the armed forces of another State;

(d) An attack by the armed forces of a State on the land, sea or air forces, or marine and air fleets of another State;

(e) The use of armed forces of one State which are within the territory of another State with the agreement of the receiving State, in contravention of the conditions provided for in the agreement or any extension of their presence in such territory beyond the termination of the agreement;

(f) The action of a State in allowing its territory, which it has placed at the disposal of another State, to be used by that other State for perpetrating an act of aggression against a third State;

(g) The sending by or on behalf of a State of armed bands, groups, irregulars or mercenaries, which carry out acts of armed force against another State of such gravity as to amount to the acts listed above, or its substantial involvement therein.

Article 4

The acts enumerated above are not exhaustive and the Security Council may determine that other acts constitute aggression under the provisions of the Charter.

Article 5

1. No consideration of whatever nature, whether political, economic, military or otherwise, may serve as a justification for aggression.

2. A war of aggression is a crime against international peace. Aggression gives rise to international responsibility.

3. No territorial acquisition or special advantage resulting from aggression is or shall be recognized as lawful.

Article 6

Nothing in this Definition shall be construed as in any way enlarging or diminishing the scope of the Charter, including its provisions concerning cases in which the use of force is lawful.

Article 7

Nothing in this Definition, and in particular article 3, could in any way prejudice the right to self-determination, freedom and independence, as derived from the Charter, of peoples forcibly deprived of that right and referred to in the Declaration on Principles of International Law concerning Friendly Relations and Cooperation among States in accordance with the Charter of the United Nations, particularly peoples under colonial and racist regimes or other forms of alien domination: nor the right of these peoples to struggle to that end and to seek and receive support, in accordance with the principles of the Charter and in conformity with the above-mentioned Declaration.

Article 8
In their interpretation and application the above provisions are interrelated and each provision should be construed in the context of the other provisions.

1984 UN Convention against Torture

Convention against Torture and Other Cruel, Inhuman or Degrading Treatment or Punishment
Adopted and opened for signature, ratification and accession by General Assembly resolution 39/46 of 10 December 1984

The States Parties to this Convention,

Considering that, in accordance with the principles proclaimed in the Charter of the United Nations, recognition of the equal and inalienable rights of all members of the human family is the foundation of freedom, justice and peace in the world,

Recognizing that those rights derive from the inherent dignity of the human person,

Considering the obligation of States under the Charter, in particular Article 55, to promote universal respect for, and observance of, human rights and fundamental freedoms,

Having regard to article 5 of the Universal Declaration of Human Rights and article 7 of the International Covenant on Civil and Political Rights, both of which provide that no one shall be subjected to torture or to cruel, inhuman or degrading treatment or punishment,

Having regard also to the Declaration on the Protection of All Persons from Being Subjected to Torture and Other Cruel, Inhuman or Degrading Treatment or Punishment, adopted by the General Assembly on 9 December 1975,

Desiring to make more effective the struggle against torture and other cruel, inhuman or degrading treatment or punishment throughout the world,

Have agreed as follows:

PART I

Article 1

1. For the purposes of this Convention, the term "torture" means any act by which severe pain or suffering, whether physical or mental, is intentionally inflicted on a person for such purposes as obtaining from him or a third person information or a confession, punishing him for an act he or a third person has committed or is suspected of having committed, or intimidating or coercing him or a third person, or for any reason based on discrimination of any kind, when such pain or suffering is inflicted by or at the instigation of or with the consent or acquiescence of a public official or other person acting in an official capacity. It does not include pain or suffering arising only from, inherent in or incidental to lawful sanctions.

2. This article is without prejudice to any international instrument or national legislation which does or may contain provisions of wider application.

Article 2

1. Each State Party shall take effective legislative, administrative, judicial or other measures to prevent acts of torture in any territory under its jurisdiction.
2. No exceptional circumstances whatsoever, whether a state of war or a threat of war, internal political instability or any other public emergency, may be invoked as a justification of torture.
3. An order from a superior officer or a public authority may not be invoked as a justification of torture.

Article 3

1. No State Party shall expel, return ("refouler") or extradite a person to another State where there are substantial grounds for believing that he would be in danger of being subjected to torture.
2. For the purpose of determining whether there are such grounds, the competent authorities shall take into account all relevant considerations including, where applicable, the existence in the State concerned of a consistent pattern of gross, flagrant or mass violations of human rights.

Article 4

1. Each State Party shall ensure that all acts of torture are offences under its criminal law. The same shall apply to an attempt to commit torture and to an act by any person which constitutes complicity or participation in torture.
2. Each State Party shall make these offences punishable by appropriate penalties which take into account their grave nature.

Article 5

1. Each State Party shall take such measures as may be necessary to establish its jurisdiction over the offences referred to in article 4 in the following cases:
   (a) When the offences are committed in any territory under its jurisdiction or on board a ship or aircraft registered in that State;
   (b) When the alleged offender is a national of that State;
   (c) When the victim is a national of that State if that State considers it appropriate.
2. Each State Party shall likewise take such measures as may be necessary to establish its jurisdiction over such offences in cases where the alleged offender is present in any territory under its jurisdiction and it does not extradite him pursuant to article 8 to any of the States mentioned in paragraph 1 of this article.
3. This Convention does not exclude any criminal jurisdiction exercised in accordance with internal law.

Article 6

1. Upon being satisfied, after an examination of information available to it, that the circumstances so warrant, any State Party in whose territory a person alleged to have committed any offence referred to in article 4 is present shall take him into custody or

10

take other legal measures to ensure his presence. The custody and other legal measures shall be as provided in the law of that State but may be continued only for such time as is necessary to enable any criminal or extradition proceedings to be instituted.

2. Such State shall immediately make a preliminary inquiry into the facts.

3. Any person in custody pursuant to paragraph 1 of this article shall be assisted in communicating immediately with the nearest appropriate representative of the State of which he is a national, or, if he is a stateless person, with the representative of the State where he usually resides.

4. When a State, pursuant to this article, has taken a person into custody, it shall immediately notify the States referred to in article 5, paragraph 1, of the fact that such person is in custody and of the circumstances which warrant his detention. The State which makes the preliminary inquiry contemplated in paragraph 2 of this article shall promptly report its findings to the said States and shall indicate whether it intends to exercise jurisdiction.

Article 7

1. The State Party in the territory under whose jurisdiction a person alleged to have committed any offence referred to in article 4 is found shall in the cases contemplated in article 5, if it does not extradite him, submit the case to its competent authorities for the purpose of prosecution.

2. These authorities shall take their decision in the same manner as in the case of any ordinary offence of a serious nature under the law of that State. In the cases referred to in article 5, paragraph 2, the standards of evidence required for prosecution and conviction shall in no way be less stringent than those which apply in the cases referred to in article 5, paragraph 1.

3. Any person regarding whom proceedings are brought in connection with any of the offences referred to in article 4 shall be guaranteed fair treatment at all stages of the proceedings.

Article 8

1. The offences referred to in article 4 shall be deemed to be included as extraditable offences in any extradition treaty existing between States Parties. States Parties undertake to include such offences as extraditable offences in every extradition treaty to be concluded between them.

2. If a State Party which makes extradition conditional on the existence of a treaty receives a request for extradition from another State Party with which it has no extradition treaty, it may consider this Convention as the legal basis for extradition in respect of such offences. Extradition shall be subject to the other conditions provided by the law of the requested State.

3. States Parties which do not make extradition conditional on the existence of a treaty shall recognize such offences as extraditable offences between themselves subject to the conditions provided by the law of the requested State.

4. Such offences shall be treated, for the purpose of extradition between States Parties, as if they had been committed not only in the place in which they occurred but also in the territories of the States required to establish their jurisdiction in accordance with article 5, paragraph 1.

Article 9

1. States Parties shall afford one another the greatest measure of assistance in connection with criminal proceedings brought in respect of any of the offences referred to in article 4, including the supply of all evidence at their disposal necessary for the proceedings.
2. States Parties shall carry out their obligations under paragraph 1 of this article in conformity with any treaties on mutual judicial assistance that may exist between them.

Article 10

1. Each State Party shall ensure that education and information regarding the prohibition against torture are fully included in the training of law enforcement personnel, civil or military, medical personnel, public officials and other persons who may be involved in the custody, interrogation or treatment of any individual subjected to any form of arrest, detention or imprisonment.
2. Each State Party shall include this prohibition in the rules or instructions issued in regard to the duties and functions of any such person.

Article 11

Each State Party shall keep under systematic review interrogation rules, instructions, methods and practices as well as arrangements for the custody and treatment of persons subjected to any form of arrest, detention or imprisonment in any territory under its jurisdiction, with a view to preventing any cases of torture.

Article 12

Each State Party shall ensure that its competent authorities proceed to a prompt and impartial investigation, wherever there is reasonable ground to believe that an act of torture has been committed in any territory under its jurisdiction.

Article 13

Each State Party shall ensure that any individual who alleges he has been subjected to torture in any territory under its jurisdiction has the right to complain to, and to have his case promptly and impartially examined by, its competent authorities. Steps shall be taken to ensure that the complainant and witnesses are protected against all ill-treatment or intimidation as a consequence of his complaint or any evidence given.

Article 14

1. Each State Party shall ensure in its legal system that the victim of an act of torture obtains redress and has an enforceable right to fair and adequate compensation, including the means for as full rehabilitation as possible. In the event of the death of the victim as a result of an act of torture, his dependants shall be entitled to compensation.
2. Nothing in this article shall affect any right of the victim or other persons to compensation which may exist under national law.

Article 15

Each State Party shall ensure that any statement which is established to have been made as a result of torture shall not be invoked as evidence in any proceedings, except against a person accused of torture as evidence that the statement was made.

Article 16

1. Each State Party shall undertake to prevent in any territory under its jurisdiction other acts of cruel, inhuman or degrading treatment or punishment which do not amount to torture as defined in article I, when such acts are committed by or at the instigation of or with the consent or acquiescence of a public official or other person acting in an official capacity. In particular, the obligations contained in articles 10, 11, 12 and 13 shall apply with the substitution for references to torture of references to other forms of cruel, inhuman or degrading treatment or punishment.

2. The provisions of this Convention are without prejudice to the provisions of any other international instrument or national law which prohibits cruel, inhuman or degrading treatment or punishment or which relates to extradition or expulsion.

PART II

Article 17

1. There shall be established a Committee against Torture (hereinafter referred to as the Committee) which shall carry out the functions hereinafter provided. The Committee shall consist of ten experts of high moral standing and recognized competence in the field of human rights, who shall serve in their personal capacity. The experts shall be elected by the States Parties, consideration being given to equitable geographical distribution and to the usefulness of the participation of some persons having legal experience.

2. The members of the Committee shall be elected by secret ballot from a list of persons nominated by States Parties. Each State Party may nominate one person from among its own nationals. States Parties shall bear in mind the usefulness of nominating persons who are also members of the Human Rights Committee established under the International Covenant on Civil and Political Rights and who are willing to serve on the Committee against Torture.

3. Elections of the members of the Committee shall be held at biennial meetings of States Parties convened by the Secretary-General of the United Nations. At those meetings, for which two thirds of the States Parties shall constitute a quorum, the persons elected to the Committee shall be those who obtain the largest number of votes and an absolute majority of the votes of the representatives of States Parties present and voting.

4. The initial election shall be held no later than six months after the date of the entry into force of this Convention. At least four months before the date of each election, the Secretary-General of the United Nations shall address a letter to the States Parties inviting them to submit their nominations within three months. The Secretary-General shall prepare a list in alphabetical order of all persons thus nominated, indicating the States Parties which have nominated them, and shall submit it to the States Parties.

5. The members of the Committee shall be elected for a term of four years. They shall be eligible for re-election if renominated. However, the term of five of the members elected at the first election shall expire at the end of two years; immediately after the first election the names of these five members shall be chosen by lot by the chairman of the meeting referred to in paragraph 3 of this article.

6. If a member of the Committee dies or resigns or for any other cause can no longer perform his Committee duties, the State Party which nominated him shall appoint another expert from among its nationals to serve for the remainder of his term, subject to the approval of the majority of the States Parties. The approval shall be considered given unless half or more of the States Parties respond negatively within six weeks after having been informed by the Secretary-General of the United Nations of the proposed appointment.

7. States Parties shall be responsible for the expenses of the members of the Committee while they are in performance of Committee duties.

Article 18

1. The Committee shall elect its officers for a term of two years. They may be re-elected.
2. The Committee shall establish its own rules of procedure, but these rules shall provide, inter alia, that:
   (a) Six members shall constitute a quorum;
   (b) Decisions of the Committee shall be made by a majority vote of the members present.
3. The Secretary-General of the United Nations shall provide the necessary staff and facilities for the effective performance of the functions of the Committee under this Convention.
4. The Secretary-General of the United Nations shall convene the initial meeting of the Committee. After its initial meeting, the Committee shall meet at such times as shall be provided in its rules of procedure.
5. The States Parties shall be responsible for expenses incurred in connection with the holding of meetings of the States Parties and of the Committee, including reimbursement to the United Nations for any expenses, such as the cost of staff and facilities, incurred by the United Nations pursuant to paragraph 3 of this article.

Article 19

1. The States Parties shall submit to the Committee, through the Secretary-General of the United Nations, reports on the measures they have taken to give effect to their undertakings under this Convention, within one year after the entry into force of the Convention for the State Party concerned. Thereafter the States Parties shall submit supplementary reports every four years on any new measures taken and such other reports as the Committee may request.
2. The Secretary-General of the United Nations shall transmit the reports to all States Parties.
3. Each report shall be considered by the Committee which may make such general comments on the report as it may consider appropriate and shall forward these to the State Party concerned. That State Party may respond with any observations it chooses to the Committee.
4. The Committee may, at its discretion, decide to include any comments made by it in accordance with paragraph 3 of this article, together with the observations thereon received from the State Party concerned, in its annual report made in accordance with article 24. If so requested by the State Party concerned, the Committee may also include a copy of the report submitted under paragraph 1 of this article.

10

Article 20

1. If the Committee receives reliable information which appears to it to contain well-founded indications that torture is being systematically practised in the territory of a State Party, the Committee shall invite that State Party to co-operate in the examination of the information and to this end to submit observations with regard to the information concerned.

2. Taking into account any observations which may have been submitted by the State Party concerned, as well as any other relevant information available to it, the Committee may, if it decides that this is warranted, designate one or more of its members to make a confidential inquiry and to report to the Committee urgently.

3. If an inquiry is made in accordance with paragraph 2 of this article, the Committee shall seek the co-operation of the State Party concerned. In agreement with that State Party, such an inquiry may include a visit to its territory.

4. After examining the findings of its member or members submitted in accordance with paragraph 2 of this article, the Commission shall transmit these findings to the State Party concerned together with any comments or suggestions which seem appropriate in view of the situation.

5. All the proceedings of the Committee referred to in paragraphs 1 to 4 of this article shall be confidential, and at all stages of the proceedings the co-operation of the State Party shall be sought. After such proceedings have been completed with regard to an inquiry made in accordance with paragraph 2, the Committee may, after consultations with the State Party concerned, decide to include a summary account of the results of the proceedings in its annual report made in accordance with article 24.

Article 21

1. A State Party to this Convention may at any time declare under this article that it recognizes the competence of the Committee to receive and consider communications to the effect that a State Party claims that another State Party is not fulfilling its obligations under this Convention. Such communications may be received and considered according to the procedures laid down in this article only if submitted by a State Party which has made a declaration recognizing in regard to itself the competence of the Committee. No communication shall be dealt with by the Committee under this article if it concerns a State Party which has not made such a declaration. Communications received under this article shall be dealt with in accordance with the following procedure;

   (a) If a State Party considers that another State Party is not giving effect to the provisions of this Convention, it may, by written communication, bring the matter to the attention of that State Party. Within three months after the receipt of the communication the receiving State shall afford the State which sent the communication an explanation or any other statement in writing clarifying the matter, which should include, to the extent possible and pertinent, reference to domestic procedures and remedies taken, pending or available in the matter;

   (b) If the matter is not adjusted to the satisfaction of both States Parties concerned within six months after the receipt by the receiving State of the initial communication, either State shall have the right to refer the matter to the Committee, by notice given to the Committee and to the other State;

(c) The Committee shall deal with a matter referred to it under this article only after it has ascertained that all domestic remedies have been invoked and exhausted in the matter, in conformity with the generally recognized principles of international law. This shall not be the rule where the application of the remedies is unreasonably prolonged or is unlikely to bring effective relief to the person who is the victim of the violation of this Convention;

(d) The Committee shall hold closed meetings when examining communications under this article; Subject to the provisions of subparagraph (e),

(e) The Committee shall make available its good offices to the States Parties concerned with a view to a friendly solution of the matter on the basis of respect for the obligations provided for in this Convention. For this purpose, the Committee may, when appropriate, set up an ad hoc conciliation commission;

(f) In any matter referred to it under this article, the Committee may call upon the States Parties concerned, referred to in subparagraph (b), to supply any relevant information;

(g) The States Parties concerned, referred to in subparagraph (b), shall have the right to be represented when the matter is being considered by the Committee and to make submissions orally and/or in writing;

(h) The Committee shall, within twelve months after the date of receipt of notice under subparagraph (b), submit a report:

  (i) If a solution within the terms of subparagraph (e) is reached, the Committee shall confine its report to a brief statement of the facts and of the solution reached;

  (ii) If a solution within the terms of subparagraph (e) is not reached, the Committee shall confine its report to a brief statement of the facts; the written submissions and record of the oral submissions made by the States Parties concerned shall be attached to the report.

In every matter, the report shall be communicated to the States Parties concerned.

2. The provisions of this article shall come into force when five States Parties to this Convention have made declarations under paragraph 1 of this article. Such declarations shall be deposited by the States Parties with the Secretary-General of the United Nations, who shall transmit copies thereof to the other States Parties. A declaration may be withdrawn at any time by notification to the Secretary-General. Such a withdrawal shall not prejudice the consideration of any matter which is the subject of a communication already transmitted under this article; no further communication by any State Party shall be received under this article after the notification of withdrawal of the declaration has been received by the Secretary-General, unless the State Party concerned has made a new declaration.

Article 22

1. A State Party to this Convention may at any time declare under this article that it recognizes the competence of the Committee to receive and consider communications from or on behalf of individuals subject to its jurisdiction who claim to be victims of a violation by a State Party of the provisions of the Convention. No communication shall be received by the Committee if it concerns a State Party which has not made such a declaration.

2. The Committee shall consider inadmissible any communication under this article which is anonymous or which it considers to be an abuse of the right of submission of such communications or to be incompatible with the provisions of this Convention.

3. Subject to the provisions of paragraph 2, the Committee shall bring any communications submitted to it under this article to the attention of the State Party to this Convention which has made a declaration under paragraph 1 and is alleged to be violating any provisions of the Convention. Within six months, the receiving State shall submit to the Committee written explanations or statements clarifying the matter and the remedy, if any, that may have been taken by that State.

4. The Committee shall consider communications received under this article in the light of all information made available to it by or on behalf of the individual and by the State Party concerned.

5. The Committee shall not consider any communications from an individual under this article unless it has ascertained that:
   (a) The same matter has not been, and is not being, examined under another procedure of international investigation or settlement;
   (b) The individual has exhausted all available domestic remedies; this shall not be the rule where the application of the remedies is unreasonably prolonged or is unlikely to bring effective relief to the person who is the victim of the violation of this Convention.

6. The Committee shall hold closed meetings when examining communications under this article.

7. The Committee shall forward its views to the State Party concerned and to the individual.

8. The provisions of this article shall come into force when five States Parties to this Convention have made declarations under paragraph 1 of this article. Such declarations shall be deposited by the States Parties with the Secretary-General of the United Nations, who shall transmit copies thereof to the other States Parties. A declaration may be withdrawn at any time by notification to the Secretary-General. Such a withdrawal shall not prejudice the consideration of any matter which is the subject of a communication already transmitted under this article; no further communication by or on behalf of an individual shall be received under this article after the notification of withdrawal of the declaration has been received by the Secretary General, unless the State Party has made a new declaration.

Article 23

The members of the Committee and of the ad hoc conciliation commissions which may be appointed under article 21, paragraph 1 (e), shall be entitled to the facilities, privileges and immunities of experts on mission for the United Nations as laid down in the relevant sections of the Convention on the Privileges and Immunities of the United Nations.

Article 24

The Committee shall submit an annual report on its activities under this Convention to the States Parties and to the General Assembly of the United Nations.

PART III

Article 25

1. This Convention is open for signature by all States.
2. This Convention is subject to ratification. Instruments of ratification shall be deposited with the Secretary-General of the United Nations.

Article 26

This Convention is open to accession by all States. Accession shall be effected by the deposit of an instrument of accession with the Secretary-General of the United Nations.

Article 27

1. This Convention shall enter into force on the thirtieth day after the date of the deposit with the Secretary-General of the United Nations of the twentieth instrument of ratification or accession.
2. For each State ratifying this Convention or acceding to it after the deposit of the twentieth instrument of ratification or accession, the Convention shall enter into force on the thirtieth day after the date of the deposit of its own instrument of ratification or accession.

Article 28

1. Each State may, at the time of signature or ratification of this Convention or accession thereto, declare that it does not recognize the competence of the Committee provided for in article 20.
2. Any State Party having made a reservation in accordance with paragraph 1 of this article may, at any time, withdraw this reservation by notification to the Secretary-General of the United Nations.

Article 29

1. Any State Party to this Convention may propose an amendment and file it with the Secretary-General of the United Nations. The Secretary-General shall thereupon communicate the proposed amendment to the States Parties with a request that they notify him whether they favour a conference of States Parties for the purpose of considering and voting upon the proposal. In the event that within four months from the date of such communication at least one third of the States Parties favours such a conference, the Secretary-General shall convene the conference under the auspices of the United Nations. Any amendment adopted by a majority of the States Parties present and voting at the conference shall be submitted by the Secretary-General to all the States Parties for acceptance.
2. An amendment adopted in accordance with paragraph 1 of this article shall enter into force when two thirds of the States Parties to this Convention have notified the Secretary-General of the United Nations that they have accepted it in accordance with their respective constitutional processes.
3. When amendments enter into force, they shall be binding on those States Parties which have accepted them, other States Parties still being bound by the provisions of this Convention and any earlier amendments which they have accepted.

Article 30

1. Any dispute between two or more States Parties concerning the interpretation or application of this Convention which cannot be settled through negotiation shall, at the request of one of them, be submitted to arbitration. If within six months from the date of the request for arbitration the Parties are unable to agree on the organization of the arbitration, any one of those Parties may refer the dispute to the International Court of Justice by request in conformity with the Statute of the Court.

2. Each State may, at the time of signature or ratification of this Convention or accession thereto, declare that it does not consider itself bound by paragraph 1 of this article. The other States Parties shall not be bound by paragraph 1 of this article with respect to any State Party having made such a reservation.

3. Any State Party having made a reservation in accordance with paragraph 2 of this article may at any time withdraw this reservation by notification to the Secretary-General of the United Nations.

Article 31

1. A State Party may denounce this Convention by written notification to the Secretary-General of the United Nations. Denunciation becomes effective one year after the date of receipt of the notification by the Secretary-General.

2. Such a denunciation shall not have the effect of releasing the State Party from its obligations under this Convention in regard to any act or omission which occurs prior to the date at which the denunciation becomes effective, nor shall denunciation prejudice in any way the continued consideration of any matter which is already under consideration by the Committee prior to the date at which the denunciation becomes effective.

3. Following the date at which the denunciation of a State Party becomes effective, the Committee shall not commence consideration of any new matter regarding that State.

Article 32

The Secretary-General of the United Nations shall inform all States Members of the United Nations and all States which have signed this Convention or acceded to it of the following:

(a) Signatures, ratifications and accessions under articles 25 and 26;

(b) The date of entry into force of this Convention under article 27 and the date of the entry into force of any amendments under article 29;

(c) Denunciations under article 31.

Article 33

1. This Convention, of which the Arabic, Chinese, English, French, Russian and Spanish texts are equally authentic, shall be deposited with the Secretary-General of the United Nations.

2. The Secretary-General of the United Nations shall transmit certified copies of this Convention to all States.

1993 Secretary-General's Report Pursuant to Security Council Resolution No. 808

Report of the Secretary-General Pursuant to Paragraph 2 of Security Council Resolution 808 (1993)

INTRODUCTION

1. By paragraph 1 of resolution 808 (1993) of 22 February 1993, the Security Council decided "that an international tribunal shall be established for the prosecution of persons responsible for serious violations of international humanitarian law committed in the territory of the former Yugoslavia since 1991".

2. By paragraph 2 of the resolution, the Secretary-General was requested "to submit for consideration by the Council at the earliest possible date, and if possible no later than 60 days after the adoption of the present resolution, a report on all aspects of this matter, including specific proposals and where appropriate options for the effective and expeditious implementation of the decision [to establish an international tribunal], taking into account suggestions put forward in this regard by Member States."

3. The present report is presented pursuant to that request.

4. Resolution 808 (1993) represents a further step taken by the Security Council in a series of resolutions concerning serious violations of international humanitarian law occurring in the territory of the former Yugoslavia.

5. In resolution 764 (1992) of 13 July 1992, the Security Council reaffirmed that all parties to the conflict are bound to comply with their obligations under international humanitarian law and in particular the Geneva Conventions of 12 August 1949, and that persons who commit or order the commission of grave breaches of the Conventions are individually responsible in respect of such breaches.

6. In resolution 771 (1992) of 13 August 1992, the Security Council expressed grave alarm at continuing reports of widespread violations of international humanitarian law occurring within the territory of the former Yugoslavia and especially in Bosnia and Herzegovina, including reports of mass forcible expulsion and deportation of civilians, imprisonment and abuse of civilians in detention centres, deliberate attacks on non-combatants, hospitals and ambulances, impeding the delivery of food and medical supplies to the civilian population, and wanton devastation and destruction of property. The Council strongly condemned any violations of international humanitarian law, including those involved in the practice of "ethnic cleansing", and demanded that all parties to the conflict in the former Yugoslavia cease and desist from all breaches of international humanitarian law. It called upon States and international humanitarian organizations to collate substantiated information relating to the

violations of humanitarian law, including grave breaches of the Geneva Conventions, being committed in the territory of the former Yugoslavia and to make this information available to the Council. Furthermore, the Council decided, acting under Chapter VII of the Charter of the United Nations, that all parties and others concerned in the former Yugoslavia, and all military forces in Bosnia and Herzegovina, should comply with the provisions of that resolution, failing which the Council would need to take further measures under the Charter.

7. In resolution 780 (1992) of 6 October 1992, the Security Council requested the Secretary-General to establish an impartial commission of Experts to examine and analyse the information as requested by resolution 771 (1992), together with such further information as the Commission may obtain through its own investigations or efforts, of other persons or bodies pursuant to resolution 771 (1992), with a view to providing the Secretary-General with its conclusions on the evidence of grave breaches of the Geneva Conventions and other violations of international humanitarian law committed in the territory of the former Yugoslavia.

8. On 14 October 1992 the Secretary-General submitted a report to the Security Council pursuant to paragraph 3 of resolution 780 (1992) in which he outlined his decision to establish a five-member Commission of Experts (S/24657). On 26 October 1992, the Secretary-General announced the appointment of the Chairman and members of the Commission of Experts.

9. By a letter dated 9 February 1993, the Secretary-General submitted to the President of the Security Council an interim report of the Commission of Experts (S/25274), which concluded that grave breaches and other violations of international humanitarian law had been committed in the territory of the former Yugoslavia, including wilful killing, "ethnic cleansing", mass killings, torture, rape, pillage and destruction of civilian property, destruction of cultural and religious property and arbitrary arrests. In its report, the Commission noted that should the Security Council or another competent organ of the United Nations decide to establish an ad hoc international tribunal, such a decision would be consistent with the direction of its work.

10. It was against this background that the Security Council considered and adopted resolution 808 (1993). After recalling the provisions of resolutions 764 (1992), 771 (1992) and 780 (1992) and, taking into consideration the interim report of the Commission of Experts, the Security Council expressed once again its grave alarm at continuing reports of widespread violations of international humanitarian law occurring within the territory of the former Yugoslavia, including reports of mass killings and the continuation of the practice of "ethnic cleansing". The Council determined that this situation constituted a threat to international peace and security, and stated that it was determined to put an end to such crimes and to take effective measures to bring to justice the persons who are responsible for them. The Security Council stated its conviction that in the particular circumstances of the former Yugoslavia the establishment of an international tribunal would enable this aim to be achieved and would contribute to the restoration and maintenance of peace.

11. The Secretary-General wishes to recall that in resolution 820 (1993) of 17 April 1993, the Security Council condemned once again all violations of international humanitarian law, including in particular, the practice of "ethnic cleansing" and the massive, organized and systematic detention and rape of women, and reaffirmed that those

who commit or have committed or order or have ordered the commission of such acts will be held individually responsible in respect of such acts.

12. The Security Council's decision in resolution 808 (1993) to establish an international tribunal is circumscribed in scope and purpose: the prosecution of persons responsible for serious violations of international humanitarian law committed in the territory of the former Yugoslavia since 1991. The decision does not relate to the establishment of an international criminal jurisdiction in general nor to the creation of an international criminal court of a permanent nature, issues which are and remain under active consideration by the International Law Commission and the General Assembly.

13. In accordance with the request of the Security Council, the Secretary-General has taken into account in the preparation of the present report the suggestions put forward by Member States, in particular those reflected in the following Security Council documents submitted by Member States and noted by the Council in its resolution 808 (1993): the report of the committee of jurists submitted by France (S/25266), the report of the commission of jurists submitted by Italy (S/25300), and the report submitted by the Permanent Representative of Sweden on behalf of the Chairman-in-Office of the Conference on Security and Cooperation in Europe (CSCE) (S/25307). The Secretary-General has also sought the views of the Commission of Experts established pursuant to Security Council resolution 780 (1992) and has made use of the information gathered by that Commission. In addition, the Secretary-General has taken into account suggestions or comments put forward formally or informally by the following Member States since the adoption of resolution 808 (1993): Australia, Austria, Belgium, Brazil, Canada, Chile, China, Denmark, Egypt,[1] Germany, Iran (Islamic Republic of), Ireland, Italy, Malaysia, Mexico, Netherlands, New Zealand, Pakistan, Portugal, Russian Federation, Saudi Arabia, Senegal, Slovenia, Spain, Sweden, Turkey, United Kingdom of Great Britain and Northern Ireland, United States of America and Yugoslavia. He has also received suggestions or comments from a non-member State (Switzerland).

14. The Secretary-General has also received comments from the International Committee of the Red Cross (ICRC) and from the following non-governmental organizations: Amnesty International, Association Internationale des Jeunes Avocats, Ethnic Minorities Barristers' Association, Federation internationale des femmes des carrieres juridiques, International Criminal Police Organization, Jacob Blaustein Institution for the Advancement of Human Rights, Lawyers Committee for Human Rights, National Alliance of Women' s Organisations (NAWO), and Parliamentarians for Global Action. Observations have also been received from international meetings and individual experts in relevant fields.

15. The Secretary-General wishes to place on record his appreciation for the interest shown by all the Governments, organizations and individuals who have offered valuable suggestions and comments.

16. In the main body of the report which follows, the Secretary-General first examines the legal basis for the establishment of the International Tribunal foreseen in resolution 808 (1993). The Secretary-General then sets out in detail the competence of the

---

[1] On behalf of the members of the Organization of the Islamic Conference (OIC) and as members of the Contact Group of OIC on Bosnia and Herzegovina.

International Tribunal as regards the law it will apply, the persons to whom the law will be applied, including considerations as to the principle of individual criminal responsibility, its territorial and temporal reach and the relation of its work to that of national courts. In succeeding chapters, the Secretary-General sets out detailed views on the organization of the international tribunal, the investigation and pre-trial proceedings, trial and post-trial proceedings, and cooperation and judicial assistance. A concluding chapter deals with a number of general and organizational issues such as privileges and immunities, the seat of the international tribunal, working languages and financial arrangements.

17. In response to the Security Council's request to include in the report specific proposals, the Secretary-General has decided to incorporate into the report specific language for inclusion in a statute of the International Tribunal. The formulations are based upon provisions found in existing international instruments, particularly with regard to competence ratione materiae of the International Tribunal. Suggestions and comments, including suggested draft articles, received from States, organizations and individuals as noted in paragraphs 13 and 14 above, also formed the basis upon which the Secretary-General prepared the statute. Texts prepared in the past by United Nations or other bodies for the establishment of international criminal courts were consulted by the Secretary-General, including texts prepared by the United Nations Committee on International Criminal Jurisdiction, the International Law Commission, and the International Law Association. Proposals regarding individual articles are, therefore, made throughout the body of the report; the full text of the statute of the International Tribunal is contained in the annex to the present report.

I. THE LEGAL BASIS FOR THE ESTABLISHMENT OF THE INTERNATIONAL TRIBUNAL

18. Security Council resolution 808 (1993) states that an international tribunal shall be established for the prosecution of persons responsible for serious violations of international humanitarian law committed in the territory of the former Yugoslavia since 1991. It does not, however, indicate how such an international tribunal is to be established or on what legal basis.

19. The approach which, in the normal course of events, would be followed in establishing an international tribunal would be the conclusion of a treaty by which the States parties would establish a tribunal and approve its statute. This treaty would be drawn up and adopted by an appropriate international body (e.g., the General Assembly or a specially convened conference), following which it would be opened for signature and ratification. Such an approach would have the advantage of allowing for a detailed examination and elaboration of all the issues pertaining to the establishment of the international tribunal. It also would allow the States participating in the negotiation and conclusion of the treaty fully to exercise their sovereign will, in particular whether they wish to become parties to the treaty or not.

20. As has been pointed out in many of the comments received, the treaty approach incurs the disadvantage of requiring considerable time to establish an instrument and then to achieve the required number of ratifications for entry into force. Even then, there could be no guarantee that ratifications will be received from those States which should be parties to the treaty if it is to be truly effective.

21. A number of suggestions have been put forward to the effect that the General Assembly, as the most representative organ of the United Nations, should have a role in the establishment of the international tribunal in addition to its role in the administrative and budgetary aspects of the question. The involvement of the General Assembly in the drafting or the review of the statute of the International Tribunal would not be reconcilable with the urgency expressed by the Security Council in resolution 808 (1993). The Secretary-General believes that there are other ways of involving the authority and prestige of the General Assembly in the establishment of the International Tribunal.

22. In the light of the disadvantages of the treaty approach in this particular case and of the need indicated in resolution 808 (1993) for an effective and expeditious implementation of the decision to establish an international tribunal, the Secretary-General believes that the International Tribunal should be established by a decision of the Security Council on the basis of Chapter VII of the Charter of the United Nations. Such a decision would constitute a measure to maintain or restore international peace and security, following the requisite determination of the existence of a threat to the peace, breach of the peace or act of aggression.

23. This approach would have the advantage of being expeditious and of being immediately effective as all states would be under a binding obligation to take whatever action is required to carry out a decision taken as an enforcement measure under Chapter VII.

24. In the particular case of the former Yugoslavia, the Secretary-General believes that the establishment of the International Tribunal by means of a Chapter VII decision would be legally justified, both in terms of the object and purpose of the decision, as indicated in the preceding paragraphs, and of past Security Council practice.

25. As indicated in paragraph 10 above, the Security Council has already determined that the situation posed by continuing reports of widespread violations of international humanitarian law occurring in the former Yugoslavia constitutes a threat to international peace and security. The Council has also decided under Chapter VII of the Charter that all parties and others concerned in the former Yugoslavia, and all military forces in Bosnia and Herzegovina, shall comply with the provisions of resolution 771 (1992), failing which it would need to take further measures under the Charter. Furthermore, the Council has repeatedly reaffirmed that all parties in the former Yugoslavia are bound to comply with the obligations under international humanitarian law and in particular the Geneva Conventions of 12 August 1949, and that persons who commit or order the commission of grave breaches of the Conventions are individually responsible in respect of such breaches.

26. Finally, the Security Council stated in resolution 808 (1993) that it was convinced that in the particular circumstances of the former Yugoslavia, the establishment of an international tribunal would bring about the achievement of the aim of putting an end to such crimes and of taking effective measures to bring to justice the persons responsible for them, and would contribute to the restoration and maintenance of peace.

27. The Security Council has on various occasions adopted decisions under Chapter VII aimed at restoring and maintaining international peace and security, which have involved the establishment of subsidiary organs for a variety of purposes. Reference

may be made in this regard to Security Council resolution 687 (1991) and subsequent resolutions relating to the situation between Iraq and Kuwait.

28. In this particular case, the Security Council would be establishing, as an enforcement measure under Chapter VII, a subsidiary organ within the terms of Article 29 of the Charter, but one of a judicial nature. This organ would, of course, have to perform its functions independently of political considerations; it would not be subject to the authority or control of the Security Council with regard to the performance of its judicial functions. As an enforcement measure under Chapter VII, however, the life span of the international tribunal would be linked to the restoration and maintenance of international peace and security in the territory of the former Yugoslavia, and Security Council decisions related thereto.

29. It should be pointed out that, in assigning to the International Tribunal the task of prosecuting persons responsible for serious violations of international humanitarian law, the Security Council would not be creating or purporting to "legislate" that law. Rather, the International Tribunal would have the task of applying existing international humanitarian law.

30. On the basis of the foregoing considerations, the Secretary-General proposes that the Security Council, acting under Chapter VII of the Charter, establish the International Tribunal. The resolution so adopted would have annexed to it a statute the opening passage of which would read as follows:

> Having been established by the Security Council acting under Chapter VII of the Charter of the United Nations, the International Tribunal for the Prosecution of Persons Responsible for Serious Violations of International Humanitarian Law Committed in the Territory of the Former Yugoslavia since 1991 (hereinafter referred to as "the International Tribunal") shall function in accordance with the provisions of the present Statute.

II. COMPETENCE OF THE INTERNATIONAL TRIBUNAL

31. The competence of the International Tribunal derives from the mandate set out in paragraph 1 of resolution 808 (1993). This part of the report will examine and make proposals regarding these fundamental elements of its competence: ratione materiae (subject-matter jurisdiction), ratione personae (personal jurisdiction), ratione loci (territorial jurisdiction) and ratione temporis (temporal jurisdiction), as well as the question of the concurrent jurisdiction of the International Tribunal and national courts.

32. The statute should begin with a general article on the competence of the International Tribunal which would read as follows:

Article 1: Competence of the International Tribunal

The International Tribunal shall have the power to prosecute persons responsible for serious violations of international humanitarian law committed in the territory of the former Yugoslavia since 1991 in accordance with the provisions of the present Statute.

A. Competence ratione materiae (subject-matter jurisdiction)

33. According to paragraph 1 of resolution 808 (1993), the international tribunal shall prosecute persons responsible for serious violations of international humanitarian

law committed in the territory of the former Yugoslavia since 1991. This body of law exists in the form of both conventional law and customary law. While there is international customary law which is not laid down in conventions, some of the major conventional humanitarian law has become part of customary international law.

34. In the view of the Secretary-General, the application of the principle nullum crimen sine lege requires that the international tribunal should apply rules of international humanitarian law which are beyond any doubt part of customary law so that the problem of adherence of some but not all States to specific conventions does not arise. This would appear to be particularly important in the context of an international tribunal prosecuting persons responsible for serious violations of international humanitarian law.

35. The part of conventional international humanitarian law which has beyond doubt become part of international customary law is the law applicable in armed conflict as embodied in the Geneva Conventions of 12 August 1949 for the Protection of War Victims; the Hague Convention (IV) Respecting the Laws and Customs of War on Land and the Regulations annexed thereto of 17 October 1907; the Convention on the Prevention and Punishment of the Crime of Genocide of 9 December 1948; and the Charter of the International Military Tribunal of 8 August 1945.

36. Suggestions have been made that the international tribunal should apply domestic law in so far as it incorporates customary international humanitarian law. While international humanitarian law as outlined above provides a sufficient basis for subject-matter jurisdiction, there is one related issue which would require reference to domestic practice, namely, penalties (see para. 111 below).

Grave breaches of the 1949 Geneva Conventions

11

37. The Geneva Conventions constitute rules of international humanitarian law and provide the core of the customary law applicable in international armed conflicts. These Conventions regulate the conduct of war from the humanitarian perspective by protecting certain categories of persons: namely, wounded and sick members of armed forces in the field; wounded, sick and shipwrecked members of armed forces at sea; prisoners of war, and civilians in time of war.

38. Each Convention contains a provision listing the particularly serious violations that qualify as "grave breaches" or war crimes. Persons committing or ordering grave breaches are subject to trial and punishment. The lists of grave breaches contained in the Geneva Conventions are reproduced in the article which follows.

39. The Security Council has reaffirmed on several occasions that persons who commit or order the commission of grave breaches of the 1949 Geneva Conventions in the territory of the former Yugoslavia are individually responsible for such breaches as serious violations of international humanitarian law.

40. The corresponding article of the statute would read:

Article 2: Grave breaches of the Geneva Conventions of 1949
The International Tribunal shall have the power to prosecute persons committing or ordering to be committed grave breaches of the Geneva Conventions of 12 August 1949, namely the following acts against persons or property protected under the provisions of the relevant Geneva Convention:

(a) wilful killing;

(b) torture or inhuman treatment, including biological experiments;

(c) wilfully causing great suffering or serious injury to body or health;

(d) extensive destruction and appropriation of property, not justified by military necessity and carried out unlawfully and wantonly;

(e) compelling a prisoner of war or a civilian to serve in the forces of a hostile power;

(f) wilfully depriving a prisoner of war or a civilian of the rights of fair and regular trial;

(g) unlawful deportation or transfer or unlawful confinement of a civilian;

(h) taking civilians as hostages.

Violations of the laws or customs of war

41. The 1907 Hague Convention (IV) Respecting the Laws and Customs of War on Land and the Regulations annexed thereto comprise a second important area of conventional humanitarian international law which has become part of the body of international customary law.

42. The Nürnberg Tribunal recognized that many of the provisions contained in the Hague Regulations, although innovative at the time of their adoption were, by 1939, recognized by all civilized nations and were regarded as being declaratory of the laws and customs of war. The Nürnberg Tribunal also recognized that war crimes defined in article 6(b) of the Nürnberg Charter were already recognized as war crimes under international law, and covered in the Hague Regulations, for which guilty individuals were punishable.

43. The Hague Regulations cover aspects of international humanitarian law which are also covered by the 1949 Geneva Conventions. However, the Hague Regulations also recognize that the right of belligerents to conduct warfare is not unlimited and that resort to certain methods of waging war is prohibited under the rules of land warfare.

44. These rules of customary law, as interpreted and applied by the Nürnberg Tribunal, provide the basis for the corresponding article of the statute which would read as follows:

Article 3: Violations of the laws or customs of war

The International Tribunal shall have the power to prosecute persons violating the laws or customs of war. Such violations shall include, but not be limited to:

(a) employment of poisonous weapons or other weapons calculated to cause unnecessary suffering;

(b) wanton destruction of cities, towns or villages, or devastation not justified by military necessity;

(c) attack, or bombardment, by whatever means, of undefended towns, villages, dwellings, or buildings;

(d) seizure of, destruction or wilful damage done to institutions dedicated to religion, charity and education, the arts and sciences, historic monuments and works of art and science;

(e) plunder of public or private property.

Genocide

45. The 1948 Convention on the Prevention and Punishment of the Crime of Genocide confirms that genocide, whether committed in time of peace or in time of war, is a crime under international law for which individuals shall be tried and punished. The Convention is today considered part of international customary law as evidenced by the International Court of Justice in its Advisory Opinion on Reservations to the Convention on the Prevention and Punishment of the Crime of Genocide, 1951.

46. The relevant provisions of the Genocide Convention are reproduced in the corresponding article of the statute, which would read as follows:

Article 4: Genocide

1. The International Tribunal shall have the power to prosecute persons committing genocide as defined in paragraph 2 of this article or of committing any of the other acts enumerated in paragraph 3 of this article.
2. Genocide means any of the following acts committed with intent to destroy, in whole or in part, a national, ethnical, racial or religious group, as such:
   (a) killing members of the group;
   (b) causing serious bodily or mental harm to members of the group;
   (c) deliberately inflicting on the group conditions of life calculated to bring about its physical destruction in whole or in part;
   (d) imposing measures intended to prevent births within the group;
   (e) forcibly transferring children of the group to another group.
3. The following acts shall be punishable:
   (a) genocide;
   (b) conspiracy to commit genocide;
   (c) direct and public incitement to commit genocide;
   (d) attempt to commit genocide;
   (e) complicity in genocide.

Crimes against humanity

47. Crimes against humanity were first recognized in the Charter and Judgement of the Nürnberg Tribunal, as well as in Law No. 10 of the Control Council for Germany. Crimes against humanity are aimed at any civilian population and are prohibited regardless of whether they are committed in an armed conflict, international or internal in character.

48. Crimes against humanity refer to inhumane acts of a very serious nature, such as wilful killing, torture or rape, committed as part of a widespread or systematic attack against any civilian population on national, political, ethnic, racial or religious grounds. In the conflict in the territory of the former Yugoslavia, such inhumane acts have taken the form of so-called "ethnic cleansing" and widespread and systematic rape and other forms of sexual assault, including enforced prostitution.

49. The corresponding article of the statute would read as follows:

11

Article 5: Crimes against humanity

The International Tribunal shall have the power to prosecute persons responsible for the following crimes when committed in armed conflict, whether international or internal in character, and directed against any civilian population:

(a) murder;

(b) extermination;

(c) enslavement;

(d) deportation;

(e) imprisonment;

(f) torture;

(g) rape;

(h) persecutions on political, racial and religious grounds;

(i) other inhumane acts.

B. Competence ratione personae (personal jurisdiction) and individual criminal responsibility

50. By paragraph 1 of resolution 808 (1993), the Security Council decided that the International Tribunal shall be established for the prosecution of persons responsible for serious violations of international humanitarian law committed in the territory of the former Yugoslavia since 1991. In the light of the complex of resolutions leading up to resolution 808 (1993) (see paras. 5–7 above), the ordinary meaning of the term "persons responsible for serious violations of international humanitarian law" would be natural persons to the exclusion of juridical persons.

51. The question arises, however, whether a juridical person, such as an association or organization, may be considered criminal as such and thus its members, for that reason alone, be made subject to the jurisdiction of the International Tribunal. The Secretary-General believes that this concept should not be retained in regard to the International Tribunal. The criminal acts set out in this statute are carried out by natural persons; such persons would be subject to the jurisdiction of the International Tribunal irrespective of membership in groups.

52. The corresponding article of the statute would read:

Article 6: Personal jurisdiction

The International Tribunal shall have jurisdiction over natural persons pursuant to the provisions of the present Statute.

Individual criminal responsibility

53. An important element in relation to the competence ratione personae (personal jurisdiction) of the International Tribunal is the principle of individual criminal responsibility. As noted above, the Security Council has reaffirmed in a number of resolutions that persons committing serious violations of international humanitarian law in the former Yugoslavia are individually responsible for such violations.

54. The Secretary-General believes that all persons who participate in the planning, preparation or execution of serious violations of international humanitarian law in

the former Yugoslavia contribute to the commission of the violation and are, therefore, individually responsible.

55. Virtually all of the written comments received by the Secretary-General have suggested that the statute of the International Tribunal should contain provisions with regard to the individual criminal responsibility of heads of State, government officials and persons acting in an official capacity. These suggestions draw upon the precedents following the Second World War. The Statute should, therefore, contain provisions which specify that a plea of head of State immunity or that an act was committed in the official capacity of the accused will not constitute a defence, nor will it mitigate punishment.

56. A person in a position of superior authority should, therefore, be held individually responsible for giving the unlawful order to commit a crime under the present statute. But he should also be held responsible for failure to prevent a crime or to deter the unlawful behaviour of his subordinates. This imputed responsibility or criminal negligence is engaged if the person in superior authority knew or had reason to know that his subordinates were about to commit or had committed crimes and yet failed to take the necessary and reasonable steps to prevent or repress the commission of such crimes or to punish those who had committed them.

57. Acting upon an order of a Government or a superior cannot relieve the perpetrator of the crime of his criminal responsibility and should not be a defence. Obedience to superior orders may, however, be considered a mitigating factor, should the International Tribunal determine that justice so requires. For example, the International Tribunal may consider the factor of superior orders in connection with other defences such as coercion or lack of moral choice.

58. The International Tribunal itself will have to decide on various personal defences which may relieve a person of individual criminal responsibility, such as minimum age or mental incapacity, drawing upon general principles of law recognized by all nations.

59. The corresponding article of the statute would read:

Article 7: Individual criminal responsibility

1. A person who planned, instigated, ordered, committed or otherwise aided and abetted in the planning, preparation or execution of a crime referred to in articles 2 to 5 of the present Statute, shall be individually responsible for the crime.

2. The official position of any accused person, whether as Head of as a responsible Government official, shall not relieve such person of criminal responsibility nor mitigate punishment.

3. The fact that any of the acts referred to in articles 2 to 5 of the present Statute was committed by a subordinate does not relieve his superior of criminal responsibility if he knew or had reason to know that the subordinate was about to commit such acts or had done so and the superior failed to take the necessary and reasonable measures to prevent such acts or to punish the perpetrators thereof.

4. The fact that an accused person acted pursuant to an order of a Government or of a superior shall not relieve him of criminal responsibility, but may be considered in mitigation of punishment if the International Tribunal determines that justice so requires.

C. Competence <u>ratione loci</u> (territorial jurisdiction) and <u>ratione temporis</u> (temporal jurisdiction)

60. Pursuant to paragraph 1 of resolution 808 (1993), the territorial and temporal jurisdiction of the International Tribunal extends to serious violations of international humanitarian law to the extent that they have been "committed in the territory of the former Yugoslavia since 1991".

61. As far as the territorial jurisdiction of the International Tribunal is concerned, the territory of the former Yugoslavia means the territory of the former Socialist Federal Republic of Yugoslavia, including its land surface, airspace and territorial waters.

62. With regard to temporal jurisdiction, Security Council resolution 808 (1993) extends the jurisdiction of the International Tribunal to violations committed "since 1991". The Secretary-General understands this to mean any time on or after 1 January 1991. This is a neutral date which is not tied to any specific event and is clearly intended to convey the notion that no judgement as to the international or internal character of the conflict is being exercised.

63. The corresponding article of the statute would read:

Article 8: Territorial and temporal jurisdiction

The territorial jurisdiction of the International Tribunal shall extend to the territory of the former Socialist Federal Republic of Yugoslavia, including its land surface, airspace and territorial waters. The temporal jurisdiction of the International Tribunal shall extend to a period beginning on 1 January 1991.

D. Concurrent jurisdiction and the principle of non-bis-in-idem

64. In establishing an international tribunal for the prosecution of persons responsible for serious violations committed in the territory of the former Yugoslavia since 1991, it was not the intention of the Security Council to preclude or prevent the exercise of jurisdiction by national courts with respect to such acts. Indeed national courts should be encouraged to exercise their jurisdiction in accordance with their relevant national laws and procedures.

65. It follows therefore that there is concurrent jurisdiction of the International Tribunal and national courts. This concurrent jurisdiction, however, should be subject to the primacy of the International Tribunal. At any stage of the procedure, the International Tribunal may formally request the national courts to defer to the competence of the International Tribunal. The details of how the primacy will be asserted shall be set out in the rules of procedure and evidence of the International Tribunal.

66. According to the principle of <u>non-bis-in-idem</u>, a person shall not be tried twice for the same crime. In the present context, given the primacy of the International Tribunal, the principle of <u>non-bis-in-idem</u> would preclude subsequent trial before a national court. However, the principle of <u>non-bis-in idem</u> should not preclude a subsequent trial before the International Tribunal in the following two circumstances:

    (a) The characterization of the act by the national court did not correspond to its characterization under the statute; or

    (b) Conditions of impartiality, independence or effective means of adjudication were not guaranteed in the proceedings before the national courts.

67. Should the International Tribunal decide to assume jurisdiction over a person who has already been convicted by a national court, it should take into consideration the extent to which any penalty imposed by the national court has already been served.

68. The corresponding articles of the statute would read:

Article 9: Concurrent jurisdiction

1. The International Tribunal and national courts shall have concurrent jurisdiction to prosecute persons for serious violations of international humanitarian law committed in the territory of the former Yugoslavia since 1 January 1991.

2. The International Tribunal shall have primacy over national courts. At any stage of the procedure, the International Tribunal may formally request national courts to defer to the competence of the International Tribunal in accordance with the present Statute and the Rules of Procedure and Evidence of the International Tribunal.

Article 10: Non-bis-in-idem

1. No person shall be tried before a national court for acts constituting serious violations of international humanitarian law under the present Statute, for which he or she has already been tried by the International Tribunal.

2. A person who has been tried by a national court for acts constituting serious violations of international humanitarian law may be subsequently tried by the International Tribunal only if:
   (a) the act for which he or she was tried was characterized as an ordinary crime; or
   (b) the national court proceedings were not impartial or independent, were designed to shield the accused from international criminal responsibility, or the case was not diligently prosecuted.

3. In considering the penalty to be imposed on a person convicted of a crime under the present Statute, the International Tribunal shall take into account the extent to which any penalty imposed by a national court on the same person for the same act has already been served.

III. THE ORGANIZATION OF THE INTERNATIONAL TRIBUNAL

69. The organization of the International Tribunal should reflect the functions to be performed by it. Since the International Tribunal is established for the prosecution of persons responsible for serious violations of international humanitarian law committed in the territory of the former Yugoslavia, this presupposes an international tribunal composed of a judicial organ, a prosecutorial organ and a secretariat. It would be the function of the prosecutorial organ to investigate cases, prepare indictments and prosecute persons responsible for committing the violations referred to above. The judicial organ would hear the cases presented to its Trial Chambers, and consider appeals from the Trial Chambers in its Appeals Chamber. A secretariat or Registry would be required to service both the prosecutorial and judicial organs.

70. The International Tribunal should therefore consist of the following organs: the Chambers, comprising two Trial Chambers and one Appeals Chamber; a Prosecutor; and a Registry.

71. The corresponding article of the statute would read as follows:

Article 11: Organization of the International Tribunal

The International Tribunal shall consist of the following organs:

(a)   The Chambers, comprising two Trial Chambers and an Appeals Chamber;

(b)   The Prosecutor; and

(c)   A Registry, servicing both the Chambers and the Prosecutor.

A. The Chambers

1. Composition of the Chambers

72. The Chambers should be composed of 11 independent judges, no 2 of whom may be nationals of the same State. Three judges would serve in each of the two Trial Chambers and five judges would serve in the Appeals Chamber.

73. The corresponding article of the statute would read as follows:

Article 12: Composition of the Chambers

The Chambers shall be composed of eleven independent judges, no two of whom may be nationals of the same State, who shall serve as follows:

(a)   Three judges shall serve in each of the Trial Chambers;

(b)   Five judges shall serve in the Appeals Chamber.

2. Qualifications and election of judges

74. The judges of the International Tribunal should be persons of high moral character, impartiality and integrity who possess the qualifications required in their respective countries for appointment to the highest judicial offices. Impartiality in this context includes impartiality with respect to the acts falling within the competence of the International Tribunal. In the overall composition of the Chambers, due account should be taken of the experience of the judges in criminal law, international law, including international humanitarian law and human rights law.

75. The judges should be elected by the General Assembly from a list submitted by the Security Council. The Secretary-General would invite nominations for judges from States Members of the United Nations as well as non-member States maintaining permanent observer missions at United Nations Headquarters. Within 60 days of the date of the invitation of the Secretary-General, each State would nominate up to two candidates meeting the qualifications mentioned in paragraph 74 above, who must not be of the same nationality. The Secretary-General would forward the nominations received to the Security Council. The Security Council would, as speedily as possible, establish from the nominations transmitted by the Secretary-General, a list of not less than 22 and not more than 33 candidates, taking due account of the adequate representation of the principal legal systems of the world. The President of the Security Council would then transmit the list to the General Assembly. From that list, the General Assembly would proceed as speedily as possible to elect the 11 judges of the International Tribunal. The candidates declared elected shall be those who have received an absolute majority of the votes of the States Members of the United Nations and of the States maintaining permanent observer missions at United

Nations Headquarters. Should two candidates of the same nationality obtain the required majority vote, the one who received the higher number of votes shall be considered elected.

76. The judges shall be elected for a term of four years. The terms and conditions of service shall be those of the Judges of the International Court of Justice. They shall be eligible for re-election.

77. In the event of a vacancy occurring in the Chambers, the Secretary-General, after consultation with the Presidents of the Security Council and the General Assembly, would appoint a person meeting the qualifications of paragraph 74 above, for the remainder of the term of office concerned.

78. The corresponding article of the statute would read as follows:

Article 13: Qualifications election of judges

1. The judges shall be persons of high moral character, impartiality and integrity who possess the qualifications required in their respective countries for appointment to the highest judicial offices. In the overall composition of the Chambers due account shall be taken of the experience of the judges in criminal law, international law, including international humanitarian law and human rights law.

2. The judges of the International Tribunal shall be elected by the General Assembly from a list submitted by the Security Council, in the following manner:

    (a) The Secretary-General shall invite nominations for judges of the International Tribunal from States Members of the United Nations and non-member States maintaining permanent observer missions at United Nations Headquarters;

    (b) Within sixty days of the date of the invitation of the Secretary-General, each state may nominate up to two candidates meeting the qualifications set out in paragraph 1 above, no two of whom shall be of the same nationality;

    (c) The Secretary-General shall forward the nominations received to the Security Council. From the nominations received the Security Council shall establish a list of not less than twenty-two and not more than thirty-three candidates, taking due account of the adequate representation of the principal legal systems of the world;

    (d) The President of the Security Council shall transmit the list of candidates to the President of the General Assembly. From that list the General Assembly shall elect the eleven judges of the International Tribunal. The candidates who receive an absolute majority of the votes of States Members of the United Nations and of the non-member States maintaining permanent observer missions at United Nations Headquarters, shall be declared elected. Should two candidates of the same nationality obtain the required majority vote, the one who received the higher number of votes shall be considered elected.

3. In the event of a vacancy in the Chambers, after consultation with the Presidents of the Security Council and of the General Assembly, the Secretary-General shall appoint a person meeting the qualifications of paragraph 1 above, for the remainder of the term of office concerned.

4. The judges shall be elected for a term of four years. The terms and conditions of service shall be those of the Judges of the International Court of Justice. They shall be eligible for re-election.

3. Officers and members of the Chambers

79. The judges would elect a President of the International Tribunal from among their members who would be a member of the Appeals Chamber and would preside over the appellate proceedings.
80. Following consultation with the members of the Chambers, the President would assign the judges to the Appeals Chamber and to the Trial Chambers. Each judge would serve only in the chamber to which he or she was assigned.
81. The members of each Trial Chamber should elect a presiding judge who would conduct all of the proceedings before the Trial Chamber as a whole.
82. The corresponding article of the statute would read as follows:

Article 14: Officers and members of the Chambers
1.. The judges of the International Tribunal shall elect a President.
2. The President of the International Tribunal shall be a member of the Appeals Chamber and shall preside over its proceedings.
3. After consultation with the judges of the International Tribunal, the President shall assign the judges to the Appeals Chamber and to the Trial Chambers. A judge shall serve only in the Chamber to which he or she was assigned.
4. The judges of each Trial Chamber shall elect a Presiding Judge, who shall conduct all of the proceedings of the Trial Chamber as a whole.

4. Rules of procedure and evidence

83. The judges of the International Tribunal as a whole should draft and adopt the rules of procedure and evidence of the International Tribunal governing the pre-trial phase of the proceedings, the conduct of trials and appeals, the admission of evidence, the protection of victims and witnesses and other appropriate matters.
84. The corresponding article of the statute would read as follows:

Article 15: Rules of procedure and evidence
The judges of the International Tribunal shall adopt rules of procedure and evidence for the conduct of the pre-trial phase of the proceedings, trials and appeals, the admission of evidence, the protection of victims and witnesses and other appropriate matters.

B. The Prosecutor

85. Responsibility for the conduct of all investigations and prosecutions of persons responsible for serious violations of international humanitarian law committed in the territory of the former Yugoslavia since 1 January 1991 should be entrusted to an independent Prosecutor. The Prosecutor should act independently as a separate organ of the International Tribunal. He or she shall not seek or receive instructions from any Government or from any other source.
86. The Prosecutor should be appointed by the Security Council, upon nomination by the Secretary-General. He or she should possess the highest level of professional competence and have extensive experience in the conduct of investigations and prosecutions of criminal cases. The Prosecutor should be appointed for a four-year

term of office and be eligible for reappointment. The terms and conditions of service of the Prosecutor shall be those of an Under-Secretary-General of the United Nations.

87. The Prosecutor would be assisted by such other staff as may be required to perform effectively and efficiently the functions entrusted to him or her. Such staff would be appointed by the Secretary-General on the recommendation of the Prosecutor. The Office of the Prosecutor should be composed of an investigation unit and a prosecution unit.

88. Staff appointed to the Office of the Prosecutor should meet rigorous criteria of professional experience and competence in their field. Persons should be sought who have had relevant experience in their own countries as investigators, prosecutors, criminal lawyers, law enforcement personnel or medical experts. Given the nature of the crimes committed and the sensitivities of victims of rape and sexual assault, due consideration should be given in the appointment of staff to the employment of qualified women.

89. The corresponding article of the statute would read as follows:

Article 16: The Prosecutor

1. The Prosecutor shall be responsible for the investigation and prosecution of persons responsible for serious violations of international humanitarian law committed in the territory of the former Yugoslavia since 1 January 1991.

2. The Prosecutor shall act independently as a separate organ of the International Tribunal. He or she shall not seek or receive instructions from any Government or from any other source.

3. The Office of the Prosecutor shall be composed of a Prosecutor and such other qualified staff as may be required.

4. The Prosecutor shall be appointed by the Security Council on nomination by the Secretary-General. He or she shall be of high moral character and possess the highest level of competence and experience in the conduct of investigations and prosecutions of criminal cases. The Prosecutor shall serve for a four-year term and be eligible for reappointment. The terms and conditions of service of the Prosecutor shall be those of an Under-Secretary-General of the United Nations.

5. The staff of the Office of the Prosecutor shall be appointed by the Secretary-General on the recommendation of the Prosecutor.

C. The Registry

90. As indicated in paragraph 69 above, a Registry would be responsible for the servicing of the International Tribunal. The Registry would be headed by a Registrar, whose responsibilities shall include but should not be limited to the following:
   (a) Public information and external relations;
   (b) Preparation of minutes of meetings;
   (c) Conference-service facilities;
   (d) Printing and publication of all documents;
   (e) All administrative work, budgetary and personnel matters; and
   (f) Serving as the channel of communications to and from the International Tribunal.

91. The Registrar should be appointed by the Secretary-General after consultation with the President of the International Tribunal. He or she would be appointed to serve for a four-year term and be eligible for reappointment. The terms and conditions of service of the Registrar shall be those of an Assistant Secretary-General of the United Nations.

92. The corresponding article of the statute would read as follows:

Article 17: The Registry

1. The Registry shall be responsible for the administration and servicing of the International Tribunal.
2. The Registry shall consist of a Registrar and such other staff as may be required.
3. The Registrar shall be appointed by the Secretary-General after consultation with the President of the International Tribunal. He or she shall serve for a four-year term and be eligible for reappointment. The terms and conditions of service of the Registrar shall be those of an Assistant Secretary-General of the United Nations.
4. The staff of the Registry shall be appointed by the Secretary-General on the recommendation of the Registrar.

IV. INVESTIGATION AND PRE-TRIAL PROCEEDINGS

93. The Prosecutor would initiate investigations ex officio, or on the basis of information obtained from any source, particularly from Governments or United Nations organs, intergovernmental and non-governmental organizations. The Prosecutor would assess the information received or obtained and decide whether there is a sufficient basis to proceed.

94. In conducting his investigations, the Prosecutor should have the power to question suspects, victims and witnesses, to collect evidence and to conduct on-site investigations. In carrying out these tasks, the Prosecutor may, as appropriate, seek the assistance of the State authorities concerned.

95. Upon the completion of the investigation, if the Prosecutor has determined that a prima facie case exists for prosecution, he would prepare an indictment containing a concise statement of the facts and the crimes with which the accused is charged under the statute. The indictment would be transmitted to a judge of a Trial Chamber, who would review it and decide whether to confirm or to dismiss the indictment.

96. If the investigation includes questioning of the suspect, then he should have the right to be assisted by counsel of his own choice, including the right to have legal assistance assigned to him without payment by him in any such case if he does not have sufficient means to pay for it. He shall also be entitled to the necessary translation into and from a language he speaks and understands.

97. Upon confirmation of the indictment, the judge would, at the request of the Prosecutor, issue such orders and warrants for the arrest, detention, surrender and transfer of persons, or any other orders as may be necessary for the conduct of the trial.

98. The corresponding articles of the statute would read as follows:

Article 18: Investigation and preparation of indictment

1. The Prosecutor shall initiate investigations ex officio or on the basis of information obtained from any source, particularly from Governments, United Nations organs, intergovernmental and non-governmental organizations. The Prosecutor shall assess the information received or obtained and decide whether there is sufficient basis to proceed.

2. The Prosecutor shall have the power to question suspects, victims and witnesses, to collect evidence and to conduct on-site investigations. In carrying out these tasks the Prosecutor may, as appropriate, seek the assistance of the State authorities concerned.

3. If questioned, the suspect shall be entitled to be assisted by counsel of his own choice, including the right to have legal assistance assigned to him without payment by him in any such case if he does not have sufficient means to pay for it, as well as to necessary translation into and from a language he speaks and understands.

4. Upon a determination that a prima facie case exists, the Prosecutor shall prepare an indictment containing a concise statement of the facts and the crime or crimes with which the accused is charged under the Statute. The indictment shall be transmitted to a judge of the Trial Chamber.

Article 19: Review of the indictment

1. The judge of the Trial Chamber to whom the indictment has been transmitted shall review it. If satisfied that a prima facie case has been established by the Prosecutor, he shall confirm the indictment. If not so satisfied, the indictment shall be dismissed.

2. Upon confirmation of an indictment, the judge may, at the request of the Prosecutor, issue such orders and warrants for the arrest, detention, surrender or transfer of persons, and any other orders as may be required for the conduct of the trial.

V. TRIAL AND POST-TRIAL PROCEEDINGS

A. Commencement and conduct of trial proceedings

99. The Trial Chambers should ensure that a trial is fair and expeditious and that proceedings are conducted in accordance with the rules of procedure and evidence and with full respect for the rights of the accused. The Trial Chamber should also provide appropriate protection for victims and witnesses during the proceedings.

100. A person against whom an indictment has been confirmed would, pursuant to an order or a warrant of the International Tribunal, be informed of the contents of the indictment and taken into custody.

101. A trial should not commence until the accused is physically present before the International Tribunal. There is a widespread perception that trials in absentia should not be provided for in the statute as this would not be consistent with article 14 of the International Covenant on Civil and Political Rights, which provides that the accused shall be entitled to be tried in his presence.

102. The person against whom an indictment has been confirmed would be transferred to the seat of the International Tribunal and brought before a Trial Chamber without undue delay and formally charged. The Trial Chamber would read the indictment,

satisfy itself that the rights of the accused are respected, confirm that the accused understands the indictment, and instruct the accused to enter a plea. After the plea has been entered, the Trial Chamber would set the date for trial.

103. The hearings should be held in public unless the Trial Chamber decides otherwise in accordance with its rules of procedure and evidence.

104. After hearing the submissions of the parties and examining the witnesses and evidence presented to it, the Trial Chamber would close the hearing and retire for private deliberations.

105. The corresponding article of the statute would read:

Article 20: Commencement and conduct of trial proceedings

1. The Trial Chambers shall ensure that a trial is fair and expeditious and that proceedings are conducted in accordance with the rules of procedure and evidence, with full respect for the rights of the accused and due regard for the protection of victims and witnesses.

2. A person against whom an indictment has been confirmed shall, pursuant to an order or an arrest warrant of the International Tribunal, be taken into custody, immediately informed of the charges against him and transferred to the International Tribunal.

3. The Trial Chamber shall read the indictment, satisfy itself that the rights of the accused are respected, confirm that the accused understands the indictment, and instruct the accused to enter a plea. The Trial Chamber shall then set the date for trial.

4. The hearings shall be public unless the Trial Chamber decides to close the proceedings in accordance with its rules of procedure and evidence.

B. Rights of the accused

106. It is axiomatic that the International Tribunal must fully respect internationally recognized standards regarding the rights of the accused at all stages of its proceedings. In the view of the Secretary-General, such internationally recognized standards are, in particular, contained in article 14 of the International Covenant on Civil and Political Rights.

107. The corresponding article of the statute would read as follows:

Article 21: Rights of the accused

1. All persons shall be equal before the International Tribunal.

2. In the determination of charges against him, the accused shall be entitled to a fair and public hearing, subject to article 22 of the Statute.

3. The accused shall be presumed innocent until proved guilty according to the provisions of the present Statute.

4. In the determination of any charge against the accused pursuant to the present Statute, the accused shall be entitled to the following minimum guarantees, in full equality:

    (a) to be informed promptly and in detail in a language which he understands of the nature and cause of the charge against him;

    (b) to have adequate time and facilities for the preparation of his defence and to communicate with counsel of his own choosing;

    (c) to be tried without undue delay;

    (d) to be tried in his presence, and to defend himself in person or through legal assistance of his own choosing; to be informed, if he does not have legal assistance, of this right; and to have legal assistance assigned to him, in any case where the interests of justice so require, and without payment by him in any such case if he does not have sufficient means to pay for it;

    (e) to examine, or have examined, the witnesses against him and to obtain the attendance and examination of witnesses on his behalf under the same conditions as witnesses against him;

    (f) to have the free assistance of an interpreter if he cannot understand or speak the language used in the International Tribunal;

    (g) not to be compelled to testify against himself or to confess guilt.

C. Protection of victims and witnesses

108. In the light of the particular nature of the crimes committed in the former Yugoslavia, it will be necessary for the International Tribunal to ensure the protection of victims and witnesses. Necessary protection measures should therefore be provided in the rules of procedure and evidence for victims and witnesses, especially in cases of rape or sexual assault. Such measures should include, but should not be limited to the conduct of in camera proceedings, and the protection of the victim' s identity.

109. The corresponding article of the statute would read as follows:

Article 22: Protection of victims and witnesses

The International Tribunal shall provide in its rules of procedure and evidence for the protection of victims and witnesses. Such protection measures shall include, but shall not be limited to, the conduct of in camera proceedings and the protection of the victim's identity.

D. Judgement and penalties

110. The Trial Chambers would have the power to pronounce judgements and impose sentences and penalties on persons convicted of serious violations of international humanitarian law. A judgement would be rendered by a majority of the judges of the Chamber and delivered in public. It should be written and accompanied by a reasoned opinion. Separate or dissenting opinions should be permitted.

111. The penalty to be imposed on a convicted person would be limited to imprisonment. In determining the term of imprisonment, the Trial Chambers should have recourse to the general practice of prison sentences applicable in the courts of the former Yugoslavia.

112. The International Tribunal should not be empowered to impose the death penalty.

113. In imposing sentences, the Trial Chambers should take into account such factors as the gravity of the offence and the individual circumstances of the convicted person.

114. In addition to imprisonment, property and proceeds acquired by criminal conduct should be confiscated and returned to their rightful owners. This would include the return of property wrongfully acquired by means of duress. In this connection the Secretary-General recalls that in resolution 779 (1992) of 6 October 1992, the Security Council endorsed the principle that all statements or commitments made

under duress, particularly those relating to land and property, are wholly null and void.

115. The corresponding articles of the statute would read as follows:

Article 23: Judgement

1. The Trial Chambers shall pronounce judgements and impose sentences and penalties on persons convicted of serious violations of international humanitarian law.
2. The judgement shall be rendered by a majority of the judges of the Trial Chamber, and shall be delivered by the Trial Chamber in public. It shall be accompanied by a reasoned opinion in writing, to which separate or dissenting opinions may be appended.

Article 24: Penalties

1. The penalty imposed by the Trial Chamber shall be limited to imprisonment. In determining the terms of imprisonment, the Trial Chambers shall have recourse to the general practice regarding prison sentences in the courts of the former Yugoslavia.
2. In imposing the sentences, the Trial Chambers should take into account such factors as the gravity of the offence and the individual circumstances of the convicted person.
3. In addition to imprisonment, the Trial Chambers may order the return of any property and proceeds acquired by criminal conduct, including by means of duress, to their rightful owners.

E. Appellate and review proceedings

116. The Secretary-General is of the view that the right of appeal should be provided for under the Statute. Such a right is a fundamental element of individual civil and political rights and has, <u>inter alia</u>, been incorporated in the International Covenant on Civil and Political Rights. For this reason, the Secretary-General has proposed that there should be an Appeals Chamber.

117. The right of appeal should be exercisable on two grounds: an error on a question of law invalidating the decision or, an error of fact which has occasioned a miscarriage of justice. The Prosecutor should also be entitled to initiate appeal proceedings on the same grounds.

118. The judgement of the Appeals Chamber affirming, reversing or revising the judgement of the Trial Chamber would be final. It would be delivered by the Appeals Chamber in public and be accompanied by a reasoned opinion to which separate or dissenting opinions may be appended.

119. Where a new fact has come to light which was not known at the time of the proceedings before the Trial Chambers or the Appeals Chamber, and which could have been a decisive factor in reaching the decision, the convicted person or the Prosecutor should be authorized to submit to the International Tribunal an application for review of the judgement.

120. The corresponding articles of the statute would read as follows:

Article 25: Appellate proceedings

1. The Appeals Chamber shall hear appeals from persons convicted by the Trial Chambers or from the Prosecutor on the following grounds:
   (a) an error on a question of law invalidating the decision; or
   (b) an error of fact which has occasioned a miscarriage of justice.

2. The Appeals Chamber may affirm, reverse or revise the decisions taken by the Trial Chambers.

Article 26: Review proceedings

Where a new fact has been discovered which was not known at the time of the proceedings before the Trial Chambers or the Appeals Chamber and which could have been a decisive factor in reaching the decision, the convicted person or the Prosecutor may submit to the International Tribunal an application for review of the judgement.

F. Enforcement of sentences

121. The Secretary-General is of the view that, given the nature of the crimes in question and the international character of the tribunal, the enforcement of sentences should take place outside the territory of the former Yugoslavia. States should be encouraged to declare their readiness to carry out the enforcement of prison sentences in accordance with their domestic laws and procedures, under the supervision of the International Tribunal.

122. The Security Council would make appropriate arrangements to obtain from States an indication of their willingness to accept convicted persons. This information would be communicated to the Registrar, who would prepare a list of States in which the enforcement of sentences would be carried out.

123. The accused would be eligible for pardon or commutation of sentence in accordance with the laws of the State in which sentence is served. In such an event, the State concerned would notify the International Tribunal, which would decide the matter in accordance with the interests of justice and the general principles of law.

124. The corresponding article of the statute would read as follows:

Article 27: Enforcement of sentences

Imprisonment shall be served in a State designated by the International Tribunal from a list of States which have indicated to the Security Council their willingness to accept convicted persons. Such imprisonment shall be in accordance with the applicable law of the State concerned, subject to the supervision of the International Tribunal.

Article 28: Pardon or commutation of sentences

If, pursuant to the applicable law of the State in which the convicted person is imprisoned, he or she is eligible for pardon or commutation of sentence, the State concerned shall notify the International Tribunal accordingly. The President of the International Tribunal, in consultation with the judges, shall decide the matter on the basis of the interests of justice and the general principles of law.

VI. COOPERATION AND JUDICIAL ASSISTANCE

125. As pointed out in paragraph 23 above, the establishment of the International Tribunal on the basis of a Chapter VII decision creates a binding obligation on all States to take whatever steps are required to implement the decision. In practical terms, this means that all States would be under an obligation to cooperate with the International Tribunal and to assist it in all stages of the proceedings to ensure

compliance with requests for assistance in the gathering of evidence, hearing of witnesses, suspects and experts, identification and location of persons and the service of documents. Effect shall also be given to orders issued by the Trial Chambers, such as warrants of arrest, search warrants, warrants for surrender or transfer of persons, and any other orders necessary for the conduct of the trial.

126. In this connection, an order by a Trial Chamber for the surrender or transfer of persons to the custody of the International Tribunal shall be considered to be the application of an enforcement measure under Chapter VII of the Charter of the United Nations.

127. The corresponding article of the statute would read as follows:

Article 29: Cooperation and judicial assistance

1. States shall cooperate with the International Tribunal in the investigation and prosecution of persons accused of committing serious violations of international humanitarian law.

2. States shall comply without undue delay with any request for assistance or an order issued by a Trial Chamber, including, but not limited to:
   (a) the identification and location of persons;
   (b) the taking of testimony and the production of evidence;
   (c) the service of documents;
   (d) the arrest or detention of persons;
   (e) the surrender or the transfer of the accused to the International Tribunal.

VII. GENERAL PROVISIONS

A. The status, privileges and immunities of the International Tribunal

128. The Convention on the Privileges and Immunities of the United Nations of 13 February 1946 would apply to the International Tribunal, the judges, the Prosecutor and his staff, and the Registrar and his staff. The judges, the Prosecutor, and the Registrar would be granted the privileges and immunities, exemptions and facilities accorded to diplomatic envoys in accordance with international law. The staff of the Prosecutor and the Registrar would enjoy the privileges and immunities of officials of the United Nations within the meaning of articles V and VII of the Convention.

129. Other persons, including the accused, required at the seat of the International Tribunal would be accorded such treatment as is necessary for the proper functioning of the International Tribunal.

130. The corresponding article of the statute would read:

Article 30: The status, privileges and immunities of the International Tribunal

1. The Convention on the Privileges and Immunities of the United Nations of 13 February 1946 shall apply to the International Tribunal, the judges, the Prosecutor and his staff, and the Registrar and his staff.

2. The judges, the Prosecutor and the Registrar shall enjoy the privileges and immunities, exemptions and facilities accorded to diplomatic envoys, in accordance with international law.

3. The staff of the Prosecutor and of the Registrar shall enjoy the privileges and immunities accorded to officials of the United Nations under articles V and VII of the Convention referred to in paragraph 1 of this article.

4. Other persons, including the accused, required at the seat of the International Tribunal shall be accorded such treatment as is necessary for the proper functioning of the International Tribunal.

B. Seat of the International Tribunal

131. While it will be for the Security Council to determine the location of the seat of the International Tribunal, in the view of the Secretary-General, there are a number of elementary considerations of justice and fairness, as well as administrative efficiency and economy which should be taken into account. As a matter of justice and fairness, it would not be appropriate for the International Tribunal to have its seat in the territory of the former Yugoslavia or in any State neighbouring upon the former Yugoslavia. For reasons of administrative efficiency and economy, it would be desirable to establish the seat of the International Tribunal at a European location in which the United Nations already has an important presence. The two locations which fulfil these requirements are Geneva and The Hague. Provided that the necessary arrangements can be made with the host country, the Secretary-General believes that the seat of the International Tribunal should be at The Hague.

132. The corresponding article of the statute would read:

Article 31: Seat of the International Tribunal

The International Tribunal shall have its seat at The Hague.

C. Financial arrangements

133. The expenses of the International Tribunal should be borne by the regular budget of the United Nations in accordance with Article 17 of the Charter of the United Nations.

134. The corresponding article of the statute would read:

Article 32: Expenses of the International Tribunal

The expenses of the International Tribunal shall be borne by the regular budget of the United Nations in accordance with Article 17 of the Charter of the United Nations.

D. Working languages

135. The working languages of the Tribunal should be English and French.

136. The corresponding article of the statute would read as follows:

Article 33: Working languages

The working languages of the International Tribunal shall be English and French.

E. Annual report

137. The International Tribunal should submit an annual report on its activities to the Security Council and the General Assembly.

138. The corresponding article of the statute would read:

Article 34: Annual report

The President of the International Tribunal shall submit an annual report of the International Tribunal to the Security Council and to the General Assembly.

...

ANNEX

Statute of the International Tribunal

Having been established by the Security Council acting under Chapter VII of the Charter of the United Nations, the International Tribunal for the Prosecution of Persons Responsible for Serious Violations of International Humanitarian Law Committed in the Territory of the Former Yugoslavia since 1991 (hereinafter referred to as "the International Tribunal") shall function in accordance with the provisions of the present Statute.

Article 1
Competence of the International Tribunal

The International Tribunal shall have the power to prosecute persons responsible for serious violations of international humanitarian law committed in the territory of the former Yugoslavia since 1991 in accordance with the provisions of the present Statute.

Article 2
Grave breaches of the Geneva Conventions of 1949

The International Tribunal shall have the power to prosecute persons committing or ordering to be committed grave breaches of the Geneva Conventions of 12 August 1949, namely the following acts against persons or property protected under the provisions of the relevant Geneva Convention:
(a) wilful killing;
(b) torture or inhuman treatment, including biological experiments;
(c) wilfully causing great suffering or serious injury to body or health;
(d) extensive destruction and appropriation of property, not justified by military necessity and carried out unlawfully and wantonly;
(e) compelling a prisoner of war or a civilian to serve in the forces of a hostile power;
(f) wilfully depriving a prisoner of war or a civilian of the rights of fair and regular trial;
(g) unlawful deportation or transfer or unlawful confinement of a civilian;
(h) taking civilians as hostages.

Article 3
Violations of the laws or customs of war

The International Tribunal shall have the power to prosecute persons violating the laws or customs of war. Such violations shall include, but not be limited to:
(a) employment of poisonous weapons or other weapons calculated to cause unnecessary suffering;
(b) wanton destruction of cities, towns or villages, or devastation not justified by military necessity;

(c) attack, or bombardment, by whatever means, of undefended towns, villages, dwellings, or buildings;

(d) seizure of, destruction or wilful damage done to institutions dedicated to religion, charity and education, the arts and sciences, historic monuments and works of art and science;

(e) plunder of public or private property.

Article 4
Genocide

1. The International Tribunal shall have the power to prosecute persons committing genocide as defined in paragraph 2 of this article or of committing any of the other acts enumerated in paragraph 3 of this article.

2. Genocide means any of the following acts committed with intent to destroy, in whole or in part, a national, ethnical, racial or religious group, as such:

    (a) killing members of the group;
    (b) causing serious bodily or mental harm to members of the group;
    (c) deliberately inflicting on the group conditions of life calculated to bring about its physical destruction in whole or in part;
    (d) imposing measures intended to prevent births within the group;
    (e) forcibly transferring children of the group to another group.

3. The following acts shall be punishable:

    (a) genocide;
    (b) conspiracy to commit genocide;
    (c) direct and public incitement to commit genocide;
    (d) attempt to commit genocide;
    (e) complicity in genocide.

Article 5
Crimes against humanity

The International Tribunal shall have the power to prosecute persons responsible for the following crimes when committed in armed conflict, whether international or internal in character, and directed against any civilian population:

(a) murder;
(b) extermination;
(c) enslavement;
(d) deportation;
(e) imprisonment;
(f) torture;
(g) rape;
(h) persecutions on political, racial and religious grounds;
(i) other inhumane acts.

Article 6
Personal jurisdiction

The International Tribunal shall have jurisdiction over natural persons pursuant to the provisions of the present Statute.

Article 7
Individual criminal responsibility

1. A person who planned, instigated, ordered, committed or otherwise aided and abetted in the planning, preparation or execution of a crime referred to in articles 2 to 5 of the present Statute, shall be individually responsible for the crime.
2. The official position of any accused person, whether as Head of State or Government or as a responsible Government official, shall not relieve such person of criminal responsibility nor mitigate punishment.
3. The fact that any of the acts referred to in articles 2 to 5 of the present Statute was committed by a subordinate does not relieve his superior of criminal responsibility if he knew or had reason to know that the subordinate was about to commit such acts or had done so and the superior failed to take the necessary and reasonable measures to prevent such acts or to punish the perpetrators thereof.
4. The fact that an accused person acted pursuant to an order of a Government or of a superior shall not relieve him of criminal responsibility, but may be considered in mitigation of punishment if the International Tribunal determines that justice so requires.

Article 8
Territorial and temporal jurisdiction

The territorial jurisdiction of the International Tribunal shall extend to the territory of the former Socialist Federal Republic of Yugoslavia, including its land surface, airspace and territorial waters. The temporal jurisdiction of the International Tribunal shall extend to a period beginning on 1 January 1991.

Article 9
Concurrent jurisdiction

1. The International Tribunal and national courts shall have concurrent jurisdiction to prosecute persons for serious violations of international humanitarian law committed in the territory of the former Yugoslavia since 1 January 1991.
2. The International Tribunal shall have primacy over national courts. At any stage of the procedure, the International Tribunal may formally request national courts to defer to the competence of the International Tribunal in accordance with the present Statute and the Rules of Procedure and Evidence of the International Tribunal.

Article 10
Non-bis-in-idem

1. No person shall be tried before a national court for acts constituting serious violations of international humanitarian law under the present Statute, for which he or she has already been tried by the International Tribunal.
2. A person who has been tried by a national court for acts constituting serious violations of international humanitarian law may be subsequently tried by the International Tribunal only if:
    (a) the act for which he or she was tried was characterized as an ordinary crime; or
    (b) the national court proceedings were not impartial or independent, were designed to shield the accused from international criminal responsibility, or the case was not diligently prosecuted.

3. In considering the penalty to be imposed on a person convicted of a crime under the present Statute, the International Tribunal shall take into account the extent to which any penalty imposed by a national court on the same person for the same act has already been served.

Article 11
Organization of the International Tribunal
The International Tribunal shall consist of the following organs:
(a) The Chambers, comprising two Trial Chambers and an Appeals Chamber;
(b) The Prosecutor, and
(c) A Registry, servicing both the Chambers and the Prosecutor.

Article 12
Composition of the Chambers
The Chambers shall be composed of eleven independent judges, no two of whom may be nationals of the same State, who shall serve as follows:
(a) Three judges shall serve in each of the Trial Chambers;
(b) Five judges shall serve in the Appeals Chamber.

Article 13
Qualifications and election of judges
1. The judges shall be persons of high moral character, impartiality and integrity who possess the qualifications required in their respective countries for appointment to the highest judicial offices. In the overall composition of the Chambers due account shall be taken of the experience of the judges in criminal law, international law, including international humanitarian law and human rights law.
2. The judges of the International Tribunal shall be elected by the General Assembly from a list submitted by the Security Council, in the following manner:
    (a) The Secretary-General shall invite nominations for judges of the International Tribunal from States Members of the United Nations and non-member States maintaining permanent observer missions at United Nations Headquarters;
    (b) Within sixty days of the date of the invitation of the Secretary-General, each State may nominate up to two candidates meeting the qualifications set out in paragraph 1 above, no two of whom shall be of the same nationality;
    (c) The Secretary-General shall forward the nominations received to the Security Council. From the nominations received the Security Council shall establish a list of not less than twenty-two and not more than thirty-three candidates, taking due account of the adequate representation of the principal legal systems of the world;
    (d) The President of the Security Council shall transmit the list of candidates to the President of the General Assembly. From that list the General Assembly shall elect the eleven judges of the International Tribunal. The candidates who receive an absolute majority of the votes of the States Members of the United Nations and of the non-Member States maintaining permanent observer missions at United Nations Headquarters, shall be declared elected. Should two candidates

of the same nationality obtain the required majority vote, the one who received the higher number of votes shall be considered elected.

3. In the event of a vacancy in the Chambers, after consultation with the Presidents of the Security Council and of the General Assembly, the Secretary-General shall appoint a person meeting the qualifications of paragraph 1 above, for the remainder of the term of office concerned.

4. The judges shall be elected for a term of four years. The terms and conditions of service shall be those of the judges of the International Court of Justice. They shall be eligible for re-election.

Article 14
Officers and members of the Chambers

1. The judges of the International Tribunal shall elect a President.

2. The President of the International Tribunal shall be a member of the Appeals Chamber and shall preside over its proceedings.

3. After consultation with the judges of the International Tribunal, the President shall assign the judges to the Appeals Chamber and to the Trial Chambers. A judge shall serve only in the Chamber to which he or she was assigned.

4. The judges of each Trial Chamber shall elect a Presiding Judge, who shall conduct all of the proceedings of the Trial Chamber as a whole.

Article 15
Rules of procedure and evidence

The judges of the International Tribunal shall adopt rules of procedure and evidence for the conduct of the pre-trial phase of the proceedings, trials and appeals, the admission of evidence, the protection of victims and witnesses and other appropriate matters.

Article 16
The Prosecutor

1. The Prosecutor shall be responsible for the investigation and prosecution of persons responsible for serious violations of international humanitarian law committed in the territory of the former Yugoslavia since 1 January 1991.

2. The Prosecutor shall act independently as a separate organ of the International Tribunal. He or she shall not seek or receive instructions from any Government or from any other source.

3. The Office of the Prosecutor shall be composed of a Prosecutor and such other qualified staff as may be required.

4. The Prosecutor shall be appointed by the Security Council on nomination by the Secretary-General. He or she shall be of high moral character and possess the highest level of competence and experience in the conduct of investigations and prosecutions of criminal cases. The Prosecutor shall serve for a four-year term and be eligible for reappointment. The terms and conditions of service of the Prosecutor shall be those of an Under-Secretary-General of the United Nations.

5. The staff of the Office of the Prosecutor shall be appointed by the Secretary-General on the recommendation of the Prosecutor.

Article 17

The Registry

1. The Registry shall be responsible for the administration and servicing of the International Tribunal.
2. The Registry shall consist of a Registrar and such other staff as may be required.
3. The Registrar shall be appointed by the Secretary-General after consultation with the President of the International Tribunal. He or she shall serve for a four-year term and be eligible for reappointment. The terms and conditions of service of the Registrar shall be those of an Assistant Secretary-General of the United Nations.
4. The staff of the Registry shall be appointed by the Secretary-General on the recommendation of the Registrar.

Article 18

Investigation and preparation of indictment

1. The Prosecutor shall initiate investigations ex-officio or on the basis of information obtained from any source, particularly from Governments, United Nations organs, intergovernmental and non-governmental organizations. The Prosecutor shall assess the information received or obtained and decide whether there is sufficient basis to proceed.
2. The Prosecutor shall have the power to question suspects, victims and witnesses, to collect evidence and to conduct on-site investigations. In carrying out these tasks, the Prosecutor may, as appropriate, seek the assistance of the State authorities concerned.
3. If questioned, the suspect shall be entitled to be assisted by counsel of his own choice, including the right to have legal assistance assigned to him without payment by him in any such case if he does not have sufficient means to pay for it, as well as to necessary translation into and from a language he speaks and understands.
4. Upon a determination that a prima facie case exists, the Prosecutor shall prepare an indictment containing a concise statement of the facts and the crime or crimes with which the accused is charged under the Statute. The indictment shall be transmitted to a judge of the Trial Chamber.

Article 19

Review of the indictment

1. The judge of the Trial Chamber to whom the indictment has been transmitted shall review it. If satisfied that a prima facie case has been established by the Prosecutor, he shall confirm the indictment. If not so satisfied, the indictment shall be dismissed.
2. Upon confirmation of an indictment, the judge may, at the request of the Prosecutor, issue such orders and warrants for the arrest, detention, surrender or transfer of persons, and any other orders as may be required for the conduct of the trial.

Article 20

Commencement and conduct of trial proceedings

1. The Trial Chambers shall ensure that a trial is fair and expeditious and that proceedings are conducted in accordance with the rules of procedure and evidence, with full respect for the rights of the accused and due regard for the protection of victims and witnesses.

2. A person against whom an indictment has been confirmed shall, pursuant to an order or an arrest warrant of the International Tribunal, be taken into custody, immediately informed of the charges against him and transferred to the International Tribunal.

3. The Trial Chamber shall read the indictment, satisfy itself that the rights of the accused are respected, confirm that the accused understands the indictment, and instruct the accused to enter a plea. The Trial Chamber shall then set the date for trial.

4. The hearings shall be public unless the Trial Chamber decides to close the proceedings in accordance with its rules of procedure and evidence.

Article 21
Rights of the accused

1. All persons shall be equal before the International Tribunal.

2. In the determination of charges against him, the accused shall be entitled to a fair and public hearing, subject to article 22 of the Statute.

3. The accused shall be presumed innocent until proved guilty according to the provisions of the present Statute.

4. In the determination of any charge against the accused pursuant to the present Statute, the accused shall be entitled to the following minimum guarantees, in full equality:

   (a) to be informed promptly and in detail in a language which he understands of the nature and cause of the charge against him;

   (b) to have adequate time and facilities for the preparation of his defence and to communicate with counsel of his own choosing;

   (c) to be tried without undue delay;

   (d) to be tried in his presence, and to defend himself in person or through legal assistance of his own choosing; to be informed, if he does not have legal assistance, of this right; and to have legal assistance assigned to him, in any case where the interests of justice so require, and without payment by him in any such case if he does not have sufficient means to pay for it;

   (e) to examine, or have examined, the witnesses against him and to obtain the attendance and examination of witnesses on his behalf under the same conditions as witnesses against him;

   (f) to have the free assistance of an interpreter if he cannot understand or speak the language used in the International Tribunal;

   (g) not to be compelled to testify against himself or to confess guilt.

Article 22
Protection of victims and witnesses

The International Tribunal shall provide in its rules of procedure and evidence for the protection of victims and witnesses. Such protection measures shall include, but shall not be limited to, the conduct of in camera proceedings and the protection of the victim' s identity.

Article 23
Judgement

1. The Trial Chambers shall pronounce judgements and impose sentences and penalties on persons convicted of serious violations of international humanitarian law.

2. The judgement shall be rendered by a majority of the judges of the Trial Chamber, and shall be delivered by the Trial Chamber in public. It shall be accompanied by a reasoned opinion in writing, to which separate or dissenting opinions may be appended.

Article 24
Penalties

1. The penalty imposed by the Trial Chamber shall be limited to imprisonment. In determining the terms of imprisonment, the Trial Chambers shall have recourse to the general practice regarding prison sentences in the courts of the former Yugoslavia.
2. In imposing the sentences, the Trial Chambers should take into account such factors as the gravity of the offence and the individual circumstances of the convicted person.
3. In addition to imprisonment, the Trial Chambers may order the return of any property and proceeds acquired by criminal conduct, including by means of duress, to their rightful owners.

Article 25
Appellate proceedings

1. The Appeals Chamber shall hear appeals from persons convicted by the Trial Chambers or from the Prosecutor on the following grounds:
    (a) an error on a question of law invalidating the decision; or
    (b) an error of fact which has occasioned a miscarriage of justice.
2. The Appeals Chamber may affirm, reverse or revise the decisions taken by the Trial Chambers.

Article 26
Review proceedings

Where a new fact has been discovered which was not known at the time of the proceedings before the Trial Chambers or the Appeals Chamber and which could have been a decisive factor in reaching the decision, the convicted person or the Prosecutor may submit to the International Tribunal an application for review of the judgement.

Article 27
Enforcement of sentences

Imprisonment shall be served in a State designated by the International Tribunal from a list of States which have indicated to the Security Council their willingness to accept convicted persons. Such imprisonment shall be in accordance with the applicable law of the State concerned, subject to the supervision of the International Tribunal.

Article 28
Pardon or commutation of sentences

If, pursuant to the applicable law of the State in which the convicted person is imprisoned, he or she is eligible for pardon or commutation of sentence, the State concerned shall notify the International Tribunal accordingly. The President of the International Tribunal, in consultation with the judges, shall decide the matter on the basis of the interests of justice and the general principles of law.

Article 29
Cooperation and judicial assistance

1. States shall cooperate with the International Tribunal in the investigation and prosecution of persons accused of committing serious violations of international humanitarian law.
2. States shall comply without undue delay with any request for assistance or an order issued by a Trial Chamber, including, but not limited to:
   (a) the identification and location of persons;
   (b) the taking of testimony and the production of evidence;
   (c) the service of documents;
   (d) the arrest or detention of persons;
   (e) the surrender or the transfer of the accused to the International Tribunal.

Article 30
The status, privileges and immunities of the International Tribunal

1. The Convention on the Privileges and Immunities of the United Nations of 13 February 1946 shall apply to the International Tribunal, the judges, the Prosecutor and his staff, and the Registrar and his staff.
2. The judges, the Prosecutor and the Registrar shall enjoy the privileges and immunities, exemptions and facilities accorded to diplomatic envoys, in accordance with international law.
3. The staff of the Prosecutor and of the Registrar shall enjoy the privileges and immunities accorded to officials of the United Nations under articles V and VII of the Convention referred to in paragraph 1 of this article.
4. Other persons, including the accused, required at the seat of the International Tribunal shall be accorded such treatment as is necessary for the proper functioning of the International Tribunal.

Article 31
Seat of the International Tribunal

The International Tribunal shall have its seat at The Hague.

Article 32
Expenses of the International Tribunal

The expenses of the International Tribunal shall be borne by the regular budget of the United Nations in accordance with Article 17 of the Charter of the United Nations.

Article 33
Working languages

The working languages of the International Tribunal shall be English and French.

Article 34
Annual report

The President of the International Tribunal shall submit an annual report of the International Tribunal to the Security Council and to the General Assembly.

1993 International Criminal Tribunal for Former Yugoslavia (ICTY); UN Security Council Resolution No. 827; Updated Statute of the ICTY; UN Security Council Resolution No. 1966 and 2010 Residual Mechanism for the International Criminal Tribunals (MICT Statute)

United Nations Security Council Resolution 827 (1993)

The Security Council,

Reaffirming its resolution 713 (1991) of 25 September 1991 and all subsequent relevant resolutions,

Having considered the report of the Secretary-General (S/25704 and Add.l) pursuant to paragraph 2 of resolution 808 (1993),

Expressing once again its grave alarm at continuing reports of widespread and flagrant violations of international humanitarian law occurring within the territory of the former Yugoslavia, and especially in the Republic of Bosnia and Herzegovina, including reports of mass killings, massive, organized and systematic detention and rape of women, and the continuance of the practice of "ethnic cleansing", including for the acquisition and the holding of territory,

Determining that this situation continues to constitute a threat to international peace and security,

Determined to put an end to such crimes and to take effective measures to bring to justice the persons who are responsible for them,

Convinced that in the particular circumstances of the former Yugoslavia the establishment as an ad hoc measure by the Council of an international tribunal and the prosecution of persons responsible for serious violations of international humanitarian law would enable this aim to be achieved and would contribute to the restoration and maintenance of peace,

Believing that the establishment of an international tribunal and the prosecution of persons responsible for the above-mentioned violations of international humanitarian law will contribute to ensuring that such violations are halted and effectively redressed,

Noting in this regard the recommendation by the Co-Chairmen of the Steering Committee of the International Conference on the Former Yugoslavia for the establishment of such a tribunal

Reaffirming in this regard its decision in resolution 808 (1993) that an international tribunal shall be established for the prosecution of persons responsible for serious violations of international humanitarian law committed in the territory of the former Yugoslavia since 1991,

Considering that, pending the appointment of the Prosecutor of the International Tribunal, the Commission of Experts established pursuant to resolution 780 (1992) should continue on an urgent basis the collection of information relating to evidence of grave breaches of the Geneva Conventions and other violations of international humanitarian law as proposed in its interim report (S/25274),

Acting under Chapter VII of the Charter of the United Nations,

1. Approves the report of the Secretary-General;
2. Decides hereby to establish an international tribunal for the sole purpose of prosecuting persons responsible for serious violations of international humanitarian law committed in the territory of the former Yugoslavia between 1 January 1991 and a date to be determined by the Security Council upon the restoration of peace and to this end to adopt the Statute of the International Tribunal annexed to the above-mentioned report;
3. Requests the Secretary-General to submit to the judges of the International Tribunal, upon their election, any suggestions received from states for the rules of procedure and evidence called for in Article 15 of the Statute of the International Tribunal;
4. Decides that all States shall cooperate fully with the International Tribunal and its organs in accordance with the present resolution and the Statute of the International Tribunal and that consequently all States shall take any measures necessary under their domestic law to implement the provisions of the present resolution and the Statute, including the obligation of States to comply with requests for assistance or orders issued by a Trial Chamber under Article 29 of the Statute;
5. Urges States and intergovernmental and non-governmental organizations to contribute funds, equipment and services to the International Tribunal, including the offer of expert personnel.
6. Decides that the determination of the seat of the International Tribunal is subject to the conclusion of appropriate arrangements between the United Nations and the Netherlands acceptable to the Council, and that the International Tribunal may sit elsewhere when it considers it necessary for the efficient exercise of its functions;
7. Decides also that the work of the International Tribunal shall be carried out without prejudice to the right of the victims to seek, through appropriate means, compensation for damages incurred as a result of violations of international humanitarian law;
8. Requests the Secretary-General to implement urgently the present resolution and in particular to make practical arrangements for the effective functioning of the International Tribunal at the earliest time and to report periodically to the Council;
9. Decides to remain actively seized of the matter.

Updated Statute of the International Criminal Tribunal for the Former Yugoslavia

Having been established by the Security Council acting under Chapter VII of the Charter of the United Nations, the International Tribunal for the Prosecution of Persons Responsible for Serious Violations of International Humanitarian Law Committed in the Territory of the Former Yugoslavia since 1991 (hereinafter referred to as "the International Tribunal") shall function in accordance with the provisions of the present Statute.

Article 1
Competence of the International Tribunal
The International Tribunal shall have the power to prosecute persons responsible for serious violations of international humanitarian law committed in the territory of the former Yugoslavia since 1991 in accordance with the provisions of the present Statute.

Article 2
Grave breaches of the Geneva Conventions of 1949
The International Tribunal shall have the power to prosecute persons committing or ordering to be committed grave breaches of the Geneva Conventions of 12 August 1949, namely the following acts against persons or property protected under the provisions of the relevant Geneva Convention:
(a) wilful killing;
(b) torture or inhuman treatment, including biological experiments;
(c) wilfully causing great suffering or serious injury to body or health;
(d) extensive destruction and appropriation of property, not justified by military necessity and carried out unlawfully and wantonly;
(e) compelling a prisoner of war or a civilian to serve in the forces of a hostile power;
(f) wilfully depriving a prisoner of war or a civilian of the rights of fair and regular trial;
(g) unlawful deportation or transfer or unlawful confinement of a civilian;
(h) taking civilians as hostages.

Article 3
Violations of the laws or customs of war
The International Tribunal shall have the power to prosecute persons violating the laws or customs of war. Such violations shall include, but not be limited to:
(a) employment of poisonous weapons or other weapons calculated to cause unnecessary suffering;
(b) wanton destruction of cities, towns or villages, or devastation not justified by military necessity;
(c) attack, or bombardment, by whatever means, of undefended towns, villages, dwellings, or buildings;
(d) seizure of, destruction or wilful damage done to institutions dedicated to religion, charity and education, the arts and sciences, historic monuments and works of art and science;
(e) plunder of public or private property.

Article 4
Genocide
1. The International Tribunal shall have the power to prosecute persons committing genocide as defined in paragraph 2 of this article or of committing any of the other acts enumerated in paragraph 3 of this article.
2. Genocide means any of the following acts committed with intent to destroy, in whole or in part, a national, ethnical, racial or religious group, as such:
   (a) killing members of the group;
   (b) causing serious bodily or mental harm to members of the group;

(c) deliberately inflicting on the group conditions of life calculated to bring about its physical destruction in whole or in part;

(d) imposing measures intended to prevent births within the group;

(e) forcibly transferring children of the group to another group.

3. The following acts shall be punishable:

    (a) genocide;

    (b) conspiracy to commit genocide;

    (c) direct and public incitement to commit genocide;

    (d) attempt to commit genocide;

    (e) complicity in genocide.

Article 5
Crimes against humanity

The International Tribunal shall have the power to prosecute persons responsible for the following crimes when committed in armed conflict, whether international or internal in character, and directed against any civilian population:

(a) murder;

(b) extermination;

(c) enslavement;

(d) deportation;

(e) imprisonment;

(f) torture;

(g) rape;

(h) persecutions on political, racial and religious grounds;

(i) other inhumane acts.

Article 6
Personal jurisdiction

The International Tribunal shall have jurisdiction over natural persons pursuant to the provisions of the present Statute.

Article 7
Individual criminal responsibility

1. A person who planned, instigated, ordered, committed or otherwise aided and abetted in the planning, preparation or execution of a crime referred to in articles 2 to 5 of the present Statute, shall be individually responsible for the crime.

2. The official position of any accused person, whether as Head of State or Government or as a responsible Government official, shall not relieve such person of criminal responsibility nor mitigate punishment.

3. The fact that any of the acts referred to in articles 2 to 5 of the present Statute was committed by a subordinate does not relieve his superior of criminal responsibility if he knew or had reason to know that the subordinate was about to commit such acts or had done so and the superior failed to take the necessary and reasonable measures to prevent such acts or to punish the perpetrators thereof.

4. The fact that an accused person acted pursuant to an order of a Government or of a superior shall not relieve him of criminal responsibility, but may be considered in mitigation of punishment if the International Tribunal determines that justice so requires.

Article 8
Territorial and temporal jurisdiction
The territorial jurisdiction of the International Tribunal shall extend to the territory of the former Socialist Federal Republic of Yugoslavia, including its land surface, airspace and territorial waters. The temporal jurisdiction of the International Tribunal shall extend to a period beginning on 1 January 1991.

Article 9
Concurrent jurisdiction
1. The International Tribunal and national courts shall have concurrent jurisdiction to prosecute persons for serious violations of international humanitarian law committed in the territory of the former Yugoslavia since 1 January 1991.
2. The International Tribunal shall have primacy over national courts. At any stage of the procedure, the International Tribunal may formally request national courts to defer to the competence of the International Tribunal in accordance with the present Statute and the Rules of Procedure and Evidence of the International Tribunal.

Article 10
Non-bis-in-idem
1. No person shall be tried before a national court for acts constituting serious violations of international humanitarian law under the present Statute, for which he or she has already been tried by the International Tribunal.
2. A person who has been tried by a national court for acts constituting serious violations of international humanitarian law may be subsequently tried by the International Tribunal only if:
   (a) the act for which he or she was tried was characterized as an ordinary crime; or
   (b) the national court proceedings were not impartial or independent, were designed to shield the accused from international criminal responsibility, or the case was not diligently prosecuted.
3. In considering the penalty to be imposed on a person convicted of a crime under the present Statute, the International Tribunal shall take into account the extent to which any penalty imposed by a national court on the same person for the same act has already been served.

Article 11
Organization of the International Tribunal
The International Tribunal shall consist of the following organs:
(a) the Chambers, comprising three Trial Chambers and an Appeals Chamber;
(b) the Prosecutor; and
(c) a Registry, servicing both the Chambers and the Prosecutor.

Article 12
Composition of the Chambers

1. The Chambers shall be composed of a maximum of sixteen permanent independent judges, no two of whom may be nationals of the same State, and a maximum at any one time of twelve *ad litem* independent judges appointed in accordance with article 13 *ter*, paragraph 2, of the Statute, no two of whom may be nationals of the same State.

2. A maximum at any one time of three permanent judges and six *ad litem* judges shall be members of each Trial Chamber. Each Trial Chamber to which *ad litem* judges are assigned may be divided into sections of three judges each, composed of both permanent and *ad litem* judges, except in the circumstances specified in paragraph 5 below. A section of a Trial Chamber shall have the same powers and responsibilities as a Trial Chamber under the Statute and shall render judgement in accordance with the same rules.

3. Seven of the permanent judges shall be members of the Appeals Chamber. The Appeals Chamber shall, for each appeal, be composed of five of its members.

4. A person who for the purposes of membership of the Chambers of the International Tribunal could be regarded as a national of more than one State shall be deemed to be a national of the State in which that person ordinarily exercises civil and political rights.

5. The Secretary-General may, at the request of the President of the International Tribunal appoint, from among the *ad litem* judges elected in accordance with Article 13 *ter*, reserve judges to be present at each stage of a trial to which they have been appointed and to replace a judge if that judge is unable to continue sitting.

6. Without prejudice to paragraph 2 above, in the event that exceptional circumstances require for a permanent judge in a section of a Trial Chamber to be replaced resulting in a section solely comprised of *ad litem* judges, that section may continue to hear the case, notwithstanding that its composition no longer includes a permanent judge.

Article 13
Qualifications of judges

The permanent and *ad litem* judges shall be persons of high moral character, impartiality and integrity who possess the qualifications required in their respective countries for appointment to the highest judicial offices. In the overall composition of the Chambers and sections of the Trial Chambers, due account shall be taken of the experience of the judges in criminal law, international law, including international humanitarian law and human rights law.

Article 13 *bis*
Election of permanent judges

1. Fourteen of the permanent judges of the International Tribunal shall be elected by the General Assembly from a list submitted by the Security Council, in the following manner:

    (a) The Secretary-General shall invite nominations for judges of the International Tribunal from States Members of the United Nations and non-member States maintaining permanent observer missions at United Nations Headquarters;

    (b) Within sixty days of the date of the invitation of the Secretary-General, each State may nominate up to two candidates meeting the qualifications set out in article 13 of the Statute, no two of whom shall be of the same nationality and neither of whom shall be of the same nationality as any judge who is a member of the Appeals Chamber and who was elected or appointed a permanent judge of the International Criminal Tribunal for the Prosecution of Persons Responsible for Genocide and Other Serious Violations of International Humanitarian Law Committed in the Territory of Rwanda and Rwandan Citizens Responsible for Genocide and Other Such Violations Committed in the Territory of Neighbouring States, between 1 January 1994 and 31 December 1994 (hereinafter referred to as "The International Tribunal for Rwanda") in accordance with article 12 *bis* of the Statute of that Tribunal;

(c) The Secretary-General shall forward the nominations received to the Security Council. From the nominations received the Security Council shall establish a list of not less than twenty-eight and not more than forty-two candidates, taking due account of the adequate representation of the principal legal systems of the world;

(d) The President of the Security Council shall transmit the list of candidates to the President of the General Assembly. From that list the General Assembly shall elect fourteen permanent judges of the International Tribunal. The candidates who receive an absolute majority of the votes of the States Members of the United Nations and of the non-member States maintaining permanent observer missions at United Nations Headquarters, shall be declared elected. Should two candidates of the same nationality obtain the required majority vote, the one who received the higher number of votes shall be considered elected.

2. In the event of a vacancy in the Chambers amongst the permanent judges elected or appointed in accordance with this article, after consultation with the Presidents of the Security Council and of the General Assembly, the Secretary-General shall appoint a person meeting the qualifications of article 13 of the Statute, for the remainder of the term of office concerned.

3. The permanent judges elected in accordance with this article shall be elected for a term of four years. The terms and conditions of service shall be those of the judges of the International Court of Justice. They shall be eligible for re-election.

Article 13 *ter*
Election and appointment of *ad litem* judges
1. The *ad litem* judges of the International Tribunal shall be elected by the General Assembly from a list submitted by the Security Council, in the following manner:

(a) The Secretary-General shall invite nominations for *ad litem* judges of the International Tribunal from States Members of the United Nations and non-member States maintaining permanent observer missions at United Nations Headquarters.

(b) Within sixty days of the date of the invitation of the Secretary-General, each State may nominate up to four candidates meeting the qualifications set out in article 13 of the Statute, taking into account the importance of a fair representation of female and male candidates.

(c) The Secretary-General shall forward the nominations received to the Security Council. From the nominations received the Security Council shall establish a list of not less than fifty-four candidates, taking due account of the adequate representation of the principal legal systems of the world and bearing in mind the importance of equitable geographical distribution.

(d) The President of the Security Council shall transmit the list of candidates to the President of the General Assembly. From that list the General Assembly shall elect the twenty-seven *ad litem* judges of the International Tribunal. The candidates who receive an absolute majority of the votes of the States Members of the United Nations and of the non-member States maintaining permanent observer missions at United Nations Headquarters shall be declared elected.

(e) The *ad litem* judges shall be elected for a term of four years. They shall be eligible for re-election.

2. During any term, *ad litem* judges will be appointed by the Secretary-General, upon request of the President of the International Tribunal, to serve in the Trial Chambers for one or more trials, for a cumulative period of up to, but not including, three years. When requesting the appointment of any particular *ad litem* judge, the President of the International Tribunal shall bear in mind the criteria set out in article 13 of the Statute regarding the composition of the Chambers and sections of the Trial Chambers, the considerations set out in paragraphs 1(b) and (c) above and the number of votes the *ad litem* judge received in the General Assembly.

Article 13 *quater*
Status of *ad litem* judges

1. During the period in which they are appointed to serve in the International Tribunal, *ad litem* judges shall:
   (a) Benefit from the same terms and conditions of service *mutatis mutandis* as the permanent judges of the International Tribunal;
   (b) Enjoy, subject to paragraph 2 below, the same powers as the permanent judges of the International Tribunal;
   (c) Enjoy the privileges and immunities, exemptions and facilities of a judge of the International Tribunal;
   (d) Enjoy the power to adjudicate in pre-trial proceedings in cases other than those that they have been appointed to try.

2. During the period in which they are appointed to serve in the International Tribunal, *ad litem* judges shall not:
   (a) Be eligible for election as, or to vote in the election of, the President of the Tribunal or the Presiding Judge of a Trial Chamber pursuant to article 14 of the Statute;
   (b) Have power:
      (i) To adopt rules of procedure and evidence pursuant to article 15 of the Statute. They shall, however, be consulted before the adoption of those rules;
      (ii) To review an indictment pursuant to article 19 of the Statute;
      (iii) To consult with the President in relation to the assignment of judges pursuant to article 14 of the Statute or in relation to a pardon or commutation of sentence pursuant to article 28 of the Statute.

3. Notwithstanding paragraphs 1 and 2 above, an *ad litem* judge who is serving as a reserve judge shall, during such time as he or she so serves:
   (a) Benefit from the same terms and conditions of service *mutatis mutandis* as the permanent judges of the International Tribunal;

(b) Enjoy the privileges and immunities, exemptions and facilities of a judge of the International Tribunal;

(c) Enjoy the power to adjudicate in pre-trial proceedings in cases other than those that they have been appointed to and for that purpose to enjoy subject to paragraph 2 above, the same powers as permanent judges.

4. In the event that a reserve judge replaces a judge who is unable to continue sitting, he or she will, as of that time, benefit from the provisions of paragraph 1 above.

Article 14
Officers and members of the Chambers

1. The permanent judges of the International Tribunal shall elect a President from amongst their number.

2. The President of the International Tribunal shall be a member of the Appeals Chamber and shall preside over its proceedings.

3. After consultation with the permanent judges of the International Tribunal, the President shall assign four of the permanent judges elected or appointed in accordance with article 13 *bis* of the Statute to the Appeals Chamber and nine to the Trial Chambers. Notwithstanding the provisions of article 12, paragraph 1, and article 12, paragraph 3, the President may assign to the Appeals Chamber up to four additional permanent judges serving in the Trial Chambers, on the completion of the cases to which each judge is assigned. The term of office of each judge redeployed to the Appeals Chamber shall be the same as the term of office of the judges serving in the Appeals Chamber.

4. Two of the permanent judges of the International Tribunal for Rwanda elected or appointed in accordance with article 12 *bis* of the Statute of that Tribunal shall be assigned by the President of that Tribunal, in consultation with the President of the International Tribunal, to be members of the Appeals Chamber and permanent judges of the International Tribunal. Notwithstanding the provisions of article 12, paragraph 1, and article 12, paragraph 3, up to four additional permanent judges serving in the Trial Chambers of the International Criminal Tribunal for Rwanda may be assigned to the Appeals Chamber by the President of that Tribunal, on the completion of the cases to which each judge is assigned. The term of office of each judge redeployed to the Appeals Chamber shall be the same as the term of office of the judges serving in the Appeals Chamber.

5. After consultation with the permanent judges of the International Tribunal, the President shall assign such *ad litem* judges as may from time to time be appointed to serve in the International Tribunal to the Trial Chambers.

6. A judge shall serve only in the Chamber to which he or she was assigned.

7. The permanent judges of each Trial Chamber shall elect a Presiding Judge from amongst their number, who shall oversee the work of the Trial Chamber as a whole.

Article 15
Rules of procedure and evidence

The judges of the International Tribunal shall adopt rules of procedure and evidence for the conduct of the pre-trial phase of the proceedings, trials and appeals, the admission of evidence, the protection of victims and witnesses and other appropriate matters.

12

Article 16
The Prosecutor

1. The Prosecutor shall be responsible for the investigation and prosecution of persons responsible for serious violations of international humanitarian law committed in the territory of the former Yugoslavia since 1 January 1991.
2. The Prosecutor shall act independently as a separate organ of the International Tribunal. He or she shall not seek or receive instructions from any Government or from any other source.
3. The Office of the Prosecutor shall be composed of a Prosecutor and such other qualified staff as may be required.
4. The Prosecutor shall be appointed by the Security Council on nomination by the Secretary-General. He or she shall be of high moral character and possess the highest level of competence and experience in the conduct of investigations and prosecutions of criminal cases. The Prosecutor shall serve for a four-year term and be eligible for reappointment. The terms and conditions of service of the Prosecutor shall be those of an Under-Secretary-General of the United Nations.
5. The staff of the Office of the Prosecutor shall be appointed by the Secretary-General on the recommendation of the Prosecutor.

Article 17
The Registry

1. The Registry shall be responsible for the administration and servicing of the International Tribunal.
2. The Registry shall consist of a Registrar and such other staff as may be required.
3. The Registrar shall be appointed by the Secretary-General after consultation with the President of the International Tribunal. He or she shall serve for a four-year term and be eligible for reappointment. The terms and conditions of service of the Registrar shall be those of an Assistant Secretary-General of the United Nations.
4. The staff of the Registry shall be appointed by the Secretary-General on the recommendation of the Registrar.

Article 18
Investigation and preparation of indictment

1. The Prosecutor shall initiate investigations *ex-officio* or on the basis of information obtained from any source, particularly from Governments, United Nations organs, intergovernmental and non-governmental organisations. The Prosecutor shall assess the information received or obtained and decide whether there is sufficient basis to proceed.
2. The Prosecutor shall have the power to question suspects, victims and witnesses, to collect evidence and to conduct on-site investigations. In carrying out these tasks, the Prosecutor may, as appropriate, seek the assistance of the State authorities concerned.
3. If questioned, the suspect shall be entitled to be assisted by counsel of his own choice, including the right to have legal assistance assigned to him without payment by him in any such case if he does not have sufficient means to pay for it, as well as to necessary translation into and from a language he speaks and understands.

4. Upon a determination that a *prima facie* case exists, the Prosecutor shall prepare an indictment containing a concise statement of the facts and the crime or crimes with which the accused is charged under the Statute. The indictment shall be transmitted to a judge of the Trial Chamber.

Article 19
Review of the indictment
1. The judge of the Trial Chamber to whom the indictment has been transmitted shall review it. If satisfied that a *prima facie* case has been established by the Prosecutor, he shall confirm the indictment. If not so satisfied, the indictment shall be dismissed.
2. Upon confirmation of an indictment, the judge may, at the request of the Prosecutor, issue such orders and warrants for the arrest, detention, surrender or transfer of persons, and any other orders as may be required for the conduct of the trial.

Article 20
Commencement and conduct of trial proceedings
1. The Trial Chambers shall ensure that a trial is fair and expeditious and that proceedings are conducted in accordance with the rules of procedure and evidence, with full respect for the rights of the accused and due regard for the protection of victims and witnesses.
2. A person against whom an indictment has been confirmed shall, pursuant to an order or an arrest warrant of the International Tribunal, be taken into custody, immediately informed of the charges against him and transferred to the International Tribunal.
3. The Trial Chamber shall read the indictment, satisfy itself that the rights of the accused are respected, confirm that the accused understands the indictment, and instruct the accused to enter a plea. The Trial Chamber shall then set the date for trial.
4. The hearings shall be public unless the Trial Chamber decides to close the proceedings in accordance with its rules of procedure and evidence.

Article 21
Rights of the accused
1. All persons shall be equal before the International Tribunal.
2. In the determination of charges against him, the accused shall be entitled to a fair and public hearing, subject to article 22 of the Statute.
3. The accused shall be presumed innocent until proved guilty according to the provisions of the present Statute.
4. In the determination of any charge against the accused pursuant to the present Statute, the accused shall be entitled to the following minimum guarantees, in full equality:
   (a) to be informed promptly and in detail in a language which he understands of the nature and cause of the charge against him;
   (b) to have adequate time and facilities for the preparation of his defence and to communicate with counsel of his own choosing;
   (c) to be tried without undue delay;
   (d) to be tried in his presence, and to defend himself in person or through legal assistance of his own choosing; to be informed, if he does not have legal assistance, of this right; and to have legal assistance assigned to him, in any case where the

interests of justice so require, and without payment by him in any such case if he does not have sufficient means to pay for it;

(e) to examine, or have examined, the witnesses against him and to obtain the attendance and examination of witnesses on his behalf under the same conditions as witnesses against him;

(f) to have the free assistance of an interpreter if he cannot understand or speak the language used in the International Tribunal;

(g) not to be compelled to testify against himself or to confess guilt.

Article 22
Protection of victims and witnesses

The International Tribunal shall provide in its rules of procedure and evidence for the protection of victims and witnesses. Such protection measures shall include, but shall not be limited to, the conduct of in camera proceedings and the protection of the victim's identity.

Article 23
Judgement

1. The Trial Chambers shall pronounce judgements and impose sentences and penalties on persons convicted of serious violations of international humanitarian law.

2. The judgement shall be rendered by a majority of the judges of the Trial Chamber, and shall be delivered by the Trial Chamber in public. It shall be accompanied by a reasoned opinion in writing, to which separate or dissenting opinions may be appended.

Article 24
Penalties

1. The penalty imposed by the Trial Chamber shall be limited to imprisonment. In determining the terms of imprisonment, the Trial Chambers shall have recourse to the general practice regarding prison sentences in the courts of the former Yugoslavia.

2. In imposing the sentences, the Trial Chambers should take into account such factors as the gravity of the offence and the individual circumstances of the convicted person.

3. In addition to imprisonment, the Trial Chambers may order the return of any property and proceeds acquired by criminal conduct, including by means of duress, to their rightful owners.

Article 25
Appellate proceedings

1. The Appeals Chamber shall hear appeals from persons convicted by the Trial Chambers or from the Prosecutor on the following grounds:

   (a) an error on a question of law invalidating the decision; or

   (b) an error of fact which has occasioned a miscarriage of justice.

2. The Appeals Chamber may affirm, reverse or revise the decisions taken by the Trial Chambers.

Article 26
Review proceedings
Where a new fact has been discovered which was not known at the time of the proceedings before the Trial Chambers or the Appeals Chamber and which could have been a decisive factor in reaching the decision, the convicted person or the Prosecutor may submit to the International Tribunal an application for review of the judgement.

Article 27
Enforcement of sentences
Imprisonment shall be served in a State designated by the International Tribunal from a list of States which have indicated to the Security Council their willingness to accept convicted persons. Such imprisonment shall be in accordance with the applicable law of the State concerned, subject to the supervision of the International Tribunal.

Article 28
Pardon or commutation of sentences
If, pursuant to the applicable law of the State in which the convicted person is imprisoned, he or she is eligible for pardon or commutation of sentence, the State concerned shall notify the International Tribunal accordingly. The President of the International Tribunal, in consultation with the judges, shall decide the matter on the basis of the interests of justice and the general principles of law.

Article 29
Co-operation and judicial assistance
1. States shall co-operate with the International Tribunal in the investigation and prosecution of persons accused of committing serious violations of international humanitarian law.
2. States shall comply without undue delay with any request for assistance or an order issued by a Trial Chamber, including, but not limited to:
   (a) the identification and location of persons;
   (b) the taking of testimony and the production of evidence;
   (c) the service of documents;
   (d) the arrest or detention of persons;
   (e) the surrender or the transfer of the accused to the International Tribunal.

Article 30
The status, privileges and immunities of the International Tribunal
1. The Convention on the Privileges and Immunities of the United Nations of 13 February 1946 shall apply to the International Tribunal, the judges, the Prosecutor and his staff, and the Registrar and his staff.
2. The judges, the Prosecutor and the Registrar shall enjoy the privileges and immunities, exemptions and facilities accorded to diplomatic envoys, in accordance with international law.

3. The staff of the Prosecutor and of the Registrar shall enjoy the privileges and immunities accorded to officials of the United Nations under articles V and VII of the Convention referred to in paragraph 1 of this article.

4. Other persons, including the accused, required at the seat of the International Tribunal shall be accorded such treatment as is necessary for the proper functioning of the International Tribunal.

Article 31
Seat of the International Tribunal
The International Tribunal shall have its seat at The Hague.

Article 32
Expenses of the International Tribunal
The expenses of the International Tribunal shall be borne by the regular budget of the United Nations in accordance with Article 17 of the Charter of the United Nations.

Article 33
Working languages
The working languages of the International Tribunal shall be English and French.

Article 34
Annual report
The President of the International Tribunal shall submit an annual report of the International Tribunal to the Security Council and to the General Assembly.

United Nations Security Council Resolution 1966 (2010)

The Security Council,

Recalling Security Council resolution 827 (1993) of 25 May 1993, which established the International Tribunal for the former Yugoslavia ("ICTY"), and resolution 955 (1994) of 8 November 1994, which established the International Criminal Tribunal for Rwanda ("ICTR"), and all subsequent relevant resolutions,

Recalling in particular Security Council resolutions 1503 (2003) of 28 August 2003 and 1534 (2004) of 26 March 2004, which called on the Tribunals to take all possible measures to complete investigations by the end of 2004, to complete all trial activities at first instance by the end of 2008, and to complete all work in 2010 ("completion strategy"), and *noting* that those envisaged dates have not been met,

Acknowledging the considerable contribution the Tribunals have made to international criminal justice and accountability for serious international crimes, and the re-establishment of the rule of law in the countries of the former Yugoslavia and in Rwanda,

Recalling that the Tribunals were established in the particular circumstances of the former Yugoslavia and Rwanda as *ad hoc* measures contributing to the restoration and maintenance of peace,

Reaffirming its determination to combat impunity for those responsible for serious violations of international humanitarian law and the necessity that all persons indicted by the ICTY and ICTR are brought to justice,

Recalling the statement of the President of the Security Council of 19 December 2008 (S/PRST/2008/47), and *reaffirming* the need to establish an *ad hoc* mechanism to carry out a number of essential functions of the Tribunals, including the trial of fugitives who are among the most senior leaders suspected of being most responsible for crimes, after the closure of the Tribunals,

Emphasizing that, in view of the substantially reduced nature of the residual functions, the international residual mechanism should be a small, temporary and efficient structure, whose functions and size will diminish over time, with a small number of staff commensurate with its reduced functions,

Welcoming the Report of the Secretary-General (S/2009/258) on the administrative and budgetary aspects of the options for possible locations for the archives of the International Tribunal for the former Yugoslavia and the International Criminal Tribunal for Rwanda and the seat of the residual mechanism(s) for the Tribunals,

Acting under Chapter VII of the Charter of the United Nations,

1. *Decides* to establish the International Residual Mechanism for Criminal Tribunals ("the Mechanism") with two branches, which shall commence functioning on 1 July 2012 (branch for the ICTR) and 1 July 2013 (branch for the ICTY), respectively ("commencement dates"), and to this end *decides* to adopt the Statute of the Mechanism in Annex 1 to this resolution;

2. *Decides* that the provisions of this resolution and the Statutes of the Mechanism and of the ICTY and ICTR shall be subject to the transitional arrangements set out in Annex 2 to this resolution;

3. *Requests* the ICTY and the ICTR to take all possible measures to expeditiously complete all their remaining work as provided by this resolution no later than 31 December 2014, to prepare their closure and to ensure a smooth transition to the Mechanism, including through advance teams in each of the Tribunals;

4. *Decides* that, as of the commencement date of each branch referred to in paragraph 1, the Mechanism shall continue the jurisdiction, rights and obligations and essential functions of the ICTY and the ICTR, respectively, subject to the provisions of this resolution and the Statute of the Mechanism, and all contracts and international agreements concluded by the United Nations in relation to the ICTY and the ICTR, and still in force as of the relevant commencement date, shall continue in force *mutatis mutandis* in relation to the Mechanism;

5. *Requests* the Secretary-General to submit at the earliest possible date, but no later than 30 June 2011, draft Rules of Procedure and Evidence of the Mechanism, which shall be based on the Tribunals' Rules of Procedure and Evidence subject to the provisions of this resolution and the Statute of the Mechanism, for consideration and adoption by the judges of the Mechanism;

6. *Decides* that the Rules of Procedure and Evidence of the Mechanism and any amendments thereto shall take effect upon adoption by the judges of the Mechanism unless the Security Council decides otherwise;

7. *Decides* that the determination of the seats of the branches of the Mechanism is subject to the conclusion of appropriate arrangements between the United Nations and the host countries of the branches of the Mechanism acceptable to the Security Council;

8. *Recalls* the obligation of States to cooperate with the Tribunals, and in particular to comply without undue delay with requests for assistance in the location, arrest, detention, surrender and transfer of accused persons;

12

9. *Decides* that all States shall cooperate fully with the Mechanism in accordance with the present resolution and the Statute of the Mechanism and that consequently all States shall take any measures necessary under their domestic law to implement the provisions of the present resolution and the Statute of the assistance or orders issued by the Mechanism pursuant to its Statute;

10. *Urges* all States, especially States where fugitives are suspected to be at large, to further intensify cooperation with and render all necessary assistance to the Tribunals and the Mechanism, as appropriate, in particular to achieve the arrest and surrender of all remaining fugitives as soon as possible;

11. *Urges* the Tribunals and the Mechanism to actively undertake every effort to refer those cases which do not involve the most senior leaders suspected of being most responsible for crimes to competent national jurisdictions in accordance with their respective Statutes and Rules of Procedure and Evidence;

12. *Calls upon* all States to cooperate to the maximum extent possible in order to receive referred cases from the Tribunals and the Mechanism;

13. *Requests* the Secretary-General to implement the present resolution and to make practical arrangements for the effective functioning of the Mechanism from the first commencement date referred to in paragraph 1, in particular to initiate no later than 30 June 2011 the procedures for the selection of the roster of judges of the Mechanism, as provided in its Statute;

14. *Requests* the Secretary-General to prepare, in consultation with the Security Council, an information security and access regime for the archives of the Tribunals and the Mechanism prior to the first commencement date referred to in paragraph 1;

15. *Requests* the Tribunals and the Mechanism to cooperate with the countries of the former Yugoslavia and with Rwanda, as well as with interested entities to facilitate the establishment of information and documentation centres by providing access to copies of public records of the archives of the Tribunals and the Mechanism, including through their websites;

16. *Requests* the President of the Mechanism to submit an annual report to the Security Council and to the General Assembly, and the President and the Prosecutor of the Mechanism to submit six-monthly reports to the Security Council on the progress of the work of the Mechanism;

17. *Decides* that the Mechanism shall operate for an initial period of four years from the first commencement date referred to in paragraph 1, and to review the progress of the work of the Mechanism, including in completing its functions, before the end of this initial period and every two years thereafter, and further *decides* that the Mechanism shall continue to operate for subsequent periods of two years following each such review, unless the Security Council decides otherwise;

18. *Underlines* its intention to decide on the modalities for the exercise of any remaining residual functions of the Mechanism upon the completion of its operation;

19. *Decides* to remain seized of the matter.

Statute of the International Residual Mechanism for Criminal Tribunals (IRMCT)

PREAMBLE

Having been established by the Security Council acting under Chapter VII of the Charter of the United Nations to carry out residual functions of the International Tribunal for the Prosecution of Persons Responsible for Serious Violations of International Humanitarian Law Committed in the Territory of the Former Yugoslavia since 1991 (hereinafter "ICTY") and the International Criminal Tribunal for the Prosecution of Persons Responsible for Genocide and Other Serious Violations of International Humanitarian Law Committed in the Territory of Rwanda and Rwandan citizens responsible for genocide and other such violations committed in the territory of neighbouring States, between 1 January 1994 and 31 December 1994 (hereinafter "ICTR"), the International Residual Mechanism for Criminal Tribunals (hereinafter "the Mechanism") shall function in accordance with the provisions of the present Statute.

Article 1: Competence of the Mechanism
1. The Mechanism shall continue the material, territorial, temporal and personal jurisdiction of the ICTY and the ICTR as set out in Articles 1 to 8 of the ICTY Statute and Articles 1 to 7 of the ICTR Statute, as well as the rights and obligations, of the ICTY and the ICTR, subject to the provisions of the present Statute.
2. The Mechanism shall have the power to prosecute, in accordance with the provisions of the present Statute, the persons indicted by the ICTY or the ICTR who are among the most senior leaders suspected of being most responsible for the crimes covered by paragraph 1 of this Article, considering the gravity of the crimes charged and the level of responsibility of the accused.
3. The Mechanism shall have the power to prosecute, in accordance with the provisions of the present Statute, the persons indicted by the ICTY or the ICTR who are not among the most senior leaders covered by paragraph 2 of this Article, provided that the Mechanism may only, in accordance with the provisions of the present Statute, proceed to try such persons itself after it has exhausted all reasonable efforts to refer the case as provided in Article 6 of the present Statute.
4. The Mechanism shall have the power to prosecute, in accordance with the provisions of the present Statute,
   (a) any person who knowingly and wilfully interferes or has interfered with the administration of justice by the Mechanism or the Tribunals, and to hold such person in contempt; or
   (b) a witness who knowingly and wilfully gives or has given false testimony before the Mechanism or the Tribunals. Before proceeding to try such persons, the Mechanism shall consider referring the case to the authorities of a State in accordance with Article 6 of the present Statute, taking into account the interests of justice and expediency.
5. The Mechanism shall not have the power to issue any new indictments against persons other than those covered by this Article.

Article 2: Functions of the Mechanism

The Mechanism shall continue the functions of the ICTY and of the ICTR, as set out in the present Statute ("residual functions"), during the period of its operation.

Article 3: Structure and Seats of the Mechanism

The Mechanism shall have two branches, one branch for the ICTY and one branch for the ICTR, respectively. The branch for the ICTY shall have its seat in The Hague. The branch for the ICTR shall have its seat in Arusha.

Article 4: Organization of the Mechanism

The Mechanism shall consist of the following organs:

(a) The Chambers, comprising a Trial Chamber for each branch of the Mechanism and an Appeals Chamber common to both branches of the Mechanism;

(b) The Prosecutor common to both branches of the Mechanism;

(c) The Registry, common to both branches of the Mechanism, to provide administrative services for the Mechanism, including the Chambers and the Prosecutor.

Article 5: Concurrent Jurisdiction

1. The Mechanism and national courts shall have concurrent jurisdiction to prosecute persons covered by Article 1 of this Statute.

2. The Mechanism shall have primacy over national courts in accordance with the present Statute. At any stage of the procedure involving a person covered by Article 1 paragraph 2 of this Statute, the Mechanism may formally request national courts to defer to its competence in accordance with the present Statute and the Rules of Procedure and Evidence of the Mechanism.

Article 6: Referral of Cases to National Jurisdictions

1. The Mechanism shall have the power, and shall undertake every effort, to refer cases involving persons covered by paragraph 3 of Article 1 of this Statute to the authorities of a State in accordance with paragraphs 2 and 3 of this Article. The Mechanism shall have the power also to refer cases involving persons covered by paragraph 4 of Article 1 of this Statute.

2. After an indictment has been confirmed and prior to the commencement of trial, irrespective of whether or not the accused is in the custody of the Mechanism, the President may designate a Trial Chamber which shall determine whether the case should be referred to the authorities of a State:

(i) in whose territory the crime was committed; or

(ii) in which the accused was arrested; or

(iii) having jurisdiction and being willing and adequately prepared to accept such a case, so that those authorities should forthwith refer the case to the appropriate court for trial within that State.

3. In determining whether to refer a case involving a person covered by paragraph 3 of Article 1 of this Statute in accordance with paragraph 2 above, the Trial Chamber shall, consistent with Security Council resolution 1534 (2004), consider the gravity of the crimes charged and the level of responsibility of the accused.

4. The Trial Chamber may order such referral *proprio motu* or at the request of the Prosecutor, after having given to the Prosecutor and, where applicable, the accused, the opportunity to be heard and after being satisfied that the accused will receive a fair trial and that the death penalty will not be imposed or carried out.

5. The Mechanism shall monitor cases referred to national courts by the ICTY, the ICTR, and those referred in accordance with this Article, with the assistance of international and regional organisations and bodies.

6. After an order referring a case has been issued by the ICTY, the ICTR or the Mechanism and before the accused is found guilty or acquitted by a national court, where it is clear that the conditions for referral of the case are no longer met and it is in the interests of justice, the Trial Chamber may, at the request of the Prosecutor or *proprio motu* and upon having given to the State authorities concerned the opportunity to be heard, revoke the order and make a formal request for deferral.

Article 7: *Non bis in Idem*

1. No person shall be tried before a national court for acts constituting serious violations of international humanitarian law under the present Statute, for which he or she has already been tried by the ICTY, the ICTR or the Mechanism.

2. A person covered by Article 1 of this Statute who has been tried before a national court for acts constituting serious violations of international humanitarian law may be subsequently tried by the Mechanism only if:
   (a) The act for which he or she was tried was characterized as an ordinary crime; or
   (b) The national court proceedings were not impartial or independent, were designed to shield the accused from international criminal responsibility, or the case was not diligently prosecuted.

3. In considering the penalty to be imposed on a person convicted of a crime under the present Statute, the Mechanism shall take into account the extent to which any penalty imposed by a national court on the same person for the same act has already been served.

Article 8: Roster of Judges

1. The Mechanism shall have a roster of 25 independent judges ("judges of the Mechanism"), not more than two of whom may be nationals of the same State.

2. A person who for the purposes of membership of the roster could be regarded as a national of more than one State shall be deemed to be a national of the State in which that person ordinarily exercises civil and political rights.

3. The judges of the Mechanism shall only be present at the seats of the branches of the Mechanism as necessary at the request of the President to exercise the functions requiring their presence. In so far as possible, and as decided by the President, the functions may be exercised remotely, away from the seats of the branches of the Mechanism.

4. The judges of the Mechanism shall not receive any remuneration or other benefits for being on the roster. The terms and conditions of service of the judges for each day on which they exercise their functions for the Mechanism shall be those of the judges ad hoc of the International Court of Justice. The terms and conditions of service of the President of the Mechanism shall be those of the judges of the International Court of Justice.

Article 9: Qualification of Judges

1. The judges shall be persons of high moral character, impartiality and integrity who possess the qualifications required in their respective countries for appointment to the highest judicial offices. Particular account shall be taken of experience as judges of the ICTY or the ICTR.

2. In the composition of the Trial and Appeals Chambers, due account shall be taken of the experience of the judges in criminal law, international law, including international humanitarian law and human rights law.

Article 10: Election of Judges

1. The judges of the Mechanism shall be elected by the General Assembly from a list submitted by the Security Council, in the following manner:

    (a) The Secretary-General shall invite nominations for judges, preferably from among persons with experience as judges of the ICTY or the ICTR, from States Members of the United Nations and non-member States maintaining permanent observer missions at United Nations Headquarters;

    (b) Within sixty days of the date of the invitation of the Secretary-General, each State may nominate up to two candidates meeting the qualifications set out in Article 9 paragraph 1 of the Statute;

    (c) The Secretary-General shall forward the nominations received to the Security Council. From the nominations received the Security Council shall establish a list of not less than 30 candidates, taking due account of the qualifications set out in Article 9 paragraph 1 and adequate representation of the principal legal systems of the world;

    (d) The President of the Security Council shall transmit the list of candidates to the President of the General Assembly. From that list the General Assembly shall elect 25 judges of the Mechanism. The candidates who receive an absolute majority of the votes of the States Members of the United Nations and of the non-member States maintaining permanent observer missions at United Nations Headquarters, shall be declared elected. Should more than two candidates of the same nationality obtain the required majority vote, the two who received the highest number of votes shall be considered elected.

2. In the event of a vacancy in the roster, after consultation with the Presidents of the Security Council and of the General Assembly, the Secretary-General shall appoint a person meeting the qualifications of Article 9 paragraph 1 of the Statute, for the remainder of the term of office concerned.

3. The judges of the Mechanism shall be elected for a term of four years and shall be eligible for reappointment by the Secretary-General after consultation with the Presidents of the Security Council and of the General Assembly.

4. If there are no judges remaining on the roster or if no judge on the roster is available for appointment, and if it is not possible to assign a judge currently serving at the Mechanism, and all practical alternatives having been explored, the Secretary-General may, at the request of the President of the Mechanism and after consultation with the Presidents of the Security Council and of the General Assembly, appoint a person meeting the qualifications of Article 9 paragraph 1 of the Statute, to serve as a judge of the Mechanism.

Article 11: The President

1. After consultation with the President of the Security Council and the judges of the Mechanism, the Secretary-General shall appoint a full-time President from among the judges of the Mechanism.
2. The President shall be present at either seat of the branches of the Mechanism as necessary to exercise his or her functions.

Article 12: Assignment of Judges and Composition of the Chambers

1. In the event of a trial of a case pursuant to paragraphs 2 and 3 of Article 1 of this Statute, or to consider the referral of such a case to a national jurisdiction, the President shall appoint three judges from the roster to compose a Trial Chamber and the Presiding Judge from amongst their number to oversee the work of that Trial Chamber. In all other circumstances, including trials pursuant to paragraph 4 of Article 1 of this Statute, the President shall appoint a Single Judge from the roster to deal with the matter.
2. The President may designate a duty judge from the roster for each branch of the Mechanism, who will be available at short notice, to serve as a Single Judge and to whom indictments, warrants, and other matters not assigned to a Trial Chamber, may be transmitted for decision.
3. The President of the Mechanism shall be a member of the Appeals Chamber, appoint the other members and preside over its proceedings. In the event of an appeal against a decision by a Single Judge, the Appeals Chamber shall be composed of three judges. In the event of an appeal against a decision by a Trial Chamber, the Appeals Chamber shall be composed of five judges.
4. In the event of an application for review in accordance with Article 24 of this Statute of a judgment rendered by a single Judge or by a Trial Chamber, the President shall appoint three judges to compose a Trial Chamber on review. In the event of an application for review of a judgment rendered by the Appeals Chamber, the Appeals Chamber on review shall be composed of five judges.
5. The President may appoint, from among the judges of the Mechanism, a reserve judge to be present at each stage of a trial and to replace a judge if that judge is unable to continue sitting.

Article 13: Rules of Procedure and Evidence

1. The judges of the Mechanism shall adopt Rules of Procedure and Evidence for the conduct of the pre-trial phase of the proceedings, trials and appeals, the admission of evidence, the protection of victims and witnesses and other appropriate matters.
2. Amendments of the Rules of Procedure and Evidence may be decided remotely by the judges of the Mechanism by written procedure.
3. The Rules of Procedure and Evidence and any amendments thereto shall take effect upon adoption by the judges of the Mechanism unless the Security Council decides otherwise.
4. The Rules of Procedure and Evidence and amendments thereto shall be consistent with this Statute.

Article 14: The Prosecutor

1. The Prosecutor shall be responsible for the investigation and prosecution of persons covered by Article 1 of this Statute.
2. The Prosecutor shall act independently as a separate organ of the Mechanism. He or she shall not seek or receive instructions from any government or from any other source.
3. The Office of the Prosecutor shall be composed of a Prosecutor, an officer in charge at the seat of each branch of the Mechanism designated by the Prosecutor, and such other qualified staff as may be required, in accordance with paragraph 5 of this Article. The Prosecutor shall be present at either seat of the branches of the Mechanism as necessary to exercise his or her functions.
4. The Prosecutor shall be appointed by the Security Council on nomination by the Secretary-General. He or she shall be of high moral character and possess the highest level of competence and experience in the conduct of investigations and prosecutions of criminal cases. The Prosecutor shall serve for a four-year term and be eligible for reappointment. The terms and conditions of service of the Prosecutor shall be those of an Under-Secretary-General of the United Nations.
5. The Office of the Prosecutor shall retain a small number of staff commensurate with the reduced functions of the Mechanism, who shall serve at the seats of the branches of the Mechanism. The Office shall maintain a roster of qualified potential staff, preferably from among persons with experience at the ICTY or the ICTR, to enable it to recruit additional staff rapidly as may be required to perform its functions. The staff of the Office of the Prosecutor shall be appointed by the Secretary-General on the recommendation of the Prosecutor.

Article 15: The Registry

1. The Registry shall be responsible for the administration and servicing of the branches of the Mechanism.
2. The Registry shall consist of a Registrar, an officer in charge at the seat of each branch of the Mechanism designated by the Registrar, and such other qualified staff as may be required in accordance with paragraph 4 of this Article. The Registrar shall be present at either seat of the branches of the Mechanism as necessary to exercise his or her functions.
3. The Registrar shall be appointed by the Secretary-General for a four-year term and be eligible for reappointment. The terms and conditions of service of the Registrar shall be those of an Assistant Secretary-General of the United Nations.
4. The Registry shall retain a small number of staff commensurate with the reduced functions of the Mechanism, who shall serve at the seat of the respective branches of the Mechanism. The Registry shall maintain a roster of qualified potential staff, preferably from among persons with experience at the ICTY or the ICTR, to enable it to recruit additional staff rapidly as may be required to perform its functions. The Staff of the Registry shall be appointed by the Secretary-General on the recommendation of the Registrar.

Article 16: Investigation and Preparation of Indictment

1. The Prosecutor shall have the power to conduct investigations against persons covered by Article 1 of this Statute. The Prosecutor shall not have the power to prepare new indictments against persons other than those covered by Article 1 of this Statute.
2. The Prosecutor shall have the power to question suspects, victims and witnesses, to collect evidence and to conduct on-site investigations. In carrying out these tasks, the Prosecutor may, as appropriate, seek the assistance of the State authorities concerned.
3. If questioned, the suspect shall be entitled to be assisted by Counsel of his or her own choice, including the right to have legal assistance assigned to the suspect without payment by him or her in any such case if he or she does not have sufficient means to pay for it, as well as necessary translation into and from a language he or she speaks and understands.
4. Upon a determination that a prima facie case exists, the Prosecutor shall prepare an indictment containing a concise statement of the facts and the crime or crimes with which the accused is charged under the Statute. The indictment shall be transmitted to the duty judge or a Single Judge designated by the President.

Article 17: Review of the Indictment

1. The indictment shall be reviewed by the duty judge or a Single Judge designated by the President. If satisfied that a prima facie case has been established by the Prosecutor, he or she shall confirm the indictment. If not so satisfied, the indictment shall be dismissed.
2. Upon confirmation of an indictment, the judge may, at the request of the Prosecutor, issue such orders and warrants for the arrest, detention, surrender or transfer of persons, and any other orders as may be required for the conduct of the trial.

Article 18: Commencement and Conduct of Trial Proceedings

1. The Single Judge or Trial Chambers conducting a trial shall ensure that the trial is fair and expeditious and that proceedings are conducted in accordance with the Rules of Procedure and Evidence, with full respect for the rights of the accused and due regard for the protection of victims and witnesses.
2. A person against whom an indictment has been confirmed shall, pursuant to an order or an arrest warrant of the Mechanism, be taken into custody, immediately informed of the charges against him or her and transferred to the Mechanism.
3. The Single Judge or judge of the Trial Chamber designated by the President shall read the indictment, ensure that the rights of the accused are respected, confirm that the accused understands the indictment, and instruct the accused to enter a plea. The Single Judge or Trial Chamber shall then set the date for trial.
4. The hearings shall be public unless the Single Judge or Trial Chamber decides to close the proceedings in accordance with its Rules of Procedure and Evidence.

Article 19: Rights of the Accused

1. All persons shall be equal before the Mechanism.
2. In the determination of charges against him or her, the accused shall be entitled to a fair and public hearing, subject to Article 20 of the Statute.

12

3. The accused shall be presumed innocent until proved guilty according to the provisions of the present Statute.

4. In the determination of any charge against the accused pursuant to the present Statute, the accused shall be entitled to the following minimum guarantees, in full equality:

   (a) to be informed promptly and in detail in a language which he or she understands of the nature and cause of the charge against him or her;

   (b) to have adequate time and facilities for the preparation of his or her defence and to communicate with counsel of his or her own choosing;

   (c) to be tried without undue delay;

   (d) to be tried in his or her presence, and to defend himself or herself in person or through legal assistance of his own choosing; to be informed, if he or she does not have legal assistance, of this right; and to have legal assistance assigned to him or her, in any case where the interests of justice so require, and without payment by him or her in any such case if he or she does not have sufficient means to pay for it;

   (e) to examine, or have examined, the witnesses against him or her and to obtain the attendance and examination of witnesses on his or her behalf under the same conditions as witnesses against him or her;

   (f) to have the free assistance of an interpreter if he or she cannot understand or speak the language used in the Mechanism;

   (g) not to be compelled to testify against himself or herself or to confess guilt.

   ...

1994 International Criminal Tribunal for Rwanda Statute

Statute of the International Criminal Tribunal for the Prosecution of Persons Responsible for Genocide and Other Serious Violations of International Humanitarian Law Committed in the Territory of Rwanda and Rwandan Citizens Responsible for Genocide and Other Such Violations Committed in the Territory of Neighbouring States, between 1 January 1994 and 31 December 1994

Having been established by the Security Council acting under Chapter VII of the Charter of the United Nations, the International Criminal Tribunal for the Prosecution of Persons Responsible for Genocide and Other Serious Violations of International Humanitarian Law Committed in the Territory of Rwanda and Rwandan citizens responsible for genocide and other such violations committed in the territory of neighbouring States, between 1 January 1994 and 31 December 1994 (hereinafter referred to as "the International Tribunal for Rwanda") shall function in accordance with the provisions of the present Statute.

Article 1
Competence of the International Tribunal for Rwanda
The International Tribunal for Rwanda shall have the power to prosecute persons responsible for serious violations of international humanitarian law committed in the territory of Rwanda and Rwandan citizens responsible for such violations committed in the territory of neighbouring States, between 1 January 1994 and 31 December 1994, in accordance with the provisions of the present Statute.

Article 2
Genocide
1. The International Tribunal for Rwanda shall have the power to prosecute persons committing genocide as defined in paragraph 2 of this article or of committing any of the other acts enumerated in paragraph 3 of this article.
2. Genocide means any of the following acts committed with intent to destroy, in whole or in part, a national, ethnical, racial or religious group, as such:
   (a) Killing members of the group;
   (b) Causing serious bodily or mental harm to members of the group;
   (c) Deliberately inflicting on the group conditions of life calculated to bring about its physical destruction in whole or in part;
   (d) Imposing measures intended to prevent births within the group;
   (e) Forcibly transferring children of the group to another group.

3. The following acts shall be punishable:
    (a) Genocide;
    (b) Conspiracy to commit genocide;
    (c) Direct and public incitement to commit genocide;
    (d) Attempt to commit genocide;
    (e) Complicity in genocide.

Article 3
Crimes against humanity

The International Tribunal for Rwanda shall have the power to prosecute persons responsible for the following crimes when committed as part of a widespread or systematic attack against any civilian population on national, political, ethnic, racial or religious grounds:
    (a) Murder;
    (b) Extermination;
    (c) Enslavement;
    (d) Deportation;
    (e) Imprisonment;
    (f) Torture;
    (g) Rape;
    (h) Persecutions on political, racial and religious grounds;
    (i) Other inhumane acts.

Article 4
Violations of Article 3 common to the Geneva Conventions and of Additional Protocol II

The International Tribunal for Rwanda shall have the power to prosecute persons committing or ordering to be committed serious violations of Article 3 common to the Geneva Conventions of 12 August 1949 for the Protection of War Victims, and of Additional Protocol II thereto of 8 June 1977. These violations shall include, but shall not be limited to:
    (a) Violence to life, health and physical or mental well-being of persons, in particular murder as well as cruel treatment such as torture, mutilation or any form of corporal punishment;
    (b) Collective punishments;
    (c) Taking of hostages;
    (d) Acts of terrorism;
    (e) Outrages upon personal dignity, in particular humiliating and degrading treatment, rape, enforced prostitution and any form of indecent assault;
    (f) Pillage;
    (g) The passing of sentences and the carrying out of executions without previous judgement pronounced by a regularly constituted court, affording all the judicial guarantees which are recognized as indispensable by civilized peoples;
    (h) Threats to commit any of the foregoing acts.

Article 5
Personal jurisdiction
The International Tribunal for Rwanda shall have jurisdiction over natural persons pursuant to the provisions of the present Statute.

Article 6
Individual criminal responsibility
1. A person who planned, instigated, ordered, committed or otherwise aided and abetted in the planning, preparation or execution of a crime referred to in articles 2 to 4 of the present Statute, shall be individually responsible for the crime.
2. The official position of any accused person, whether as Head of State or Government or as a responsible Government official, shall not relieve such person of criminal responsibility nor mitigate punishment.
3. The fact that any of the acts referred to in articles 2 to 4 of the present Statute was committed by a subordinate does not relieve his or her superior of criminal responsibility if he or she knew or had reason to know that the subordinate was about to commit such acts or had done so and the superior failed to take the necessary and reasonable measures to prevent such acts or to punish the perpetrators thereof.
4. The fact that an accused person acted pursuant to an order of a Government or of a superior shall not relieve him or her of criminal responsibility, but may be considered in mitigation of punishment if the International Tribunal for Rwanda determines that justice so requires.

Article 7
Territorial and temporal jurisdiction
The territorial jurisdiction of the International Tribunal for Rwanda shall extend to the territory of Rwanda including its land surface and airspace as well as to the territory of neighbouring States in respect of serious violations of international humanitarian law committed by Rwandan citizens. The temporal jurisdiction of the International Tribunal for Rwanda shall extend to a period beginning on 1 January 1994 and ending on 31 December 1994.

Article 8
Concurrent jurisdiction
1. The International Tribunal for Rwanda and national courts shall have concurrent jurisdiction to prosecute persons for serious violations of international humanitarian law committed in the territory of Rwanda and Rwandan citizens for such violations committed in the territory of neighbouring States, between 1 January 1994 and 31 December 1994.
2. The International Tribunal for Rwanda shall have primacy over the national courts of all States. At any stage of the procedure, the International Tribunal for Rwanda may formally request national courts to defer to its competence in accordance with the present Statute and the Rules of Procedure and Evidence of the International Tribunal for Rwanda.

Article 9
Non bis in idem

1. No person shall be tried before a national court for acts constituting serious violations of international humanitarian law under the present Statute, for which he or she has already been tried by the International Tribunal for Rwanda.

2. A person who has been tried by a national court for acts constituting serious violations of international humanitarian law may be subsequently tried by the International Tribunal for Rwanda only if:

    (a) The act for which he or she was tried was characterized as an ordinary crime; or

    (b) The national court proceedings were not impartial or independent, were designed to shield the accused from international criminal responsibility, or the case was not diligently prosecuted.

3. In considering the penalty to be imposed on a person convicted of a crime under the present Statute, the International Tribunal for Rwanda shall take into account the extent to which any penalty imposed by a national court on the same person for the same act has already been served.

Article 10
Organization of the International Tribunal for Rwanda

The International Tribunal for Rwanda shall consist of the following organs:

(a) The Chambers, comprising three Trial Chambers and an Appeals Chamber;

(b) The Prosecutor;

(c) A Registry.

Article 11
Composition of the Chambers

1. The Chambers shall be composed of sixteen permanent independent judges, no two of whom may be nationals of the same State, and a maximum at any one time of four *ad litem* independent judges appointed in accordance with article 12 *ter*, paragraph 2, of the present Statute, no two of whom may be nationals of the same State.

2. Three permanent judges and a maximum at any one time of four *ad litem* judges shall be members of each Trial Chamber. Each Trial Chamber to which *ad litem* judges are assigned may be divided into sections of three judges each, composed of both permanent and *ad litem* judges. A section of a Trial Chamber shall have the same powers and responsibilities as a Trial Chamber under the present Statute and shall render judgement in accordance with the same rules.

3. Seven of the permanent judges shall be members of the Appeals Chamber. The Appeals Chamber shall, for each appeal, be composed of five of its members.

4. A person who for the purposes of membership of the Chambers of the International Tribunal for Rwanda could be regarded as a national of more than one State shall be deemed to be a national of the State in which that person ordinarily exercises civil and political rights.

Article 12
Qualifications of judges

The permanent and *ad litem* judges shall be persons of high moral character, impartiality and integrity who possess the qualifications required in their respective countries for appointment to the highest judicial offices. In the overall composition of the Chambers and sections of the Trial Chambers, due account shall be taken of the experience of the judges in criminal law, international law, including international humanitarian law and human rights law.

Article 12 *bis*
Election of permanent judges

1. Eleven of the permanent judges of the International Tribunal for Rwanda shall be elected by the General Assembly from a list submitted by the Security Council, in the following manner:

   (a) The Secretary-General shall invite nominations for permanent judges of the International Tribunal for Rwanda from States Members of the United Nations and non-member States maintaining permanent observer missions at United Nations Headquarters;

   (b) Within sixty days of the date of the invitation of the Secretary-General, each State may nominate up to two candidates meeting the qualifications set out in article 12 of the present Statute, no two of whom shall be of the same nationality and neither of whom shall be of the same nationality as any judge who is a member of the Appeals Chamber and who was elected or appointed a permanent judge of the International Tribunal for the Prosecution of Persons Responsible for Serious Violations of International Humanitarian Law Committed in the Territory of the former Yugoslavia since 1991 (hereinafter referred to as "the International Tribunal for the Former Yugoslavia") in accordance with article 13 *bis* of the Statute of that Tribunal;

   (c) The Secretary-General shall forward the nominations received to the Security Council. From the nominations received the Security Council shall establish a list of not less than twenty-two and not more than thirty-three candidates, taking due account of the adequate representation on the International Tribunal for Rwanda of the principal legal systems of the world;

   (d) The President of the Security Council shall transmit the list of candidates to the President of the General Assembly. From that list the General Assembly shall elect eleven permanent judges of the International Tribunal for Rwanda. The candidates who receive an absolute majority of the votes of the States Members of the United Nations and of the non-member States maintaining permanent observer missions at United Nations Headquarters, shall be declared elected. Should two candidates of the same nationality obtain the required majority vote, the one who received the higher number of votes shall be considered elected.

2. In the event of a vacancy in the Chambers amongst the permanent judges elected or appointed in accordance with this article, after consultation with the Presidents of the Security Council and of the General Assembly, the Secretary-General shall appoint a person meeting the qualifications of article 12 of the present Statute, for the remainder of the term of office concerned.

3. The permanent judges elected in accordance with this article shall be elected for a term of four years. The terms and conditions of service shall be those of the permanent judges of the International Tribunal for the Former Yugoslavia. They shall be eligible for re-election.

Article 12 *ter*

Election and appointment of *ad litem* judges

1. The *ad litem* judges of the International Tribunal for Rwanda shall be elected by the General Assembly from a list submitted by the Security Council, in the following manner:

   (a) The Secretary-General shall invite nominations for *ad litem* judges of the International Tribunal for Rwanda from States Members of the United Nations and non-member States maintaining permanent observer missions at United Nations Headquarters;

   (b) Within sixty days of the date of the invitation of the Secretary-General, each State may nominate up to four candidates meeting the qualifications set out in article 12 of the present Statute, taking into account the importance of a fair representation of female and male candidates;

   (c) The Secretary-General shall forward the nominations received to the Security Council. From the nominations received the Security Council shall establish a list of not less than thirty-six candidates, taking due account of the adequate representation of the principal legal systems of the world and bearing in mind the importance of equitable geographical distribution;

   (d) The President of the Security Council shall transmit the list of candidates to the President of the General Assembly. From that list the General Assembly shall elect the eighteen *ad litem* judges of the International Tribunal for Rwanda. The candidates who receive an absolute majority of the votes of the States Members of the United Nations and of the non-member States maintaining permanent observer missions at United Nations Headquarters shall be declared elected;

   (e) The *ad litem* judges shall be elected for a term of four years. They shall not be eligible for re-election.

2. During their term, *ad litem* judges will be appointed by the Secretary-General, upon request of the President of the International Tribunal for Rwanda, to serve in the Trial Chambers for one or more trials, for a cumulative period of up to, but not including, three years. When requesting the appointment of any particular *ad litem* judge, the President of the International Tribunal for Rwanda shall bear in mind the criteria set out in article 12 of the present Statute regarding the composition of the Chambers and sections of the Trial Chambers, the considerations set out in paragraphs 1(b) and (c) above and the number of votes the *ad litem* judge received in the General Assembly.

Article 12 *quater*

Status of *ad litem* judges

1. During the period in which they are appointed to serve in the International Tribunal for Rwanda, *ad litem* judges shall:

   (a) Benefit from the same terms and conditions of service *mutatis mutandis* as the permanent judges of the International Tribunal for Rwanda;

   (b) Enjoy, subject to paragraph 2 below, the same powers as the permanent judges of the International Tribunal for Rwanda;

   (c) Enjoy the privileges and immunities, exemptions and facilities of a judge of the International Tribunal for Rwanda.

2. During the period in which they are appointed to serve in the International Tribunal for Rwanda, *ad litem* judges shall not:
   (a) Be eligible for election as, or to vote in the election of, the President of the International Tribunal for Rwanda or the Presiding Judge of a Trial Chamber pursuant to article 13 of the present Statute;
   (b) Have power:
      (i) To adopt rules of procedure and evidence pursuant to article 14 of the present Statute. They shall, however, be consulted before the adoption of those rules;
      (ii) To review an indictment pursuant to Article 18 of the present Statute;
      (iii) To consult with the President of the International Tribunal for Rwanda in relation to the assignment of judges pursuant to article 13 of the present Statute or in relation to a pardon or commutation of sentence pursuant to article 27 of the present Statute;
      (iv) To adjudicate in pre-trial proceedings.

Article 13
Officers and members of the Chambers
1. The permanent judges of the International Tribunal for Rwanda shall elect a President from amongst their number.
2. The President of the International Tribunal for Rwanda shall be a member of one of its Trial Chambers.
3. After consultation with the permanent judges of the International Tribunal for Rwanda, the President shall assign two of the permanent judges elected or appointed in accordance with Article 12 *bis* of the present Statute to be members of the Appeals Chamber of the International Tribunal for the Former Yugoslavia and eight to the Trial Chambers of the International Tribunal for Rwanda.
4. The members of the Appeals Chamber of the International Tribunal for the Former Yugoslavia shall also serve as the members of the Appeals Chamber of the International Tribunal for Rwanda.
5. After consultation with the permanent judges of the International Tribunal for Rwanda, the President shall assign such *ad litem* judges as may from time to time be appointed to serve in the International Tribunal for Rwanda to the Trial Chambers.
6. A judge shall serve only in the Chamber to which he or she was assigned.
7. The permanent judges of each Trial Chamber shall elect a Presiding Judge from amongst their number, who shall oversee the work of that Trial Chamber as a whole.

Article 14
Rules of procedure and evidence
The judges of the International Tribunal for Rwanda shall adopt, for the purpose of proceedings before the International Tribunal for Rwanda, the rules of procedure and evidence for the conduct of the pre-trial phase of the proceedings, trials and appeals, the admission of evidence, the protection of victims and witnesses and other appropriate matters of the International Tribunal for the Former Yugoslavia with such changes as they deem necessary.

13

Article 15
The Prosecutor

1. The Prosecutor shall be responsible for the investigation and prosecution of persons responsible for serious violations of international humanitarian law committed in the territory of Rwanda and Rwandan citizens responsible for such violations committed in the territory of neighbouring States, between 1 January 1994 and 31 December 1994.

2. The Prosecutor shall act independently as a separate organ of the International Tribunal for Rwanda. He or she shall not seek or receive instructions from any Government or from any other source.

3. The Prosecutor of the International Tribunal for the Former Yugoslavia shall also serve as the Prosecutor of the International Tribunal for Rwanda. He or she shall have additional staff, including an additional Deputy Prosecutor, to assist with prosecutions before the International Tribunal for Rwanda. Such staff shall be appointed by the Secretary-General on the recommendation of the Prosecutor.

Article 16
The Registry

1. The Registry shall be responsible for the administration and servicing of the International Tribunal for Rwanda.

2. The Registry shall consist of a Registrar and such other staff as may be required.

3. The Registrar shall be appointed by the Secretary-General after consultation with the President of the International Tribunal for Rwanda. He or she shall serve for a four-year term and be eligible for reappointment. The terms and conditions of service of the Registrar shall be those of an Assistant Secretary-General of the United Nations.

4. The staff of the Registry shall be appointed by the Secretary-General on the recommendation of the Registrar.

Article 17
Investigation and preparation of indictment

1. The Prosecutor shall initiate investigations ex-officio or on the basis of information obtained from any source, particularly from governments, United Nations organs, intergovernmental and non-governmental organizations. The Prosecutor shall assess the information received or obtained and decide whether there is sufficient basis to proceed.

2. The Prosecutor shall have the power to question suspects, victims and witnesses, to collect evidence and to conduct on-site investigations. In carrying out these tasks, the Prosecutor may, as appropriate, seek the assistance of the State authorities concerned.

3. If questioned, the suspect shall be entitled to be assisted by counsel of his or her own choice, including the right to have legal assistance assigned to the suspect without payment by him or her in any such case if he or she does not have sufficient means to pay for it, as well as to necessary translation into and from a language he or she speaks and understands.

4. Upon a determination that a prima facie case exists, the Prosecutor shall prepare an indictment containing a concise statement of the facts and the crime or crimes with

which the accused is charged under the Statute. The indictment shall be transmitted to a judge of the Trial Chamber.

Article 18
Review of the indictment

1. The judge of the Trial Chamber to whom the indictment has been transmitted shall review it. If satisfied that a prima facie case has been established by the Prosecutor, he or she shall confirm the indictment. If not so satisfied, the indictment shall be dismissed.
2. Upon confirmation of an indictment, the judge may, at the request of the Prosecutor, issue such orders and warrants for the arrest, detention, surrender or transfer of persons, and any other orders as may be required for the conduct of the trial.

Article 19
Commencement and conduct of trial proceedings

1. The Trial Chambers shall ensure that a trial is fair and expeditious and that proceedings are conducted in accordance with the rules of procedure and evidence, with full respect for the rights of the accused and due regard for the protection of victims and witnesses.
2. A person against whom an indictment has been confirmed shall, pursuant to an order or an arrest warrant of the International Tribunal for Rwanda, be taken into custody, immediately informed of the charges against him or her and transferred to the International Tribunal for Rwanda.
3. The Trial Chamber shall read the indictment, satisfy itself that the rights of the accused are respected, confirm that the accused understands the indictment, and instruct the accused to enter a plea. The Trial Chamber shall then set the date for trial.
4. The hearings shall be public unless the Trial Chamber decides to close the proceedings in accordance with its rules of procedure and evidence.

Article 20
Rights of the accused

1. All persons shall be equal before the International Tribunal for Rwanda.
2. In the determination of charges against him or her, the accused shall be entitled to a fair and public hearing, subject to article 21 of the Statute.
3. The accused shall be presumed innocent until proved guilty according to the provisions of the present Statute.
4. In the determination of any charge against the accused pursuant to the present Statute, the accused shall be entitled to the following minimum guarantees, in full equality:
   (a) To be informed promptly and in detail in a language which he or she understands of the nature and cause of the charge against him or her;
   (b) To have adequate time and facilities for the preparation of his or her defence and to communicate with counsel of his or her own choosing;
   (c) To be tried without undue delay;
   (d) To be tried in his or her presence, and to defend himself or herself in person or through legal assistance of his or her own choosing; to be informed, if he or she does not have legal assistance, of this right; and to have legal assistance assigned

to him or her, in any case where the interests of justice so require, and without payment by him or her in any such case if he or she does not have sufficient means to pay for it;

(e) To examine, or have examined, the witnesses against him or her and to obtain the attendance and examination of witnesses on his or her behalf under the same conditions as witnesses against him or her;

(f) To have the free assistance of an interpreter if he or she cannot understand or speak the language used in the International Tribunal for Rwanda;

(g) Not to be compelled to testify against himself or herself or to confess guilt.

Article 21
Protection of victims and witnesses

The International Tribunal for Rwanda shall provide in its rules of procedure and evidence for the protection of victims and witnesses. Such protection measures shall include, but shall not be limited to, the conduct of in camera proceedings and the protection of the victim's identity.

Article 22
Judgement

1. The Trial Chambers shall pronounce judgements and impose sentences and penalties on persons convicted of serious violations of international humanitarian law.
2. The judgement shall be rendered by a majority of the judges of the Trial Chamber, and shall be delivered by the Trial Chamber in public. It shall be accompanied by a reasoned opinion in writing, to which separate or dissenting opinions may be appended.

Article 23
Penalties

1. The penalty imposed by the Trial Chamber shall be limited to imprisonment. In determining the terms of imprisonment, the Trial Chambers shall have recourse to the general practice regarding prison sentences in the courts of Rwanda.
2. In imposing the sentences, the Trial Chambers should take into account such factors as the gravity of the offence and the individual circumstances of the convicted person.
3. In addition to imprisonment, the Trial Chambers may order the return of any property and proceeds acquired by criminal conduct, including by means of duress, to their rightful owners.

Article 24
Appellate proceedings

1. The Appeals Chamber shall hear appeals from persons convicted by the Trial Chambers or from the Prosecutor on the following grounds:
   (a) An error on a question of law invalidating the decision; or
   (b) An error of fact which has occasioned a miscarriage of justice.
2. The Appeals Chamber may affirm, reverse or revise the decisions taken by the Trial Chambers.

Article 25
Review proceedings
Where a new fact has been discovered which was not known at the time of the proceedings before the Trial Chambers or the Appeals Chamber and which could have been a decisive factor in reaching the decision, the convicted person or the Prosecutor may submit to the International Tribunal for Rwanda an application for review of the judgement.

Article 26
Enforcement of sentences
Imprisonment shall be served in Rwanda or any of the States on a list of States which have indicated to the Security Council their willingness to accept convicted persons, as designated by the International Tribunal for Rwanda. Such imprisonment shall be in accordance with the applicable law of the State concerned, subject to the supervision of the International Tribunal for Rwanda.

Article 27
Pardon or commutation of sentences
If, pursuant to the applicable law of the State in which the convicted person is imprisoned, he or she is eligible for pardon or commutation of sentence, the State concerned shall notify the International Tribunal for Rwanda accordingly. There shall only be pardon or commutation of sentence if the President of the International Tribunal for Rwanda, in consultation with the judges, so decides on the basis of the interests of justice and the general principles of law.

Article 28
Cooperation and judicial assistance
1. States shall cooperate with the International Tribunal for Rwanda in the investigation and prosecution of persons accused of committing serious violations of international humanitarian law.
2. States shall comply without undue delay with any request for assistance or an order issued by a Trial Chamber, including, but not limited to:
   (a) The identification and location of persons;
   (b) The taking of testimony and the production of evidence;
   (c) The service of documents;
   (d) The arrest or detention of persons;
   (e) The surrender or the transfer of the accused to the International Tribunal for Rwanda.

Article 29
The status, privileges and immunities of the International Tribunal for Rwanda
1. The Convention on the Privileges and Immunities of the United Nations of 13 February 1946 shall apply to the International Tribunal for Rwanda, the judges, the Prosecutor and his or her staff, and the Registrar and his or her staff.
2. The judges, the Prosecutor and the Registrar shall enjoy the privileges and immunities, exemptions and facilities accorded to diplomatic envoys, in accordance with international law.

3. The staff of the Prosecutor and of the Registrar shall enjoy the privileges and immunities accorded to officials of the United Nations under articles V and VII of the Convention referred to in paragraph 1 of this article.

4. Other persons, including the accused, required at the seat or meeting place of the International Tribunal for Rwanda shall be accorded such treatment as is necessary for the proper functioning of the International Tribunal for Rwanda.

Article 30
Expenses of the International Tribunal for Rwanda
The expenses of the International Tribunal for Rwanda shall be expenses of the Organization in accordance with Article 17 of the Charter of the United Nations.

Article 31
Working languages
The working languages of the International Tribunal shall be English and French.

Article 32
Annual report
The President of the International Tribunal for Rwanda shall submit an annual report of the International Tribunal for Rwanda to the Security Council and to the General Assembly.

13

1994 International Law Commission Draft Statute of an International Criminal Court

Draft Statute for an International Criminal Court, including Annex

(A) DRAFT STATUTE FOR AN INTERNATIONAL CRIMINAL COURT

The States Parties to this Statute,

Desiring to further international cooperation to enhance the effective prosecution and suppression of crimes of international concern, and for that purpose to establish an international criminal court;

Emphasizing that such a court is intended to exercise jurisdiction only over the most serious crimes of concern to the international community as a whole;

Emphasizing further that such a court is intended to be complementary to national criminal justice systems in cases where such trial procedures may not be available or may be ineffective;

Have agreed as follows:

PART ONE: ESTABLISHMENT OF THE COURT

Article 1
The Court
There is established an International Criminal Court ("the Court"), whose jurisdiction and functioning shall be governed by the provisions of this Statute.

Article 2
Relationship of the Court to the United Nations
The President, with the approval of the States Parties to this Statute ("States Parties"), may conclude an agreement establishing an appropriate relationship between the Court and the United Nations.

Article 3
Seat of the Court
1. The seat of the Court shall be established at ... in ... ("the host State").
2. The President, with the approval of the States Parties, may conclude an agreement with the host State establishing the relationship between that State and the Court.
3. The Court may exercise its powers and functions on the territory of any State Party and, by special agreement, on the territory of any other State.

Article 4
Status and legal capacity

1. The Court is a permanent institution open to States Parties in accordance with this Statute. It shall act when required to consider a case submitted to it.
2. The Court shall enjoy in the territory of each State Party such legal capacity as may be necessary for the exercise of its functions and the fulfilment of its purposes.

PART TWO: COMPOSITION AND ADMINISTRATION OF THE COURT

Article 5
Organs of the Court

The Court consists of the following organs:
(a) a Presidency, as provided in article 8;
(b) an Appeals Chamber, Trial Chambers and other chambers, as provided in article 9;
(c) a Procuracy, as provided in article 12;
(d) a Registry, as provided in article 13.

Article 6
Qualification and election of judges

1. The judges of the Court shall be persons of high moral character, impartiality and integrity who possess the qualifications required in their respective countries for appointment to the highest judicial offices, and have, in addition:
    (a) criminal trial experience;
    (b) recognized competence in international law.
2. Each State Party may nominate for election not more than two persons, of different nationality, who possess the qualification referred to in paragraph 1(*a*) or that referred to in paragraph 1(*b*), and who are willing to serve as may be required on the Court.
3. Eighteen judges shall be elected by an absolute majority vote of the States Parties by secret ballot. Ten judges shall first be elected, from among the persons nominated as having the qualification referred to in paragraph 1(*a*). Eight judges shall then be elected, from among the persons nominated as having the qualification referred to in paragraph 1(*b*).
4. No two judges may be nationals of the same State.
5. States Parties should bear in mind in the election of the judges that the representation of the principal legal systems of the world should be assured.
6. Judges hold office for a term of nine years and, subject to paragraph 7 and article 7, paragraph 2, are not eligible for re-election. A judge shall, however, continue in office in order to complete any case the hearing of which has commenced.
7. At the first election, six judges chosen by lot shall serve for a term of three years and are eligible for re-election; six judges chosen by lot shall serve for a term of six years; and the remainder shall serve for a term of nine years.
8. Judges nominated as having the qualification referred to in paragraphs 1(*a*) or 1(*b*), as the case may be, shall be replaced by persons nominated as having the same qualification.

Article 7
Judicial vacancies
1. In the event of a vacancy, a replacement judge shall be elected in accordance with article 6.
2. A judge elected to fill a vacancy shall serve for the remainder of the predecessor's term, and if that period is less than five years is eligible for re-election for a further term.

Article 8
The Presidency
1. The President, the first and second Vice-Presidents and two alternate Vice-Presidents shall be elected by an absolute majority of the judges. They shall serve for a term of three years or until the end of their term of office as judges, whichever is earlier.
2. The first or second Vice-President, as the case may be, may act in place of the President in the event that the President is unavailable or disqualified. An alternate Vice-President may act in place of either Vice-President as required.
3. The President and the Vice-Presidents shall constitute the Presidency which shall be responsible for:
   (a) the due administration of the Court;
   (b) the other functions conferred on it by this Statute.
4. Unless otherwise indicated, pre-trial and other procedural functions conferred under this Statute on the Court may be exercised by the Presidency in any case where a chamber of the Court is not seized of the matter.
5. The Presidency may, in accordance with the Rules, delegate to one or more judges the exercise of a power vested in it under article 26, paragraphs 3, 27, paragraphs 5, 28, 29 or 30, paragraph 3, in relation to a case, during the period before a trial chamber is established for that case.

Article 9
Chambers
1. As soon as possible after each election of judges to the Court, the Presidency shall in accordance with the Rules constitute an Appeals Chamber consisting of the President and six other judges, of whom at least three shall be judges elected from among the persons nominated as having the qualification referred to in article 6, paragraph 1(*b*). The President shall preside over the Appeals Chamber.
2. The Appeals Chamber shall be constituted for a term of three years. Members of the Appeals Chamber shall, however, continue to sit on the Chamber in order to complete any case the hearing of which has commenced.
3. Judges may be renewed as members of the Appeals Chamber for a second or subsequent term.
4. Judges not members of the Appeals Chamber shall be available to serve on Trial Chambers and other chambers required by this Statute, and to act as substitute members of the Appeals Chamber in the event that a member of that Chamber is unavailable or disqualified.
5. The Presidency shall nominate in accordance with the Rules five such judges to be members of the Trial Chamber for a given case. A Trial Chamber shall include at least

three judges elected from among the persons nominated as having the qualification referred to in article 6, paragraph 1(*a*).

6. The Rules may provide for alternate judges to be nominated to attend a trial and to act as members of the Trial Chamber in the event that a judge dies or becomes unavailable during the course of the trial.

7. No judge who is a national of a complainant State or of a State of which the accused is a national shall be a member of a chamber dealing with the case.

Article 10
Independence of the judges

1. In performing their functions, the judges shall be independent.

2. Judges shall not engage in any activity which is likely to interfere with their judicial functions or to affect confidence in their independence. In particular, they shall not while holding the office of judge be a member of the legislative or executive branches of the Government of a State, or of a body responsible for the investigation or prosecution of crimes.

3. Any question as to the application of paragraph 2 shall be decided by the Presidency.

4. On the recommendation of the Presidency, the States Parties may by a two-thirds majority decide that the workload of the Court requires that the judges should serve on a full-time basis. In that case:

   (a) existing judges who elect to serve on a full-time basis shall not hold any other office or employment;

   (b) judges subsequently elected shall not hold any other office or employment.

Article 11
Excusing and disqualification of judges

1. The Presidency at the request of a judge may excuse that judge from the exercise of a function under this Statute.

2. Judges shall not participate in any case in which they have previously been involved in any capacity or in which their impartiality might reasonably be doubted on any ground, including an actual, apparent or potential conflict of interest.

3. The Prosecutor or the accused may request the disqualification of a judge under paragraph 2.

4. Any question as to the disqualification of a judge shall be decided by an absolute majority of the members of the Chamber concerned. The challenged judge shall not take part in the decision.

Article 12
The Procuracy

1. The Procuracy is an independent organ of the Court responsible for the investigation of complaints brought in accordance with this Statute and for the conduct of prosecutions. A member of the Procuracy shall not seek or act on instructions from any external source.

2. The Procuracy shall be headed by the Prosecutor, assisted by one or more Deputy Prosecutors, who may act in place of the Prosecutor in the event that the Prosecutor is

unavailable. The Prosecutor and the Deputy Prosecutors shall be of different nationalities. The Prosecutor may appoint such other qualified staff as may be required.

3. The Prosecutor and Deputy Prosecutors shall be persons of high moral character and have high competence and experience in the prosecution of criminal cases. They shall be elected by secret ballot by an absolute majority of the States Parties, from among candidates nominated by States Parties. Unless a shorter term is otherwise decided on at the time of their election, they shall hold office for a term of five years and are eligible for re-election.

4. The States Parties may elect the Prosecutor and Deputy Prosecutors on the basis that they are willing to serve as required.

5. The Prosecutor and Deputy Prosecutors shall not act in relation to a complaint involving a person of their own nationality.

6. The Presidency may excuse the Prosecutor or a Deputy Prosecutor at their request from acting in a particular case, and shall decide any question raised in a particular case as to the disqualification of the Prosecutor or a Deputy Prosecutor.

7. The staff of the Procuracy shall be subject to Staff Regulations drawn up by the Prosecutor.

Article 13
The Registry

1. On the proposal of the Presidency, the judges by an absolute majority by secret ballot shall elect a Registrar, who shall be the principal administrative officer of the Court. They may in the same manner elect a Deputy Registrar.

2. The Registrar shall hold office for a term of five years, is eligible for re-election and shall be available on a full-time basis. The Deputy Registrar shall hold office for a term of five years or such shorter term as may be decided on, and may be elected on the basis that the Deputy Registrar is willing to serve as required.

3. The Presidency may appoint or authorize the Registrar to appoint such other staff of the Registry as may be necessary.

4. The staff of the Registry shall be subject to Staff Regulations drawn up by the Registrar.

Article 14
Solemn undertaking

Before first exercising their functions under this Statute, judges and other officers of the Court shall make a public and solemn undertaking to do so impartially and conscientiously.

Article 15
Loss of office

1. A judge, the Prosecutor or other officer of the Court who is found to have committed misconduct or a serious breach of this Statute, or to be unable to exercise the functions required by this Statute because of long-term illness or disability, shall cease to hold office.

2. A decision as to the loss of office under paragraph 1 shall be made by secret ballot:
   (a) in the case of the Prosecutor or a Deputy Prosecutor, by an absolute majority of the States Parties;
   (b) in any other case, by a two-thirds majority of the judges.

3. The judge, the Prosecutor or any other officer whose conduct or fitness for office is impugned shall have full opportunity to present evidence and to make submissions but shall not otherwise participate in the discussion of the question.

Article 16
Privileges and immunities

1. The judges, the Prosecutor, the Deputy Prosecutors and the staff of the Procuracy, the Registrar and the Deputy Registrar shall enjoy the privileges, immunities and facilities of a diplomatic agent within the meaning of the Vienna Convention on Diplomatic Relations of 16 April 1961.
2. The staff of the Registry shall enjoy the privileges, immunities and facilities necessary to the performance of their functions.
3. Counsel, experts and witnesses before the Court shall enjoy the privileges and immunities necessary to the independent exercise of their duties.
4. The judges may by an absolute majority decide to revoke a privilege or waive an immunity conferred by this article, other than an immunity of a judge, the Prosecutor or Registrar as such. In the case of other officers and staff of the Procuracy or Registry, they may do so only on the recommendation of the Prosecutor or Registrar, as the case may be.

Article 17
Allowances and expenses

1. The President shall receive an annual allowance.
2. The Vice-Presidents shall receive a special allowance for each day they exercise the functions of the President.
3. Subject to paragraph 4, the judges shall receive a daily allowance during the period in which they exercise their functions. They may continue to receive a salary payable in respect of another position occupied by them consistently with article 10.
4. If it is decided under article 10, paragraph 4, that judges shall thereafter serve on a full-time basis, existing judges who elect to serve on a full-time basis, and all judges subsequently elected, shall be paid a salary.

Article 18
Working languages

The working languages of the Court shall be English and French.

Article 19
Rules of the Court

1. Subject to paragraphs 2 and 3, the judges may by an absolute majority make rules for the functioning of the Court in accordance with this Statute, including rules regulating:
    (a) the conduct of investigations;
    (b) the procedure to be followed and the rules of evidence to be applied;
    (c) any other matter which is necessary for the implementation of this Statute.
2. The initial Rules of the Court shall be drafted by the judges within six months of the first elections for the Court, and submitted to a conference of States Parties for

approval. The judges may decide that a rule subsequently made under paragraph 1 should also be submitted to a conference of States Parties for approval.

3. In any case to which paragraph 2 does not apply, rules made under paragraph 1 shall be transmitted to States Parties and may be confirmed by the Presidency unless, within six months after transmission, a majority of States Parties have communicated in writing their objections.

4. A rule may provide for its provisional application in the period prior to its approval or confirmation. A rule not approved or confirmed shall lapse.

PART THREE: JURISDICTION OF THE COURT

Article 20
Crimes within the jurisdiction of the Court

The Court has jurisdiction in accordance with this Statute with respect to the following crimes:

(a) the crime of genocide;

(b) the crime of aggression;

(c) serious violations of the laws and customs applicable in armed conflict;

(d) crimes against humanity;

(e) crimes, established under or pursuant to the treaty provisions listed in the Annex, which, having regard to the conduct alleged, constitute exceptionally serious crimes of international concern.

Article 21
Preconditions to the exercise of jurisdiction

1. The Court may exercise its jurisdiction over a person with respect to a crime referred to in article 20 if:

(a) in a case of genocide, a complaint is brought under article 25, paragraph 1;

(b) in any other case, a complaint is brought under article 25, paragraph 2, and the jurisdiction of the Court with respect to the crime is accepted under article 22:

    (i) by the State which has custody of the suspect with respect to the crime ("the custodial State");

    (ii) by the State on the territory of which the act or omission in question occurred.

2. If, with respect to a crime to which paragraph 1(*b*) applies, the custodial State has received, under an international agreement, a request from another State to surrender a suspect for the purposes of prosecution, then, unless the request is rejected, the acceptance by the requesting State of the Court's jurisdiction with respect to the crime is also required.

Article 22
Acceptance of the jurisdiction of the Court for the purposes of article 21

1. A State Party to this Statute may:

(a) at the time it expresses its consent to be bound by the Statute, by declaration lodged with the depositary; or

(b) at a later time, by declaration lodged with the Registrar;

accept the jurisdiction of the Court with respect to such of the crimes referred to in article 20 as it specifies in the declaration.

2. A declaration may be of general application, or may be limited to particular conduct or to conduct committed during a particular period of time.

3. A declaration may be made for a specified period, in which case it may not be withdrawn before the end of that period, or for an unspecified period, in which case it may be withdrawn only upon giving six months' notice of withdrawal to the Registrar. Withdrawal does not affect proceedings already commenced under this Statute.

4. If under article 21 the acceptance of a State which is not a party to this Statute is required, that State may, by declaration lodged with the Registrar, consent to the Court exercising jurisdiction with respect to the crime.

Article 23
Action by the Security Council

1. Notwithstanding article 21, the Court has jurisdiction in accordance with this Statute with respect to crimes referred to in article 20 as a consequence of the referral of a matter to the Court by the Security Council acting under Chapter VII of the Charter of the United Nations.

2. A complaint of or directly related to an act of aggression may not be brought under this Statute unless the Security Council has first determined that a State has committed the act of aggression which is the subject of the complaint.

3. No prosecution may be commenced under this Statute arising from a situation which is being dealt with by the Security Council as a threat to or breach of the peace or an act of aggression under Chapter VII of the Charter, unless the Security Council otherwise decides.

Article 24
Duty of the Court as to jurisdiction

The Court shall satisfy itself that it has jurisdiction in any case brought before it.

PART FOUR: INVESTIGATION AND PROSECUTION

Article 25
Complaint

1. A State Party which is also a Contracting Party to the Convention on the Prevention and Punishment of the Crime of Genocide of 9 December 1948 may lodge a complaint with the Prosecutor alleging that a crime of genocide appears to have been committed.

2. A State Party which accepts the jurisdiction of the Court under article 22 with respect to a crime may lodge a complaint with the Prosecutor alleging that such a crime appears to have been committed.

3. As far as possible a complaint shall specify the circumstances of the alleged crime and the identity and whereabouts of any suspect, and be accompanied by such supporting documentation as is available to the complainant State.

4. In a case to which article 23, paragraph 1, applies, a complaint is not required for the initiation of an investigation.

Article 26
Investigation of alleged crimes

1. On receiving a complaint or upon notification of a decision of the Security Council referred to in article 23, paragraph 1, the Prosecutor shall initiate an investigation unless the Prosecutor concludes that there is no possible basis for a prosecution under this Statute and decides not to initiate an investigation, in which case the Prosecutor shall so inform the Presidency.
2. The Prosecutor may:
   (a) request the presence of and question suspects, victims and witnesses;
   (b) collect documentary and other evidence;
   (c) conduct on-site investigations;
   (d) take necessary measures to ensure the confidentiality of information or the protection of any person;
   (e) as appropriate, seek the cooperation of any State or of the United Nations.
3. The Presidency may, at the request of the Prosecutor, issue such subpoenas and warrants as may be required for the purposes of an investigation, including a warrant under article 28, paragraph 1, for the provisional arrest of a suspect.
4. If, upon investigation and having regard, inter alia, to the matters referred to in article 35, the Prosecutor concludes that there is no sufficient basis for a prosecution under this Statute and decides not to file an indictment, the Prosecutor shall so inform the Presidency giving details of the nature and basis of the complaint and of the reasons for not filing an indictment.
5. At the request of a complainant State or, in a case to which article 23, paragraph 1, applies, at the request of the Security Council, the Presidency shall review a decision of the Prosecutor not to initiate an investigation or not to file an indictment, and may request the Prosecutor to reconsider the decision.
6. A person suspected of a crime under this Statute shall:
   (a) prior to being questioned, be informed that the person is a suspect and of the rights:
       (i) to remain silent, without such silence being a consideration in the determination of guilt or innocence;
       (ii) to have the assistance of counsel of the suspect's choice or, if the suspect lacks the means to retain counsel, to have legal assistance assigned by the Court;
   (b) not be compelled to testify or to confess guilt;
   (c) if questioned in a language other than a language the suspect understands and speaks, be provided with competent interpretation services and with a translation of any document on which the suspect is to be questioned.

Article 27
Commencement of prosecution

1. If upon investigation the Prosecutor concludes that there is a prima facie case, the Prosecutor shall file with the Registrar an indictment containing a concise statement of the allegations of fact and of the crime or crimes with which the suspect is charged.
2. The Presidency shall examine the indictment and any supporting material and determine:

(a) whether a prima facie case exists with respect to a crime within the jurisdiction of the Court; and

(b) whether, having regard, inter alia, to the matters referred to in article 35, the case should on the information available be heard by the Court.

If so, it shall confirm the indictment and establish a trial chamber in accordance with article 9.

3. If, after any adjournment that may be necessary to allow additional material to be produced, the Presidency decides not to confirm the indictment, it shall so inform the complainant State or, in a case to which article 23, paragraph 1, applies, the Security Council.

4. The Presidency may at the request of the Prosecutor amend the indictment, in which case it shall make any necessary orders to ensure that the accused is notified of the amendment and has adequate time to prepare a defence.

5. The Presidency may make any further orders required for the conduct of the trial, including an order:

(a) determining the language or languages to be used during the trial;

(b) requiring the disclosure to the defence, within a sufficient time before the trial to enable the preparation of the defence, of documentary or other evidence available to the Prosecutor, whether or not the Prosecutor intends to rely on that evidence;

(c) providing for the exchange of information between the Prosecutor and the defence, so that both parties are sufficiently aware of the issues to be decided at the trial;

(d) providing for the protection of the accused, victims and witnesses and of confidential information.

Article 28
Arrest

1. At any time after an investigation has been initiated, the Presidency may at the request of the Prosecutor issue a warrant for the provisional arrest of a suspect if:

(a) there is probable cause to believe that the suspect may have committed a crime within the jurisdiction of the Court; and

(b) the suspect may not be available to stand trial unless provisionally arrested.

2. A suspect who has been provisionally arrested is entitled to release from arrest if the indictment has not been confirmed within 90 days of the arrest, or such longer time as the Presidency may allow.

3. As soon as practicable after the confirmation of the indictment, the Prosecutor shall seek from the Presidency a warrant for the arrest and transfer of the accused. The Presidency shall issue such a warrant unless it is satisfied that:

(a) the accused will voluntarily appear for trial; or

(b) there are special circumstances making it unnecessary for the time being to issue the warrant.

4. A person arrested shall be informed at the time of arrest of the reasons for the arrest and shall be promptly informed of any charges.

Article 29
Pre-trial detention or release

1. A person arrested shall be brought promptly before a judicial officer of the State where the arrest occurred. The judicial officer shall determine, in accordance with the

procedures applicable in that State, that the warrant has been duly served and that the rights of the accused have been respected.

2. A person arrested may apply to the Presidency for release pending trial. The Presidency may release the person unconditionally or on bail if it is satisfied that the accused will appear at the trial.

3. A person arrested may apply to the Presidency for a determination of the lawfulness under this Statute of the arrest or detention. If the Presidency decides that the arrest or detention was unlawful, it shall order the release of the accused, and may award compensation.

4. A person arrested shall be held, pending trial or release on bail, in an appropriate place of detention in the arresting State, in the State in which the trial is to be held or if necessary, in the host State.

Article 30
Notification of the indictment

1. The Prosecutor shall ensure that a person who has been arrested is personally served, as soon as possible after being taken into custody, with certified copies of the following documents, in a language understood by that person:
   (a) in the case of a suspect provisionally arrested, a statement of the grounds for the arrest;
   (b) in any other case, the confirmed indictment;
   (c) a statement of the accused's rights under this Statute.

2. In any case to which paragraph 1(*a*) applies, the indictment shall be served on the accused as soon as possible after it has been confirmed.

3. If, 60 days after the indictment has been confirmed, the accused is not in custody pursuant to a warrant issued under article 28, paragraph 3, or for some reason the requirements of paragraph 1 cannot be complied with, the Presidency may on the application of the Prosecutor prescribe some other manner of bringing the indictment to the attention of the accused.

Article 31
Persons made available to assist in a prosecution

1. The Prosecutor may request a State Party to make persons available to assist in a prosecution in accordance with paragraph 2.

2. Such persons should be available for the duration of the prosecution, unless otherwise agreed. They shall serve at the direction of the Prosecutor, and shall not seek or receive instructions from any Government or source other than the Prosecutor in relation to their exercise of functions under this article.

3. The terms and conditions on which persons may be made available under this article shall be approved by the Presidency on the recommendation of the Prosecutor.

PART FIVE: THE TRIAL

Article 32
Place of trial

Unless otherwise decided by the Presidency, the place of the trial will be the seat of the Court.

Article 33
Applicable law
The Court shall apply:
(a) this Statute;
(b) applicable treaties and the principles and rules of general international law;
(c) to the extent applicable, any rule of national law.

Article 34
Challenges to jurisdiction
Challenges to the jurisdiction of the Court may be made, in accordance with the Rules:
(a) prior to or at the commencement of the hearing, by an accused or any interested State; and
(b) at any later stage of the trial, by an accused.

Article 35
Issues of admissibility
The Court may, on application by the accused or at the request of an interested State at any time prior to the commencement of the trial, or of its own motion, decide, having regard to the purposes of this Statute set out in the preamble, that a case before it is inadmissible on the ground that the crime in question:
(a) has been duly investigated by a State with jurisdiction over it, and the decision of that State not to proceed to a prosecution is apparently well-founded;
(b) is under investigation by a State which has or may have jurisdiction over it, and there is no reason for the Court to take any further action for the time being with respect to the crime; or
(c) is not of such gravity to justify further action by the Court.

Article 36
Procedure under articles 34 and 35
1. In proceedings under articles 34 and 35, the accused and the complainant State have the right to be heard.
2. Proceedings under articles 34 and 35 shall be decided by the Trial Chamber, unless it considers, having regard to the importance of the issues involved, that the matter should be referred to the Appeals Chamber.

Article 37
Trial in the presence of the accused
1. As a general rule, the accused should be present during the trial.
2. The Trial Chamber may order that the trial proceed in the absence of the accused if:
(a) the accused is in custody, or has been released pending trial, and for reasons of security or the ill-health of the accused it is undesirable for the accused to be present;
(b) the accused is continuing to disrupt the trial; or
(c) the accused has escaped from lawful custody under this Statute or has broken bail.

3. The Chamber shall, if it makes an order under paragraph 2, ensure that the rights of the accused under this Statute are respected, and in particular:
   (a) that all reasonable steps have been taken to inform the accused of the charge; and
   (b) that the accused is legally represented, if necessary by a lawyer appointed by the Court.
4. In cases where a trial cannot be held because of the deliberate absence of an accused, the Court may establish, in accordance with the Rules, an Indictment Chamber for the purpose of:
   (a) recording the evidence;
   (b) considering whether the evidence establishes a prima facie case of a crime within the jurisdiction of the Court; and
   (c) issuing and publishing a warrant of arrest in respect of an accused against whom a prima facie case is established.
5. If the accused is subsequently tried under this Statute:
   (a) the record of evidence before the Indictment Chamber shall be admissible;
   (b) any judge who was a member of the Indictment Chamber may not be a member of the Trial Chamber.

Article 38
Functions and powers of the Trial Chamber
1. At the commencement of the trial, the Trial Chamber shall:
   (a) have the indictment read;
   (b) ensure that articles 27, paragraph 5(b), and 30 have been complied with sufficiently in advance of the trial to enable adequate preparation of the defence;
   (c) satisfy itself that the other rights of the accused under this Statute have been respected; and
   (d) allow the accused to enter a plea of guilty or not guilty.
2. The Chamber shall ensure that a trial is fair and expeditious and is conducted in accordance with this Statute and the Rules, with full respect for the rights of the accused and due regard for the protection of victims and witnesses.
3. The Chamber may, subject to the Rules, hear charges against more than one accused arising out of the same factual situation.
4. The trial shall be held in public, unless the Chamber determines that certain proceedings be in closed session in accordance with article 43, or for the purpose of protecting confidential or sensitive information which is to be given in evidence.
5. The Chamber shall, subject to this Statute and the Rules have, inter alia, the power on the application of a party or of its own motion, to:
   (a) issue a warrant for the arrest and transfer of an accused who is not already in the custody of the Court;
   (b) require the attendance and testimony of witnesses;
   (c) require the production of documentary and other evidentiary materials;
   (d) rule on the admissibility or relevance of evidence;
   (e) protect confidential information;
   (f) maintain order in the course of a hearing.

6. The Chamber shall ensure that a complete record of the trial, which accurately reflects the proceedings, is maintained and preserved by the Registrar.

Article 39
Principle of legality (*nullum crimen sine lege*)
An accused shall not be held guilty:

(a) in the case of a prosecution with respect to a crime referred to in article 20, subparagraphs (*a*) to (*d*), unless the act or omission in question constituted a crime under international law;

(b) in the case of a prosecution with respect to a crime referred to in article 20, subparagraph (*e*), unless the treaty in question was applicable to the conduct of the accused;

at the time the act or omission occurred.

Article 40
Presumption of innocence
An accused shall be presumed innocent until proved guilty in accordance with the law. The onus is on the Prosecutor to establish the guilt of the accused beyond reasonable doubt.

Article 41
Rights of the accused
1. In the determination of any charge under this Statute, the accused is entitled to a fair and public hearing, subject to article 43, and to the following minimum guarantees:

   (a) to be informed promptly and in detail, in a language which the accused understands, of the nature and cause of the charge;

   (b) to have adequate time and facilities for the preparation of the defence, and to communicate with counsel of the accused's choosing;

   (c) to be tried without undue delay;

   (d) subject to article 37, paragraph 2, to be present at the trial, to conduct the defence in person or through legal assistance of the accused's choosing, to be informed, if the accused does not have legal assistance, of this right and to have legal assistance assigned by the Court, without payment if the accused lacks sufficient means to pay for such assistance;

   (e) to examine, or have examined, the prosecution witnesses and to obtain the attendance and examination of witnesses for the defence under the same conditions as witnesses for the prosecution;

   (f) if any of the proceedings of or documents presented to the Court are not in a language the accused understands and speaks, to have, free of any cost, the assistance of a competent interpreter and such translations as are necessary to meet the requirements of fairness;

   (g) not to be compelled to testify or to confess guilt.

2. Exculpatory evidence that becomes available to the Procuracy prior to the conclusion of the trial shall be made available to the defence. In case of doubt as to the application of this paragraph or as to the admissibility of the evidence, the Trial Chamber shall decide.

Article 42
Non bis in idem
1. No person shall be tried before any other court for acts constituting a crime of the kind referred to in article 20 for which that person has already been tried by the Court.
2. A person who has been tried by another court for acts constituting a crime of the kind referred to in article 20 may be tried under this Statute only if:
   (a) the acts in question were characterized by that court as an ordinary crime and not as a crime which is within the jurisdiction of the Court; or
   (b) the proceedings in the other court were not impartial or independent or were designed to shield the accused from international criminal responsibility or the case was not diligently prosecuted.
3. In considering the penalty to be imposed on a person convicted under this Statute, the Court shall take into account the extent to which a penalty imposed by another court on the same person for the same act has already been served.

Article 43
Protection of the accused, victims and witnesses
The Court shall take necessary measures available to it to protect the accused, victims and witnesses and may to that end conduct closed proceedings or allow the presentation of evidence by electronic or other special means.

Article 44
Evidence
1. Before testifying, each witness shall, in accordance with the Rules, give an undertaking as to the truthfulness of the evidence to be given by that witness.
2. States Parties shall extend their laws of perjury to cover evidence given under this Statute by their nationals, and shall cooperate with the Court in investigating and where appropriate prosecuting any case of suspected perjury.
3. The Court may require to be informed of the nature of any evidence before it is offered so that it may rule on its relevance or admissibility.
4. The Court shall not require proof of facts of common knowledge but may take judicial notice of them.
5. Evidence obtained by means of a serious violation of this Statute or of other rules of international law shall not be admissible.

Article 45
Quorum and judgement
1. At least four members of the Trial Chamber must be present at each stage of the trial.
2. The decisions of the Trial Chamber shall be taken by a majority of the judges. At least three judges must concur in a decision as to conviction or acquittal and as to the sentence to be imposed.
3. If after sufficient time for deliberation a Chamber which has been reduced to four judges is unable to agree on a decision, it may order a new trial.
4. The deliberations of the Court shall be and remain secret.

5. The judgement shall be in writing and shall contain a full and reasoned statement of the findings and conclusions. It shall be the sole judgement issued, and shall be delivered in open court.

Article 46
Sentencing

1. In the event of a conviction, the Trial Chamber shall hold a further hearing to hear any evidence relevant to sentence, to allow the Prosecutor and the defence to make submissions and to consider the appropriate sentence to be imposed.
2. In imposing sentence, the Trial Chamber should take into account such factors as the gravity of the crime and the individual circumstances of the convicted person.

Article 47
Applicable penalties

1. The Court may impose on a person convicted of a crime under this Statute one or more of the following penalties:
    (a) a term of life imprisonment, or of imprisonment for a specified number of years;
    (b) a fine.
2. In determining the length of a term of imprisonment or the amount of a fine to be imposed, the Court may have regard to the penalties provided for by the law of:
    (a) the State of which the convicted person is a national;
    (b) the State where the crime was committed;
    (c) the State which had custody of and jurisdiction over the accused.
3. Fines paid may be transferred, by order of the Court, to one or more of the following:
    (a) the Registrar, to defray the costs of the trial;
    (b) a State of which the nationals were the victims of the crime;
    (c) a trust fund established by the Secretary-General of the United Nations for the benefit of victims of crime.

PART SIX: APPEAL AND REVIEW

Article 48
Appeal against judgement or sentence

1. The Prosecutor and the convicted person may, in accordance with the Rules, appeal against a decision under articles 45 or 47 on grounds of procedural error, error of fact or of law, or disproportion between the crime and the sentence.
2. Unless the Trial Chamber otherwise orders, a convicted person shall remain in custody pending an appeal.

Article 49
Proceedings on appeal

1. The Appeals Chamber has all the powers of the Trial Chamber.
2. If the Appeals Chamber finds that the proceedings appealed from were unfair or that the decision is vitiated by error of fact or law, it may:

(a) if the appeal is brought by the convicted person, reverse or amend the decision, or, if necessary, order a new trial;

(b) if the appeal is brought by the Prosecutor against an acquittal, order a new trial.

3. If in an appeal against sentence the Chamber finds that the sentence is manifestly disproportionate to the crime, it may vary the sentence in accordance with article 47.

4. The decision of the Chamber shall be taken by a majority of the judges, and shall be delivered in open court. Six judges constitute a quorum.

5. Subject to article 50, the decision of the Chamber shall be final.

Article 50
Revision

1. The convicted person or the Prosecutor may, in accordance with the Rules, apply to the Presidency for revision of a conviction on the ground that evidence has been discovered which was not available to the applicant at the time the conviction was pronounced or affirmed and which could have been a decisive factor in the conviction.

2. The Presidency shall request the Prosecutor or the convicted person, as the case may be, to present written observations on whether the application should be accepted.

3. If the Presidency is of the view that the new evidence could lead to the revision of the conviction, it may:

(a) reconvene the Trial Chamber;

(b) constitute a new Trial Chamber; or

(c) refer the matter to the Appeals Chamber;

with a view to the Chamber determining, after hearing the parties, whether the new evidence should lead to a revision of the conviction.

PART SEVEN: INTERNATIONAL COOPERATION AND JUDICIAL ASSISTANCE

Article 51
Cooperation and judicial assistance

1. States Parties shall cooperate with the Court in connection with criminal investigations and proceedings under this Statute.

2. The Registrar may transmit to any State a request for cooperation and judicial assistance with respect to a crime, including, but not limited to:

(a) the identification and location of persons;

(b) the taking of testimony and the production of evidence;

(c) the service of documents;

(d) the arrest or detention of persons;

(e) any other request which may facilitate the administration of justice, including provisional measures as required.

3. Upon receipt of a request under paragraph 2:

(a) in a case covered by article 21, paragraph 1(*a*), all States Parties;

(b) in any other case, States Parties which have accepted the jurisdiction of the Court with respect to the crime in question;

shall respond without undue delay to the request.

Article 52
Provisional measures

1. In case of need, the Court may request a State to take necessary provisional measures, including the following:
   (a) to provisionally arrest a suspect;
   (b) to seize documents or other evidence; or
   (c) to prevent injury to or the intimidation of a witness or the destruction of evidence.
2. The Court shall follow up a request under paragraph 1 by providing, as soon as possible and in any case within 28 days, a formal request for assistance complying with article 57.

Article 53
Transfer of an accused to the Court

1. The Registrar shall transmit to any State on the territory of which the accused may be found a warrant for the arrest and transfer of an accused issued under article 28, and shall request the cooperation of that State in the arrest and transfer of the accused.
2. Upon receipt of a request under paragraph 1:
   (a) all States Parties:
      (i)   in a case covered by article 21, paragraph 1(*a*); or
      (ii) which have accepted the jurisdiction of the Court with respect to the crime in question;
      shall, subject to paragraphs 5 and 6, take immediate steps to arrest and transfer the accused to the Court;
   (b) in the case of a crime to which article 20, subparagraph (*e*), applies, a State Party which is a party to the treaty in question but which has not accepted the Court's jurisdiction with respect to that crime shall, if it decides not to transfer the accused to the Court, forthwith take all necessary steps to extradite the accused to a requesting State or refer the case to its competent authorities for the purpose of prosecution;
   (c) in any other case, a State Party shall consider whether it can, in accordance with its legal procedures, take steps to arrest and transfer the accused to the Court, or whether it should take steps to extradite the accused to a requesting State or refer the case to its competent authorities for the purpose of prosecution.
3. The transfer of an accused to the Court constitutes, as between States Parties which accept the jurisdiction of the Court with respect to the crime, sufficient compliance with a provision of any treaty requiring that a suspect be extradited or the case referred to the competent authorities of the requested State for the purpose of prosecution.
4. A State Party which accepts the jurisdiction of the Court with respect to the crime shall, as far as possible, give priority to a request under paragraph 1 over requests for extradition from other States.
5. A State Party may delay complying with paragraph 2 if the accused is in its custody or control and is being proceeded against for a serious crime, or serving a sentence imposed by a court for a crime. It shall within 45 days of receiving the request inform the Registrar of the reasons for the delay. In such cases, the requested State:

(a) may agree to the temporary transfer of the accused for the purpose of standing trial under this Statute; or

(b) shall comply with paragraph 2 after the prosecution has been completed or abandoned or the sentence has been served, as the case may be.

6. A State Party may, within 45 days of receiving a request under paragraph 1, file a written application with the Registrar requesting the Court to set aside the request on specified grounds. Pending a decision of the Court on the application, the State concerned may delay complying with paragraph 2 but shall take any provisional measures necessary to ensure that the accused remains in its custody or control.

Article 54
Obligation to extradite or prosecute
In a case of a crime referred to in article 20, subparagraph (e), a custodial State Party to this Statute which is a party to the treaty in question but which has not accepted the Court's jurisdiction with respect to the crime for the purposes of article 21, paragraph 1(b)(i), shall either take all necessary steps to extradite the suspect to a requesting State for the purpose of prosecution or refer the case to its competent authorities for that purpose.

Article 55
Rule of speciality
1. A person transferred to the Court under article 53 shall not be subject to prosecution or punishment for any crime other than that for which the person was transferred.
2. Evidence provided under this Part shall not, if the State when providing it so requests, be used as evidence for any purpose other than that for which it was provided, unless this is necessary to preserve the right of an accused under article 41, paragraph 2.
3. The Court may request the State concerned to waive the requirements of paragraphs 1 or 2, for the reasons and purposes specified in the request.

Article 56
Cooperation with States not parties to this Statute
States not parties to this Statute may assist in relation to the matters referred to in this Part on the basis of comity, a unilateral declaration, an ad hoc arrangement or other agreement with the Court.

Article 57
Communications and documentation
1. Requests under this Part shall be in writing, or be forthwith reduced to writing, and shall be between the competent national authority and the Registrar. States Parties shall inform the Registrar of the name and address of their national authority for this purpose.
2. When appropriate, communications may also be made through the International Criminal Police Organization.
3. A request under this Part shall include the following, as applicable:

(a) a brief statement of the purpose of the request and of the assistance sought, including the legal basis and grounds for the request;

(b) information concerning the person who is the subject of the request on the evidence sought, in sufficient detail to enable identification;

(c) a brief description of the essential facts underlying the request; and

(d) information concerning the complaint or charge to which the request relates and of the basis for the Court's jurisdiction.

4. A requested State which considers the information provided insufficient to enable the request to be complied with may seek further particulars.

PART EIGHT: ENFORCEMENT

Article 58
Recognition of judgements

States Parties undertake to recognize the judgements of the Court.

Article 59
Enforcement of sentences

1. A sentence of imprisonment shall be served in a State designated by the Court from a list of States which have indicated to the Court their willingness to accept convicted persons.

2. If no State is designated under paragraph 1, the sentence of imprisonment shall be served in a prison facility made available by the host State.

3. A sentence of imprisonment shall be subject to the supervision of the Court in accordance with the Rules.

Article 60
Pardon, parole and commutation of sentences

1. If, under a generally applicable law of the State of imprisonment, a person in the same circumstances who had been convicted for the same conduct by a court of that State would be eligible for pardon, parole or commutation of sentence, the State shall so notify the Court.

2. If a notification has been given under paragraph 1, the prisoner may apply to the Court in accordance with the Rules, seeking an order for pardon, parole or commutation of the sentence.

3. If the Presidency decides that an application under paragraph 2 is apparently well-founded, it shall convene a Chamber of five judges to consider and decide whether in the interests of justice the person convicted should be pardoned or paroled or the sentence commuted, and on what basis.

4. When imposing a sentence of imprisonment, a Chamber may stipulate that the sentence is to be served in accordance with specified laws as to pardon, parole or commutation of sentence of the State of imprisonment. The consent of the Court is not required to subsequent action by that State in conformity with those laws, but the Court shall be given at least 45 days' notice of any decision which might materially affect the terms or extent of the imprisonment.

5. Except as provided in paragraphs 3 and 4, a person serving a sentence imposed by the Court is not to be released before the expiry of the sentence.

(B) ANNEX CRIMES PURSUANT TO TREATIES (SEE ART. 20, SUBPARA. (*e*))

1. Grave breaches of:
   (a) the Geneva Convention for the Amelioration of the Condition of the Wounded and Sick in Armed Forces in the Field of 12 August 1949, as defined by article 50 of that Convention;
   (b) the Geneva Convention for the Amelioration of the Condition of Wounded, Sick and Shipwrecked Members of Armed Forces at Sea of 12 August 1949, as defined by article 51 of that Convention;
   (c) the Geneva Convention relative to the Treatment of Prisoners of War of 12 August 1949, as defined by article 130 of that Convention;
   (d) the Geneva Convention relative to the Protection of Civilian Persons in Time of War of 12 August 1949, as defined by article 147 of that Convention;
   (e) Protocol Additional to the Geneva Conventions of 12 August 1949, and relating to the protection of victims of international armed conflicts (Protocol I) of 8 June 1977, as defined by article 85 of that Protocol.
2. The unlawful seizure of aircraft as defined by article 1 of the Convention for the Suppression of Unlawful Seizure of Aircraft of 16 December 1970.
3. The crimes defined by article 1 of the Convention for the Suppression of Unlawful Acts against the Safety of Civil Aviation of 23 September 1971.
4. *Apartheid* and related crimes as defined by article II of the International Convention on the Suppression and Punishment of the Crime of *Apartheid* of 30 November 1973.
5. The crimes defined by article 2 of the Convention on the Prevention and Punishment of Crimes against Internationally Protected Persons, including Diplomatic Agents of 14 December 1973.
6. Hostage-taking and related crimes as defined by article 1 of the International Convention against the Taking of Hostages of 17 December 1979.
7. The crime of torture made punishable pursuant to article 4 of the Convention against Torture and Other Cruel, Inhuman or Degrading Treatment or Punishment of 10 December 1984.
8. The crimes defined by article 3 of the Convention for the Suppression of Unlawful Acts against the Safety of Maritime Navigation and by article 2 of the Protocol for the Suppression of Unlawful Acts against the Safety of Fixed Platforms located on the Continental Shelf, both of 10 March 1988.
9. Crimes involving illicit traffic in narcotic drugs and psychotropic substances as envisaged by article 3, paragraph 1, of the United Nations Convention against Illicit Traffic in Narcotic Drugs and Psychotropic Substances of 20 December 1988 which, having regard to article 2 of the Convention, are crimes with an international dimension.

14

1996 International Law Commission Draft Code of Crimes against the Peace and Security of Mankind

Draft Code of Crimes against the Peace and Security of Mankind (1996)

PART ONE GENERAL PROVISIONS

Article 1
Scope and application of the present Code
1. The present Code applies to the crimes against the peace and security of mankind set out in part two.
2. Crimes against the peace and security of mankind are crimes under international law and punishable as such, whether or not they are punishable under national law.

Article 2
Individual responsibility
1. A crime against the peace and security of mankind entails individual responsibility.
2. An individual shall be responsible for the crime of aggression in accordance with article 16.
3. An individual shall be responsible for a crime set out in article 17, 18, 19 or 20 if that individual:
   (a) intentionally commits such a crime;
   (b) orders the commission of such a crime which in fact occurs or is attempted;
   (c) fails to prevent or repress the commission of such a crime in the circumstances set out in article 6;
   (d) knowingly aids, abets or otherwise assists, directly and substantially, in the commission of such a crime, including providing the means for its commission;
   (e) directly participates in planning or conspiring to commit such a crime which in fact occurs;
   (f) directly and publicly incites another individual to commit such a crime which in fact occurs;
   (g) attempts to commit such a crime by taking action commencing the execution of a crime which does not in fact occur because of circumstances independent of his intentions.

Article 3
Punishment
An individual who is responsible for a crime against the peace and security of mankind shall be liable to punishment. The punishment shall be commensurate with the character and gravity of the crime.

Article 4
Responsibility of States
The fact that the present Code provides for the responsibility of individuals for crimes against the peace and security of mankind is without prejudice to any question of the responsibility of States under international law.

Article 5
Order of a Government or a superior
The fact that an individual charged with a crime against the peace and security of mankind acted pursuant to an order of a Government or a superior does not relieve him of criminal responsibility, but may be considered in mitigation of punishment if justice so requires.

Article 6
Responsibility of the superior
The fact that a crime against the peace and security of mankind was committed by a subordinate does not relieve his superiors of criminal responsibility, if they knew or had reason to know, in the circumstances at the time, that the subordinate was committing or was going to commit such a crime and if they did not take all necessary measures within their power to prevent or repress the crime.

Article 7
Official position and responsibility
The official position of an individual who commits a crime against the peace and security of mankind, even if he acted as head of State or Government, does not relieve him of criminal responsibility or mitigate punishment.

Article 8
Establishment of jurisdiction
Without prejudice to the jurisdiction of an international criminal court, each State Party shall take such measures as may be necessary to establish its jurisdiction over the crimes set out in articles 17, 18, 19 and 20, irrespective of where or by whom those crimes were committed. Jurisdiction over the crime set out in article 16 shall rest with an international criminal court. However, a State referred to in article 16 is not precluded from trying its nationals for the crime set out in that article.

Article 9
Obligation to extradite or prosecute
Without prejudice to the jurisdiction of an international criminal court, the State Party in the territory of which an individual alleged to have committed a crime set out in article 17, 18, 19 or 20 is found shall extradite or prosecute that individual.

15

Article 10
Extradition of alleged offenders

1. To the extent that the crimes set out in articles 17, 18, 19 and 20 are not extraditable offences in any extradition treaty existing between States Parties, they shall be deemed to be included as such therein. States Parties undertake to include those crimes as extraditable offences in every extradition treaty to be concluded between them.
2. If a State Party which makes extradition conditional on the existence of a treaty receives a request for extradition from another State Party with which it has no extradition treaty, it may at its option consider the present Code as the legal basis for extradition in respect of those crimes. Extradition shall be subject to the conditions provided in the law of the requested State.
3. States Parties which do not make extradition conditional on the existence of a treaty shall recognize those crimes as extraditable offences between themselves subject to the conditions provided in the law of the requested State.
4. Each of those crimes shall be treated, for the purpose of extradition between States Parties, as if it had been committed not only in the place in which it occurred but also in the territory of any other State Party.

Article 11
Judicial guarantees

1. An individual charged with a crime against the peace and security of mankind shall be presumed innocent until proved guilty and shall be entitled without discrimination to the minimum guarantees due to all human beings with regard to the law and the facts and shall have the rights:
   (a) in the determination of any charge against him, to have a fair and public hearing by a competent, independent and impartial tribunal duly established by law;
   (b) to be informed promptly and in detail in a language which he understands of the nature and cause of the charge against him;
   (c) to have adequate time and facilities for the preparation of his defence and to communicate with counsel of his own choosing;
   (d) to be tried without undue delay;
   (e) to be tried in his presence, and to defend himself in person or through legal assistance of his own choosing; to be informed, if he does not have legal assistance, of this right; and to have legal assistance assigned to him and without payment by him if he does not have sufficient means to pay for it;
   (f) to examine, or have examined, the witnesses against him and to obtain the attendance and examination of witnesses on his behalf under the same conditions as witnesses against him;
   (g) to have the free assistance of an interpreter if he cannot understand or speak the language used in court;
   (h) not to be compelled to testify against himself or to confess guilt.
2. An individual convicted of a crime shall have the right to his conviction and sentence being reviewed according to law.

Article 12
Non bis in idem

1. No one shall be tried for a crime against the peace and security of mankind of which he has already been finally convicted or acquitted by an international criminal court.
2. An individual may not be tried again for a crime of which he has been finally convicted or acquitted by a national court except in the following cases:
   (a) by an international criminal court, if:
      (i) the act which was the subject of the judgement in the national court was characterized by that court as an ordinary crime and not as a crime against the peace and security of mankind; or
      (ii) the national court proceedings were not impartial or independent or were designed to shield the accused from international criminal responsibility or the case was not diligently prosecuted;
   (b) by a national court of another State, if:
      (i) the act which was the subject of the previous judgement took place in the territory of that State; or
      (ii) that State was the main victim of the crime.
3. In the case of a subsequent conviction under the present Code, the court, in passing sentence, shall take into account the extent to which any penalty imposed by a national court on the same person for the same act has already been served.

Article 13
Non-retroactivity

1. No one shall be convicted under the present Code for acts committed before its entry into force.
2. Nothing in this article precludes the trial of anyone for any act which, at the time when it was committed, was criminal in accordance with international law or national law.

Article 14
Defences

The competent court shall determine the admissibility of defences in accordance with the general principles of law, in the light of the character of each crime.

Article 15
Extenuating circumstances

In passing sentence, the court shall, where appropriate, take into account extenuating circumstances in accordance with the general principles of law.

PART TWO CRIMES AGAINST THE PEACE AND SECURITY OF MANKIND

Article 16
Crime of aggression

An individual who, as leader or organizer, actively participates in or orders the planning, preparation, initiation or waging of aggression committed by a State shall be responsible for a crime of aggression.

Article 17
Crime of genocide

A crime of genocide means any of the following acts committed with intent to destroy, in whole or in part, a national, ethnic, racial or religious group, as such:

(a) killing members of the group;

(b) causing serious bodily or mental harm to members of the group;

(c) deliberately inflicting on the group conditions of life calculated to bring about its physical destruction in whole or in part;

(d) imposing measures intended to prevent births within the group;

(e) forcibly transferring children of the group to another group.

Article 18
Crimes against humanity

A crime against humanity means any of the following acts, when committed in a systematic manner or on a large scale and instigated or directed by a Government or by any organization or group:

(a) murder;

(b) extermination;

(c) torture;

(d) enslavement;

(e) persecution on political, racial, religious or ethnic grounds;

(f) institutionalized discrimination on racial, ethnic or religious grounds involving the violation of fundamental human rights and freedoms and resulting in seriously disadvantaging a part of the population;

(g) arbitrary deportation or forcible transfer of population;

(h) arbitrary imprisonment;

(i) forced disappearance of persons;

(j) rape, enforced prostitution and other forms of sexual abuse;

(k) other inhumane acts which severely damage physical or mental integrity, health or human dignity, such as mutilation and severe bodily harm.

Article 19
Crimes against United Nations and associated personnel

1. The following crimes constitute crimes against the peace and security of mankind when committed intentionally and in a systematic manner or on a large scale against United Nations and associated personnel involved in a United Nations operation with a view to preventing or impeding that operation from fulfilling its mandate:

   (a) murder, kidnapping or other attack upon the person or liberty of any such personnel;

   (b) violent attack upon the official premises, the private accommodation or the means of transportation of any such personnel likely to endanger his or her person or liberty.

2. This article shall not apply to a United Nations operation authorized by the Security Council as an enforcement action under Chapter VII of the Charter of the United Nations in which any of the personnel are engaged as combatants against organized armed forces and to which the law of international armed conflict applies.

Article 20

War crimes

Any of the following war crimes constitutes a crime against the peace and security of mankind when committed in a systematic manner or on a large scale:

(a) any of the following acts committed in violation of international humanitarian law:

    (i) wilful killing;

    (ii) torture or inhuman treatment, including biological experiments;

    (iii) wilfully causing great suffering or serious injury to body or health;

    (iv) extensive destruction and appropriation of property, not justified by military necessity and carried out unlawfully and wantonly;

    (v) compelling a prisoner of war or other protected person to serve in the forces of a hostile Power;

    (vi) wilfully depriving a prisoner of war or other protected person of the rights of fair and regular trial;

    (vii) unlawful deportation or transfer of unlawful confinement of protected persons;

    (viii) taking of hostages;

(b) any of the following acts committed wilfully in violation of international humanitarian law and causing death or serious injury to body or health:

    (i) making the civilian population or individual civilians the object of attack;

    (ii) launching an indiscriminate attack affecting the civilian population or civilian objects in the knowledge that such attack will cause excessive loss of life, injury to civilians or damage to civilian objects;

    (iii) launching an attack against works or installations containing dangerous forces in the knowledge that such attack will cause excessive loss of life, injury to civilians or damage to civilian objects;

    (iv) making a person the object of attack in the knowledge that he is hors de combat;

    (v) the perfidious use of the distinctive emblem of the red cross, red crescent or red lion and sun or of other recognized protective signs;

(c) any of the following acts committed wilfully in violation of international humanitarian law:

    (i) the transfer by the Occupying Power of parts of its own civilian population into the territory it occupies;

    (ii) unjustifiable delay in the repatriation of prisoners of war or civilians;

(d) outrages upon personal dignity in violation of international humanitarian law, in particular humiliating and degrading treatment, rape, enforced prostitution and any form of indecent assault;

(e) any of the following acts committed in violation of the laws or customs of war:

    (i) employment of poisonous weapons or other weapons calculated to cause unnecessary suffering;

    (ii) wanton destruction of cities, towns or villages, or devastation not justified by military necessity;

    (iii) attack, or bombardment, by whatever means, of undefended towns, villages, dwellings or buildings or of demilitarized zones;

      (iv)   seizure of, destruction of or wilful damage done to institutions dedicated to religion, charity and education, the arts and sciences, historic monuments and works of art and science;

      (v)   plunder of public or private property;

(f) any of the following acts committed in violation of international humanitarian law applicable in armed conflict not of an international character:

      (i)   violence to the life, health and physical or mental well-being of persons, in particular murder as well as cruel treatment such as torture, mutilation or any form of corporal punishment;

      (ii)   collective punishments;

      (iii)   taking of hostages;

      (iv)   acts of terrorism;

      (v)   outrages upon personal dignity, in particular humiliating and degrading treatment, rape, enforced prostitution and any form of indecent assault;

      (vi)   pillage;

      (vii)   the passing of sentences and the carrying out of executions without previous judgement pronounced by a regularly constituted court, affording all the judicial guarantees which are generally recognized as indispensable;

(g) in the case of armed conflict, using methods or means of warfare not justified by military necessity with the intent to cause widespread, long-term and severe damage to the natural environment and thereby gravely prejudice the health or survival of the population and such damage occurs.

1998 Rome Statute of the International Criminal Court (ICC) including 2010 Kampala Amendments; 2002 ICC Rules of Procedure and Evidence; 2002 ICC Elements of Crimes; 2004 United Nations-ICC Relationship Agreement

Rome Statute of the International Criminal Court[1]

PREAMBLE

The States Parties to this Statute,

Conscious that all peoples are united by common bonds, their cultures pieced together in a shared heritage, and concerned that this delicate mosaic may be shattered at any time,

Mindful that during this century millions of children, women and men have been victims of unimaginable atrocities that deeply shock the conscience of humanity,

Recognizing that such grave crimes threaten the peace, security and well-being of the world,

Affirming that the most serious crimes of concern to the international community as a whole must not go unpunished and that their effective prosecution must be ensured by taking measures at the national level and by enhancing international cooperation,

Determined to put an end to impunity for the perpetrators of these crimes and thus to contribute to the prevention of such crimes,

Recalling that it is the duty of every State to exercise its criminal jurisdiction over those responsible for international crimes,

Reaffirming the Purposes and Principles of the Charter of the United Nations, and in particular that all States shall refrain from the threat or use of force against the territorial integrity or political independence of any State, or in any other manner inconsistent with the Purposes of the United Nations,

---

[1] Italicised parts of the Statute reflect the changes made pursuant to the Kampala Amendments of 2010. Such changes are in force for their parties to those amendments. Later amendments that relate to the addition of certain weapons crimes and the deletion of Article 124 have been omitted as they are not in force, thus not part of the Statute.

Emphasizing in this connection that nothing in this Statute shall be taken as authorizing any State Party to intervene in an armed conflict or in the internal affairs of any State,

Determined to these ends and for the sake of present and future generations, to establish an independent permanent International Criminal Court in relationship with the United Nations system, with jurisdiction over the most serious crimes of concern to the international community as a whole,

Emphasizing that the International Criminal Court established under this Statute shall be complementary to national criminal jurisdictions,

Resolved to guarantee lasting respect for and the enforcement of international justice,

Have agreed as follows

PART 1. ESTABLISHMENT OF THE COURT

Article 1
The Court

An International Criminal Court ("the Court") is hereby established. It shall be a permanent institution and shall have the power to exercise its jurisdiction over persons for the most serious crimes of international concern, as referred to in this Statute, and shall be complementary to national criminal jurisdictions. The jurisdiction and functioning of the Court shall be governed by the provisions of this Statute.

Article 2
Relationship of the Court with the United Nations

The Court shall be brought into relationship with the United Nations through an agreement to be approved by the Assembly of States Parties to this Statute and thereafter concluded by the President of the Court on its behalf.

Article 3
Seat of the Court

1. The seat of the Court shall be established at The Hague in the Netherlands ("the host State").
2. The Court shall enter into a headquarters agreement with the host State, to be approved by the Assembly of States Parties and thereafter concluded by the President of the Court on its behalf.
3. The Court may sit elsewhere, whenever it considers it desirable, as provided in this Statute.

Article 4
Legal status and powers of the Court

1. The Court shall have international legal personality. It shall also have such legal capacity as may be necessary for the exercise of its functions and the fulfilment of its purposes.
2. The Court may exercise its functions and powers, as provided in this Statute, on the territory of any State Party and, by special agreement, on the territory of any other State.

PART 2. JURISDICTION, ADMISSIBILITY AND APPLICABLE LAW

Article 5
Crimes within the jurisdiction of the Court

1. The jurisdiction of the Court shall be limited to the most serious crimes of concern to the international community as a whole. The Court has jurisdiction in accordance with this Statute with respect to the following crimes:
   - (a) The crime of genocide;
   - (b) Crimes against humanity;
   - (c) War crimes;
   - (d) The crime of aggression.
2. The Court shall exercise jurisdiction over the crime of aggression once a provision is adopted in accordance with articles 121 and 123 defining the crime and setting out the conditions under which the Court shall exercise jurisdiction with respect to this crime. Such a provision shall be consistent with the relevant provisions of the Charter of the United Nations.[2]

Article 6
Genocide

For the purpose of this Statute, "genocide" means any of the following acts committed with intent to destroy, in whole or in part, a national, ethnical, racial or religious group, as such:

- (a) Killing members of the group;
- (b) Causing serious bodily or mental harm to members of the group;
- (c) Deliberately inflicting on the group conditions of life calculated to bring about its physical destruction in whole or in part;
- (d) Imposing measures intended to prevent births within the group;
- (e) Forcibly transferring children of the group to another group.

Article 7
Crimes against humanity

1. For the purpose of this Statute, "crime against humanity" means any of the following acts when committed as part of a widespread or systematic attack directed against any civilian population, with knowledge of the attack:
   - (a) Murder;
   - (b) Extermination;
   - (c) Enslavement;
   - (d) Deportation or forcible transfer of population;
   - (e) Imprisonment or other severe deprivation of physical liberty in violation of fundamental rules of international law;
   - (f) Torture;
   - (g) Rape, sexual slavery, enforced prostitution, forced pregnancy, enforced sterilization, or any other form of sexual violence of comparable gravity;

---

[2] The Kampala Amendments delete this provision.

(h) Persecution against any identifiable group or collectivity on political, racial, national, ethnic, cultural, religious, gender as defined in paragraph 3, or other grounds that are universally recognized as impermissible under international law, in connection with any act referred to in this paragraph or any crime within the jurisdiction of the Court;

(i) Enforced disappearance of persons;

(j) The crime of apartheid;

(k) Other inhumane acts of a similar character intentionally causing great suffering, or serious injury to body or to mental or physical health.

2. For the purpose of paragraph 1:

(a) "Attack directed against any civilian population" means a course of conduct involving the multiple commission of acts referred to in paragraph 1 against any civilian population, pursuant to or in furtherance of a State or organizational policy to commit such attack;

(b) "Extermination" includes the intentional infliction of conditions of life, *inter alia* the deprivation of access to food and medicine, calculated to bring about the destruction of part of a population;

(c) "Enslavement" means the exercise of any or all of the powers attaching to the right of ownership over a person and includes the exercise of such power in the course of trafficking in persons, in particular women and children;

(d) "Deportation or forcible transfer of population" means forced displacement of the persons concerned by expulsion or other coercive acts from the area in which they are lawfully present, without grounds permitted under international law;

(e) "Torture" means the intentional infliction of severe pain or suffering, whether physical or mental, upon a person in the custody or under the control of the accused; except that torture shall not include pain or suffering arising only from, inherent in or incidental to, lawful sanctions;

(f) "Forced pregnancy" means the unlawful confinement of a woman forcibly made pregnant, with the intent of affecting the ethnic composition of any population or carrying out other grave violations of international law. This definition shall not in any way be interpreted as affecting national laws relating to pregnancy;

(g) "Persecution" means the intentional and severe deprivation of fundamental rights contrary to international law by reason of the identity of the group or collectivity;

(h) "The crime of apartheid" means inhumane acts of a character similar to those referred to in paragraph 1, committed in the context of an institutionalized regime of systematic oppression and domination by one racial group over any other racial group or groups and committed with the intention of maintaining that regime;

(i) "Enforced disappearance of persons" means the arrest, detention or abduction of persons by, or with the authorization, support or acquiescence of, a State or a political organization, followed by a refusal to acknowledge that deprivation of freedom or to give information on the fate or whereabouts of those persons, with the intention of removing them from the protection of the law for a prolonged period of time.

3. For the purpose of this Statute, it is understood that the term "gender" refers to the two sexes, male and female, within the context of society. The term "gender" does not indicate any meaning different from the above.

Article 8

War crimes

1. The Court shall have jurisdiction in respect of war crimes in particular when committed as part of a plan or policy or as part of a large-scale commission of such crimes.

2. For the purpose of this Statute, "war crimes" means:

(a) Grave breaches of the Geneva Conventions of 12 August 1949, namely, any of the following acts against persons or property protected under the provisions of the relevant Geneva Convention:

    (i) Wilful killing;

    (ii) Torture or inhuman treatment, including biological experiments;

    (iii) Wilfully causing great suffering, or serious injury to body or health;

    (iv) Extensive destruction and appropriation of property, not justified by military necessity and carried out unlawfully and wantonly;

    (v) Compelling a prisoner of war or other protected person to serve in the forces of a hostile Power;

    (vi) Wilfully depriving a prisoner of war or other protected person of the rights of fair and regular trial;

    (vii) Unlawful deportation or transfer or unlawful confinement;

    (viii) Taking of hostages.

(b) Other serious violations of the laws and customs applicable in international armed conflict, within the established framework of international law, namely, any of the following acts:

    (i) Intentionally directing attacks against the civilian population as such or against individual civilians not taking direct part in hostilities;

    (ii) Intentionally directing attacks against civilian objects, that is, objects which are not military objectives;

    (iii) Intentionally directing attacks against personnel, installations, material, units or vehicles involved in a humanitarian assistance or peacekeeping mission in accordance with the Charter of the United Nations, as long as they are entitled to the protection given to civilians or civilian objects under the international law of armed conflict;

    (iv) Intentionally launching an attack in the knowledge that such attack will cause incidental loss of life or injury to civilians or damage to civilian objects or widespread, long-term and severe damage to the natural environment which would be clearly excessive in relation to the concrete and direct overall military advantage anticipated;

    (v) Attacking or bombarding, by whatever means, towns, villages, dwellings or buildings which are undefended and which are not military objectives;

    (vi) Killing or wounding a combatant who, having laid down his arms or having no longer means of defence, has surrendered at discretion;

    (vii) Making improper use of a flag of truce, of the flag or of the military insignia and uniform of the enemy or of the United Nations, as well as of the distinctive emblems of the Geneva Conventions, resulting in death or serious personal injury;

    (viii) The transfer, directly or indirectly, by the Occupying Power of parts of its own civilian population into the territory it occupies, or the deportation or transfer of all or parts of the population of the occupied territory within or outside this territory;

(ix) Intentionally directing attacks against buildings dedicated to religion, education, art, science or charitable purposes, historic monuments, hospitals and places where the sick and wounded are collected, provided they are not military objectives;

(x) Subjecting persons who are in the power of an adverse party to physical mutilation or to medical or scientific experiments of any kind which are neither justified by the medical, dental or hospital treatment of the person concerned nor carried out in his or her interest, and which cause death to or seriously endanger the health of such person or persons;

(xi) Killing or wounding treacherously individuals belonging to the hostile nation or army;

(xii) Declaring that no quarter will be given;

(xiii) Destroying or seizing the enemy's property unless such destruction or seizure be imperatively demanded by the necessities of war;

(xiv) Declaring abolished, suspended or inadmissible in a court of law the rights and actions of the nationals of the hostile party;

(xv) Compelling the nationals of the hostile party to take part in the operations of war directed against their own country, even if they were in the belligerent's service before the commencement of the war;

(xvi) Pillaging a town or place, even when taken by assault;

(xvii) Employing poison or poisoned weapons;

(xviii) Employing asphyxiating, poisonous or other gases, and all analogous liquids, materials or devices;

(xix) Employing bullets which expand or flatten easily in the human body, such as bullets with a hard envelope which does not entirely cover the core or is pierced with incisions;

(xx) Employing weapons, projectiles and material and methods of warfare which are of a nature to cause superfluous injury or unnecessary suffering or which are inherently indiscriminate in violation of the international law of armed conflict, provided that such weapons, projectiles and material and methods of warfare are the subject of a comprehensive prohibition and are included in an annex to this Statute, by an amendment in accordance with the relevant provisions set forth in articles 121 and 123;

(xxi) Committing outrages upon personal dignity, in particular humiliating and degrading treatment;

(xxii) Committing rape, sexual slavery, enforced prostitution, forced pregnancy, as defined in article 7, paragraph 2(f), enforced sterilization, or any other form of sexual violence also constituting a grave breach of the Geneva Conventions;

(xxiii) Utilizing the presence of a civilian or other protected person to render certain points, areas or military forces immune from military operations;

(xxiv) Intentionally directing attacks against buildings, material, medical units and transport, and personnel using the distinctive emblems of the Geneva Conventions in conformity with international law;

(xxv) Intentionally using starvation of civilians as a method of warfare by depriving them of objects indispensable to their survival, including wilfully impeding relief supplies as provided for under the Geneva Conventions;

(xxvi) Conscripting or enlisting children under the age of fifteen years into the national armed forces or using them to participate actively in hostilities.

(c) In the case of an armed conflict not of an international character, serious violations of article 3 common to the four Geneva Conventions of 12 August 1949, namely, any of the following acts committed against persons taking no active part in the hostilities, including members of armed forces who have laid down their arms and those placed hors de combat by sickness, wounds, detention or any other cause:

(i) Violence to life and person, in particular murder of all kinds, mutilation, cruel treatment and torture;

(ii) Committing outrages upon personal dignity, in particular humiliating and degrading treatment;

(iii) Taking of hostages;

(iv) The passing of sentences and the carrying out of executions without previous judgement pronounced by a regularly constituted court, affording all judicial guarantees which are generally recognized as indispensable.

(d) Paragraph 2(c) applies to armed conflicts not of an international character and thus does not apply to situations of internal disturbances and tensions, such as riots, isolated and sporadic acts of violence or other acts of a similar nature.

(e) Other serious violations of the laws and customs applicable in armed conflicts not of an international character, within the established framework of international law, namely, any of the following acts:

(i) Intentionally directing attacks against the civilian population as such or against individual civilians not taking direct part in hostilities;

(ii) Intentionally directing attacks against buildings, material, medical units and transport, and personnel using the distinctive emblems of the Geneva Conventions in conformity with international law;

(iii) Intentionally directing attacks against personnel, installations, material, units or vehicles involved in a humanitarian assistance or peacekeeping mission in accordance with the Charter of the United Nations, as long as they are entitled to the protection given to civilians or civilian objects under the international law of armed conflict;

(iv) Intentionally directing attacks against buildings dedicated to religion, education, art, science or charitable purposes, historic monuments, hospitals and places where the sick and wounded are collected, provided they are not military objectives;

(v) Pillaging a town or place, even when taken by assault;

(vi) Committing rape, sexual slavery, enforced prostitution, forced pregnancy, as defined in article 7, paragraph 2(f), enforced sterilization, and any other form of sexual violence also constituting a serious violation of article 3 common to the four Geneva Conventions;

16

(vii) Conscripting or enlisting children under the age of fifteen years into armed forces or groups or using them to participate actively in hostilities;

(viii) Ordering the displacement of the civilian population for reasons related to the conflict, unless the security of the civilians involved or imperative military reasons so demand;

(ix) Killing or wounding treacherously a combatant adversary;

(x) Declaring that no quarter will be given;

(xi) Subjecting persons who are in the power of another party to the conflict to physical mutilation or to medical or scientific experiments of any kind which are neither justified by the medical, dental or hospital treatment of the person concerned nor carried out in his or her interest, and which cause death to or seriously endanger the health of such person or persons;

(xii) Destroying or seizing the property of an adversary unless such destruction or seizure be imperatively demanded by the necessities of the conflict;

(xiii) *Employing poison or poisoned weapons;*

(xiv) *Employing asphyxiating, poisonous or other gases, and all analogous liquids, materials or devices;*

(xv) *Employing bullets which expand or flatten easily in the human body, such as bullets with a hard envelope which does not entirely cover the core or is pierced with incisions.*

(f) Paragraph 2(e) applies to armed conflicts not of an international character and thus does not apply to situations of internal disturbances and tensions, such as riots, isolated and sporadic acts of violence or other acts of a similar nature. It applies to armed conflicts that take place in the territory of a State when there is protracted armed conflict between governmental authorities and organized armed groups or between such groups.

3. Nothing in paragraph 2(c) and (e) shall affect the responsibility of a Government to maintain or re-establish law and order in the State or to defend the unity and territorial integrity of the State, by all legitimate means.

Article 8 bis
Crime of aggression

1. *For the purpose of this Statute, "crime of aggression" means the planning, preparation, initiation or execution, by a person in a position effectively to exercise control over or to direct the political or military action of a State, of an act of aggression which, by its character, gravity and scale, constitutes a manifest violation of the Charter of the United Nations.*

2. *For the purpose of paragraph 1, "act of aggression" means the use of armed force by a State against the sovereignty, territorial integrity or political independence of another State, or in any other manner inconsistent with the Charter of the United Nations.*

   Any of the following acts, regardless of a declaration of war, shall, in accordance with United Nations General Assembly resolution 3314 (XXIX) of 14 December 1974, qualify as an act of aggression:

   (a) *The invasion or attack by the armed forces of a State of the territory of another State, or any military occupation, however temporary, resulting from such invasion* or attack, or any annexation by the use of force of the territory of another State or part thereof;

(b) *Bombardment by the armed forces of a State against the territory of another State or the use of any weapons by a State against the territory of another State;*

(c) *The blockade of the ports or coasts of a State by the armed forces of another State;*

(d) *An attack by the armed forces of a State on the land, sea or air forces, or marine and air fleets of another State;*

(e) *The use of armed forces of one State which are within the territory of another State with the agreement of the receiving State, in contravention of the conditions provided for in the agreement or any extension of their presence in such territory beyond the termination of the agreement;*

(f) *The action of a State in allowing its territory, which it has placed at the disposal of another State, to be used by that other State for perpetrating an act of aggression against a third State;*

(g) *The sending by or on behalf of a State of armed bands, groups, irregulars or merce-naries, which carry out acts of armed force against another State of such gravity as to amount to the acts listed above, or its substantial involvement therein.*

Article 9
Elements of Crimes

1. Elements of Crimes shall assist the Court in the interpretation and application of arti-cles 6, 7 and 8. They shall be adopted by a two-thirds majority of the members of the Assembly of States Parties.

2. Amendments to the Elements of Crimes may be proposed by:
   (a) Any State Party;
   (b) The judges acting by an absolute majority;
   (c) The Prosecutor.
   Such amendments shall be adopted by a two-thirds majority of the members of the Assembly of States Parties.

3. The Elements of Crimes and amendments thereto shall be consistent with this Statute.

Article 10

Nothing in this Part shall be interpreted as limiting or prejudicing in any way existing or developing rules of international law for purposes other than this Statute.

Article 11
Jurisdiction ratione temporis

1. The Court has jurisdiction only with respect to crimes committed after the entry into force of this Statute.

2. If a State becomes a Party to this Statute after its entry into force, the Court may exercise its jurisdiction only with respect to crimes committed after the entry into force of this Statute for that State, unless that State has made a declaration under article 12, paragraph 3.

Article 12
Preconditions to the exercise of jurisdiction

1. A State which becomes a Party to this Statute thereby accepts the jurisdiction of the Court with respect to the crimes referred to in article 5.

2. In the case of article 13, paragraph (a) or (c), the Court may exercise its jurisdiction if one or more of the following States are Parties to this Statute or have accepted the jurisdiction of the Court in accordance with paragraph 3:

    (a) The State on the territory of which the conduct in question occurred or, if the crime was committed on board a vessel or aircraft, the State of registration of that vessel or aircraft;

    (b) The State of which the person accused of the crime is a national.

3. If the acceptance of a State which is not a Party to this Statute is required under paragraph 2, that State may, by declaration lodged with the Registrar, accept the exercise of jurisdiction by the Court with respect to the crime in question. The accepting State shall cooperate with the Court without any delay or exception in accordance with Part 9.

Article 13
Exercise of jurisdiction

The Court may exercise its jurisdiction with respect to a crime referred to in article 5 in accordance with the provisions of this Statute if:

(a) A situation in which one or more of such crimes appears to have been committed is referred to the Prosecutor by a State Party in accordance with article 14;

(b) A situation in which one or more of such crimes appears to have been committed is referred to the Prosecutor by the Security Council acting under Chapter VII of the Charter of the United Nations; or

(c) The Prosecutor has initiated an investigation in respect of such a crime in accordance with article 15.

Article 14
Referral of a situation by a State Party

1. A State Party may refer to the Prosecutor a situation in which one or more crimes within the jurisdiction of the Court appear to have been committed requesting the Prosecutor to investigate the situation for the purpose of determining whether one or more specific persons should be charged with the commission of such crimes.

2. As far as possible, a referral shall specify the relevant circumstances and be accompanied by such supporting documentation as is available to the State referring the situation.

Article 15
Prosecutor

1. The Prosecutor may initiate investigations *proprio motu* on the basis of information on crimes within the jurisdiction of the Court.

2. The Prosecutor shall analyse the seriousness of the information received. For this purpose, he or she may seek additional information from States, organs of the United Nations, intergovernmental or non-governmental organizations, or other reliable sources that he or she deems appropriate, and may receive written or oral testimony at the seat of the Court.

3. If the Prosecutor concludes that there is a reasonable basis to proceed with an investigation, he or she shall submit to the Pre-Trial Chamber a request for authorization of an

investigation, together with any supporting material collected. Victims may make representations to the Pre-Trial Chamber, in accordance with the Rules of Procedure and Evidence.

4. If the Pre-Trial Chamber, upon examination of the request and the supporting material, considers that there is a reasonable basis to proceed with an investigation, and that the case appears to fall within the jurisdiction of the Court, it shall authorize the commencement of the investigation, without prejudice to subsequent determinations by the Court with regard to the jurisdiction and admissibility of a case.

5. The refusal of the Pre-Trial Chamber to authorize the investigation shall not preclude the presentation of a subsequent request by the Prosecutor based on new facts or evidence regarding the same situation.

6. If, after the preliminary examination referred to in paragraphs 1 and 2, the Prosecutor concludes that the information provided does not constitute a reasonable basis for an investigation, he or she shall inform those who provided the information. This shall not preclude the Prosecutor from considering further information submitted to him or her regarding the same situation in the light of new facts or evidence.

Article 15 bis
Exercise of jurisdiction over the crime of aggression (State referral, proprio motu)

1. *The Court may exercise jurisdiction over the crime of aggression in accordance with article 13, paragraphs (a) and (c), subject to the provisions of this article.*

2. *The Court may exercise jurisdiction only with respect to crimes of aggression committed one year after the ratification or acceptance of the amendments by thirty States Parties.*

3. *The Court shall exercise jurisdiction over the crime of aggression in accordance with this article, subject to a decision to be taken after 1 January 2017 by the same majority of States Parties as is required for the adoption of an amendment to the Statute.*

4. *The Court may, in accordance with article 12, exercise jurisdiction over a crime of aggression, arising from an act of aggression committed by a State Party, unless that State Party has previously declared that it does not accept such jurisdiction by lodging a declaration with the Registrar. The withdrawal of such a declaration may be effected at any time and shall be considered by the State Party within three years.*

5. *In respect of a State that is not a party to this Statute, the Court shall not exercise its jurisdiction over the crime of aggression when committed by that State's nationals or on its territory. Where the Prosecutor concludes that there is a reasonable basis to proceed with an investigation in respect of a crime of aggression, he or she shall first ascertain whether the Security Council has made a determination of an act of aggression committed by the State concerned. The Prosecutor shall notify the Secretary-General of the United Nations of the situation before the Court, including any relevant information and documents.*

7. *Where the Security Council has made such a determination, the Prosecutor may proceed with the investigation in respect of a crime of aggression.*

8. *Where no such determination is made within six months after the date of notification, the Prosecutor may proceed with the investigation in respect of a crime of aggression, provided that the Pre-Trial Division has authorized the commencement of the investigation in respect of a crime of aggression in accordance with the procedure contained*

16

in article 15, and the Security Council has not decided otherwise in accordance with article16.

9. A determination of an act of aggression by an organ outside the Court shall be without prejudice to the Court's own findings under this Statute.

10. This article is without prejudice to the provisions relating to the exercise of jurisdiction with respect to other crimes referred to in article 5.

Article 15 ter
Exercise of jurisdiction over the crime of aggression (Security Council referral)

1. The Court may exercise jurisdiction over the crime of aggression in accordance with article 13, paragraph (b), subject to the provisions of this article.

2. The Court may exercise jurisdiction only with respect to crimes of aggression committed one year after the ratification or acceptance of the amendments by thirty States Parties.

3. The Court shall exercise jurisdiction over the crime of aggression in accordance with this article, subject to a decision to be taken after 1 January 2017 by the same majority of States Parties as is required for the adoption of an amendment to the Statute.

4. A determination of an act of aggression by an organ outside the Court shall be without prejudice to the Court's own findings under this Statute.

5. This article is without prejudice to the provisions relating to the exercise of jurisdiction with respect to other crimes referred to in article 5.

Article 16
Deferral of investigation or prosecution

No investigation or prosecution may be commenced or proceeded with under this Statute for a period of 12 months after the Security Council, in a resolution adopted under Chapter VII of the Charter of the United Nations, has requested the Court to that effect; that request may be renewed by the Council under the same conditions.

Article 17
Issues of admissibility

1. Having regard to paragraph 10 of the Preamble and article 1, the Court shall determine that a case is inadmissible where:

    (a) The case is being investigated or prosecuted by a State which has jurisdiction over it, unless the State is unwilling or unable genuinely to carry out the investigation or prosecution;

    (b) The case has been investigated by a State which has jurisdiction over it and the State has decided not to prosecute the person concerned, unless the decision resulted from the unwillingness or inability of the State genuinely to prosecute;

    (c) The person concerned has already been tried for conduct which is the subject of the complaint, and a trial by the Court is not permitted under article 20, paragraph 3;

    (d) The case is not of sufficient gravity to justify further action by the Court.

2. In order to determine unwillingness in a particular case, the Court shall consider, having regard to the principles of due process recognized by international law, whether one or more of the following exist, as applicable:

(a) The proceedings were or are being undertaken or the national decision was made for the purpose of shielding the person concerned from criminal responsibility for crimes within the jurisdiction of the Court referred to in article 5;

(b) There has been an unjustified delay in the proceedings which in the circumstances is inconsistent with an intent to bring the person concerned to justice;

(c) The proceedings were not or are not being conducted independently or impartially, and they were or are being conducted in a manner which, in the circumstances, is inconsistent with an intent to bring the person concerned to justice.

3. In order to determine inability in a particular case, the Court shall consider whether, due to a total or substantial collapse or unavailability of its national judicial system, the State is unable to obtain the accused or the necessary evidence and testimony or otherwise unable to carry out its proceedings.

Article 18
Preliminary rulings regarding admissibility

1. When a situation has been referred to the Court pursuant to article 13(a) and the Prosecutor has determined that there would be a reasonable basis to commence an investigation, or the Prosecutor initiates an investigation pursuant to articles 13(c) and 15, the Prosecutor shall notify all States Parties and those States which, taking into account the information available, would normally exercise jurisdiction over the crimes concerned. The Prosecutor may notify such States on a confidential basis and, where the Prosecutor believes it necessary to protect persons, prevent destruction of evidence or prevent the absconding of persons, may limit the scope of the information provided to States.

2. Within one month of receipt of that notification, a State may inform the Court that it is investigating or has investigated its nationals or others within its jurisdiction with respect to criminal acts which may constitute crimes referred to in article 5 and which relate to the information provided in the notification to States. At the request of that State, the Prosecutor shall defer to the State's investigation of those persons unless the Pre-Trial Chamber, on the application of the Prosecutor, decides to authorize the investigation.

3. The Prosecutor's deferral to a State's investigation shall be open to review by the Prosecutor six months after the date of deferral or at any time when there has been a significant change of circumstances based on the State's unwillingness or inability genuinely to carry out the investigation.

4. The State concerned or the Prosecutor may appeal to the Appeals Chamber against a ruling of the Pre-Trial Chamber, in accordance with article 82. The appeal may be heard on an expedited basis.

5. When the Prosecutor has deferred an investigation in accordance with paragraph 2, the Prosecutor may request that the State concerned periodically inform the Prosecutor of the progress of its investigations and any subsequent prosecutions. States Parties shall respond to such requests without undue delay.

6. Pending a ruling by the Pre-Trial Chamber, or at any time when the Prosecutor has deferred an investigation under this article, the Prosecutor may, on an exceptional basis, seek authority from the Pre-Trial Chamber to pursue necessary investigative steps for the purpose of preserving evidence where there is a unique opportunity to

obtain important evidence or there is a significant risk that such evidence may not be subsequently available.

7. A State which has challenged a ruling of the Pre-Trial Chamber under this article may challenge the admissibility of a case under article 19 on the grounds of additional significant facts or significant change of circumstances.

Article 19
Challenges to the jurisdiction of the Court or the admissibility of a case

1. The Court shall satisfy itself that it has jurisdiction in any case brought before it. The Court may, on its own motion, determine the admissibility of a case in accordance with article 17.

2. Challenges to the admissibility of a case on the grounds referred to in article 17 or challenges to the jurisdiction of the Court may be made by:

    (a) An accused or a person for whom a warrant of arrest or a summons to appear has been issued under article 58;

    (b) A State which has jurisdiction over a case, on the ground that it is investigating or prosecuting the case or has investigated or prosecuted; or

    (c) A State from which acceptance of jurisdiction is required under article 12.

3. The Prosecutor may seek a ruling from the Court regarding a question of jurisdiction or admissibility. In proceedings with respect to jurisdiction or admissibility, those who have referred the situation under article 13, as well as victims, may also submit observations to the Court.

4. The admissibility of a case or the jurisdiction of the Court may be challenged only once by any person or State referred to in paragraph 2. The challenge shall take place prior to or at the commencement of the trial. In exceptional circumstances, the Court may grant leave for a challenge to be brought more than once or at a time later than the commencement of the trial. Challenges to the admissibility of a case, at the commencement of a trial, or subsequently with the leave of the Court, may be based only on article 17, paragraph 1(c).

5. A State referred to in paragraph 2(b) and (c) shall make a challenge at the earliest opportunity.

6. Prior to the confirmation of the charges, challenges to the admissibility of a case or challenges to the jurisdiction of the Court shall be referred to the Pre-Trial Chamber. After confirmation of the charges, they shall be referred to the Trial Chamber. Decisions with respect to jurisdiction or admissibility may be appealed to the Appeals Chamber in accordance with article 82.

7. If a challenge is made by a State referred to in paragraph 2(b) or (c), the Prosecutor shall suspend the investigation until such time as the Court makes a determination in accordance with article 17.

8. Pending a ruling by the Court, the Prosecutor may seek authority from the Court:

    (a) To pursue necessary investigative steps of the kind referred to in article 18, paragraph 6;

    (b) To take a statement or testimony from a witness or complete the collection and examination of evidence which had begun prior to the making of the challenge; and

(c) In cooperation with the relevant States, to prevent the absconding of persons in respect of whom the Prosecutor has already requested a warrant of arrest under article 58.

9. The making of a challenge shall not affect the validity of any act performed by the Prosecutor or any order or warrant issued by the Court prior to the making of the challenge.

10. If the Court has decided that a case is inadmissible under article 17, the Prosecutor may submit a request for a review of the decision when he or she is fully satisfied that new facts have arisen which negate the basis on which the case had previously been found inadmissible under article 17.

11. If the Prosecutor, having regard to the matters referred to in article 17, defers an investigation, the Prosecutor may request that the relevant State make available to the Prosecutor information on the proceedings. That information shall, at the request of the State concerned, be confidential. If the Prosecutor thereafter decides to proceed with an investigation, he or she shall notify the State to which deferral of the proceedings has taken place.

Article 20
Ne bis in idem

1. Except as provided in this Statute, no person shall be tried before the Court with respect to conduct which formed the basis of crimes for which the person has been convicted or acquitted by the Court.

2. No person shall be tried by another court for a crime referred to in article 5 for which that person has already been convicted or acquitted by the Court.

3. No person who has been tried by another court for conduct also proscribed under article 6, 7 or 8 shall be tried by the Court with respect to the same conduct unless the proceedings in the other court:
   (a) Were for the purpose of shielding the person concerned from criminal responsibility for crimes within the jurisdiction of the Court; or
   (b) Otherwise were not conducted independently or impartially in accordance with the norms of due process recognized by international law and were conducted in a manner which, in the circumstances, was inconsistent with an intent to bring the person concerned to justice.

Article 21
Applicable law

1. The Court shall apply:
   (a) In the first place, this Statute, Elements of Crimes and its Rules of Procedure and Evidence;
   (b) In the second place, where appropriate, applicable treaties and the principles and rules of international law, including the established principles of the international law of armed conflict;
   (c) Failing that, general principles of law derived by the Court from national laws of legal systems of the world including, as appropriate, the national laws of States that would normally exercise jurisdiction over the crime, provided that those

principles are not inconsistent with this Statute and with international law and internationally recognized norms and standards.

2. The Court may apply principles and rules of law as interpreted in its previous decisions.

3. The application and interpretation of law pursuant to this article must be consistent with internationally recognized human rights, and be without any adverse distinction founded on grounds such as gender as defined in article 7, paragraph 3, age, race, colour, language, religion or belief, political or other opinion, national, ethnic or social origin, wealth, birth or other status.

PART 3. GENERAL PRINCIPLES OF CRIMINAL LAW

Article 22
Nullum crimen sine lege

1. A person shall not be criminally responsible under this Statute unless the conduct in question constitutes, at the time it takes place, a crime within the jurisdiction of the Court.

2. The definition of a crime shall be strictly construed and shall not be extended by analogy. In case of ambiguity, the definition shall be interpreted in favour of the person being investigated, prosecuted or convicted.

3. This article shall not affect the characterization of any conduct as criminal under international law independently of this Statute.

Article 23
Nulla poena sine lege

A person convicted by the Court may be punished only in accordance with this Statute.

Article 24
Non-retroactivity ratione personae

1. No person shall be criminally responsible under this Statute for conduct prior to the entry into force of the Statute.

2. In the event of a change in the law applicable to a given case prior to a final judgement, the law more favourable to the person being investigated, prosecuted or convicted shall apply.

Article 25
Individual criminal responsibility

1. The Court shall have jurisdiction over natural persons pursuant to this Statute.

2. A person who commits a crime within the jurisdiction of the Court shall be individually responsible and liable for punishment in accordance with this Statute.

3. In accordance with this Statute, a person shall be criminally responsible and liable for punishment for a crime within the jurisdiction of the Court if that person:
   (a) Commits such a crime, whether as an individual, jointly with another or through another person, regardless of whether that other person is criminally responsible;
   (b) Orders, solicits or induces the commission of such a crime which in fact occurs or is attempted;

(c) For the purpose of facilitating the commission of such a crime, aids, abets or otherwise assists in its commission or its attempted commission, including providing the means for its commission;

(d) In any other way contributes to the commission or attempted commission of such a crime by a group of persons acting with a common purpose. Such contribution shall be intentional and shall either:

(i) Be made with the aim of furthering the criminal activity or criminal purpose of the group, where such activity or purpose involves the commission of a crime within the jurisdiction of the Court; or

(ii) Be made in the knowledge of the intention of the group to commit the crime;

(e) In respect of the crime of genocide, directly and publicly incites others to commit genocide;

(f) Attempts to commit such a crime by taking action that commences its execution by means of a substantial step, but the crime does not occur because of circumstances independent of the person's intentions. However, a person who abandons the effort to commit the crime or otherwise prevents the completion of the crime shall not be liable for punishment under this Statute for the attempt to commit that crime if that person completely and voluntarily gave up the criminal purpose.

3bis. In respect of the crime of aggression, the provisions of this article shall apply only to persons in a position effectively to exercise control over or to direct the political or military action of a State.

4. No provision in this Statute relating to individual criminal responsibility shall affect the responsibility of States under international law.

Article 26
Exclusion of jurisdiction over persons under eighteen
The Court shall have no jurisdiction over any person who was under the age of 18 at the time of the alleged commission of a crime.

Article 27
Irrelevance of official capacity
1. This Statute shall apply equally to all persons without any distinction based on official capacity. In particular, official capacity as a Head of State or Government, a member of a Government or parliament, an elected representative or a government official shall in no case exempt a person from criminal responsibility under this Statute, nor shall it, in and of itself, constitute a ground for reduction of sentence.

2. Immunities or special procedural rules which may attach to the official capacity of a person, whether under national or international law, shall not bar the Court from exercising its jurisdiction over such a person.

Article 28
Responsibility of commanders and other superiors
In addition to other grounds of criminal responsibility under this Statute for crimes within the jurisdiction of the Court:

(a) A military commander or person effectively acting as a military commander shall be criminally responsible for crimes within the jurisdiction of the Court committed by forces under his or her effective command and control, or effective authority and control as the case may be, as a result of his or her failure to exercise control properly over such forces, where:

    (i) That military commander or person either knew or, owing to the circumstances at the time, should have known that the forces were committing or about to commit such crimes; and

    (ii) That military commander or person failed to take all necessary and reasonable measures within his or her power to prevent or repress their commission or to submit the matter to the competent authorities for investigation and prosecution.

(b) With respect to superior and subordinate relationships not described in paragraph (a), a superior shall be criminally responsible for crimes within the jurisdiction of the Court committed by subordinates under his or her effective authority and control, as a result of his or her failure to exercise control properly over such subordinates, where:

    (i) The superior either knew, or consciously disregarded information which clearly indicated, that the subordinates were committing or about to commit such crimes;

    (ii) The crimes concerned activities that were within the effective responsibility and control of the superior; and

    (iii) The superior failed to take all necessary and reasonable measures within his or her power to prevent or repress their commission or to submit the matter to the competent authorities for investigation and prosecution.

Article 29
Non-applicability of statute of limitations

The crimes within the jurisdiction of the Court shall not be subject to any statute of limitations.

Article 30
Mental element

1. Unless otherwise provided, a person shall be criminally responsible and liable for punishment for a crime within the jurisdiction of the Court only if the material elements are committed with intent and knowledge.

2. For the purposes of this article, a person has intent where:
   (a) In relation to conduct, that person means to engage in the conduct;
   (b) In relation to a consequence, that person means to cause that consequence or is aware that it will occur in the ordinary course of events.

3. For the purposes of this article, "knowledge" means awareness that a circumstance exists or a consequence will occur in the ordinary course of events. "Know" and "knowingly" shall be construed accordingly.

Article 31
Grounds for excluding criminal responsibility

1. In addition to other grounds for excluding criminal responsibility provided for in this Statute, a person shall not be criminally responsible if, at the time of that person's conduct:
   (a) The person suffers from a mental disease or defect that destroys that person's capacity to appreciate the unlawfulness or nature of his or her conduct, or capacity to control his or her conduct to conform to the requirements of law;

(b) The person is in a state of intoxication that destroys that person's capacity to appreciate the unlawfulness or nature of his or her conduct, or capacity to control his or her conduct to conform to the requirements of law, unless the person has become voluntarily intoxicated under such circumstances that the person knew, or disregarded the risk, that, as a result of the intoxication, he or she was likely to engage in conduct constituting a crime within the jurisdiction of the Court;

(c) The person acts reasonably to defend himself or herself or another person or, in the case of war crimes, property which is essential for the survival of the person or another person or property which is essential for accomplishing a military mission, against an imminent and unlawful use of force in a manner proportionate to the degree of danger to the person or the other person or property protected. The fact that the person was involved in a defensive operation conducted by forces shall not in itself constitute a ground for excluding criminal responsibility under this subparagraph;

(d) The conduct which is alleged to constitute a crime within the jurisdiction of the Court has been caused by duress resulting from a threat of imminent death or of continuing or imminent serious bodily harm against that person or another person, and the person acts necessarily and reasonably to avoid this threat, provided that the person does not intend to cause a greater harm than the one sought to be avoided. Such a threat may either be:

  (i) Made by other persons; or

  (ii) Constituted by other circumstances beyond that person's control.

2. The Court shall determine the applicability of the grounds for excluding criminal responsibility provided for in this Statute to the case before it.

3. At trial, the Court may consider a ground for excluding criminal responsibility other than those referred to in paragraph 1 where such a ground is derived from applicable law as set forth in article 21. The procedures relating to the consideration of such a ground shall be provided for in the Rules of Procedure and Evidence.

Article 32
Mistake of fact or mistake of law

1. A mistake of fact shall be a ground for excluding criminal responsibility only if it negates the mental element required by the crime.

2. A mistake of law as to whether a particular type of conduct is a crime within the jurisdiction of the Court shall not be a ground for excluding criminal responsibility. A mistake of law may, however, be a ground for excluding criminal responsibility if it negates the mental element required by such a crime, or as provided for in article 33.

Article 33
Superior orders and prescription of law

1. The fact that a crime within the jurisdiction of the Court has been committed by a person pursuant to an order of a Government or of a superior, whether military or civilian, shall not relieve that person of criminal responsibility unless:

(a) The person was under a legal obligation to obey orders of the Government or the superior in question;

(b) The person did not know that the order was unlawful; and

(c) The order was not manifestly unlawful.

2. For the purposes of this article, orders to commit genocide or crimes against humanity are manifestly unlawful.

PART 4. COMPOSITION AND ADMINISTRATION OF THE COURT

Article 34
Organs of the Court
The Court shall be composed of the following organs:
(a) The Presidency;
(b) An Appeals Division, a Trial Division and a Pre-Trial Division;
(c) The Office of the Prosecutor;
(d) The Registry.

Article 35
Service of judges
1. All judges shall be elected as full-time members of the Court and shall be available to serve on that basis from the commencement of their terms of office.
2. The judges composing the Presidency shall serve on a full-time basis as soon as they are elected.
3. The Presidency may, on the basis of the workload of the Court and in consultation with its members, decide from time to time to what extent the remaining judges shall be required to serve on a full-time basis. Any such arrangement shall be without prejudice to the provisions of article 40.
4. The financial arrangements for judges not required to serve on a full-time basis shall be made in accordance with article 49.

Article 36
Qualifications, nomination and election of judges
1. Subject to the provisions of paragraph 2, there shall be 18 judges of the Court.
2.
   (a) The Presidency, acting on behalf of the Court, may propose an increase in the number of judges specified in paragraph 1, indicating the reasons why this is considered necessary and appropriate. The Registrar shall promptly circulate any such proposal to all States Parties.
   (b) Any such proposal shall then be considered at a meeting of the Assembly of States Parties to be convened in accordance with article 112. The proposal shall be considered adopted if approved at the meeting by a vote of two thirds of the members of the Assembly of States Parties and shall enter into force at such time as decided by the Assembly of States Parties.
   (c)
      (i) Once a proposal for an increase in the number of judges has been adopted under subparagraph (b), the election of the additional judges shall take place at the next session of the Assembly of States Parties in accordance with paragraphs 3 to 8, and article 37, paragraph 2;
      (ii) Once a proposal for an increase in the number of judges has been adopted and brought into effect under subparagraphs (b) and (c)(i), it shall be open to the Presidency at any time thereafter, if the workload of the Court justifies it,

to propose a reduction in the number of judges, provided that the number of judges shall not be reduced below that specified in paragraph 1. The proposal shall be dealt with in accordance with the procedure laid down in subparagraphs (a) and (b). In the event that the proposal is adopted, the number of judges shall be progressively decreased as the terms of office of serving judges expire, until the necessary number has been reached.

3.

(a) The judges shall be chosen from among persons of high moral character, impartiality and integrity who possess the qualifications required in their respective States for appointment to the highest judicial offices.

(b) Every candidate for election to the Court shall:

(i) Have established competence in criminal law and procedure, and the necessary relevant experience, whether as judge, prosecutor, advocate or in other similar capacity, in criminal proceedings; or

(ii) Have established competence in relevant areas of international law such as international humanitarian law and the law of human rights, and extensive experience in a professional legal capacity which is of relevance to the judicial work of the Court;

(c) Every candidate for election to the Court shall have an excellent knowledge of and be fluent in at least one of the working languages of the Court.

4.

(a) Nominations of candidates for election to the Court may be made by any State Party to this Statute, and shall be made either:

(i) By the procedure for the nomination of candidates for appointment to the highest judicial offices in the State in question; or

(ii) By the procedure provided for the nomination of candidates for the International Court of Justice in the Statute of that Court.

Nominations shall be accompanied by a statement in the necessary detail specifying how the candidate fulfils the requirements of paragraph 3.

(b) Each State Party may put forward one candidate for any given election who need not necessarily be a national of that State Party but shall in any case be a national of a State Party.

(c) The Assembly of States Parties may decide to establish, if appropriate, an Advisory Committee on nominations. In that event, the Committee's composition and mandate shall be established by the Assembly of States Parties.

5. For the purposes of the election, there shall be two lists of candidates:

List A containing the names of candidates with the qualifications specified in paragraph 3(b)(i); and

List B containing the names of candidates with the qualifications specified in paragraph 3(b)(ii).

A candidate with sufficient qualifications for both lists may choose on which list to appear. At the first election to the Court, at least nine judges shall be elected from list A and at least five judges from list B. Subsequent elections shall be so organized as to maintain the equivalent proportion on the Court of judges qualified on the two lists.

6.

(a) The judges shall be elected by secret ballot at a meeting of the Assembly of States Parties convened for that purpose under article 112. Subject to paragraph 7, the persons elected to the Court shall be the 18 candidates who obtain the highest number of votes and a two-thirds majority of the States Parties present and voting.

    (b) In the event that a sufficient number of judges is not elected on the first ballot, successive ballots shall be held in accordance with the procedures laid down in subparagraph (a) until the remaining places have been filled.

7. No two judges may be nationals of the same State. A person who, for the purposes of membership of the Court, could be regarded as a national of more than one State shall be deemed to be a national of the State in which that person ordinarily exercises civil and political rights.

8.
    (a) The States Parties shall, in the selection of judges, take into account the need, within the membership of the Court, for:
       (i) The representation of the principal legal systems of the world;
      (ii) Equitable geographical representation; and
     (iii) A fair representation of female and male judges.
    (b) States Parties shall also take into account the need to include judges with legal expertise on specific issues, including, but not limited to, violence against women or children.

9.
    (a) Subject to subparagraph (b), judges shall hold office for a term of nine years and, subject to subparagraph (c) and to article 37, paragraph 2, shall not be eligible for re-election.
    (b) At the first election, one third of the judges elected shall be selected by lot to serve for a term of three years; one third of the judges elected shall be selected by lot to serve for a term of six years; and the remainder shall serve for a term of nine years.
    (c) A judge who is selected to serve for a term of three years under subparagraph (b) shall be eligible for re-election for a full term.

10. Notwithstanding paragraph 9, a judge assigned to a Trial or Appeals Chamber in accordance with article 39 shall continue in office to complete any trial or appeal the hearing of which has already commenced before that Chamber.

Article 37
Judicial vacancies

1. In the event of a vacancy, an election shall be held in accordance with article 36 to fill the vacancy.

2. A judge elected to fill a vacancy shall serve for the remainder of the predecessor's term and, if that period is three years or less, shall be eligible for re-election for a full term under article 36.

Article 38
The Presidency

1. The President and the First and Second Vice-Presidents shall be elected by an absolute majority of the judges. They shall each serve for a term of three years or until the end of their respective terms of office as judges, whichever expires earlier. They shall be eligible for re-election once.

2. The First Vice-President shall act in place of the President in the event that the President is unavailable or disqualified. The Second Vice-President shall act in place of the President in the event that both the President and the First Vice-President are unavailable or disqualified.

3. The President, together with the First and Second Vice-Presidents, shall constitute the Presidency, which shall be responsible for:

   (a) The proper administration of the Court, with the exception of the Office of the Prosecutor; and

   (b) The other functions conferred upon it in accordance with this Statute.

4. In discharging its responsibility under paragraph 3(a), the Presidency shall coordinate with and seek the concurrence of the Prosecutor on all matters of mutual concern.

Article 39
Chambers

1. As soon as possible after the election of the judges, the Court shall organize itself into the divisions specified in article 34, paragraph (b). The Appeals Division shall be composed of the President and four other judges, the Trial Division of not less than six judges and the Pre-Trial Division of not less than six judges. The assignment of judges to divisions shall be based on the nature of the functions to be performed by each division and the qualifications and experience of the judges elected to the Court, in such a way that each division shall contain an appropriate combination of expertise in criminal law and procedure and in international law. The Trial and Pre-Trial Divisions shall be composed predominantly of judges with criminal trial experience.

2.
   (a) The judicial functions of the Court shall be carried out in each division by Chambers.

   (b)
      (i) The Appeals Chamber shall be composed of all the judges of the Appeals Division;

      (ii) The functions of the Trial Chamber shall be carried out by three judges of the Trial Division;

      (iii) The functions of the Pre-Trial Chamber shall be carried out either by three judges of the Pre-Trial Division or by a single judge of that division in accordance with this Statute and the Rules of Procedure and Evidence;

   (c) Nothing in this paragraph shall preclude the simultaneous constitution of more than one Trial Chamber or Pre-Trial Chamber when the efficient management of the Court's workload so requires.

3.
   (a) Judges assigned to the Trial and Pre-Trial Divisions shall serve in those divisions for a period of three years, and thereafter until the completion of any case the hearing of which has already commenced in the division concerned.

   (b) Judges assigned to the Appeals Division shall serve in that division for their entire term of office.

4. Judges assigned to the Appeals Division shall serve only in that division. Nothing in this article shall, however, preclude the temporary attachment of judges from the Trial Division to the Pre-Trial Division or vice versa, if the Presidency considers that the efficient management of the Court's workload so requires, provided that under no

16

circumstances shall a judge who has participated in the pre-trial phase of a case be eligible to sit on the Trial Chamber hearing that case.

Article 40
Independence of the judges
1. The judges shall be independent in the performance of their functions.
2. Judges shall not engage in any activity which is likely to interfere with their judicial functions or to affect confidence in their independence.
3. Judges required to serve on a full-time basis at the seat of the Court shall not engage in any other occupation of a professional nature.
4. Any question regarding the application of paragraphs 2 and 3 shall be decided by an absolute majority of the judges. Where any such question concerns an individual judge, that judge shall not take part in the decision.

Article 41
Excusing and disqualification of judges
1. The Presidency may, at the request of a judge, excuse that judge from the exercise of a function under this Statute, in accordance with the Rules of Procedure and Evidence.
2.
    (a) A judge shall not participate in any case in which his or her impartiality might reasonably be doubted on any ground. A judge shall be disqualified from a case in accordance with this paragraph if, *inter alia*, that judge has previously been involved in any capacity in that case before the Court or in a related criminal case at the national level involving the person being investigated or prosecuted. A judge shall also be disqualified on such other grounds as may be provided for in the Rules of Procedure and Evidence.
    (b) The Prosecutor or the person being investigated or prosecuted may request the disqualification of a judge under this paragraph.
    (c) Any question as to the disqualification of a judge shall be decided by an absolute majority of the judges. The challenged judge shall be entitled to present his or her comments on the matter, but shall not take part in the decision.

Article 42
The Office of the Prosecutor
1. The Office of the Prosecutor shall act independently as a separate organ of the Court. It shall be responsible for receiving referrals and any substantiated information on crimes within the jurisdiction of the Court, for examining them and for conducting investigations and prosecutions before the Court. A member of the Office shall not seek or act on instructions from any external source.
2. The Office shall be headed by the Prosecutor. The Prosecutor shall have full authority over the management and administration of the Office, including the staff, facilities and other resources thereof. The Prosecutor shall be assisted by one or more Deputy Prosecutors, who shall be entitled to carry out any of the acts required of the Prosecutor under this Statute. The Prosecutor and the Deputy Prosecutors shall be of different nationalities. They shall serve on a full-time basis.
3. The Prosecutor and the Deputy Prosecutors shall be persons of high moral character, be highly competent in and have extensive practical experience in the prosecution or

trial of criminal cases. They shall have an excellent knowledge of and be fluent in at least one of the working languages of the Court.

4. The Prosecutor shall be elected by secret ballot by an absolute majority of the members of the Assembly of States Parties. The Deputy Prosecutors shall be elected in the same way from a list of candidates provided by the Prosecutor. The Prosecutor shall nominate three candidates for each position of Deputy Prosecutor to be filled. Unless a shorter term is decided upon at the time of their election, the Prosecutor and the Deputy Prosecutors shall hold office for a term of nine years and shall not be eligible for re-election.

5. Neither the Prosecutor nor a Deputy Prosecutor shall engage in any activity which is likely to interfere with his or her prosecutorial functions or to affect confidence in his or her independence. They shall not engage in any other occupation of a professional nature.

6. The Presidency may excuse the Prosecutor or a Deputy Prosecutor, at his or her request, from acting in a particular case.

7. Neither the Prosecutor nor a Deputy Prosecutor shall participate in any matter in which their impartiality might reasonably be doubted on any ground. They shall be disqualified from a case in accordance with this paragraph if, *inter alia*, they have previously been involved in any capacity in that case before the Court or in a related criminal case at the national level involving the person being investigated or prosecuted.

8. Any question as to the disqualification of the Prosecutor or a Deputy Prosecutor shall be decided by the Appeals Chamber.

   (a) The person being investigated or prosecuted may at any time request the disqualification of the Prosecutor or a Deputy Prosecutor on the grounds set out in this article;

   (b) The Prosecutor or the Deputy Prosecutor, as appropriate, shall be entitled to present his or her comments on the matter.

9. The Prosecutor shall appoint advisers with legal expertise on specific issues, including, but not limited to, sexual and gender violence and violence against children.

Article 43
The Registry

1. The Registry shall be responsible for the non-judicial aspects of the administration and servicing of the Court, without prejudice to the functions and powers of the Prosecutor in accordance with article 42.

2. The Registry shall be headed by the Registrar, who shall be the principal administrative officer of the Court. The Registrar shall exercise his or her functions under the authority of the President of the Court.

3. The Registrar and the Deputy Registrar shall be persons of high moral character, be highly competent and have an excellent knowledge of and be fluent in at least one of the working languages of the Court.

4. The judges shall elect the Registrar by an absolute majority by secret ballot, taking into account any recommendation by the Assembly of States Parties. If the need arises and upon the recommendation of the Registrar, the judges shall elect, in the same manner, a Deputy Registrar.

5. The Registrar shall hold office for a term of five years, shall be eligible for re-election once and shall serve on a full-time basis. The Deputy Registrar shall hold office for a

term of five years or such shorter term as may be decided upon by an absolute majority of the judges, and may be elected on the basis that the Deputy Registrar shall be called upon to serve as required.

6. The Registrar shall set up a Victims and Witnesses Unit within the Registry. This Unit shall provide, in consultation with the Office of the Prosecutor, protective measures and security arrangements, counselling and other appropriate assistance for witnesses, victims who appear before the Court, and others who are at risk on account of testimony given by such witnesses. The Unit shall include staff with expertise in trauma, including trauma related to crimes of sexual violence.

Article 44
Staff

1. The Prosecutor and the Registrar shall appoint such qualified staff as may be required to their respective offices. In the case of the Prosecutor, this shall include the appointment of investigators.

2. In the employment of staff, the Prosecutor and the Registrar shall ensure the highest standards of efficiency, competency and integrity, and shall have regard, *mutatis mutandis*, to the criteria set forth in article 36, paragraph 8.

3. The Registrar, with the agreement of the Presidency and the Prosecutor, shall propose Staff Regulations which include the terms and conditions upon which the staff of the Court shall be appointed, remunerated and dismissed. The Staff Regulations shall be approved by the Assembly of States Parties.

4. The Court may, in exceptional circumstances, employ the expertise of gratis personnel offered by States Parties, intergovernmental organizations or non-governmental organizations to assist with the work of any of the organs of the Court. The Prosecutor may accept any such offer on behalf of the Office of the Prosecutor. Such gratis personnel shall be employed in accordance with guidelines to be established by the Assembly of States Parties.

Article 45
Solemn undertaking

Before taking up their respective duties under this Statute, the judges, the Prosecutor, the Deputy Prosecutors, the Registrar and the Deputy Registrar shall each make a solemn undertaking in open court to exercise his or her respective functions impartially and conscientiously.

Article 46
Removal from office

1. A judge, the Prosecutor, a Deputy Prosecutor, the Registrar or the Deputy Registrar shall be removed from office if a decision to this effect is made in accordance with paragraph 2, in cases where that person:

   (a) Is found to have committed serious misconduct or a serious breach of his or her duties under this Statute, as provided for in the Rules of Procedure and Evidence; or

   (b) Is unable to exercise the functions required by this Statute.

2. A decision as to the removal from office of a judge, the Prosecutor or a Deputy Prosecutor under paragraph 1 shall be made by the Assembly of States Parties, by secret ballot:

(a) In the case of a judge, by a two-thirds majority of the States Parties upon a recommendation adopted by a two-thirds majority of the other judges;

(b) In the case of the Prosecutor, by an absolute majority of the States Parties;

(c) In the case of a Deputy Prosecutor, by an absolute majority of the States Parties upon the recommendation of the Prosecutor.

3. A decision as to the removal from office of the Registrar or Deputy Registrar shall be made by an absolute majority of the judges.

4. A judge, Prosecutor, Deputy Prosecutor, Registrar or Deputy Registrar whose conduct or ability to exercise the functions of the office as required by this Statute is challenged under this article shall have full opportunity to present and receive evidence and to make submissions in accordance with the Rules of Procedure and Evidence. The person in question shall not otherwise participate in the consideration of the matter.

Article 47
Disciplinary measures

A judge, Prosecutor, Deputy Prosecutor, Registrar or Deputy Registrar who has committed misconduct of a less serious nature than that set out in article 46, paragraph 1, shall be subject to disciplinary measures, in accordance with the Rules of Procedure and Evidence.

Article 48
Privileges and immunities

1. The Court shall enjoy in the territory of each State Party such privileges and immunities as are necessary for the fulfilment of its purposes.

2. The judges, the Prosecutor, the Deputy Prosecutors and the Registrar shall, when engaged on or with respect to the business of the Court, enjoy the same privileges and immunities as are accorded to heads of diplomatic missions and shall, after the expiry of their terms of office, continue to be accorded immunity from legal process of every kind in respect of words spoken or written and acts performed by them in their official capacity.

3. The Deputy Registrar, the staff of the Office of the Prosecutor and the staff of the Registry shall enjoy the privileges and immunities and facilities necessary for the performance of their functions, in accordance with the agreement on the privileges and immunities of the Court.

4. Counsel, experts, witnesses or any other person required to be present at the seat of the Court shall be accorded such treatment as is necessary for the proper functioning of the Court, in accordance with the agreement on the privileges and immunities of the Court.

5. The privileges and immunities of:

(a) A judge or the Prosecutor may be waived by an absolute majority of the judges;

(b) The Registrar may be waived by the Presidency;

(c) The Deputy Prosecutors and staff of the Office of the Prosecutor may be waived by the Prosecutor;

(d) The Deputy Registrar and staff of the Registry may be waived by the Registrar.

16

Article 49
Salaries, allowances and expenses

The judges, the Prosecutor, the Deputy Prosecutors, the Registrar and the Deputy Registrar shall receive such salaries, allowances and expenses as may be decided upon by the Assembly of States Parties. These salaries and allowances shall not be reduced during their terms of office.

Article 50
Official and working languages

1. The official languages of the Court shall be Arabic, Chinese, English, French, Russian and Spanish. The judgements of the Court, as well as other decisions resolving fundamental issues before the Court, shall be published in the official languages. The Presidency shall, in accordance with the criteria established by the Rules of Procedure and Evidence, determine which decisions may be considered as resolving fundamental issues for the purposes of this paragraph.
2. The working languages of the Court shall be English and French. The Rules of Procedure and Evidence shall determine the cases in which other official languages may be used as working languages.
3. At the request of any party to a proceeding or a State allowed to intervene in a proceeding, the Court shall authorize a language other than English or French to be used by such a party or State, provided that the Court considers such authorization to be adequately justified.

Article 51
Rules of Procedure and Evidence

1. The Rules of Procedure and Evidence shall enter into force upon adoption by a two-thirds majority of the members of the Assembly of States Parties.
2. Amendments to the Rules of Procedure and Evidence may be proposed by:
    (a) Any State Party;
    (b) The judges acting by an absolute majority; or
    (c) The Prosecutor.
    Such amendments shall enter into force upon adoption by a two-thirds majority of the members of the Assembly of States Parties.
3. After the adoption of the Rules of Procedure and Evidence, in urgent cases where the Rules do not provide for a specific situation before the Court, the judges may, by a two-thirds majority, draw up provisional Rules to be applied until adopted, amended or rejected at the next ordinary or special session of the Assembly of States Parties.
4. The Rules of Procedure and Evidence, amendments thereto and any provisional Rule shall be consistent with this Statute. Amendments to the Rules of Procedure and Evidence as well as provisional Rules shall not be applied retroactively to the detriment of the person who is being investigated or prosecuted or who has been convicted.
5. In the event of conflict between the Statute and the Rules of Procedure and Evidence, the Statute shall prevail.

Article 52
Regulations of the Court
1. The judges shall, in accordance with this Statute and the Rules of Procedure and Evidence, adopt, by an absolute majority, the Regulations of the Court necessary for its routine functioning.
2. The Prosecutor and the Registrar shall be consulted in the elaboration of the Regulations and any amendments thereto.
3. The Regulations and any amendments thereto shall take effect upon adoption unless otherwise decided by the judges. Immediately upon adoption, they shall be circulated to States Parties for comments. If within six months there are no objections from a majority of States Parties, they shall remain in force.

PART 5. INVESTIGATION AND PROSECUTION

Article 53
Initiation of an investigation
1. The Prosecutor shall, having evaluated the information made available to him or her, initiate an investigation unless he or she determines that there is no reasonable basis to proceed under this Statute. In deciding whether to initiate an investigation, the Prosecutor shall consider whether:
   (a) The information available to the Prosecutor provides a reasonable basis to believe that a crime within the jurisdiction of the Court has been or is being committed;
   (b) The case is or would be admissible under article 17; and
   (c) Taking into account the gravity of the crime and the interests of victims, there are nonetheless substantial reasons to believe that an investigation would not serve the interests of justice.
   If the Prosecutor determines that there is no reasonable basis to proceed and his or her determination is based solely on subparagraph (c) above, he or she shall inform the Pre-Trial Chamber.
2. If, upon investigation, the Prosecutor concludes that there is not a sufficient basis for a prosecution because:
   (a) There is not a sufficient legal or factual basis to seek a warrant or summons under article 58;
   (b) The case is inadmissible under article 17; or
   (c) A prosecution is not in the interests of justice, taking into account all the circumstances, including the gravity of the crime, the interests of victims and the age or infirmity of the alleged perpetrator, and his or her role in the alleged crime;
   the Prosecutor shall inform the Pre-Trial Chamber and the State making a referral under article 14 or the Security Council in a case under article 13, paragraph (b), of his or her conclusion and the reasons for the conclusion.
3.
   (a) At the request of the State making a referral under article 14 or the Security Council under article 13, paragraph (b), the Pre-Trial Chamber may review a decision of the Prosecutor under paragraph 1 or 2 not to proceed and may request the Prosecutor to reconsider that decision.

(b) In addition, the Pre-Trial Chamber may, on its own initiative, review a decision of the Prosecutor not to proceed if it is based solely on paragraph 1(c) or 2(c). In such a case, the decision of the Prosecutor shall be effective only if confirmed by the Pre-Trial Chamber.

4. The Prosecutor may, at any time, reconsider a decision whether to initiate an investigation or prosecution based on new facts or information.

Article 54
Duties and powers of the Prosecutor with respect to investigations

1. The Prosecutor shall:
   (a) In order to establish the truth, extend the investigation to cover all facts and evidence relevant to an assessment of whether there is criminal responsibility under this Statute, and, in doing so, investigate incriminating and exonerating circumstances equally;
   (b) Take appropriate measures to ensure the effective investigation and prosecution of crimes within the jurisdiction of the Court, and in doing so, respect the interests and personal circumstances of victims and witnesses, including age, gender as defined in article 7, paragraph 3, and health, and take into account the nature of the crime, in particular where it involves sexual violence, gender violence or violence against children; and
   (c) Fully respect the rights of persons arising under this Statute.
2. The Prosecutor may conduct investigations on the territory of a State:
   (a) In accordance with the provisions of Part 9; or
   (b) As authorized by the Pre-Trial Chamber under article 57, paragraph 3(d).
3. The Prosecutor may:
   (a) Collect and examine evidence;
   (b) Request the presence of and question persons being investigated, victims and witnesses;
   (c) Seek the cooperation of any State or intergovernmental organization or arrangement in accordance with its respective competence and/or mandate;
   (d) Enter into such arrangements or agreements, not inconsistent with this Statute, as may be necessary to facilitate the cooperation of a State, intergovernmental organization or person;
   (e) Agree not to disclose, at any stage of the proceedings, documents or information that the Prosecutor obtains on the condition of confidentiality and solely for the purpose of generating new evidence, unless the provider of the information consents; and
   (f) Take necessary measures, or request that necessary measures be taken, to ensure the confidentiality of information, the protection of any person or the preservation of evidence.

Article 55
Rights of persons during an investigation

1. In respect of an investigation under this Statute, a person:
   (a) Shall not be compelled to incriminate himself or herself or to confess guilt;

(b) Shall not be subjected to any form of coercion, duress or threat, to torture or to any other form of cruel, inhuman or degrading treatment or punishment;

(c) Shall, if questioned in a language other than a language the person fully understands and speaks, have, free of any cost, the assistance of a competent interpreter and such translations as are necessary to meet the requirements of fairness; and

(d) Shall not be subjected to arbitrary arrest or detention, and shall not be deprived of his or her liberty except on such grounds and in accordance with such procedures as are established in this Statute.

2. Where there are grounds to believe that a person has committed a crime within the jurisdiction of the Court and that person is about to be questioned either by the Prosecutor, or by national authorities pursuant to a request made under Part 9, that person shall also have the following rights of which he or she shall be informed prior to being questioned:

(a) To be informed, prior to being questioned, that there are grounds to believe that he or she has committed a crime within the jurisdiction of the Court;

(b) To remain silent, without such silence being a consideration in the determination of guilt or innocence;

(c) To have legal assistance of the person's choosing, or, if the person does not have legal assistance, to have legal assistance assigned to him or her, in any case where the interests of justice so require, and without payment by the person in any such case if the person does not have sufficient means to pay for it; and

(d) To be questioned in the presence of counsel unless the person has voluntarily waived his or her right to counsel.

Article 56
Role of the Pre-Trial Chamber in relation to a unique investigative opportunity

1.
(a) Where the Prosecutor considers an investigation to present a unique opportunity to take testimony or a statement from a witness or to examine, collect or test evidence, which may not be available subsequently for the purposes of a trial, the Prosecutor shall so inform the Pre-Trial Chamber.

(b) In that case, the Pre-Trial Chamber may, upon request of the Prosecutor, take such measures as may be necessary to ensure the efficiency and integrity of the proceedings and, in particular, to protect the rights of the defence.

(c) Unless the Pre-Trial Chamber orders otherwise, the Prosecutor shall provide the relevant information to the person who has been arrested or appeared in response to a summons in connection with the investigation referred to in subparagraph (a), in order that he or she may be heard on the matter.

2. The measures referred to in paragraph 1(b) may include:
(a) Making recommendations or orders regarding procedures to be followed;
(b) Directing that a record be made of the proceedings;
(c) Appointing an expert to assist;
(d) Authorizing counsel for a person who has been arrested, or appeared before the Court in response to a summons, to participate, or where there has not yet been

16

such an arrest or appearance or counsel has not been designated, appointing another counsel to attend and represent the interests of the defence;

(e) Naming one of its members or, if necessary, another available judge of the Pre-Trial or Trial Division to observe and make recommendations or orders regarding the collection and preservation of evidence and the questioning of persons;

(f) Taking such other action as may be necessary to collect or preserve evidence.

3.

   (a) Where the Prosecutor has not sought measures pursuant to this article but the Pre-Trial Chamber considers that such measures are required to preserve evidence that it deems would be essential for the defence at trial, it shall consult with the Prosecutor as to whether there is good reason for the Prosecutor's failure to request the measures. If upon consultation, the Pre-Trial Chamber concludes that the Prosecutor's failure to request such measures is unjustified, the Pre-Trial Chamber may take such measures on its own initiative.

   (b) A decision of the Pre-Trial Chamber to act on its own initiative under this paragraph may be appealed by the Prosecutor. The appeal shall be heard on an expedited basis.

4. The admissibility of evidence preserved or collected for trial pursuant to this article, or the record thereof, shall be governed at trial by article 69, and given such weight as determined by the Trial Chamber.

Article 57
Functions and powers of the Pre-Trial Chamber

1. Unless otherwise provided in this Statute, the Pre-Trial Chamber shall exercise its functions in accordance with the provisions of this article.

2.

   (a) Orders or rulings of the Pre-Trial Chamber issued under articles 15, 18, 19, 54, paragraph 2, 61, paragraph 7, and 72 must be concurred in by a majority of its judges.

   (b) In all other cases, a single judge of the Pre-Trial Chamber may exercise the functions provided for in this Statute, unless otherwise provided for in the Rules of Procedure and Evidence or by a majority of the Pre-Trial Chamber.

3. In addition to its other functions under this Statute, the Pre-Trial Chamber may:

   (a) At the request of the Prosecutor, issue such orders and warrants as may be required for the purposes of an investigation;

   (b) Upon the request of a person who has been arrested or has appeared pursuant to a summons under article 58, issue such orders, including measures such as those described in article 56, or seek such cooperation pursuant to Part 9 as may be necessary to assist the person in the preparation of his or her defence;

   (c) Where necessary, provide for the protection and privacy of victims and witnesses, the preservation of evidence, the protection of persons who have been arrested or appeared in response to a summons, and the protection of national security information;

   (d) Authorize the Prosecutor to take specific investigative steps within the territory of a State Party without having secured the cooperation of that State under Part 9 if, whenever possible having regard to the views of the State concerned, the Pre-Trial Chamber has determined in that case that the State is clearly unable to execute a request for cooperation due to the unavailability of any authority or any component of its judicial system competent to execute the request for cooperation under Part 9.

(e) Where a warrant of arrest or a summons has been issued under article 58, and having due regard to the strength of the evidence and the rights of the parties concerned, as provided for in this Statute and the Rules of Procedure and Evidence, seek the cooperation of States pursuant to article 93, paragraph 1(k), to take protective measures for the purpose of forfeiture, in particular for the ultimate benefit of victims.

Article 58
Issuance by the Pre-Trial Chamber of a warrant of arrest or a summons to appear

1. At any time after the initiation of an investigation, the Pre-Trial Chamber shall, on the application of the Prosecutor, issue a warrant of arrest of a person if, having examined the application and the evidence or other information submitted by the Prosecutor, it is satisfied that:
   (a) There are reasonable grounds to believe that the person has committed a crime within the jurisdiction of the Court; and
   (b) The arrest of the person appears necessary:
      (i) To ensure the person's appearance at trial,
      (ii) To ensure that the person does not obstruct or endanger the investigation or the court proceedings, or
      (iii) Where applicable, to prevent the person from continuing with the commission of that crime or a related crime which is within the jurisdiction of the Court and which arises out of the same circumstances.
2. The application of the Prosecutor shall contain:
   (a) The name of the person and any other relevant identifying information;
   (b) A specific reference to the crimes within the jurisdiction of the Court which the person is alleged to have committed;
   (c) A concise statement of the facts which are alleged to constitute those crimes;
   (d) A summary of the evidence and any other information which establish reasonable grounds to believe that the person committed those crimes; and
   (e) The reason why the Prosecutor believes that the arrest of the person is necessary.
3. The warrant of arrest shall contain:
   (a) The name of the person and any other relevant identifying information;
   (b) A specific reference to the crimes within the jurisdiction of the Court for which the person's arrest is sought; and
   (c) A concise statement of the facts which are alleged to constitute those crimes.
4. The warrant of arrest shall remain in effect until otherwise ordered by the Court.
5. On the basis of the warrant of arrest, the Court may request the provisional arrest or the arrest and surrender of the person under Part 9.
6. The Prosecutor may request the Pre-Trial Chamber to amend the warrant of arrest by modifying or adding to the crimes specified therein. The Pre-Trial Chamber shall so

amend the warrant if it is satisfied that there are reasonable grounds to believe that the person committed the modified or additional crimes.

7. As an alternative to seeking a warrant of arrest, the Prosecutor may submit an application requesting that the Pre-Trial Chamber issue a summons for the person to appear. If the Pre-Trial Chamber is satisfied that there are reasonable grounds to believe that the person committed the crime alleged and that a summons is sufficient to ensure the person's appearance, it shall issue the summons, with or without conditions restricting liberty (other than detention) if provided for by national law, for the person to appear. The summons shall contain:

   (a) The name of the person and any other relevant identifying information;

   (b) The specified date on which the person is to appear;

   (c) A specific reference to the crimes within the jurisdiction of the Court which the person is alleged to have committed; and

   (d) A concise statement of the facts which are alleged to constitute the crime.

   The summons shall be served on the person.

Article 59
Arrest proceedings in the custodial State

1. A State Party which has received a request for provisional arrest or for arrest and surrender shall immediately take steps to arrest the person in question in accordance with its laws and the provisions of Part 9.

2. A person arrested shall be brought promptly before the competent judicial authority in the custodial State which shall determine, in accordance with the law of that State, that:

   (a) The warrant applies to that person;

   (b) The person has been arrested in accordance with the proper process; and

   (c) The person's rights have been respected.

3. The person arrested shall have the right to apply to the competent authority in the custodial State for interim release pending surrender.

4. In reaching a decision on any such application, the competent authority in the custodial State shall consider whether, given the gravity of the alleged crimes, there are urgent and exceptional circumstances to justify interim release and whether necessary safeguards exist to ensure that the custodial State can fulfil its duty to surrender the person to the Court. It shall not be open to the competent authority of the custodial State to consider whether the warrant of arrest was properly issued in accordance with article 58, paragraph 1(a) and (b).

5. The Pre-Trial Chamber shall be notified of any request for interim release and shall make recommendations to the competent authority in the custodial State. The competent authority in the custodial State shall give full consideration to such recommendations, including any recommendations on measures to prevent the escape of the person, before rendering its decision.

6. If the person is granted interim release, the Pre-Trial Chamber may request periodic reports on the status of the interim release.

7. Once ordered to be surrendered by the custodial State, the person shall be delivered to the Court as soon as possible.

Article 60
Initial proceedings before the Court

1. Upon the surrender of the person to the Court, or the person's appearance before the Court voluntarily or pursuant to a summons, the Pre-Trial Chamber shall satisfy itself that the person has been informed of the crimes which he or she is alleged to have committed, and of his or her rights under this Statute, including the right to apply for interim release pending trial.

2. A person subject to a warrant of arrest may apply for interim release pending trial. If the Pre-Trial Chamber is satisfied that the conditions set forth in article 58, paragraph 1, are met, the person shall continue to be detained. If it is not so satisfied, the Pre-Trial Chamber shall release the person, with or without conditions.

3. The Pre-Trial Chamber shall periodically review its ruling on the release or detention of the person, and may do so at any time on the request of the Prosecutor or the person. Upon such review, it may modify its ruling as to detention, release or conditions of release, if it is satisfied that changed circumstances so require.

4. The Pre-Trial Chamber shall ensure that a person is not detained for an unreasonable period prior to trial due to inexcusable delay by the Prosecutor. If such delay occurs, the Court shall consider releasing the person, with or without conditions.

5. If necessary, the Pre-Trial Chamber may issue a warrant of arrest to secure the presence of a person who has been released.

Article 61
Confirmation of the charges before trial

1. Subject to the provisions of paragraph 2, within a reasonable time after the person's surrender or voluntary appearance before the Court, the Pre-Trial Chamber shall hold a hearing to confirm the charges on which the Prosecutor intends to seek trial. The hearing shall be held in the presence of the Prosecutor and the person charged, as well as his or her counsel.

2. The Pre-Trial Chamber may, upon request of the Prosecutor or on its own motion, hold a hearing in the absence of the person charged to confirm the charges on which the Prosecutor intends to seek trial when the person has:

    (a) Waived his or her right to be present; or

    (b) Fled or cannot be found and all reasonable steps have been taken to secure his or her appearance before the Court and to inform the person of the charges and that a hearing to confirm those charges will be held.

    In that case, the person shall be represented by counsel where the Pre-Trial Chamber determines that it is in the interests of justice.

3. Within a reasonable time before the hearing, the person shall:

    (a) Be provided with a copy of the document containing the charges on which the Prosecutor intends to bring the person to trial; and

    (b) Be informed of the evidence on which the Prosecutor intends to rely at the hearing.

    The Pre-Trial Chamber may issue orders regarding the disclosure of information for the purposes of the hearing.

4. Before the hearing, the Prosecutor may continue the investigation and may amend or withdraw any charges. The person shall be given reasonable notice before the hearing of any amendment to or withdrawal of charges. In case of a withdrawal of charges, the Prosecutor shall notify the Pre-Trial Chamber of the reasons for the withdrawal.

16

5. At the hearing, the Prosecutor shall support each charge with sufficient evidence to establish substantial grounds to believe that the person committed the crime charged. The Prosecutor may rely on documentary or summary evidence and need not call the witnesses expected to testify at the trial.

6. At the hearing, the person may:
   (a) Object to the charges;
   (b) Challenge the evidence presented by the Prosecutor; and
   (c) Present evidence.

7. The Pre-Trial Chamber shall, on the basis of the hearing, determine whether there is sufficient evidence to establish substantial grounds to believe that the person committed each of the crimes charged. Based on its determination, the Pre-Trial Chamber shall:
   (a) Confirm those charges in relation to which it has determined that there is sufficient evidence, and commit the person to a Trial Chamber for trial on the charges as confirmed;
   (b) Decline to confirm those charges in relation to which it has determined that there is insufficient evidence;
   (c) Adjourn the hearing and request the Prosecutor to consider:
      (i) Providing further evidence or conducting further investigation with respect to a particular charge; or
      (ii) Amending a charge because the evidence submitted appears to establish a different crime within the jurisdiction of the Court.

8. Where the Pre-Trial Chamber declines to confirm a charge, the Prosecutor shall not be precluded from subsequently requesting its confirmation if the request is supported by additional evidence.

9. After the charges are confirmed and before the trial has begun, the Prosecutor may, with the permission of the Pre-Trial Chamber and after notice to the accused, amend the charges. If the Prosecutor seeks to add additional charges or to substitute more serious charges, a hearing under this article to confirm those charges must be held. After commencement of the trial, the Prosecutor may, with the permission of the Trial Chamber, withdraw the charges.

10. Any warrant previously issued shall cease to have effect with respect to any charges which have not been confirmed by the Pre-Trial Chamber or which have been withdrawn by the Prosecutor.

11. Once the charges have been confirmed in accordance with this article, the Presidency shall constitute a Trial Chamber which, subject to paragraph 9 and to article 64, paragraph 4, shall be responsible for the conduct of subsequent proceedings and may exercise any function of the Pre-Trial Chamber that is relevant and capable of application in those proceedings.

PART 6. THE TRIAL

Article 62
Place of trial
Unless otherwise decided, the place of the trial shall be the seat of the Court.

Article 63
Trial in the presence of the accused

1. The accused shall be present during the trial.
2. If the accused, being present before the Court, continues to disrupt the trial, the Trial Chamber may remove the accused and shall make provision for him or her to observe the trial and instruct counsel from outside the courtroom, through the use of communications technology, if required. Such measures shall be taken only in exceptional circumstances after other reasonable alternatives have proved inadequate, and only for such duration as is strictly required.

Article 64
Functions and powers of the Trial Chamber

1. The functions and powers of the Trial Chamber set out in this article shall be exercised in accordance with this Statute and the Rules of Procedure and Evidence.
2. The Trial Chamber shall ensure that a trial is fair and expeditious and is conducted with full respect for the rights of the accused and due regard for the protection of victims and witnesses.
3. Upon assignment of a case for trial in accordance with this Statute, the Trial Chamber assigned to deal with the case shall:
   (a) Confer with the parties and adopt such procedures as are necessary to facilitate the fair and expeditious conduct of the proceedings;
   (b) Determine the language or languages to be used at trial; and
   (c) Subject to any other relevant provisions of this Statute, provide for disclosure of documents or information not previously disclosed, sufficiently in advance of the commencement of the trial to enable adequate preparation for trial.
4. The Trial Chamber may, if necessary for its effective and fair functioning, refer preliminary issues to the Pre-Trial Chamber or, if necessary, to another available judge of the Pre-Trial Division.
5. Upon notice to the parties, the Trial Chamber may, as appropriate, direct that there be joinder or severance in respect of charges against more than one accused.
6. In performing its functions prior to trial or during the course of a trial, the Trial Chamber may, as necessary:
   (a) Exercise any functions of the Pre-Trial Chamber referred to in article 61, paragraph 11;
   (b) Require the attendance and testimony of witnesses and production of documents and other evidence by obtaining, if necessary, the assistance of States as provided in this Statute;
   (c) Provide for the protection of confidential information;
   (d) Order the production of evidence in addition to that already collected prior to the trial or presented during the trial by the parties;
   (e) Provide for the protection of the accused, witnesses and victims; and
   (f) Rule on any other relevant matters.
7. The trial shall be held in public. The Trial Chamber may, however, determine that special circumstances require that certain proceedings be in closed session for the

purposes set forth in article 68, or to protect confidential or sensitive information to be given in evidence.

8.

(a) At the commencement of the trial, the Trial Chamber shall have read to the accused the charges previously confirmed by the Pre-Trial Chamber. The Trial Chamber shall satisfy itself that the accused understands the nature of the charges. It shall afford him or her the opportunity to make an admission of guilt in accordance with article 65 or to plead not guilty.

(b) At the trial, the presiding judge may give directions for the conduct of proceedings, including to ensure that they are conducted in a fair and impartial manner. Subject to any directions of the presiding judge, the parties may submit evidence in accordance with the provisions of this Statute.

9. The Trial Chamber shall have, *inter alia*, the power on application of a party or on its own motion to:

(a) Rule on the admissibility or relevance of evidence; and

(b) Take all necessary steps to maintain order in the course of a hearing.

10. The Trial Chamber shall ensure that a complete record of the trial, which accurately reflects the proceedings, is made and that it is maintained and preserved by the Registrar.

Article 65
Proceedings on an admission of guilt

1. Where the accused makes an admission of guilt pursuant to article 64, paragraph 8(a), the Trial Chamber shall determine whether:

(a) The accused understands the nature and consequences of the admission of guilt;

(b) The admission is voluntarily made by the accused after sufficient consultation with defence counsel; and

(c) The admission of guilt is supported by the facts of the case that are contained in:

(i) The charges brought by the Prosecutor and admitted by the accused;

(ii) Any materials presented by the Prosecutor which supplement the charges and which the accused accepts; and

(iii) Any other evidence, such as the testimony of witnesses, presented by the Prosecutor or the accused.

2. Where the Trial Chamber is satisfied that the matters referred to in paragraph 1 are established, it shall consider the admission of guilt, together with any additional evidence presented, as establishing all the essential facts that are required to prove the crime to which the admission of guilt relates, and may convict the accused of that crime.

3. Where the Trial Chamber is not satisfied that the matters referred to in paragraph 1 are established, it shall consider the admission of guilt as not having been made, in which case it shall order that the trial be continued under the ordinary trial procedures provided by this Statute and may remit the case to another Trial Chamber.

4. Where the Trial Chamber is of the opinion that a more complete presentation of the facts of the case is required in the interests of justice, in particular the interests of the victims, the Trial Chamber may:

(a) Request the Prosecutor to present additional evidence, including the testimony of witnesses; or

(b) Order that the trial be continued under the ordinary trial procedures provided by this Statute, in which case it shall consider the admission of guilt as not having been made and may remit the case to another Trial Chamber.

5. Any discussions between the Prosecutor and the defence regarding modification of the charges, the admission of guilt or the penalty to be imposed shall not be binding on the Court.

Article 66
Presumption of innocence

1. Everyone shall be presumed innocent until proved guilty before the Court in accordance with the applicable law.

2. The onus is on the Prosecutor to prove the guilt of the accused.

3. In order to convict the accused, the Court must be convinced of the guilt of the accused beyond reasonable doubt.

Article 67
Rights of the accused

1. In the determination of any charge, the accused shall be entitled to a public hearing, having regard to the provisions of this Statute, to a fair hearing conducted impartially, and to the following minimum guarantees, in full equality:

(a) To be informed promptly and in detail of the nature, cause and content of the charge, in a language which the accused fully understands and speaks;

(b) To have adequate time and facilities for the preparation of the defence and to communicate freely with counsel of the accused's choosing in confidence;

(c) To be tried without undue delay;

(d) Subject to article 63, paragraph 2, to be present at the trial, to conduct the defence in person or through legal assistance of the accused's choosing, to be informed, if the accused does not have legal assistance, of this right and to have legal assistance assigned by the Court in any case where the interests of justice so require, and without payment if the accused lacks sufficient means to pay for it;

(e) To examine, or have examined, the witnesses against him or her and to obtain the attendance and examination of witnesses on his or her behalf under the same conditions as witnesses against him or her. The accused shall also be entitled to raise defences and to present other evidence admissible under this Statute;

(f) To have, free of any cost, the assistance of a competent interpreter and such translations as are necessary to meet the requirements of fairness, if any of the proceedings of or documents presented to the Court are not in a language which the accused fully understands and speaks;

(g) Not to be compelled to testify or to confess guilt and to remain silent, without such silence being a consideration in the determination of guilt or innocence;

(h) To make an unsworn oral or written statement in his or her defence; and

(i) Not to have imposed on him or her any reversal of the burden of proof or any onus of rebuttal.

2. In addition to any other disclosure provided for in this Statute, the Prosecutor shall, as soon as practicable, disclose to the defence evidence in the Prosecutor's possession or control which he or she believes shows or tends to show the innocence of the accused, or to mitigate the guilt of the accused, or which may affect the credibility of prosecution evidence. In case of doubt as to the application of this paragraph, the Court shall decide.

Article 68
Protection of the victims and witnesses and their participation in the proceedings

1. The Court shall take appropriate measures to protect the safety, physical and psychological well-being, dignity and privacy of victims and witnesses. In so doing, the Court shall have regard to all relevant factors, including age, gender as defined in article 7, paragraph 3, and health, and the nature of the crime, in particular, but not limited to, where the crime involves sexual or gender violence or violence against children. The Prosecutor shall take such measures particularly during the investigation and prosecution of such crimes. These measures shall not be prejudicial to or inconsistent with the rights of the accused and a fair and impartial trial.

2. As an exception to the principle of public hearings provided for in article 67, the Chambers of the Court may, to protect victims and witnesses or an accused, conduct any part of the proceedings *in camera* or allow the presentation of evidence by electronic or other special means. In particular, such measures shall be implemented in the case of a victim of sexual violence or a child who is a victim or a witness, unless otherwise ordered by the Court, having regard to all the circumstances, particularly the views of the victim or witness.

3. Where the personal interests of the victims are affected, the Court shall permit their views and concerns to be presented and considered at stages of the proceedings determined to be appropriate by the Court and in a manner which is not prejudicial to or inconsistent with the rights of the accused and a fair and impartial trial. Such views and concerns may be presented by the legal representatives of the victims where the Court considers it appropriate, in accordance with the Rules of Procedure and Evidence.

4. The Victims and Witnesses Unit may advise the Prosecutor and the Court on appropriate protective measures, security arrangements, counselling and assistance as referred to in article 43, paragraph 6.

5. Where the disclosure of evidence or information pursuant to this Statute may lead to the grave endangerment of the security of a witness or his or her family, the Prosecutor may, for the purposes of any proceedings conducted prior to the commencement of the trial, withhold such evidence or information and instead submit a summary thereof. Such measures shall be exercised in a manner which is not prejudicial to or inconsistent with the rights of the accused and a fair and impartial trial.

6. A State may make an application for necessary measures to be taken in respect of the protection of its servants or agents and the protection of confidential or sensitive information.

Article 69
Evidence

1. Before testifying, each witness shall, in accordance with the Rules of Procedure and Evidence, give an undertaking as to the truthfulness of the evidence to be given by that witness.
2. The testimony of a witness at trial shall be given in person, except to the extent provided by the measures set forth in article 68 or in the Rules of Procedure and Evidence. The Court may also permit the giving of *viva voce* (oral) or recorded testimony of a witness by means of video or audio technology, as well as the introduction of documents or written transcripts, subject to this Statute and in accordance with the Rules of Procedure and Evidence. These measures shall not be prejudicial to or inconsistent with the rights of the accused.
3. The parties may submit evidence relevant to the case, in accordance with article 64. The Court shall have the authority to request the submission of all evidence that it considers necessary for the determination of the truth.
4. The Court may rule on the relevance or admissibility of any evidence, taking into account, *inter alia*, the probative value of the evidence and any prejudice that such evidence may cause to a fair trial or to a fair evaluation of the testimony of a witness, in accordance with the Rules of Procedure and Evidence.
5. The Court shall respect and observe privileges on confidentiality as provided for in the Rules of Procedure and Evidence.
6. The Court shall not require proof of facts of common knowledge but may take judicial notice of them.
7. Evidence obtained by means of a violation of this Statute or internationally recognized human rights shall not be admissible if:
   (a) The violation casts substantial doubt on the reliability of the evidence; or
   (b) The admission of the evidence would be antithetical to and would seriously damage the integrity of the proceedings.
8. When deciding on the relevance or admissibility of evidence collected by a State, the Court shall not rule on the application of the State's national law.

Article 70
Offences against the administration of justice

1. The Court shall have jurisdiction over the following offences against its administration of justice when committed intentionally:
   (a) Giving false testimony when under an obligation pursuant to article 69, paragraph 1, to tell the truth;
   (b) Presenting evidence that the party knows is false or forged;
   (c) Corruptly influencing a witness, obstructing or interfering with the attendance or testimony of a witness, retaliating against a witness for giving testimony or destroying, tampering with or interfering with the collection of evidence;
   (d) Impeding, intimidating or corruptly influencing an official of the Court for the purpose of forcing or persuading the official not to perform, or to perform improperly, his or her duties;
   (e) Retaliating against an official of the Court on account of duties performed by that or another official;

(f) Soliciting or accepting a bribe as an official of the Court in connection with his or her official duties.

2. The principles and procedures governing the Court's exercise of jurisdiction over offences under this article shall be those provided for in the Rules of Procedure and Evidence. The conditions for providing international cooperation to the Court with respect to its proceedings under this article shall be governed by the domestic laws of the requested State.

3. In the event of conviction, the Court may impose a term of imprisonment not exceeding five years, or a fine in accordance with the Rules of Procedure and Evidence, or both.

4.

(a) Each State Party shall extend its criminal laws penalizing offences against the integrity of its own investigative or judicial process to offences against the administration of justice referred to in this article, committed on its territory, or by one of its nationals;

(b) Upon request by the Court, whenever it deems it proper, the State Party shall submit the case to its competent authorities for the purpose of prosecution. Those authorities shall treat such cases with diligence and devote sufficient resources to enable them to be conducted effectively.

Article 71
Sanctions for misconduct before the Court

1. The Court may sanction persons present before it who commit misconduct, including disruption of its proceedings or deliberate refusal to comply with its directions, by administrative measures other than imprisonment, such as temporary or permanent removal from the courtroom, a fine or other similar measures provided for in the Rules of Procedure and Evidence.

2. The procedures governing the imposition of the measures set forth in paragraph 1 shall be those provided for in the Rules of Procedure and Evidence.

Article 72
Protection of national security information

1. This article applies in any case where the disclosure of the information or documents of a State would, in the opinion of that State, prejudice its national security interests. Such cases include those falling within the scope of article 56, paragraphs 2 and 3, article 61, paragraph 3, article 64, paragraph 3, article 67, paragraph 2, article 68, paragraph 6, article 87, paragraph 6 and article 93, as well as cases arising at any other stage of the proceedings where such disclosure may be at issue.

2. This article shall also apply when a person who has been requested to give information or evidence has refused to do so or has referred the matter to the State on the ground that disclosure would prejudice the national security interests of a State and the State concerned confirms that it is of the opinion that disclosure would prejudice its national security interests.

3. Nothing in this article shall prejudice the requirements of confidentiality applicable under article 54, paragraph 3(e) and (f), or the application of article 73.

4. If a State learns that information or documents of the State are being, or are likely to be, disclosed at any stage of the proceedings, and it is of the opinion that disclosure would

prejudice its national security interests, that State shall have the right to intervene in order to obtain resolution of the issue in accordance with this article.

5. If, in the opinion of a State, disclosure of information would prejudice its national security interests, all reasonable steps will be taken by the State, acting in conjunction with the Prosecutor, the defence or the Pre-Trial Chamber or Trial Chamber, as the case may be, to seek to resolve the matter by cooperative means. Such steps may include:

(a) Modification or clarification of the request;

(b) A determination by the Court regarding the relevance of the information or evidence sought, or a determination as to whether the evidence, though relevant, could be or has been obtained from a source other than the requested State;

(c) Obtaining the information or evidence from a different source or in a different form; or

(d) Agreement on conditions under which the assistance could be provided including, among other things, providing summaries or redactions, limitations on disclosure, use of *in camera* or *ex parte* proceedings, or other protective measures permissible under the Statute and the Rules of Procedure and Evidence.

6. Once all reasonable steps have been taken to resolve the matter through cooperative means, and if the State considers that there are no means or conditions under which the information or documents could be provided or disclosed without prejudice to its national security interests, it shall so notify the Prosecutor or the Court of the specific reasons for its decision, unless a specific description of the reasons would itself necessarily result in such prejudice to the State's national security interests.

7. Thereafter, if the Court determines that the evidence is relevant and necessary for the establishment of the guilt or innocence of the accused, the Court may undertake the following actions:

(a) Where disclosure of the information or document is sought pursuant to a request for cooperation under Part 9 or the circumstances described in paragraph 2, and the State has invoked the ground for refusal referred to in article 93, paragraph 4:

(i) The Court may, before making any conclusion referred to in subparagraph 7(a)(ii), request further consultations for the purpose of considering the State's representations, which may include, as appropriate, hearings *in camera* and *ex parte*;

(ii) If the Court concludes that, by invoking the ground for refusal under article 93, paragraph 4, in the circumstances of the case, the requested State is not acting in accordance with its obligations under this Statute, the Court may refer the matter in accordance with article 87, paragraph 7, specifying the reasons for its conclusion; and

(iii) The Court may make such inference in the trial of the accused as to the existence or non-existence of a fact, as may be appropriate in the circumstances; or

(b) In all other circumstances:

(i) Order disclosure; or

(ii) To the extent it does not order disclosure, make such inference in the trial of the accused as to the existence or non-existence of a fact, as may be appropriate in the circumstances.

Article 73
Third-party information or documents

If a State Party is requested by the Court to provide a document or information in its custody, possession or control, which was disclosed to it in confidence by a State, inter-governmental organization or international organization, it shall seek the consent of the originator to disclose that document or information. If the originator is a State Party, it shall either consent to disclosure of the information or document or undertake to resolve the issue of disclosure with the Court, subject to the provisions of article 72. If the originator is not a State Party and refuses to consent to disclosure, the requested State shall inform the Court that it is unable to provide the document or information because of a pre-existing obligation of confidentiality to the originator.

Article 74
Requirements for the decision

1. All the judges of the Trial Chamber shall be present at each stage of the trial and throughout their deliberations. The Presidency may, on a case-by-case basis, designate, as available, one or more alternate judges to be present at each stage of the trial and to replace a member of the Trial Chamber if that member is unable to continue attending.
2. The Trial Chamber's decision shall be based on its evaluation of the evidence and the entire proceedings. The decision shall not exceed the facts and circumstances described in the charges and any amendments to the charges. The Court may base its decision only on evidence submitted and discussed before it at the trial.
3. The judges shall attempt to achieve unanimity in their decision, failing which the decision shall be taken by a majority of the judges.
4. The deliberations of the Trial Chamber shall remain secret.
5. The decision shall be in writing and shall contain a full and reasoned statement of the Trial Chamber's findings on the evidence and conclusions. The Trial Chamber shall issue one decision. When there is no unanimity, the Trial Chamber's decision shall contain the views of the majority and the minority. The decision or a summary thereof shall be delivered in open court.

Article 75
Reparations to victims

1. The Court shall establish principles relating to reparations to, or in respect of, victims, including restitution, compensation and rehabilitation. On this basis, in its decision the Court may, either upon request or on its own motion in exceptional circumstances, determine the scope and extent of any damage, loss and injury to, or in respect of, victims and will state the principles on which it is acting.
2. The Court may make an order directly against a convicted person specifying appropriate reparations to, or in respect of, victims, including restitution, compensation and rehabilitation. Where appropriate, the Court may order that the award for reparations be made through the Trust Fund provided for in article 79.
3. Before making an order under this article, the Court may invite and shall take account of representations from or on behalf of the convicted person, victims, other interested persons or interested States.
4. In exercising its power under this article, the Court may, after a person is convicted of a crime within the jurisdiction of the Court, determine whether, in order to give

effect to an order which it may make under this article, it is necessary to seek measures under article 93, paragraph 1.

5. A State Party shall give effect to a decision under this article as if the provisions of article 109 were applicable to this article.

6. Nothing in this article shall be interpreted as prejudicing the rights of victims under national or international law.

Article 76
Sentencing

1. In the event of a conviction, the Trial Chamber shall consider the appropriate sentence to be imposed and shall take into account the evidence presented and submissions made during the trial that are relevant to the sentence.

2. Except where article 65 applies and before the completion of the trial, the Trial Chamber may on its own motion and shall, at the request of the Prosecutor or the accused, hold a further hearing to hear any additional evidence or submissions relevant to the sentence, in accordance with the Rules of Procedure and Evidence.

3. Where paragraph 2 applies, any representations under article 75 shall be heard during the further hearing referred to in paragraph 2 and, if necessary, during any additional hearing.

4. The sentence shall be pronounced in public and, wherever possible, in the presence of the accused.

PART 7. PENALTIES

Article 77
Applicable penalties

1. Subject to article 110, the Court may impose one of the following penalties on a person convicted of a crime referred to in article 5 of this Statute:

   (a) Imprisonment for a specified number of years, which may not exceed a maximum of 30 years; or

   (b) A term of life imprisonment when justified by the extreme gravity of the crime and the individual circumstances of the convicted person.

2. In addition to imprisonment, the Court may order:

   (a) A fine under the criteria provided for in the Rules of Procedure and Evidence;

   (b) A forfeiture of proceeds, property and assets derived directly or indirectly from that crime, without prejudice to the rights of bona fide third parties.

Article 78
Determination of the sentence

1. In determining the sentence, the Court shall, in accordance with the Rules of Procedure and Evidence, take into account such factors as the gravity of the crime and the individual circumstances of the convicted person.

2. In imposing a sentence of imprisonment, the Court shall deduct the time, if any, previously spent in detention in accordance with an order of the Court. The Court may deduct any time otherwise spent in detention in connection with conduct underlying the crime.

3. When a person has been convicted of more than one crime, the Court shall pronounce a sentence for each crime and a joint sentence specifying the total period of

16

imprisonment. This period shall be no less than the highest individual sentence pronounced and shall not exceed 30 years imprisonment or a sentence of life imprisonment in conformity with article 77, paragraph 1(b).

Article 79
Trust Fund

1. A Trust Fund shall be established by decision of the Assembly of States Parties for the benefit of victims of crimes within the jurisdiction of the Court, and of the families of such victims.
2. The Court may order money and other property collected through fines or forfeiture to be transferred, by order of the Court, to the Trust Fund.
3. The Trust Fund shall be managed according to criteria to be determined by the Assembly of States Parties.

Article 80
Non-prejudice to national application of penalties and national laws

Nothing in this Part affects the application by States of penalties prescribed by their national law, nor the law of States which do not provide for penalties prescribed in this Part.

PART 8. APPEAL AND REVISION

Article 81
Appeal against decision of acquittal or conviction or against sentence

1. A decision under article 74 may be appealed in accordance with the Rules of Procedure and Evidence as follows:
   (a) The Prosecutor may make an appeal on any of the following grounds:
       (i) Procedural error,
       (ii) Error of fact, or
       (iii) Error of law;
   (b) The convicted person, or the Prosecutor on that person's behalf, may make an appeal on any of the following grounds:
       (i) Procedural error,
       (ii) Error of fact,
       (iii) Error of law, or
       (iv) Any other ground that affects the fairness or reliability of the proceedings or decision.
2.
   (a) A sentence may be appealed, in accordance with the Rules of Procedure and Evidence, by the Prosecutor or the convicted person on the ground of disproportion between the crime and the sentence;
   (b) If on an appeal against sentence the Court considers that there are grounds on which the conviction might be set aside, wholly or in part, it may invite the Prosecutor and the convicted person to submit grounds under article 81, paragraph 1(a) or (b), and may render a decision on conviction in accordance with article 83;
   (c) The same procedure applies when the Court, on an appeal against conviction only, considers that there are grounds to reduce the sentence under paragraph 2(a).

3.
    (a) Unless the Trial Chamber orders otherwise, a convicted person shall remain in custody pending an appeal;

    (b) When a convicted person's time in custody exceeds the sentence of imprisonment imposed, that person shall be released, except that if the Prosecutor is also appealing, the release may be subject to the conditions under subparagraph (c) below;

    (c) In case of an acquittal, the accused shall be released immediately, subject to the following:

        (i) Under exceptional circumstances, and having regard, *inter alia*, to the concrete risk of flight, the seriousness of the offence charged and the probability of success on appeal, the Trial Chamber, at the request of the Prosecutor, may maintain the detention of the person pending appeal;

        (ii) A decision by the Trial Chamber under subparagraph (c)(i) may be appealed in accordance with the Rules of Procedure and Evidence.

4. Subject to the provisions of paragraph 3(a) and (b), execution of the decision or sentence shall be suspended during the period allowed for appeal and for the duration of the appeal proceedings.

Article 82
Appeal against other decisions

1. Either party may appeal any of the following decisions in accordance with the Rules of Procedure and Evidence:

    (a) A decision with respect to jurisdiction or admissibility;

    (b) A decision granting or denying release of the person being investigated or prosecuted;

    (c) A decision of the Pre-Trial Chamber to act on its own initiative under article 56, paragraph 3;

    (d) A decision that involves an issue that would significantly affect the fair and expeditious conduct of the proceedings or the outcome of the trial, and for which, in the opinion of the Pre-Trial or Trial Chamber, an immediate resolution by the Appeals Chamber may materially advance the proceedings.

2. A decision of the Pre-Trial Chamber under article 57, paragraph 3(d), may be appealed against by the State concerned or by the Prosecutor, with the leave of the Pre-Trial Chamber. The appeal shall be heard on an expedited basis.

3. An appeal shall not of itself have suspensive effect unless the Appeals Chamber so orders, upon request, in accordance with the Rules of Procedure and Evidence.

4. A legal representative of the victims, the convicted person or a bona fide owner of property adversely affected by an order under article 75 may appeal against the order for reparations, as provided in the Rules of Procedure and Evidence.

Article 83
Proceedings on appeal

1. For the purposes of proceedings under article 81 and this article, the Appeals Chamber shall have all the powers of the Trial Chamber.

2. If the Appeals Chamber finds that the proceedings appealed from were unfair in a way that affected the reliability of the decision or sentence, or that the decision or sentence appealed from was materially affected by error of fact or law or procedural error, it may:

(a) Reverse or amend the decision or sentence; or

(b) Order a new trial before a different Trial Chamber.

For these purposes, the Appeals Chamber may remand a factual issue to the original Trial Chamber for it to determine the issue and to report back accordingly, or may itself call evidence to determine the issue. When the decision or sentence has been appealed only by the person convicted, or the Prosecutor on that person's behalf, it cannot be amended to his or her detriment.

3. If in an appeal against sentence the Appeals Chamber finds that the sentence is disproportionate to the crime, it may vary the sentence in accordance with Part 7.

4. The judgement of the Appeals Chamber shall be taken by a majority of the judges and shall be delivered in open court. The judgement shall state the reasons on which it is based. When there is no unanimity, the judgement of the Appeals Chamber shall contain the views of the majority and the minority, but a judge may deliver a separate or dissenting opinion on a question of law.

5. The Appeals Chamber may deliver its judgement in the absence of the person acquitted or convicted.

Article 84
Revision of conviction or sentence

1. The convicted person or, after death, spouses, children, parents or one person alive at the time of the accused's death who has been given express written instructions from the accused to bring such a claim, or the Prosecutor on the person's behalf, may apply to the Appeals Chamber to revise the final judgement of conviction or sentence on the grounds that:

(a) New evidence has been discovered that:

   (i) Was not available at the time of trial, and such unavailability was not wholly or partially attributable to the party making application; and

   (ii) Is sufficiently important that had it been proved at trial it would have been likely to have resulted in a different verdict;

(b) It has been newly discovered that decisive evidence, taken into account at trial and upon which the conviction depends, was false, forged or falsified;

(c) One or more of the judges who participated in conviction or confirmation of the charges has committed, in that case, an act of serious misconduct or serious breach of duty of sufficient gravity to justify the removal of that judge or those judges from office under article 46.

2. The Appeals Chamber shall reject the application if it considers it to be unfounded. If it determines that the application is meritorious, it may, as appropriate:

(a) Reconvene the original Trial Chamber;

(b) Constitute a new Trial Chamber; or

(c) Retain jurisdiction over the matter,

with a view to, after hearing the parties in the manner set forth in the Rules of Procedure and Evidence, arriving at a determination on whether the judgement should be revised.

Article 85
Compensation to an arrested or convicted person

1. Anyone who has been the victim of unlawful arrest or detention shall have an enforceable right to compensation.
2. When a person has by a final decision been convicted of a criminal offence, and when subsequently his or her conviction has been reversed on the ground that a new or newly discovered fact shows conclusively that there has been a miscarriage of justice, the person who has suffered punishment as a result of such conviction shall be compensated according to law, unless it is proved that the non-disclosure of the unknown fact in time is wholly or partly attributable to him or her.
3. In exceptional circumstances, where the Court finds conclusive facts showing that there has been a grave and manifest miscarriage of justice, it may in its discretion award compensation, according to the criteria provided in the Rules of Procedure and Evidence, to a person who has been released from detention following a final decision of acquittal or a termination of the proceedings for that reason.

PART 9. INTERNATIONAL COOPERATION AND JUDICIAL ASSISTANCE

Article 86
General obligation to cooperate

States Parties shall, in accordance with the provisions of this Statute, cooperate fully with the Court in its investigation and prosecution of crimes within the jurisdiction of the Court.

Article 87
Requests for cooperation: general provisions

1.
   (a) The Court shall have the authority to make requests to States Parties for cooperation. The requests shall be transmitted through the diplomatic channel or any other appropriate channel as may be designated by each State Party upon ratification, acceptance, approval or accession.
   Subsequent changes to the designation shall be made by each State Party in accordance with the Rules of Procedure and Evidence.
   (b) When appropriate, without prejudice to the provisions of subparagraph (a), requests may also be transmitted through the International Criminal Police Organization or any appropriate regional organization.
2. Requests for cooperation and any documents supporting the request shall either be in or be accompanied by a translation into an official language of the requested State or one of the working languages of the Court, in accordance with the choice made by that State upon ratification, acceptance, approval or accession.
   Subsequent changes to this choice shall be made in accordance with the Rules of Procedure and Evidence.
3. The requested State shall keep confidential a request for cooperation and any documents supporting the request, except to the extent that the disclosure is necessary for execution of the request.
4. In relation to any request for assistance presented under this Part, the Court may take such measures, including measures related to the protection of information, as may be

necessary to ensure the safety or physical or psychological well-being of any victims, potential witnesses and their families. The Court may request that any information that is made available under this Part shall be provided and handled in a manner that protects the safety and physical or psychological well-being of any victims, potential witnesses and their families.

5.

    (a) The Court may invite any State not party to this Statute to provide assistance under this Part on the basis of an *ad hoc* arrangement, an agreement with such State or any other appropriate basis.

    (b) Where a State not party to this Statute, which has entered into an *ad hoc* arrangement or an agreement with the Court, fails to cooperate with requests pursuant to any such arrangement or agreement, the Court may so inform the Assembly of States Parties or, where the Security Council referred the matter to the Court, the Security Council.

6. The Court may ask any intergovernmental organization to provide information or documents. The Court may also ask for other forms of cooperation and assistance which may be agreed upon with such an organization and which are in accordance with its competence or mandate.

7. Where a State Party fails to comply with a request to cooperate by the Court contrary to the provisions of this Statute, thereby preventing the Court from exercising its functions and powers under this Statute, the Court may make a finding to that effect and refer the matter to the Assembly of States Parties or, where the Security Council referred the matter to the Court, to the Security Council.

Article 88
Availability of procedures under national law

States Parties shall ensure that there are procedures available under their national law for all of the forms of cooperation which are specified under this Part.

Article 89
Surrender of persons to the Court

1. The Court may transmit a request for the arrest and surrender of a person, together with the material supporting the request outlined in article 91, to any State on the territory of which that person may be found and shall request the cooperation of that State in the arrest and surrender of such a person. States Parties shall, in accordance with the provisions of this Part and the procedure under their national law, comply with requests for arrest and surrender.

2. Where the person sought for surrender brings a challenge before a national court on the basis of the principle of *ne bis in idem* as provided in article 20, the requested State shall immediately consult with the Court to determine if there has been a relevant ruling on admissibility. If the case is admissible, the requested State shall proceed with the execution of the request. If an admissibility ruling is pending, the requested State may postpone the execution of the request for surrender of the person until the Court makes a determination on admissibility.

3.

    (a) A State Party shall authorize, in accordance with its national procedural law, transportation through its territory of a person being surrendered to the Court by another State, except where transit through that State would impede or delay the surrender.

(b) A request by the Court for transit shall be transmitted in accordance with article 87. The request for transit shall contain:

    (i) A description of the person being transported;

    (ii) A brief statement of the facts of the case and their legal characterization; and

    (iii) The warrant for arrest and surrender;

(c) A person being transported shall be detained in custody during the period of transit;

(d) No authorization is required if the person is transported by air and no landing is scheduled on the territory of the transit State;

(e) If an unscheduled landing occurs on the territory of the transit State, that State may require a request for transit from the Court as provided for in subparagraph (b). The transit State shall detain the person being transported until the request for transit is received and the transit is effected, provided that detention for purposes of this subparagraph may not be extended beyond 96 hours from the unscheduled landing unless the request is received within that time.

4. If the person sought is being proceeded against or is serving a sentence in the requested State for a crime different from that for which surrender to the Court is sought, the requested State, after making its decision to grant the request, shall consult with the Court.

Article 90
Competing requests

1. A State Party which receives a request from the Court for the surrender of a person under article 89 shall, if it also receives a request from any other State for the extradition of the same person for the same conduct which forms the basis of the crime for which the Court seeks the person's surrender, notify the Court and the requesting State of that fact.

2. Where the requesting State is a State Party, the requested State shall give priority to the request from the Court if:

(a) The Court has, pursuant to article 18 or 19, made a determination that the case in respect of which surrender is sought is admissible and that determination takes into account the investigation or prosecution conducted by the requesting State in respect of its request for extradition; or

(b) The Court makes the determination described in subparagraph (a) pursuant to the requested State's notification under paragraph 1.

3. Where a determination under paragraph 2(a) has not been made, the requested State may, at its discretion, pending the determination of the Court under paragraph 2(b), proceed to deal with the request for extradition from the requesting State but shall not extradite the person until the Court has determined that the case is inadmissible. The Court's determination shall be made on an expedited basis.

4. If the requesting State is a State not Party to this Statute the requested State, if it is not under an international obligation to extradite the person to the requesting State, shall give priority to the request for surrender from the Court, if the Court has determined that the case is admissible.

16

5. Where a case under paragraph 4 has not been determined to be admissible by the Court, the requested State may, at its discretion, proceed to deal with the request for extradition from the requesting State.

6. In cases where paragraph 4 applies except that the requested State is under an existing international obligation to extradite the person to the requesting State not Party to this Statute, the requested State shall determine whether to surrender the person to the Court or extradite the person to the requesting State. In making its decision, the requested State shall consider all the relevant factors, including but not limited to:

   (a) The respective dates of the requests;

   (b) The interests of the requesting State including, where relevant, whether the crime was committed in its territory and the nationality of the victims and of the person sought; and

   (c) The possibility of subsequent surrender between the Court and the requesting State.

7. Where a State Party which receives a request from the Court for the surrender of a person also receives a request from any State for the extradition of the same person for conduct other than that which constitutes the crime for which the Court seeks the person's surrender:

   (a) The requested State shall, if it is not under an existing international obligation to extradite the person to the requesting State, give priority to the request from the Court;

   (b) The requested State shall, if it is under an existing international obligation to extradite the person to the requesting State, determine whether to surrender the person to the Court or to extradite the person to the requesting State. In making its decision, the requested State shall consider all the relevant factors, including but not limited to those set out in paragraph 6, but shall give special consideration to the relative nature and gravity of the conduct in question.

8. Where pursuant to a notification under this article, the Court has determined a case to be inadmissible, and subsequently extradition to the requesting State is refused, the requested State shall notify the Court of this decision.

Article 91
Contents of request for arrest and surrender

1. A request for arrest and surrender shall be made in writing. In urgent cases, a request may be made by any medium capable of delivering a written record, provided that the request shall be confirmed through the channel provided for in article 87, paragraph 1(a).

2. In the case of a request for the arrest and surrender of a person for whom a warrant of arrest has been issued by the Pre-Trial Chamber under article 58, the request shall contain or be supported by:

   (a) Information describing the person sought, sufficient to identify the person, and information as to that person's probable location;

   (b) A copy of the warrant of arrest; and

   (c) Such documents, statements or information as may be necessary to meet the requirements for the surrender process in the requested State, except that those requirements should not be more burdensome than those applicable to requests for extradition pursuant to treaties or arrangements between the requested State and other States and should, if possible, be less burdensome, taking into account the distinct nature of the Court.

3. In the case of a request for the arrest and surrender of a person already convicted, the request shall contain or be supported by:

(a) A copy of any warrant of arrest for that person;

(b) A copy of the judgement of conviction;

(c) Information to demonstrate that the person sought is the one referred to in the judgement of conviction; and

(d) If the person sought has been sentenced, a copy of the sentence imposed and, in the case of a sentence for imprisonment, a statement of any time already served and the time remaining to be served.

4. Upon the request of the Court, a State Party shall consult with the Court, either generally or with respect to a specific matter, regarding any requirements under its national law that may apply under paragraph 2(c). During the consultations, the State Party shall advise the Court of the specific requirements of its national law.

Article 92
Provisional arrest

1. In urgent cases, the Court may request the provisional arrest of the person sought, pending presentation of the request for surrender and the documents supporting the request as specified in article 91.

2. The request for provisional arrest shall be made by any medium capable of delivering a written record and shall contain:

(a) Information describing the person sought, sufficient to identify the person, and information as to that person's probable location;

(b) A concise statement of the crimes for which the person's arrest is sought and of the facts which are alleged to constitute those crimes, including, where possible, the date and location of the crime;

(c) A statement of the existence of a warrant of arrest or a judgement of conviction against the person sought; and

(d) A statement that a request for surrender of the person sought will follow.

3. A person who is provisionally arrested may be released from custody if the requested State has not received the request for surrender and the documents supporting the request as specified in article 91 within the time limits specified in the Rules of Procedure and Evidence. However, the person may consent to surrender before the expiration of this period if permitted by the law of the requested State. In such a case, the requested State shall proceed to surrender the person to the Court as soon as possible.

4. The fact that the person sought has been released from custody pursuant to paragraph 3 shall not prejudice the subsequent arrest and surrender of that person if the request for surrender and the documents supporting the request are delivered at a later date.

Article 93
Other forms of cooperation

1. States Parties shall, in accordance with the provisions of this Part and under procedures of national law, comply with requests by the Court to provide the following assistance in relation to investigations or prosecutions:

(a) The identification and whereabouts of persons or the location of items;

    (b) The taking of evidence, including testimony under oath, and the production of evidence, including expert opinions and reports necessary to the Court;

    (c) The questioning of any person being investigated or prosecuted;

    (d) The service of documents, including judicial documents;

    (e) Facilitating the voluntary appearance of persons as witnesses or experts before the Court;

    (f) The temporary transfer of persons as provided in paragraph 7;

    (g) The examination of places or sites, including the exhumation and examination of grave sites;

    (h) The execution of searches and seizures;

    (i) The provision of records and documents, including official records and documents;

    (j) The protection of victims and witnesses and the preservation of evidence;

    (k) The identification, tracing and freezing or seizure of proceeds, property and assets and instrumentalities of crimes for the purpose of eventual forfeiture, without prejudice to the rights of bona fide third parties; and

    (l) Any other type of assistance which is not prohibited by the law of the requested State, with a view to facilitating the investigation and prosecution of crimes within the jurisdiction of the Court.

2. The Court shall have the authority to provide an assurance to a witness or an expert appearing before the Court that he or she will not be prosecuted, detained or subjected to any restriction of personal freedom by the Court in respect of any act or omission that preceded the departure of that person from the requested State.

3. Where execution of a particular measure of assistance detailed in a request presented under paragraph 1, is prohibited in the requested State on the basis of an existing fundamental legal principle of general application, the requested State shall promptly consult with the Court to try to resolve the matter. In the consultations, consideration should be given to whether the assistance can be rendered in another manner or subject to conditions. If after consultations the matter cannot be resolved, the Court shall modify the request as necessary.

4. In accordance with article 72, a State Party may deny a request for assistance, in whole or in part, only if the request concerns the production of any documents or disclosure of evidence which relates to its national security.

5. Before denying a request for assistance under paragraph 1(l), the requested State shall consider whether the assistance can be provided subject to specified conditions, or whether the assistance can be provided at a later date or in an alternative manner, provided that if the Court or the Prosecutor accepts the assistance subject to conditions, the Court or the Prosecutor shall abide by them.

6. If a request for assistance is denied, the requested State Party shall promptly inform the Court or the Prosecutor of the reasons for such denial.

7.

    (a) The Court may request the temporary transfer of a person in custody for purposes of identification or for obtaining testimony or other assistance. The person may be transferred if the following conditions are fulfilled:

       (i) The person freely gives his or her informed consent to the transfer; and

       (ii) The requested State agrees to the transfer, subject to such conditions as that State and the Court may agree.

(b) The person being transferred shall remain in custody. When the purposes of the transfer have been fulfilled, the Court shall return the person without delay to the requested State.

8.

    (a) The Court shall ensure the confidentiality of documents and information, except as required for the investigation and proceedings described in the request.

    (b) The requested State may, when necessary, transmit documents or information to the Prosecutor on a confidential basis. The Prosecutor may then use them solely for the purpose of generating new evidence.

    (c) The requested State may, on its own motion or at the request of the Prosecutor, subsequently consent to the disclosure of such documents or information. They may then be used as evidence pursuant to the provisions of Parts 5 and 6 and in accordance with the Rules of Procedure and Evidence.

9.

    (a)

      (i) In the event that a State Party receives competing requests, other than for surrender or extradition, from the Court and from another State pursuant to an international obligation, the State Party shall endeavour, in consultation with the Court and the other State, to meet both requests, if necessary by postponing or attaching conditions to one or the other request.

      (ii) Failing that, competing requests shall be resolved in accordance with the principles established in article 90.

    (b) Where, however, the request from the Court concerns information, property or persons which are subject to the control of a third State or an international organization by virtue of an international agreement, the requested States shall so inform the Court and the Court shall direct its request to the third State or international organization.

10.

    (a) The Court may, upon request, cooperate with and provide assistance to a State Party conducting an investigation into or trial in respect of conduct which constitutes a crime within the jurisdiction of the Court or which constitutes a serious crime under the national law of the requesting State.

    (b)

      (i) The assistance provided under subparagraph (a) shall include, *inter alia*:

        a. The transmission of statements, documents or other types of evidence obtained in the course of an investigation or a trial conducted by the Court; and

        b. The questioning of any person detained by order of the Court;

      (ii) In the case of assistance under subparagraph (b)(i) a:

        a. If the documents or other types of evidence have been obtained with the assistance of a State, such transmission shall require the consent of that State;

        b. If the statements, documents or other types of evidence have been provided by a witness or expert, such transmission shall be subject to the provisions of article 68.

    (c) The Court may, under the conditions set out in this paragraph, grant a request for assistance under this paragraph from a State which is not a Party to this Statute.

Article 94
Postponement of execution of a request in respect of ongoing investigation or prosecution

1. If the immediate execution of a request would interfere with an ongoing investigation or prosecution of a case different from that to which the request relates, the requested State may postpone the execution of the request for a period of time agreed upon with the Court. However, the postponement shall be no longer than is necessary to complete the relevant investigation or prosecution in the requested State. Before making a decision to postpone, the requested State should consider whether the assistance may be immediately provided subject to certain conditions.
2. If a decision to postpone is taken pursuant to paragraph 1, the Prosecutor may, however, seek measures to preserve evidence, pursuant to article 93, paragraph 1(j).

Article 95
Postponement of execution of a request in respect of an admissibility challenge

Where there is an admissibility challenge under consideration by the Court pursuant to article 18 or 19, the requested State may postpone the execution of a request under this Part pending a determination by the Court, unless the Court has specifically ordered that the Prosecutor may pursue the collection of such evidence pursuant to article 18 or 19.

Article 96
Contents of request for other forms of assistance under article 93

1. A request for other forms of assistance referred to in article 93 shall be made in writing. In urgent cases, a request may be made by any medium capable of delivering a written record, provided that the request shall be confirmed through the channel provided for in article 87, paragraph 1(a).
2. The request shall, as applicable, contain or be supported by the following:
   (a) A concise statement of the purpose of the request and the assistance sought, including the legal basis and the grounds for the request;
   (b) As much detailed information as possible about the location or identification of any person or place that must be found or identified in order for the assistance sought to be provided;
   (c) A concise statement of the essential facts underlying the request;
   (d) The reasons for and details of any procedure or requirement to be followed;
   (e) Such information as may be required under the law of the requested State in order to execute the request; and
   (f) Any other information relevant in order for the assistance sought to be provided.
3. Upon the request of the Court, a State Party shall consult with the Court, either generally or with respect to a specific matter, regarding any requirements under its national law that may apply under paragraph 2(e). During the consultations, the State Party shall advise the Court of the specific requirements of its national law.
4. The provisions of this article shall, where applicable, also apply in respect of a request for assistance made to the Court.

Article 97
Consultations

Where a State Party receives a request under this Part in relation to which it identifies problems which may impede or prevent the execution of the request, that State shall consult with the Court without delay in order to resolve the matter. Such problems may include, *inter alia*:

(a) Insufficient information to execute the request;
(b) In the case of a request for surrender, the fact that despite best efforts, the person sought cannot be located or that the investigation conducted has determined that the person in the requested State is clearly not the person named in the warrant; or
(c) The fact that execution of the request in its current form would require the requested State to breach a pre-existing treaty obligation undertaken with respect to another State.

Article 98
Cooperation with respect to waiver of immunity and consent to surrender

1. The Court may not proceed with a request for surrender or assistance which would require the requested State to act inconsistently with its obligations under international law with respect to the State or diplomatic immunity of a person or property of a third State, unless the Court can first obtain the cooperation of that third State for the waiver of the immunity.
2. The Court may not proceed with a request for surrender which would require the requested State to act inconsistently with its obligations under international agreements pursuant to which the consent of a sending State is required to surrender a person of that State to the Court, unless the Court can first obtain the cooperation of the sending State for the giving of consent for the surrender.

Article 99
Execution of requests under articles 93 and 96

1. Requests for assistance shall be executed in accordance with the relevant procedure under the law of the requested State and, unless prohibited by such law, in the manner specified in the request, including following any procedure outlined therein or permitting persons specified in the request to be present at and assist in the execution process.
2. In the case of an urgent request, the documents or evidence produced in response shall, at the request of the Court, be sent urgently.
3. Replies from the requested State shall be transmitted in their original language and form.
4. Without prejudice to other articles in this Part, where it is necessary for the successful execution of a request which can be executed without any compulsory measures, including specifically the interview of or taking evidence from a person on a voluntary basis, including doing so without the presence of the authorities of the requested State Party if it is essential for the request to be executed, and the examination without modification of a public site or other public place, the Prosecutor may execute such request directly on the territory of a State as follows:

(a) When the State Party requested is a State on the territory of which the crime is alleged to have been committed, and there has been a determination of admissibility pursuant to article 18 or 19, the Prosecutor may directly execute such request following all possible consultations with the requested State Party;

(b) In other cases, the Prosecutor may execute such request following consultations with the requested State Party and subject to any reasonable conditions or concerns raised by that State Party. Where the requested State Party identifies problems with the execution of a request pursuant to this subparagraph it shall, without delay, consult with the Court to resolve the matter.

5. Provisions allowing a person heard or examined by the Court under article 72 to invoke restrictions designed to prevent disclosure of confidential information connected with national security shall also apply to the execution of requests for assistance under this article.

Article 100
Costs

1. The ordinary costs for execution of requests in the territory of the requested State shall be borne by that State, except for the following, which shall be borne by the Court:

    (a) Costs associated with the travel and security of witnesses and experts or the transfer under article 93 of persons in custody;

    (b) Costs of translation, interpretation and transcription;

    (c) Travel and subsistence costs of the judges, the Prosecutor, the Deputy Prosecutors, the Registrar, the Deputy Registrar and staff of any organ of the Court;

    (d) Costs of any expert opinion or report requested by the Court;

    (e) Costs associated with the transport of a person being surrendered to the Court by a custodial State; and

    (f) Following consultations, any extraordinary costs that may result from the execution of a request.

2. The provisions of paragraph 1 shall, as appropriate, apply to requests from States Parties to the Court. In that case, the Court shall bear the ordinary costs of execution.

Article 101
Rule of speciality

1. A person surrendered to the Court under this Statute shall not be proceeded against, punished or detained for any conduct committed prior to surrender, other than the conduct or course of conduct which forms the basis of the crimes for which that person has been surrendered.

2. The Court may request a waiver of the requirements of paragraph 1 from the State which surrendered the person to the Court and, if necessary, the Court shall provide additional information in accordance with article 91. States Parties shall have the authority to provide a waiver to the Court and should endeavour to do so.

Article 102
Use of terms

For the purposes of this Statute:

(a) "surrender" means the delivering up of a person by a State to the Court, pursuant to this Statute.

(b) "extradition" means the delivering up of a person by one State to another as provided by treaty, convention or national legislation.

PART 10. ENFORCEMENT

Article 103
Role of States in enforcement of sentences of imprisonment

1.
(a) A sentence of imprisonment shall be served in a State designated by the Court from a list of States which have indicated to the Court their willingness to accept sentenced persons.

(b) At the time of declaring its willingness to accept sentenced persons, a State may attach conditions to its acceptance as agreed by the Court and in accordance with this Part.

(c) A State designated in a particular case shall promptly inform the Court whether it accepts the Court's designation.

2.
(a) The State of enforcement shall notify the Court of any circumstances, including the exercise of any conditions agreed under paragraph 1, which could materially affect the terms or extent of the imprisonment. The Court shall be given at least 45 days' notice of any such known or foreseeable circumstances. During this period, the State of enforcement shall take no action that might prejudice its obligations under article 110.

(b) Where the Court cannot agree to the circumstances referred to in subparagraph (a), it shall notify the State of enforcement and proceed in accordance with article 104, paragraph 1.

3. In exercising its discretion to make a designation under paragraph 1, the Court shall take into account the following:

(a) The principle that States Parties should share the responsibility for enforcing sentences of imprisonment, in accordance with principles of equitable distribution, as provided in the Rules of Procedure and Evidence;

(b) The application of widely accepted international treaty standards governing the treatment of prisoners;

(c) The views of the sentenced person;

(d) The nationality of the sentenced person;

(e) Such other factors regarding the circumstances of the crime or the person sentenced, or the effective enforcement of the sentence, as may be appropriate in designating the State of enforcement.

4. If no State is designated under paragraph 1, the sentence of imprisonment shall be served in a prison facility made available by the host State, in accordance with the conditions set out in the headquarters agreement referred to in article 3, paragraph 2. In such a case, the costs arising out of the enforcement of a sentence of imprisonment shall be borne by the Court.

Article 104
Change in designation of State of enforcement

1. The Court may, at any time, decide to transfer a sentenced person to a prison of another State.
2. A sentenced person may, at any time, apply to the Court to be transferred from the State of enforcement.

Article 105
Enforcement of the sentence

1. Subject to conditions which a State may have specified in accordance with article 103, paragraph 1(b), the sentence of imprisonment shall be binding on the States Parties, which shall in no case modify it.
2. The Court alone shall have the right to decide any application for appeal and revision. The State of enforcement shall not impede the making of any such application by a sentenced person.

Article 106
Supervision of enforcement of sentences and conditions of imprisonment

1. The enforcement of a sentence of imprisonment shall be subject to the supervision of the Court and shall be consistent with widely accepted international treaty standards governing treatment of prisoners.
2. The conditions of imprisonment shall be governed by the law of the State of enforcement and shall be consistent with widely accepted international treaty standards governing treatment of prisoners; in no case shall such conditions be more or less favourable than those available to prisoners convicted of similar offences in the State of enforcement.
3. Communications between a sentenced person and the Court shall be unimpeded and confidential.

Article 107
Transfer of the person upon completion of sentence

1. Following completion of the sentence, a person who is not a national of the State of enforcement may, in accordance with the law of the State of enforcement, be transferred to a State which is obliged to receive him or her, or to another State which agrees to receive him or her, taking into account any wishes of the person to be transferred to that State, unless the State of enforcement authorizes the person to remain in its territory.
2. If no State bears the costs arising out of transferring the person to another State pursuant to paragraph 1, such costs shall be borne by the Court.
3. Subject to the provisions of article 108, the State of enforcement may also, in accordance with its national law, extradite or otherwise surrender the person to a State which has requested the extradition or surrender of the person for purposes of trial or enforcement of a sentence.

Article 108
Limitation on the prosecution or punishment of other offences

1. A sentenced person in the custody of the State of enforcement shall not be subject to prosecution or punishment or to extradition to a third State for any conduct engaged

in prior to that person's delivery to the State of enforcement, unless such prosecution, punishment or extradition has been approved by the Court at the request of the State of enforcement.

2. The Court shall decide the matter after having heard the views of the sentenced person.

3. Paragraph 1 shall cease to apply if the sentenced person remains voluntarily for more than 30 days in the territory of the State of enforcement after having served the full sentence imposed by the Court, or returns to the territory of that State after having left it.

Article 109
Enforcement of fines and forfeiture measures

1. States Parties shall give effect to fines or forfeitures ordered by the Court under Part 7, without prejudice to the rights of bona fide third parties, and in accordance with the procedure of their national law.

2. If a State Party is unable to give effect to an order for forfeiture, it shall take measures to recover the value of the proceeds, property or assets ordered by the Court to be forfeited, without prejudice to the rights of bona fide third parties.

3. Property, or the proceeds of the sale of real property or, where appropriate, the sale of other property, which is obtained by a State Party as a result of its enforcement of a judgement of the Court shall be transferred to the Court.

Article 110
Review by the Court concerning reduction of sentence

1. The State of enforcement shall not release the person before expiry of the sentence pronounced by the Court.

2. The Court alone shall have the right to decide any reduction of sentence, and shall rule on the matter after having heard the person.

3. When the person has served two thirds of the sentence, or 25 years in the case of life imprisonment, the Court shall review the sentence to determine whether it should be reduced. Such a review shall not be conducted before that time.

4. In its review under paragraph 3, the Court may reduce the sentence if it finds that one or more of the following factors are present:

   (a) The early and continuing willingness of the person to cooperate with the Court in its investigations and prosecutions;

   (b) The voluntary assistance of the person in enabling the enforcement of the judgements and orders of the Court in other cases, and in particular providing assistance in locating assets subject to orders of fine, forfeiture or reparation which may be used for the benefit of victims; or

   (c) Other factors establishing a clear and significant change of circumstances sufficient to justify the reduction of sentence, as provided in the Rules of Procedure and Evidence.

5. If the Court determines in its initial review under paragraph 3 that it is not appropriate to reduce the sentence, it shall thereafter review the question of reduction of sentence at such intervals and applying such criteria as provided for in the Rules of Procedure and Evidence.

16

Article 111
Escape

If a convicted person escapes from custody and flees the State of enforcement, that State may, after consultation with the Court, request the person's surrender from the State in which the person is located pursuant to existing bilateral or multilateral arrangements, or may request that the Court seek the person's surrender, in accordance with Part 9. It may direct that the person be delivered to the State in which he or she was serving the sentence or to another State designated by the Court.

PART 11. ASSEMBLY OF STATES PARTIES

Article 112
Assembly of States Parties

1. An Assembly of States Parties to this Statute is hereby established. Each State Party shall have one representative in the Assembly who may be accompanied by alternates and advisers. Other States which have signed this Statute or the Final Act may be observers in the Assembly.

2. The Assembly shall:
   (a) Consider and adopt, as appropriate, recommendations of the Preparatory Commission;
   (b) Provide management oversight to the Presidency, the Prosecutor and the Registrar regarding the administration of the Court;
   (c) Consider the reports and activities of the Bureau established under paragraph 3 and take appropriate action in regard thereto;
   (d) Consider and decide the budget for the Court;
   (e) Decide whether to alter, in accordance with article 36, the number of judges;
   (f) Consider pursuant to article 87, paragraphs 5 and 7, any question relating to non-cooperation;
   (g) Perform any other function consistent with this Statute or the Rules of Procedure and Evidence.

3.
   (a) The Assembly shall have a Bureau consisting of a President, two Vice-Presidents and 18 members elected by the Assembly for three-year terms.
   (b) The Bureau shall have a representative character, taking into account, in particular, equitable geographical distribution and the adequate representation of the principal legal systems of the world.
   (c) The Bureau shall meet as often as necessary, but at least once a year. It shall assist the Assembly in the discharge of its responsibilities.

4. The Assembly may establish such subsidiary bodies as may be necessary, including an independent oversight mechanism for inspection, evaluation and investigation of the Court, in order to enhance its efficiency and economy.

5. The President of the Court, the Prosecutor and the Registrar or their representatives may participate, as appropriate, in meetings of the Assembly and of the Bureau.

6. The Assembly shall meet at the seat of the Court or at the Headquarters of the United Nations once a year and, when circumstances so require, hold special sessions. Except as otherwise specified in this Statute, special sessions shall be convened by the Bureau on its own initiative or at the request of one third of the States Parties.

7. Each State Party shall have one vote. Every effort shall be made to reach decisions by consensus in the Assembly and in the Bureau. If consensus cannot be reached, except as otherwise provided in the Statute:

   (a) Decisions on matters of substance must be approved by a two-thirds majority of those present and voting provided that an absolute majority of States Parties constitutes the quorum for voting;

   (b) Decisions on matters of procedure shall be taken by a simple majority of States Parties present and voting.

8. A State Party which is in arrears in the payment of its financial contributions towards the costs of the Court shall have no vote in the Assembly and in the Bureau if the amount of its arrears equals or exceeds the amount of the contributions due from it for the preceding two full years. The Assembly may, nevertheless, permit such a State Party to vote in the Assembly and in the Bureau if it is satisfied that the failure to pay is due to conditions beyond the control of the State Party.

9. The Assembly shall adopt its own rules of procedure.

10. The official and working languages of the Assembly shall be those of the General Assembly of the United Nations.

PART 12. FINANCING

Article 113
Financial Regulations

Except as otherwise specifically provided, all financial matters related to the Court and the meetings of the Assembly of States Parties, including its Bureau and subsidiary bodies, shall be governed by this Statute and the Financial Regulations and Rules adopted by the Assembly of States Parties.

Article 114
Payment of expenses

Expenses of the Court and the Assembly of States Parties, including its Bureau and subsidiary bodies, shall be paid from the funds of the Court.

Article 115
Funds of the Court and of the Assembly of States Parties

The expenses of the Court and the Assembly of States Parties, including its Bureau and subsidiary bodies, as provided for in the budget decided by the Assembly of States Parties, shall be provided by the following sources:

(a) Assessed contributions made by States Parties;

(b) Funds provided by the United Nations, subject to the approval of the General Assembly, in particular in relation to the expenses incurred due to referrals by the Security Council.

Article 116
Voluntary contributions

Without prejudice to article 115, the Court may receive and utilize, as additional funds, voluntary contributions from Governments, international organizations, individuals, corporations and other entities, in accordance with relevant criteria adopted by the Assembly of States Parties.

Article 117
Assessment of contributions
The contributions of States Parties shall be assessed in accordance with an agreed scale of assessment, based on the scale adopted by the United Nations for its regular budget and adjusted in accordance with the principles on which that scale is based.

Article 118
Annual audit
The records, books and accounts of the Court, including its annual financial statements, shall be audited annually by an independent auditor.

PART 13. FINAL CLAUSES

Article 119
Settlement of disputes
1. Any dispute concerning the judicial functions of the Court shall be settled by the decision of the Court.
2. Any other dispute between two or more States Parties relating to the interpretation or application of this Statute which is not settled through negotiations within three months of their commencement shall be referred to the Assembly of States Parties. The Assembly may itself seek to settle the dispute or may make recommendations on further means of settlement of the dispute, including referral to the International Court of Justice in conformity with the Statute of that Court.

Article 120
Reservations
No reservations may be made to this Statute.

Article 121
Amendments
1. After the expiry of seven years from the entry into force of this Statute, any State Party may propose amendments thereto. The text of any proposed amendment shall be submitted to the Secretary-General of the United Nations, who shall promptly circulate it to all States Parties.
2. No sooner than three months from the date of notification, the Assembly of States Parties, at its next meeting, shall, by a majority of those present and voting, decide whether to take up the proposal. The Assembly may deal with the proposal directly or convene a Review Conference if the issue involved so warrants.
3. The adoption of an amendment at a meeting of the Assembly of States Parties or at a Review Conference on which consensus cannot be reached shall require a two-thirds majority of States Parties.
4. Except as provided in paragraph 5, an amendment shall enter into force for all States Parties one year after instruments of ratification or acceptance have been deposited with the Secretary-General of the United Nations by seven-eighths of them.
5. Any amendment to articles 5, 6, 7 and 8 of this Statute shall enter into force for those States Parties which have accepted the amendment one year after the deposit of their

instruments of ratification or acceptance. In respect of a State Party which has not accepted the amendment, the Court shall not exercise its jurisdiction regarding a crime covered by the amendment when committed by that State Party's nationals or on its territory.

6. If an amendment has been accepted by seven-eighths of States Parties in accordance with paragraph 4, any State Party which has not accepted the amendment may withdraw from this Statute with immediate effect, notwithstanding article 127, paragraph 1, but subject to article 127, paragraph 2, by giving notice no later than one year after the entry into force of such amendment.

7. The Secretary-General of the United Nations shall circulate to all States Parties any amendment adopted at a meeting of the Assembly of States Parties or at a Review Conference.

Article 122
Amendments to provisions of an institutional nature

1. Amendments to provisions of this Statute which are of an exclusively institutional nature, namely, article 35, article 36, paragraphs 8 and 9, article 37, article 38, article 39, paragraphs 1 (first two sentences), 2 and 4, article 42, paragraphs 4 to 9, article 43, paragraphs 2 and 3, and articles 44, 46, 47 and 49, may be proposed at any time, notwithstanding article 121, paragraph 1, by any State Party. The text of any proposed amendment shall be submitted to the Secretary-General of the United Nations or such other person designated by the Assembly of States Parties who shall promptly circulate it to all States Parties and to others participating in the Assembly.

2. Amendments under this article on which consensus cannot be reached shall be adopted by the Assembly of States Parties or by a Review Conference, by a two-thirds majority of States Parties. Such amendments shall enter into force for all States Parties six months after their adoption by the Assembly or, as the case may be, by the Conference.

Article 123
Review of the Statute

1. Seven years after the entry into force of this Statute the Secretary-General of the United Nations shall convene a Review Conference to consider any amendments to this Statute. Such review may include, but is not limited to, the list of crimes contained in article 5. The Conference shall be open to those participating in the Assembly of States Parties and on the same conditions.

2. At any time thereafter, at the request of a State Party and for the purposes set out in paragraph 1, the Secretary-General of the United Nations shall, upon approval by a majority of States Parties, convene a Review Conference.

3. The provisions of article 121, paragraphs 3 to 7, shall apply to the adoption and entry into force of any amendment to the Statute considered at a Review Conference.

Article 124
Transitional Provision

Notwithstanding article 12, paragraphs 1 and 2, a State, on becoming a party to this Statute, may declare that, for a period of seven years after the entry into force of this Statute for the State concerned, it does not accept the jurisdiction of the Court with

16

respect to the category of crimes referred to in article 8 when a crime is alleged to have been committed by its nationals or on its territory. A declaration under this article may be withdrawn at any time. The provisions of this article shall be reviewed at the Review Conference convened in accordance with article 123, paragraph 1.

Article 125
Signature, ratification, acceptance, approval or accession

1. This Statute shall be open for signature by all States in Rome, at the headquarters of the Food and Agriculture Organization of the United Nations, on 17 July 1998. Thereafter, it shall remain open for signature in Rome at the Ministry of Foreign Affairs of Italy until 17 October 1998. After that date, the Statute shall remain open for signature in New York, at United Nations Headquarters, until 31 December 2000.
2. This Statute is subject to ratification, acceptance or approval by signatory States. Instruments of ratification, acceptance or approval shall be deposited with the Secretary-General of the United Nations.
3. This Statute shall be open to accession by all States. Instruments of accession shall be deposited with the Secretary-General of the United Nations.

Article 126
Entry into force

1. This Statute shall enter into force on the first day of the month after the 60th day following the date of the deposit of the 60th instrument of ratification, acceptance, approval or accession with the Secretary-General of the United Nations.
2. For each State ratifying, accepting, approving or acceding to this Statute after the deposit of the 60th instrument of ratification, acceptance, approval or accession, the Statute shall enter into force on the first day of the month after the 60th day following the deposit by such State of its instrument of ratification, acceptance, approval or accession.

Article 127
Withdrawal

1. A State Party may, by written notification addressed to the Secretary-General of the United Nations, withdraw from this Statute. The withdrawal shall take effect one year after the date of receipt of the notification, unless the notification specifies a later date.
2. A State shall not be discharged, by reason of its withdrawal, from the obligations arising from this Statute while it was a Party to the Statute, including any financial obligations which may have accrued. Its withdrawal shall not affect any cooperation with the Court in connection with criminal investigations and proceedings in relation to which the withdrawing State had a duty to cooperate and which were commenced prior to the date on which the withdrawal became effective, nor shall it prejudice in any way the continued consideration of any matter which was already under consideration by the Court prior to the date on which the withdrawal became effective.

Article 128
Authentic texts

The original of this Statute, of which the Arabic, Chinese, English, French, Russian and Spanish texts are equally authentic, shall be deposited with the Secretary-General of the United Nations, who shall send certified copies thereof to all States.

Amendments to the Rome Statute (Kampala, 2010) in force for parties to them.

International Criminal Court Rules of Procedure and Evidence

CHAPTER 1. GENERAL PROVISIONS

Rule 1
Use of terms

In the present document:

(a) "article" refers to articles of the Rome Statute;

(b) "Chamber" refers to a Chamber of the Court;

(c) "Part" refers to the Parts of the Rome Statute;

(d) "Presiding Judge" refers to the Presiding Judge of a Chamber;

(e) "the President" refers to the President of the Court;

(f) "the Regulations" refers to the Regulations of the Court;

(g) "the Rules" refers to the Rules of Procedure and Evidence.

Rule 2
Authentic texts

The Rules have been adopted in the official languages of the Court established by article 50, paragraph 1. All texts are equally authentic.

Rule 3
Amendments

1. Amendments to the rules that are proposed in accordance with article 51, paragraph 2, shall be forwarded to the President of the Bureau of the Assembly of States Parties.

2. The President of the Bureau of the Assembly of States Parties shall ensure that all proposed amendments are translated into the official languages of the Court and are transmitted to the States Parties.

3. The procedure described in sub-rules 1 and 2 shall also apply to the provisional rules referred to in article 51, paragraph 3.

CHAPTER 2. COMPOSITION AND ADMINISTRATION OF THE COURT

SECTION I. GENERAL PROVISIONS RELATING TO THE COMPOSITION AND ADMINISTRATION OF THE COURT

Rule 4[1]
Plenary sessions

1. The judges shall meet in plenary session after having made their solemn undertaking, in conformity with rule 5. At that session the judges shall elect the President and Vice-Presidents.

2. The judges shall meet subsequently in plenary session at least once a year to exercise their functions under the Statute, the Rules and the Regulations and, if necessary, in

---

[1] As amended by resolution ICC-ASP/10/Res.1.

special plenary sessions convened by the President on his or her own motion or at the request of one half of the judges.

3. The quorum for each plenary session shall be two-thirds of the judges.

4. Unless otherwise provided in the Statute or the Rules, the decisions of the plenary sessions shall be taken by the majority of the judges present. In the event of an equality of votes, the President, or the judge acting in the place of the President, shall have a casting vote.

5. The Regulations shall be adopted as soon as possible in plenary sessions.

Rule 4 *bis*[2]
The Presidency

1. Pursuant to article 38, paragraph 3, the Presidency is established upon election by the plenary session of the judges.

2. As soon as possible following its establishment, the Presidency shall, after consultation with the judges, decide on the assignment of judges to divisions in accordance with article 39, paragraph 1.

Rule 5
Solemn undertaking under article 45

1. As provided in article 45, before exercising their functions under the Statute, the following solemn undertakings shall be made:

   a. In the case of a judge:

   "I solemnly undertake that I will perform my duties and exercise my powers as a judge of the International Criminal Court honourably, faithfully, impartially and conscientiously, and that I will respect the confidentiality of investigations and prosecutions and the secrecy of deliberations.";

   b. In the case of the Prosecutor, a Deputy Prosecutor, the Registrar and the Deputy Registrar of the Court:

   "I solemnly undertake that I will perform my duties and exercise my powers as (title) of the International Criminal Court honourably, faithfully, impartially and conscientiously, and that I will respect the confidentiality of investigations and prosecutions."

2. The undertaking, signed by the person making it and witnessed by the President or a Vice-President of the Bureau of the Assembly of States Parties, shall be filed with the Registry and kept in the records of the Court.

Rule 6
Solemn undertaking by the staff of the Office of the Prosecutor, the Registry, interpreters and translators

1. Upon commencing employment, every staff member of the Office of the Prosecutor and the Registry shall make the following undertaking:

   "I solemnly undertake that I will perform my duties and exercise my powers as (title) of the International Criminal Court honourably, faithfully, impartially and conscientiously, and that I will respect the confidentiality of investigations and prosecutions.";

---

[2] As amended by resolution ICC-ASP/10/Res.1

The undertaking, signed by the person making it and witnessed, as appropriate, by the Prosecutor, the Deputy Prosecutor, the Registrar or the Deputy Registrar, shall be filed with the Registry and kept in the records of the Court.

2. Before performing any duties, an interpreter or a translator shall make the following undertaking:

"I solemnly declare that I will perform my duties faithfully, impartially and with full respect for the duty of confidentiality.";

The undertaking, signed by the person making it and witnessed by the President of the Court or his or her representative, shall be filed with the Registry and kept in the records of the Court.

Rule 7

Single judge under article 39, paragraph 2(b)(iii)

1. Whenever the Pre-Trial Chamber designates a judge as a single judge in accordance with article 39, paragraph 2(b)(iii), it shall do so on the basis of objective pre-established criteria.
2. The designated judge shall make the appropriate decisions on those questions on which decision by the full Chamber is not expressly provided for in the Statute or the Rules.
3. The Pre-Trial Chamber, on its own motion or, if appropriate, at the request of a party, may decide that the functions of the single judge be exercised by the full Chamber.

Rule 8

Code of Professional Conduct

1. The Presidency, on the basis of a proposal made by the Registrar, shall draw up a draft Code of Professional Conduct for counsel, after having consulted the Prosecutor. In the preparation of the proposal, the Registrar shall conduct the consultations in accordance with rule 20, sub-rule 3.
2. The draft Code shall then be transmitted to the Assembly of States Parties, for the purpose of adoption, according to article 112, paragraph 7.
3. The Code shall contain procedures for its amendment.

SECTION II. THE OFFICE OF THE PROSECUTOR

Rule 9

Operation of the Office of the Prosecutor

In discharging his or her responsibility for the management and administration of the Office of the Prosecutor, the Prosecutor shall put in place regulations to govern the operation of the Office. In preparing or amending these regulations, the Prosecutor shall consult with the Registrar on any matters that may affect the operation of the Registry.

Rule 10

Retention of information and evidence

The Prosecutor shall be responsible for the retention, storage and security of information and physical evidence obtained in the course of the investigations by his or her Office.

Rule 11

Delegation of the Prosecutor's functions

Except for the inherent powers of the Prosecutor set forth in the Statute, *inter alia*, those described in articles 15 and 53, the Prosecutor or a Deputy Prosecutor may authorize staff members of the Office of the Prosecutor, other than those referred to in article 44, paragraph 4, to represent him or her in the exercise of his or her functions.

SECTION III. THE REGISTRY
SUBSECTION 1. *GENERAL PROVISIONS RELATING TO THE REGISTRY*

Rule 12

Qualifications and election of the Registrar and the Deputy Registrar

1. As soon as it is elected, the Presidency shall establish a list of candidates who satisfy the criteria laid down in article 43, paragraph 3, and shall transmit the list to the Assembly of States Parties with a request for any recommendations.
2. Upon receipt of any recommendations from the Assembly of States Parties, the President shall, without delay, transmit the list together with the recommendations to the plenary session.
3. As provided for in article 43, paragraph 4, the Court, meeting in plenary session, shall, as soon as possible, elect the Registrar by an absolute majority, taking into account any recommendations by the Assembly of States Parties. In the event that no candidate obtains an absolute majority on the first ballot, successive ballots shall be held until one candidate obtains an absolute majority.
4. If the need for a Deputy Registrar arises, the Registrar may make a recommendation to the President to that effect. The President shall convene a plenary session to decide on the matter. If the Court, meeting in plenary session, decides by an absolute majority that a Deputy Registrar is to be elected, the Registrar shall submit a list of candidates to the Court.
5. The Deputy Registrar shall be elected by the Court, meeting in plenary session, in the same manner as the Registrar.

Rule 13

Functions of the Registrar

1. Without prejudice to the authority of the Office of the Prosecutor under the Statute to receive, obtain and provide information and to establish channels of communication for this purpose, the Registrar shall serve as the channel of communication of the Court.
2. The Registrar shall also be responsible for the internal security of the Court in consultation with the Presidency and the Prosecutor, as well as the host State.

Rule 14

Operation of the Registry

1. In discharging his or her responsibility for the organization and management of the Registry, the Registrar shall put in place regulations to govern the operation of the Registry. In preparing or amending these regulations, the Registrar shall consult with the Prosecutor on any matters which may affect the operation of the Office of the Prosecutor. The regulations shall be approved by the Presidency.
2. The regulations shall provide for defence counsel to have access to appropriate and reasonable administrative assistance from the Registry.

Rule 15

Records

1. The Registrar shall keep a database containing all the particulars of each case brought before the Court, subject to any order of a judge or Chamber providing for the non-disclosure of any document or information, and to the protection of sensitive personal data. Information on the database shall be available to the public in the working languages of the Court.

2. The Registrar shall also maintain the other records of the Court.

SUBSECTION 2. *VICTIMS AND WITNESSES UNIT*

Rule 16

Responsibilities of the Registrar relating to victims and witnesses

1. In relation to victims, the Registrar shall be responsible for the performance of the following functions in accordance with the Statute and these Rules:

   (a) Providing notice or notification to victims or their legal representatives;

   (b) Assisting them in obtaining legal advice and organizing their legal representation, and providing their legal representatives with adequate support, assistance and information, including such facilities as may be necessary for the direct performance of their duty, for the purpose of protecting their rights during all stages of the proceedings in accordance with rules 89 to 91;

   (c) Assisting them in participating in the different phases of the proceedings in accordance with rules 89 to 91;

   (d) Taking gender-sensitive measures to facilitate the participation of victims of sexual violence at all stages of the proceedings.

2. In relation to victims, witnesses and others who are at risk on account of testimony given by such witnesses, the Registrar shall be responsible for the performance of the following functions in accordance with the Statute and these Rules:

   (a) Informing them of their rights under the Statute and the Rules, and of the existence, functions and availability of the Victims and Witnesses Unit;

   (b) Ensuring that they are aware, in a timely manner, of the relevant decisions of the Court that may have an impact on their interests, subject to provisions on confidentiality.

3. For the fulfilment of his or her functions, the Registrar may keep a special register for victims who have expressed their intention to participate in relation to a specific case.

4. Agreements on relocation and provision of support services on the territory of a State of traumatized or threatened victims, witnesses and others who are at risk on account of testimony given by such witnesses may be negotiated with the States by the Registrar on behalf of the Court. Such agreements may remain confidential.

Rule 17

Functions of the Unit

1. The Victims and Witnesses Unit shall exercise its functions in accordance with article 43, paragraph 6.

2. The Victims and Witnesses Unit shall, *inter alia*, perform the following functions, in accordance with the Statute and the Rules, and in consultation with the Chamber, the Prosecutor and the defence, as appropriate:

(a) With respect to all witnesses, victims who appear before the Court, and others who are at risk on account of testimony given by such witnesses, in accordance with their particular needs and circumstances:

   (i) Providing them with adequate protective and security measures and formulating long- and short-term plans for their protection;

   (ii) Recommending to the organs of the Court the adoption of protection measures and also advising relevant States of such measures;

   (iii) Assisting them in obtaining medical, psychological and other appropriate assistance;

   (iv) Making available to the Court and the parties training in issues of trauma, sexual violence, security and confidentiality;

   (v) Recommending, in consultation with the Office of the Prosecutor, the elaboration of a code of conduct, emphasizing the vital nature of security and confidentiality for investigators of the Court and of the defence and all intergovernmental and non-governmental organizations acting at the request of the Court, as appropriate;

   (vi) Cooperating with States, where necessary, in providing any of the measures stipulated in this rule;

(b) With respect to witnesses:

   (i) Advising them where to obtain legal advice for the purpose of protecting their rights, in particular in relation to their testimony;

   (ii) Assisting them when they are called to testify before the Court;

   (iii) Taking gender-sensitive measures to facilitate the testimony of victims of sexual violence at all stages of the proceedings.

3. In performing its functions, the Unit shall give due regard to the particular needs of children, elderly persons and persons with disabilities. In order to facilitate the participation and protection of children as witnesses, the Unit may assign, as appropriate, and with the agreement of the parents or the legal guardian, a child-support person to assist a child through all stages of the proceedings.

Rule 18
Responsibilities of the Unit

For the efficient and effective performance of its work, the Victims and Witnesses Unit shall:

(a) Ensure that the staff in the Unit maintain confidentiality at all times;

(b) While recognizing the specific interests of the Office of the Prosecutor, the defence and the witnesses, respect the interests of the witness, including, where necessary, by maintaining an appropriate separation of the services provided to the prosecution and defence witnesses, and act impartially when cooperating with all parties and in accordance with the rulings and decisions of the Chambers;

(c) Have administrative and technical assistance available for witnesses, victims who appear before the Court, and others who are at risk on account of testimony given by such witnesses, during all stages of the proceedings and thereafter, as reasonably appropriate;

(d) Ensure training of its staff with respect to victims' and witnesses' security, integrity and dignity, including matters related to gender and cultural sensitivity;

(e) Where appropriate, cooperate with intergovernmental and non-governmental organizations.

Rule 19
Expertise in the Unit
In addition to the staff mentioned in article 43, paragraph 6, and subject to article 44, the Victims and Witnesses Unit may include, as appropriate, persons with expertise, *inter alia*, in the following areas:
(a) Witness protection and security;
(b) Legal and administrative matters, including areas of humanitarian and criminal law;
(c) Logistics administration;
(d) Psychology in criminal proceedings;
(e) Gender and cultural diversity;
(f) Children, in particular traumatized children;
(g) Elderly persons, in particular in connection with armed conflict and exile trauma;
(h) Persons with disabilities;
(i) Social work and counselling;
(j) Health care;
(k) Interpretation and translation.

SUBSECTION 3. *COUNSEL FOR THE DEFENCE*

Rule 20
Responsibilities of the Registrar relating to the rights of the defence
1. In accordance with article 43, paragraph 1, the Registrar shall organize the staff of the Registry in a manner that promotes the rights of the defence, consistent with the principle of fair trial as defined in the Statute. For that purpose, the Registrar shall, *inter alia*:
   (a) Facilitate the protection of confidentiality, as defined in article 67, paragraph 1(b);
   (b) Provide support, assistance, and information to all defence counsel appearing before the Court and, as appropriate, support for professional investigators necessary for the efficient and effective conduct of the defence;
   (c) Assist arrested persons, persons to whom article 55, paragraph 2, applies and the accused in obtaining legal advice and the assistance of legal counsel;
   (d) Advise the Prosecutor and the Chambers, as necessary, on relevant defence-related issues;
   (e) Provide the defence with such facilities as may be necessary for the direct performance of the duty of the defence;
   (f) Facilitate the dissemination of information and case law of the Court to defence counsel and, as appropriate, cooperate with national defence and bar associations or any independent representative body of counsel and legal associations referred to in sub-rule 3 to promote the specialization and training of lawyers in the law of the Statute and the Rules.
2. The Registrar shall carry out the functions stipulated in sub-rule 1, including the financial administration of the Registry, in such a manner as to ensure the professional independence of defence counsel.
3. For purposes such as the management of legal assistance in accordance with rule 21 and the development of a Code of Professional Conduct in accordance with rule 8, the Registrar shall consult, as appropriate, with any independent representative body of counsel or legal associations, including any such body the establishment of which may be facilitated by the Assembly of States Parties.

16

Rule 21
Assignment of legal assistance

1. Subject to article 55, paragraph 2(c), and article 67, paragraph 1(d), criteria and proce-dures for assignment of legal assistance shall be established in the Regulations, based on a proposal by the Registrar, following consultations with any independent repre-sentative body of counsel or legal associations, as referred to in rule 20, sub-rule 3.

2. The Registrar shall create and maintain a list of counsel who meet the criteria set forth in rule 22 and the Regulations. The person shall freely choose his or her counsel from this list or other counsel who meets the required criteria and is willing to be included in the list.

3. A person may seek from the Presidency a review of a decision to refuse a request for assignment of counsel. The decision of the Presidency shall be final. If a request is refused, a further request may be made by a person to the Registrar, upon showing a change in circumstances.

4. A person choosing to represent himself or herself shall so notify the Registrar in writ-ing at the first opportunity.

5. Where a person claims to have insufficient means to pay for legal assistance and this is subsequently found not to be so, the Chamber dealing with the case at that time may make an order of contribution to recover the cost of providing counsel.

Rule 22
Appointment and qualifications of Counsel for the defence

1. A counsel for the defence shall have established competence in international or crim-inal law and procedure, as well as the necessary relevant experience, whether as judge, prosecutor, advocate or in other similar capacity, in criminal proceedings. A counsel for the defence shall have an excellent knowledge of and be fluent in at least one of the working languages of the Court. Counsel for the defence may be assisted by other persons, including professors of law, with relevant expertise.

2. Counsel for the defence engaged by a person exercising his or her right under the Statute to retain legal counsel of his or her choosing shall file a power of attorney with the Registrar at the earliest opportunity.

3. In the performance of their duties, Counsel for the defence shall be subject to the Statute, the Rules, the Regulations, the Code of Professional Conduct for Counsel adopted in accordance with rule 8 and any other document adopted by the Court that may be relevant to the performance of their duties.

SECTION IV. SITUATIONS THAT MAY AFFECT THE FUNCTIONING OF THE COURT
SUBSECTION 1. *REMOVAL FROM OFFICE AND DISCIPLINARY MEASURES*

Rule 23
General principle

A judge, the Prosecutor, a Deputy Prosecutor, the Registrar and a Deputy Registrar shall be removed from office or shall be subject to disciplinary measures in such cases and with such guarantees as are established in the Statute and the Rules.

Rule 24

Definition of serious misconduct and serious breach of duty

1. For the purposes of article 46, paragraph 1(a), "serious misconduct" shall be constituted by conduct that:

   (a) If it occurs in the course of official duties, is incompatible with official functions, and causes or is likely to cause serious harm to the proper administration of justice before the Court or the proper internal functioning of the Court, such as:

      (i) Disclosing facts or information that he or she has acquired in the course of his or her duties or on a matter which is *sub judice*, where such disclosure is seriously prejudicial to the judicial proceedings or to any person;

      (ii) Concealing information or circumstances of a nature sufficiently serious to have precluded him or her from holding office;

      (iii) Abuse of judicial office in order to obtain unwarranted favourable treatment from any authorities, officials or professionals; or

   (b) If it occurs outside the course of official duties, is of a grave nature that causes or is likely to cause serious harm to the standing of the Court.

2. For the purposes of article 46, paragraph 1(a), a "serious breach of duty" occurs where a person has been grossly negligent in the performance of his or her duties or has knowingly acted in contravention of those duties. This may include, *inter alia*, situations where the person:

   (a) Fails to comply with the duty to request to be excused, knowing that there are grounds for doing so;

   (b) Repeatedly causes unwarranted delay in the initiation, prosecution or trial of cases, or in the exercise of judicial powers.

Rule 25

Definition of misconduct of a less serious nature

1. For the purposes of article 47, "misconduct of a less serious nature" shall be constituted by conduct that:

   (a) If it occurs in the course of official duties, causes or is likely to cause harm to the proper administration of justice before the Court or the proper internal functioning of the Court, such as:

      (i) Interfering in the exercise of the functions of a person referred to in article 47;

      (ii) Repeatedly failing to comply with or ignoring requests made by the Presiding Judge or by the Presidency in the exercise of their lawful authority;

      (iii) Failing to enforce the disciplinary measures to which the Registrar or a Deputy Registrar and other officers of the Court are subject when a judge knows or should know of a serious breach of duty on their part; or

   (b) If it occurs outside the course of official duties, causes or is likely to cause harm to the standing of the Court.

2. Nothing in this rule precludes the possibility of the conduct set out in sub-rule 1(a) constituting "serious misconduct" or "serious breach of duty" for the purposes of article 46, paragraph 1(a).

Rule 26

Receipt of complaints

1. For the purposes of article 46, paragraph 1, and article 47, any complaint concerning any conduct defined under rules 24 and 25 shall include the grounds on which it is based, the identity of the complainant and, if available, any relevant evidence. The complaint shall remain confidential.

2. All complaints shall be transmitted to the Presidency, which may also initiate proceedings on its own motion, and which shall, pursuant to the Regulations, set aside anonymous or manifestly unfounded complaints and transmit the other complaints to the competent organ. The Presidency shall be assisted in this task by one or more judges, appointed on the basis of automatic rotation, in accordance with the Regulations.

Rule 27

Common provisions on the rights of the defence

1. In any case in which removal from office under article 46 or disciplinary measures under article 47 is under consideration, the person concerned shall be so informed in a written statement.

2. The person concerned shall be afforded full opportunity to present and receive evidence, to make written submissions and to supply answers to any questions put to him or her.

3. The person may be represented by counsel during the process established under this rule.

Rule 28

Suspension from duty

Where an allegation against a person who is the subject of a complaint is of a sufficiently serious nature, the person may be suspended from duty pending the final decision of the competent organ.

Rule 29

Procedure in the event of a request for removal from office

1. In the case of a judge, the Registrar or a Deputy Registrar, the question of removal from office shall be put to a vote at a plenary session.

2. The Presidency shall advise the President of the Bureau of the Assembly of States Parties in writing of any recommendation adopted in the case of a judge, and any decision adopted in the case of the Registrar or a Deputy Registrar.

3. The Prosecutor shall advise the President of the Bureau of the Assembly of States Parties in writing of any recommendation he or she makes in the case of a Deputy Prosecutor.

4. Where the conduct is found not to amount to serious misconduct or a serious breach of duty, it may be decided in accordance with article 47 that the person concerned has engaged in misconduct of a less serious nature and a disciplinary measure imposed.

Rule 30

Procedure in the event of a request for disciplinary measures

1. In the case of a judge, the Registrar or a Deputy Registrar, any decision to impose a disciplinary measure shall be taken by the Presidency.

2. In the case of the Prosecutor, any decision to impose a disciplinary measure shall be taken by an absolute majority of the Bureau of the Assembly of States Parties.
3. In the case of a Deputy Prosecutor:
   (a) Any decision to give a reprimand shall be taken by the Prosecutor;
   (b) Any decision to impose a pecuniary sanction shall be taken by an absolute majority of the Bureau of the Assembly of States Parties upon the recommendation of the Prosecutor.
4. Reprimands shall be recorded in writing and shall be transmitted to the President of the Bureau of the Assembly of States Parties.

Rule 31
Removal from office
Once removal from office has been pronounced, it shall take effect immediately. The person concerned shall cease to form part of the Court, including for unfinished cases in which he or she was taking part.

Rule 32
Disciplinary measures
The disciplinary measures that may be imposed are:
(a) A reprimand; or
(b) A pecuniary sanction that may not exceed six months of the salary paid by the Court to the person concerned.

SUBSECTION 2. EXCUSING, DISQUALIFICATION, DEATH AND RESIGNATION

Rule 33
Excusing of a judge, the Prosecutor or a Deputy Prosecutor
1. A judge, the Prosecutor or a Deputy Prosecutor seeking to be excused from his or her functions shall make a request in writing to the Presidency, setting out the grounds upon which he or she should be excused.
2. The Presidency shall treat the request as confidential and shall not make public the reasons for its decision without the consent of the person concerned.

Rule 34
Disqualification of a judge, the Prosecutor or a Deputy Prosecutor
1. In addition to the grounds set out in article 41, paragraph 2, and article 42, paragraph 7, the grounds for disqualification of a judge, the Prosecutor or a Deputy Prosecutor shall include, *inter alia*, the following:
   (a) Personal interest in the case, including a spousal, parental or other close family, personal or professional relationship, or a subordinate relationship, with any of the parties;
   (b) Involvement, in his or her private capacity, in any legal proceedings initiated prior to his or her involvement in the case, or initiated by him or her subsequently, in which the person being investigated or prosecuted was or is an opposing party;
   (c) Performance of functions, prior to taking office, during which he or she could be expected to have formed an opinion on the case in question, on the parties or

16

on their legal representatives that, objectively, could adversely affect the required impartiality of the person concerned;

    (d) Expression of opinions, through the communications media, in writing or in public actions, that, objectively, could adversely affect the required impartiality of the person concerned.

2. Subject to the provisions set out in article 41, paragraph 2, and article 42, paragraph 8, a request for disqualification shall be made in writing as soon as there is knowledge of the grounds on which it is based. The request shall state the grounds and attach any relevant evidence, and shall be transmitted to the person concerned, who shall be entitled to present written submissions.

3. Any question relating to the disqualification of the Prosecutor or a Deputy Prosecutor shall be decided by a majority of the judges of the Appeals Chamber.

Rule 35

Duty of a judge, the Prosecutor or a Deputy Prosecutor to request to be excused

Where a judge, the Prosecutor or a Deputy Prosecutor has reason to believe that a ground for disqualification exists in relation to him or her, he or she shall make a request to be excused and shall not wait for a request for disqualification to be made in accordance with article 41, paragraph 2, or article 42, paragraph 7, and rule 34. The request shall be made and the Presidency shall deal with it in accordance with rule 33.

Rule 36

Death of a judge, the Prosecutor, a Deputy Prosecutor, the Registrar or a Deputy Registrar

The Presidency shall inform, in writing, the President of the Bureau of the Assembly of States Parties of the death of a judge, the Prosecutor, a Deputy Prosecutor, the Registrar or a Deputy Registrar.

Rule 37

Resignation of a judge, the Prosecutor, a Deputy Prosecutor, the Registrar or a Deputy Registrar

1. A judge, the Prosecutor, a Deputy Prosecutor, the Registrar or a Deputy Registrar shall communicate to the Presidency, in writing, his or her decision to resign. The Presidency shall inform, in writing, the President of the Bureau of the Assembly of States Parties.

2. A judge, the Prosecutor, a Deputy Prosecutor, the Registrar or a Deputy Registrar shall endeavour to give notice of the date on which his or her resignation will take effect at least six months in advance. Before the resignation of a judge takes effect, he or she shall make every effort to discharge his or her outstanding responsibilities.

SUBSECTION 3. *REPLACEMENTS AND ALTERNATE JUDGES*

Rule 38
Replacements

1. A judge may be replaced for objective and justified reasons, *inter alia*:

    (a) Resignation;

    (b) Accepted excuse;

   (c) Disqualification;

   (d) Removal from office;

   (e) Death.

2. Replacement shall take place in accordance with the pre-established procedure in the Statute, the Rules and the Regulations.

Rule 39
Alternate judges

Where an alternate judge has been assigned by the Presidency to a Trial Chamber pursuant to article 74, paragraph 1, he or she shall sit through all proceedings and deliberations of the case, but may not take any part therein and shall not exercise any of the functions of the members of the Trial Chamber hearing the case, unless and until he or she is required to replace a member of the Trial Chamber if that member is unable to continue attending. Alternate judges shall be designated in accordance with a procedure pre-established by the Court.

SECTION V. PUBLICATION, LANGUAGES AND TRANSLATION

Rule 40
Publication of decisions in official languages of the Court

1. For the purposes of article 50, paragraph 1, the following decisions shall be considered as resolving fundamental issues:

   (a) All decisions of the Appeals Division;

   (b) All decisions of the Court on its jurisdiction or on the admissibility of a case pursuant to articles 17, 18, 19 and 20;

   (c) All decisions of a Trial Chamber on guilt or innocence, sentencing and reparations to victims pursuant to articles 74, 75 and 76;

   (d) All decisions of a Pre-Trial Chamber pursuant to article 57, paragraph 3(d).

2. Decisions on confirmation of charges under article 61, paragraph 7, and on offences against the administration of justice under article 70, paragraph 3, shall be published in all the official languages of the Court when the Presidency determines that they resolve fundamental issues.

3. The Presidency may decide to publish other decisions in all the official languages when such decisions concern major issues relating to the interpretation or the implementation of the Statute or concern a major issue of general interest.

Rule 41
Working languages of the Court

1. For the purposes of article 50, paragraph 2, the Presidency shall authorize the use of an official language of the Court as a working language when:

   (a) That language is understood and spoken by the majority of those involved in a case before the Court and any of the participants in the proceedings so requests; or

   (b) The Prosecutor and the defence so request.

2. The Presidency may authorize the use of an official language of the Court as a working language if it considers that it would facilitate the efficiency of the proceedings.

16

Rule 42

Translation and interpretation services

The Court shall arrange for the translation and interpretation services necessary to ensure the implementation of its obligations under the Statute and the Rules.

Rule 43

Procedure applicable to the publication of documents of the Court

The Court shall ensure that all documents subject to publication in accordance with the Statute and the Rules respect the duty to protect the confidentiality of the proceedings and the security of victims and witnesses.

CHAPTER 3. JURISDICTION AND ADMISSIBILITY

SECTION I. DECLARATIONS AND REFERRALS RELATING TO ARTICLES 11, 12, 13 AND 14

Rule 44

Declaration provided for in article 12, paragraph 3

1. The Registrar, at the request of the Prosecutor, may inquire of a State that is not a Party to the Statute or that has become a Party to the Statute after its entry into force, on a confidential basis, whether it intends to make the declaration provided for in article 12, paragraph 3.
2. When a State lodges, or declares to the Registrar its intent to lodge, a declaration with the Registrar pursuant to article 12, paragraph 3, or when the Registrar acts pursuant to sub-rule 1, the Registrar shall inform the State concerned that the declaration under article 12, paragraph 3, has as a consequence the acceptance of jurisdiction with respect to the crimes referred to in article 5 of relevance to the situation and the provisions of Part 9, and any rules thereunder concerning States Parties, shall apply.

Rule 45

Referral of a situation to the Prosecutor

A referral of a situation to the Prosecutor shall be in writing.

SECTION II. INITIATION OF INVESTIGATIONS UNDER ARTICLE 15

Rule 46

Information provided to the Prosecutor under article 15, paragraphs 1 and 2

Where information is submitted under article 15, paragraph 1, or where oral or written testimony is received pursuant to article 15, paragraph 2, at the seat of the Court, the Prosecutor shall protect the confidentiality of such information and testimony or take any other necessary measures, pursuant to his or her duties under the Statute.

Rule 47

Testimony under article 15, paragraph 2

1. The provisions of rules 111 and 112 shall apply, *mutatis mutandis*, to testimony received by the Prosecutor pursuant to article 15, paragraph 2.

2. When the Prosecutor considers that there is a serious risk that it might not be possible for the testimony to be taken subsequently, he or she may request the Pre-Trial Chamber to take such measures as may be necessary to ensure the efficiency and integrity of the proceedings and, in particular, to appoint a counsel or a judge from the Pre-Trial Chamber to be present during the taking of the testimony in order to protect the rights of the defence. If the testimony is subsequently presented in the proceedings, its admissibility shall be governed by article 69, paragraph 4, and given such weight as determined by the relevant Chamber.

Rule 48
Determination of reasonable basis to proceed with an investigation under article 15, paragraph 3
In determining whether there is a reasonable basis to proceed with an investigation under article 15, paragraph 3, the Prosecutor shall consider the factors set out in article 53, paragraph 1(a) to (c).

Rule 49
Decision and notice under article 15, paragraph 6
1. Where a decision under article 15, paragraph 6, is taken, the Prosecutor shall promptly ensure that notice is provided, including reasons for his or her decision, in a manner that prevents any danger to the safety, well-being and privacy of those who provided information to him or her under article 15, paragraphs 1 and 2, or the integrity of investigations or proceedings.
2. The notice shall also advise of the possibility of submitting further information regarding the same situation in the light of new facts and evidence.

Rule 50
Procedure for authorization by the Pre-Trial Chamber of the commencement of the investigation
1. When the Prosecutor intends to seek authorization from the Pre-Trial Chamber to initiate an investigation pursuant to article 15, paragraph 3, the Prosecutor shall inform victims, known to him or her or to the Victims and Witnesses Unit, or their legal representatives, unless the Prosecutor decides that doing so would pose a danger to the integrity of the investigation or the life or well-being of victims and witnesses. The Prosecutor may also give notice by general means in order to reach groups of victims if he or she determines in the particular circumstances of the case that such notice could not pose a danger to the integrity and effective conduct of the investigation or to the security and well-being of victims and witnesses. In performing these functions, the Prosecutor may seek the assistance of the Victims and Witnesses Unit as appropriate.
2. A request for authorization by the Prosecutor shall be in writing.
3. Following information given in accordance with sub-rule 1, victims may make representations in writing to the Pre-Trial Chamber within such time limit as set forth in the Regulations.
4. The Pre-Trial Chamber, in deciding on the procedure to be followed, may request additional information from the Prosecutor and from any of the victims who have made representations, and, if it considers it appropriate, may hold a hearing.

16

5. The Pre-Trial Chamber shall issue its decision, including its reasons, as to whether to authorize the commencement of the investigation in accordance with article 15, paragraph 4, with respect to all or any part of the request by the Prosecutor. The Chamber shall give notice of the decision to victims who have made representations.

6. The above procedure shall also apply to a new request to the Pre-Trial Chamber pursuant to article 15, paragraph 5.

SECTION III. CHALLENGES AND PRELIMINARY RULINGS UNDER ARTICLES 17, 18 AND 19

Rule 51
Information provided under article 17

In considering the matters referred to in article 17, paragraph 2, and in the context of the circumstances of the case, the Court may consider, *inter alia*, information that the State referred to in article 17, paragraph 1, may choose to bring to the attention of the Court showing that its courts meet internationally recognized norms and standards for the independent and impartial prosecution of similar conduct, or that the State has confirmed in writing to the Prosecutor that the case is being investigated or prosecuted.

Rule 52
Notification provided for in article 18, paragraph 1

1. Subject to the limitations provided for in article 18, paragraph 1, the notification shall contain information about the acts that may constitute crimes referred to in article 5, relevant for the purposes of article 18, paragraph 2.

2. A State may request additional information from the Prosecutor to assist it in the application of article 18, paragraph 2. Such a request shall not affect the one-month time limit provided for in article 18, paragraph 2, and shall be responded to by the Prosecutor on an expedited basis.

Rule 53
Deferral provided for in article 18, paragraph 2

When a State requests a deferral pursuant to article 18, paragraph 2, that State shall make this request in writing and provide information concerning its investigation, taking into account article 18, paragraph 2. The Prosecutor may request additional information from that State.

Rule 54
Application by the Prosecutor under article 18, paragraph 2

1. An application submitted by the Prosecutor to the Pre-Trial Chamber in accordance with article 18, paragraph 2, shall be in writing and shall contain the basis for the application. The information provided by the State under rule 53 shall be communicated by the Prosecutor to the Pre-Trial Chamber.

2. The Prosecutor shall inform that State in writing when he or she makes an application to the Pre-Trial Chamber under article 18, paragraph 2, and shall include in the notice a summary of the basis of the application.

Rule 55
Proceedings concerning article 18, paragraph 2

1. The Pre-Trial Chamber shall decide on the procedure to be followed and may take appropriate measures for the proper conduct of the proceedings. It may hold a hearing.
2. The Pre-Trial Chamber shall examine the Prosecutor's application and any observations submitted by a State that requested a deferral in accordance with article 18, paragraph 2, and shall consider the factors in article 17 in deciding whether to authorize an investigation.
3. The decision and the basis for the decision of the Pre-Trial Chamber shall be communicated as soon as possible to the Prosecutor and to the State that requested a deferral of an investigation.

Rule 56
Application by the Prosecutor following review under article 18, paragraph 3

1. Following a review by the Prosecutor as set forth in article 18, paragraph 3, the Prosecutor may apply to the Pre-Trial Chamber for authorization in accordance with article 18, paragraph 2. The application to the Pre-Trial Chamber shall be in writing and shall contain the basis for the application.
2. Any further information provided by the State under article 18, paragraph 5, shall be communicated by the Prosecutor to the Pre-Trial Chamber.
3. The proceedings shall be conducted in accordance with rules 54, sub-rule 2, and 55.

Rule 57
Provisional measures under article 18, paragraph 6

An application to the Pre-Trial Chamber by the Prosecutor in the circumstances provided for in article 18, paragraph 6, shall be considered *ex parte* and *in camera*. The Pre-Trial Chamber shall rule on the application on an expedited basis.

Rule 58
Proceedings under article 19

1. A request or application made under article 19 shall be in writing and contain the basis for it.
2. When a Chamber receives a request or application raising a challenge or question concerning its jurisdiction or the admissibility of a case in accordance with article 19, paragraph 2 or 3, or is acting on its own motion as provided for in article 19, paragraph 1, it shall decide on the procedure to be followed and may take appropriate measures for the proper conduct of the proceedings. It may hold a hearing. It may join the challenge or question to a confirmation or a trial proceeding as long as this does not cause undue delay, and in this circumstance shall hear and decide on the challenge or question first.
3. The Court shall transmit a request or application received under sub-rule 2 to the Prosecutor and to the person referred to in article 19, paragraph 2, who has been surrendered to the Court or who has appeared voluntarily or pursuant to a summons, and shall allow them to submit written observations to the request or application within a period of time determined by the Chamber.
4. The Court shall rule on any challenge or question of jurisdiction first and then on any challenge or question of admissibility.

16

Rule 59
Participation in proceedings under article 19, paragraph 3

1. For the purpose of article 19, paragraph 3, the Registrar shall inform the following of any question or challenge of jurisdiction or admissibility which has arisen pursuant to article 19, paragraphs 1, 2 and 3:

    (a) Those who have referred a situation pursuant to article 13;

    (b) The victims who have already communicated with the Court in relation to that case or their legal representatives.

2. The Registrar shall provide those referred to in sub-rule 1, in a manner consistent with the duty of the Court regarding the confidentiality of information, the protection of any person and the preservation of evidence, with a summary of the grounds on which the jurisdiction of the Court or the admissibility of the case has been challenged.

3. Those receiving the information, as provided for in sub-rule 1, may make representation in writing to the competent Chamber within such time limit as it considers appropriate.

Rule 60
Competent organ to receive challenges

If a challenge to the jurisdiction of the Court or to the admissibility of a case is made after a confirmation of the charges but before the constitution or designation of the Trial Chamber, it shall be addressed to the Presidency, which shall refer it to the Trial Chamber as soon as the latter is constituted or designated in accordance with rule 130.

Rule 61
Provisional measures under article 19, paragraph 8

When the Prosecutor makes application to the competent Chamber in the circumstances provided for in article 19, paragraph 8, rule 57 shall apply.

Rule 62
Proceedings under article 19, paragraph 10

1. If the Prosecutor makes a request under article 19, paragraph 10, he or she shall make the request to the Chamber that made the latest ruling on admissibility. The provisions of rules 58, 59 and 61 shall be applicable.

2. The State or States whose challenge to admissibility under article 19, paragraph 2, provoked the decision of inadmissibility provided for in article 19, paragraph 10, shall be notified of the request of the Prosecutor and shall be given a time limit within which to make representations.

CHAPTER 4. PROVISIONS RELATING TO VARIOUS STAGES OF THE PROCEEDINGS

SECTION I. EVIDENCE

Rule 63
General provisions relating to evidence

1. The rules of evidence set forth in this chapter, together with article 69, shall apply in proceedings before all Chambers.

2. A Chamber shall have the authority, in accordance with the discretion described in article 64, paragraph 9, to assess freely all evidence submitted in order to determine its relevance or admissibility in accordance with article 69.

3. A Chamber shall rule on an application of a party or on its own motion, made under article 64, subparagraph 9(a), concerning admissibility when it is based on the grounds set out in article 69, paragraph 7.

4. Without prejudice to article 66, paragraph 3, a Chamber shall not impose a legal requirement that corroboration is required in order to prove any crime within the jurisdiction of the Court, in particular, crimes of sexual violence.

5. The Chambers shall not apply national laws governing evidence, other than in accordance with article 21.

Rule 64
Procedure relating to the relevance or admissibility of evidence

1. An issue relating to relevance or admissibility must be raised at the time when the evidence is submitted to a Chamber. Exceptionally, when those issues were not known at the time when the evidence was submitted, it may be raised immediately after the issue has become known. The Chamber may request that the issue be raised in writing. The written motion shall be communicated by the Court to all those who participate in the proceedings, unless otherwise decided by the Court.

2. A Chamber shall give reasons for any rulings it makes on evidentiary matters. These reasons shall be placed in the record of the proceedings if they have not already been incorporated into the record during the course of the proceedings in accordance with article 64, paragraph 10, and rule 137, sub-rule 1.

3. Evidence ruled irrelevant or inadmissible shall not be considered by the Chamber.

Rule 65
Compellability of witnesses

1. A witness who appears before the Court is compellable by the Court to provide testimony, unless otherwise provided for in the Statute and the Rules, in particular rules 73, 74 and 75.

2. Rule 171 applies to a witness appearing before the Court who is compellable to provide testimony under sub-rule 1.

Rule 66
Solemn undertaking

1. Except as described in sub-rule 2, every witness shall, in accordance with article 69, paragraph 1, make the following solemn undertaking before testifying:
"I solemnly declare that I will speak the truth, the whole truth and nothing but the truth."

2. A person under the age of 18 or a person whose judgement has been impaired and who, in the opinion of the Chamber, does not understand the nature of a solemn undertaking may be allowed to testify without this solemn undertaking if the Chamber considers that the person is able to describe matters of which he or she has knowledge and that the person understands the meaning of the duty to speak the truth.

3. Before testifying, the witness shall be informed of the offence defined in article 70, paragraph 1(a).

Rule 67
Live testimony by means of audio or video-link technology

1. In accordance with article 69, paragraph 2, a Chamber may allow a witness to give *viva voce* (oral) testimony before the Chamber by means of audio or video technology, provided that such technology permits the witness to be examined by the Prosecutor, the defence, and by the Chamber itself, at the time that the witness so testifies.

2. The examination of a witness under this rule shall be conducted in accordance with the relevant rules of this chapter.

3. The Chamber, with the assistance of the Registry, shall ensure that the venue chosen for the conduct of the audio or video-link testimony is conducive to the giving of truthful and open testimony and to the safety, physical and psychological well-being, dignity and privacy of the witness.

Rule 68[3]
Prior recorded testimony

1. When the Pre-Trial Chamber has not taken measures under article 56, the Trial Chamber may, in accordance with article 69, paragraphs 2 and 4, and after hearing the parties, allow the introduction of previously recorded audio or video testimony of a witness, or the transcript or other documented evidence of such testimony, provided that this would not be prejudicial to or inconsistent with the rights of the accused and that the requirements of one or more of the following sub-rules are met.

2. If the witness who gave the previously recorded testimony is not present before the Trial Chamber, the Chamber may allow the introduction of that previously recorded testimony in any one of the following instances:

   (a) Both the Prosecutor and the defence had the opportunity to examine the witness during the recording.

   (b) The prior recorded testimony goes to proof of a matter other than the acts and conduct of the accused. In such a case:

      (i) In determining whether introduction of prior recorded testimony falling under sub-rule (b) may be allowed, the Chamber shall consider, *inter alia*, whether the prior recorded testimony in question:
         – relates to issues that are not materially in dispute;
         – is of a cumulative or corroborative nature, in that other witnesses will give or have given oral testimony of similar facts;
         – relates to background information;
         – is such that the interests of justice are best served by its introduction; and
         – has sufficient indicia of reliability.

      (ii) Prior recorded testimony falling under sub-rule (b) may only be introduced if it is accompanied by a declaration by the testifying person that the contents of the prior recorded testimony are true and correct to the best of that person's knowledge and belief. Accompanying declarations may not contain any new information and must be made reasonably close in time to when the prior recorded testimony is being submitted.

---

[3] As amended by resolution ICC-ASP/12/Res.7.

(iii) Accompanying declarations must be witnessed by a person authorised to witness such a declaration by the relevant Chamber or in accordance with the law and procedure of a State. The person witnessing the declaration must verify in writing the date and place of the declaration, and that the person making the declaration:

- is the person identified in the prior recorded testimony;
- assures that he or she is making the declaration voluntarily and without undue influence;
- states that the contents of the prior recorded testimony are, to the best of that person's knowledge and belief, true and correct; and
- was informed that if the contents of the prior recorded testimony are not true then he or she may be subject to proceedings for having given false testimony.

(c) The prior recorded testimony comes from a person who has subsequently died, must be presumed dead, or is, due to obstacles that cannot be overcome with reasonable diligence, unavailable to testify orally. In such a case:

(i) Prior recorded testimony falling under sub-rule (c) may only be introduced if the Chamber is satisfied that the person is unavailable as set out above, that the necessity of measures under article 56 could not be anticipated, and that the prior recorded testimony has sufficient indicia of reliability.

(ii) The fact that the prior recorded testimony goes to proof of acts and conduct of an accused may be a factor against its introduction, or part of it.

(d) The prior recorded testimony comes from a person who has been subjected to interference. In such a case:

(i) Prior recorded testimony falling under sub-rule (d) may only be introduced if the Chamber is satisfied that:

- the person has failed to attend as a witness or, having attended, has failed to give evidence with respect to a material aspect included in his or her prior recorded testimony;
- the failure of the person to attend or to give evidence has been materially influenced by improper interference, including threats, intimidation, or coercion;
- reasonable efforts have been made to secure the attendance of the person as a witness or, if in attendance, to secure from the witness all material facts known to the witness;
- the interests of justice are best served by the prior recorded testimony being introduced; and
- the prior recorded testimony has sufficient indicia of reliability.

(ii) For the purposes of sub-rule (d)(i), an improper interference may relate, *inter alia*, to the physical, psychological, economic or other interests of the person.

(iii) When prior recorded testimony submitted under sub-rule (d)(i) relates to completed proceedings for offences defined in article 70, the Chamber may consider adjudicated facts from these proceedings in its assessment.

(iv) The fact that the prior recorded testimony goes to proof of acts and conduct of an accused may be a factor against its introduction, or part of it.

16

3. If the witness who gave the previously recorded testimony is present before the Trial Chamber, the Chamber may allow the introduction of that previously recorded testimony if he or she does not object to the submission of the previously recorded testimony and the Prosecutor, the defence and the Chamber have the opportunity to examine the witness during the proceedings.

Rule 69
Agreements as to evidence

The Prosecutor and the defence may agree that an alleged fact, which is contained in the charges, the contents of a document, the expected testimony of a witness or other evidence is not contested and, accordingly, a Chamber may consider such alleged fact as being proven, unless the Chamber is of the opinion that a more complete presentation of the alleged facts is required in the interests of justice, in particular the interests of the victims.

Rule 70
Principles of evidence in cases of sexual violence

In cases of sexual violence, the Court shall be guided by and, where appropriate, apply the following principles:
(a) Consent cannot be inferred by reason of any words or conduct of a victim where force, threat of force, coercion or taking advantage of a coercive environment undermined the victim's ability to give voluntary and genuine consent;
(b) Consent cannot be inferred by reason of any words or conduct of a victim where the victim is incapable of giving genuine consent;
(c) Consent cannot be inferred by reason of the silence of, or lack of resistance by, a victim to the alleged sexual violence;
(d) Credibility, character or predisposition to sexual availability of a victim or witness cannot be inferred by reason of the sexual nature of the prior or subsequent conduct of a victim or witness.

Rule 71
Evidence of other sexual conduct

In the light of the definition and nature of the crimes within the jurisdiction of the Court, and subject to article 69, paragraph 4, a Chamber shall not admit evidence of the prior or subsequent sexual conduct of a victim or witness.

Rule 72
In camera procedure to consider relevance or admissibility of evidence

1. Where there is an intention to introduce or elicit, including by means of the questioning of a victim or witness, evidence that the victim consented to an alleged crime of sexual violence, or evidence of the words, conduct, silence or lack of resistance of a victim or witness as referred to in principles (a) through (d) of rule 70, notification shall be provided to the Court which shall describe the substance of the evidence intended to be introduced or elicited and the relevance of the evidence to the issues in the case.
2. In deciding whether the evidence referred to in sub-rule 1 is relevant or admissible, a Chamber shall hear *in camera* the views of the Prosecutor, the defence, the witness and

the victim or his or her legal representative, if any, and shall take into account whether that evidence has a sufficient degree of probative value to an issue in the case and the prejudice that such evidence may cause, in accordance with article 69, paragraph 4. For this purpose, the Chamber shall have regard to article 21, paragraph 3, and articles 67 and 68, and shall be guided by principles (a) to (d) of rule 70, especially with respect to the proposed questioning of a victim.

3. Where the Chamber determines that the evidence referred to in sub-rule 2 is admissible in the proceedings, the Chamber shall state on the record the specific purpose for which the evidence is admissible. In evaluating the evidence during the proceedings, the Chamber shall apply principles (a) to (d) of rule 70.

Rule 73
Privileged communications and information

1. Without prejudice to article 67, paragraph 1(b), communications made in the context of the professional relationship between a person and his or her legal counsel shall be regarded as privileged, and consequently not subject to disclosure, unless:
   (a) The person consents in writing to such disclosure; or
   (b) The person voluntarily disclosed the content of the communication to a third party, and that third party then gives evidence of that disclosure.
2. Having regard to rule 63, sub-rule 5, communications made in the context of a class of professional or other confidential relationships shall be regarded as privileged, and consequently not subject to disclosure, under the same terms as in sub-rules 1 (a) and 1(b) if a Chamber decides in respect of that class that:
   (a) Communications occurring within that class of relationship are made in the course of a confidential relationship producing a reasonable expectation of privacy and non-disclosure;
   (b) Confidentiality is essential to the nature and type of relationship between the person and the confidant; and
   (c) Recognition of the privilege would further the objectives of the Statute and the Rules.
3. In making a decision under sub-rule 2, the Court shall give particular regard to recognizing as privileged those communications made in the context of the professional relationship between a person and his or her medical doctor, psychiatrist, psychologist or counsellor, in particular those related to or involving victims, or between a person and a member of a religious clergy; and in the latter case, the Court shall recognize as privileged those communications made in the context of a sacred confession where it is an integral part of the practice of that religion.
4. The Court shall regard as privileged, and consequently not subject to disclosure, including by way of testimony of any present or past official or employee of the International Committee of the Red Cross (ICRC), any information, documents or other evidence which it came into the possession of in the course, or as a consequence, of the performance by ICRC of its functions under the Statutes of the International Red Cross and Red Crescent Movement, unless:
   (a) After consultations undertaken pursuant to sub-rule 6, ICRC does not object in writing to such disclosure, or otherwise has waived this privilege; or
   (b) Such information, documents or other evidence is contained in public statements and documents of ICRC.

5. Nothing in sub-rule 4 shall affect the admissibility of the same evidence obtained from a source other than ICRC and its officials or employees when such evidence has also been acquired by this source independently of ICRC and its officials or employees.

6. If the Court determines that ICRC information, documents or other evidence are of great importance for a particular case, consultations shall be held between the Court and ICRC in order to seek to resolve the matter by cooperative means, bearing in mind the circumstances of the case, the relevance of the evidence sought, whether the evidence could be obtained from a source other than ICRC, the interests of justice and of victims, and the performance of the Court's and ICRC's functions.

Rule 74

Self-incrimination by a witness

1. Unless a witness has been notified pursuant to rule 190, the Chamber shall notify a witness of the provisions of this rule before his or her testimony.

2. Where the Court determines that an assurance with respect to self-incrimination should be provided to a particular witness, it shall provide the assurances under sub-rule 3, paragraph (c), before the witness attends, directly or pursuant to a request under article 93, paragraph (1)(e).

3. (a) A witness may object to making any statement that might tend to incriminate him or her.

   (b) Where the witness has attended after receiving an assurance under sub-rule 2, the Court may require the witness to answer the question or questions.

   (c) In the case of other witnesses, the Chamber may require the witness to answer the question or questions, after assuring the witness that the evidence provided in response to the questions:

   (i) Will be kept confidential and will not be disclosed to the public or any State; and

   (ii) Will not be used either directly or indirectly against that person in any subsequent prosecution by the Court, except under articles 70 and 71.

4. Before giving such an assurance, the Chamber shall seek the views of the Prosecutor, *ex parte*, to determine if the assurance should be given to this particular witness.

5. In determining whether to require the witness to answer, the Chamber shall consider:

   (a) The importance of the anticipated evidence;

   (b) Whether the witness would be providing unique evidence;

   (c) The nature of the possible incrimination, if known; and

   (d) The sufficiency of the protections for the witness, in the particular circumstances.

6. If the Chamber determines that it would not be appropriate to provide an assurance to this witness, it shall not require the witness to answer the question. If the Chamber determines not to require the witness to answer, it may still continue the questioning of the witness on other matters.

7. In order to give effect to the assurance, the Chamber shall:

   (a) Order that the evidence of the witness be given *in camera*;

   (b) Order that the identity of the witness and the content of the evidence given shall not be disclosed, in any manner, and provide that the breach of any such order will be subject to sanction under article 71;

    (c) Specifically advise the Prosecutor, the accused, the defence counsel, the legal representative of the victim and any Court staff present of the consequences of a breach of the order under subparagraph (b);

    (d) Order the sealing of any record of the proceedings; and

    (e) Use protective measures with respect to any decision of the Court to ensure that the identity of the witness and the content of the evidence given are not disclosed.

8. Where the Prosecutor is aware that the testimony of any witness may raise issues with respect to self-incrimination, he or she shall request an *in camera* hearing and advise the Chamber of this, in advance of the testimony of the witness. The Chamber may impose the measures outlined in sub-rule 7 for all or a part of the testimony of that witness.

9. The accused, the defence counsel or the witness may advise the Prosecutor or the Chamber that the testimony of a witness will raise issues of self-incrimination before the witness testifies and the Chamber may take the measures outlined in sub-rule 7.

10. If an issue of self-incrimination arises in the course of the proceedings, the Chamber shall suspend the taking of the testimony and provide the witness with an opportunity to obtain legal advice if he or she so requests for the purpose of the application of the rule.

Rule 75
Incrimination by family members

1. A witness appearing before the Court, who is a spouse, child or parent of an accused person, shall not be required by a Chamber to make any statement that might tend to incriminate that accused person. However, the witness may choose to make such a statement.

2. In evaluating the testimony of a witness, a Chamber may take into account that the witness, referred to in sub-rule 1, objected to reply to a question which was intended to contradict a previous statement made by the witness, or the witness was selective in choosing which questions to answer.

SECTION II. DISCLOSURE

Rule 76
Pre-trial disclosure relating to prosecution witnesses

1. The Prosecutor shall provide the defence with the names of witnesses whom the Prosecutor intends to call to testify and copies of any prior statements made by those witnesses. This shall be done sufficiently in advance to enable the adequate preparation of the defence.

2. The Prosecutor shall subsequently advise the defence of the names of any additional prosecution witnesses and provide copies of their statements when the decision is made to call those witnesses.

3. The statements of prosecution witnesses shall be made available in original and in a language which the accused fully understands and speaks.

4. This rule is subject to the protection and privacy of victims and witnesses and the protection of confidential information as provided for in the Statute and rules 81 and 82.

16

Rule 77

Inspection of material in possession or control of the Prosecutor

The Prosecutor shall, subject to the restrictions on disclosure as provided for in the Statute and in rules 81 and 82, permit the defence to inspect any books, documents, photographs and other tangible objects in the possession or control of the Prosecutor, which are material to the preparation of the defence or are intended for use by the Prosecutor as evidence for the purposes of the confirmation hearing or at trial, as the case may be, or were obtained from or belonged to the person.

Rule 78

Inspection of material in possession or control of the defence

The defence shall permit the Prosecutor to inspect any books, documents, photographs and other tangible objects in the possession or control of the defence, which are intended for use by the defence as evidence for the purposes of the confirmation hearing or at trial.

Rule 79

Disclosure by the defence

1. The defence shall notify the Prosecutor of its intent to:
   (a) Raise the existence of an alibi, in which case the notification shall specify the place or places at which the accused claims to have been present at the time of the alleged crime and the names of witnesses and any other evidence upon which the accused intends to rely to establish the alibi; or
   (b) Raise a ground for excluding criminal responsibility provided for in article 31, paragraph 1, in which case the notification shall specify the names of witnesses and any other evidence upon which the accused intends to rely to establish the ground.
2. With due regard to time limits set forth in other rules, notification under sub-rule 1 shall be given sufficiently in advance to enable the Prosecutor to prepare adequately and to respond. The Chamber dealing with the matter may grant the Prosecutor an adjournment to address the issue raised by the defence.
3. Failure of the defence to provide notice under this rule shall not limit its right to raise matters dealt with in sub-rule 1 and to present evidence.
4. This rule does not prevent a Chamber from ordering disclosure of any other evidence.

Rule 80

Procedures for raising a ground for excluding criminal responsibility under article 31, paragraph 3

1. The defence shall give notice to both the Trial Chamber and the Prosecutor if it intends to raise a ground for excluding criminal responsibility under article 31, paragraph 3. This shall be done sufficiently in advance of the commencement of the trial to enable the Prosecutor to prepare adequately for trial.
2. Following notice given under sub-rule 1, the Trial Chamber shall hear both the Prosecutor and the defence before deciding whether the defence can raise a ground for excluding criminal responsibility.
3. If the defence is permitted to raise the ground, the Trial Chamber may grant the Prosecutor an adjournment to address that ground.

Rule 81
Restrictions on disclosure

1. Reports, memoranda or other internal documents prepared by a party, its assistants or representatives in connection with the investigation or preparation of the case are not subject to disclosure.

2. Where material or information is in the possession or control of the Prosecutor which must be disclosed in accordance with the Statute, but disclosure may prejudice further or ongoing investigations, the Prosecutor may apply to the Chamber dealing with the matter for a ruling as to whether the material or information must be disclosed to the defence. The matter shall be heard on an *ex parte* basis by the Chamber. However, the Prosecutor may not introduce such material or information into evidence during the confirmation hearing or the trial without adequate prior disclosure to the accused.

3. Where steps have been taken to ensure the confidentiality of information, in accordance with articles 54, 57, 64, 72 and 93, and, in accordance with article 68, to protect the safety of witnesses and victims and members of their families, such information shall not be disclosed, except in accordance with those articles. When the disclosure of such information may create a risk to the safety of the witness, the Court shall take measures to inform the witness in advance.

4. The Chamber dealing with the matter shall, on its own motion or at the request of the Prosecutor, the accused or any State, take the necessary steps to ensure the confidentiality of information, in accordance with articles 54, 72 and 93, and, in accordance with article 68, to protect the safety of witnesses and victims and members of their families, including by authorizing the non-disclosure of their identity prior to the commencement of the trial.

5. Where material or information is in the possession or control of the Prosecutor which is withheld under article 68, paragraph 5, such material and information may not be subsequently introduced into evidence during the confirmation hearing or the trial without adequate prior disclosure to the accused.

6. Where material or information is in the possession or control of the defence which is subject to disclosure, it may be withheld in circumstances similar to those which would allow the Prosecutor to rely on article 68, paragraph 5, and a summary thereof submitted instead. Such material and information may not be subsequently introduced into evidence during the confirmation hearing or the trial without adequate prior disclosure to the Prosecutor.

Rule 82
Restrictions on disclosure of material and information protected under article 54, paragraph 3(e)

1. Where material or information is in the possession or control of the Prosecutor which is protected under article 54, paragraph 3(e), the Prosecutor may not subsequently introduce such material or information into evidence without the prior consent of the provider of the material or information and adequate prior disclosure to the accused.

2. If the Prosecutor introduces material or information protected under article 54, paragraph 3(e), into evidence, a Chamber may not order the production of additional evidence received from the provider of the initial material or information, nor may a Chamber for the purpose of obtaining such additional evidence itself summon the provider or a representative of the provider as a witness or order their attendance.

16

3. If the Prosecutor calls a witness to introduce in evidence any material or information which has been protected under article 54, paragraph 3(e), a Chamber may not compel that witness to answer any question relating to the material or information or its origin, if the witness declines to answer on grounds of confidentiality.

4. The right of the accused to challenge evidence which has been protected under article 54, paragraph 3(e), shall remain unaffected subject only to the limitations contained in sub-rules 2 and 3.

5. A Chamber dealing with the matter may order, upon application by the defence, that, in the interests of justice, material or information in the possession of the accused, which has been provided to the accused under the same conditions as set forth in article 54, paragraph 3(e), and which is to be introduced into evidence, shall be subject *mutatis mutandis* to sub-rules 1, 2 and 3.

Rule 83
Ruling on exculpatory evidence under article 67, paragraph 2
The Prosecutor may request as soon as practicable a hearing on an *ex parte* basis before the Chamber dealing with the matter for the purpose of obtaining a ruling under article 67, paragraph 2.

Rule 84
Disclosure and additional evidence for trial
In order to enable the parties to prepare for trial and to facilitate the fair and expeditious conduct of the proceedings, the Trial Chamber shall, in accordance with article 64, paragraphs 3(c) and 6(d), and article 67, paragraph (2), and subject to article 68, paragraph 5, make any necessary orders for the disclosure of documents or information not previously disclosed and for the production of additional evidence. To avoid delay and to ensure that the trial commences on the set date, any such orders shall include strict time limits which shall be kept under review by the Trial Chamber.

SECTION III. VICTIMS AND WITNESSES
SUBSECTION 1. *DEFINITION AND GENERAL PRINCIPLE RELATING TO VICTIMS*

Rule 85
Definition of victims
For the purposes of the Statute and the Rules of Procedure and Evidence:
(a) "Victims" means natural persons who have suffered harm as a result of the commission of any crime within the jurisdiction of the Court;
(b) Victims may include organizations or institutions that have sustained direct harm to any of their property which is dedicated to religion, education, art or science or charitable purposes, and to their historic monuments, hospitals and other places and objects for humanitarian purposes.

Rule 86
General principle
A Chamber in making any direction or order, and other organs of the Court in performing their functions under the Statute or the Rules, shall take into account the needs of

all victims and witnesses in accordance with article 68, in particular, children, elderly persons, persons with disabilities and victims of sexual or gender violence.

SUBSECTION 2. *PROTECTION OF VICTIMS AND WITNESSES*

Rule 87
Protective measures

1. Upon the motion of the Prosecutor or the defence or upon the request of a witness or a victim or his or her legal representative, if any, or on its own motion, and after having consulted with the Victims and Witnesses Unit, as appropriate, a Chamber may order measures to protect a victim, a witness or another person at risk on account of testimony given by a witness pursuant to article 68, paragraphs 1 and 2. The Chamber shall seek to obtain, whenever possible, the consent of the person in respect of whom the protective measure is sought prior to ordering the protective measure.

2. A motion or request under sub-rule 1 shall be governed by rule 134, provided that:
    (a) Such a motion or request shall not be submitted *ex parte*;
    (b) A request by a witness or by a victim or his or her legal representative, if any, shall be served on both the Prosecutor and the defence, each of whom shall have the opportunity to respond;
    (c) A motion or request affecting a particular witness or a particular victim shall be served on that witness or victim or his or her legal representative, if any, in addition to the other party, each of whom shall have the opportunity to respond;
    (d) When the Chamber proceeds on its own motion, notice and opportunity to respond shall be given to the Prosecutor and the defence, and to any witness or any victim or his or her legal representative, if any, who would be affected by such protective measure; and
    (e) A motion or request may be filed under seal, and, if so filed, shall remain sealed until otherwise ordered by a Chamber. Responses to motions or requests filed under seal shall also be filed under seal.

3. A Chamber may, on a motion or request under sub-rule 1, hold a hearing, which shall be conducted *in camera*, to determine whether to order measures to prevent the release to the public or press and information agencies, of the identity or the location of a victim, a witness or other person at risk on account of testimony given by a witness by ordering, *inter alia*:
    (a) That the name of the victim, witness or other person at risk on account of testimony given by a witness or any information which could lead to his or her identification, be expunged from the public records of the Chamber;
    (b) That the Prosecutor, the defence or any other participant in the proceedings be prohibited from disclosing such information to a third party;
    (c) That testimony be presented by electronic or other special means, including the use of technical means enabling the alteration of pictures or voice, the use of audio-visual technology, in particular videoconferencing and closed-circuit television, and the exclusive use of the sound media;
    (d) That a pseudonym be used for a victim, a witness or other person at risk on account of testimony given by a witness; or
    (e) That a Chamber conducts part of its proceedings *in camera*.

16

Rule 88
Special measures

1. Upon the motion of the Prosecutor or the defence, or upon the request of a witness or a victim or his or her legal representative, if any, or on its own motion, and after having consulted with the Victims and Witnesses Unit, as appropriate, a Chamber may, taking into account the views of the victim or witness, order special measures such as, but not limited to, measures to facilitate the testimony of a traumatized victim or witness, a child, an elderly person or a victim of sexual violence, pursuant to article 68, paragraphs 1 and 2. The Chamber shall seek to obtain, whenever possible, the consent of the person in respect of whom the special measure is sought prior to ordering that measure.

2. A Chamber may hold a hearing on a motion or a request under sub-rule 1, if necessary *in camera* or *ex parte*, to determine whether to order any such special measure, including but not limited to an order that a counsel, a legal representative, a psychologist or a family member be permitted to attend during the testimony of the victim or the witness.

3. For *inter partes* motions or requests filed under this rule, the provisions of rule 87, sub-rules 2(b) to (d), shall apply *mutatis mutandis*.

4. A motion or request filed under this rule may be filed under seal, and if so filed shall remain sealed until otherwise ordered by a Chamber. Any responses to *inter partes* motions or requests filed under seal shall also be filed under seal.

5. Taking into consideration that violations of the privacy of a witness or victim may create risk to his or her security, a Chamber shall be vigilant in controlling the manner of questioning a witness or victim so as to avoid any harassment or intimidation, paying particular attention to attacks on victims of crimes of sexual violence.

SUBSECTION 3. *PARTICIPATION OF VICTIMS IN THE PROCEEDINGS*

Rule 89
Application for participation of victims in the proceedings

1. In order to present their views and concerns, victims shall make written application to the Registrar, who shall transmit the application to the relevant Chamber. Subject to the provisions of the Statute, in particular article 68, paragraph 1, the Registrar shall provide a copy of the application to the Prosecutor and the defence, who shall be entitled to reply within a time limit to be set by the Chamber. Subject to the provisions of sub-rule 2, the Chamber shall then specify the proceedings and manner in which participation is considered appropriate, which may include making opening and closing statements.

2. The Chamber, on its own initiative or on the application of the Prosecutor or the defence, may reject the application if it considers that the person is not a victim or that the criteria set forth in article 68, paragraph 3, are not otherwise fulfilled. A victim whose application has been rejected may file a new application later in the proceedings.

3. An application referred to in this rule may also be made by a person acting with the consent of the victim, or a person acting on behalf of a victim, in the case of a victim who is a child or, when necessary, a victim who is disabled.

4. Where there are a number of applications, the Chamber may consider the applications in such a manner as to ensure the effectiveness of the proceedings and may issue one decision.

Rule 90
Legal representatives of victims
1. A victim shall be free to choose a legal representative.
2. Where there are a number of victims, the Chamber may, for the purposes of ensuring the effectiveness of the proceedings, request the victims or particular groups of victims, if necessary with the assistance of the Registry, to choose a common legal representative or representatives. In facilitating the coordination of victim representation, the Registry may provide assistance, *inter alia*, by referring the victims to a list of counsel, maintained by the Registry, or suggesting one or more common legal representatives.
3. If the victims are unable to choose a common legal representative or representatives within a time limit that the Chamber may decide, the Chamber may request the Registrar to choose one or more common legal representatives.
4. The Chamber and the Registry shall take all reasonable steps to ensure that in the selection of common legal representatives, the distinct interests of the victims, particularly as provided in article 68, paragraph 1, are represented and that any conflict of interest is avoided.
5. A victim or group of victims who lack the necessary means to pay for a common legal representative chosen by the Court may receive assistance from the Registry, including, as appropriate, financial assistance.
6. A legal representative of a victim or victims shall have the qualifications set forth in rule 22, sub-rule 1.

Rule 91
Participation of legal representatives in the proceedings
1. A Chamber may modify a previous ruling under rule 89.
2. A legal representative of a victim shall be entitled to attend and participate in the proceedings in accordance with the terms of the ruling of the Chamber and any modification thereof given under rules 89 and 90. This shall include participation in hearings unless, in the circumstances of the case, the Chamber concerned is of the view that the representative's intervention should be confined to written observations or submissions. The Prosecutor and the defence shall be allowed to reply to any oral or written observation by the legal representative for victims.
3.
  (a) When a legal representative attends and participates in accordance with this rule, and wishes to question a witness, including questioning under rules 67 and 68, an expert or the accused, the legal representative must make application to the Chamber. The Chamber may require the legal representative to provide a written note of the questions and in that case the questions shall be communicated to the Prosecutor and, if appropriate, the defence, who shall be allowed to make observations within a time limit set by the Chamber.
  (b) The Chamber shall then issue a ruling on the request, taking into account the stage of the proceedings, the rights of the accused, the interests of witnesses, the need for a fair, impartial and expeditious trial and in order to give effect to article 68, paragraph 3. The ruling may include directions on the manner and order of the questions and the production of documents in accordance with the powers of the Chamber under article 64. The Chamber may, if it considers it appropriate,

put the question to the witness, expert or accused on behalf of the victim's legal representative.

4. For a hearing limited to reparations under article 75, the restrictions on questioning by the legal representative set forth in sub-rule 2 shall not apply. In that case, the legal representative may, with the permission of the Chamber concerned, question witnesses, experts and the person concerned.

Rule 92
Notification to victims and their legal representatives

1. This rule on notification to victims and their legal representatives shall apply to all proceedings before the Court, except in proceedings provided for in Part 2.

2. In order to allow victims to apply for participation in the proceedings in accordance with rule 89, the Court shall notify victims concerning the decision of the Prosecutor not to initiate an investigation or not to prosecute pursuant to article 53. Such a notification shall be given to victims or their legal representatives who have already participated in the proceedings or, as far as possible, to those who have communicated with the Court in respect of the situation or case in question. The Chamber may order the measures outlined in sub-rule 8 if it considers it appropriate in the particular circumstances.

3. In order to allow victims to apply for participation in the proceedings in accordance with rule 89, the Court shall notify victims regarding its decision to hold a hearing to confirm charges pursuant to article 61. Such a notification shall be given to victims or their legal representatives who have already participated in the proceedings or, as far as possible, to those who have communicated with the Court in respect of the case in question.

4. When a notification for participation as provided for in sub-rules 2 and 3 has been given, any subsequent notification as referred to in sub-rules 5 and 6 shall only be provided to victims or their legal representatives who may participate in the proceedings in accordance with a ruling of the Chamber pursuant to rule 89 and any modification thereof.

5. In a manner consistent with the ruling made under rules 89 to 91, victims or their legal representatives participating in proceedings shall, in respect of those proceedings, be notified by the Registrar in a timely manner of:

   (a) Proceedings before the Court, including the date of hearings and any postponements thereof, and the date of delivery of the decision;

   (b) Requests, submissions, motions and other documents relating to such requests, submissions or motions.

6. Where victims or their legal representatives have participated in a certain stage of the proceedings, the Registrar shall notify them as soon as possible of the decisions of the Court in those proceedings.

7. Notifications as referred to in sub-rules 5 and 6 shall be in writing or, where written notification is not possible, in any other form as appropriate. The Registry shall keep a record of all notifications. Where necessary, the Registrar may seek the cooperation of States Parties in accordance with article 93, paragraph 1(d) and (l).

8. For notification as referred to in sub-rule 3 and otherwise at the request of a Chamber, the Registrar shall take necessary measures to give adequate publicity to

the proceedings. In doing so, the Registrar may seek, in accordance with Part 9, the cooperation of relevant States Parties, and seek the assistance of intergovernmental organizations.

Rule 93
Views of victims or their legal representatives

A Chamber may seek the views of victims or their legal representatives participating pursuant to rules 89 to 91 on any issue, *inter alia*, in relation to issues referred to in rules 107, 109, 125, 128, 136, 139 and 191. In addition, a Chamber may seek the views of other victims, as appropriate.

SUBSECTION 4. *REPARATIONS TO VICTIMS*

Rule 94
Procedure upon request

1. A victim's request for reparations under article 75 shall be made in writing and filed with the Registrar. It shall contain the following particulars:
   (a) The identity and address of the claimant;
   (b) A description of the injury, loss or harm;
   (c) The location and date of the incident and, to the extent possible, the identity of the person or persons the victim believes to be responsible for the injury, loss or harm;
   (d) Where restitution of assets, property or other tangible items is sought, a description of them;
   (e) Claims for compensation;
   (f) Claims for rehabilitation and other forms of remedy;
   (g) To the extent possible, any relevant supporting documentation, including names and addresses of witnesses.
2. At commencement of the trial and subject to any protective measures, the Court shall ask the Registrar to provide notification of the request to the person or persons named in the request or identified in the charges and, to the extent possible, to any interested persons or any interested States. Those notified shall file with the Registry any representation made under article 75, paragraph 3.

Rule 95
Procedure on the motion of the Court

1. In cases where the Court intends to proceed on its own motion pursuant to article 75, paragraph 1, it shall ask the Registrar to provide notification of its intention to the person or persons against whom the Court is considering making a determination, and, to the extent possible, to victims, interested persons and interested States. Those notified shall file with the Registry any representation made under article 75, paragraph 3.
2. If, as a result of notification under sub-rule 1:
   (a) A victim makes a request for reparations, that request will be determined as if it had been brought under rule 94;
   (b) A victim requests that the Court does not make an order for reparations, the Court shall not proceed to make an individual order in respect of that victim.

Rule 96
Publication of reparation proceedings

1. Without prejudice to any other rules on notification of proceedings, the Registrar shall, insofar as practicable, notify the victims or their legal representatives and the person or persons concerned. The Registrar shall also, having regard to any information provided by the Prosecutor, take all the necessary measures to give adequate publicity of the reparation proceedings before the Court, to the extent possible, to other victims, interested persons and interested States.

2. In taking the measures described in sub-rule 1, the Court may seek, in accordance with Part 9, the cooperation of relevant States Parties, and seek the assistance of intergovernmental organizations in order to give publicity, as widely as possible and by all possible means, to the reparation proceedings before the Court.

Rule 97
Assessment of reparations

1. Taking into account the scope and extent of any damage, loss or injury, the Court may award reparations on an individualized basis or, where it deems it appropriate, on a collective basis or both.

2. At the request of victims or their legal representatives, or at the request of the convicted person, or on its own motion, the Court may appoint appropriate experts to assist it in determining the scope, extent of any damage, loss and injury to, or in respect of victims and to suggest various options concerning the appropriate types and modalities of reparations. The Court shall invite, as appropriate, victims or their legal representatives, the convicted person as well as interested persons and interested States to make observations on the reports of the experts.

3. In all cases, the Court shall respect the rights of victims and the convicted person.

Rule 98
Trust Fund

1. Individual awards for reparations shall be made directly against a convicted person.

2. The Court may order that an award for reparations against a convicted person be deposited with the Trust Fund where at the time of making the order it is impossible or impracticable to make individual awards directly to each victim. The award for reparations thus deposited in the Trust Fund shall be separated from other resources of the Trust Fund and shall be forwarded to each victim as soon as possible.

3. The Court may order that an award for reparations against a convicted person be made through the Trust Fund where the number of the victims and the scope, forms and modalities of reparations makes a collective award more appropriate.

4. Following consultations with interested States and the Trust Fund, the Court may order that an award for reparations be made through the Trust Fund to an intergovernmental, international or national organization approved by the Trust Fund.

5. Other resources of the Trust Fund may be used for the benefit of victims subject to the provisions of article 79.

Rule 99

Cooperation and protective measures for the purpose of forfeiture under articles 57, paragraph 3(e), and 75, paragraph 4

1. The Pre-Trial Chamber, pursuant to article 57, paragraph 3(e), or the Trial Chamber, pursuant to article 75, paragraph 4, may, on its own motion or on the application of the Prosecutor or at the request of the victims or their legal representatives who have made a request for reparations or who have given a written undertaking to do so, determine whether measures should be requested.

2. Notice is not required unless the Court determines, in the particular circumstances of the case, that notification could not jeopardize the effectiveness of the measures requested. In the latter case, the Registrar shall provide notification of the proceedings to the person against whom a request is made and so far as is possible to any interested persons or interested States.

3. If an order is made without prior notification, the relevant Chamber shall request the Registrar, as soon as is consistent with the effectiveness of the measures requested, to notify those against whom a request is made and, to the extent possible, to any interested persons or any interested States and invite them to make observations as to whether the order should be revoked or otherwise modified.

4. The Court may make orders as to the timing and conduct of any proceedings necessary to determine these issues.

SECTION IV. MISCELLANEOUS PROVISIONS

Rule 100[4]

Place of the proceedings

1. In a particular case, where the Court considers that it would be in the interests of justice, it may decide to sit in a State other than the host State, for such period or periods as may be required, to hear the case in whole or in part.

2. The Chamber, at any time after the initiation of an investigation, may *proprio motu* or at the request of the Prosecutor or the defence, decide to make a recommendation changing the place where the Chamber sits. The judges of the Chamber shall attempt to achieve unanimity in their recommendation, failing which the recommendation shall be made by a majority of the judges. Such a recommendation shall take account of the views of the parties, of the victims and an assessment prepared by the Registry and shall be addressed to the Presidency. It shall be made in writing and specify in which State the Chamber would sit. The assessment prepared by the Registry shall be annexed to the recommendation.

3. The Presidency shall consult the State where the Chamber intends to sit. If that State agrees that the Chamber can sit in that State, then the decision to sit in a State other than the host State shall be taken by the Presidency in consultation with the Chamber. Thereafter, the Chamber or any designated Judge shall sit at the location decided upon.

---

[4] As amended by resolution ICC-ASP/12/Res.7.

Rule 101

Time limits

1. In making any order setting time limits regarding the conduct of any proceedings, the Court shall have regard to the need to facilitate fair and expeditious proceedings, bearing in mind in particular the rights of the defence and the victims.

2. Taking into account the rights of the accused, in particular under article 67, paragraph (1)(c), all those participating in the proceedings to whom any order is directed shall endeavour to act as expeditiously as possible, within the time limit ordered by the Court.

Rule 102

Communications other than in writing

Where a person is unable, due to a disability or illiteracy, to make a written request, application, observation or other communication to the Court, the person may make such request, application, observation or communication in audio, video or other electronic form.

Rule 103

***Amicus curiae* and other forms of submission**

1. At any stage of the proceedings, a Chamber may, if it considers it desirable for the proper determination of the case, invite or grant leave to a State, organization or person to submit, in writing or orally, any observation on any issue that the Chamber deems appropriate.

2. The Prosecutor and the defence shall have the opportunity to respond to the observations submitted under sub-rule 1.

3. A written observation submitted under sub-rule 1 shall be filed with the Registrar, who shall provide copies to the Prosecutor and the defence. The Chamber shall determine what time limits shall apply to the filing of such observations.

CHAPTER 5. INVESTIGATION AND PROSECUTION

SECTION I. DECISION OF THE PROSECUTOR REGARDING THE INITIATION OF AN INVESTIGATION UNDER ARTICLE 53, PARAGRAPHS 1 AND 2

Rule 104

Evaluation of information by the Prosecutor

1. In acting pursuant to article 53, paragraph 1, the Prosecutor shall, in evaluating the information made available to him or her, analyse the seriousness of the information received.

2. For the purposes of sub-rule 1, the Prosecutor may seek additional information from States, organs of the United Nations, intergovernmental and non-governmental organizations, or other reliable sources that he or she deems appropriate, and may receive written or oral testimony at the seat of the Court. The procedure set out in rule 47 shall apply to the receiving of such testimony.

Rule 105

Notification of a decision by the Prosecutor not to initiate an investigation

1. When the Prosecutor decides not to initiate an investigation under article 53, paragraph 1, he or she shall promptly inform in writing the State or States that referred a

situation under article 14, or the Security Council in respect of a situation covered by article 13, paragraph (b).

2. When the Prosecutor decides not to submit to the Pre-Trial Chamber a request for authorization of an investigation, rule 49 shall apply.

3. The notification referred to in sub-rule 1 shall contain the conclusion of the Prosecutor and, having regard to article 68, paragraph 1, the reasons for the conclusion.

4. In case the Prosecutor decides not to investigate solely on the basis of article 53, paragraph 1(c), he or she shall inform in writing the Pre-Trial Chamber promptly after making that decision.

5. The notification shall contain the conclusion of the Prosecutor and the reasons for the conclusion.

Rule 106
Notification of a decision by the Prosecutor not to prosecute

1. When the Prosecutor decides that there is not a sufficient basis for prosecution under article 53, paragraph 2, he or she shall promptly inform in writing the Pre-Trial Chamber, together with the State or States that referred a situation under article 14, or the Security Council in respect of a situation covered by article 13, paragraph (b).

2. The notifications referred to in sub-rule 1 shall contain the conclusion of the Prosecutor and, having regard to article 68, paragraph 1, the reasons for the conclusion.

SECTION II. PROCEDURE UNDER ARTICLE 53, PARAGRAPH 3

Rule 107
Request for review under article 53, paragraph 3(a)

1. A request under article 53, paragraph 3, for a review of a decision by the Prosecutor not to initiate an investigation or not to prosecute shall be made in writing, and be supported with reasons, within 90 days following the notification given under rule 105 or 106.

2. The Pre-Trial Chamber may request the Prosecutor to transmit the information or documents in his or her possession, or summaries thereof, that the Chamber considers necessary for the conduct of the review.

3. The Pre-Trial Chamber shall take such measures as are necessary under articles 54, 72 and 93 to protect the information and documents referred to in sub-rule 2 and, under article 68, paragraph 5, to protect the safety of witnesses and victims and members of their families.

4. When a State or the Security Council makes a request referred to in sub-rule 1, the Pre-Trial Chamber may seek further observations from them.

5. Where an issue of jurisdiction or admissibility of the case is raised, rule 59 shall apply.

Rule 108
Decision of the Pre-Trial Chamber under article 53, paragraph 3(a)

1. A decision of the Pre-Trial Chamber under article 53, paragraph 3(a), must be concurred in by a majority of its judges and shall contain reasons. It shall be communicated to all those who participated in the review.

2. Where the Pre-Trial Chamber requests the Prosecutor to review, in whole or in part, his or her decision not to initiate an investigation or not to prosecute, the Prosecutor shall reconsider that decision as soon as possible.

3. Once the Prosecutor has taken a final decision, he or she shall notify the Pre-Trial Chamber in writing. This notification shall contain the conclusion of the Prosecutor and the reasons for the conclusion. It shall be communicated to all those who participated in the review.

Rule 109
Review by the Pre-Trial Chamber under article 53, paragraph 3(b)

1. Within 180 days following a notification given under rule 105 or 106, the Pre-Trial Chamber may on its own initiative decide to review a decision of the Prosecutor taken solely under article 53, paragraph 1(c) or 2(c). The Pre-Trial Chamber shall inform the Prosecutor of its intention to review his or her decision and shall establish a time limit within which the Prosecutor may submit observations and other material.

2. In cases where a request has been submitted to the Pre-Trial Chamber by a State or by the Security Council, they shall also be informed and may submit observations in accordance with rule 107.

Rule 110
Decision by the Pre-Trial Chamber under article 53, paragraph 3(b)

1. A decision by the Pre-Trial Chamber to confirm or not to confirm a decision taken by the Prosecutor solely under article 53, paragraph 1(c) or 2(c), must be concurred in by a majority of its judges and shall contain reasons. It shall be communicated to all those who participated in the review.

2. When the Pre-Trial Chamber does not confirm the decision by the Prosecutor referred to in sub-rule 1, he or she shall proceed with the investigation or prosecution.

SECTION III. COLLECTION OF EVIDENCE

Rule 111
Record of questioning in general

1. A record shall be made of formal statements made by any person who is questioned in connection with an investigation or with proceedings. The record shall be signed by the person who records and conducts the questioning and by the person who is questioned and his or her counsel, if present, and, where applicable, the Prosecutor or the judge who is present. The record shall note the date, time and place of, and all persons present during the questioning. It shall also be noted when someone has not signed the record as well as the reasons therefor.

2. When the Prosecutor or national authorities question a person, due regard shall be given to article 55. When a person is informed of his or her rights under article 55, paragraph 2, the fact that this information has been provided shall be noted in the record.

Rule 112
Recording of questioning in particular cases

1. Whenever the Prosecutor questions a person to whom article 55, paragraph 2, applies, or for whom a warrant of arrest or a summons to appear has been issued under article 58, paragraph 7, the questioning shall be audio- or video-recorded, in accordance with the following procedure:

(a) The person questioned shall be informed, in a language he or she fully understands and speaks, that the questioning is to be audio- or video-recorded, and that the person concerned may object if he or she so wishes. The fact that this information has been provided and the response given by the person concerned shall be noted in the record. The person may, before replying, speak in private with his or her counsel, if present. If the person questioned refuses to be audio- or video-recorded, the procedure in rule 111 shall be followed;

(b) A waiver of the right to be questioned in the presence of counsel shall be recorded in writing and, if possible, be audio- or video-recorded;

(c) In the event of an interruption in the course of questioning, the fact and the time of the interruption shall be recorded before the audio- or video-recording ends as well as the time of resumption of the questioning;

(d) At the conclusion of the questioning, the person questioned shall be offered the opportunity to clarify anything he or she has said and to add anything he or she may wish. The time of conclusion of the questioning shall be noted;

(e) The tape shall be transcribed as soon as practicable after the conclusion of the questioning and a copy of the transcript supplied to the person questioned together with a copy of the recorded tape or, if multiple recording apparatus was used, one of the original recorded tapes;

(f) The original tape or one of the original tapes shall be sealed in the presence of the person questioned and his or her counsel, if present, under the signature of the Prosecutor and the person questioned and the counsel, if present.

2. The Prosecutor shall make every reasonable effort to record the questioning in accordance with sub-rule 1. As an exception, a person may be questioned without the questioning being audio- or video-recorded where the circumstances prevent such recording taking place. In this case, the reasons for not recording the questioning shall be stated in writing and the procedure in rule 111 shall be followed.

3. When, pursuant to sub-rule 1(a) or 2, the questioning is not audio- or video-recorded, the person questioned shall be provided with a copy of his or her statement.

4. The Prosecutor may choose to follow the procedure in this rule when questioning other persons than those mentioned in sub-rule 1, in particular where the use of such procedures could assist in reducing any subsequent traumatization of a victim of sexual or gender violence, a child or a person with disabilities in providing their evidence. The Prosecutor may make an application to the relevant Chamber.

5. The Pre-Trial Chamber may, in pursuance of article 56, paragraph 2, order that the procedure in this rule be applied to the questioning of any person.

Rule 113
Collection of information regarding the state of health of the person concerned

1. The Pre-Trial Chamber may, on its own initiative or at the request of the Prosecutor, the person concerned or his or her counsel, order that a person having the rights in article 55, paragraph 2, be given a medical, psychological or psychiatric examination. In making its determination, the Pre-Trial Chamber shall consider the nature and purpose of the examination and whether the person consents to the examination.

2. The Pre-Trial Chamber shall appoint one or more experts from the list of experts approved by the Registrar, or an expert approved by the Pre-Trial Chamber at the request of a party.

Rule 114
Unique investigative opportunity under article 56

1. Upon being advised by the Prosecutor in accordance with article 56, paragraph 1(a), the Pre-Trial Chamber shall hold consultations without delay with the Prosecutor and, subject to the provisions of article 56, paragraph 1(c), with the person who has been arrested or who has appeared before the Court pursuant to summons and his or her counsel, in order to determine the measures to be taken and the modalities of their implementation, which may include measures to ensure that the right to communicate under article 67, paragraph 1(b), is protected.
2. A decision of the Pre-Trial Chamber to take measures pursuant to article 56, paragraph 3, must be concurred in by a majority of its judges after consultations with the Prosecutor. During the consultations, the Prosecutor may advise the Pre-Trial Chamber that intended measures could jeopardize the proper conduct of the investigation.

Rule 115
Collection of evidence in the territory of a State Party under article 57, paragraph 3(d)

1. Where the Prosecutor considers that article 57, paragraph 3(d), applies, the Prosecutor may submit a written request to the Pre-Trial Chamber for authorization to take certain measures in the territory of the State Party in question. After a submission of such a request, the Pre-Trial Chamber shall, whenever possible, inform and invite views from the State Party concerned.
2. In arriving at its determination as to whether the request is well founded, the Pre-Trial Chamber shall take into account any views expressed by the State Party concerned. The Pre-Trial Chamber may, on its own initiative or at the request of the Prosecutor or the State Party concerned, decide to hold a hearing.
3. An authorization under article 57, paragraph 3(d), shall be issued in the form of an order and shall state the reasons, based on the criteria set forth in that paragraph. The order may specify procedures to be followed in carrying out such collection of evidence.

Rule 116
Collection of evidence at the request of the defence under article 57, paragraph 3(b)

1. The Pre-Trial Chamber shall issue an order or seek cooperation under article 57, paragraph 3(b), where it is satisfied:
   (a) That such an order would facilitate the collection of evidence that may be material to the proper determination of the issues being adjudicated, or to the proper preparation of the person's defence; and
   (b) In a case of cooperation under Part 9, that sufficient information to comply with article 96, paragraph 2, has been provided.
2. Before taking a decision whether to issue an order or seek cooperation under article 57, paragraph 3(b), the Pre-Trial Chamber may seek the views of the Prosecutor.

SECTION IV. PROCEDURES IN RESPECT OF RESTRICTION AND DEPRIVATION OF LIBERTY

Rule 117
Detention in the custodial State

1. The Court shall take measures to ensure that it is informed of the arrest of a person in response to a request made by the Court under article 89 or 92. Once so informed, the Court shall ensure that the person receives a copy of the arrest warrant issued by the Pre-Trial Chamber under article 58 and any relevant provisions of the Statute. The documents shall be made available in a language that the person fully understands and speaks.
2. At any time after arrest, the person may make a request to the Pre-Trial Chamber for the appointment of counsel to assist with proceedings before the Court and the Pre-Trial Chamber shall take a decision on such request.
3. A challenge as to whether the warrant of arrest was properly issued in accordance with article 58, paragraph 1(a) and (b), shall be made in writing to the Pre-Trial Chamber. The application shall set out the basis for the challenge. After having obtained the views of the Prosecutor, the Pre-Trial Chamber shall decide on the application without delay.
4. When the competent authority of the custodial State notifies the Pre-Trial Chamber that a request for release has been made by the person arrested, in accordance with article 59, paragraph 5, the Pre-Trial Chamber shall provide its recommendations within any time limit set by the custodial State.
5. When the Pre-Trial Chamber is informed that the person has been granted interim release by the competent authority of the custodial State, the Pre-Trial Chamber shall inform the custodial State how and when it would like to receive periodic reports on the status of the interim release.

Rule 118
Pre-trial detention at the seat of the Court

1. If the person surrendered to the Court makes an initial request for interim release pending trial, either upon first appearance in accordance with rule 121 or subsequently, the Pre-Trial Chamber shall decide upon the request without delay, after seeking the views of the Prosecutor.
2. The Pre-Trial Chamber shall review its ruling on the release or detention of a person in accordance with article 60, paragraph 3, at least every 120 days and may do so at any time on the request of the person or the Prosecutor.
3. After the first appearance, a request for interim release must be made in writing. The Prosecutor shall be given notice of such a request. The Pre-Trial Chamber shall decide after having received observations in writing of the Prosecutor and the detained person. The Pre-Trial Chamber may decide to hold a hearing, at the request of the Prosecutor or the detained person or on its own initiative. A hearing must be held at least once every year.

Rule 119
Conditional release

1. The Pre-Trial Chamber may set one or more conditions restricting liberty, including the following:
   (a) The person must not travel beyond territorial limits set by the Pre-Trial Chamber without the explicit agreement of the Chamber;

    (b) The person must not go to certain places or associate with certain persons as specified by the Pre-Trial Chamber;

    (c) The person must not contact directly or indirectly victims or witnesses;

    (d) The person must not engage in certain professional activities;

    (e) The person must reside at a particular address as specified by the Pre-Trial Chamber;

    (f) The person must respond when summoned by an authority or qualified person designated by the Pre-Trial Chamber;

    (g) The person must post bond or provide real or personal security or surety, for which the amount and the schedule and mode of payment shall be determined by the Pre-Trial Chamber;

    (h) The person must supply the Registrar with all identity documents, particularly his or her passport.

2. At the request of the person concerned or the Prosecutor or on its own initiative, the Pre-Trial Chamber may at any time decide to amend the conditions set pursuant to sub-rule 1.

3. Before imposing or amending any conditions restricting liberty, the Pre-Trial Chamber shall seek the views of the Prosecutor, the person concerned, any relevant State and victims that have communicated with the Court in that case and whom the Chamber considers could be at risk as a result of a release or conditions imposed.

4. If the Pre-Trial Chamber is convinced that the person concerned has failed to comply with one or more of the obligations imposed, it may, on such basis, at the request of the Prosecutor or on its own initiative, issue a warrant of arrest in respect of the person.

5. When the Pre-Trial Chamber issues a summons to appear pursuant to article 58, paragraph 7, and intends to set conditions restricting liberty, it shall ascertain the relevant provisions of the national law of the State receiving the summons. In a manner that is in keeping with the national law of the State receiving the summons, the Pre-Trial Chamber shall proceed in accordance with sub-rules 1, 2 and 3. If the Pre-Trial Chamber receives information that the person concerned has failed to comply with conditions imposed, it shall proceed in accordance with sub-rule 4.

Rule 120
Instruments of restraint
Personal instruments of restraint shall not be used except as a precaution against escape, for the protection of the person in the custody of the Court and others or for other security reasons, and shall be removed when the person appears before a Chamber.

SECTION V. PROCEEDINGS WITH REGARD TO THE CONFIRMATION OF CHARGES UNDER ARTICLE 61

Rule 121
Proceedings before the confirmation hearing

1. A person subject to a warrant of arrest or a summons to appear under article 58 shall appear before the Pre-Trial Chamber, in the presence of the Prosecutor, promptly upon arriving at the Court. Subject to the provisions of articles 60 and 61, the person shall enjoy the rights set forth in article 67. At this first appearance, the Pre-Trial

Chamber shall set the date on which it intends to hold a hearing to confirm the charges. It shall ensure that this date, and any postponements under sub-rule 7, are made public.

2. In accordance with article 61, paragraph 3, the Pre-Trial Chamber shall take the necessary decisions regarding disclosure between the Prosecutor and the person in respect of whom a warrant of arrest or a summons to appear has been issued. During disclosure:

   (a) The person concerned may be assisted or represented by the counsel of his or her choice or by a counsel assigned to him or her;

   (b) The Pre-Trial Chamber shall hold status conferences to ensure that disclosure takes place under satisfactory conditions. For each case, a judge of the Pre-Trial Chamber shall be appointed to organize such status conferences, on his or her own motion, or at the request of the Prosecutor or the person;

   (c) All evidence disclosed between the Prosecutor and the person for the purposes of the confirmation hearing shall be communicated to the Pre-Trial Chamber.

3. The Prosecutor shall provide to the Pre-Trial Chamber and the person, no later than 30 days before the date of the confirmation hearing, a detailed description of the charges together with a list of the evidence which he or she intends to present at the hearing.

4. Where the Prosecutor intends to amend the charges pursuant to article 61, paragraph 4, he or she shall notify the Pre-Trial Chamber and the person no later than 15 days before the date of the hearing of the amended charges together with a list of evidence that the Prosecutor intends to bring in support of those charges at the hearing.

5. Where the Prosecutor intends to present new evidence at the hearing, he or she shall provide the Pre-Trial Chamber and the person with a list of that evidence no later than 15 days before the date of the hearing.

6. If the person intends to present evidence under article 61, paragraph 6, he or she shall provide a list of that evidence to the Pre-Trial Chamber no later than 15 days before the date of the hearing. The Pre-Trial Chamber shall transmit the list to the Prosecutor without delay. The person shall provide a list of evidence that he or she intends to present in response to any amended charges or a new list of evidence provided by the Prosecutor.

7. The Prosecutor or the person may ask the Pre-Trial Chamber to postpone the date of the confirmation hearing. The Pre-Trial Chamber may also, on its own motion, decide to postpone the hearing.

8. The Pre-Trial Chamber shall not take into consideration charges and evidence presented after the time limit, or any extension thereof, has expired.

9. The Prosecutor and the person may lodge written submissions with the Pre-Trial Chamber, on points of fact and on law, including grounds for excluding criminal responsibility set forth in article 31, paragraph 1, no later than three days before the date of the hearing. A copy of these submissions shall be transmitted immediately to the Prosecutor or the person, as the case may be.

10. The Registry shall create and maintain a full and accurate record of all proceedings before the Pre-Trial Chamber, including all documents transmitted to the Chamber pursuant to this rule. Subject to any restrictions concerning confidentiality and the protection of national security information, the record may be consulted by the

Prosecutor, the person and victims or their legal representatives participating in the proceedings pursuant to rules 89 to 91.

Rule 122
Proceedings at the confirmation hearing in the presence of the person charged

1. The Presiding Judge of the Pre-Trial Chamber shall ask the officer of the Registry assisting the Chamber to read out the charges as presented by the Prosecutor. The Presiding Judge shall determine how the hearing is to be conducted and, in particular, may establish the order and the conditions under which he or she intends the evidence contained in the record of the proceedings to be presented.
2. If a question or challenge concerning jurisdiction or admissibility arises, rule 58 applies.
3. Before hearing the matter on the merits, the Presiding Judge of the Pre-Trial Chamber shall ask the Prosecutor and the person whether they intend to raise objections or make observations concerning an issue related to the proper conduct of the proceedings prior to the confirmation hearing.
4. At no subsequent point may the objections and observations made under sub-rule 3 be raised or made again in the confirmation or trial proceedings.
5. If objections or observations referred to in sub-rule 3 are presented, the Presiding Judge of the Pre-Trial Chamber shall invite those referred to in sub-rule 3 to present their arguments, in the order which he or she shall establish. The person shall have the right to reply.
6. If the objections raised or observations made are those referred to in sub-rule 3, the Pre-Trial Chamber shall decide whether to join the issue raised with the examination of the charges and the evidence, or to separate them, in which case it shall adjourn the confirmation hearing and render a decision on the issues raised.
7. During the hearing on the merits, the Prosecutor and the person shall present their arguments in accordance with article 61, paragraphs 5 and 6.
8. The Pre-Trial Chamber shall permit the Prosecutor and the person, in that order, to make final observations.
9. Subject to the provisions of article 61, article 69 shall apply *mutatis mutandis* at the confirmation hearing.

Rule 123
Measures to ensure the presence of the person concerned at the confirmation hearing

1. When a warrant of arrest or summons to appear in accordance with article 58, paragraph 7, has been issued for a person by the Pre-Trial Chamber and the person is arrested or served with the summons, the Pre-Trial Chamber shall ensure that the person is notified of the provisions of article 61, paragraph 2.
2. The Pre-Trial Chamber may hold consultations with the Prosecutor, at the request of the latter or on its own initiative, in order to determine whether there is cause to hold a hearing on confirmation of charges under the conditions set forth in article 61, paragraph 2(b). When the person concerned has a counsel known to the Court, the consultations shall be held in the presence of the counsel unless the Pre-Trial Chamber decides otherwise.

3. The Pre-Trial Chamber shall ensure that a warrant of arrest for the person concerned has been issued and, if the warrant of arrest has not been executed within a reasonable period of time after the issuance of the warrant, that all reasonable measures have been taken to locate and arrest the person.

Rule 124
Waiver of the right to be present at the confirmation hearing

1. If the person concerned is available to the Court but wishes to waive the right to be present at the hearing on confirmation of charges, he or she shall submit a written request to the Pre-Trial Chamber, which may then hold consultations with the Prosecutor and the person concerned, assisted or represented by his or her counsel.
2. A confirmation hearing pursuant to article 61, paragraph 2(a), shall only be held when the Pre-Trial Chamber is satisfied that the person concerned understands the right to be present at the hearing and the consequences of waiving this right.
3. The Pre-Trial Chamber may authorize and make provision for the person to observe the hearing from outside the courtroom through the use of communications technology, if required.
4. The waiving of the right to be present at the hearing does not prevent the Pre-Trial Chamber from receiving written observations on issues before the Chamber from the person concerned.

Rule 125
Decision to hold the confirmation hearing in the absence of the person concerned

1. After holding consultations under rules 123 and 124, the Pre-Trial Chamber shall decide whether there is cause to hold a hearing on confirmation of charges in the absence of the person concerned, and in that case, whether the person may be represented by counsel. The Pre-Trial Chamber shall, when appropriate, set a date for the hearing and make the date public.
2. The decision of the Pre-Trial Chamber shall be notified to the Prosecutor and, if possible, to the person concerned or his or her counsel.
3. If the Pre-Trial Chamber decides not to hold a hearing on confirmation of charges in the absence of the person concerned, and the person is not available to the Court, the confirmation of charges may not take place until the person is available to the Court. The Pre-Trial Chamber may review its decision at any time, at the request of the Prosecutor or on its own initiative.
4. If the Pre-Trial Chamber decides not to hold a hearing on confirmation of charges in the absence of the person concerned, and the person is available to the Court, it shall order the person to appear.

Rule 126
Confirmation hearing in the absence of the person concerned

1. The provisions of rules 121 and 122 shall apply *mutatis mutandis* to the preparation for and holding of a hearing on confirmation of charges in the absence of the person concerned.

2. If the Pre-Trial Chamber has determined that the person concerned shall be represented by counsel, the counsel shall have the opportunity to exercise the rights of that person.

3. When the person who has fled is subsequently arrested and the Court has confirmed the charges upon which the Prosecutor intends to pursue the trial, the person charged shall be committed to the Trial Chamber established under article 61, paragraph 11. The person charged may request in writing that the Trial Chamber refer issues to the Pre-Trial Chamber that are necessary for the Chamber's effective and fair functioning in accordance with article 64, paragraph 4.

SECTION VI. CLOSURE OF THE PRE-TRIAL PHASE

Rule 127
Procedure in the event of different decisions on multiple charges
If the Pre-Trial Chamber is ready to confirm some of the charges but adjourns the hearing on other charges under article 61, paragraph 7(c), it may decide that the committal of the person concerned to the Trial Chamber on the charges that it is ready to confirm shall be deferred pending the continuation of the hearing. The Pre-Trial Chamber may then establish a time limit within which the Prosecutor may proceed in accordance with article 61, paragraph 7(c)(i) or (ii).

Rule 128
Amendment of the charges
1. If the Prosecutor seeks to amend charges already confirmed before the trial has begun, in accordance with article 61, the Prosecutor shall make a written request to the Pre-Trial Chamber, and that Chamber shall so notify the accused.

2. Before deciding whether to authorize the amendment, the Pre-Trial Chamber may request the accused and the Prosecutor to submit written observations on certain issues of fact or law.

3. If the Pre-Trial Chamber determines that the amendments proposed by the Prosecutor constitute additional or more serious charges, it shall proceed, as appropriate, in accordance with rules 121 and 122 or rules 123 to 126.

Rule 129
Notification of the decision on the confirmation of charges
The decision of the Pre-Trial Chamber on the confirmation of charges and the committal of the accused to the Trial Chamber shall be notified, if possible, to the Prosecutor, the person concerned and his or her counsel. Such decision and the record of the proceedings of the Pre-Trial Chamber shall be transmitted to the Presidency.

Rule 130
Constitution of the Trial Chamber
When the Presidency constitutes a Trial Chamber and refers the case to it, the Presidency shall transmit the decision of the Pre-Trial Chamber and the record of the proceedings to the Trial Chamber. The Presidency may also refer the case to a previously constituted Trial Chamber.

CHAPTER 6. TRIAL PROCEDURE

Rule 131

Record of the proceedings transmitted by the Pre-Trial Chamber

1. The Registrar shall maintain the record of the proceedings transmitted by the Pre-Trial Chamber, pursuant to rule 121, sub-rule 10.

2. Subject to any restrictions concerning confidentiality and the protection of national security information, the record may be consulted by the Prosecutor, the defence, the representatives of States when they participate in the proceedings, and the victims or their legal representatives participating in the proceedings pursuant to rules 89 to 91.

Rule 132

Status conferences

1. Promptly after it is constituted, the Trial Chamber shall hold a status conference in order to set the date of the trial. The Trial Chamber, on its own motion, or at the request of the Prosecutor or the defence, may postpone the date of the trial. The Trial Chamber shall notify the trial date to all those participating in the proceedings. The Trial Chamber shall ensure that this date and any postponements are made public.

2. In order to facilitate the fair and expeditious conduct of the proceedings, the Trial Chamber may confer with the parties by holding status conferences as necessary.

Rule 132 *bis*[5]

Designation of a judge for the preparation of the trial

1. In exercising its authority under article 64, paragraph 3(a), a Trial Chamber may designate one or more of its members for the purposes of ensuring the preparation of the trial.

2. The judge shall take all necessary preparatory measures in order to facilitate the fair and expeditious conduct of the trial proceedings, in consultation with the Trial Chamber.

3. The judge may at any time, *proprio motu* or, if appropriate, at the request of a party, refer specific issues to the Trial Chamber for its decision. A majority of the Trial Chamber may also decide *proprio motu* or, if appropriate, at the request of a party, to deal with issues that could otherwise be dealt with by the judge.

4. In order to fulfil his or her responsibilities for the preparation of the trial, the judge may hold status conferences and render orders and decisions. The judge may also establish a work plan indicating the obligations the parties are required to meet pursuant to this rule and the dates by which these obligations must be fulfilled.

5. The functions of the judge may be performed in relation to preparatory issues, whether or not they arise before or after the commencement of the trial. These issues may include:

    (a) Ensuring proper disclosure between the parties;

    (b) Ordering protective measures where necessary;

    (c) Dealing with applications by victims for participation in the trial, as referred to in article 68, paragraph 3;

---

[5] As amended by resolution ICC-ASP/11/Res.2.

(d) Conferring with the parties regarding issues referred to in regulation 54 of the Regulations of the Court, decisions thereon being taken by the Trial Chamber;

(e) Scheduling matters, with the exception of setting the date of the trial, as referred to in rule 132, sub-rule 1;

(f) Dealing with the conditions of detention and related matters; and

(g) Dealing with any other preparatory matters that must be resolved which do not otherwise fall within the exclusive competence of the Trial Chamber.

6. The judge shall not render decisions which significantly affect the rights of the accused or which touch upon the central legal and factual issues in the case, nor shall he or she, subject to sub-rule 5, make decisions that affect the substantive rights of victims.

Rule 133
Motions challenging admissibility or jurisdiction

Challenges to the jurisdiction of the Court or the admissibility of the case at the commencement of the trial, or subsequently with the leave of the Court, shall be dealt with by the Presiding Judge and the Trial Chamber in accordance with rule 58.

Rule 134
Motions relating to the trial proceedings

1. Prior to the commencement of the trial, the Trial Chamber on its own motion, or at the request of the Prosecutor or the defence, may rule on any issue concerning the conduct of the proceedings. Any request from the Prosecutor or the defence shall be in writing and, unless the request is for an *ex parte* procedure, served on the other party. For all requests other than those submitted for an *ex parte* procedure, the other party shall have the opportunity to file a response.

2. At the commencement of the trial, the Trial Chamber shall ask the Prosecutor and the defence whether they have any objections or observations concerning the conduct of the proceedings which have arisen since the confirmation hearings. Such objections or observations may not be raised or made again on a subsequent occasion in the trial proceedings, without leave of the Trial Chamber in this proceeding.

3. After the commencement of the trial, the Trial Chamber, on its own motion, or at the request of the Prosecutor or the defence, may rule on issues that arise during the course of the trial.

Rule 134 *bis*[6]
Presence through the use of video technology

1. An accused subject to a summons to appear may submit a written request to the Trial Chamber to be allowed to be present through the use of video technology during part or parts of his or her trial.

2. The Trial Chamber shall rule on the request on a case-by-case basis, with due regard to the subject matter of the specific hearings in question.

---

[6] As amended by resolution ICC-ASP/12/Res.7.

Rule 134 *ter*[7]

Excusal from presence at trial

1. An accused subject to a summons to appear may submit a written request to the Trial Chamber to be excused and to be represented by counsel only during part or parts of his or her trial.
2. The Trial Chamber shall only grant the request if it is satisfied that:
   (a) exceptional circumstances exist to justify such an absence;
   (b) alternative measures, including changes to the trial schedule or a short adjournment of the trial, would be inadequate;
   (c) the accused has explicitly waived his or her right to be present at the trial; and
   (d) the rights of the accused will be fully ensured in his or her absence.
3. The Trial Chamber shall rule on the request on a case-by-case basis, with due regard to the subject matter of the specific hearings in question. Any absence must be limited to what is strictly necessary and must not become the rule.

Rule 134 *quater*[8]

Excusal from presence at trial due to extraordinary public duties

1. An accused subject to a summons to appear who is mandated to fulfill extraordinary public duties at the highest national level may submit a written request to the Trial Chamber to be excused and to be represented by counsel only; the request must specify that the accused explicitly waives the right to be present at the trial.
2. The Trial Chamber shall consider the request expeditiously and, if alternative measures are inadequate, shall grant the request where it determines that it is in the interests of justice and provided that the rights of the accused are fully ensured. The decision shall be taken with due regard to the subject matter of the specific hearings in question and is subject to review at any time.

Rule 135

Medical examination of the accused

1. The Trial Chamber may, for the purpose of discharging its obligations under article 64, paragraph 8(a), or for any other reasons, or at the request of a party, order a medical, psychiatric or psychological examination of the accused, under the conditions set forth in rule 113.
2. The Trial Chamber shall place its reasons for any such order on the record.
3. The Trial Chamber shall appoint one or more experts from the list of experts approved by the Registrar, or an expert approved by the Trial Chamber at the request of a party.
4. Where the Trial Chamber is satisfied that the accused is unfit to stand trial, it shall order that the trial be adjourned. The Trial Chamber may, on its own motion or at the request of the prosecution or the defence, review the case of the accused. In any event, the case shall be reviewed every 120 days unless there are reasons to do otherwise. If necessary, the Trial Chamber may order further examinations of the accused. When the Trial Chamber is satisfied that the accused has become fit to stand trial, it shall proceed in accordance with rule 132.

---

[7] As amended by resolution ICC-ASP/12/Res.7.
[8] As amended by resolution ICC-ASP/12/Res.7.

Rule 136
Joint and separate trials

1. Persons accused jointly shall be tried together unless the Trial Chamber, on its own motion or at the request of the Prosecutor or the defence, orders that separate trials are necessary, in order to avoid serious prejudice to the accused, to protect the interests of justice or because a person jointly accused has made an admission of guilt and can be proceeded against in accordance with article 65, paragraph 2.
2. In joint trials, each accused shall be accorded the same rights as if such accused were being tried separately.

Rule 137
Record of the trial proceedings

1. In accordance with article 64, paragraph 10, the Registrar shall take measures to make, and preserve, a full and accurate record of all proceedings, including transcripts, audio- and video-recordings and other means of capturing sound or image.
2. A Trial Chamber may order the disclosure of all or part of the record of closed proceedings when the reasons for ordering its non-disclosure no longer exist.
3. The Trial Chamber may authorize persons other than the Registrar to take photographs, audio- and video-recordings and other means of capturing the sound or image of the trial.

Rule 138
Custody of evidence

The Registrar shall retain and preserve, as necessary, all the evidence and other materials offered during the hearing, subject to any order of the Trial Chamber.

Rule 139
Decision on admission of guilt

1. After having proceeded in accordance with article 65, paragraph 1, the Trial Chamber, in order to decide whether to proceed in accordance with article 65, paragraph 4, may invite the views of the Prosecutor and the defence.
2. The Trial Chamber shall then make its decision on the admission of guilt and shall give reasons for this decision, which shall be placed on the record.

Rule 140
Directions for the conduct of the proceedings and testimony

1. If the Presiding Judge does not give directions under article 64, paragraph 8, the Prosecutor and the defence shall agree on the order and manner in which the evidence shall be submitted to the Trial Chamber. If no agreement can be reached, the Presiding Judge shall issue directions.
2. In all cases, subject to article 64, paragraphs 8(b) and 9, article 69, paragraph 4, and rule 88, sub-rule 5, a witness may be questioned as follows:
   (a) A party that submits evidence in accordance with article 69, paragraph 3, by way of a witness, has the right to question that witness;
   (b) The prosecution and the defence have the right to question that witness about relevant matters related to the witness's testimony and its reliability, the credibility of the witness and other relevant matters;

(c) The Trial Chamber has the right to question a witness before or after a witness is questioned by a participant referred to in sub-rules 2(a) or (b);

(d) The defence shall have the right to be the last to examine a witness.

3. Unless otherwise ordered by the Trial Chamber, a witness other than an expert, or an investigator if he or she has not yet testified, shall not be present when the testimony of another witness is given. However, a witness who has heard the testimony of another witness shall not for that reason alone be disqualified from testifying. When a witness testifies after hearing the testimony of others, this fact shall be noted in the record and considered by the Trial Chamber when evaluating the evidence.

Rule 141
Closure of evidence and closing statements
1. The Presiding Judge shall declare when the submission of evidence is closed.
2. The Presiding Judge shall invite the Prosecutor and the defence to make their closing statements. The defence shall always have the opportunity to speak last.

Rule 142
Deliberations
1. After the closing statements, the Trial Chamber shall retire to deliberate, *in camera*. The Trial Chamber shall inform all those who participated in the proceedings of the date on which the Trial Chamber will pronounce its decision. The pronouncement shall be made within a reasonable period of time after the Trial Chamber has retired to deliberate.
2. When there is more than one charge, the Trial Chamber shall decide separately on each charge. When there is more than one accused, the Trial Chamber shall decide separately on the charges against each accused.

Rule 143
Additional hearings on matters related to sentence or reparations
Pursuant to article 76, paragraphs 2 and 3, for the purpose of holding a further hearing on matters related to sentence and, if applicable, reparations, the Presiding Judge shall set the date of the further hearing. This hearing can be postponed, in exceptional circumstances, by the Trial Chamber, on its own motion or at the request of the Prosecutor, the defence or the legal representatives of the victims participating in the proceedings pursuant to rules 89 to 91 and, in respect of reparations hearings, those victims who have made a request under rule 94.

Rule 144
Delivery of the decisions of the Trial Chamber
1. Decisions of the Trial Chamber concerning admissibility of a case, the jurisdiction of the Court, criminal responsibility of the accused, sentence and reparations shall be pronounced in public and, wherever possible, in the presence of the accused, the Prosecutor, the victims or the legal representatives of the victims participating in the proceedings pursuant to rules 89 to 91, and the representatives of the States which have participated in the proceedings.
2. Copies of all the above-mentioned decisions shall be provided as soon as possible to:
   (a) All those who participated in the proceedings, in a working language of the Court;

(b) The accused, in a language he or she fully understands or speaks, if necessary to meet the requirements of fairness under article 67, paragraph 1(f).

CHAPTER 7. PENALTIES

Rule 145

Determination of sentence

1. In its determination of the sentence pursuant to article 78, paragraph 1, the Court shall:

    (a) Bear in mind that the totality of any sentence of imprisonment and fine, as the case may be, imposed under article 77 must reflect the culpability of the convicted person;

    (b) Balance all the relevant factors, including any mitigating and aggravating factors and consider the circumstances both of the convicted person and of the crime;

    (c) In addition to the factors mentioned in article 78, paragraph 1, give consideration, *inter alia*, to the extent of the damage caused, in particular the harm caused to the victims and their families, the nature of the unlawful behaviour and the means employed to execute the crime; the degree of participation of the convicted person; the degree of intent; the circumstances of manner, time and location; and the age, education, social and economic condition of the convicted person.

2. In addition to the factors mentioned above, the Court shall take into account, as appropriate:

    (a) Mitigating circumstances such as:

      (i) The circumstances falling short of constituting grounds for exclusion of criminal responsibility, such as substantially diminished mental capacity or duress;

      (ii) The convicted person's conduct after the act, including any efforts by the person to compensate the victims and any cooperation with the Court;

    (b) As aggravating circumstances:

      (i) Any relevant prior criminal convictions for crimes under the jurisdiction of the Court or of a similar nature;

      (ii) Abuse of power or official capacity;

      (iii) Commission of the crime where the victim is particularly defenceless;

      (iv) Commission of the crime with particular cruelty or where there were multiple victims;

      (v) Commission of the crime for any motive involving discrimination on any of the grounds referred to in article 21, paragraph 3;

      (vi) Other circumstances which, although not enumerated above, by virtue of their nature are similar to those mentioned.

3. Life imprisonment may be imposed when justified by the extreme gravity of the crime and the individual circumstances of the convicted person, as evidenced by the existence of one or more aggravating circumstances.

Rule 146

Imposition of fines under article 77

1. In determining whether to order a fine under article 77, paragraph 2(a), and in fixing the amount of the fine, the Court shall determine whether imprisonment is a

sufficient penalty. The Court shall give due consideration to the financial capacity of the convicted person, including any orders for forfeiture in accordance with article 77, paragraph 2(b), and, as appropriate, any orders for reparation in accordance with article 75. The Court shall take into account, in addition to the factors referred to in rule 145, whether and to what degree the crime was motivated by personal financial gain.

2. A fine imposed under article 77, paragraph 2(a), shall be set at an appropriate level. To this end, the Court shall, in addition to the factors referred to above, in particular take into consideration the damage and injuries caused as well as the proportionate gains derived from the crime by the perpetrator. Under no circumstances may the total amount exceed 75 per cent of the value of the convicted person's identifiable assets, liquid or realizable, and property, after deduction of an appropriate amount that would satisfy the financial needs of the convicted person and his or her dependants.

3. In imposing a fine, the Court shall allow the convicted person a reasonable period in which to pay the fine. The Court may provide for payment of a lump sum or by way of instalments during that period.

4. In imposing a fine, the Court may, as an option, calculate it according to a system of daily fines. In such cases, the minimum duration shall be 30 days and the maximum duration five years. The Court shall decide the total amount in accordance with sub-rules 1 and 2. It shall determine the amount of daily payment in the light of the individual circumstances of the convicted person, including the financial needs of his or her dependants.

5. If the convicted person does not pay the fine imposed in accordance with the conditions set above, appropriate measures may be taken by the Court pursuant to rules 217 to 222 and in accordance with article 109. Where, in cases of continued wilful non-payment, the Presidency, on its own motion or at the request of the Prosecutor, is satisfied that all available enforcement measures have been exhausted, it may as a last resort extend the term of imprisonment for a period not to exceed a quarter of such term or five years, whichever is less. In the determination of such period of extension, the Presidency shall take into account the amount of the fine, imposed and paid. Any such extension shall not apply in the case of life imprisonment. The extension may not lead to a total period of imprisonment in excess of 30 years.

6. In order to determine whether to order an extension and the period involved, the Presidency shall sit *in camera* for the purpose of obtaining the views of the sentenced person and the Prosecutor. The sentenced person shall have the right to be assisted by counsel.

7. In imposing a fine, the Court shall warn the convicted person that failure to pay the fine in accordance with the conditions set out above may result in an extension of the period of imprisonment as described in this rule.

Rule 147
Orders of forfeiture

1. In accordance with article 76, paragraphs 2 and 3, and rules 63, sub-rule 1, and 143, at any hearing to consider an order of forfeiture, Chamber shall hear evidence as to the identification and location of specific proceeds, property or assets which have been derived directly or indirectly from the crime.

2. If before or during the hearing, a Chamber becomes aware of any bona fide third party who appears to have an interest in relevant proceeds, property or assets, it shall give notice to that third party.

3. The Prosecutor, the convicted person and any bona fide third party with an interest in the relevant proceeds, property or assets may submit evidence relevant to the issue.

4. After considering any evidence submitted, a Chamber may issue an order of forfeiture in relation to specific proceeds, property or assets if it is satisfied that these have been derived directly or indirectly from the crime.

Rule 148
Orders to transfer fines or forfeitures to the Trust Fund

Before making an order pursuant to article 79, paragraph 2, a Chamber may request the representatives of the Fund to submit written or oral observations to it.

CHAPTER 8. APPEAL AND REVISION

SECTION I. GENERAL PROVISIONS

Rule 149
Rules governing proceedings in the Appeals Chamber

Parts 5 and 6 and rules governing proceedings and the submission of evidence in the Pre-Trial and Trial Chambers shall apply *mutatis mutandis* to proceedings in the Appeals Chamber.

SECTION II. APPEALS AGAINST CONVICTIONS, ACQUITTALS, SENTENCES AND REPARATION ORDERS

Rule 150
Appeal

1. Subject to sub-rule 2, an appeal against a decision of conviction or acquittal under article 74, a sentence under article 76 or a reparation order under article 75 may be filed not later than 30 days from the date on which the party filing the appeal is notified of the decision, the sentence or the reparation order.

2. The Appeals Chamber may extend the time limit set out in sub-rule 1, for good cause, upon the application of the party seeking to file the appeal.

3. The appeal shall be filed with the Registrar.

4. If an appeal is not filed as set out in sub-rules 1 to 3, the decision, the sentence or the reparation order of the Trial Chamber shall become final.

Rule 151
Procedure for the appeal

1. Upon the filing of an appeal under rule 150, the Registrar shall transmit the trial record to the Appeals Chamber.

2. The Registrar shall notify all parties who participated in the proceedings before the Trial Chamber that an appeal has been filed.

Rule 152

Discontinuance of the appeal

1. Any party who has filed an appeal may discontinue the appeal at any time before judgement has been delivered. In such case, the party shall file with the Registrar a written notice of discontinuance of appeal. The Registrar shall inform the other parties that such a notice has been filed.
2. If the Prosecutor has filed an appeal on behalf of a convicted person in accordance with article 81, paragraph 1(b), before filing any notice of discontinuance, the Prosecutor shall inform the convicted person that he or she intends to discontinue the appeal in order to give him or her the opportunity to continue the appeal proceedings.

Rule 153

Judgement on appeals against reparation orders

1. The Appeals Chamber may confirm, reverse or amend a reparation order made under article 75.
2. The judgement of the Appeals Chamber shall be delivered in accordance with article 83, paragraphs 4 and 5.

SECTION III. APPEALS AGAINST OTHER DECISIONS

Rule 154

Appeals that do not require the leave of the Court

1. An appeal may be filed under article 81, paragraph 3(c)(ii), or article 82, paragraph 1 (a) or (b), not later than five days from the date upon which the party filing the appeal is notified of the decision.
2. An appeal may be filed under article 82, paragraph 1(c), not later than two days from the date upon which the party filing the appeal is notified of the decision.
3. Rule 150, sub-rules 3 and 4, shall apply to appeals filed under sub-rules 1 and 2 of this rule.

Rule 155

Appeals that require leave of the Court

1. When a party wishes to appeal a decision under article 82, paragraph 1(d), or article 82, paragraph 2, that party shall, within five days of being notified of that decision, make a written application to the Chamber that gave the decision, setting out the reasons for the request for leave to appeal.
2. The Chamber shall render a decision and shall notify all parties who participated in the proceedings that gave rise to the decision referred to in sub-rule 1.

Rule 156

Procedure for the appeal

1. As soon as an appeal has been filed under rule 154 or as soon as leave to appeal has been granted under rule 155, the Registrar shall transmit to the Appeals Chamber the record of the proceedings of the Chamber that made the decision that is the subject of the appeal.

2. The Registrar shall give notice of the appeal to all parties who participated in the proceedings before the Chamber that gave the decision that is the subject of the appeal, unless they have already been notified by the Chamber under rule 155, sub-rule 2.

3. The appeal proceedings shall be in writing unless the Appeals Chamber decides to convene a hearing.

4. The appeal shall be heard as expeditiously as possible.

5. When filing the appeal, the party appealing may request that the appeal have suspensive effect in accordance with article 82, paragraph 3.

Rule 157
Discontinuance of the appeal

Any party who has filed an appeal under rule 154 or who has obtained the leave of a Chamber to appeal a decision under rule 155 may discontinue the appeal at any time before judgement has been delivered. In such case, the party shall file with the Registrar a written notice of discontinuance of appeal. The Registrar shall inform the other parties that such a notice has been filed.

Rule 158
Judgement on the appeal

1. An Appeals Chamber which considers an appeal referred to in this section may confirm, reverse or amend the decision appealed.

2. The judgement of the Appeals Chamber shall be delivered in accordance with article 83, paragraph 4.

SECTION IV. REVISION OF CONVICTION OR SENTENCE

Rule 159
Application for revision

1. An application for revision provided for in article 84, paragraph 1, shall be in writing and shall set out the grounds on which the revision is sought. It shall as far as possible be accompanied by supporting material.

2. The determination on whether the application is meritorious shall be taken by a majority of the judges of the Appeals Chamber and shall be supported by reasons in writing.

3. Notification of the decision shall be sent to the applicant and, as far as possible, to all the parties who participated in the proceedings related to the initial decision.

Rule 160
Transfer for the purpose of revision

1. For the conduct of the hearing provided for in rule 161, the relevant Chamber shall issue its order sufficiently in advance to enable the transfer of the sentenced person to the seat of the Court, as appropriate.

2. The determination of the Court shall be communicated without delay to the State of enforcement.

3. The provisions of rule 206, sub-rule 3, shall be applicable.

Rule 161
Determination on revision

1. On a date which it shall determine and shall communicate to the applicant and to all those having received notification under rule 159, sub-rule 3, the relevant Chamber shall hold a hearing to determine whether the conviction or sentence should be revised.

2. For the conduct of the hearing, the relevant Chamber shall exercise, *mutatis mutandis*, all the powers of the Trial Chamber pursuant to Part 6 and the rules governing proceedings and the submission of evidence in the Pre-Trial and Trial Chambers.

3. The determination on revision shall be governed by the applicable provisions of article 83, paragraph 4.

CHAPTER 9. OFFENCES AND MISCONDUCT AGAINST THE COURT

SECTION I. OFFENCES AGAINST THE ADMINISTRATION OF JUSTICE UNDER ARTICLE 70

Rule 162
Exercise of jurisdiction

1. Before deciding whether to exercise jurisdiction, the Court may consult with States Parties that may have jurisdiction over the offence.

2. In making a decision whether or not to exercise jurisdiction, the Court may consider, in particular:
   (a) The availability and effectiveness of prosecution in a State Party;
   (b) The seriousness of an offence;
   (c) The possible joinder of charges under article 70 with charges under articles 5 to 8;
   (d) The need to expedite proceedings;
   (e) Links with an ongoing investigation or a trial before the Court; and
   (f) Evidentiary considerations.

3. The Court shall give favourable consideration to a request from the host State for a waiver of the power of the Court to exercise jurisdiction in cases where the host State considers such a waiver to be of particular importance.

4. If the Court decides not to exercise its jurisdiction, it may request a State Party to exercise jurisdiction pursuant to article 70, paragraph 4.

Rule 163
Application of the Statute and the Rules

1. Unless otherwise provided in sub-rules 2 and 3, rule 162 and rules 164 to 169, the Statute and the Rules shall apply *mutatis mutandis* to the Court's investigation, prosecution and punishment of offences defined in article 70.

2. The provisions of Part 2, and any rules thereunder, shall not apply, with the exception of article 21.

3. The provisions of Part 10, and any rules thereunder, shall not apply, with the exception of articles 103, 107, 109 and 111.

Rule 164
Periods of limitation

1. If the Court exercises jurisdiction in accordance with rule 162, it shall apply the periods of limitation set forth in this rule.
2. Offences defined in article 70 shall be subject to a period of limitation of five years from the date on which the offence was committed, provided that during this period no investigation or prosecution has been initiated. The period of limitation shall be interrupted if an investigation or prosecution has been initiated during this period, either before the Court or by a State Party with jurisdiction over the case pursuant to article 70, paragraph 4(a).
3. Enforcement of sanctions imposed with respect to offences defined in article 70 shall be subject to a period of limitation of 10 years from the date on which the sanction has become final. The period of limitation shall be interrupted with the detention of the convicted person or while the person concerned is outside the territory of the States Parties.

Rule 165
Investigation, prosecution and trial

1. The Prosecutor may initiate and conduct investigations with respect to the offences defined in article 70 on his or her own initiative, on the basis of information communicated by a Chamber or any reliable source.
2. Articles 53 and 59, and any rules thereunder, shall not apply.
3. For purposes of article 61, the Pre-Trial Chamber may make any of the determinations set forth in that article on the basis of written submissions, without a hearing, unless the interests of justice otherwise require.
4. A Trial Chamber may, as appropriate and taking into account the rights of the defence, direct that there be joinder of charges under article 70 with charges under articles 5 to 8.

Rule 166
Sanctions under article 70

1. If the Court imposes sanctions with respect to article 70, this rule shall apply.
2. Article 77, and any rules thereunder, shall not apply, with the exception of an order of forfeiture under article 77, paragraph 2(b), which may be ordered in addition to imprisonment or a fine or both.
3. Each offence may be separately fined and those fines may be cumulative. Under no circumstances may the total amount exceed 50 per cent of the value of the convicted person's identifiable assets, liquid or realizable, and property, after deduction of an appropriate amount that would satisfy the financial needs of the convicted person and his or her dependants.
4. In imposing a fine the Court shall allow the convicted person a reasonable period in which to pay the fine. The Court may provide for payment of a lump sum or by way of instalments during that period.
5. If the convicted person does not pay a fine imposed in accordance with the conditions set forth in sub-rule 4, appropriate measures may be taken by the Court pursuant to rules 217 to 222 and in accordance with article 109. Where, in cases of continued wilful non-payment, the Court, on its own motion or at the request of the Prosecutor, is

satisfied that all available enforcement measures have been exhausted, it may as a last resort impose a term of imprisonment in accordance with article 70, paragraph 3. In the determination of such term of imprisonment, the Court shall take into account the amount of fine paid.

Rule 167
International cooperation and judicial assistance
1. With regard to offences under article 70, the Court may request a State to provide any form of international cooperation or judicial assistance corresponding to those forms set forth in Part 9. In any such request, the Court shall indicate that the basis for the request is an investigation or prosecution of offences under article 70.
2. The conditions for providing international cooperation or judicial assistance to the Court with respect to offences under article 70 shall be those set forth in article 70, paragraph 2.

Rule 168
Ne bis in idem
In respect of offences under article 70, no person shall be tried before the Court with respect to conduct which formed the basis of an offence for which the person has already been convicted or acquitted by the Court or another court.

Rule 169
Immediate arrest
In the case of an alleged offence under article 70 committed in the presence of a Chamber, the Prosecutor may orally request that Chamber to order the immediate arrest of the person concerned.

SECTION II. MISCONDUCT BEFORE THE COURT UNDER ARTICLE 71

Rule 170
Disruption of proceedings
Having regard to article 63, paragraph 2, the Presiding Judge of the Chamber dealing with the matter may, after giving a warning:
(a) Order a person disrupting the proceedings of the Court to leave or be removed from the courtroom; or,
(b) In case of repeated misconduct, order the interdiction of that person from attending the proceedings.

Rule 171
Refusal to comply with a direction by the Court
1. When the misconduct consists of deliberate refusal to comply with an oral or written direction by the Court, not covered by rule 170, and that direction is accompanied by a warning of sanctions in case of breach, the Presiding Judge of the Chamber dealing with the matter may order the interdiction of that person from the proceedings for a period not exceeding 30 days or, if the misconduct is of a more serious nature, impose a fine.

2. If the person committing misconduct as described in sub-rule 1 is an official of the Court, or a defence counsel, or a legal representative of victims, the Presiding Judge of the Chamber dealing with the matter may also order the interdiction of that person from exercising his or her functions before the Court for a period not exceeding 30 days.

3. If the Presiding Judge in cases under sub-rules 1 and 2 considers that a longer period of interdiction is appropriate, the Presiding Judge shall refer the matter to the Presidency, which may hold a hearing to determine whether to order a longer or permanent period of interdiction.

4. A fine imposed under sub-rule 1 shall not exceed 2,000 euros, or the equivalent amount in any currency, provided that in cases of continuing misconduct, a new fine may be imposed on each day that the misconduct continues, and such fines shall be cumulative.

5. The person concerned shall be given an opportunity to be heard before a sanction for misconduct, as described in this rule, is imposed.

Rule 172

Conduct covered by both articles 70 and 71

If conduct covered by article 71 also constitutes one of the offences defined in article 70, the Court shall proceed in accordance with article 70 and rules 162 to 169.

CHAPTER 10. COMPENSATION TO AN ARRESTED OR CONVICTED PERSON

Rule 173

Request for compensation

1. Anyone seeking compensation on any of the grounds indicated in article 85 shall submit a request, in writing, to the Presidency, which shall designate a Chamber composed of three judges to consider the request. These judges shall not have participated in any earlier judgement of the Court regarding the person making the request.

2. The request for compensation shall be submitted not later than six months from the date the person making the request was notified of the decision of the Court concerning:
   (a) The unlawfulness of the arrest or detention under article 85, paragraph 1;
   (b) The reversal of the conviction under article 85, paragraph 2;
   (c) The existence of a grave and manifest miscarriage of justice under article 85, paragraph 3.

3. The request shall contain the grounds and the amount of compensation requested.

4. The person requesting compensation shall be entitled to legal assistance.

Rule 174

Procedure for seeking compensation

1. A request for compensation and any other written observation by the person filing the request shall be transmitted to the Prosecutor, who shall have an opportunity to respond in writing. Any observations by the Prosecutor shall be notified to the person filing the request.

2. The Chamber designated under rule 173, sub-rule 1, may either hold a hearing or determine the matter on the basis of the request and any written observations by the

Prosecutor and the person filing the request. A hearing shall be held if the Prosecutor or the person seeking compensation so requests.

3. The decision shall be taken by the majority of the judges. The decision shall be notified to the Prosecutor and to the person filing the request.

Rule 175
Amount of compensation

In establishing the amount of any compensation in conformity with article 85, paragraph 3, the Chamber designated under rule 173, sub-rule 1, shall take into consideration the consequences of the grave and manifest miscarriage of justice on the personal, family, social and professional situation of the person filing the request.

CHAPTER 11. INTERNATIONAL COOPERATION AND JUDICIAL ASSISTANCE

SECTION I. REQUESTS FOR COOPERATION UNDER ARTICLE 87

Rule 176
Organs of the Court responsible for the transmission and receipt of any communications relating to international cooperation and judicial assistance

1. Upon and subsequent to the establishment of the Court, the Registrar shall obtain from the Secretary-General of the United Nations any communication made by States pursuant to article 87, paragraphs 1(a) and 2.
2. The Registrar shall transmit the requests for cooperation made by the Chambers and shall receive the responses, information and documents from requested States. The Office of the Prosecutor shall transmit the requests for cooperation made by the Prosecutor and shall receive the responses, information and documents from requested States.
3. The Registrar shall be the recipient of any communication from States concerning subsequent changes in the designation of the national channels charged with receiving requests for cooperation, as well as of any change in the language in which requests for cooperation should be made, and shall, upon request, make such information available to States Parties as may be appropriate.
4. The provisions of sub-rule 2 are applicable *mutatis mutandis* where the Court requests information, documents or other forms of cooperation and assistance from an intergovernmental organization.
5. The Registrar shall transmit any communications referred to in sub-rules 1 and 3 and rule 177, sub-rule 2, as appropriate, to the Presidency or the Office of the Prosecutor, or both.

Rule 177
Channels of communication

1. Communications concerning the national authority charged with receiving requests for cooperation made upon ratification, acceptance, approval or accession shall provide all relevant information about such authorities.
2. When an intergovernmental organization is asked to assist the Court under article 87, paragraph 6, the Registrar shall, when necessary, ascertain its designated channel of communication and obtain all relevant information relating thereto.

16

Rule 178
Language chosen by States Parties under article 87, paragraph 2

1. When a requested State Party has more than one official language, it may indicate upon ratification, acceptance, approval or accession that requests for cooperation and any supporting documents can be drafted in any one of its official languages.
2. When the requested State Party has not chosen a language for communication with the Court upon ratification, acceptance, accession or approval, the request for cooperation shall either be in or be accompanied by a translation into one of the working languages of the Court pursuant to article 87, paragraph 2.

Rule 179
Language of requests directed to States not party to the Statute

When a State not party to the Statute has agreed to provide assistance to the Court under article 87, paragraph 5, and has not made a choice of language for such requests, the requests for cooperation shall either be in or be accompanied by a translation into one of the working languages of the Court.

Rule 180
Changes in the channels of communication or the languages of requests for cooperation

1. Changes concerning the channel of communication or the language a State has chosen under article 87, paragraph 2, shall be communicated in writing to the Registrar at the earliest opportunity.
2. Such changes shall take effect in respect of requests for cooperation made by the Court at a time agreed between the Court and the State or, in the absence of such an agreement, 45 days after the Court has received the communication and, in all cases, without prejudice to current requests or requests in progress.

SECTION II. SURRENDER, TRANSIT AND COMPETING REQUESTS UNDER ARTICLES 89 AND 90

Rule 181
Challenge to admissibility of a case before a national court

When a situation described in article 89, paragraph 2, arises, and without prejudice to the provisions of article 19 and of rules 58 to 62 on procedures applicable to challenges to the jurisdiction of the Court or the admissibility of a case, the Chamber dealing with the case, if the admissibility ruling is still pending, shall take steps to obtain from the requested State all the relevant information about the *ne bis in idem* challenge brought by the person.

Rule 182
Request for transit under article 89, paragraph 3(e)

1. In situations described in article 89, paragraph 3(e), the Court may transmit the request for transit by any medium capable of delivering a written record.
2. When the time limit provided for in article 89, paragraph 3(e), has expired and the person concerned has been released, such a release is without prejudice to a subsequent arrest of the person in accordance with the provisions of article 89 or article 92.

Rule 183
Possible temporary surrender
Following the consultations referred to in article 89, paragraph 4, the requested State may temporarily surrender the person sought in accordance with conditions determined between the requested State and the Court. In such case the person shall be kept in custody during his or her presence before the Court and shall be transferred to the requested State once his or her presence before the Court is no longer required, at the latest when the proceedings have been completed.

Rule 184
Arrangements for surrender
1. The requested State shall immediately inform the Registrar when the person sought by the Court is available for surrender.
2. The person shall be surrendered to the Court by the date and in the manner agreed upon between the authorities of the requested State and the Registrar.
3. If circumstances prevent the surrender of the person by the date agreed, the authorities of the requested State and the Registrar shall agree upon a new date and manner by which the person shall be surrendered.
4. The Registrar shall maintain contact with the authorities of the host State in relation to the arrangements for the surrender of the person to the Court.

Rule 185
Release of a person from the custody of the Court other than upon completion of sentence
1. Subject to sub-rule 2, where a person surrendered to the Court is released from the custody of the Court because the Court does not have jurisdiction, the case is inadmissible under article 17, paragraph 1(b), (c) or (d), the charges have not been confirmed under article 61, the person has been acquitted at trial or on appeal, or for any other reason, the Court shall, as soon as possible, make such arrangements as it considers appropriate for the transfer of the person, taking into account the views of the person, to a State which is obliged to receive him or her, to another State which agrees to receive him or her, or to a State which has requested his or her extradition with the consent of the original surrendering State. In this case, the host State shall facilitate the transfer in accordance with the agreement referred to in article 3, paragraph 2, and the related arrangements.
2. Where the Court has determined that the case is inadmissible under article 17, paragraph 1(a), the Court shall make arrangements, as appropriate, for the transfer of the person to a State whose investigation or prosecution has formed the basis of the successful challenge to admissibility, unless the State that originally surrendered the person requests his or her return.

Rule 186
Competing requests in the context of a challenge to the admissibility of the case
In situations described in article 90, paragraph 8, the requested State shall provide the notification of its decision to the Prosecutor in order to enable him or her to act in accordance with article 19, paragraph 10.

16

SECTION III. DOCUMENTS FOR ARREST AND SURRENDER UNDER ARTICLES 91 AND 92

Rule 187
Translation of documents accompanying request for surrender

For the purposes of article 67, paragraph 1(a), and in accordance with rule 117, sub-rule 1, the request under article 91 shall be accompanied, as appropriate, by a translation of the warrant of arrest or of the judgement of conviction and by a translation of the text of any relevant provisions of the Statute, in a language that the person fully understands and speaks.

Rule 188
Time limit for submission of documents after provisional arrest

For the purposes of article 92, paragraph 3, the time limit for receipt by the requested State of the request for surrender and the documents supporting the request shall be 60 days from the date of the provisional arrest.

Rule 189
Transmission of documents supporting the request

When a person has consented to surrender in accordance with the provisions of article 92, paragraph 3, and the requested State proceeds to surrender the person to the Court, the Court shall not be required to provide the documents described in article 91 unless the requested State indicates otherwise.

SECTION IV. COOPERATION UNDER ARTICLE 93

Rule 190
Instruction on self-incrimination accompanying request for witness

When making a request under article 93, paragraph 1(e), with respect to a witness, the Court shall annex an instruction, concerning rule 74 relating to self-incrimination, to be provided to the witness in question, in a language that the person fully understands and speaks.

Rule 191
Assurance provided by the Court under article 93, paragraph 2

The Chamber dealing with the case, on its own motion or at the request of the Prosecutor, defence or witness or expert concerned, may decide, after taking into account the views of the Prosecutor and the witness or expert concerned, to provide the assurance described in article 93, paragraph 2.

Rule 192
Transfer of a person in custody

1. Transfer of a person in custody to the Court in accordance with article 93, paragraph 7, shall be arranged by the national authorities concerned in liaison with the Registrar and the authorities of the host State.
2. The Registrar shall ensure the proper conduct of the transfer, including the supervision of the person while in the custody of the Court.

3. The person in custody before the Court shall have the right to raise matters concerning the conditions of his or her detention with the relevant Chamber.

4. In accordance with article 93, paragraph 7(b), when the purposes of the transfer have been fulfilled, the Registrar shall arrange for the return of the person in custody to the requested State.

Rule 193
Temporary transfer of the person from the State of enforcement

1. The Chamber that is considering the case may order the temporary transfer from the State of enforcement to the seat of the Court of any person sentenced by the Court whose testimony or other assistance is necessary to the Court. The provisions of article 93, paragraph 7, shall not apply.

2. The Registrar shall ensure the proper conduct of the transfer, in liaison with the authorities of the State of enforcement and the authorities of the host State. When the purposes of the transfer have been fulfilled, the Court shall return the sentenced person to the State of enforcement.

3. The person shall be kept in custody during his or her presence before the Court. The entire period of detention spent at the seat of the Court shall be deducted from the sentence remaining to be served.

Rule 194
Cooperation requested from the Court

1. In accordance with article 93, paragraph 10, and consistent with article 96, *mutatis mutandis*, a State may transmit to the Court a request for cooperation or assistance to the Court, either in or accompanied by a translation into one of the working languages of the Court.

2. Requests described in sub-rule 1 are to be sent to the Registrar, which shall transmit them, as appropriate, either to the Prosecutor or to the Chamber concerned.

3. If protective measures within the meaning of article 68 have been adopted, the Prosecutor or Chamber, as appropriate, shall consider the views of the Chamber which ordered the measures as well as those of the relevant victim or witness, before deciding on the request.

4. If the request relates to documents or evidence as described in article 93, paragraph 10(b)(ii), the Prosecutor or Chamber, as appropriate, shall obtain the written consent of the relevant State before proceeding with the request.

5. When the Court decides to grant the request for cooperation or assistance from a State, the request shall be executed, insofar as possible, following any procedure outlined therein by the requesting State and permitting persons specified in the request to be present.

SECTION V. COOPERATION UNDER ARTICLE 98

Rule 195
Provision of information

1. When a requested State notifies the Court that a request for surrender or assistance raises a problem of execution in respect of article 98, the requested State shall provide any

information relevant to assist the Court in the application of article 98. Any concerned third State or sending State may provide additional information to assist the Court.

2. The Court may not proceed with a request for the surrender of a person without the consent of a sending State if, under article 98, paragraph 2, such a request would be inconsistent with obligations under an international agreement pursuant to which the consent of a sending State is required prior to the surrender of a person of that State to the Court.

SECTION VI. RULE OF SPECIALITY UNDER ARTICLE 101

Rule 196
Provision of views on article 101, paragraph 1
A person surrendered to the Court may provide views on a perceived violation of the provisions of article 101, paragraph 1.

Rule 197
Extension of the surrender
When the Court has requested a waiver of the requirements of article 101, paragraph 1, the requested State may ask the Court to obtain and provide the views of the person surrendered to the Court.

CHAPTER 12. ENFORCEMENT

SECTION I. ROLE OF STATES IN ENFORCEMENT OF SENTENCES OF IMPRISONMENT AND CHANGE IN DESIGNATION OF STATE OF ENFORCEMENT UNDER ARTICLES 103 AND 104

Rule 198
Communications between the Court and States
Unless the context otherwise requires, article 87 and rules 176 to 180 shall apply, as appropriate, to communications between the Court and a State on matters relating to enforcement of sentences.

Rule 199
Organ responsible under Part 10
Unless provided otherwise in the Rules, the functions of the Court under Part 10 shall be exercised by the Presidency.

Rule 200
List of States of enforcement
1. A list of States that have indicated their willingness to accept sentenced persons shall be established and maintained by the Registrar.
2. The Presidency shall not include a State on the list provided for in article 103, paragraph 1(a), if it does not agree with the conditions that such a State attaches to its acceptance. The Presidency may request any additional information from that State prior to taking a decision.

3. A State that has attached conditions of acceptance may at any time withdraw such conditions. Any amendments or additions to such conditions shall be subject to confirmation by the Presidency.

4. A State may at any time inform the Registrar of its withdrawal from the list. Such withdrawal shall not affect the enforcement of the sentences in respect of persons that the State has already accepted.

5. The Court may enter bilateral arrangements with States with a view to establishing a framework for the acceptance of prisoners sentenced by the Court. Such arrangements shall be consistent with the Statute.

Rule 201
Principles of equitable distribution
Principles of equitable distribution for purposes of article 103, paragraph 3, shall include:
(a) The principle of equitable geographical distribution;
(b) The need to afford each State on the list an opportunity to receive sentenced persons;
(c) The number of sentenced persons already received by that State and other States of enforcement;
(d) Any other relevant factors.

Rule 202
Timing of delivery of the sentenced person to the State of enforcement
The delivery of a sentenced person from the Court to the designated State of enforcement shall not take place unless the decision on the conviction and the decision on the sentence have become final.

Rule 203
Views of the sentenced person
1. The Presidency shall give notice in writing to the sentenced person that it is addressing the designation of a State of enforcement. The sentenced person shall, within such time limit as the Presidency shall prescribe, submit in writing his or her views on the question to the Presidency.
2. The Presidency may allow the sentenced person to make oral presentations.
3. The Presidency shall allow the sentenced person:
   (a) To be assisted, as appropriate, by a competent interpreter and to benefit from any translation necessary for the presentation of his or her views;
   (b) To be granted adequate time and facilities necessary to prepare for the presentation of his or her views.

Rule 204
Information relating to designation
When the Presidency notifies the designated State of its decision, it shall also transmit the following information and documents:
(a) The name, nationality, date and place of birth of the sentenced person;
(b) A copy of the final judgement of conviction and of the sentence imposed;
(c) The length and commencement date of the sentence and the time remaining to be served;

(d) After having heard the views of the sentenced person, any necessary information concerning the state of his or her health, including any medical treatment that he or she is receiving.

Rule 205
Rejection of designation in a particular case

Where a State in a particular case rejects the designation by the Presidency, the Presidency may designate another State.

Rule 206
Delivery of the sentenced person to the State of enforcement

1. The Registrar shall inform the Prosecutor and the sentenced person of the State designated to enforce the sentence.
2. The sentenced person shall be delivered to the State of enforcement as soon as possible after the designated State of enforcement accepts.
3. The Registrar shall ensure the proper conduct of the delivery of the person in consultation with the authorities of the State of enforcement and the host State.

Rule 207
Transit

1. No authorization is required if the sentenced person is transported by air and no landing is scheduled on the territory of the transit State. If an unscheduled landing occurs on the territory of the transit State, that State shall, to the extent possible under the procedure of national law, detain the sentenced person in custody until a request for transit as provided in sub-rule 2 or a request under article 89, paragraph 1, or article 92 is received.
2. To the extent possible under the procedure of national law, a State Party shall authorize the transit of a sentenced person through its territory and the provisions of article 89, paragraph 3(b) and (c), and articles 105 and 108 and any rules relating thereto shall, as appropriate, apply. A copy of the final judgement of conviction and of the sentence imposed shall be attached to such request for transit.

Rule 208 Costs

1. The ordinary costs for the enforcement of the sentence in the territory of the State of enforcement shall be borne by that State.
2. Other costs, including those for the transport of the sentenced person and those referred to in article 100, paragraph 1(c), (d) and (e), shall be borne by the Court.

Rule 209
Change in designation of State of enforcement

1. The Presidency, acting on its own motion or at the request of the sentenced person or the Prosecutor, may at any time act in accordance with article 104, paragraph 1.
2. The request of the sentenced person or of the Prosecutor shall be made in writing and shall set out the grounds upon which the transfer is sought.

Rule 210
Procedure for change in the designation of a State of enforcement

1. Before deciding to change the designation of a State of enforcement, the Presidency may:
   (a) Request views from the State of enforcement;
   (b) Consider written or oral presentations of the sentenced person and the Prosecutor;
   (c) Consider written or oral expert opinion concerning, *inter alia*, the sentenced person;
   (d) Obtain any other relevant information from any reliable sources.
2. The provisions of rule 203, sub-rule 3, shall apply, as appropriate.
3. If the Presidency refuses to change the designation of the State of enforcement, it shall, as soon as possible, inform the sentenced person, the Prosecutor and the Registrar of its decision and of the reasons therefor. It shall also inform the State of enforcement.

SECTION II. ENFORCEMENT, SUPERVISION AND TRANSFER UNDER ARTICLES 105, 106 AND 107

Rule 211
Supervision of enforcement of sentences and conditions of imprisonment

1. In order to supervise the enforcement of sentences of imprisonment, the Presidency:
   (a) Shall, in consultation with the State of enforcement, ensure that in establishing appropriate arrangements for the exercise by any sentenced person of his or her right to communicate with the Court about the conditions of imprisonment, the provisions of article 106, paragraph 3, shall be respected;
   (b) May, when necessary, request any information, report or expert opinion from the State of enforcement or from any reliable sources;
   (c) May, where appropriate, delegate a judge of the Court or a member of the staff of the Court who will be responsible, after notifying the State of enforcement, for meeting the sentenced person and hearing his or her views, without the presence of national authorities;
   (d) May, where appropriate, give the State of enforcement an opportunity to comment on the views expressed by the sentenced person under sub-rule 1(c).
2. When a sentenced person is eligible for a prison programme or benefit available under the domestic law of the State of enforcement which may entail some activity outside the prison facility, the State of enforcement shall communicate that fact to the Presidency, together with any relevant information or observation, to enable the Court to exercise its supervisory function.

Rule 212
Information on location of the person for enforcement of fines, forfeitures or reparation measures

For the purpose of enforcement of fines and forfeiture measures and of reparation measures ordered by the Court, the Presidency may, at any time or at least 30 days before the scheduled completion of the sentence served by the sentenced person, request the State of enforcement to transmit to it the relevant information concerning the intention of that

State to authorize the person to remain in its territory or the location where it intends to transfer the person.

Rule 213

Procedure for article 107, paragraph 3

With respect to article 107, paragraph 3, the procedure set out in rules 214 and 215 shall apply, as appropriate.

SECTION III. LIMITATION ON THE PROSECUTION OR PUNISHMENT OF OTHER OFFENCES UNDER ARTICLE 108

Rule 214

Request to prosecute or enforce a sentence for prior conduct

1. For the application of article 108, when the State of enforcement wishes to prosecute or enforce a sentence against the sentenced person for any conduct engaged in prior to that person's transfer, it shall notify its intention to the Presidency and transmit to it the following documents:

   (a) A statement of the facts of the case and their legal characterization;

   (b) A copy of any applicable legal provisions, including those concerning the statute of limitation and the applicable penalties;

   (c) A copy of any sentence, warrant of arrest or other document having the same force, or of any other legal writ which the State intends to enforce;

   (d) A protocol containing views of the sentenced person obtained after the person has been informed sufficiently about the proceedings.

2. In the event of a request for extradition made by another State, the State of enforcement shall transmit the entire request to the Presidency with a protocol containing the views of the sentenced person obtained after informing the person sufficiently about the extradition request.

3. The Presidency may in all cases request any document or additional information from the State of enforcement or the State requesting extradition.

4. If the person was surrendered to the Court by a State other than the State of enforcement or the State seeking extradition, the Presidency shall consult with the State that surrendered the person and take into account any views expressed by that State.

5. Any information or documents transmitted to the Presidency under sub-rules 1 to 4 shall be transmitted to the Prosecutor, who may comment.

6. The Presidency may decide to conduct a hearing.

Rule 215

Decision on request to prosecute or enforce a sentence

1. The Presidency shall make a determination as soon as possible. This determination shall be notified to all those who have participated in the proceedings.

2. If the request submitted under sub-rules 1 or 2 of rule 214 concerns the enforcement of a sentence, the sentenced person may serve that sentence in the State designated by the Court to enforce the sentence pronounced by it or be extradited to a third State only after having served the full sentence pronounced by the Court, subject to the provisions of article 110.

3. The Presidency may authorize the temporary extradition of the sentenced person to a third State for prosecution only if it has obtained assurances which it deems to be sufficient that the sentenced person will be kept in custody in the third State and transferred back to the State responsible for enforcement of the sentence pronounced by the Court, after the prosecution.

Rule 216
Information on enforcement
The Presidency shall request the State of enforcement to inform it of any important event concerning the sentenced person, and of any prosecution of that person for events subsequent to his or her transfer.

SECTION IV. ENFORCEMENT OF FINES, FORFEITURE MEASURES AND REPARATION ORDERS

Rule 217
Cooperation and measures for enforcement of fines, forfeiture or reparation orders
For the enforcement of fines, forfeiture or reparation orders, the Presidency shall, as appropriate, seek cooperation and measures for enforcement in accordance with Part 9, as well as transmit copies of relevant orders to any State with which the sentenced person appears to have direct connection by reason of either nationality, domicile or habitual residence or by virtue of the location of the sentenced person's assets and property or with which the victim has such connection. The Presidency shall, as appropriate, inform the State of any third-party claims or of the fact that no claim was presented by a person who received notification of any proceedings conducted pursuant to article 75.

Rule 218
Orders for forfeiture and reparations
1. In order to enable States to give effect to an order for forfeiture, the order shall specify:
   (a) The identity of the person against whom the order has been issued;
   (b) The proceeds, property and assets that have been ordered by the Court to be forfeited; and
   (c) That if the State Party is unable to give effect to the order for forfeiture in relation to the specified proceeds, property or assets, it shall take measures to recover the value of the same.
2. In the request for cooperation and measures for enforcement, the Court shall also provide available information as to the location of the proceeds, property and assets that are covered by the order for forfeiture.
3. In order to enable States to give effect to an order for reparations, the order shall specify:
   (a) The identity of the person against whom the order has been issued;
   (b) In respect of reparations of a financial nature, the identity of the victims to whom individual reparations have been granted, and, where the award for reparations shall be deposited with the Trust Fund, the particulars of the Trust Fund for the deposit of the award; and
   (c) The scope and nature of the reparations ordered by the Court, including, where applicable, the property and assets for which restitution has been ordered.

16

4. Where the Court awards reparations on an individual basis, a copy of the reparation order shall be transmitted to the victim concerned.

Rule 219
Non-modification of orders for reparation

The Presidency shall, when transmitting copies of orders for reparations to States Parties under rule 217, inform them that, in giving effect to an order for reparations, the national authorities shall not modify the reparations specified by the Court, the scope or the extent of any damage, loss or injury determined by the Court or the principles stated in the order, and shall facilitate the enforcement of such order.

Rule 220
Non-modification of judgements in which fines were imposed

When transmitting copies of judgements in which fines were imposed to States Parties for the purpose of enforcement in accordance with article 109 and rule 217, the Presidency shall inform them that in enforcing the fines imposed, national authorities shall not modify them.

Rule 221
Decision on disposition or allocation of property or assets

1. The Presidency shall, after having consulted, as appropriate, with the Prosecutor, the sentenced person, the victims or their legal representatives, the national authorities of the State of enforcement or any relevant third party, or representatives of the Trust Fund provided for in article 79, decide on all matters related to the disposition or allocation of property or assets realized through enforcement of an order of the Court.

2. In all cases, when the Presidency decides on the disposition or allocation of property or assets belonging to the sentenced person, it shall give priority to the enforcement of measures concerning reparations to victims.

Rule 222
Assistance for service or any other measure

The Presidency shall assist the State in the enforcement of fines, forfeiture or reparation orders, as requested, with the service of any relevant notification on the sentenced person or any other relevant persons, or the carrying out of any other measures necessary for the enforcement of the order under the procedure of the national law of the enforcement State.

SECTION V. REVIEW CONCERNING REDUCTION OF SENTENCE UNDER ARTICLE 110

Rule 223
Criteria for review concerning reduction of sentence

In reviewing the question of reduction of sentence pursuant to article 110, paragraphs 3 and 5, the three judges of the Appeals Chamber shall take into account the criteria listed in article 110, paragraph 4(a) and (b), and the following criteria:

(a) The conduct of the sentenced person while in detention, which shows a genuine dissociation from his or her crime;

(b) The prospect of the resocialization and successful resettlement of the sentenced person;

(c) Whether the early release of the sentenced person would give rise to significant social instability;

(d) Any significant action taken by the sentenced person for the benefit of the victims as well as any impact on the victims and their families as a result of the early release;

(e) Individual circumstances of the sentenced person, including a worsening state of physical or mental health or advanced age.

Rule 224

Procedure for review concerning reduction of sentence

1. For the application of article 110, paragraph 3, three judges of the Appeals Chamber appointed by that Chamber shall conduct a hearing, unless they decide otherwise in a particular case, for exceptional reasons. The hearing shall be conducted with the sentenced person, who may be assisted by his or her counsel, with interpretation, as may be required. Those three judges shall invite the Prosecutor, the State of enforcement of any penalty under article 77 or any reparation order pursuant to article 75 and, to the extent possible, the victims or their legal representatives who participated in the proceedings, to participate in the hearing or to submit written observations. Under exceptional circumstances, this hearing may be conducted by way of a videoconference or in the State of enforcement by a judge delegated by the Appeals Chamber.

2. The same three judges shall communicate the decision and the reasons for it to all those who participated in the review proceedings as soon as possible.

3. For the application of article 110, paragraph 5, three judges of the Appeals Chamber appointed by that Chamber shall review the question of reduction of sentence every three years, unless it establishes a shorter interval in its decision taken pursuant to article 110, paragraph 3. In case of a significant change in circumstances, those three judges may permit the sentenced person to apply for a review within the three-year period or such shorter period as may have been set by the three judges.

4. For any review under article 110, paragraph 5, three judges of the Appeals Chamber appointed by that Chamber shall invite written representations from the sentenced person or his or her counsel, the Prosecutor, the State of enforcement of any penalty under article 77 and any reparation order pursuant to article 75 and, to the extent possible, the victims or their legal representatives who participated in the proceedings. The three judges may also decide to hold a hearing.

5. The decision and the reasons for it shall be communicated to all those who participated in the review proceedings as soon as possible.

SECTION VI. ESCAPE

Rule 225

Measures under article 111 in the event of escape

1. If the sentenced person has escaped, the State of enforcement shall, as soon as possible, advise the Registrar by any medium capable of delivering a written record. The Presidency shall then proceed in accordance with Part 9.

16

2. However, if the State in which the sentenced person is located agrees to surrender him or her to the State of enforcement, pursuant to either international agreements or its national legislation, the State of enforcement shall so advise the Registrar in writing. The person shall be surrendered to the State of enforcement as soon as possible, if necessary in consultation with the Registrar, who shall provide all necessary assistance, including, if necessary, the presentation of requests for transit to the States concerned, in accordance with rule 207. The costs associated with the surrender of the sentenced person shall be borne by the Court if no State assumes responsibility for them.

3. If the sentenced person is surrendered to the Court pursuant to Part 9, the Court shall transfer him or her to the State of enforcement. Nevertheless, the Presidency may, acting on its own motion or at the request of the Prosecutor or of the initial State of enforcement and in accordance with article 103 and rules 203 to 206, designate another State, including the State to the territory of which the sentenced person has fled.

4. In all cases, the entire period of detention in the territory of the State in which the sentenced person was in custody after his or her escape and, where sub-rule 3 is applicable, the period of detention at the seat of the Court following the surrender of the sentenced person from the State in which he or she was located shall be deducted from the sentence remaining to be served.

International Criminal Court Elements of Crimes

GENERAL INTRODUCTION

1. Pursuant to article 9, the following Elements of Crimes shall assist the Court in the interpretation and application of articles 6, 7 and 8, consistent with the Statute. The provisions of the Statute, including article 21 and the general principles set out in Part 3, are applicable to the Elements of Crimes.

2. As stated in article 30, unless otherwise provided, a person shall be criminally responsible and liable for punishment for a crime within the jurisdiction of the Court only if the material elements are committed with intent and knowledge. Where no reference is made in the Elements of Crimes to a mental element for any particular conduct, consequence or circumstance listed, it is understood that the relevant mental element, i.e., intent, knowledge or both, set out in article 30 applies. Exceptions to the article 30 standard, based on the Statute, including applicable law under its relevant provisions, are indicated below.

3. Existence of intent and knowledge can be inferred from relevant facts and circumstances.

4. With respect to mental elements associated with elements involving value judgement, such as those using the terms "inhumane" or "severe", it is not necessary that the perpetrator personally completed a particular value judgement, unless otherwise indicated.

5. Grounds for excluding criminal responsibility or the absence thereof are generally not specified in the elements of crimes listed under each crime.[1]

---

[1] This paragraph is without prejudice to the obligation of the Prosecutor under article 54, paragraph 1, of the Statute.

6. The requirement of "unlawfulness" found in the Statute or in other parts of international law, in particular international humanitarian law, is generally not specified in the elements of crimes.
7. The elements of crimes are generally structured in accordance with the following principles:
   (a) As the elements of crimes focus on the conduct, consequences and circumstances associated with each crime, they are generally listed in that order;
   (b) When required, a particular mental element is listed after the affected conduct, consequence or circumstance;
   (c) Contextual circumstances are listed last.
8. As used in the Elements of Crimes, the term "perpetrator" is neutral as to guilt or innocence. The elements, including the appropriate mental elements, apply, *mutatis mutandis*, to all those whose criminal responsibility may fall under articles 25 and 28 of the Statute.
9. A particular conduct may constitute one or more crimes.
10. The use of short titles for the crimes has no legal effect.

Article 6
Genocide

Introduction

With respect to the last element listed for each crime:
(a) The term "in the context of" would include the initial acts in an emerging pattern;
(b) The term "manifest" is an objective qualification;
(c) Notwithstanding the normal requirement for a mental element provided for in article 30, and recognizing that knowledge of the circumstances will usually be addressed in proving genocidal intent, the appropriate requirement, if any, for a mental element regarding this circumstance will need to be decided by the Court on a case-by-case basis.

Article 6(a)
Genocide by killing

Elements

1. The perpetrator killed[2] one or more persons.
2. Such person or persons belonged to a particular national, ethnical, racial or religious group.
3. The perpetrator intended to destroy, in whole or in part, that national, ethnical, racial or religious group, as such.
4. The conduct took place in the context of a manifest pattern of similar conduct directed against that group or was conduct that could itself effect such destruction.

---

[2] The term "killed" is interchangeable with the term "caused death".

Article 6(b)
Genocide by causing serious bodily or mental harm
Elements

1. The perpetrator caused serious bodily or mental harm to one or more persons.[3]
2. Such person or persons belonged to a particular national, ethnical, racial or religious group.
3. The perpetrator intended to destroy, in whole or in part, that national, ethnical, racial or religious group, as such.
4. The conduct took place in the context of a manifest pattern of similar conduct directed against that group or was conduct that could itself effect such destruction.

Article 6(c)
Genocide by deliberately inflicting conditions of life calculated to bring about physical destruction
Elements

1. The perpetrator inflicted certain conditions of life upon one or more persons.
2. Such person or persons belonged to a particular national, ethnical, racial or religious group.
3. The perpetrator intended to destroy, in whole or in part, that national, ethnical, racial or religious group, as such.
4. The conditions of life were calculated to bring about the physical destruction of that group, in whole or in part.[4]
5. The conduct took place in the context of a manifest pattern of similar conduct directed against that group or was conduct that could itself effect such destruction.

Article 6(d)
Genocide by imposing measures intended to prevent births
Elements

1. The perpetrator imposed certain measures upon one or more persons.
2. Such person or persons belonged to a particular national, ethnical, racial or religious group.
3. The perpetrator intended to destroy, in whole or in part, that national, ethnical, racial or religious group, as such.
4. The measures imposed were intended to prevent births within that group.
5. The conduct took place in the context of a manifest pattern of similar conduct directed against that group or was conduct that could itself effect such destruction.

---

[3] This conduct may include, but is not necessarily restricted to, acts of torture, rape, sexual violence or inhuman or degrading treatment.

[4] The term "conditions of life" may include, but is not necessarily restricted to, deliberate deprivation of resources indispensable for survival, such as food or medical services, or systematic expulsion from homes.

Article 6(e)
Genocide by forcibly transferring children
Elements

1. The perpetrator forcibly transferred one or more persons.[5]
2. Such person or persons belonged to a particular national, ethnical, racial or religious group.
3. The perpetrator intended to destroy, in whole or in part, that national, ethnical, racial or religious group, as such.
4. The transfer was from that group to another group.
5. The person or persons were under the age of 18 years.
6. The perpetrator knew, or should have known, that the person or persons were under the age of 18 years.
7. The conduct took place in the context of a manifest pattern of similar conduct directed against that group or was conduct that could itself effect such destruction.

Article 7
Crimes against humanity
Introduction

1. Since article 7 pertains to international criminal law, its provisions, consistent with article 22, must be strictly construed, taking into account that crimes against humanity as defined in article 7 are among the most serious crimes of concern to the international community as a whole, warrant and entail individual criminal responsibility, and require conduct which is impermissible under generally applicable international law, as recognized by the principal legal systems of the world.
2. The last two elements for each crime against humanity describe the context in which the conduct must take place. These elements clarify the requisite participation in and knowledge of a widespread or systematic attack against a civilian population. However, the last element should not be interpreted as requiring proof that the perpetrator had knowledge of all characteristics of the attack or the precise details of the plan or policy of the State or organization. In the case of an emerging widespread or systematic attack against a civilian population, the intent clause of the last element indicates that this mental element is satisfied if the perpetrator intended to further such an attack.
3. "Attack directed against a civilian population" in these context elements is understood to mean a course of conduct involving the multiple commission of acts referred to in article 7, paragraph 1, of the Statute against any civilian population, pursuant to or in furtherance of a State or organizational policy to commit such attack. The acts need not constitute a military attack. It is understood that "policy to commit such attack"

---

[5] The term "forcibly" is not restricted to physical force, but may include threat of force or coercion, such as that caused by fear of violence, duress, detention, psychological oppression or abuse of power, against such person or persons or another person, or by taking advantage of a coercive environment.

requires that the State or organization actively promote or encourage such an attack against a civilian population.[6]

Article 7(1)(a)
Crime against humanity of murder
Elements

1. The perpetrator killed[7] one or more persons.
2. The conduct was committed as part of a widespread or systematic attack directed against a civilian population.
3. The perpetrator knew that the conduct was part of or intended the conduct to be part of a widespread or systematic attack against a civilian population.

Article 7(1)(b)
Crime against humanity of extermination
Elements

1. The perpetrator killed[8] one or more persons, including by inflicting conditions of life calculated to bring about the destruction of part of a population.[9]
2. The conduct constituted, or took place as part of,[10] a mass killing of members of a civilian population.
3. The conduct was committed as part of a widespread or systematic attack directed against a civilian population.
4. The perpetrator knew that the conduct was part of or intended the conduct to be part of a widespread or systematic attack directed against a civilian population.

Article 7(1)(c)
Crime against humanity of enslavement
Elements

1. The perpetrator exercised any or all of the powers attaching to the right of ownership over one or more persons, such as by purchasing, selling, lending or bartering such a person or persons, or by imposing on them a similar deprivation of liberty.[11]
2. The conduct was committed as part of a widespread or systematic attack directed against a civilian population.

---

[6] A policy which has a civilian population as the object of the attack would be implemented by State or organizational action. Such a policy may, in exceptional circumstances, be implemented by a deliberate failure to take action, which is consciously aimed at encouraging such attack. The existence of such a policy cannot be inferred solely from the absence of governmental or organizational action.

[7] The term "killed" is interchangeable with the term "caused death". This footnote applies to all elements which use either of these concepts.

[8] The conduct could be committed by different methods of killing, either directly or indirectly.

[9] The infliction of such conditions could include the deprivation of access to food and medicine.

[10] The term "as part of" would include the initial conduct in a mass killing.

[11] It is understood that such deprivation of liberty may, in some circumstances, include exacting forced labour or otherwise reducing a person to a servile status as defined in the Supplementary Convention on the Abolition of Slavery, the Slave Trade, and Institutions and Practices Similar to Slavery of 1956. It is also understood that the conduct described in this element includes trafficking in persons, in particular women and children.

3. The perpetrator knew that the conduct was part of or intended the conduct to be part of a widespread or systematic attack directed against a civilian population.

Article 7(1)(d)
Crime against humanity of deportation or forcible transfer of population
Elements

1. The perpetrator deported or forcibly[12] transferred,[13] without grounds permitted under international law, one or more persons to another State or location, by expulsion or other coercive acts.
2. Such person or persons were lawfully present in the area from which they were so deported or transferred.
3. The perpetrator was aware of the factual circumstances that established the lawfulness of such presence.
4. The conduct was committed as part of a widespread or systematic attack directed against a civilian population.
5. The perpetrator knew that the conduct was part of or intended the conduct to be part of a widespread or systematic attack directed against a civilian population.

Article 7(1)(e)
Crime against humanity of imprisonment or other severe deprivation of physical liberty
Elements

1. The perpetrator imprisoned one or more persons or otherwise severely deprived one or more persons of physical liberty.
2. The gravity of the conduct was such that it was in violation of fundamental rules of international law.
3. The perpetrator was aware of the factual circumstances that established the gravity of the conduct.
4. The conduct was committed as part of a widespread or systematic attack directed against a civilian population.
5. The perpetrator knew that the conduct was part of or intended the conduct to be part of a widespread or systematic attack directed against a civilian population.

Article 7(1)(f)
Crime against humanity of torture[14]
Elements

1. The perpetrator inflicted severe physical or mental pain or suffering upon one or more persons.

---

[12] The term "forcibly" is not restricted to physical force, but may include threat of force or coercion, such as that caused by fear of violence, duress, detention, psychological oppression or abuse of power against such person or persons or another person, or by taking advantage of a coercive environment.

[13] "Deported or forcibly transferred" is interchangeable with "forcibly displaced".

[14] It is understood that no specific purpose need be proved for this crime.

2. Such person or persons were in the custody or under the control of the perpetrator.
3. Such pain or suffering did not arise only from, and was not inherent in or incidental to, lawful sanctions.
4. The conduct was committed as part of a widespread or systematic attack directed against a civilian population.
5. The perpetrator knew that the conduct was part of or intended the conduct to be part of a widespread or systematic attack directed against a civilian population.

Article 7(1)(g)-1
Crime against humanity of rape

Elements

1. The perpetrator invaded[15] the body of a person by conduct resulting in penetration, however slight, of any part of the body of the victim or of the perpetrator with a sexual organ, or of the anal or genital opening of the victim with any object or any other part of the body.
2. The invasion was committed by force, or by threat of force or coercion, such as that caused by fear of violence, duress, detention, psychological oppression or abuse of power, against such person or another person, or by taking advantage of a coercive environment, or the invasion was committed against a person incapable of giving genuine consent.[16]
3. The conduct was committed as part of a widespread or systematic attack directed against a civilian population.
4. The perpetrator knew that the conduct was part of or intended the conduct to be part of a widespread or systematic attack directed against a civilian population.

Article 7(1)(g)-2
Crime against humanity of sexual slavery[17]

Elements

1. The perpetrator exercised any or all of the powers attaching to the right of ownership over one or more persons, such as by purchasing, selling, lending or bartering such a person or persons, or by imposing on them a similar deprivation of liberty.[18]
2. The perpetrator caused such person or persons to engage in one or more acts of a sexual nature.
3. The conduct was committed as part of a widespread or systematic attack directed against a civilian population.

---

[15] The concept of "invasion" is intended to be broad enough to be gender-neutral.

[16] It is understood that a person may be incapable of giving genuine consent if affected by natural, induced or age-related incapacity. This footnote also applies to the corresponding elements of article 7(1)(g)-3, 5 and 6.

[17] Given the complex nature of this crime, it is recognized that its commission could involve more than one perpetrator as a part of a common criminal purpose.

[18] It is understood that such deprivation of liberty may, in some circumstances, include exacting forced labour or otherwise reducing a person to a servile status as defined in the Supplementary Convention on the Abolition of Slavery, the Slave Trade, and Institutions and Practices Similar to Slavery of 1956. It is also understood that the conduct described in this element includes trafficking in persons, in particular women and children.

4. The perpetrator knew that the conduct was part of or intended the conduct to be part of a widespread or systematic attack directed against a civilian population.

Article 7(1)(g)-3
Crime against humanity of enforced prostitution
Elements

1. The perpetrator caused one or more persons to engage in one or more acts of a sexual nature by force, or by threat of force or coercion, such as that caused by fear of violence, duress, detention, psychological oppression or abuse of power, against such person or persons or another person, or by taking advantage of a coercive environment or such person's or persons' incapacity to give genuine consent.
2. The perpetrator or another person obtained or expected to obtain pecuniary or other advantage in exchange for or in connection with the acts of a sexual nature.
3. The conduct was committed as part of a widespread or systematic attack directed against a civilian population.
4. The perpetrator knew that the conduct was part of or intended the conduct to be part of a widespread or systematic attack directed against a civilian population.

Article 7(1)(g)-4
Crime against humanity of forced pregnancy
Elements

1. The perpetrator confined one or more women forcibly made pregnant, with the intent of affecting the ethnic composition of any population or carrying out other grave violations of international law.
2. The conduct was committed as part of a widespread or systematic attack directed against a civilian population.
3. The perpetrator knew that the conduct was part of or intended the conduct to be part of a widespread or systematic attack directed against a civilian population.

Article 7(1)(g)-5
Crime against humanity of enforced sterilization
Elements

1. The perpetrator deprived one or more persons of biological reproductive capacity.[19]
2. The conduct was neither justified by the medical or hospital treatment of the person or persons concerned nor carried out with their genuine consent.[20]
3. The conduct was committed as part of a widespread or systematic attack directed against a civilian population.

---

[19] The deprivation is not intended to include birth-control measures which have a non-permanent effect in practice.

[20] It is understood that "genuine consent" does not include consent obtained through deception.

4. The perpetrator knew that the conduct was part of or intended the conduct to be part of a widespread or systematic attack directed against a civilian population.

Article 7(1)(g)-6
Crime against humanity of sexual violence
Elements

1. The perpetrator committed an act of a sexual nature against one or more persons or caused such person or persons to engage in an act of a sexual nature by force, or by threat of force or coercion, such as that caused by fear of violence, duress, detention, psychological oppression or abuse of power, against such person or persons or another person, or by taking advantage of a coercive environment or such person's or persons' incapacity to give genuine consent.
2. Such conduct was of a gravity comparable to the other offences in article 7, paragraph 1(g), of the Statute.
3. The perpetrator was aware of the factual circumstances that established the gravity of the conduct.
4. The conduct was committed as part of a widespread or systematic attack directed against a civilian population.
5. The perpetrator knew that the conduct was part of or intended the conduct to be part of a widespread or systematic attack directed against a civilian population.

Article 7(1)(h)
Crime against humanity of persecution
Elements

1. The perpetrator severely deprived, contrary to international law,[21] one or more persons of fundamental rights.
2. The perpetrator targeted such person or persons by reason of the identity of a group or collectivity or targeted the group or collectivity as such.
3. Such targeting was based on political, racial, national, ethnic, cultural, religious, gender as defined in article 7, paragraph 3, of the Statute, or other grounds that are universally recognized as impermissible under international law.
4. The conduct was committed in connection with any act referred to in article 7, paragraph 1, of the Statute or any crime within the jurisdiction of the Court.[22]
5. The conduct was committed as part of a widespread or systematic attack directed against a civilian population.
6. The perpetrator knew that the conduct was part of or intended the conduct to be part of a widespread or systematic attack directed against a civilian population.

---

[21] This requirement is without prejudice to paragraph 6 of the General Introduction to the Elements of Crimes.
[22] It is understood that no additional mental element is necessary for this element other than that inherent in element 6.

Article 7(1)(i)
Crime against humanity of enforced disappearance of persons[23, 24]
Elements

1. The perpetrator:
   (a) Arrested, detained[25, 26] or abducted one or more persons; or
   (b) Refused to acknowledge the arrest, detention or abduction, or to give information on the fate or whereabouts of such person or persons.
2.
   (a) Such arrest, detention or abduction was followed or accompanied by a refusal to acknowledge that deprivation of freedom or to give information on the fate or whereabouts of such person or persons; or
   (b) Such refusal was preceded or accompanied by that deprivation of freedom.
3. The perpetrator was aware that:[27]
   (a) Such arrest, detention or abduction would be followed in the ordinary course of events by a refusal to acknowledge that deprivation of freedom or to give information on the fate or whereabouts of such person or persons;[28] or
   (b) Such refusal was preceded or accompanied by that deprivation of freedom.
4. Such arrest, detention or abduction was carried out by, or with the authorization, support or acquiescence of, a State or a political organization.
5. Such refusal to acknowledge that deprivation of freedom or to give information on the fate or whereabouts of such person or persons was carried out by, or with the authorization or support of, such State or political organization.
6. The perpetrator intended to remove such person or persons from the protection of the law for a prolonged period of time.
7. The conduct was committed as part of a widespread or systematic attack directed against a civilian population.
8. The perpetrator knew that the conduct was part of or intended the conduct to be part of a widespread or systematic attack directed against a civilian population.

Article 7(1)(j)
Crime against humanity of apartheid
Elements

1. The perpetrator committed an inhumane act against one or more persons.

---

[23] Given the complex nature of this crime, it is recognized that its commission will normally involve more than one perpetrator as a part of a common criminal purpose.

[24] This crime falls under the jurisdiction of the Court only if the attack referred to in elements 7 and 8 occurs after the entry into force of the Statute.

[25] The word "detained" would include a perpetrator who maintained an existing detention.

[26] It is understood that under certain circumstances an arrest or detention may have been lawful.

[27] This element, inserted because of the complexity of this crime, is without prejudice to the General Introduction to the Elements of Crimes.

[28] It is understood that, in the case of a perpetrator who maintained an existing detention, this element would be satisfied if the perpetrator was aware that such a refusal had already taken place.

2. Such act was an act referred to in article 7, paragraph 1, of the Statute, or was an act of a character similar to any of those acts.[29]
3. The perpetrator was aware of the factual circumstances that established the character of the act.
4. The conduct was committed in the context of an institutionalized regime of systematic oppression and domination by one racial group over any other racial group or groups.
5. The perpetrator intended to maintain such regime by that conduct.
6. The conduct was committed as part of a widespread or systematic attack directed against a civilian population.
7. The perpetrator knew that the conduct was part of or intended the conduct to be part of a widespread or systematic attack directed against a civilian population.

Article 7(1)(k)
Crime against humanity of other inhumane acts
Elements

1. The perpetrator inflicted great suffering, or serious injury to body or to mental or physical health, by means of an inhumane act.
2. Such act was of a character similar to any other act referred to in article 7, paragraph 1, of the Statute.[30]
3. The perpetrator was aware of the factual circumstances that established the character of the act.
4. The conduct was committed as part of a widespread or systematic attack directed against a civilian population.
5. The perpetrator knew that the conduct was part of or intended the conduct to be part of a widespread or systematic attack directed against a civilian population.

Article 8
War crimes
Introduction

The elements for war crimes under article 8, paragraph 2(c) and (e), are subject to the limitations addressed in article 8, paragraph 2(d) and (f), which are not elements of crimes.

The elements for war crimes under article 8, paragraph 2, of the Statute shall be interpreted within the established framework of the international law of armed conflict including, as appropriate, the international law of armed conflict applicable to armed conflict at sea.

With respect to the last two elements listed for each crime:

(a) There is no requirement for a legal evaluation by the perpetrator as to the existence of an armed conflict or its character as international or non-international;
(b) In that context there is no requirement for awareness by the perpetrator of the facts that established the character of the conflict as international or non-international;

---

[29] It is understood that "character" refers to the nature and gravity of the act.
[30] It is understood that "character" refers to the nature and gravity of the act.

(c) There is only a requirement for the awareness of the factual circumstances that estab-lished the existence of an armed conflict that is implicit in the terms "took place in the context of and was associated with".

Article 8(2)(a)
Article 8(2)(a)(i)
War crime of wilful killing

Elements

1. The perpetrator killed one or more persons.[31]
2. Such person or persons were protected under one or more of the Geneva Conventions of 1949.
3. The perpetrator was aware of the factual circumstances that established that protected status.[32, 33]
4. The conduct took place in the context of and was associated with an international armed conflict.[34]
5. The perpetrator was aware of factual circumstances that established the existence of an armed conflict.

Article 8(2)(a)(ii)-1
War crime of torture

Elements[35]

1. The perpetrator inflicted severe physical or mental pain or suffering upon one or more persons.
2. The perpetrator inflicted the pain or suffering for such purposes as: obtaining infor-mation or a confession, punishment, intimidation or coercion or for any reason based on discrimination of any kind.
3. Such person or persons were protected under one or more of the Geneva Conventions of 1949.
4. The perpetrator was aware of the factual circumstances that established that protected status.
5. The conduct took place in the context of and was associated with an international armed conflict.

---

[31] The term "killed" is interchangeable with the term "caused death". This footnote applies to all elements which use either of these concepts.

[32] This mental element recognizes the interplay between articles 30 and 32. This footnote also applies to the corresponding element in each crime under article 8(2)(a), and to the element in other crimes in article 8(2) concerning the awareness of factual circumstances that establish the status of persons or property protected under the relevant international law of armed conflict.

[33] With respect to nationality, it is understood that the perpetrator needs only to know that the victim belonged to an adverse party to the conflict. This footnote also applies to the corresponding element in each crime under article 8(2)(a).

[34] The term "international armed conflict" includes military occupation. This footnote also applies to the corre-sponding element in each crime under article 8(2)(a).

[35] As element 3 requires that all victims must be "protected persons" under one or more of the Geneva Con-ventions of 1949, these elements do not include the custody or control requirement found in the elements of article 7(1)(e).

16

6. The perpetrator was aware of factual circumstances that established the existence of an armed conflict.

Article 8(2)(a)(ii)-2
War crime of inhuman treatment

Elements

1. The perpetrator inflicted severe physical or mental pain or suffering upon one or more persons.
2. Such person or persons were protected under one or more of the Geneva Conventions of 1949.
3. The perpetrator was aware of the factual circumstances that established that protected status.
4. The conduct took place in the context of and was associated with an international armed conflict.
5. The perpetrator was aware of factual circumstances that established the existence of an armed conflict.

Article 8(2)(a)(ii)-3
War crime of biological experiments

Elements

1. The perpetrator subjected one or more persons to a particular biological experiment.
2. The experiment seriously endangered the physical or mental health or integrity of such person or persons.
3. The intent of the experiment was non-therapeutic and it was neither justified by medical reasons nor carried out in such person's or persons' interest.
4. Such person or persons were protected under one or more of the Geneva Conventions of 1949.
5. The perpetrator was aware of the factual circumstances that established that protected status.
6. The conduct took place in the context of and was associated with an international armed conflict.
7. The perpetrator was aware of factual circumstances that established the existence of an armed conflict.

Article 8(2)(a)(iii)
War crime of wilfully causing great suffering

Elements

1. The perpetrator caused great physical or mental pain or suffering to, or serious injury to body or health of, one or more persons.
2. Such person or persons were protected under one or more of the Geneva Conventions of 1949.
3. The perpetrator was aware of the factual circumstances that established that protected status.

4. The conduct took place in the context of and was associated with an international armed conflict.
5. The perpetrator was aware of factual circumstances that established the existence of an armed conflict.

Article 8(2)(a)(iv)
War crime of destruction and appropriation of property
Elements

1. The perpetrator destroyed or appropriated certain property.
2. The destruction or appropriation was not justified by military necessity.
3. The destruction or appropriation was extensive and carried out wantonly.
4. Such property was protected under one or more of the Geneva Conventions of 1949.
5. The perpetrator was aware of the factual circumstances that established that protected status.
6. The conduct took place in the context of and was associated with an international armed conflict.
7. The perpetrator was aware of factual circumstances that established the existence of an armed conflict.

Article 8(2)(a)(v)
War crime of compelling service in hostile forces
Elements

1. The perpetrator coerced one or more persons, by act or threat, to take part in military operations against that person's own country or forces or otherwise serve in the forces of a hostile power.
2. Such person or persons were protected under one or more of the Geneva Conventions of 1949.
3. The perpetrator was aware of the factual circumstances that established that protected status.
4. The conduct took place in the context of and was associated with an international armed conflict.
5. The perpetrator was aware of factual circumstances that established the existence of an armed conflict.

Article 8(2)(a)(vi)
War crime of denying a fair trial
Elements

1. The perpetrator deprived one or more persons of a fair and regular trial by denying judicial guarantees as defined, in particular, in the third and the fourth Geneva Conventions of 1949.
2. Such person or persons were protected under one or more of the Geneva Conventions of 1949.

3. The perpetrator was aware of the factual circumstances that established that protected status.
4. The conduct took place in the context of and was associated with an international armed conflict.
5. The perpetrator was aware of factual circumstances that established the existence of an armed conflict.

Article 8(2)(a)(vii)-1
War crime of unlawful deportation and transfer
Elements

1. The perpetrator deported or transferred one or more persons to another State or to another location.
2. Such person or persons were protected under one or more of the Geneva Conventions of 1949.
3. The perpetrator was aware of the factual circumstances that established that protected status.
4. The conduct took place in the context of and was associated with an international armed conflict.
5. The perpetrator was aware of factual circumstances that established the existence of an armed conflict.

Article 8(2)(a)(vii)-2
War crime of unlawful confinement
Elements

1. The perpetrator confined or continued to confine one or more persons to a certain location.
2. Such person or persons were protected under one or more of the Geneva Conventions of 1949.
3. The perpetrator was aware of the factual circumstances that established that protected status.
4. The conduct took place in the context of and was associated with an international armed conflict.
5. The perpetrator was aware of factual circumstances that established the existence of an armed conflict.

Article 8(2)(a)(viii)
War crime of taking hostages
Elements

1. The perpetrator seized, detained or otherwise held hostage one or more persons.
2. The perpetrator threatened to kill, injure or continue to detain such person or persons.
3. The perpetrator intended to compel a State, an international organization, a natural or legal person or a group of persons to act or refrain from acting as an explicit or implicit condition for the safety or the release of such person or persons.

4. Such person or persons were protected under one or more of the Geneva Conventions of 1949.
5. The perpetrator was aware of the factual circumstances that established that protected status.
6. The conduct took place in the context of and was associated with an international armed conflict.
7. The perpetrator was aware of factual circumstances that established the existence of an armed conflict.

Article 8(2)(b)
Article 8(2)(b)(i)
War crime of attacking civilians

Elements

1. The perpetrator directed an attack.
2. The object of the attack was a civilian population as such or individual civilians not taking direct part in hostilities.
3. The perpetrator intended the civilian population as such or individual civilians not taking direct part in hostilities to be the object of the attack.
4. The conduct took place in the context of and was associated with an international armed conflict.
5. The perpetrator was aware of factual circumstances that established the existence of an armed conflict.

Article 8(2)(b)(ii)
War crime of attacking civilian objects

Elements

1. The perpetrator directed an attack.
2. The object of the attack was civilian objects, that is, objects which are not military objectives.
3. The perpetrator intended such civilian objects to be the object of the attack.
4. The conduct took place in the context of and was associated with an international armed conflict.
5. The perpetrator was aware of factual circumstances that established the existence of an armed conflict.

Article 8(2)(b)(iii)
War crime of attacking personnel or objects involved in a humanitarian assistance or peacekeeping mission

Elements

1. The perpetrator directed an attack.
2. The object of the attack was personnel, installations, material, units or vehicles involved in a humanitarian assistance or peacekeeping mission in accordance with the Charter of the United Nations.
3. The perpetrator intended such personnel, installations, material, units or vehicles so involved to be the object of the attack.

4. Such personnel, installations, material, units or vehicles were entitled to that protection given to civilians or civilian objects under the international law of armed conflict.
5. The perpetrator was aware of the factual circumstances that established that protection.
6. The conduct took place in the context of and was associated with an international armed conflict.
7. The perpetrator was aware of factual circumstances that established the existence of an armed conflict.

Article 8(2)(b)(iv)
War crime of excessive incidental death, injury, or damage
Elements

1. The perpetrator launched an attack.
2. The attack was such that it would cause incidental death or injury to civilians or damage to civilian objects or widespread, long-term and severe damage to the natural environment and that such death, injury or damage would be of such an extent as to be clearly excessive in relation to the concrete and direct overall military advantage anticipated.[36]
3. The perpetrator knew that the attack would cause incidental death or injury to civilians or damage to civilian objects or widespread, long-term and severe damage to the natural environment and that such death, injury or damage would be of such an extent as to be clearly excessive in relation to the concrete and direct overall military advantage anticipated.[37]
4. The conduct took place in the context of and was associated with an international armed conflict.
5. The perpetrator was aware of factual circumstances that established the existence of an armed conflict.

Article 8(2)(b)(v)
War crime of attacking undefended places[38]
Elements

1. The perpetrator attacked one or more towns, villages, dwellings or buildings.
2. Such towns, villages, dwellings or buildings were open for unresisted occupation.
3. Such towns, villages, dwellings or buildings did not constitute military objectives.

---

[36] The expression "concrete and direct overall military advantage" refers to a military advantage that is foreseeable by the perpetrator at the relevant time. Such advantage may or may not be temporally or geographically related to the object of the attack. The fact that this crime admits the possibility of lawful incidental injury and collateral damage does not in any way justify any violation of the law applicable in armed conflict. It does not address justifications for war or other rules related to *jus ad bellum*. It reflects the proportionality requirement inherent in determining the legality of any military activity undertaken in the context of an armed conflict.

[37] As opposed to the general rule set forth in paragraph 4 of the General Introduction, this knowledge element requires that the perpetrator make the value judgement as described therein. An evaluation of that value judgement must be based on the requisite information available to the perpetrator at the time.

[38] The presence in the locality of persons specially protected under the Geneva Conventions of 1949 or of police forces retained for the sole purpose of maintaining law and order does not by itself render the locality a military objective.

4. The conduct took place in the context of and was associated with an international armed conflict.
5. The perpetrator was aware of factual circumstances that established the existence of an armed conflict.

Article 8(2)(b)(vi)
War crime of killing or wounding a person *hors de combat*
Elements

1. The perpetrator killed or injured one or more persons.
2. Such person or persons were *hors de combat.*
3. The perpetrator was aware of the factual circumstances that established this status.
4. The conduct took place in the context of and was associated with an international armed conflict.
5. The perpetrator was aware of factual circumstances that established the existence of an armed conflict.

Article 8(2)(b)(vii)-1
War crime of improper use of a flag of truce
Elements

1. The perpetrator used a flag of truce.
2. The perpetrator made such use in order to feign an intention to negotiate when there was no such intention on the part of the perpetrator.
3. The perpetrator knew or should have known of the prohibited nature of such use.[39]
4. The conduct resulted in death or serious personal injury.
5. The perpetrator knew that the conduct could result in death or serious personal injury.
6. The conduct took place in the context of and was associated with an international armed conflict.
7. The perpetrator was aware of factual circumstances that established the existence of an armed conflict.

Article 8(2)(b)(vii)-2
War crime of improper use of a flag, insignia or uniform of the hostile party
Elements

1. The perpetrator used a flag, insignia or uniform of the hostile party.
2. The perpetrator made such use in a manner prohibited under the international law of armed conflict while engaged in an attack.
3. The perpetrator knew or should have known of the prohibited nature of such use.[40]
4. The conduct resulted in death or serious personal injury.

---

[39] This mental element recognizes the interplay between article 30 and article 32. The term "prohibited nature" denotes illegality.
[40] This mental element recognizes the interplay between article 30 and article 32. The term "prohibited nature" denotes illegality.

5. The perpetrator knew that the conduct could result in death or serious personal injury.
6. The conduct took place in the context of and was associated with an international armed conflict.
7. The perpetrator was aware of factual circumstances that established the existence of an armed conflict.

Article 8(2)(b)(vii)-3
War crime of improper use of a flag, insignia or uniform of the United Nations
Elements

1. The perpetrator used a flag, insignia or uniform of the United Nations.
2. The perpetrator made such use in a manner prohibited under the international law of armed conflict.
3. The perpetrator knew of the prohibited nature of such use.[41]
4. The conduct resulted in death or serious personal injury.
5. The perpetrator knew that the conduct could result in death or serious personal injury.
6. The conduct took place in the context of and was associated with an international armed conflict.
7. The perpetrator was aware of factual circumstances that established the existence of an armed conflict.

Article 8(2)(b)(vii)-4
War crime of improper use of the distinctive emblems of the Geneva Conventions
Elements

1. The perpetrator used the distinctive emblems of the Geneva Conventions.
2. The perpetrator made such use for combatant purposes[42] in a manner prohibited under the international law of armed conflict.
3. The perpetrator knew or should have known of the prohibited nature of such use.[43]
4. The conduct resulted in death or serious personal injury.
5. The perpetrator knew that the conduct could result in death or serious personal injury.
6. The conduct took place in the context of and was associated with an international armed conflict.
7. The perpetrator was aware of factual circumstances that established the existence of an armed conflict.

---

[41] This mental element recognizes the interplay between article 30 and article 32. The "should have known" test required in the other offences found in article 8(2)(b)(vii) is not applicable here because of the variable and regulatory nature of the relevant prohibitions.

[42] "Combatant purposes" in these circumstances means purposes directly related to hostilities and not including medical, religious or similar activities.

[43] This mental element recognizes the interplay between article 30 and article 32. The term "prohibited nature" denotes illegality.

Article 8(2)(b)(viii)
The transfer, directly or indirectly, by the Occupying Power of parts of its own civilian population into the territory it occupies, or the deportation or transfer of all or parts of the population of the occupied territory within or outside this territory

Elements

1. The perpetrator:
   (a) Transferred,[44] directly or indirectly, parts of its own population into the territory it occupies; or
   (b) Deported or transferred all or parts of the population of the occupied territory within or outside this territory.
2. The conduct took place in the context of and was associated with an international armed conflict.
3. The perpetrator was aware of factual circumstances that established the existence of an armed conflict.

Article 8(2)(b)(ix)
War crime of attacking protected objects[45]

Elements

1. The perpetrator directed an attack.
2. The object of the attack was one or more buildings dedicated to religion, education, art, science or charitable purposes, historic monuments, hospitals or places where the sick and wounded are collected, which were not military objectives.
3. The perpetrator intended such building or buildings dedicated to religion, education, art, science or charitable purposes, historic monuments, hospitals or places where the sick and wounded are collected, which were not military objectives, to be the object of the attack.
4. The conduct took place in the context of and was associated with an international armed conflict.
5. The perpetrator was aware of factual circumstances that established the existence of an armed conflict.

Article 8(2)(b)(x)-1
War crime of mutilation

Elements

1. The perpetrator subjected one or more persons to mutilation, in particular by permanently disfiguring the person or persons, or by permanently disabling or removing an organ or appendage.

---

[44] The term "transfer" needs to be interpreted in accordance with the relevant provisions of international humanitarian law.

[45] The presence in the locality of persons specially protected under the Geneva Conventions of 1949 or of police forces retained for the sole purpose of maintaining law and order does not by itself render the locality a military objective.

2. The conduct caused death or seriously endangered the physical or mental health of such person or persons.

3. The conduct was neither justified by the medical, dental or hospital treatment of the person or persons concerned nor carried out in such person's or persons' interest.[46]

4. Such person or persons were in the power of an adverse party.

5. The conduct took place in the context of and was associated with an international armed conflict.

6. The perpetrator was aware of factual circumstances that established the existence of an armed conflict.

Article 8(2)(b)(x)-2
War crime of medical or scientific experiments
Elements

1. The perpetrator subjected one or more persons to a medical or scientific experiment.

2. The experiment caused death or seriously endangered the physical or mental health or integrity of such person or persons.

3. The conduct was neither justified by the medical, dental or hospital treatment of such person or persons concerned nor carried out in such person's or persons' interest.

4. Such person or persons were in the power of an adverse party.

5. The conduct took place in the context of and was associated with an international armed conflict.

6. The perpetrator was aware of factual circumstances that established the existence of an armed conflict.

Article 8(2)(b)(xi)
War crime of treacherously killing or wounding
Elements

1. The perpetrator invited the confidence or belief of one or more persons that they were entitled to, or were obliged to accord, protection under rules of international law applicable in armed conflict.

2. The perpetrator intended to betray that confidence or belief.

3. The perpetrator killed or injured such person or persons.

4. The perpetrator made use of that confidence or belief in killing or injuring such person or persons.

5. Such person or persons belonged to an adverse party.

6. The conduct took place in the context of and was associated with an international armed conflict.

7. The perpetrator was aware of factual circumstances that established the existence of an armed conflict.

---

[46] Consent is not a defence to this crime. The crime prohibits any medical procedure which is not indicated by the state of health of the person concerned and which is not consistent with generally accepted medical standards which would be applied under similar medical circumstances to persons who are nationals of the party conducting the procedure and who are in no way deprived of liberty. This footnote also applies to the same element for article 8(2)(b)(x)-2.

Article 8(2)(b)(xii)
War crime of denying quarter
Elements

1. The perpetrator declared or ordered that there shall be no survivors.
2. Such declaration or order was given in order to threaten an adversary or to conduct hostilities on the basis that there shall be no survivors.
3. The perpetrator was in a position of effective command or control over the subordinate forces to which the declaration or order was directed.
4. The conduct took place in the context of and was associated with an international armed conflict.
5. The perpetrator was aware of factual circumstances that established the existence of an armed conflict.

Article 8(2)(b)(xiii)
War crime of destroying or seizing the enemy's property
Elements

1. The perpetrator destroyed or seized certain property.
2. Such property was property of a hostile party.
3. Such property was protected from that destruction or seizure under the international law of armed conflict.
4. The perpetrator was aware of the factual circumstances that established the status of the property.
5. The destruction or seizure was not justified by military necessity.
6. The conduct took place in the context of and was associated with an international armed conflict.
7. The perpetrator was aware of factual circumstances that established the existence of an armed conflict.

Article 8(2)(b)(xiv)
War crime of depriving the nationals of the hostile power of rights or actions
Elements

1. The perpetrator effected the abolition, suspension or termination of admissibility in a court of law of certain rights or actions.
2. The abolition, suspension or termination was directed at the nationals of a hostile party.
3. The perpetrator intended the abolition, suspension or termination to be directed at the nationals of a hostile party.
4. The conduct took place in the context of and was associated with an international armed conflict.
5. The perpetrator was aware of factual circumstances that established the existence of an armed conflict.

Article 8(2)(b)(xv)
War crime of compelling participation in military operations
Elements

1. The perpetrator coerced one or more persons by act or threat to take part in military operations against that person's own country or forces.
2. Such person or persons were nationals of a hostile party.
3. The conduct took place in the context of and was associated with an international armed conflict.
4. The perpetrator was aware of factual circumstances that established the existence of an armed conflict.

Article 8(2)(b)(xvi)
War crime of pillaging

Elements

1. The perpetrator appropriated certain property.
2. The perpetrator intended to deprive the owner of the property and to appropriate it for private or personal use.[47]
3. The appropriation was without the consent of the owner.
4. The conduct took place in the context of and was associated with an international armed conflict.
5. The perpetrator was aware of factual circumstances that established the existence of an armed conflict.

Article 8(2)(b)(xvii)
War crime of employing poison or poisoned weapons
Elements

1. The perpetrator employed a substance or a weapon that releases a substance as a result of its employment.
2. The substance was such that it causes death or serious damage to health in the ordinary course of events, through its toxic properties.
3. The conduct took place in the context of and was associated with an international armed conflict.
4. The perpetrator was aware of factual circumstances that established the existence of an armed conflict.

Article 8(2)(b)(xviii)
War crime of employing prohibited gases, liquids, materials or devices
Elements

1. The perpetrator employed a gas or other analogous substance or device.

---

[47] As indicated by the use of the term "private or personal use", appropriations justified by military necessity cannot constitute the crime of pillaging.

2. The gas, substance or device was such that it causes death or serious damage to health in the ordinary course of events, through its asphyxiating or toxic properties.[48]
3. The conduct took place in the context of and was associated with an international armed conflict.
4. The perpetrator was aware of factual circumstances that established the existence of an armed conflict.

Article 8(2)(b)(xix)
War crime of employing prohibited bullets
Elements

1. The perpetrator employed certain bullets.
2. The bullets were such that their use violates the international law of armed conflict because they expand or flatten easily in the human body.
3. The perpetrator was aware that the nature of the bullets was such that their employment would uselessly aggravate suffering or the wounding effect.
4. The conduct took place in the context of and was associated with an international armed conflict.
5. The perpetrator was aware of factual circumstances that established the existence of an armed conflict.

Article 8(2)(b)(xx)
War crime of employing weapons, projectiles or materials or methods of warfare listed in the Annex to the Statute
Elements

[Elements will have to be drafted once weapons, projectiles or material or methods of warfare have been included in an annex to the Statute.]

Article 8(2)(b)(xxi)
War crime of outrages upon personal dignity
Elements

1. The perpetrator humiliated, degraded or otherwise violated the dignity of one or more persons.[49]
2. The severity of the humiliation, degradation or other violation was of such degree as to be generally recognized as an outrage upon personal dignity.
3. The conduct took place in the context of and was associated with an international armed conflict.
4. The perpetrator was aware of factual circumstances that established the existence of an armed conflict.

---

[48] Nothing in this element shall be interpreted as limiting or prejudicing in any way existing or developing rules of international law with respect to the development, production, stockpiling and use of chemical weapons.
[49] For this crime, "persons" can include dead persons. It is understood that the victim need not personally be aware of the existence of the humiliation or degradation or other violation. This element takes into account relevant aspects of the cultural background of the victim.

Article 8(2)(b)(xxii)-1
War crime of rape

Elements

1. The perpetrator invaded[50] the body of a person by conduct resulting in penetration, however slight, of any part of the body of the victim or of the perpetrator with a sexual organ, or of the anal or genital opening of the victim with any object or any other part of the body.
2. The invasion was committed by force, or by threat of force or coercion, such as that caused by fear of violence, duress, detention, psychological oppression or abuse of power, against such person or another person, or by taking advantage of a coercive environment, or the invasion was committed against a person incapable of giving genuine consent.[51]
3. The conduct took place in the context of and was associated with an international armed conflict.
4. The perpetrator was aware of factual circumstances that established the existence of an armed conflict.

Article 8(2)(b)(xxii)-2
War crime of sexual slavery[52]

Elements

1. The perpetrator exercised any or all of the powers attaching to the right of ownership over one or more persons, such as by purchasing, selling, lending or bartering such a person or persons, or by imposing on them a similar deprivation of liberty.[53]
2. The perpetrator caused such person or persons to engage in one or more acts of a sexual nature.
3. The conduct took place in the context of and was associated with an international armed conflict.
4. The perpetrator was aware of factual circumstances that established the existence of an armed conflict.

Article 8(2)(b)(xxii)-3
War crime of enforced prostitution

Elements

1. The perpetrator caused one or more persons to engage in one or more acts of a sexual nature by force, or by threat of force or coercion, such as that caused by fear of violence,

---

[50] The concept of "invasion" is intended to be broad enough to be gender-neutral.

[51] It is understood that a person may be incapable of giving genuine consent if affected by natural, induced or age-related incapacity. This footnote also applies to the corresponding elements of article 8(2)(b)(xxii)-3, 5 and 6.

[52] Given the complex nature of this crime, it is recognized that its commission could involve more than one perpetrator as a part of a common criminal purpose.

[53] It is understood that such deprivation of liberty may, in some circumstances, include exacting forced labour or otherwise reducing a person to servile status as defined in the Supplementary Convention on the Abolition of Slavery, the Slave Trade, and Institutions and Practices Similar to Slavery of 1956. It is also understood that the conduct described in this element includes trafficking in persons, in particular women and children.

duress, detention, psychological oppression or abuse of power, against such person or persons or another person, or by taking advantage of a coercive environment or such person's or persons' incapacity to give genuine consent.
2. The perpetrator or another person obtained or expected to obtain pecuniary or other advantage in exchange for or in connection with the acts of a sexual nature.
3. The conduct took place in the context of and was associated with an international armed conflict.
4. The perpetrator was aware of factual circumstances that established the existence of an armed conflict.

Article 8(2)(b)(xxii)-4
War crime of forced pregnancy

Elements

1. The perpetrator confined one or more women forcibly made pregnant, with the intent of affecting the ethnic composition of any population or carrying out other grave violations of international law.
2. The conduct took place in the context of and was associated with an international armed conflict.
3. The perpetrator was aware of factual circumstances that established the existence of an armed conflict.

Article 8(2)(b)(xxii)-5
War crime of enforced sterilization

Elements

1. The perpetrator deprived one or more persons of biological reproductive capacity.[54]
2. The conduct was neither justified by the medical or hospital treatment of the person or persons concerned nor carried out with their genuine consent.[55]
3. The conduct took place in the context of and was associated with an international armed conflict.
4. The perpetrator was aware of factual circumstances that established the existence of an armed conflict.

Article 8(2)(b)(xxii)-6
War crime of sexual violence

Elements

1. The perpetrator committed an act of a sexual nature against one or more persons or caused such person or persons to engage in an act of a sexual nature by force, or by threat of force or coercion, such as that caused by fear of violence, duress, detention, psychological oppression or abuse of power, against such person or persons or another

---

[54] The deprivation is not intended to include birth-control measures which have a non-permanent effect in practice.
[55] It is understood that "genuine consent" does not include consent obtained through deception.

person, or by taking advantage of a coercive environment or such person's or persons' incapacity to give genuine consent.

2. The conduct was of a gravity comparable to that of a grave breach of the Geneva Conventions.

3. The perpetrator was aware of the factual circumstances that established the gravity of the conduct.

4. The conduct took place in the context of and was associated with an international armed conflict.

5. The perpetrator was aware of factual circumstances that established the existence of an armed conflict.

Article 8(2)(b)(xxiii)
War crime of using protected persons as shields
Elements

1. The perpetrator moved or otherwise took advantage of the location of one or more civilians or other persons protected under the international law of armed conflict.

2. The perpetrator intended to shield a military objective from attack or shield, favour or impede military operations.

3. The conduct took place in the context of and was associated with an international armed conflict.

4. The perpetrator was aware of factual circumstances that established the existence of an armed conflict.

Article 8(2)(b)(xxiv)
War crime of attacking objects or persons using the distinctive emblems of the Geneva Conventions
Elements

1. The perpetrator attacked one or more persons, buildings, medical units or transports or other objects using, in conformity with international law, a distinctive emblem or other method of identification indicating protection under the Geneva Conventions.

2. The perpetrator intended such persons, buildings, units or transports or other objects so using such identification to be the object of the attack.

3. The conduct took place in the context of and was associated with an international armed conflict.

4. The perpetrator was aware of factual circumstances that established the existence of an armed conflict.

Article 8(2)(b)(xxv)
War crime of starvation as a method of warfare
Elements

1. The perpetrator deprived civilians of objects indispensable to their survival.

2. The perpetrator intended to starve civilians as a method of warfare.

3. The conduct took place in the context of and was associated with an international armed conflict.
4. The perpetrator was aware of factual circumstances that established the existence of an armed conflict.

Article 8(2)(b)(xxvi)
War crime of using, conscripting or enlisting children
Elements

1. The perpetrator conscripted or enlisted one or more persons into the national armed forces or used one or more persons to participate actively in hostilities.
2. Such person or persons were under the age of 15 years.
3. The perpetrator knew or should have known that such person or persons were under the age of 15 years.
4. The conduct took place in the context of and was associated with an international armed conflict.
5. The perpetrator was aware of factual circumstances that established the existence of an armed conflict.

Article 8(2)(c)
Article 8(2)(c)(i)-1
War crime of murder

Elements

1. The perpetrator killed one or more persons.
2. Such person or persons were either *hors de combat*, or were civilians, medical personnel, or religious personnel[56] taking no active part in the hostilities.
3. The perpetrator was aware of the factual circumstances that established this status.
4. The conduct took place in the context of and was associated with an armed conflict not of an international character.
5. The perpetrator was aware of factual circumstances that established the existence of an armed conflict.

Article 8(2)(c)(i)-2
War crime of mutilation

Elements

1. The perpetrator subjected one or more persons to mutilation, in particular by permanently disfiguring the person or persons, or by permanently disabling or removing an organ or appendage.
2. The conduct was neither justified by the medical, dental or hospital treatment of the person or persons concerned nor carried out in such person's or persons' interests.
3. Such person or persons were either *hors de combat*, or were civilians, medical personnel or religious personnel taking no active part in the hostilities.

---

[56] The term "religious personnel" includes those non-confessional non-combatant military personnel carrying out a similar function.

4. The perpetrator was aware of the factual circumstances that established this status.
5. The conduct took place in the context of and was associated with an armed conflict not of an international character.
6. The perpetrator was aware of factual circumstances that established the existence of an armed conflict.

Article 8(2)(c)(i)-3
War crime of cruel treatment

Elements

1. The perpetrator inflicted severe physical or mental pain or suffering upon one or more persons.
2. Such person or persons were either *hors de combat*, or were civilians, medical personnel, or religious personnel taking no active part in the hostilities.
3. The perpetrator was aware of the factual circumstances that established this status.
4. The conduct took place in the context of and was associated with an armed conflict not of an international character.
5. The perpetrator was aware of factual circumstances that established the existence of an armed conflict.

Article 8(2)(c)(i)-4
War crime of torture

Elements

1. The perpetrator inflicted severe physical or mental pain or suffering upon one or more persons.
2. The perpetrator inflicted the pain or suffering for such purposes as: obtaining information or a confession, punishment, intimidation or coercion or for any reason based on discrimination of any kind.
3. Such person or persons were either *hors de combat*, or were civilians, medical personnel or religious personnel taking no active part in the hostilities.
4. The perpetrator was aware of the factual circumstances that established this status.
5. The conduct took place in the context of and was associated with an armed conflict not of an international character.
6. The perpetrator was aware of factual circumstances that established the existence of an armed conflict.

Article 8(2)(c)(ii)
War crime of outrages upon personal dignity

Elements

1. The perpetrator humiliated, degraded or otherwise violated the dignity of one or more persons.[57]

---

[57] For this crime, "persons" can include dead persons. It is understood that the victim need not personally be aware of the existence of the humiliation or degradation or other violation. This element takes into account relevant aspects of the cultural background of the victim.

2. The severity of the humiliation, degradation or other violation was of such degree as to be generally recognized as an outrage upon personal dignity.
3. Such person or persons were either *hors de combat*, or were civilians, medical personnel or religious personnel taking no active part in the hostilities.
4. The perpetrator was aware of the factual circumstances that established this status.
5. The conduct took place in the context of and was associated with an armed conflict not of an international character.
6. The perpetrator was aware of factual circumstances that established the existence of an armed conflict.

Article 8(2)(c)(iii)
War crime of taking hostages

Elements

1. The perpetrator seized, detained or otherwise held hostage one or more persons.
2. The perpetrator threatened to kill, injure or continue to detain such person or persons.
3. The perpetrator intended to compel a State, an international organization, a natural or legal person or a group of persons to act or refrain from acting as an explicit or implicit condition for the safety or the release of such person or persons.
4. Such person or persons were either *hors de combat*, or were civilians, medical personnel or religious personnel taking no active part in the hostilities.
5. The perpetrator was aware of the factual circumstances that established this status.
6. The conduct took place in the context of and was associated with an armed conflict not of an international character.
7. The perpetrator was aware of factual circumstances that established the existence of an armed conflict.

Article 8(2)(c)(iv)
War crime of sentencing or execution without due process

Elements

1. The perpetrator passed sentence or executed one or more persons.[58]
2. Such person or persons were either *hors de combat*, or were civilians, medical personnel or religious personnel taking no active part in the hostilities.
3. The perpetrator was aware of the factual circumstances that established this status.
4. There was no previous judgement pronounced by a court, or the court that rendered judgement was not "regularly constituted", that is, it did not afford the essential guarantees of independence and impartiality, or the court that rendered judgement did not afford all other judicial guarantees generally recognized as indispensable under international law.[59]
5. The perpetrator was aware of the absence of a previous judgement or of the denial of relevant guarantees and the fact that they are essential or indispensable to a fair trial.

---

[58] The elements laid down in these documents do not address the different forms of individual criminal responsibility, as enunciated in articles 25 and 28 of the Statute.

[59] With respect to elements 4 and 5, the Court should consider whether, in the light of all relevant circumstances, the cumulative effect of factors with respect to guarantees deprived the person or persons of a fair trial.

6. The conduct took place in the context of and was associated with an armed conflict not of an international character.
7. The perpetrator was aware of factual circumstances that established the existence of an armed conflict.

Article 8(2)(e)[60]
Article 8(2)(e)(i)
War crime of attacking civilians

Elements

1. The perpetrator directed an attack.
2. The object of the attack was a civilian population as such or individual civilians not taking direct part in hostilities.
3. The perpetrator intended the civilian population as such or individual civilians not taking direct part in hostilities to be the object of the attack.
4. The conduct took place in the context of and was associated with an armed conflict not of an international character.
5. The perpetrator was aware of factual circumstances that established the existence of an armed conflict.

Article 8(2)(e)(ii)
War crime of attacking objects or persons using the distinctive emblems of the Geneva Conventions

Elements

1. The perpetrator attacked one or more persons, buildings, medical units or transports or other objects using, in conformity with international law, a distinctive emblem or other method of identification indicating protection under the Geneva Conventions.
2. The perpetrator intended such persons, buildings, units or transports or other objects so using such identification to be the object of the attack.
3. The conduct took place in the context of and was associated with an armed conflict not of an international character.
4. The perpetrator was aware of factual circumstances that established the existence of an armed conflict.

Article 8(2)(e)(iii)
War crime of attacking personnel or objects involved in a humanitarian assistance or peacekeeping mission

Elements

1. The perpetrator directed an attack.
2. The object of the attack was personnel, installations, material, units or vehicles involved in a humanitarian assistance or peacekeeping mission in accordance with the Charter of the United Nations.

---

[60] As amended by resolution RC/Res.5.

3. The perpetrator intended such personnel, installations, material, units or vehicles so involved to be the object of the attack.
4. Such personnel, installations, material, units or vehicles were entitled to that protection given to civilians or civilian objects under the international law of armed conflict.
5. The perpetrator was aware of the factual circumstances that established that protection.
6. The conduct took place in the context of and was associated with an armed conflict not of an international character.
7. The perpetrator was aware of factual circumstances that established the existence of an armed conflict.

Article 8(2)(e)(iv)
War crime of attacking protected objects[61]

Elements

1. The perpetrator directed an attack.
2. The object of the attack was one or more buildings dedicated to religion, education, art, science or charitable purposes, historic monuments, hospitals or places where the sick and wounded are collected, which were not military objectives.
3. The perpetrator intended such building or buildings dedicated to religion, education, art, science or charitable purposes, historic monuments, hospitals or places where the sick and wounded are collected, which were not military objectives, to be the object of the attack.
4. The conduct took place in the context of and was associated with an armed conflict not of an international character.
5. The perpetrator was aware of factual circumstances that established the existence of an armed conflict.

Article 8(2)(e)(v)
War crime of pillaging

Elements

1. The perpetrator appropriated certain property.
2. The perpetrator intended to deprive the owner of the property and to appropriate it for private or personal use.[62]
3. The appropriation was without the consent of the owner.
4. The conduct took place in the context of and was associated with an armed conflict not of an international character.
5. The perpetrator was aware of factual circumstances that established the existence of an armed conflict.

---

[61] The presence in the locality of persons specially protected under the Geneva Conventions of 1949 or of police forces retained for the sole purpose of maintaining law and order does not by itself render the locality a military objective.

[62] As indicated by the use of the term "private or personal use", appropriations justified by military necessity cannot constitute the crime of pillaging.

Article 8(2)(e)(vi)-1
War crime of rape

Elements

1. The perpetrator invaded[63] the body of a person by conduct resulting in penetration, however slight, of any part of the body of the victim or of the perpetrator with a sexual organ, or of the anal or genital opening of the victim with any object or any other part of the body.
2. The invasion was committed by force, or by threat of force or coercion, such as that caused by fear of violence, duress, detention, psychological oppression or abuse of power, against such person or another person, or by taking advantage of a coercive environment, or the invasion was committed against a person incapable of giving genuine consent.[64]
3. The conduct took place in the context of and was associated with an armed conflict not of an international character.
4. The perpetrator was aware of factual circumstances that established the existence of an armed conflict.

Article 8(2)(e)(vi)-2
War crime of sexual slavery[65]

Elements

1. The perpetrator exercised any or all of the powers attaching to the right of ownership over one or more persons, such as by purchasing, selling, lending or bartering such a person or persons, or by imposing on them a similar deprivation of liberty.[66]
2. The perpetrator caused such person or persons to engage in one or more acts of a sexual nature.
3. The conduct took place in the context of and was associated with an armed conflict not of an international character.
4. The perpetrator was aware of factual circumstances that established the existence of an armed conflict.

Article 8(2)(e)(vi)-3
War crime of enforced prostitution

Elements

1. The perpetrator caused one or more persons to engage in one or more acts of a sexual nature by force, or by threat of force or coercion, such as that caused by fear of violence,

---

[63] The concept of "invasion" is intended to be broad enough to be gender-neutral.

[64] It is understood that a person may be incapable of giving genuine consent if affected by natural, induced or age-related incapacity. This footnote also applies to the corresponding elements in article 8(2)(e)(vi)-3, 5 and 6.

[65] Given the complex nature of this crime, it is recognized that its commission could involve more than one perpetrator as a part of a common criminal purpose.

[66] It is understood that such deprivation of liberty may, in some circumstances, include exacting forced labour or otherwise reducing a person to servile status as defined in the Supplementary Convention on the Abolition of Slavery, the Slave Trade, and Institutions and Practices Similar to Slavery of 1956. It is also understood that the conduct described in this element includes trafficking in persons, in particular women and children.

duress, detention, psychological oppression or abuse of power, against such person or persons or another person, or by taking advantage of a coercive environment or such person's or persons' incapacity to give genuine consent.
2. The perpetrator or another person obtained or expected to obtain pecuniary or other advantage in exchange for or in connection with the acts of a sexual nature.
3. The conduct took place in the context of and was associated with an armed conflict not of an international character.
4. The perpetrator was aware of factual circumstances that established the existence of an armed conflict.

Article 8(2)(e)(vi)-4
War crime of forced pregnancy

Elements

1. The perpetrator confined one or more women forcibly made pregnant, with the intent of affecting the ethnic composition of any population or carrying out other grave violations of international law.
2. The conduct took place in the context of and was associated with an armed conflict not of an international character.
3. The perpetrator was aware of factual circumstances that established the existence of an armed conflict.

Article 8(2)(e)(vi)-5
War crime of enforced sterilization

Elements

1. The perpetrator deprived one or more persons of biological reproductive capacity.[67]
2. The conduct was neither justified by the medical or hospital treatment of the person or persons concerned nor carried out with their genuine consent.[68]
3. The conduct took place in the context of and was associated with an armed conflict not of an international character.
4. The perpetrator was aware of factual circumstances that established the existence of an armed conflict.

Article 8(2)(e)(vi)-6
War crime of sexual violence

Elements

1. The perpetrator committed an act of a sexual nature against one or more persons or caused such person or persons to engage in an act of a sexual nature by force, or by threat of force or coercion, such as that caused by fear of violence, duress, detention, psychological oppression or abuse of power, against such person or persons or another

---

[67] The deprivation is not intended to include birth-control measures which have a non-permanent effect in practice.

[68] It is understood that "genuine consent" does not include consent obtained through deception.

person, or by taking advantage of a coercive environment or such person's or persons' incapacity to give genuine consent.

2. The conduct was of a gravity comparable to that of a serious violation of article 3 common to the four Geneva Conventions.

3. The perpetrator was aware of the factual circumstances that established the gravity of the conduct.

4. The conduct took place in the context of and was associated with an armed conflict not of an international character.

5. The perpetrator was aware of factual circumstances that established the existence of an armed conflict.

Article 8(2)(e)(vii)
War crime of using, conscripting and enlisting children
Elements

1. The perpetrator conscripted or enlisted one or more persons into an armed force or group or used one or more persons to participate actively in hostilities.

2. Such person or persons were under the age of 15 years.

3. The perpetrator knew or should have known that such person or persons were under the age of 15 years.

4. The conduct took place in the context of and was associated with an armed conflict not of an international character.

5. The perpetrator was aware of factual circumstances that established the existence of an armed conflict.

Article 8(2)(e)(viii)
War crime of displacing civilians
Elements

1. The perpetrator ordered a displacement of a civilian population.

2. Such order was not justified by the security of the civilians involved or by military necessity.

3. The perpetrator was in a position to effect such displacement by giving such order.

4. The conduct took place in the context of and was associated with an armed conflict not of an international character.

5. The perpetrator was aware of factual circumstances that established the existence of an armed conflict.

Article 8(2)(e)(ix)
War crime of treacherously killing or wounding
Elements

1. The perpetrator invited the confidence or belief of one or more combatant adversaries that they were entitled to, or were obliged to accord, protection under rules of international law applicable in armed conflict.

2. The perpetrator intended to betray that confidence or belief.

3. The perpetrator killed or injured such person or persons.
4. The perpetrator made use of that confidence or belief in killing or injuring such person or persons.
5. Such person or persons belonged to an adverse party.
6. The conduct took place in the context of and was associated with an armed conflict not of an international character.
7. The perpetrator was aware of factual circumstances that established the existence of an armed conflict.

Article 8(2)(e)(x)
War crime of denying quarter
Elements

1. The perpetrator declared or ordered that there shall be no survivors.
2. Such declaration or order was given in order to threaten an adversary or to conduct hostilities on the basis that there shall be no survivors.
3. The perpetrator was in a position of effective command or control over the subordinate forces to which the declaration or order was directed.
4. The conduct took place in the context of and was associated with an armed conflict not of an international character.
5. The perpetrator was aware of factual circumstances that established the existence of an armed conflict.

Article 8(2)(e)(xi)-1
War crime of mutilation
Elements

1. The perpetrator subjected one or more persons to mutilation, in particular by permanently disfiguring the person or persons, or by permanently disabling or removing an organ or appendage.
2. The conduct caused death or seriously endangered the physical or mental health of such person or persons.
3. The conduct was neither justified by the medical, dental or hospital treatment of the person or persons concerned nor carried out in such person's or persons' interest.[69]
4. Such person or persons were in the power of another party to the conflict.
5. The conduct took place in the context of and was associated with an armed conflict not of an international character.
6. The perpetrator was aware of factual circumstances that established the existence of an armed conflict.

---

[69] Consent is not a defence to this crime. The crime prohibits any medical procedure which is not indicated by the state of health of the person concerned and which is not consistent with generally accepted medical standards which would be applied under similar medical circumstances to persons who are nationals of the party conducting the procedure and who are in no way deprived of liberty. This footnote also applies to the similar element in article 8(2)(e)(xi)-2.

Article 8(2)(e)(xi)-2
War crime of medical or scientific experiments
Elements

1. The perpetrator subjected one or more persons to a medical or scientific experiment.
2. The experiment caused the death or seriously endangered the physical or mental health or integrity of such person or persons.
3. The conduct was neither justified by the medical, dental or hospital treatment of such person or persons concerned nor carried out in such person's or persons' interest.
4. Such person or persons were in the power of another party to the conflict.
5. The conduct took place in the context of and was associated with an armed conflict not of an international character.
6. The perpetrator was aware of factual circumstances that established the existence of an armed conflict.

Article 8(2)(e)(xii)
War crime of destroying or seizing the enemy's property
Elements

1. The perpetrator destroyed or seized certain property.
2. Such property was property of an adversary.
3. Such property was protected from that destruction or seizure under the international law of armed conflict.
4. The perpetrator was aware of the factual circumstances that established the status of the property.
5. The destruction or seizure was not required by military necessity.
6. The conduct took place in the context of and was associated with an armed conflict not of an international character.
7. The perpetrator was aware of factual circumstances that established the existence of an armed conflict.

Article 8(2)(e)(xiii)[70]
War crime of employing poison or poisoned weapons
Elements

1. The perpetrator employed a substance or a weapon that releases a substance as a result of its employment.
2. The substance was such that it causes death or serious damage to health in the ordinary course of events, through its toxic properties.
3. The conduct took place in the context of and was associated with an armed conflict not of an international character.
4. The perpetrator was aware of factual circumstances that established the existence of an armed conflict.

---

[70] As amended by resolution RC/Res.5; see *Official Records of the Review Conference of the Rome Statute of the International Criminal Court, Kampala, 31 May–11 June 2010* (International Criminal Court publication, RC/11), part II.

Article 8(2)(e)(xiv)[71]
War crime of employing prohibited gases, liquids, materials or devices
Elements

1. The perpetrator employed a gas or other analogous substance or device.
2. The gas, substance or device was such that it causes death or serious damage to health in the ordinary course of events, through its asphyxiating or toxic properties.[72]
3. The conduct took place in the context of and was associated with an armed conflict not of an international character.
4. The perpetrator was aware of factual circumstances that established the existence of an armed conflict.

Article 8(2)(e)(xv)[73]
War crime of employing prohibited bullets
Elements

1. The perpetrator employed certain bullets.
2. The bullets were such that their use violates the international law of armed conflict because they expand or flatten easily in the human body.
3. The perpetrator was aware that the nature of the bullets was such that their employment would uselessly aggravate suffering or the wounding effect.
4. The conduct took place in the context of and was associated with an armed conflict not of an international character.
5. The perpetrator was aware of factual circumstances that established the existence of an armed conflict.

Article 8 *bis*[74]
Crime of aggression
Introduction

1. It is understood that any of the acts referred to in article 8 *bis*, paragraph 2, qualify as an act of aggression.
2. There is no requirement to prove that the perpetrator has made a legal evaluation as to whether the use of armed force was inconsistent with the Charter of the United Nations.
3. The term "manifest" is an objective qualification.
4. There is no requirement to prove that the perpetrator has made a legal evaluation as to the "manifest" nature of the violation of the Charter of the United Nations.

---

[71] Ibid.

[72] Nothing in this element shall be interpreted as limiting or prejudicing in any way existing or developing rules of international law with respect to the development, production, stockpiling and use of chemical weapons.

[73] As amended by resolution RC/Res.5; see *Official Records of the Review Conference of the Rome Statute of the International Criminal Court, Kampala, 31 May–11 June 2010* (International Criminal Court publication, RC/11), part II.

[74] As amended by resolution RC/Res.6; see *Official Records of the Review Conference of the Rome Statute of the International Criminal Court, Kampala, 31 May–11 June 2010* (International Criminal Court publication, RC/11), part II.

16

Elements

1. The perpetrator planned, prepared, initiated or executed an act of aggression.
2. The perpetrator was a person[75] in a position effectively to exercise control over or to direct the political or military action of the State which committed the act of aggression.
3. The act of aggression – the use of armed force by a State against the sovereignty, territorial integrity or political independence of another State, or in any other manner inconsistent with the Charter of the United Nations – was committed.
4. The perpetrator was aware of the factual circumstances that established that such a use of armed force was inconsistent with the Charter of the United Nations.
5. The act of aggression, by its character, gravity and scale, constituted a manifest violation of the Charter of the United Nations.
6. The perpetrator was aware of the factual circumstances that established such a manifest violation of the Charter of the United Nations.

Negotiated Relationship Agreement between the International Criminal Court and the United Nations

PREAMBLE

The International Criminal Court and the United Nations,

Bearing in mind the Purposes and Principles of the Charter of the United Nations,

Recalling that the Rome Statute of the International Criminal Court reaffirms the Purposes and Principles of the Charter of the United Nations,

Noting the important role assigned to the International Criminal Court in dealing with the most serious crimes of concern to the international community as a whole, as referred to in the Rome Statute, and which threaten the peace, security and well-being of the world,

Bearing in mind that, in accordance with the Rome Statute, the International Criminal Court is established as an independent permanent institution in relationship with the United Nations system,

Recalling also that, in accordance with article 2 of the Rome Statute, the International Criminal Court shall be brought into relationship with the United Nations through an agreement to be approved by the Assembly of the States Parties to the Rome Statute and thereafter concluded by the President of the Court on its behalf,

Recalling further General Assembly resolution 58/79 of 9 December 2003 calling for the conclusion of a relationship agreement between the United Nations and the International Criminal Court,

Noting the responsibilities of the Secretary-General of the United Nations under the provisions of the Rome Statute of the International Criminal Court,

Desiring to make provision for a mutually beneficial relationship whereby the discharge of respective responsibilities of the United Nations and the International Criminal Court may be facilitated,

---

[75] With respect to an act of aggression, more than one person may be in a position that meets these criteria.

Taking into account for this purpose the provisions of the Charter of the United Nations and the provisions of the Rome Statute of the International Criminal Court,

Have agreed as follows:

I. GENERAL PROVISIONS

Article 1
Purpose of the Agreement

1. The present Agreement, which is entered into by the United Nations and the International Criminal Court ("the Court"), pursuant to the provisions of the Charter of the United Nations ("the Charter") and the Rome Statute of the International Criminal Court ("the Statute"), respectively, defines the terms on which the United Nations and the Court shall be brought into relationship.
2. For the purposes of this Agreement, "the Court" shall also include the Secretariat of the Assembly of States Parties.

Article 2
Principles

1. The United Nations recognizes the Court as an independent permanent judicial institution which, in accordance with articles 1 and 4 of the Statute, has international legal personality and such legal capacity as may be necessary for the exercise of its functions and the fulfilment of its purposes.
2. The Court recognizes the responsibilities of the United Nations under the Charter.
3. The United Nations and the Court respect each other's status and mandate.

Article 3
Obligation of cooperation and coordination

The United Nations and the Court agree that, with a view to facilitating the effective discharge of their respective responsibilities, they shall cooperate closely, whenever appropriate, with each other and consult each other on matters of mutual interest pursuant to the provisions of the present Agreement and in conformity with the respective provisions of the Charter and the Statute.

II. INSTITUTIONAL RELATIONS

Article 4
Reciprocal representation

1. Subject to the applicable provisions of the Rules of Procedure and Evidence of the Court ("the Rules of Procedure and Evidence"), the Secretary-General of the United Nations ("the Secretary-General") or his/her representative shall have a standing invitation to attend public hearings of the Chambers of the Court that relate to cases of interest to the United Nations and any public meetings of the Court.
2. The Court may attend and participate in the work of the General Assembly of the United Nations in the capacity of observer. The United Nations shall, subject to the

rules and practice of the bodies concerned, invite the Court to attend meetings and conferences convened under the auspices of the United Nations where observers are allowed and whenever matters of interest to the Court are under discussion.

3. Whenever the Security Council considers matters related to the activities of the Court, the President of the Court ("the President") or the Prosecutor of the Court ("the Prosecutor") may address the Council, at its invitation, in order to give assistance with regard to matters within the jurisdiction of the Court.

Article 5
Exchange of information

1. Without prejudice to other provisions of the present Agreement concerning the submission of documents and information concerning particular cases before the Court, the United Nations and the Court shall, to the fullest extent possible and practicable, arrange for the exchange of information and documents of mutual interest. In particular:

   (a) The Secretary-General shall:

      (i) Transmit to the Court information on developments related to the Statute which are relevant to the work of the Court, including information on communications received by the Secretary-General in the capacity of depositary of the Statute or depositary of any other agreements which relate to the exercise by the Court of its jurisdiction;

      (ii) Keep the Court informed regarding the implementation of article 123, paragraphs 1 and 2, of the Statute relating to the convening by the Secretary-General of review conferences;

      (iii) In addition to the requirement provided in article 121, paragraph 7, of the Statute, circulate to all States Members of the United Nations or members of specialized agencies or of the International Atomic Energy Agency which are not parties to the Statute the text of any amendment adopted pursuant to article 121 of the Statute;

   (b) The Registrar of the Court ("the Registrar") shall:

      (i) In accordance with the Statute and the Rules of Procedure and Evidence, provide information and documentation relating to pleadings, oral proceedings, judgements and orders of the Court in cases which may be of interest to the United Nations generally, and particularly in those cases which involve crimes committed against the personnel of the United Nations or that involve the improper use of the flag, insignia or uniform of the United Nations resulting in death or serious personal injury as well as any cases involving the circumstances referred to under article 16, 17, or 18, paragraph 1 or 2, of the present Agreement;

      (ii) Furnish to the United Nations, with the concurrence of the Court and subject to its Statute and rules, any information relating to the work of the Court requested by the International Court of Justice in accordance with its Statute;

2. The United Nations and the Court shall make every effort to achieve maximum cooperation with a view to avoiding undesirable duplication in the collection, analysis, publication and dissemination of information relating to matters of mutual interest. They

shall strive, where appropriate, to combine their efforts to secure the greatest possible usefulness and utilization of such information.

Article 6
Reports to the United Nations
The Court may, if it deems it appropriate, submit reports on its activities to the United Nations through the Secretary-General.

Article 7
Agenda items
The Court may propose items for consideration by the United Nations. In such cases, the Court shall notify the Secretary-General of its proposal and provide any relevant information. The Secretary-General shall, in accordance with his/her authority, bring such item or items to the attention of the General Assembly or the Security Council, and also to any other United Nations organ concerned, including organs of United Nations programmes and funds.

Article 8
Personnel arrangements
1. The United Nations and the Court agree to consult and cooperate as far as practicable regarding personnel standards, methods and arrangements.
2. The United Nations and the Court agree to:
   (a) Periodically consult on matters of mutual interest relating to the employment of their officers and staff, including conditions of service, the duration of appointments, classification, salary scale and allowances, retirement and pension rights and staff regulations and rules;
   (b) Cooperate in the temporary interchange of personnel, where appropriate, making due provision for the retention of seniority and pension rights;
   (c) Strive for maximum cooperation in order to achieve the most efficient use of specialized personnel, systems and services.

Article 9
Administrative cooperation
The United Nations and the Court shall consult, from time to time, concerning the most efficient use of facilities, staff and services with a view to avoiding the establishment and operation of overlapping facilities and services. They shall also consult to explore the possibility of establishing common facilities or services in specific areas, with due regard for cost savings.

Article 10
Services and facilities
1. The United Nations agrees that, upon the request of the Court, it shall, subject to availability, provide on a reimbursable basis, or as otherwise agreed, for the purposes of the Court such facilities and services as may be required, including for the meetings of the Assembly of States Parties ("the Assembly"), its Bureau or subsidiary bodies, including translation and interpretation services, documentation and conference services. When

the United Nations is unable to meet the request of the Court, it shall notify the Court accordingly, giving reasonable notice.

2. The terms and conditions on which any such facilities or services of the United Nations may be provided shall, as appropriate, be the subject of supplementary arrangements.

Article 11
Access to United Nations Headquarters
The United Nations and the Court shall endeavour, subject to their respective rules, to facilitate access by the representatives of all States Parties to the Statute, representatives of the Court and observers in the Assembly, as provided for in article 112, paragraph 1, of the Statute, to United Nations Headquarters when a meeting of the Assembly is to be held. This shall also apply, as appropriate, to meetings of the Bureau or subsidiary bodies.

Article 12
Laissez-passer
The judges, the Prosecutor, the Deputy Prosecutors, the Registrar and the staff/officials of the Office of the Prosecutor and the Registry shall be entitled, in accordance with such special arrangements as may be concluded between the Secretary-General and the Court, to use the laissez-passer of the United Nations as a valid travel document where such use is recognized by States in agreements defining the privileges and immunities of the Court. Staff of "the Registry" includes staff of the Presidency and of the Chambers, pursuant to article 44 of the Statute, and staff of the Secretariat of the Assembly of States Parties, pursuant to paragraph 3 of the Annex of Resolution ICC-ASP/2/Res.3.

Article 13
Financial matters
1. The United Nations and the Court agree that the conditions under which any funds may be provided to the Court by a decision of the General Assembly of the United Nations pursuant to article 115 of the Statute shall be subject to separate arrangements. The Registrar shall inform the Assembly of the making of such arrangements.
2. The United Nations and the Court further agree that the costs and expenses resulting from cooperation or the provision of services pursuant to the present Agreement shall be subject to separate arrangements between the United Nations and the Court. The Registrar shall inform the Assembly of the making of such arrangements.
3. The United Nations may, upon request of the Court and subject to paragraph 2 of this article, provide advice on financial and fiscal questions of interest to the Court.

Article 14
Other agreements concluded by the Court
The United Nations and the Court shall consult, when appropriate, on the registration or filing and recording with the United Nations of agreements concluded by the Court with States or international organizations.

III. COOPERATION AND JUDICIAL ASSISTANCE

Article 15
General provisions regarding cooperation between the United Nations and the Court

1. With due regard to its responsibilities and competence under the Charter and subject to its rules as defined under the applicable international law, the United Nations undertakes to cooperate with the Court and to provide to the Court such information or documents as the Court may request pursuant to article 87, paragraph 6, of the Statute.
2. The United Nations or its programmes, funds and offices concerned may agree to provide to the Court other forms of cooperation and assistance compatible with the provisions of the Charter and the Statute.
3. In the event that the disclosure of information or documents or the provision of other forms of cooperation would endanger the safety or security of current or former personnel of the United Nations or otherwise prejudice the security or proper conduct of any operation or activity of the United Nations, the Court may order, particularly at the request of the United Nations, appropriate measures of protection. In the absence of such measures, the United Nations shall endeavour to disclose the information or documents or to provide the requested cooperation, while reserving the right to take its own measures of protection, which may include withholding of some information or documents or their submission in an appropriate form, including the introduction of redactions.

Article 16
Testimony of the officials of the United Nations

1. If the Court requests the testimony of an official of the United Nations or one of its programmes, funds or offices, the United Nations undertakes to cooperate with the Court and, if necessary and with due regard to its responsibilities and competence under the Charter and the Convention on the Privileges and Immunities of the United Nations and subject to its rules, shall waive that person's obligation of confidentiality.
2. The Secretary-General shall be authorized by the Court to appoint a representative of the United Nations to assist any official of the United Nations who appears as a witness before the Court.

Article 17
Cooperation between the Security Council of the United Nations and the Court

1. When the Security Council, acting under Chapter VII of the Charter of the United Nations, decides to refer to the Prosecutor pursuant to article 13, paragraph (b), of the Statute, a situation in which one or more of the crimes referred to in article 5 of the Statute appears to have been committed, the Secretary-General shall immediately transmit the written decision of the Security Council to the Prosecutor together with documents and other materials that may be pertinent to the decision of the Council. The Court undertakes to keep the Security Council informed in this regard in accordance with the Statute and the Rules of Procedure and Evidence. Such information shall be transmitted through the Secretary-General.

2. When the Security Council adopts under Chapter VII of the Charter a resolution requesting the Court, pursuant to article 16 of the Statute, not to commence or proceed with an investigation or prosecution, this request shall immediately be transmitted by the Secretary-General to the President of the Court and the Prosecutor. The Court shall inform the Security Council through the Secretary-General of its receipt of the above request and, as appropriate, inform the Security Council through the Secretary-General of actions, if any, taken by the Court in this regard.

3. Where a matter has been referred to the Court by the Security Council and the Court makes a finding, pursuant to article 87, paragraph 5(b) or paragraph 7, of the Statute, of a failure by a State to cooperate with the Court, the Court shall inform the Security Council or refer the matter to it, as the case may be, and the Registrar shall convey to the Security Council through the Secretary-General the decision of the Court, together with relevant information in the case. The Security Council, through the Secretary-General, shall inform the Court through the Registrar of action, if any, taken by it under the circumstances.

Article 18
Cooperation between the United Nations and the Prosecutor

1. With due regard to its responsibilities and competence under the Charter of the United Nations and subject to its rules, the United Nations undertakes to cooperate with the Prosecutor and to enter with the Prosecutor into such arrangements or, as appropriate, agreements as may be necessary to facilitate such cooperation, in particular when the Prosecutor exercises, under article 54 of the Statute, his or her duties and powers with respect to investigation and seeks the cooperation of the United Nations in accordance with that article.

2. Subject to the rules of the organ concerned, the United Nations undertakes to cooperate in relation to requests from the Prosecutor in providing such additional information as he or she may seek, in accordance with article 15, paragraph 2, of the Statute, from organs of the United Nations in connection with investigations initiated *proprio motu* by the Prosecutor pursuant to that article. The Prosecutor shall address a request for such information to the Secretary-General, who shall convey it to the presiding officer or other appropriate officer of the organ concerned.

3. The United Nations and the Prosecutor may agree that the United Nations provide documents or information to the Prosecutor on condition of confidentiality and solely for the purpose of generating new evidence and that such documents or information shall not be disclosed to other organs of the Court or to third parties, at any stage of the proceedings or thereafter, without the consent of the United Nations.

4. The Prosecutor and the United Nations or its programmes, funds and offices concerned may enter into such arrangements as may be necessary to facilitate their cooperation for the implementation of this article, in particular in order to ensure the confidentiality of information, the protection of any person, including former or current United Nations personnel, and the security or proper conduct of any operation or activity of the United Nations.

Article 19
Rules concerning United Nations privileges and immunities
If the Court seeks to exercise its jurisdiction over a person who is alleged to be criminally responsible for a crime within the jurisdiction of the Court and if, in the circumstances, such person enjoys, according to the Convention on the Privileges and Immunities of the United Nations and the relevant rules of international law, any privileges and immunities as are necessary for the independent exercise of his or her work for the United Nations, the United Nations undertakes to cooperate fully with the Court and to take all necessary measures to allow the Court to exercise its jurisdiction, in particular by waiving any such privileges and immunities in accordance with the Convention on the Privileges and Immunities of the United Nations and the relevant rules of international law.

Article 20
Protection of confidentiality
If the United Nations is requested by the Court to provide information or documentation in its custody, possession or control which was disclosed to it in confidence by a State or an intergovernmental, international or non-governmental organization or an individual, the United Nations shall seek the consent of the originator to disclose that information or documentation or, where appropriate, will inform the Court that it may seek the consent of the originator for the United Nations to disclose that information or documentation. If the originator is a State Party to the Statute and the United Nations fails to obtain its consent to disclosure within a reasonable period of time, the United Nations shall inform the Court accordingly, and the issue of disclosure shall be resolved between the State Party concerned and the Court in accordance with the Statute. If the originator is not a State Party to the Statute and refuses to consent to disclosure, the United Nations shall inform the Court that it is unable to provide the requested information or documentation because of a pre-existing obligation of confidentiality to the originator.

IV. FINAL PROVISIONS

Article 21
Supplementary arrangements for the implementation of the present Agreement
The Secretary-General and the Court may, for the purpose of implementing the present Agreement, make such supplementary arrangements as may be found appropriate.

Article 22
Amendments
The present Agreement may be amended by agreement between the United Nations and the Court. Any such amendment shall be approved by the General Assembly of the United Nations and by the Assembly in accordance with article 2 of the Statute. The United Nations and the Court shall notify each other in writing of the date of such approval, and the Agreement shall enter into force on the date of the later of the said approvals.

16

Article 23
Entry into force

The present Agreement shall be approved by the General Assembly of the United Nations and by the Assembly in accordance with article 2 of the Statute. The United Nations and the Court shall notify each other in writing of the date of such approval. The Agreement shall thereafter enter into force upon signature.

2002 Special Court for Sierra Leone Statute; Agreement for the Establishment of a Residual Mechanism for the Special Court for Sierra Leone and Statute of the Residual Special Court for Sierra Leone

Statute of the Special Court for Sierra Leone

Having been established by an Agreement between the United Nations and the Government of Sierra Leone pursuant to Security Council resolution 1315 (2000) of 14 August 2000, the Special Court for Sierra Leone (hereinafter "the Special Court") shall function in accordance with the provisions of the present Statute.

Article 1
Competence of the Special Court

1. The Special Court shall, except as provided in subparagraph (2), have the power to prosecute persons who bear the greatest responsibility for serious violations of international humanitarian law and Sierra Leonean law committed in the territory of Sierra Leone since 30 November 1996, including those leaders who, in committing such crimes, have threatened the establishment of and implementation of the peace process in Sierra Leone.
2. Any transgressions by peacekeepers and related personnel present in Sierra Leone pursuant to the Status of Mission Agreement in force between the United Nations and the Government of Sierra Leone or agreements between Sierra Leone and other Governments or regional organizations, or, in the absence of such agreement, provided that the peacekeeping operations were undertaken with the consent of the Government of Sierra Leone, shall be within the primary jurisdiction of the sending State.
3. In the event the sending State is unwilling or unable genuinely to carry out an investigation or prosecution, the Court may, if authorized by the Security Council on the proposal of any State, exercise jurisdiction over such persons.

Article 2
Crimes against humanity

The Special Court shall have the power to prosecute persons who committed the following crimes as part of a widespread or systematic attack against any civilian population:

a. Murder;
b. Extermination;
c. Enslavement;
d. Deportation;
e. Imprisonment;
f. Torture;
g. Rape, sexual slavery, enforced prostitution, forced pregnancy and any other form of sexual violence;
h. Persecution on political, racial, ethnic or religious grounds;
i. Other inhumane acts.

Article 3
Violations of Article 3 common to the Geneva Conventions and of Additional Protocol II

The Special Court shall have the power to prosecute persons who committed or ordered the commission of serious violations of article 3 common to the Geneva Conventions of 12 August 1949 for the Protection of War Victims, and of Additional Protocol II thereto of 8 June 1977. These violations shall include:
a. Violence to life, health and physical or mental well-being of persons, in particular murder as well as cruel treatment such as torture, mutilation or any form of corporal punishment;
b. Collective punishments;
c. Taking of hostages;
d. Acts of terrorism;
e. Outrages upon personal dignity, in particular humiliating and degrading treatment, rape, enforced prostitution and any form of indecent assault;
f. Pillage;
g. The passing of sentences and the carrying out of executions without previous judgement pronounced by a regularly constituted court, affording all the judicial guarantees which are recognized as indispensable by civilized peoples;
h. Threats to commit any of the foregoing acts.

Article 4
Other serious violations of international humanitarian law

The Special Court shall have the power to prosecute persons who committed the following serious violations of international humanitarian law:
a. Intentionally directing attacks against the civilian population as such or against individual civilians not taking direct part in hostilities;
b. Intentionally directing attacks against personnel, installations, material, units or vehicles involved in a humanitarian assistance or peacekeeping mission in accordance with the Charter of the United Nations, as long as they are entitled to the protection given to civilians or civilian objects under the international law of armed conflict;
c. Conscripting or enlisting children under the age of 15 years into armed forces or groups or using them to participate actively in hostilities.

Article 5

Crimes under Sierra Leonean law

The Special Court shall have the power to prosecute persons who have committed the following crimes under Sierra Leonean law:

a. Offences relating to the abuse of girls under the Prevention of Cruelty to Children Act, 1926 (Cap. 31):

    i. Abusing a girl under 13 years of age, contrary to section 6;

    ii. Abusing a girl between 13 and 14 years of age, contrary to section 7;

    iii. Abduction of a girl for immoral purposes, contrary to section 12.

b. Offences relating to the wanton destruction of property under the Malicious Damage Act, 1861:

    i. Setting fire to dwelling-houses, any person being therein, contrary to section 2;

    ii. Setting fire to public buildings, contrary to sections 5 and 6;

    iii. Setting fire to other buildings, contrary to section 6.

Article 6

Individual criminal responsibility

1. A person who planned, instigated, ordered, committed or otherwise aided and abetted in the planning, preparation or execution of a crime referred to in articles 2 to 4 of the present Statute shall be individually responsible for the crime.

2. The official position of any accused persons, whether as Head of State or Government or as a responsible government official, shall not relieve such person of criminal responsibility nor mitigate punishment.

3. The fact that any of the acts referred to in articles 2 to 4 of the present Statute was committed by a subordinate does not relieve his or her superior of criminal responsibility if he or she knew or had reason to know that the subordinate was about to commit such acts or had done so and the superior had failed to take the necessary and reasonable measures to prevent such acts or to punish the perpetrators thereof.

4. The fact that an accused person acted pursuant to an order of a Government or of a superior shall not relieve him or her of criminal responsibility, but may be considered in mitigation of punishment if the Special Court determines that justice so requires.

5. Individual criminal responsibility for the crimes referred to in article 5 shall be determined in accordance with the respective laws of Sierra Leone.

Article 7

Jurisdiction over persons of 15 years of age

1. The Special Court shall have no jurisdiction over any person who was under the age of 15 at the time of the alleged commission of the crime. Should any person who was at the time of the alleged commission of the crime between 15 and 18 years of age come before the Court, he or she shall be treated with dignity and a sense of worth, taking into account his or her young age and the desirability of promoting his or her rehabilitation, reintegration into and assumption of a constructive role in society, and in accordance with international human rights standards, in particular the rights of the child.

2. In the disposition of a case against a juvenile offender, the Special Court shall order any of the following: care guidance and supervision orders, community service orders,

counselling, foster care, correctional, educational and vocational training programmes, approved schools and, as appropriate, any programmes of disarmament, demobilization and reintegration or programmes of child protection agencies.

Article 8
Concurrent jurisdiction
1. The Special Court and the national courts of Sierra Leone shall have concurrent jurisdiction.
2. The Special Court shall have primacy over the national courts of Sierra Leone. At any stage of the procedure, the Special Court may formally request a national court to defer to its competence in accordance with the present Statute and the Rules of Procedure and Evidence.

Article 9
Non bis in idem
1. No person shall be tried before a national court of Sierra Leone for acts for which he or she has already been tried by the Special Court.
2. A person who has been tried by a national court for the acts referred to in articles 2 to 4 of the present Statute may be subsequently tried by the Special Court if:
   a. The act for which he or she was tried was characterized as an ordinary crime; or
   b. The national court proceedings were not impartial or independent, were designed to shield the accused from international criminal responsibility or the case was not diligently prosecuted.
3. In considering the penalty to be imposed on a person convicted of a crime under the present Statute, the Special Court shall take into account the extent to which any penalty imposed by a national court on the same person for the same act has already been served.

Article 10
Amnesty
An amnesty granted to any person falling within the jurisdiction of the Special Court in respect of the crimes referred to in articles 2 to 4 of the present Statute shall not be a bar to prosecution.

Article 11
Organization of the Special Court
The Special Court shall consist of the following organs:
a. The Chambers, comprising one or more Trial Chambers and an Appeals Chamber;
b. The Prosecutor; and
c. The Registry.

Article 12
Composition of the Chambers
1. The Chambers shall be composed of not less than eight (8) or more than eleven (11) independent judges, who shall serve as follows:

a. Three judges shall serve in the Trial Chamber, of whom one shall be a judge appointed by the Government of Sierra Leone, and two judges appointed by the Secretary-General of the United Nations (hereinafter "the Secretary-General").

b. Five judges shall serve in the Appeals Chamber, of whom two shall be judges appointed by the Government of Sierra Leone, and three judges appointed by the Secretary-General.

2. Each judge shall serve only in the Chamber to which he or she has been appointed.

3. The judges of the Appeals Chamber and the judges of the Trial Chamber, respectively, shall elect a presiding judge who shall conduct the proceedings in the Chamber to which he or she was elected. The presiding judge of the Appeals Chamber shall be the President of the Special Court.

4. If, at the request of the President of the Special Court, an alternate judge or judges have been appointed by the Government of Sierra Leone or the Secretary-General, the presiding judge of a Trial Chamber or the Appeals Chamber shall designate such an alternate judge to be present at each stage of the trial and to replace a judge if that judge is unable to continue sitting.

Article 13

Qualification and appointment of judges

1. The judges shall be persons of high moral character, impartiality and integrity who possess the qualifications required in their respective countries for appointment to the highest judicial offices. They shall be independent in the performance of their functions, and shall not accept or seek instructions from any Government or any other source.

2. In the overall composition of the Chambers, due account shall be taken of the experience of the judges in international law, including international humanitarian law and human rights law, criminal law and juvenile justice.

3. The judges shall be appointed for a three-year period and shall be eligible for reappointment.

Article 14

Rules of Procedure and Evidence

1. The Rules of Procedure and Evidence of the International Criminal Tribunal for Rwanda obtaining at the time of the establishment of the Special Court shall be applicable *mutatis mutandis* to the conduct of the legal proceedings before the Special Court.

2. The judges of the Special Court as a whole may amend the Rules of Procedure and Evidence or adopt additional rules where the applicable Rules do not, or do not adequately, provide for a specific situation. In so doing, they may be guided, as appropriate, by the Criminal Procedure Act, 1965, of Sierra Leone.

Article 15

The Prosecutor

1. The Prosecutor shall be responsible for the investigation and prosecution of persons who bear the greatest responsibility for serious violations of international humanitarian law and crimes under Sierra Leonean law committed in the territory of Sierra

Leone since 30 November 1996. The Prosecutor shall act independently as a separate organ of the Special Court. He or she shall not seek or receive instructions from any Government or from any other source.

2. The Office of the Prosecutor shall have the power to question suspects, victims and witnesses, to collect evidence and to conduct on-site investigations. In carrying out these tasks, the Prosecutor shall, as appropriate, be assisted by the Sierra Leonean authorities concerned.

3. The Prosecutor shall be appointed by the Secretary-General for a three-year term and shall be eligible for re-appointment. He or she shall be of high moral character and possess the highest level of professional competence, and have extensive experience in the conduct of investigations and prosecutions of criminal cases.

4. The Prosecutor shall be assisted by a Sierra Leonean Deputy Prosecutor, and by such other Sierra Leonean and international staff as may be required to perform the functions assigned to him or her effectively and efficiently. Given the nature of the crimes committed and the particular sensitivities of girls, young women and children victims of rape, sexual assault, abduction and slavery of all kinds, due consideration should be given in the appointment of staff to the employment of prosecutors and investigators experienced in gender-related crimes and juvenile justice.

5. In the prosecution of juvenile offenders, the Prosecutor shall ensure that the child-rehabilitation programme is not placed at risk and that, where appropriate, resort should be had to alternative truth and reconciliation mechanisms, to the extent of their availability.

Article 16
The Registry

1. The Registry shall be responsible for the administration and servicing of the Special Court.

2. The Registry shall consist of a Registrar and such other staff as may be required.

3. The Registrar shall be appointed by the Secretary-General after consultation with the President of the Special Court and shall be a staff member of the United Nations. He or she shall serve for a three-year term and be eligible for re-appointment.

4. The Registrar shall set up a Victims and Witnesses Unit within the Registry. This Unit shall provide, in consultation with the Office of the Prosecutor, protective measures and security arrangements, counselling and other appropriate assistance for witnesses, victims who appear before the Court and others who are at risk on account of testimony given by such witnesses. The Unit personnel shall include experts in trauma, including trauma related to crimes of sexual violence and violence against children.

Article 17
Rights of the accused

1. All accused shall be equal before the Special Court.

2. The accused shall be entitled to a fair and public hearing, subject to measures ordered by the Special Court for the protection of victims and witnesses.

3. The accused shall be presumed innocent until proved guilty according to the provisions of the present Statute.

4. In the determination of any charge against the accused pursuant to the present Statute, he or she shall be entitled to the following minimum guarantees, in full equality:

   a. To be informed promptly and in detail in a language which he or she understands of the nature and cause of the charge against him or her;

   b. To have adequate time and facilities for the preparation of his or her defence and to communicate with counsel of his or her own choosing;

   c. To be tried without undue delay;

   d. To be tried in his or her presence, and to defend himself or herself in person or through legal assistance of his or her own choosing; to be informed, if he or she does not have legal assistance, of this right; and to have legal assistance assigned to him or her, in any case where the interests of justice so require, and without payment by him or her in any such case if he or she does not have sufficient means to pay for it;

   e. To examine, or have examined, the witnesses against him or her and to obtain the attendance and examination of witnesses on his or her behalf under the same conditions as witnesses against him or her;

   f. To have the free assistance of an interpreter if he or she cannot understand or speak the language used in the Special Court;

   g. Not to be compelled to testify against himself or herself or to confess guilt.

Article 18
Judgement

The judgement shall be rendered by a majority of the judges of the Trial Chamber or of the Appeals Chamber, and shall be delivered in public. It shall be accompanied by a reasoned opinion in writing, to which separate or dissenting opinions may be appended.

Article 19
Penalties

1. The Trial Chamber shall impose upon a convicted person, other than a juvenile offender, imprisonment for a specified number of years. In determining the terms of imprisonment, the Trial Chamber shall, as appropriate, have recourse to the practice regarding prison sentences in the International Criminal Tribunal for Rwanda and the national courts of Sierra Leone.

2. In imposing the sentences, the Trial Chamber should take into account such factors as the gravity of the offence and the individual circumstances of the convicted person.

3. In addition to imprisonment, the Trial Chamber may order the forfeiture of the property, proceeds and any assets acquired unlawfully or by criminal conduct, and their return to their rightful owner or to the State of Sierra Leone.

Article 20
Appellate proceedings

1. The Appeals Chamber shall hear appeals from persons convicted by the Trial Chamber or from the Prosecutor on the following grounds:

   a. A procedural error;

   b. An error on a question of law invalidating the decision;

   c. An error of fact which has occasioned a miscarriage of justice.

17

2. The Appeals Chamber may affirm, reverse or revise the decisions taken by the Trial Chamber.

3. The judges of the Appeals Chamber of the Special Court shall be guided by the decisions of the Appeals Chamber of the International Tribunals for the former Yugoslavia and for Rwanda. In the interpretation and application of the laws of Sierra Leone, they shall be guided by the decisions of the Supreme Court of Sierra Leone.

Article 21
Review proceedings

1. Where a new fact has been discovered which was not known at the time of the proceedings before the Trial Chamber or the Appeals Chamber and which could have been a decisive factor in reaching the decision, the convicted person or the Prosecutor may submit an application for review of the judgement.

2. An application for review shall be submitted to the Appeals Chamber. The Appeals Chamber may reject the application if it considers it to be unfounded. If it determines that the application is meritorious, it may, as appropriate:
   a. Reconvene the Trial Chamber;
   b. Retain jurisdiction over the matter.

Article 22
Enforcement of sentences

1. Imprisonment shall be served in Sierra Leone. If circumstances so require, imprisonment may also be served in any of the States which have concluded with the International Criminal Tribunal for Rwanda or the International Criminal Tribunal for the former Yugoslavia an agreement for the enforcement of sentences, and which have indicated to the Registrar of the Special Court their willingness to accept convicted persons. The Special Court may conclude similar agreements for the enforcement of sentences with other States.

2. Conditions of imprisonment, whether in Sierra Leone or in a third State, shall be governed by the law of the State of enforcement subject to the supervision of the Special Court. The State of enforcement shall be bound by the duration of the sentence, subject to article 23 of the present Statute.

Article 23
Pardon or commutation of sentences

If, pursuant to the applicable law of the State in which the convicted person is imprisoned, he or she is eligible for pardon or commutation of sentence, the State concerned shall notify the Special Court accordingly. There shall only be pardon or commutation of sentence if the President of the Special Court, in consultation with the judges, so decides on the basis of the interests of justice and the general principles of law.

Article 24
Working language

The working language of the Special Court shall be English.

17

Article 25
Annual Report
The President of the Special Court shall submit an annual report on the operation and activities of the Court to the Secretary-General and to the Government of Sierra Leone.

Agreement between the United Nations and the Government of Sierra Leone on the Establishment of a Residual Special Court for Sierra Leone

Whereas, pursuant to Security Council resolution 1315 (2000) adopted on 14 August 2000, the Special Court for Sierra Leone (hereinafter "the Special Court") was created by the Agreement between the United Nations and the Government of Sierra Leone on the Establishment of a Special Court for Sierra Leone to prosecute persons who bear the greatest responsibility for serious violations of international humanitarian law and Sierra Leonean law committed in the territory of Sierra Leone since 30 November 1996;

Whereas, according to Article 23 of the Agreement, the Agreement shall be terminated by agreement of the Parties upon completion of the judicial activities of the Special Court;

Whereas, in anticipation of the completion of the judicial activities of the Special Court, the United Nations and the Government of Sierra Leone are convinced of the need to establish a small and efficient residual court comprising such number of staff as is commensurate with its reduced functions, to carry out essential functions of the Special Court after its closure;

Now therefore the United Nations and the Government of Sierra Leone (hereinafter referred to jointly as "the Parties") have agreed as follows:

Article 1
Establishment and functions
1. There is hereby established a Residual Special Court for Sierra Leone (the "Residual Special Court") to carry out the functions of the Special Court for Sierra Leone that must continue after the closure of the Special Court.
2. The Residual Special Court shall be governed by the Statute annexed to this Agreement, which forms an integral part hereof.
3. The Residual Special Court shall continue the jurisdiction, functions, rights and obligations of the Special Court subject to the provisions of this Agreement and the Statute.

Article 2
Composition
The Residual Special Court shall be composed of the Chambers, consisting of the President and when necessary a Trial Chamber and Appeals Chamber, the Prosecutor, and the Registrar.

Article 3
Expenses
The expenses of the Residual Special Court shall be borne by voluntary contributions from the international community. The Parties and the oversight committee may explore alternative means of financing the Residual Special Court.

Article 4
Oversight committee

The Residual Special Court shall have an oversight committee to assist in obtaining adequate funding and to provide advice and policy direction on all non-judicial aspects of its operation. The oversight committee shall consist of the Parties and significant contributors to the Residual Special Court.

Article 5
Juridical capacity

The Residual Special Court shall possess the juridical capacity necessary to:

(a) Contract;

(b) Acquire and dispose of movable and immovable property;

(c) Institute legal proceedings;

(d) Enter into agreements with States and international organizations as may be necessary for the exercise of its functions and for its operation.

Article 6
Seat

The Residual Special Court shall have its principal seat in Sierra Leone. The Residual Special Court shall carry out its functions at an interim seat in The Netherlands, with a branch or sub-office in Sierra Leone for witness and victim protection and support, until such time as the Parties agree otherwise. The Residual Special Court may meet away from its seat if it considers it necessary for the efficient exercise of its functions.

Article 7
Archives

1. The archives and other documents of the Special Court shall be the property of the Residual Special Court, without prejudice to the rights of, and conditions imposed by, information providers and other third parties. The Residual Special Court shall maintain, as necessary, the confidentiality of the archives and shall ensure the continued protection of information that was provided by individuals, States and other entities with confidentiality restrictions under the Rules of Procedure and Evidence of the Special Court for Sierra Leone or protected by judicial orders of the Special Court.

2. The original archives shall be co-located with the Residual Special Court. In order to preserve and promote the legacy of the Special Court, electronic access to, and printed copies of, the public archives shall be available to the public in Sierra Leone.

3. The Parties may at any time agree to re-locate the original archives to Sierra Leone when there is a suitable facility for their preservation and sufficient security for maintaining the archives in accordance with international standards.

4. The Residual Special Court shall be responsible for the management, including preservation and provision of access, of its archives.

5. The archives, and in general all documents and materials made available, belonging to or used by the Residual Special Court, wherever located and by whomsoever held, shall be inviolable in Sierra Leone. Arrangements shall be made to ensure that the archives, and in general all documents and materials made available, belonging to or

used by the Residual Special Court, wherever located and by whomsoever held, shall be inviolable.

Article 8
Inviolability of premises

1. The premises of the Residual Special Court in Sierra Leone shall be inviolable. Appropriate arrangements shall also be made to ensure that any premises of the Residual Special Court elsewhere are inviolable.
2. The property, funds and assets of the Residual Special Court, wherever located and by whomsoever held, shall be immune in Sierra Leone from search, seizure, requisition, confiscation, expropriation and any other form of interference, whether by executive, administrative, judicial, or legislative action. Appropriate arrangements shall be made for such immunity at any other location of the Residual Special Court.

Article 9
Immunity of funds, assets and other property

The Residual Special Court, its funds, assets and other property, wherever located and by whomsoever held, shall enjoy immunity in Sierra Leone from every form of legal process, except insofar as in any particular case the Residual Special Court has expressly waived its immunity. A waiver of immunity does not extend to any measure of execution. Appropriate arrangements shall be made for such immunity at any other location of the Residual Special Court.

Article 10
Privileges and immunities

1. The President, judges, Prosecutor, Registrar, and staff serving with the Residual Special Court shall be accorded in Sierra Leone those privileges and immunities accorded to officials of the United Nations, *mutatis mutandis*, under Section 18 of the 1946 Convention on the Privileges and Immunities of the United Nations. Appropriate arrangements shall be made for such privileges and immunities to be accorded to those serving at other locations of the Residual Special Court.
2. These privileges and immunities will be accorded in the interest of the Residual Special Court and not for the personal benefit of the individuals themselves.
3. Other persons, including the accused, witnesses, victims and defence counsel required at the seat or other location of the Residual Special Court shall be accorded in Sierra Leone such treatment as is necessary for the proper functioning of the Residual Special Court. Appropriate arrangements shall be made for such treatment to be accorded to these persons at other locations of the Residual Special Court.

Article 11
Cooperation with the Residual Special Court

The Government of Sierra Leone shall cooperate with the Residual Special Court in all its operations. The Government shall comply without undue delay with any request for assistance by the Residual Special Court or an order issued by the Chambers, including, but not limited to:

17

(a) Identification and location of persons;
(b) Service of documents;
(c) Arrest or detention of persons;
(d) Transfer of an indictee to the Residual Special Court.

Article 12
Practical Arrangements

Appropriate arrangements shall be made to ensure that there is a coordinated transition from the activities of the Special Court to the activities of the Residual Special Court. Priority shall be given to the needs of the Residual Special Court in the liquidation of the assets of the Special Court, after which the assets shall be disposed of to the Government of Sierra Leone in accordance with the liquidation policy of the Special Court.

Article 13
Settlement of Disputes

Any dispute between the Parties concerning the interpretation or application of this Agreement shall be settled by negotiation, or by any other mutually agreed upon mode of settlement.

Article 14
Entry into force

The present Agreement shall enter into force on the day after both Parties have notified each other in writing that the legal requirements for entry into force have been complied with. The Residual Special Court shall commence operations immediately upon the closure of the Special Court.

Article 15
Amendment

This Agreement may be amended by written agreement of the Parties.

Article 16
Termination

This Agreement shall be terminated by written agreement of the Parties. The provisions relating to the inviolability of the funds, assets, archives and documents of the Residual Special Court, the privileges and immunities of those referred to in this Agreement, as well as provisions relating to the treatment of defence counsel, victims and witnesses, shall survive the termination of this Agreement.

Article 17
Disposition of assets

On the completion of the work of the Residual Special Court, any assets inherited from the Special Court or acquired by the Residual Special Court shall become the property of the Government of Sierra Leone.

Statute of the Residual Special Court for Sierra Leone

The Residual Special Court established by the Agreement between the United Nations and the Government of Sierra Leone on the Establishment of a Residual Special Court for Sierra Leone ("the Agreement") shall function in accordance with the provisions of the present Statute.

Article 1

Competence

1. The purpose of the Residual Special Court is to carry out the functions of the Special Court for Sierra Leone that must continue after the closure of the Special Court. To that end, the Residual Special Court shall: maintain, preserve and manage its archives, including the archives of the Special Court; provide for witness and victim protection and support; respond to requests for access to evidence by national prosecution authorities; supervise enforcement of sentences; review convictions and acquittals; conduct contempt of court proceedings; provide defence counsel and legal aid for the conduct of proceedings before the Residual Special Court; respond to requests from national authorities with respect to claims for compensation; and prevent double jeopardy.
2. The jurisdiction of the Residual Special Court is limited to persons who bear the greatest responsibility for serious violations of international humanitarian law and Sierra Leonean law committed in the territory of Sierra Leone since 30 November 1996. That is, the Residual Special Court shall have the power to prosecute the remaining fugitive Special Court indictee if his case has not been referred to a competent national jurisdiction, and to prosecute any cases resulting from review of convictions and acquittals.

Article 2

Crimes against humanity

The Residual Special Court shall have the power to prosecute persons who committed the following crimes as part of a widespread or systematic attack against any civilian population:

a. Murder;
b. Extermination;
c. Enslavement;
d. Deportation;
e. Imprisonment;
f. Torture;
g. Rape, sexual slavery, enforced prostitution, forced pregnancy and any other form of sexual violence;
h. Persecution on political, racial, ethnic or religious grounds;
i. Other inhumane acts.

Article 3

Violations of Article 3 common to the Geneva Conventions and of Additional Protocol II

The Residual Special Court shall have the power to prosecute persons who committed or ordered the commission of serious violations of Article 3 common to the Geneva

17

Conventions of 12 August 1949 for the Protection of War Victims, and of Additional Protocol II thereto of 8 June 1977. These violations shall include:

a. Violence to life, health and physical or mental well-being of persons, in particular murder as well as cruel treatment such as torture, mutilation or any form of corporal punishment;
b. Collective punishments;
c. Taking of hostages;
d. Acts of terrorism;
e. Outrages upon personal dignity, in particular humiliating and degrading treatment, rape, enforced prostitution and any form of indecent assault;
f. Pillage;
g. The passing of sentences and the carrying out of executions without previous judgment pronounced by a regularly constituted court, affording all the judicial guarantees which are recognized as indispensable by civilized peoples;
h. Threats to commit any of the foregoing acts.

Article 4
Other serious violations of international humanitarian law

The Residual Special Court shall have the power to prosecute persons who committed the following serious violations of international humanitarian law:

a. Intentionally directing attacks against the civilian population as such or against individual civilians not taking direct part in hostilities;
b. Intentionally directing attacks against personnel, installations, material, units or vehicles involved in a humanitarian assistance or peacekeeping mission in accordance with the Charter of the United Nations, as long as they are entitled to the protection given to civilians or civilian objects under the international law of armed conflict;
c. Conscripting or enlisting children under the age of 15 years into armed forces or groups or using them to participate actively in hostilities.

Article 5
Crimes under Sierra Leonean law

The Residual Special Court shall have the power to prosecute persons who have committed the following crimes under Sierra Leonean law:

a. Offences relating to the abuse of girls under the Prevention of Cruelty to Children Act, 1926 (Cap. 31):
    i. Abusing a girl under 13 years of age, contrary to section 6;
    ii. Abusing a girl between 13 and 14 years of age, contrary to section 7;
    iii. Abduction of a girl for immoral purposes, contrary to section 12.
b. Offences relating to the wanton destruction of property under the Malicious Damage Act, 1861:
    i. Setting fire to dwelling-houses, any person being therein, contrary to section 2;
    ii. Setting fire to public buildings, contrary to sections 5 and 6;
    iii. Setting fire to other buildings, contrary to section 6.

Article 6
Individual criminal responsibility

1. A person who planned, instigated, ordered, committed or otherwise aided and abetted in the planning, preparation or execution of a crime referred to in Articles 2 to 4 of the present Statute shall be individually responsible for the crime.
2. The official position of any accused persons, whether as Head of State or Government or as a responsible government official, shall not relieve such person of criminal responsibility nor mitigate punishment.
3. The fact that any of the acts referred to in Articles 2 to 4 of the present Statute was committed by a subordinate does not relieve his or her superior of criminal responsibility if he or she knew or had reason to know that the subordinate was about to commit such acts or had done so and the superior had failed to take the necessary and reasonable measures to prevent such acts or to punish the perpetrators thereof.
4. The fact that an accused person acted pursuant to an order of a Government or of a superior shall not relieve him or her of criminal responsibility, but may be considered in mitigation of punishment if the Residual Special Court determines that justice so requires.
5. Individual criminal responsibility for the crimes referred to in Article 5 shall be determined in accordance with the respective laws of Sierra Leone.

Article 7
Referral of cases to national jurisdictions

1. The Residual Special Court shall have power, and shall undertake every effort, to refer the case of the remaining fugitive Special Court indictee to a competent national jurisdiction for investigation and prosecution, if the Special Court has not referred the case to a national jurisdiction.
2. After the referral, the Residual Special Court shall monitor the case through cooperation with international or regional organizations.
3. The Residual Special Court may revoke the referral only if:
   a. The national jurisdiction is unwilling or unable to prosecute the accused; or
   b. The national court proceedings are not impartial or independent, are designed to shield the accused from international criminal responsibility, or the case is not diligently prosecuted; and
   c. The accused has not yet been found guilty or acquitted.

Article 8
Concurrent jurisdiction

1. The Residual Special Court and the national courts of Sierra Leone shall have concurrent jurisdiction.
2. The Residual Special Court shall have primacy over the national courts of Sierra Leone in matters falling within Article 1(2) above. At any stage of proceedings, the Residual Special Court may formally request a national court to defer to its competence in accordance with the present Statute and the Rules of Procedure and Evidence.

Article 9
Non bis in idem

1. No person shall be tried before a national court of Sierra Leone for acts for which he or she has already been tried by the Special Court for Sierra Leone or the Residual Special Court.
2. Should the remaining fugitive Special Court indictee be tried by a national court, the Residual Special Court may try him subsequently, or may refer his case to a competent national jurisdiction, only if:
    a. The act for which he was tried was characterized as an ordinary crime; or
    b. The national court proceedings were not impartial or independent, were designed to shield him from international criminal responsibility, or the case was not diligently prosecuted.
3. In considering the penalty to be imposed on a person convicted of a crime under the present Statute, the Residual Special Court shall take into account the extent to which any penalty imposed by a national court on the same person for the same act has already been served.

Article 10
Amnesty

An amnesty granted to any person falling within the jurisdiction of the Residual Special Court in respect of the crimes referred to in Articles 2 to 4 of the present Statute shall not be a bar to prosecution.

Article 11
Roster of judges

1. There shall be a roster of no fewer than 16 judges who may be assigned to the Trial Chamber and Appeals Chamber. The judges shall not receive any remuneration or other benefits for being on the roster, but shall be remunerated on a pro-rata basis if called upon by the President to serve the Residual Special Court.
2. The judges shall be persons of high moral character, impartiality and integrity who possess the qualifications required in their respective countries for appointment to the highest judicial offices. They shall be independent in the performance of their functions, and shall not accept or seek instructions from any Government or any other source.
3. Ten judges shall be appointed to the roster by the Secretary-General and six judges shall be appointed to the roster by the Government of Sierra Leone. Additional judges shall be appointed, when necessary, by the Secretary-General in consultation with the Government of Sierra Leone. In the appointment of judges, particular account shall be taken of the experience of former judges of the Special Court, the International Tribunal for the former Yugoslavia, the International Criminal Tribunal for Rwanda, the Extraordinary Chambers in the Courts of Cambodia, the International Criminal Court, and the Special Tribunal for Lebanon.
4. Judges shall be appointed to the roster for a six-year term and shall be eligible for reappointment.

17

Article 12
The President

1. The judges on the roster shall elect a President, who shall serve as the duty judge of the Residual Special Court to handle any judicial work, including but not limited to contempt proceedings, that arises but that does not require convening a Trial Chamber pursuant to Article 13(1) or Appeals Chamber pursuant to Article 13(2).

2. The President shall in as far as possible carry out his or her functions remotely and shall be present at the seat of the Residual Special Court only as necessary to carry out functions. The President shall be remunerated on a pro-rata basis.

Article 13
Assignment of judges

1. In the event that the need arises for a trial or to review a judgment, the President shall have the authority to convene a Trial Chamber consisting of two judges appointed by the Secretary-General and one judge appointed by the Government of Sierra Leone. The judges shall elect a presiding judge from amongst themselves.

2. In the event of an appeal, the President shall have the authority to convene an Appeals Chamber consisting of three judges appointed by the Secretary-General and two judges appointed by the Government of Sierra Leone. The judges shall elect a presiding judge from amongst themselves.

3. In exceptional circumstances, the President may also designate from the roster an additional duty judge to exercise judicial functions that cannot be carried out by the President or by a Trial Chamber or Appeals Chamber which has been convened already.

4. The judges assigned to the Chambers and any additional duty judge shall be present at the seat of the Residual Special Court only as necessary at the request of the President to carry out their functions. In so far as possible, they shall carry out their functions remotely.

Article 14
The Prosecutor

1. The Secretary-General, after consultation with the Government of Sierra Leone, shall appoint a Prosecutor for a three-year term. The Prosecutor shall be eligible for reappointment.

2. The Prosecutor shall be of high moral character and integrity, and shall possess the highest level of professional competence and extensive experience in the conduct of investigations and prosecutions of international criminal cases. The Prosecutor shall be independent in the performance of his or her functions and shall not accept or seek instructions from any Government or any other source.

3. The Prosecutor shall be responsible for the investigation and prosecution of the remaining fugitive Special Court indictee, of any cases of contempt of court that may arise, and of any cases resulting from review of convictions and acquittals. The Prosecutor shall act independently as a separate organ of the Residual Special Court.

4. The Prosecutor shall have the power to question suspects, victims and witnesses, to collect evidence and to conduct on-site investigations. In carrying out these tasks,

17

the Prosecutor shall, as appropriate, be assisted by the Sierra Leonean authorities concerned.

5. The Prosecutor shall in as far as possible carry out his or her functions remotely and shall be present at the seat of the Residual Special Court only as necessary to carry out functions. The Prosecutor shall be remunerated on a pro-rata basis.

Article 15
The Registrar

1. The Secretary-General, in consultation with the President of the Residual Special Court, shall appoint a Registrar for a three-year term. The Registrar shall be eligible for reappointment.

2. The Registrar shall be of high moral character and integrity, and shall possess the highest level of professional competence. The Registrar shall be independent in the performance of his or her functions and shall not accept or seek instructions from any Government or any other source.

3. The Registrar shall be responsible for the servicing of the Residual Special Court, and for the recruitment and administration of staff. The Registrar shall also administer the financial resources of the Residual Special Court.

4. The Residual Special Court shall retain a small number of staff commensurate with its functions. The Registrar shall also create and maintain a roster of suitably quali-fied potential staff who may be called on as necessary to perform functions required by the Residual Special Court. Particular account shall be taken of the experience of former staff of the Special Court, the International Tribunal for the former Yugoslavia, the International Criminal Tribunal for Rwanda, the Extraordinary Chambers in the Courts of Cambodia, the International Criminal Court, and the Special Tribunal for Lebanon.

5. The Registrar shall be based permanently at the seat of the Residual Special Court.

Article 16
Rules of Procedure and Evidence

1. The Rules of Procedure and Evidence of the Special Court for Sierra Leone obtaining at the time of the closure of the Special Court shall apply *mutatis mutandis* to the con-duct of the legal proceedings before the Residual Special Court.

2. The President may convene a plenary meeting of five international judges and three Sierra Leonean judges from the roster of the Residual Special Court to amend the Rules of Procedure and Evidence or adopt additional rules where the applicable Rules do not, or do not adequately, provide for a specific situation. In so doing, they may be guided, as appropriate, by the Criminal Procedure Act, 1965, of Sierra Leone.

Article 17
Rights of the accused

1. All accused shall be equal before the Residual Special Court.

2. The accused shall be entitled to a fair and public hearing, subject to measures ordered by the Special Court and/or the Residual Special Court, including for the protection of victims and witnesses.

3. The accused shall be presumed innocent until proven guilty pursuant to this Statute.

4. In the determination of any charge against the accused pursuant to the present Statute, he or she shall be entitled to the following minimum guarantees, in full equality:
   a. To be informed promptly and in detail in a language which he or she understands of the nature and cause of the charge against him or her;
   b. To have adequate time and facilities for the preparation of his or her defence and to communicate with counsel of his or her own choosing;
   c. To be tried without undue delay;
   d. To be tried in his or her presence, and to defend himself or herself in person or through legal assistance of his or her own choosing; to be informed, if he or she does not have legal assistance, of this right; and to have legal assistance assigned to him or her, in any case where the interests of justice so require, and without payment by him or her in any such case if he or she does not have sufficient means to pay for it;
   e. To examine, or have examined, the witnesses against him or her and to obtain the attendance and examination of witnesses on his or her behalf under the same conditions as witnesses against him or her;
   f. To have the free assistance of an interpreter if he or she cannot understand or speak the language used in the Residual Special Court;
   g. Not to be compelled to testify against himself or herself or to confess guilt.

Article 18
Protection of witnesses and victims

The Residual Special Court shall provide for protective measures and security arrangements, counseling and other appropriate assistance for witnesses and victims who appeared before the Special Court or who appear before the Residual Special Court and others who are at risk on account of testimony given by such witnesses and victims. Such protection measures shall include, but shall not be limited to, the conduct of *in camera* proceedings and the protection of the victim's identity.

Article 19
Judgment

1. The Trial Chamber shall pronounce judgments and impose sentences and penalties on persons convicted of crimes pursuant to this Statute.
2. The judgment shall be rendered by a majority of the judges of the Trial Chamber, and shall be delivered in public. It shall be accompanied by a reasoned opinion in writing, to which separate or dissenting opinions may be appended.

Article 20
Penalties

1. The Trial Chamber shall impose upon a convicted person imprisonment for a specified number of years. In determining the terms of imprisonment, the Trial Chamber shall, as appropriate, have recourse to the practice regarding prison sentences in the Special Court, the International Criminal Tribunal for Rwanda and the national courts of Sierra Leone.
2. In imposing the sentences, the Trial Chamber should take into account such factors as the gravity of the offence and the individual circumstances of the convicted person.

17

3. In addition to imprisonment, the Trial Chamber may order the forfeiture of the property, proceeds and any assets acquired unlawfully or by criminal conduct, and their return to their rightful owner or to the State of Sierra Leone.

Article 21
Appellate proceedings

1. The Appeals Chamber shall hear appeals from persons convicted by the Trial Chamber or from the Prosecutor on the following grounds:
    a. A procedural error;
    b. An error on a question of law invalidating the decision;
    c. An error of fact which has occasioned a miscarriage of justice.
2. The Appeals Chamber may affirm, reverse or revise the decisions taken by the Trial Chamber. The judgment shall be rendered by a majority of the judges of the Appeals Chamber, and shall be delivered in public. It shall be accompanied by a reasoned opinion in writing, to which separate or dissenting opinions may be appended.
3. The judges of the Appeals Chamber shall be guided by the decisions of the Appeals Chambers of the Special Court for Sierra Leone, the International Tribunal for the former Yugoslavia and the International Criminal Tribunal for Rwanda. In the interpretation and application of the laws of Sierra Leone, they shall be guided by the decisions of the Supreme Court of Sierra Leone.

Article 22
Review proceedings

1. Where a new fact has been discovered which was not known at the time of the proceedings before the Special Court or the Trial Chamber or Appeals Chamber of the Residual Special Court and which could have been a decisive factor in reaching the decision, the convicted person or the Prosecutor may submit an application for review of the judgment.
2. An application for review shall be submitted to the President. The President may reject the application if he or she considers it to be unfounded. If the President determines that the application is meritorious, he or she may, as appropriate, reconvene the original Trial Chamber; or if not possible, constitute a new Trial Chamber.

Article 23
Enforcement of sentences

1. Imprisonment may be served in Sierra Leone or in any of the States which have concluded with the Residual Special Court or the Special Court an agreement for the enforcement of sentences, and which have indicated to the Registrar their willingness to accept convicted persons.
2. Conditions of imprisonment, whether in Sierra Leone or in a third State, shall be governed by the law of the State of enforcement subject to the supervision of the Residual Special Court. The State of enforcement shall be bound by the duration of the sentence, subject to Article 24 of the present Statute.
3. The Residual Special Court shall have the power to supervise the enforcement of sentences, including the implementation of the sentence enforcement agreements, and other agreements with international and regional organizations and other appropriate organizations and bodies.

Article 24
Pardon or commutation of sentences

If, pursuant to the applicable law of the State in which the convicted person is imprisoned, he or she is eligible for pardon or commutation of sentence, the State concerned shall notify the Residual Special Court accordingly. There shall only be pardon or commutation of sentence if the President of the Residual Special Court, in consultation with the judges who imposed the sentence where possible, so decides on the basis of the interests of justice and the general principles of law.

Article 25
Working language

The working language of the Residual Special Court shall be English.

Article 26
Annual Report

1. The President of the Residual Special Court shall submit an annual report on the operation and activities of the Residual Special Court to the Secretary-General and to the Government of Sierra Leone.
2. In the event of a trial or appeal by the Residual Special Court, the President and the Prosecutor shall submit six-monthly reports to the Secretary-General and to the Government of Sierra Leone.

17

2003 Agreement between the UN and Cambodia relating to the Extraordinary Chambers in the Courts of Cambodia

Agreement between the United Nations and the Royal Government of Cambodia Concerning the Prosecution under Cambodian Law of Crimes Committed during the Period of Democratic Kampuchea

Whereas the General Assembly of the United Nations, in its resolution 57/228 of 18 December 2002, recalled that the serious violations of Cambodian and international humanitarian law during the period of Democratic Kampuchea from 1975 to 1979 continue to be matters of vitally important concern to the international community as a whole;

Whereas in the same resolution the General Assembly recognized the legitimate concern of the Government and the people of Cambodia in the pursuit of justice and national reconciliation, stability, peace and security;

Whereas the Cambodian authorities have requested assistance from the United Nations in bringing to trial senior leaders of Democratic Kampuchea and those who were most responsible for the crimes and serious violations of Cambodian penal law, international humanitarian law and custom, and international conventions recognized by Cambodia, that were committed during the period from 17 April 1975 to 6 January 1979;

Whereas prior to the negotiation of the present Agreement substantial progress had been made by the Secretary-General of the United Nations (hereinafter, "the Secretary-General") and the Royal Government of Cambodia towards the establishment, with international assistance, of Extraordinary Chambers within the existing court structure of Cambodia for the prosecution of crimes committed during the period of Democratic Kampuchea;

Whereas by its resolution 57/228, the General Assembly welcomed the promulgation of the Law on the Establishment of the Extraordinary Chambers in the Courts of Cambodia for the Prosecution of Crimes Committed during the Period of Democratic Kampuchea and requested the Secretary-General to resume negotiations, without delay, to conclude an agreement with the Government, based on previous negotiations on the establishment of the Extraordinary Chambers consistent with the provisions of the said resolution, so that the Extraordinary Chambers may begin to function promptly;

Whereas the Secretary-General and the Royal Government of Cambodia have held negotiations on the establishment of the Extraordinary Chambers;

Now Therefore the United Nations and the Royal Government of Cambodia have agreed as follows:

Article 1
Purpose

The purpose of the present Agreement is to regulate the cooperation between the United Nations and the Royal Government of Cambodia in bringing to trial senior leaders of Democratic Kampuchea and those who were most responsible for the crimes and serious violations of Cambodian penal law, international humanitarian law and custom, and international conventions recognized by Cambodia, that were committed during the period from 17 April 1975 to 6 January 1979. The Agreement provides, *inter alia*, the legal basis and the principles and modalities for such cooperation.

Article 2
The Law on the Establishment of Extraordinary Chambers

1. The present Agreement recognizes that the Extraordinary Chambers have subject matter jurisdiction consistent with that set forth in "the Law on the Establishment of the Extraordinary Chambers in the Courts of Cambodia for the Prosecution of Crimes Committed During the Period of Democratic Kampuchea" (hereinafter: "the Law on the Establishment of the Extraordinary Chambers"), as adopted and amended by the Cambodian Legislature under the Constitution of Cambodia. The present Agreement further recognizes that the Extraordinary Chambers have personal jurisdiction over senior leaders of Democratic Kampuchea and those who were most responsible for the crimes referred to in Article 1 of the Agreement.
2. The present Agreement shall be implemented in Cambodia through the Law on the Establishment of the Extraordinary Chambers as adopted and amended. The Vienna Convention on the Law of Treaties, and in particular its Articles 26 and 27, applies to the Agreement.
3. In case amendments to the Law on the Establishment of the Extraordinary Chambers are deemed necessary, such amendments shall always be preceded by consultations between the parties.

Article 3
Judges

1. Cambodian judges, on the one hand, and judges appointed by the Supreme Council of the Magistracy upon nomination by the Secretary-General of the United Nations (hereinafter: "international judges"), on the other hand, shall serve in each of the two Extraordinary Chambers.
2. The composition of the Chambers shall be as follows:
   a. The Trial Chamber: three Cambodian judges and two international judges;
   b. The Supreme Court Chamber, which shall serve as both appellate chamber and final instance: four Cambodian judges and three international judges.
3. The judges shall be persons of high moral character, impartiality and integrity who possess the qualifications required in their respective countries for appointment to judicial offices. They shall be independent in the performance of their functions and shall not accept or seek instructions from any Government or any other source.
4. In the overall composition of the Chambers due account should be taken of the experience of the judges in criminal law, international law, including international humanitarian law and human rights law.

18

5. The Secretary-General of the United Nations undertakes to forward a list of not less than seven nominees for international judges from which the Supreme Council of the Magistracy shall appoint five to serve as judges in the two Chambers. Appointment of international judges by the Supreme Council of the Magistracy shall be made only from the list submitted by the Secretary-General.

6. In the event of a vacancy of an international judge, the Supreme Council of the Magistracy shall appoint another international judge from the same list.

7. The judges shall be appointed for the duration of the proceedings.

8. In addition to the international judges sitting in the Chambers and present at every stage of the proceedings, the President of a Chamber may, on a case-by-case basis, designate from the list of nominees submitted by the Secretary-General, one or more alternate judges to be present at each stage of the proceedings, and to replace an international judge if that judge is unable to continue sitting.

Article 4
Decision-making

1. The judges shall attempt to achieve unanimity in their decisions. If this is not possible, the following shall apply:
   a. A decision by the Trial Chamber shall require the affirmative vote of at least four judges;
   b. A decision by the Supreme Court Chamber shall require the affirmative vote of at least five judges.

2. When there is no unanimity, the decision of the Chamber shall contain the views of the majority and the minority.

Article 5
Investigating judges

1. There shall be one Cambodian and one international investigating judge serving as co-investigating judges. They shall be responsible for the conduct of investigations.

2. The co-investigating judges shall be persons of high moral character, impartiality and integrity who possess the qualifications required in their respective countries for appointment to such a judicial office.

3. The co-investigating judges shall be independent in the performance of their functions and shall not accept or seek instructions from any Government or any other source. It is understood, however, that the scope of the investigation is limited to senior leaders of Democratic Kampuchea and those who were most responsible for the crimes and serious violations of Cambodian penal law, international humanitarian law and custom, and international conventions recognized by Cambodia, that were committed during the period from 17 April 1975 to 6 January 1979.

4. The co-investigating judges shall cooperate with a view to arriving at a common approach to the investigation. In case the co-investigating judges are unable to agree whether to proceed with an investigation, the investigation shall proceed unless the judges or one of them requests within thirty days that the difference shall be settled in accordance with Article 7.

5. In addition to the list of nominees provided for in Article 3, paragraph 5, the Secretary-General shall submit a list of two nominees from which the Supreme Council of the

Magistracy shall appoint one to serve as an international co-investigating judge, and one as a reserve international co-investigating judge.

6. In case there is a vacancy or a need to fill the post of the international co-investigating judge, the person appointed to fill this post must be the reserve international co-investigating judge.

7. The co-investigating judges shall be appointed for the duration of the proceedings.

Article 6
Prosecutors

1. There shall be one Cambodian prosecutor and one international prosecutor competent to appear in both Chambers, serving as co-prosecutors. They shall be responsible for the conduct of the prosecutions.

2. The co-prosecutors shall be of high moral character, and possess a high level of professional competence and extensive experience in the conduct of investigations and prosecutions of criminal cases.

3. The co-prosecutors shall be independent in the performance of their functions and shall not accept or seek instructions from any Government or any other source. It is understood, however, that the scope of the prosecution is limited to senior leaders of Democratic Kampuchea and those who were most responsible for the crimes and serious violations of Cambodian penal law, international humanitarian law and custom, and international conventions recognized by Cambodia, that were committed during the period from 17 April 1975 to 6 January 1979.

4. The co-prosecutors shall cooperate with a view to arriving at a common approach to the prosecution. In case the prosecutors are unable to agree whether to proceed with a prosecution, the prosecution shall proceed unless the prosecutors or one of them requests within thirty days that the difference shall be settled in accordance with Article 7.

5. The Secretary-General undertakes to forward a list of two nominees from which the Supreme Council of the Magistracy shall select one international co-prosecutor and one reserve international co-prosecutor.

6. In case there is a vacancy or a need to fill the post of the international co-prosecutor, the person appointed to fill this post must be the reserve international co-prosecutor.

7. The co-prosecutors shall be appointed for the duration of the proceedings.

8. Each co-prosecutor shall have one or more deputy prosecutors to assist him or her with prosecutions before the Chambers. Deputy international prosecutors shall be appointed by the international co-prosecutor from a list provided by the Secretary-General.

Article 7
Settlement of differences between the co-investigating judges or the co-prosecutors

1. In case the co-investigating judges or the co-prosecutors have made a request in accordance with Article 5, paragraph 4, or Article 6, paragraph 4, as the case may be, they shall submit written statements of facts and the reasons for their different positions to the Director of the Office of Administration.

2. The difference shall be settled forthwith by a Pre-Trial Chamber of five judges, three appointed by the Supreme Council of the Magistracy, with one as President, and

18

two appointed by the Supreme Council of the Magistracy upon nomination by the Secretary-General. Article 3, paragraph 3, shall apply to the judges.

3. Upon receipt of the statements referred to in paragraph 1, the Director of the Office of Administration shall immediately convene the Pre-Trial Chamber and communicate the statements to its members.

4. A decision of the Pre-Trial Chamber, against which there is no appeal, requires the affirmative vote of at least four judges. The decision shall be communicated to the Director of the Office of Administration, who shall publish it and communicate it to the co-investigating judges or the co-prosecutors. They shall immediately proceed in accordance with the decision of the Chamber. If there is no majority, as required for a decision, the investigation or prosecution shall proceed.

Article 8
Office of Administration

1. There shall be an Office of Administration to service the Extraordinary Chambers, the Pre-Trial Chamber, the co-investigating judges and the Prosecutors' Office.

2. There shall be a Cambodian Director of this Office, who shall be appointed by the Royal Government of Cambodia. The Director shall be responsible for the overall management of the Office of Administration, except in matters that are subject to United Nations rules and procedures.

3. There shall be an international Deputy Director of the Office of Administration, who shall be appointed by the Secretary-General. The Deputy Director shall be responsible for the recruitment of all international staff and all administration of the international components of the Extraordinary Chambers, the Pre-Trial Chamber, the co-investigating judges, the Prosecutors' Office and the Office of Administration. The United Nations and the Royal Government of Cambodia agree that, when an international Deputy Director has been appointed by the Secretary-General, the assignment of that person to that position by the Royal Government of Cambodia shall take place forthwith.

4. The Director and the Deputy Director shall cooperate in order to ensure an effective and efficient functioning of the administration.

Article 9
Crimes falling within the jurisdiction of the Extraordinary Chambers

The subject-matter jurisdiction of the Extraordinary Chambers shall be the crime of genocide as defined in the 1948 Convention on the Prevention and Punishment of the Crime of Genocide, crimes against humanity as defined in the 1998 Rome Statute of the International Criminal Court and grave breaches of the 1949 Geneva Conventions and such other crimes as defined in Chapter II of the Law on the Establishment of the Extraordinary Chambers as promulgated on 10 August 2001.

Article 10
Penalties

The maximum penalty for conviction for crimes falling within the jurisdiction of the Extraordinary Chambers shall be life imprisonment.

Article 11
Amnesty

1. The Royal Government of Cambodia shall not request an amnesty or pardon for any persons who may be investigated for or convicted of crimes referred to in the present Agreement.
2. This provision is based upon a declaration by the Royal Government of Cambodia that until now, with regard to matters covered in the law, there has been only one case, dated 14 September 1996, when a pardon was granted to only one person with regard to a 1979 conviction on the charge of genocide. The United Nations and the Royal Government of Cambodia agree that the scope of this pardon is a matter to be decided by the Extraordinary Chambers.

Article 12
Procedure

1. The procedure shall be in accordance with Cambodian law. Where Cambodian law does not deal with a particular matter, or where there is uncertainty regarding the interpretation or application of a relevant rule of Cambodian law, or where there is a question regarding the consistency of such a rule with international standards, guidance may also be sought in procedural rules established at the international level.
2. The Extraordinary Chambers shall exercise their jurisdiction in accordance with international standards of justice, fairness and due process of law, as set out in Articles 14 and 15 of the 1966 International Covenant on Civil and Political Rights, to which Cambodia is a party. In the interest of securing a fair and public hearing and credibility of the procedure, it is understood that representatives of Member States of the United Nations, of the Secretary-General, of the media and of national and international non-governmental organizations will at all times have access to the proceedings before the Extraordinary Chambers. Any exclusion from such proceedings in accordance with the provisions of Article 14 of the Covenant shall only be to the extent strictly necessary in the opinion of the Chamber concerned and where publicity would prejudice the interests of justice.

Article 13
Rights of the accused

1. The rights of the accused enshrined in Articles 14 and 15 of the 1966 International Covenant on Civil and Political Rights shall be respected throughout the trial process. Such rights shall, in particular, include the right: to a fair and public hearing; to be presumed innocent until proved guilty; to engage a counsel of his or her choice; to have adequate time and facilities for the preparation of his or her defence; to have counsel provided if he or she does not have sufficient means to pay for it; and to examine or have examined the witnesses against him or her.
2. The United Nations and the Royal Government of Cambodia agree that the provisions on the right to defence counsel in the Law on the Establishment of Extraordinary Chambers mean that the accused has the right to engage counsel of his or her own choosing as guaranteed by the International Covenant on Civil and Political Rights.

18

Article 14
Premises

The Royal Government of Cambodia shall provide at its expense the premises for the co-investigating judges, the Prosecutors' Office, the Extraordinary Chambers, the Pre-Trial Chamber and the Office of Administration. It shall also provide for such utilities, facilities and other services necessary for their operation that may be mutually agreed upon by separate agreement between the United Nations and the Government.

Article 15
Cambodian personnel

Salaries and emoluments of Cambodian judges and other Cambodian personnel shall be defrayed by the Royal Government of Cambodia.

Article 16
International personnel

Salaries and emoluments of international judges, the international co-investigating judge, the international co-prosecutor and other personnel recruited by the United Nations shall be defrayed by the United Nations.

Article 17
Financial and other assistance of the United Nations

The United Nations shall be responsible for the following:

a. remuneration of the international judges, the international co-investigating judge, the international co-prosecutor, the Deputy Director of the Office of Administration and other international personnel;
b. costs for utilities and services as agreed separately between the United Nations and the Royal Government of Cambodia;
c. remuneration of defence counsel;
d. witnesses' travel from within Cambodia and from abroad;
e. safety and security arrangements as agreed separately between the United Nations and the Government;
f. such other limited assistance as may be necessary to ensure the smooth functioning of the investigation, the prosecution and the Extraordinary Chambers.

Article 18
Inviolability of archives and documents

The archives of the co-investigating judges, the co-prosecutors, the Extraordinary Chambers, the Pre-Trial Chamber and the Office of Administration, and in general all documents and materials made available, belonging to or used by them, wherever located in Cambodia and by whomsoever held, shall be inviolable for the duration of the proceedings.

Article 19
Privileges and immunities of international judges, the international co-investigating judge, the international co-prosecutor and the Deputy Director of the Office of Administration

1. The international judges, the international co-investigating judge, the international co-prosecutor and the Deputy Director of the Office of Administration, together with

their families forming part of their household, shall enjoy the privileges and immunities, exemptions and facilities accorded to diplomatic agents in accordance with the 1961 Vienna Convention on Diplomatic Relations. They shall, in particular, enjoy:

a. personal inviolability, including immunity from arrest or detention;

b. immunity from criminal, civil and administrative jurisdiction in conformity with the Vienna Convention;

c. inviolability for all papers and documents;

d. exemption from immigration restrictions and alien registration;

e. the same immunities and facilities in respect of their personal baggage as are accorded to diplomatic agents.

2. The international judges, the international co-investigating judge, the international co-prosecutor and the Deputy Director of the Office of Administration shall enjoy exemption from taxation in Cambodia on their salaries, emoluments and allowances.

Article 20
Privileges and immunities of Cambodian and international personnel

1. Cambodian judges, the Cambodian co-investigating judge, the Cambodian co-prosecutor and other Cambodian personnel shall be accorded immunity from legal process in respect of words spoken or written and all acts performed by them in their official capacity under the present Agreement. Such immunity shall continue to be accorded after termination of employment with the co-investigating judges, the co-prosecutors, the Extraordinary Chambers, the Pre-Trial Chamber and the Office of Administration.

2. International personnel shall be accorded:

a. immunity from legal process in respect of words spoken or written and all acts performed by them in their official capacity under the present Agreement. Such immunity shall continue to be accorded after termination of employment with the co-investigating judges, the co-prosecutors, the Extraordinary Chambers, the Pre-Trial Chamber and the Office of Administration;

b. immunity from taxation on salaries, allowances and emoluments paid to them by the United Nations;

c. immunity from immigration restrictions;

d. the right to import free of duties and taxes, except for payment for services, their furniture and effects at the time of first taking up their official duties in Cambodia.

3. The United Nations and the Royal Government of Cambodia agree that the immunity granted by the Law on the Establishment of the Extraordinary Chambers in respect of words spoken or written and all acts performed by them in their official capacity under the present Agreement will apply also after the persons have left the service of the co-investigating judges, the co-prosecutors, the Extraordinary Chambers, the Pre-Trial Chamber and the Office of Administration.

Article 21
Counsel

1. The counsel of a suspect or an accused who has been admitted as such by the Extraordinary Chambers shall not be subjected by the Royal Government of Cambodia to any measure which may affect the free and independent exercise of his or her functions under the present Agreement.

18

2. In particular, the counsel shall be accorded:
   a. immunity from personal arrest or detention and from seizure of personal baggage;
   b. inviolability of all documents relating to the exercise of his or her functions as a counsel of a suspect or accused;
   c. immunity from criminal or civil jurisdiction in respect of words spoken or written and acts performed by them in their official capacity as counsel. Such immunity shall continue to be accorded to them after termination of their functions as a counsel of a suspect or accused.
3. Any counsel, whether of Cambodian or non-Cambodian nationality, engaged by or assigned to a suspect or an accused shall, in the defence of his or her client, act in accordance with the present Agreement, the Cambodian Law on the Statutes of the Bar and recognized standards and ethics of the legal profession.

Article 22
Witnesses and experts
Witnesses and experts appearing on a summons or a request of the judges, the co-investigating judges, or the co-prosecutors shall not be prosecuted, detained or subjected to any other restriction on their liberty by the Cambodian authorities. They shall not be subjected by the authorities to any measure which may affect the free and independent exercise of their functions.

Article 23
Protection of victims and witnesses
The co-investigating judges, the co-prosecutors and the Extraordinary Chambers shall provide for the protection of victims and witnesses. Such protection measures shall include, but shall not be limited to, the conduct of in camera proceedings and the protection of the identity of a victim or witness.

Article 24
Security, safety and protection of persons referred to in the present Agreement
The Royal Government of Cambodia shall take all effective and adequate actions which may be required to ensure the security, safety and protection of persons referred to in the present Agreement. The United Nations and the Government agree that the Government is responsible for the security of all accused, irrespective of whether they appear voluntarily before the Extraordinary Chambers or whether they are under arrest.

Article 25
Obligation to assist the co-investigating judges, the co-prosecutors and the Extraordinary Chambers
The Royal Government of Cambodia shall comply without undue delay with any request for assistance by the co-investigating judges, the co-prosecutors and the Extraordinary Chambers or an order issued by any of them, including, but not limited to:
a. identification and location of persons;
b. service of documents;
c. arrest or detention of persons;
d. transfer of an indictee to the Extraordinary Chambers.

Article 26
Languages

1. The official language of the Extraordinary Chambers and the Pre-Trial Chamber is Khmer.
2. The official working languages of the Extraordinary Chambers and the Pre-Trial Chamber shall be Khmer, English and French.
3. Translations of public documents and interpretation at public hearings into Russian may be provided by the Royal Government of Cambodia at its discretion and expense on condition that such services do not hinder the proceedings before the Extraordinary Chambers.

Article 27
Practical arrangements

1. With a view to achieving efficiency and cost-effectiveness in the operation of the Extraordinary Chambers, a phased-in approach shall be adopted for their establishment in accordance with the chronological order of the legal process.
2. In the first phase of the operation of the Extraordinary Chambers, the judges, the co-investigating judges and the co-prosecutors will be appointed along with investigative and prosecutorial staff, and the process of investigations and prosecutions shall be initiated.
3. The trial process of those already in custody shall proceed simultaneously with the investigation of other persons responsible for crimes falling within the jurisdiction of the Extraordinary Chambers.
4. With the completion of the investigation of persons suspected of having committed the crimes falling within the jurisdiction of the Extraordinary Chambers, arrest warrants shall be issued and submitted to the Royal Government of Cambodia to effectuate the arrest.
5. With the arrest by the Royal Government of Cambodia of indicted persons situated in its territory, the Extraordinary Chambers shall be fully operational, provided that the judges of the Supreme Court Chamber shall serve when seized with a matter. The judges of the Pre-Trial Chamber shall serve only if and when their services are needed.

Article 28
Withdrawal of cooperation

Should the Royal Government of Cambodia change the structure or organization of the Extraordinary Chambers or otherwise cause them to function in a manner that does not conform with the terms of the present Agreement, the United Nations reserves the right to cease to provide assistance, financial or otherwise, pursuant to the present Agreement.

Article 29
Settlement of disputes

Any dispute between the Parties concerning the interpretation or application of the present Agreement shall be settled by negotiation, or by any other mutually agreed upon mode of settlement.

18

Article 30
Approval
To be binding on the parties, the present Agreement must be approved by the General Assembly of the United Nations and ratified by Cambodia. The Royal Government of Cambodia will make its best endeavours to obtain this ratification by the earliest possible date.

Article 31
Application within Cambodia
The present Agreement shall apply as law within the Kingdom of Cambodia following its ratification in accordance with the relevant provisions of the internal law of the Kingdom of Cambodia regarding competence to conclude treaties.

Article 32
Entry into force
The present Agreement shall enter into force on the day after both parties have notified each other in writing that the legal requirements for entry into force have been complied with.

Done at Phnom Penh on 6 June 2003 in two copies in the English language.

Security Council Resolution No. 1757 and 2007 Special Tribunal for Lebanon Statute

United Nations Security Council Resolution 1757 (2007) Adopted by the Security Council at its 5685th meeting, on 30 May 2007

The Security Council,

Recalling all its previous relevant resolutions, in particular resolutions 1595 (2005) of 7 April 2005, 1636 (2005) of 31 October 2005, 1644 (2005) of 15 December 2005, 1664 (2006) of 29 March 2006 and 1748 (2007) of 27 March 2007,

Reaffirming its strongest condemnation of the 14 February 2005 terrorist bombings as well as other attacks in Lebanon since October 2004,

Reiterating its call for the strict respect of the sovereignty, territorial integrity, unity and political independence of Lebanon under the sole and exclusive authority of the Government of Lebanon,

Recalling the letter of the Prime Minister of Lebanon to the Secretary-General of 13 December 2005 (S/2005/783) requesting inter alia the establishment of a tribunal of an international character to try all those who are found responsible for this terrorist crime, and the request by this Council for the Secretary-General to negotiate an agreement with the Government of Lebanon aimed at establishing such a Tribunal based on the highest international standards of criminal justice,

Recalling further the report of the Secretary-General on the establishment of a special tribunal for Lebanon on 15 November 2006 (S/2006/893) reporting on the conclusion of negotiations and consultations that took place between January 2006 and September 2006 at United Nations Headquarters in New York, the Hague, and Beirut between the Legal Counsel of the United Nations and authorized representatives of the Government of Lebanon, and the letter of its President to the Secretary-General of 21 November 2006 (S/2006/911) reporting that the Members of the Security Council welcomed the conclusion of the negotiations and that they were satisfied with the Agreement annexed to the Report,

Recalling that, as set out in its letter of 21 November 2006, should voluntary contributions be insufficient for the Tribunal to implement its mandate, the Secretary-General and the Security Council shall explore alternate means of financing the Tribunal,

Recalling also that the Agreement between the United Nations and the Lebanese Republic on the establishment of a Special Tribunal for Lebanon was signed by the Government of Lebanon and the United Nations respectively on 23 January and 6 February 2007,

Referring to the letter of the Prime Minister of Lebanon to the Secretary-General of the United Nations (S/2007/281), which recalled that the parliamentary majority has expressed its support for the Tribunal, and asked that his request that the Special Tribunal be put into effect be presented to the Council as a matter of urgency,

Mindful of the demand of the Lebanese people that all those responsible for the terrorist bombing that killed former Lebanese Prime Minister Rafik Hariri and others be identified and brought to justice,

Commending the Secretary-General for his continuing efforts to proceed, together with the Government of Lebanon, with the final steps for the conclusion of the Agreement as requested in the letter of its President dated 21 November 2006 and referring in this regard to the briefing by the Legal Counsel on 2 May 2007, in which he noted that the establishment of the Tribunal through the Constitutional process is facing serious obstacles, but noting also that all parties concerned reaffirmed their agreement in principle to the establishment of the Tribunal,

Commending also the recent efforts of parties in the region to overcome these obstacles,

Willing to continue to assist Lebanon in the search for the truth and in holding all those involved in the terrorist attack accountable and reaffirming its determination to support Lebanon in its efforts to bring to justice perpetrators, organizers and sponsors of this and other assassinations,

Reaffirming its determination that this terrorist act and its implications constitute a threat to international peace and security,

1. *Decides*, acting under Chapter VII of the Charter of the United Nations, that:

   (a) The provisions of the annexed document, including its attachment, on the establishment of a Special Tribunal for Lebanon shall enter into force on 10 June 2007, unless the Government of Lebanon has provided notification under Article 19 (1) of the annexed document before that date;

   (b) If the Secretary-General reports that the Headquarters Agreement has not been concluded as envisioned under Article 8 of the annexed document, the location of the seat of the Tribunal shall be determined in consultation with the Government of Lebanon and be subject to the conclusion of a Headquarters Agreement between the United Nations and the State that hosts the Tribunal;

   (c) If the Secretary-General reports that contributions from the Government of Lebanon are not sufficient to bear the expenses described in Article 5 (b) of the annexed document, he may accept or use voluntary contributions from States to cover any shortfall;

1. *Notes* that, pursuant to Article 19 (2) of the annexed document, the Special Tribunal shall commence functioning on a date to be determined by the Secretary-General in consultation with the Government of Lebanon, taking into account the progress of the work of the International Independent Investigation Commission;

2. *Requests* the Secretary-General, in coordination, when appropriate, with the Government of Lebanon, to undertake the steps and measures necessary to establish the Special Tribunal in a timely manner and to report to the Council within 90 days and thereafter periodically on the implementation of this resolution;

3. *Decides* to remain actively seized of the matter.

ANNEX

Agreement between the United Nations and the Lebanese Republic on the establishment of a Special Tribunal for Lebanon

Whereas the Security Council, in its resolution 1664 (2006) of 29 March 2006, which responded to the request of the Government of Lebanon to establish a tribunal of an international character to try all those who are found responsible for the terrorist crime which killed the former Lebanese Prime Minister Rafik Hariri and others, recalled all its previous resolutions, in particular resolutions 1595 (2005) of 7 April 2005, 1636 (2005) of 31 October 2005 and 1644 (2005) of 15 December 2005,

Whereas the Security Council has requested the Secretary-General of the United Nations (hereinafter "the Secretary-General") "to negotiate an agreement with the Government of Lebanon aimed at establishing a tribunal of an international character based on the highest international standards of criminal justice", taking into account the recommendations of the Secretary-General's report of 21 March 2006 (S/2006/176) and the views that have been expressed by Council members,

Whereas the Secretary-General and the Government of the Lebanese Republic (hereinafter "the Government") have conducted negotiations for the establishment of a Special Tribunal for Lebanon (hereinafter "the Special Tribunal" or "the Tribunal"),

Now therefore the United Nations and the Lebanese Republic (hereinafter referred to jointly as the "Parties") have agreed as follows:

Article 1 Establishment of the Special Tribunal

1. There is hereby established a Special Tribunal for Lebanon to prosecute persons responsible for the attack of 14 February 2005 resulting in the death of former Lebanese Prime Minister Rafik Hariri and in the death or injury of other persons. If the tribunal finds that other attacks that occurred in Lebanon between 1 October 2004 and 12 December 2005, or any later date decided by the Parties and with the consent of the Security Council, are connected in accordance with the principles of criminal justice and are of a nature and gravity similar to the attack of 14 February 2005, it shall also have jurisdiction over persons responsible for such attacks. This connection includes but is not limited to a combination of the following elements: criminal intent (motive), the purpose behind the attacks, the nature of the victims targeted, the pattern of the attacks (modus operandi) and the perpetrators.
2. The Special Tribunal shall function in accordance with the Statute of the Special Tribunal for Lebanon. The Statute is attached to this Agreement and forms an integral part thereof.

Article 2 Composition of the Special Tribunal and appointment of judges

1. The Special Tribunal shall consist of the following organs: the Chambers, the Prosecutor, the Registry and the Defence Office.

2. The Chambers shall be composed of a Pre-Trial Judge, a Trial Chamber and an Appeals Chamber, with a second Trial Chamber to be created if, after the passage of at least six months from the commencement of the functioning of the Special Tribunal, the Secretary-General or the President of the Special Tribunal so requests.

3. The Chambers shall be composed of no fewer than eleven independent judges and no more than fourteen such judges, who shall serve as follows:

   (a) A single international judge shall serve as a Pre-Trial Judge;

   (b) Three judges shall serve in the Trial Chamber, of whom one shall be a Lebanese judge and two shall be international judges;

   (c) In the event of the creation of a second Trial Chamber, that Chamber shall be likewise composed in the manner contained in subparagraph (b) above;

   (d) Five judges shall serve in the Appeals Chamber, of whom two shall be Lebanese judges and three shall be international judges; and

   (e) Two alternate judges, of whom one shall be a Lebanese judge and one shall be an international judge.

The judges of the Tribunal shall be persons of high moral character, impartiality and integrity, with extensive judicial experience. They shall be independent in the performance of their functions and shall not accept or seek instructions from any Government or any other source.

1. (a) Lebanese judges shall be appointed by the Secretary-General to serve in the Trial Chamber or the Appeals Chamber or as an alternate judge from a list of twelve persons presented by the Government upon the proposal of the Lebanese Supreme Council of the Judiciary;

   (b) International judges shall be appointed by the Secretary-General to serve as Pre-Trial Judge, a Trial Chamber Judge, an Appeals Chamber Judge or an alternate judge, upon nominations forwarded by States at the invitation of the Secretary-General, as well as by competent persons;

   (c) The Government and the Secretary-General shall consult on the appointment of judges;

   (d) The Secretary-General shall appoint judges, upon the recommendation of a selection panel he has established after indicating his intentions to the Security Council. The selection panel shall be composed of two judges, currently sitting on or retired from an international tribunal, and the representative of the Secretary-General.

At the request of the presiding judge of a Trial Chamber, the President of the Special Tribunal may, in the interest of justice, assign alternate judges to be present at each stage of the trial and to replace a judge if that judge is unable to continue sitting.

1. Judges shall be appointed for a three-year period and may be eligible for reappointment for a further period to be determined by the Secretary-General in consultation with the Government.

2. Lebanese judges appointed to serve in the Special Tribunal shall be given full credit for their period of service with the Tribunal on their return to the Lebanese national judiciaries from which they were released and shall be reintegrated at a level at least comparable to that of their former position.

Article 3 Appointment of a Prosecutor and a Deputy Prosecutor

1. The Secretary-General, after consultation with the Government, shall appoint a Prosecutor for a three-year term. The Prosecutor may be eligible for reappointment for a further period to be determined by the Secretary-General in consultation with the Government.
2. The Secretary-General shall appoint the Prosecutor, upon the recommendation of a selection panel he has established after indicating his intentions to the Security Council. The selection panel shall be composed of two judges, currently sitting on or retired from an international tribunal, and the representative of the Secretary-General.
3. The Government, in consultation with the Secretary-General and the Prosecutor, shall appoint a Lebanese Deputy Prosecutor to assist the Prosecutor in the conduct of the investigations and prosecutions.
4. The Prosecutor and the Deputy Prosecutor shall be of high moral character and possess the highest level of professional competence and extensive experience in the conduct of investigations and prosecutions of criminal cases. The Prosecutor and the Deputy Prosecutor shall be independent in the performance of their functions and shall not accept or seek instructions from any Government or any other source.
5. The Prosecutor shall be assisted by such Lebanese and international staff as may be required to perform the functions assigned to him or her effectively and efficiently.

Article 4 Appointment of a Registrar

1. The Secretary-General shall appoint a Registrar who shall be responsible for the servicing of the Chambers and the Office of the Prosecutor, and for the recruitment and administration of all support staff. He or she shall also administer the financial and staff resources of the Special Tribunal.
2. The Registrar shall be a staff member of the United Nations. He or she shall serve a three-year term and may be eligible for reappointment for a further period to be determined by the Secretary-General in consultation with the Government.

Article 5 Financing of the Special Tribunal

1. The expenses of the Special Tribunal shall be borne in the following manner:
   (a) Fifty-one per cent of the expenses of the Tribunal shall be borne by voluntary contributions from States;
   (b) Forty-nine per cent of the expenses of the Tribunal shall be borne by the Government of Lebanon.
2. It is understood that the Secretary-General will commence the process of establishing the Tribunal when he has sufficient contributions in hand to finance the establishment of the Tribunal and twelve months of its operations plus pledges equal to the anticipated expenses of the following 24 months of the Tribunal's operation. Should voluntary contributions be insufficient for the Tribunal to implement its mandate, the Secretary-General and the Security Council shall explore alternate means of financing the Tribunal.

Article 6 Management Committee

The parties shall consult concerning the establishment of a Management Committee.

Article 7 Juridical capacity

The Special Tribunal shall possess the juridical capacity necessary:

(a) To contract;

(b) To acquire and dispose of movable and immovable property;

(c) To institute legal proceedings;

(d) To enter into agreements with States as may be necessary for the exercise of its functions and for the operation of the Tribunal.

Article 8 Seat of the Special Tribunal

1. The Special Tribunal shall have its seat outside Lebanon. The location of the seat shall be determined having due regard to considerations of justice and fairness as well as security and administrative efficiency, including the rights of victims and access to witnesses, and subject to the conclusion of a headquarters agreement between the United Nations, the Government and the State that hosts the Tribunal.

2. The Special Tribunal may meet away from its seat when it considers it necessary for the efficient exercise of its functions.

3. An Office of the Special Tribunal for the conduct of investigations shall be established in Lebanon subject to the conclusion of appropriate arrangements with the Government.

Article 9 Inviolability of premises, archives and all other documents

1. The Office of the Special Tribunal in Lebanon shall be inviolable. The competent authorities shall take appropriate action that may be necessary to ensure that the Tribunal shall not be dispossessed of all or any part of the premises of the Tribunal without its express consent.

2. The property, funds and assets of the Office of the Special Tribunal in Lebanon, wherever located and by whomsoever held, shall be immune from search, seizure, requisition, confiscation, expropriation and any other form of interference, whether by executive, administrative, judicial or legislative action.

3. The archives of the Office of the Special Tribunal in Lebanon, and in general all documents and materials made available, belonging to or used by it, wherever located and by whomsoever held, shall be inviolable.

Article 10 Funds, assets and other property

The Office of the Special Tribunal, its funds, assets and other property in Lebanon, wherever located and by whomsoever held, shall enjoy immunity from every form of legal process, except insofar as in any particular case the Tribunal has expressly waived its immunity. It is understood, however, that no waiver of immunity shall extend to any measure of execution.

Article 11 Privileges and immunities of the judges, the Prosecutor, the Deputy Prosecutor, the Registrar and the Head of the Defence Office

1. The judges, the Prosecutor, the Deputy Prosecutor, the Registrar and the Head of the Defence Office, while in Lebanon, shall enjoy the privileges and immunities, exemptions and facilities accorded to diplomatic agents in accordance with the Vienna Convention on Diplomatic Relations of 1961.

2. Privileges and immunities are accorded to the judges, the Prosecutor, the Deputy Prosecutor, the Registrar and the Head of the Defence Office in the interest of the Special Tribunal and not for the personal benefit of the individuals themselves. The right and the duty to waive the immunity in any case where it can be waived without prejudice to the purposes for which it is accorded shall lie with the Secretary-General, in consultation with the President of the Tribunal.

Article 12 Privileges and immunities of international and Lebanese personnel

1. Lebanese and international personnel of the Office of the Special Tribunal, while in Lebanon, shall be accorded:
   (a) Immunity from legal process in respect of words spoken or written and all acts performed by them in their official capacity. Such immunity shall continue to be accorded after termination of employment with the Office of the Special Tribunal;
   (b) Exemption from taxation on salaries, allowances and emoluments paid to them.
2. International personnel shall, in addition thereto, be accorded:
   (a) Immunity from immigration restriction;
   (b) The right to import free of duties and taxes, except for payment for services, their furniture and effects at the time of first taking up their official duties in Lebanon.
3. The privileges and immunities are granted to the officials of the Office of the Special Tribunal in the interest of the Tribunal and not for their personal benefit. The right and the duty to waive the immunity in any case where it can be waived without prejudice to the purpose for which it is accorded shall lie with the Registrar of the Tribunal.

Article 13 Defence counsel

1. The Government shall ensure that the counsel of a suspect or an accused who has been admitted as such by the Special Tribunal shall not be subjected, while in Lebanon, to any measure that may affect the free and independent exercise of his or her functions.
2. In particular, the counsel shall be accorded:
   (a) Immunity from personal arrest or detention and from seizure of personal baggage;
   (b) Inviolability of all documents relating to the exercise of his or her functions as a counsel of a suspect or accused;
   (c) Immunity from criminal or civil jurisdiction in respect of words spoken or written and acts performed in his or her capacity as counsel. Such immunity shall continue to be accorded after termination of his or her functions as a counsel of a suspect or accused;
   (d) Immunity from any immigration restrictions during his or her stay as well as during his or her journey to the Tribunal and back.

Article 14 Security, safety and protection of persons referred to in this Agreement

The Government shall take effective and adequate measures to ensure the appropriate security, safety and protection of personnel of the Office of the Special Tribunal and other persons referred to in this Agreement, while in Lebanon. It shall take all appropriate steps, within its capabilities, to protect the equipment and premises of the Office of the Special Tribunal from attack or any action that prevents the Tribunal from discharging its mandate.

19

Article 15 Cooperation with the Special Tribunal

1. The Government shall cooperate with all organs of the Special Tribunal, in particular with the Prosecutor and defence counsel, at all stages of the proceedings. It shall facilitate access of the Prosecutor and defence counsel to sites, persons and relevant documents required for the investigation.
2. The Government shall comply without undue delay with any request for assistance by the Special Tribunal or an order issued by the Chambers, including, but not limited to:
   (a) Identification and location of persons;
   (b) Service of documents;
   (c) Arrest or detention of persons;
   (d) Transfer of an indictee to the Tribunal.

Article 16 Amnesty

The Government undertakes not to grant amnesty to any person for any crime falling within the jurisdiction of the Special Tribunal. An amnesty already granted in respect of any such persons and crimes shall not be a bar to prosecution.

Article 17 Practical arrangements

With a view to achieving efficiency and cost-effectiveness in the operation of the Special Tribunal:

(a) Appropriate arrangements shall be made to ensure that there is a coordinated transition from the activities of the International Independent Investigation Commission, established by the Security Council in its resolution 1595 (2005), to the activities of the Office of the Prosecutor;
(b) Judges of the Trial Chamber and the Appeals Chamber shall take office on a date to be determined by the Secretary-General in consultation with the President of the Special Tribunal. Pending such a determination, judges of both Chambers shall be convened on an ad hoc basis to deal with organizational matters and serving, when required, to perform their duties.

Article 18 Settlement of disputes

Any dispute between the Parties concerning the interpretation or application of this Agreement shall be settled by negotiation or by any other mutually agreed upon mode of settlement.

Article 19 Entry into force and commencement of the functioning of the Special Tribunal

1. This Agreement shall enter into force on the day after the Government has notified the United Nations in writing that the legal requirements for entry into force have been complied with.
2. The Special Tribunal shall commence functioning on a date to be determined by the Secretary-General in consultation with the Government, taking into account the progress of the work of the International Independent Investigation Commission.

Article 20 Amendment

This Agreement may be amended by written agreement between the Parties.

Article 21 Duration of the Agreement

1. This Agreement shall remain in force for a period of three years from the date of the commencement of the functioning of the Special Tribunal.
2. Three years after the commencement of the functioning of the Special Tribunal the Parties shall, in consultation with the Security Council, review the progress of the work of the Special Tribunal. If at the end of this period of three years the activities of the Tribunal have not been completed, the Agreement shall be extended to allow the Tribunal to complete its work, for a further period(s) to be determined by the Secretary-General in consultation with the Government and the Security Council.
3. The provisions relating to the inviolability of the funds, assets, archives and documents of the Office of the Special Tribunal in Lebanon, the privileges and immunities of those referred to in this Agreement, as well as provisions relating to defence counsel and the protection of victims and witnesses, shall survive termination of this Agreement.

Statute of the Special Tribunal for Lebanon

Having been established by an Agreement between the United Nations and the Lebanese Republic (hereinafter "the Agreement") pursuant to Security Council resolution 1664 (2006) of 29 March 2006, which responded to the request of the Government of Lebanon to establish a tribunal of an international character to try all those who are found responsible for the terrorist crime which killed the former Lebanese Prime Minister Rafik Hariri and others, the Special Tribunal for Lebanon (hereinafter "the Special Tribunal") shall function in accordance with the provisions of this Statute.

SECTION I. JURISDICTION AND APPLICABLE LAW

Article 1 Jurisdiction of the Special Tribunal

The Special Tribunal shall have jurisdiction over persons responsible for the attack of 14 February 2005 resulting in the death of former Lebanese Prime Minister Rafik Hariri and in the death or injury of other persons. If the Tribunal finds that other attacks that occurred in Lebanon between 1 October 2004 and 12 December 2005, or any later date decided by the Parties and with the consent of the Security Council, are connected in accordance with the principles of criminal justice and are of a nature and gravity similar to the attack of 14 February 2005, it shall also have jurisdiction over persons responsible for such attacks. This connection includes but is not limited to a combination of the following elements: criminal intent (motive), the purpose behind the attacks, the nature of the victims targeted, the pattern of the attacks (modus operandi) and the perpetrators.

Article 2 Applicable criminal law

The following shall be applicable to the prosecution and punishment of the crimes referred to in article 1, subject to the provisions of this Statute:

(a) The provisions of the Lebanese Criminal Code relating to the prosecution and punishment of acts of terrorism, crimes and offences against life and personal integrity, illicit associations and failure to report crimes and offences, including the rules regarding the material elements of a crime, criminal participation and conspiracy; and
(b) Articles 6 and 7 of the Lebanese law of 11 January 1958 on "Increasing the penalties for sedition, civil war and interfaith struggle".

Article 3 Individual criminal responsibility

1. A person shall be individually responsible for crimes within the jurisdiction of the Special Tribunal if that person:

   (a) Committed, participated as accomplice, organized or directed others to commit the crime set forth in article 2 of this Statute; or

   (b) Contributed in any other way to the commission of the crime set forth in article 2 of this Statute by a group of persons acting with a common purpose, where such contribution is intentional and is either made with the aim of furthering the general criminal activity or purpose of the group or in the knowledge of the intention of the group to commit the crime.

2. With respect to superior and subordinate relationships, a superior shall be criminally responsible for any of the crimes set forth in article 2 of this Statute committed by subordinates under his or her effective authority and control, as a result of his or her failure to exercise control properly over such subordinates, where:

   (a) The superior either knew, or consciously disregarded information that clearly indicated that the subordinates were committing or about to commit such crimes;

   (b) The crimes concerned activities that were within the effective responsibility and control of the superior; and

   (c) The superior failed to take all necessary and reasonable measures within his or her power to prevent or repress their commission or to submit the matter to the competent authorities for investigation and prosecution.

3. The fact that the person acted pursuant to an order of a superior shall not relieve him or her of criminal responsibility, but may be considered in mitigation of punishment if the Special Tribunal determines that justice so requires.

Article 4 Concurrent jurisdiction

1. The Special Tribunal and the national courts of Lebanon shall have concurrent jurisdiction. Within its jurisdiction, the Tribunal shall have primacy over the national courts of Lebanon.

2. Upon the assumption of office of the Prosecutor, as determined by the Secretary-General, and no later than two months thereafter, the Special Tribunal shall request the national judicial authority seized with the case of the attack against Prime Minister Rafik Hariri and others to defer to its competence. The Lebanese judicial authority shall refer to the Tribunal the results of the investigation and a copy of the court's records, if any. Persons detained in connection with the investigation shall be transferred to the custody of the Tribunal.

3.

   (a) At the request of the Special Tribunal, the national judicial authority seized with any of the other crimes committed between 1 October 2004 and 12 December 2005, or a later date decided pursuant to article 1, shall refer to the Tribunal the results of the investigation and a copy of the court's records, if any, for review by the Prosecutor;

   (b) At the further request of the Tribunal, the national authority in question shall defer to the competence of the Tribunal. It shall refer to the Tribunal the results of the investigation and a copy of the court's records, if any, and persons detained in connection with any such case shall be transferred to the custody of the Tribunal;

(c) The national judicial authorities shall regularly inform the Tribunal of the progress of their investigation. At any stage of the proceedings, the Tribunal may formally request a national judicial authority to defer to its competence.

Article 5 Non bis in idem

1. No person shall be tried before a national court of Lebanon for acts for which he or she has already been tried by the Special Tribunal.
2. A person who has been tried by a national court may be subsequently tried by the Special Tribunal if the national court proceedings were not impartial or independent, were designed to shield the accused from criminal responsibility for crimes within the jurisdiction of the Tribunal or the case was not diligently prosecuted.
3. In considering the penalty to be imposed on a person convicted of a crime under this Statute, the Special Tribunal shall take into account the extent to which any penalty imposed by a national court on the same person for the same act has already been served.

Article 6 Amnesty

An amnesty granted to any person for any crime falling within the jurisdiction of the Special Tribunal shall not be a bar to prosecution.

SECTION II. ORGANIZATION OF THE SPECIAL TRIBUNAL

Article 7 Organs of the Special Tribunal

The Special Tribunal shall consist of the following organs:

(a) The Chambers, comprising a Pre-Trial Judge, a Trial Chamber and an Appeals Chamber;
(b) The Prosecutor;
(c) The Registry; and
(d) The Defence Office.

Article 8 Composition of the Chambers

1. The Chambers shall be composed as follows:
   (a) One international Pre-Trial Judge;
   (b) Three judges who shall serve in the Trial Chamber, of whom one shall be a Lebanese judge and two shall be international judges;
   (c) Five judges who shall serve in the Appeals Chamber, of whom two shall be Lebanese judges and three shall be international judges;
   (d) Two alternate judges, one of whom shall be a Lebanese judge and one shall be an international judge.
2. The judges of the Appeals Chamber and the judges of the Trial Chamber, respectively, shall elect a presiding judge who shall conduct the proceedings in the Chamber to which he or she was elected. The presiding judge of the Appeals Chamber shall be the President of the Special Tribunal.

19

3. At the request of the presiding judge of the Trial Chamber, the President of the Special Tribunal may, in the interest of justice, assign the alternate judges to be present at each stage of the trial and to replace a judge if that judge is unable to continue sitting.

Article 9 Qualification and appointment of judges

1. The judges shall be persons of high moral character, impartiality and integrity, with extensive judicial experience. They shall be independent in the performance of their functions and shall not accept or seek instructions from any Government or any other source.
2. In the overall composition of the Chambers, due account shall be taken of the established competence of the judges in criminal law and procedure and international law.
3. The judges shall be appointed by the Secretary-General, as set forth in article 2 of the Agreement, for a three-year period and may be eligible for reappointment for a further period to be determined by the Secretary-General in consultation with the Government.

Article 10 Powers of the President of the Special Tribunal

1. The President of the Special Tribunal, in addition to his or her judicial functions, shall represent the Tribunal and be responsible for its effective functioning and the good administration of justice.
2. The President of the Special Tribunal shall submit an annual report on the operation and activities of the Tribunal to the Secretary-General and to the Government of Lebanon.

Article 11 The Prosecutor

1. The Prosecutor shall be responsible for the investigation and prosecution of persons responsible for the crimes falling within the jurisdiction of the Special Tribunal. In the interest of proper administration of justice, he or she may decide to charge jointly persons accused of the same or different crimes committed in the course of the same transaction.
2. The Prosecutor shall act independently as a separate organ of the Special Tribunal. He or she shall not seek or receive instructions from any Government or from any other source.
3. The Prosecutor shall be appointed, as set forth in article 3 of the Agreement, by the Secretary-General for a three-year term and may be eligible for reappointment for a further period to be determined by the Secretary-General in consultation with the Government. He or she shall be of high moral character and possess the highest level of professional competence, and have extensive experience in the conduct of investigations and prosecutions of criminal cases.
4. The Prosecutor shall be assisted by a Lebanese Deputy Prosecutor and by such other Lebanese and international staff as may be required to perform the functions assigned to him or her effectively and efficiently.
5. The Office of the Prosecutor shall have the power to question suspects, victims and witnesses, to collect evidence and to conduct on-site investigations. In carrying out these tasks, the Prosecutor shall, as appropriate, be assisted by the Lebanese authorities concerned.

Article 12 The Registry

1. Under the authority of the President of the Special Tribunal, the Registry shall be responsible for the administration and servicing of the Tribunal.
2. The Registry shall consist of a Registrar and such other staff as may be required.
3. The Registrar shall be appointed by the Secretary-General and shall be a staff member of the United Nations. He or she shall serve for a three-year term and may be eligible for reappointment for a further period to be determined by the Secretary-General in consultation with the Government.
4. The Registrar shall set up a Victims and Witnesses Unit within the Registry. This Unit shall provide, in consultation with the Office of the Prosecutor, measures to protect the safety, physical and psychological well-being, dignity and privacy of victims and witnesses, and such other appropriate assistance for witnesses who appear before the Special Tribunal and others who are at risk on account of testimony given by such witnesses.

Article 13 The Defence Office

1. The Secretary-General, in consultation with the President of the Special Tribunal, shall appoint an independent Head of the Defence Office, who shall be responsible for the appointment of the Office staff and the drawing up of a list of defence counsel.
2. The Defence Office, which may also include one or more public defenders, shall protect the rights of the defence, provide support and assistance to defence counsel and to the persons entitled to legal assistance, including, where appropriate, legal research, collection of evidence and advice, and appearing before the Pre-Trial Judge or a Chamber in respect of specific issues.

Article 14 Official and working languages

The official languages of the Special Tribunal shall be Arabic, French and English. In any given case proceedings, the Pre-Trial Judge or a Chamber may decide that one or two of the languages may be used as working languages as appropriate.

SECTION III. RIGHTS OF DEFENDANTS AND VICTIMS

Article 15 Rights of suspects during investigation

A suspect who is to be questioned by the Prosecutor shall not be compelled to incriminate himself or herself or to confess guilt. He or she shall have the following rights of which he or she shall be informed by the Prosecutor prior to questioning, in a language he or she speaks and understands:

(a) The right to be informed that there are grounds to believe that he or she has committed a crime within the jurisdiction of the Special Tribunal;
(b) The right to remain silent, without such silence being considered in the determination of guilt or innocence, and to be cautioned that any statement he or she makes shall be recorded and may be used in evidence;
(c) The right to have legal assistance of his or her own choosing, including the right to have legal assistance provided by the Defence Office where the interests of justice so require and where the suspect does not have sufficient means to pay for it;
(d) The right to have the free assistance of an interpreter if he or she cannot understand or speak the language used for questioning;

(e) The right to be questioned in the presence of counsel unless the person has voluntarily waived his or her right to counsel.

Article 16 Rights of the accused

1. All accused shall be equal before the Special Tribunal.
2. The accused shall be entitled to a fair and public hearing, subject to measures ordered by the Special Tribunal for the protection of victims and witnesses.
3.
   (a) The accused shall be presumed innocent until proved guilty according to the provisions of this Statute;
   (b) The onus is on the Prosecutor to prove the guilt of the accused;
   (c) In order to convict the accused, the relevant Chamber must be convinced of the guilt of the accused beyond reasonable doubt.
4. In the determination of any charge against the accused pursuant to this Statute, he or she shall be entitled to the following minimum guarantees, in full equality:
   (a) To be informed promptly and in detail in a language which he or she understands of the nature and cause of the charge against him or her;
   (b) To have adequate time and facilities for the preparation of his or her defence and to communicate without hindrance with counsel of his or her own choosing;
   (c) To be tried without undue delay;
   (d) Subject to the provisions of article 22, to be tried in his or her presence, and to defend himself or herself in person or through legal assistance of his or her own choosing; to be informed, if he or she does not have legal assistance, of this right; and to have legal assistance assigned to him or her, in any case where the interests of justice so require and without payment by him or her in any such case if he or she does not have sufficient means to pay for it;
   (e) To examine, or have examined, the witnesses against him or her and to obtain the attendance and examination of witnesses on his or her behalf under the same conditions as witnesses against him or her;
   (f) To examine all evidence to be used against him or her during the trial in accordance with the Rules of Procedure and Evidence of the Special Tribunal;
   (g) To have the free assistance of an interpreter if he or she cannot understand or speak the language used in the Special Tribunal;
   (h) Not to be compelled to testify against himself or herself or to confess guilt.
5. The accused may make statements in court at any stage of the proceedings, provided such statements are relevant to the case at issue. The Chambers shall decide on the probative value, if any, of such statements.

Article 17 Rights of victims

Where the personal interests of the victims are affected, the Special Tribunal shall permit their views and concerns to be presented and considered at stages of the proceedings determined to be appropriate by the Pre-Trial Judge or the Chamber and in a manner that is not prejudicial to or inconsistent with the rights of the accused and a fair and impartial trial. Such views and concerns may be presented by the legal representatives of the victims where the Pre-Trial Judge or the Chamber considers it appropriate.

SECTION IV. CONDUCT OF PROCEEDINGS

Article 18 Pre-Trial proceedings

1. The Pre-Trial Judge shall review the indictment. If satisfied that a prima facie case has been established by the Prosecutor, he or she shall confirm the indictment. If he or she is not so satisfied, the indictment shall be dismissed.
2. The Pre-Trial Judge may, at the request of the Prosecutor, issue such orders and warrants for the arrest or transfer of persons, and any other orders as may be required for the conduct of the investigation and for the preparation of a fair and expeditious trial.

Article 19 Evidence collected prior to the establishment of the Special Tribunal

Evidence collected with regard to cases subject to the consideration of the Special Tribunal, prior to the establishment of the Tribunal, by the national authorities of Lebanon or by the International Independent Investigation Commission in accordance with its mandate as set out in Security Council resolution 1595 (2005) and subsequent resolutions, shall be received by the Tribunal. Its admissibility shall be decided by the Chambers pursuant to international standards on collection of evidence. The weight to be given to any such evidence shall be determined by the Chambers.

Article 20 Commencement and conduct of trial proceedings

1. The Trial Chamber shall read the indictment to the accused, satisfy itself that the rights of the accused are respected, confirm that the accused understands the indictment and instruct the accused to enter a plea.
2. Unless otherwise decided by the Trial Chamber in the interests of justice, examination of witnesses shall commence with questions posed by the presiding judge, followed by questions posed by other members of the Trial Chamber, the Prosecutor and the Defence.
3. Upon request or *proprio motu*, the Trial Chamber may at any stage of the trial decide to call additional witnesses and/or order the production of additional evidence.
4. The hearings shall be public unless the Trial Chamber decides to hold the proceedings in camera in accordance with the Rules of Procedure and Evidence.

Article 21 Powers of the Chambers

1. The Special Tribunal shall confine the trial, appellate and review proceedings strictly to an expeditious hearing of the issues raised by the charges, or the grounds for appeal or review, respectively. It shall take strict measures to prevent any action that may cause unreasonable delay.
2. A Chamber may admit any relevant evidence that it deems to have probative value and exclude such evidence if its probative value is substantially outweighed by the need to ensure a fair trial.
3. A Chamber may receive the evidence of a witness orally or, where the interests of justice allow, in written form.
4. In cases not otherwise provided for in the Rules of Procedure and Evidence, a Chamber shall apply rules of evidence that will best favour a fair determination of the matter before it and are consonant with the spirit of the Statute and the general principles of law.

Article 22 Trials in absentia

1. The Special Tribunal shall conduct trial proceedings in the absence of the accused, if he or she:
   (a) Has expressly and in writing waived his or her right to be present;
   (b) Has not been handed over to the Tribunal by the State authorities concerned;
   (c) Has absconded or otherwise cannot be found and all reasonable steps have been taken to secure his or her appearance before the Tribunal and to inform him or her of the charges confirmed by the Pre-Trial Judge.
2. When hearings are conducted in the absence of the accused, the Special Tribunal shall ensure that:
   (a) The accused has been notified, or served with the indictment, or notice has otherwise been given of the indictment through publication in the media or communication to the State of residence or nationality;
   (b) The accused has designated a defence counsel of his or her own choosing, to be remunerated either by the accused or, if the accused is proved to be indigent, by the Tribunal;
   (c) Whenever the accused refuses or fails to appoint a defence counsel, such counsel has been assigned by the Defence Office of the Tribunal with a view to ensuring full representation of the interests and rights of the accused.
3. In case of conviction in absentia, the accused, if he or she had not designated a defence counsel of his or her choosing, shall have the right to be retried in his or her presence before the Special Tribunal, unless he or she accepts the judgement.

Article 23 Judgement

The judgement shall be rendered by a majority of the judges of the Trial Chamber or of the Appeals Chamber and shall be delivered in public. It shall be accompanied by a reasoned opinion in writing, to which any separate or dissenting opinions shall be appended.

Article 24 Penalties

1. The Trial Chamber shall impose upon a convicted person imprisonment for life or for a specified number of years. In determining the terms of imprisonment for the crimes provided for in this Statute, the Trial Chamber shall, as appropriate, have recourse to international practice regarding prison sentences and to the practice of the national courts of Lebanon.
2. In imposing sentence, the Trial Chamber should take into account such factors as the gravity of the offence and the individual circumstances of the convicted person.

Article 25 Compensation to victims

1. The Special Tribunal may identify victims who have suffered harm as a result of the commission of crimes by an accused convicted by the Tribunal.
2. The Registrar shall transmit to the competent authorities of the State concerned the judgement finding the accused guilty of a crime that has caused harm to a victim.
3. Based on the decision of the Special Tribunal and pursuant to the relevant national legislation, a victim or persons claiming through the victim, whether or not such

victim had been identified as such by the Tribunal under paragraph 1 of this article, may bring an action in a national court or other competent body to obtain
compensation.
4. For the purposes of a claim made under paragraph 3 of this article, the judgement of
the Special Tribunal shall be final and binding as to the criminal responsibility of the
convicted person.

Article 26 Appellate proceedings

1. The Appeals Chamber shall hear appeals from persons convicted by the Trial Chamber
or from the Prosecutor on the following grounds:
    (a) An error on a question of law invalidating the decision;
    (b) An error of fact that has occasioned a miscarriage of justice.
2. The Appeals Chamber may affirm, reverse or revise the decisions taken by the Trial Chamber.

Article 27 Review proceedings[1]

1. Where a new fact has been discovered that was not known at the time of the proceedings before the Trial Chamber or the Appeals Chamber and that could have been a
decisive factor in reaching the decision, the convicted person or the Prosecutor may
submit an application for review of the judgement.
1. An application for review shall be submitted to the Appeals Chamber. The Appeals
Chamber may reject the application if it considers it to be unfounded. If it determines
that the application is meritorious, it may, as appropriate:
2. Reconvene the Trial Chamber;
3. Retain jurisdiction over the matter.

Article 28 Rules of Procedure and Evidence

1. The judges of the Special Tribunal shall, as soon as practicable after taking office, adopt
Rules of Procedure and Evidence for the conduct of the pre-trial, trial and appellate
proceedings, the admission of evidence, the participation of victims, the protection
of victims and witnesses and other appropriate matters and may amend them, as
appropriate.
2. In so doing, the judges shall be guided, as appropriate, by the Lebanese Code of
Criminal Procedure, as well as by other reference materials reflecting the highest
standards of international criminal procedure, with a view to ensuring a fair and expeditious trial.

Article 29 Enforcement of sentences

1. Imprisonment shall be served in a State designated by the President of the Special
Tribunal from a list of States that have indicated their willingness to accept persons
convicted by the Tribunal.
2. Conditions of imprisonment shall be governed by the law of the State of enforcement
subject to the supervision of the Special Tribunal. The State of enforcement shall be
bound by the duration of the sentence, subject to article 30 of this Statute.

---

[1] Numbering as in original.

Article 30 Pardon or commutation of sentences

If, pursuant to the applicable law of the State in which the convicted person is imprisoned, he or she is eligible for pardon or commutation of sentence, the State concerned shall notify the Special Tribunal accordingly. There shall only be pardon or commutation of sentence if the President of the Tribunal, in consultation with the judges, so decides on the basis of the interests of justice and the general principles of law.

2008 International Convention for the Protection of All Persons from Enforced Disappearances

International Convention for the Protection of All Persons from Enforced Disappearance

PREAMBLE

The States Parties to this Convention,

Considering the obligation of States under the Charter of the United Nations to promote universal respect for, and observance of, human rights and fundamental freedoms,

Having regard to the Universal Declaration of Human Rights,

Recalling the International Covenant on Economic, Social and Cultural Rights, the International Covenant on Civil and Political Rights and the other relevant international instruments in the fields of human rights, humanitarian law and international criminal law,

Also recalling the Declaration on the Protection of All Persons from Enforced Disappearance adopted by the General Assembly of the United Nations in its resolution 47/133 of 18 December 1992,

Aware of the extreme seriousness of enforced disappearance, which constitutes a crime and, in certain circumstances defined in international law, a crime against humanity,

Determined to prevent enforced disappearances and to combat impunity for the crime of enforced disappearance,

Considering the right of any person not to be subjected to enforced disappearance, the right of victims to justice and to reparation,

Affirming the right of any victim to know the truth about the circumstances of an enforced disappearance and the fate of the disappeared person, and the right to freedom to seek, receive and impart information to this end,

Have agreed on the following articles:

PART I

Article 1

1. No one shall be subjected to enforced disappearance.
2. No exceptional circumstances whatsoever, whether a state of war or a threat of war, internal political instability or any other public emergency, may be invoked as a justification for enforced disappearance.

Article 2

For the purposes of this Convention, "enforced disappearance" is considered to be the arrest, detention, abduction or any other form of deprivation of liberty by agents of the State or by persons or groups of persons acting with the authorization, support or acquiescence of the State, followed by a refusal to acknowledge the deprivation of liberty or by concealment of the fate or whereabouts of the disappeared person, which place such a person outside the protection of the law.

Article 3

Each State Party shall take appropriate measures to investigate acts defined in article 2 committed by persons or groups of persons acting without the authorization, support or acquiescence of the State and to bring those responsible to justice.

Article 4

Each State Party shall take the necessary measures to ensure that enforced disappearance constitutes an offence under its criminal law.

Article 5

The widespread or systematic practice of enforced disappearance constitutes a crime against humanity as defined in applicable international law and shall attract the consequences provided for under such applicable international law.

Article 6

1. Each State Party shall take the necessary measures to hold criminally responsible at least:
   (a) Any person who commits, orders, solicits or induces the commission of, attempts to commit, is an accomplice to or participates in an enforced disappearance;
   (b) A superior who:
       (i) Knew, or consciously disregarded information which clearly indicated, that subordinates under his or her effective authority and control were committing or about to commit a crime of enforced disappearance;
       (ii) Exercised effective responsibility for and control over activities which were concerned with the crime of enforced disappearance; and
       (iii) Failed to take all necessary and reasonable measures within his or her power to prevent or repress the commission of an enforced disappearance or to submit the matter to the competent authorities for investigation and prosecution;
   (c) Subparagraph (b) above is without prejudice to the higher standards of responsibility applicable under relevant international law to a military commander or to a person effectively acting as a military commander.
2. No order or instruction from any public authority, civilian, military or other, may be invoked to justify an offence of enforced disappearance.

Article 7

1. Each State Party shall make the offence of enforced disappearance punishable by appropriate penalties which take into account its extreme seriousness.
2. Each State Party may establish:

(a) Mitigating circumstances, in particular for persons who, having been implicated in the commission of an enforced disappearance, effectively contribute to bringing the disappeared person forward alive or make it possible to clarify cases of enforced disappearance or to identify the perpetrators of an enforced disappearance;

(b) Without prejudice to other criminal procedures, aggravating circumstances, in particular in the event of the death of the disappeared person or the commission of an enforced disappearance in respect of pregnant women, minors, persons with disabilities or other particularly vulnerable persons.

Article 8

Without prejudice to article 5,

1. A State Party which applies a statute of limitations in respect of enforced disappearance shall take the necessary measures to ensure that the term of limitation for criminal proceedings:

   (a) Is of long duration and is proportionate to the extreme seriousness of this offence;

   (b) Commences from the moment when the offence of enforced disappearance ceases, taking into account its continuous nature.

2. Each State Party shall guarantee the right of victims of enforced disappearance to an effective remedy during the term of limitation.

Article 9

1. Each State Party shall take the necessary measures to establish its competence to exercise jurisdiction over the offence of enforced disappearance:

   (a) When the offence is committed in any territory under its jurisdiction or on board a ship or aircraft registered in that State;

   (b) When the alleged offender is one of its nationals;

   (c) When the disappeared person is one of its nationals and the State Party considers it appropriate.

2. Each State Party shall likewise take such measures as may be necessary to establish its competence to exercise jurisdiction over the offence of enforced disappearance when the alleged offender is present in any territory under its jurisdiction, unless it extradites or surrenders him or her to another State in accordance with its international obligations or surrenders him or her to an international criminal tribunal whose jurisdiction it has recognized.

3. This Convention does not exclude any additional criminal jurisdiction exercised in accordance with national law.

Article 10

1. Upon being satisfied, after an examination of the information available to it, that the circumstances so warrant, any State Party in whose territory a person suspected of having committed an offence of enforced disappearance is present shall take him or her into custody or take such other legal measures as are necessary to ensure his or her presence. The custody and other legal measures shall be as provided for in the law of that State Party but may be maintained only for such time as is necessary to ensure the person's presence at criminal, surrender or extradition proceedings.

2. A State Party which has taken the measures referred to in paragraph 1 of this article shall immediately carry out a preliminary inquiry or investigations to establish the facts. It shall notify the States Parties referred to in article 9, paragraph 1, of the measures it has taken in pursuance of paragraph 1 of this article, including detention and the circumstances warranting detention, and of the findings of its preliminary inquiry or its investigations, indicating whether it intends to exercise its jurisdiction.

3. Any person in custody pursuant to paragraph 1 of this article may communicate immediately with the nearest appropriate representative of the State of which he or she is a national, or, if he or she is a stateless person, with the representative of the State where he or she usually resides.

Article 11

1. The State Party in the territory under whose jurisdiction a person alleged to have committed an offence of enforced disappearance is found shall, if it does not extradite that person or surrender him or her to another State in accordance with its international obligations or surrender him or her to an international criminal tribunal whose jurisdiction it has recognized, submit the case to its competent authorities for the purpose of prosecution.

2. These authorities shall take their decision in the same manner as in the case of any ordinary offence of a serious nature under the law of that State Party. In the cases referred to in article 9, paragraph 2, the standards of evidence required for prosecution and conviction shall in no way be less stringent than those which apply in the cases referred to in article 9, paragraph 1.

3. Any person against whom proceedings are brought in connection with an offence of enforced disappearance shall be guaranteed fair treatment at all stages of the proceedings. Any person tried for an offence of enforced disappearance shall benefit from a fair trial before a competent, independent and impartial court or tribunal established by law.

Article 12

1. Each State Party shall ensure that any individual who alleges that a person has been subjected to enforced disappearance has the right to report the facts to the competent authorities, which shall examine the allegation promptly and impartially and, where necessary, undertake without delay a thorough and impartial investigation. Appropriate steps shall be taken, where necessary, to ensure that the complainant, witnesses, relatives of the disappeared person and their defence counsel, as well as persons participating in the investigation, are protected against all ill-treatment or intimidation as a consequence of the complaint or any evidence given.

2. Where there are reasonable grounds for believing that a person has been subjected to enforced disappearance, the authorities referred to in paragraph 1 of this article shall undertake an investigation, even if there has been no formal complaint.

3. Each State Party shall ensure that the authorities referred to in paragraph 1 of this article:

   (a) Have the necessary powers and resources to conduct the investigation effectively, including access to the documentation and other information relevant to their investigation;

(b) Have access, if necessary with the prior authorization of a judicial authority, which shall rule promptly on the matter, to any place of detention or any other place where there are reasonable grounds to believe that the disappeared person may be present.

4. Each State Party shall take the necessary measures to prevent and sanction acts that hinder the conduct of an investigation. It shall ensure in particular that persons suspected of having committed an offence of enforced disappearance are not in a position to influence the progress of an investigation by means of pressure or acts of intimidation or reprisal aimed at the complainant, witnesses, relatives of the disappeared person or their defence counsel, or at persons participating in the investigation.

Article 13

1. For the purposes of extradition between States Parties, the offence of enforced disappearance shall not be regarded as a political offence or as an offence connected with a political offence or as an offence inspired by political motives. Accordingly, a request for extradition based on such an offence may not be refused on these grounds alone.

2. The offence of enforced disappearance shall be deemed to be included as an extraditable offence in any extradition treaty existing between States Parties before the entry into force of this Convention.

3. States Parties undertake to include the offence of enforced disappearance as an extraditable offence in any extradition treaty subsequently to be concluded between them.

4. If a State Party which makes extradition conditional on the existence of a treaty receives a request for extradition from another State Party with which it has no extradition treaty, it may consider this Convention as the necessary legal basis for extradition in respect of the offence of enforced disappearance.

5. States Parties which do not make extradition conditional on the existence of a treaty shall recognize the offence of enforced disappearance as an extraditable offence between themselves.

6. Extradition shall, in all cases, be subject to the conditions provided for by the law of the requested State Party or by applicable extradition treaties, including, in particular, conditions relating to the minimum penalty requirement for extradition and the grounds upon which the requested State Party may refuse extradition or make it subject to certain conditions.

7. Nothing in this Convention shall be interpreted as imposing an obligation to extradite if the requested State Party has substantial grounds for believing that the request has been made for the purpose of prosecuting or punishing a person on account of that person's sex, race, religion, nationality, ethnic origin, political opinions or membership of a particular social group, or that compliance with the request would cause harm to that person for any one of these reasons.

Article 14

1. States Parties shall afford one another the greatest measure of mutual legal assistance in connection with criminal proceedings brought in respect of an offence of enforced disappearance, including the supply of all evidence at their disposal that is necessary for the proceedings.

20

2. Such mutual legal assistance shall be subject to the conditions provided for by the domestic law of the requested State Party or by applicable treaties on mutual legal assistance, including, in particular, the conditions in relation to the grounds upon which the requested State Party may refuse to grant mutual legal assistance or may make it subject to conditions.

Article 15

States Parties shall cooperate with each other and shall afford one another the greatest measure of mutual assistance with a view to assisting victims of enforced disappearance, and in searching for, locating and releasing disappeared persons and, in the event of death, in exhuming and identifying them and returning their remains.

Article 16

1. No State Party shall expel, return ("refouler"), surrender or extradite a person to another State where there are substantial grounds for believing that he or she would be in danger of being subjected to enforced disappearance.
2. For the purpose of determining whether there are such grounds, the competent authorities shall take into account all relevant considerations, including, where applicable, the existence in the State concerned of a consistent pattern of gross, flagrant or mass violations of human rights or of serious violations of international humanitarian law.

Article 17

1. No one shall be held in secret detention.
2. Without prejudice to other international obligations of the State Party with regard to the deprivation of liberty, each State Party shall, in its legislation:
   (a) Establish the conditions under which orders of deprivation of liberty may be given;
   (b) Indicate those authorities authorized to order the deprivation of liberty;
   (c) Guarantee that any person deprived of liberty shall be held solely in officially recognized and supervised places of deprivation of liberty;
   (d) Guarantee that any person deprived of liberty shall be authorized to communicate with and be visited by his or her family, counsel or any other person of his or her choice, subject only to the conditions established by law, or, if he or she is a foreigner, to communicate with his or her consular authorities, in accordance with applicable international law;
   (e) Guarantee access by the competent and legally authorized authorities and institutions to the places where persons are deprived of liberty, if necessary with prior authorization from a judicial authority;
   (f) Guarantee that any person deprived of liberty or, in the case of a suspected enforced disappearance, since the person deprived of liberty is not able to exercise this right, any persons with a legitimate interest, such as relatives of the person deprived of liberty, their representatives or their counsel, shall, in all circumstances, be entitled to take proceedings before a court, in order that the court may decide without delay on the lawfulness of the deprivation of liberty and order the person's release if such deprivation of liberty is not lawful.

20

3. Each State Party shall assure the compilation and maintenance of one or more up-to-date official registers and/or records of persons deprived of liberty, which shall be made promptly available, upon request, to any judicial or other competent authority or institution authorized for that purpose by the law of the State Party concerned or any relevant international legal instrument to which the State concerned is a party. The information contained therein shall include, as a minimum:

(a) The identity of the person deprived of liberty;

(b) The date, time and place where the person was deprived of liberty and the identity of the authority that deprived the person of liberty;

(c) The authority that ordered the deprivation of liberty and the grounds for the deprivation of liberty;

(d) The authority responsible for supervising the deprivation of liberty;

(e) The place of deprivation of liberty, the date and time of admission to the place of deprivation of liberty and the authority responsible for the place of deprivation of liberty;

(f) Elements relating to the state of health of the person deprived of liberty;

(g) In the event of death during the deprivation of liberty, the circumstances and cause of death and the destination of the remains;

(h) The date and time of release or transfer to another place of detention, the destination and the authority responsible for the transfer.

Article 18

1. Subject to articles 19 and 20, each State Party shall guarantee to any person with a legitimate interest in this information, such as relatives of the person deprived of liberty, their representatives or their counsel, access to at least the following information:

(a) The authority that ordered the deprivation of liberty;

(b) The date, time and place where the person was deprived of liberty and admitted to the place of deprivation of liberty;

(c) The authority responsible for supervising the deprivation of liberty;

(d) The whereabouts of the person deprived of liberty, including, in the event of a transfer to another place of deprivation of liberty, the destination and the authority responsible for the transfer;

(e) The date, time and place of release;

(f) Elements relating to the state of health of the person deprived of liberty;

(g) In the event of death during the deprivation of liberty, the circumstances and cause of death and the destination of the remains.

2. Appropriate measures shall be taken, where necessary, to protect the persons referred to in paragraph 1 of this article, as well as persons participating in the investigation, from any ill-treatment, intimidation or sanction as a result of the search for information concerning a person deprived of liberty.

Article 19

1. Personal information, including medical and genetic data, which is collected and/or transmitted within the framework of the search for a disappeared person shall not be used or made available for purposes other than the search for the disappeared person. This is without prejudice to the use of such information in criminal proceedings

20

relating to an offence of enforced disappearance or the exercise of the right to obtain reparation.

2. The collection, processing, use and storage of personal information, including medical and genetic data, shall not infringe or have the effect of infringing the human rights, fundamental freedoms or human dignity of an individual.

Article 20

1. Only where a person is under the protection of the law and the deprivation of liberty is subject to judicial control may the right to information referred to in article 18 be restricted, on an exceptional basis, where strictly necessary and where provided for by law, and if the transmission of the information would adversely affect the privacy or safety of the person, hinder a criminal investigation, or for other equivalent reasons in accordance with the law, and in conformity with applicable international law and with the objectives of this Convention. In no case shall there be restrictions on the right to information referred to in article 18 that could constitute conduct defined in article 2 or be in violation of article 17, paragraph 1.

2. Without prejudice to consideration of the lawfulness of the deprivation of a person's liberty, States Parties shall guarantee to the persons referred to in article 18, paragraph 1, the right to a prompt and effective judicial remedy as a means of obtaining without delay the information referred to in article 18, paragraph 1. This right to a remedy may not be suspended or restricted in any circumstances.

Article 21

Each State Party shall take the necessary measures to ensure that persons deprived of liberty are released in a manner permitting reliable verification that they have actually been released. Each State Party shall also take the necessary measures to assure the physical integrity of such persons and their ability to exercise fully their rights at the time of release, without prejudice to any obligations to which such persons may be subject under national law.

Article 22

Without prejudice to article 6, each State Party shall take the necessary measures to prevent and impose sanctions for the following conduct:

(a) Delaying or obstructing the remedies referred to in article 17, paragraph 2(f), and article 20, paragraph 2;

(b) Failure to record the deprivation of liberty of any person, or the recording of any information which the official responsible for the official register knew or should have known to be inaccurate;

(c) Refusal to provide information on the deprivation of liberty of a person, or the provision of inaccurate information, even though the legal requirements for providing such information have been met.

Article 23

1. Each State Party shall ensure that the training of law enforcement personnel, civil or military, medical personnel, public officials and other persons who may be involved in the custody or treatment of any person deprived of liberty includes the necessary

education and information regarding the relevant provisions of this Convention, in order to:

(a) Prevent the involvement of such officials in enforced disappearances;

(b) Emphasize the importance of prevention and investigations in relation to enforced disappearances;

(c) Ensure that the urgent need to resolve cases of enforced disappearance is recognized.

2. Each State Party shall ensure that orders or instructions prescribing, authorizing or encouraging enforced disappearance are prohibited. Each State Party shall guarantee that a person who refuses to obey such an order will not be punished.

3. Each State Party shall take the necessary measures to ensure that the persons referred to in paragraph 1 of this article who have reason to believe that an enforced disappearance has occurred or is planned report the matter to their superiors and, where necessary, to the appropriate authorities or bodies vested with powers of review or remedy.

Article 24

1. For the purposes of this Convention, "victim" means the disappeared person and any individual who has suffered harm as the direct result of an enforced disappearance.

2. Each victim has the right to know the truth regarding the circumstances of the enforced disappearance, the progress and results of the investigation and the fate of the disappeared person. Each State Party shall take appropriate measures in this regard.

3. Each State Party shall take all appropriate measures to search for, locate and release disappeared persons and, in the event of death, to locate, respect and return their remains.

4. Each State Party shall ensure in its legal system that the victims of enforced disappearance have the right to obtain reparation and prompt, fair and adequate compensation.

5. The right to obtain reparation referred to in paragraph 4 of this article covers material and moral damages and, where appropriate, other forms of reparation such as:

(a) Restitution;

(b) Rehabilitation;

(c) Satisfaction, including restoration of dignity and reputation;

(d) Guarantees of non-repetition.

6. Without prejudice to the obligation to continue the investigation until the fate of the disappeared person has been clarified, each State Party shall take the appropriate steps with regard to the legal situation of disappeared persons whose fate has not been clarified and that of their relatives, in fields such as social welfare, financial matters, family law and property rights.

7. Each State Party shall guarantee the right to form and participate freely in organizations and associations concerned with attempting to establish the circumstances of enforced disappearances and the fate of disappeared persons, and to assist victims of enforced disappearance.

Article 25

1. Each State Party shall take the necessary measures to prevent and punish under its criminal law:

20

    (a) The wrongful removal of children who are subjected to enforced disappearance, children whose father, mother or legal guardian is subjected to enforced disappearance or children born during the captivity of a mother subjected to enforced disappearance;

    (b) The falsification, concealment or destruction of documents attesting to the true identity of the children referred to in subparagraph (a) above.

2. Each State Party shall take the necessary measures to search for and identify the children referred to in paragraph 1(a) of this article and to return them to their families of origin, in accordance with legal procedures and applicable international agreements.

3. States Parties shall assist one another in searching for, identifying and locating the children referred to in paragraph 1(a) of this article.

4. Given the need to protect the best interests of the children referred to in paragraph 1(a) of this article and their right to preserve, or to have re-established, their identity, including their nationality, name and family relations as recognized by law, States Parties which recognize a system of adoption or other form of placement of children shall have legal procedures in place to review the adoption or placement procedure, and, where appropriate, to annul any adoption or placement of children that originated in an enforced disappearance.

5. In all cases, and in particular in all matters relating to this article, the best interests of the child shall be a primary consideration, and a child who is capable of forming his or her own views shall have the right to express those views freely, the views of the child being given due weight in accordance with the age and maturity of the child.

PART II

Article 26

1. A Committee on Enforced Disappearances (hereinafter referred to as "the Committee") shall be established to carry out the functions provided for under this Convention. The Committee shall consist of ten experts of high moral character and recognized competence in the field of human rights, who shall serve in their personal capacity and be independent and impartial. The members of the Committee shall be elected by the States Parties according to equitable geographical distribution. Due account shall be taken of the usefulness of the participation in the work of the Committee of persons having relevant legal experience and of balanced gender representation.

2. The members of the Committee shall be elected by secret ballot from a list of persons nominated by States Parties from among their nationals, at biennial meetings of the States Parties convened by the Secretary-General of the United Nations for this purpose. At those meetings, for which two thirds of the States Parties shall constitute a quorum, the persons elected to the Committee shall be those who obtain the largest number of votes and an absolute majority of the votes of the representatives of States Parties present and voting.

3. The initial election shall be held no later than six months after the date of entry into force of this Convention. Four months before the date of each election, the Secretary-General of the United Nations shall address a letter to the States Parties inviting them to submit nominations within three months. The Secretary-General shall prepare a list

in alphabetical order of all persons thus nominated, indicating the State Party which nominated each candidate, and shall submit this list to all States Parties.

4. The members of the Committee shall be elected for a term of four years. They shall be eligible for re-election once. However, the term of five of the members elected at the first election shall expire at the end of two years; immediately after the first election, the names of these five members shall be chosen by lot by the chairman of the meeting referred to in paragraph 2 of this article.

5. If a member of the Committee dies or resigns or for any other reason can no longer perform his or her Committee duties, the State Party which nominated him or her shall, in accordance with the criteria set out in paragraph 1 of this article, appoint another candidate from among its nationals to serve out his or her term, subject to the approval of the majority of the States Parties. Such approval shall be considered to have been obtained unless half or more of the States Parties respond negatively within six weeks of having been informed by the Secretary-General of the United Nations of the proposed appointment.

6. The Committee shall establish its own rules of procedure.

7. The Secretary-General of the United Nations shall provide the Committee with the necessary means, staff and facilities for the effective performance of its functions. The Secretary-General of the United Nations shall convene the initial meeting of the Committee.

8. The members of the Committee shall be entitled to the facilities, privileges and immunities of experts on mission for the United Nations, as laid down in the relevant sections of the Convention on the Privileges and Immunities of the United Nations.

9. Each State Party shall cooperate with the Committee and assist its members in the fulfilment of their mandate, to the extent of the Committee's functions that the State Party has accepted.

Article 27

A Conference of the States Parties will take place at the earliest four years and at the latest six years following the entry into force of this Convention to evaluate the functioning of the Committee and to decide, in accordance with the procedure described in article 44, paragraph 2, whether it is appropriate to transfer to another body – without excluding any possibility – the monitoring of this Convention, in accordance with the functions defined in articles 28 to 36.

Article 28

1. In the framework of the competencies granted by this Convention, the Committee shall cooperate with all relevant organs, offices and specialized agencies and funds of the United Nations, with the treaty bodies instituted by international instruments, with the special procedures of the United Nations and with the relevant regional intergovernmental organizations or bodies, as well as with all relevant State institutions, agencies or offices working towards the protection of all persons against enforced disappearances.

2. As it discharges its mandate, the Committee shall consult other treaty bodies instituted by relevant international human rights instruments, in particular the Human Rights Committee instituted by the International Covenant on Civil and Political

20

Rights, with a view to ensuring the consistency of their respective observations and recommendations.

Article 29

1. Each State Party shall submit to the Committee, through the Secretary-General of the United Nations, a report on the measures taken to give effect to its obligations under this Convention, within two years after the entry into force of this Convention for the State Party concerned.
2. The Secretary-General of the United Nations shall make this report available to all States Parties.
3. Each report shall be considered by the Committee, which shall issue such comments, observations or recommendations as it may deem appropriate. The comments, observations or recommendations shall be communicated to the State Party concerned, which may respond to them, on its own initiative or at the request of the Committee.
4. The Committee may also request States Parties to provide additional information on the implementation of this Convention.

Article 30

1. A request that a disappeared person should be sought and found may be submitted to the Committee, as a matter of urgency, by relatives of the disappeared person or their legal representatives, their counsel or any person authorized by them, as well as by any other person having a legitimate interest.
2. If the Committee considers that a request for urgent action submitted in pursuance of paragraph 1 of this article:
   (a) Is not manifestly unfounded;
   (b) Does not constitute an abuse of the right of submission of such requests;
   (c) Has already been duly presented to the competent bodies of the State Party concerned, such as those authorized to undertake investigations, where such a possibility exists;
   (d) Is not incompatible with the provisions of this Convention; and
   (e) The same matter is not being examined under another procedure of international investigation or settlement of the same nature;
   it shall request the State Party concerned to provide it with information on the situation of the persons sought, within a time limit set by the Committee.
3. In the light of the information provided by the State Party concerned in accordance with paragraph 2 of this article, the Committee may transmit recommendations to the State Party, including a request that the State Party should take all the necessary measures, including interim measures, to locate and protect the person concerned in accordance with this Convention and to inform the Committee, within a specified period of time, of measures taken, taking into account the urgency of the situation. The Committee shall inform the person submitting the urgent action request of its recommendations and of the information provided to it by the State as it becomes available.
4. The Committee shall continue its efforts to work with the State Party concerned for as long as the fate of the person sought remains unresolved. The person presenting the request shall be kept informed.

Article 31

1. A State Party may at the time of ratification of this Convention or at any time afterwards declare that it recognizes the competence of the Committee to receive and consider communications from or on behalf of individuals subject to its jurisdiction claiming to be victims of a violation by this State Party of provisions of this Convention. The Committee shall not admit any communication concerning a State Party which has not made such a declaration.

2. The Committee shall consider a communication inadmissible where:

    (a) The communication is anonymous;

    (b) The communication constitutes an abuse of the right of submission of such communications or is incompatible with the provisions of this Convention;

    (c) The same matter is being examined under another procedure of international investigation or settlement of the same nature; or where

    (d) All effective available domestic remedies have not been exhausted. This rule shall not apply where the application of the remedies is unreasonably prolonged.

3. If the Committee considers that the communication meets the requirements set out in paragraph 2 of this article, it shall transmit the communication to the State Party concerned, requesting it to provide observations and comments within a time limit set by the Committee.

4. At any time after the receipt of a communication and before a determination on the merits has been reached, the Committee may transmit to the State Party concerned for its urgent consideration a request that the State Party will take such interim measures as may be necessary to avoid possible irreparable damage to the victims of the alleged violation. Where the Committee exercises its discretion, this does not imply a determination on admissibility or on the merits of the communication.

5. The Committee shall hold closed meetings when examining communications under the present article. It shall inform the author of a communication of the responses provided by the State Party concerned. When the Committee decides to finalize the procedure, it shall communicate its views to the State Party and to the author of the communication.

Article 32

A State Party to this Convention may at any time declare that it recognizes the competence of the Committee to receive and consider communications in which a State Party claims that another State Party is not fulfilling its obligations under this Convention. The Committee shall not receive communications concerning a State Party which has not made such a declaration, nor communications from a State Party which has not made such a declaration.

Article 33

1. If the Committee receives reliable information indicating that a State Party is seriously violating the provisions of this Convention, it may, after consultation with the State Party concerned, request one or more of its members to undertake a visit and report back to it without delay.

2. The Committee shall notify the State Party concerned, in writing, of its intention to organize a visit, indicating the composition of the delegation and the purpose of the visit. The State Party shall answer the Committee within a reasonable time.

20

3. Upon a substantiated request by the State Party, the Committee may decide to postpone or cancel its visit.
4. If the State Party agrees to the visit, the Committee and the State Party concerned shall work together to define the modalities of the visit and the State Party shall provide the Committee with all the facilities needed for the successful completion of the visit.
5. Following its visit, the Committee shall communicate to the State Party concerned its observations and recommendations.

Article 34

If the Committee receives information which appears to it to contain well-founded indications that enforced disappearance is being practised on a widespread or systematic basis in the territory under the jurisdiction of a State Party, it may, after seeking from the State Party concerned all relevant information on the situation, urgently bring the matter to the attention of the General Assembly of the United Nations, through the Secretary-General of the United Nations.

Article 35

1. The Committee shall have competence solely in respect of enforced disappearances which commenced after the entry into force of this Convention.
2. If a State becomes a party to this Convention after its entry into force, the obligations of that State vis-à-vis the Committee shall relate only to enforced disappearances which commenced after the entry into force of this Convention for the State concerned.

Article 36

1. The Committee shall submit an annual report on its activities under this Convention to the States Parties and to the General Assembly of the United Nations.
2. Before an observation on a State Party is published in the annual report, the State Party concerned shall be informed in advance and shall be given reasonable time to answer. This State Party may request the publication of its comments or observations in the report.

PART III

Article 37

Nothing in this Convention shall affect any provisions which are more conducive to the protection of all persons from enforced disappearance and which may be contained in:
(a) The law of a State Party;
(b) International law in force for that State.

Article 38

1. This Convention is open for signature by all Member States of the United Nations.
2. This Convention is subject to ratification by all Member States of the United Nations. Instruments of ratification shall be deposited with the Secretary-General of the United Nations.
3. This Convention is open to accession by all Member States of the United Nations. Accession shall be effected by the deposit of an instrument of accession with the Secretary-General.

Article 39

1. This Convention shall enter into force on the thirtieth day after the date of deposit with the Secretary-General of the United Nations of the twentieth instrument of ratification or accession.
2. For each State ratifying or acceding to this Convention after the deposit of the twentieth instrument of ratification or accession, this Convention shall enter into force on the thirtieth day after the date of the deposit of that State's instrument of ratification or accession.

Article 40

The Secretary-General of the United Nations shall notify all States Members of the United Nations and all States which have signed or acceded to this Convention of the following:
(a) Signatures, ratifications and accessions under article 38;
(b) The date of entry into force of this Convention under article 39.

Article 41

The provisions of this Convention shall apply to all parts of federal States without any limitations or exceptions.

Article 42

1. Any dispute between two or more States Parties concerning the interpretation or application of this Convention which cannot be settled through negotiation or by the procedures expressly provided for in this Convention shall, at the request of one of them, be submitted to arbitration. If within six months from the date of the request for arbitration the Parties are unable to agree on the organization of the arbitration, any one of those Parties may refer the dispute to the International Court of Justice by request in conformity with the Statute of the Court.
2. A State may, at the time of signature or ratification of this Convention or accession thereto, declare that it does not consider itself bound by paragraph 1 of this article. The other States Parties shall not be bound by paragraph 1 of this article with respect to any State Party having made such a declaration.
3. Any State Party having made a declaration in accordance with the provisions of paragraph 2 of this article may at any time withdraw this declaration by notification to the Secretary-General of the United Nations.

Article 43

This Convention is without prejudice to the provisions of international humanitarian law, including the obligations of the High Contracting Parties to the four Geneva Conventions of 12 August 1949 and the two Additional Protocols thereto of 8 June 1977, or to the opportunity available to any State Party to authorize the International Committee of the Red Cross to visit places of detention in situations not covered by international humanitarian law.

Article 44

1. Any State Party to this Convention may propose an amendment and file it with the Secretary-General of the United Nations. The Secretary-General shall thereupon communicate the proposed amendment to the States Parties to this Convention with a request that they indicate whether they favour a conference of States Parties for the

purpose of considering and voting upon the proposal. In the event that within four months from the date of such communication at least one third of the States Parties favour such a conference, the Secretary-General shall convene the conference under the auspices of the United Nations.

2. Any amendment adopted by a majority of two thirds of the States Parties present and voting at the conference shall be submitted by the Secretary-General of the United Nations to all the States Parties for acceptance.

3. An amendment adopted in accordance with paragraph 1 of this article shall enter into force when two thirds of the States Parties to this Convention have accepted it in accordance with their respective constitutional processes.

4. When amendments enter into force, they shall be binding on those States Parties which have accepted them, other States Parties still being bound by the provisions of this Convention and any earlier amendment which they have accepted.

Article 45

1. This Convention, of which the Arabic, Chinese, English, French, Russian and Spanish texts are equally authentic, shall be deposited with the Secretary-General of the United Nations.

2. The Secretary-General of the United Nations shall transmit certified copies of this Convention to all States referred to in article 38.

Index

Printed in the United States
by Baker & Taylor Publisher Services